D1369458

Professional DevExpress™ ASP.NET Controls

Professional
DevExpress™ ASP.NET Controls

Professional
DevExpress™ ASP.NET Controls

Paul Kimmel
with Julian Bucknall and Joe Kunk

WILEY

Wiley Publishing, Inc.

Professional DevExpress™ ASP.NET Controls

Published by
Wiley Publishing, Inc.
10475 Crosspoint Boulevard
Indianapolis, IN 46256

www.wiley.com

Copyright © 2010 by Wiley Publishing, Inc., Indianapolis, Indiana

Published by Wiley Publishing, Inc., Indianapolis, Indiana

Published simultaneously in Canada

ISBN: 978-0-470-50083-5

Manufactured in the United States of America

10 9 8 7 6 5 4 3 2 1

For general information on our other products and services please contact our Customer Care Department within the United States at (877) 762-2974, outside the United States at (317) 572-3993 or fax (317) 572-4002.

Wiley also publishes its books in a variety of electronic formats. Some content that appears in print may not be available in electronic books.

Library of Congress Control Number: 2009930063

For Alex and Noah

About the Authors

Paul Kimmel is a technical Evangelist for DevExpress and loving every minute of it. Paul started programming in 1988 when Donald Gardener and Mike Groher let him write some Databus code and has been writing code ever since. Paul has twenty plus years of experience writing software, writing books on object-oriented languages and UML, presenting at national conferences and local user groups, and is the co-founder of two .NET User Groups (Greater Lansing Area .NET User Group in Flint and East Lansing, Michigan). Paul is a five-time Microsoft MVP and the VB Today columnist for codeguru .com and is frequent contributor to InformIT.com, developer.com, devsource.com, and *Dr. Dobbs Journal*.

Julian Bucknall is the Chief Technology Officer for DevExpress, a software company that writes some great controls and tools for .NET and Delphi. He is responsible for technology oversight at DevExpress. Julian is the author of the *Tomes of Delphi: Algorithms and Data Structures* from WordWare Publishing, Inc, the author of blog.boyet.com and the ctodx blog at DevExpress.

Julian is an ex-Brit, residing in Colorado with his beautiful wife and considers himself a programmer by trade, an actor by ambition, and an algorithm guy by osmosis as well as a contributor to *PCPlus*, the UK's premier technology magazine.

Joe Kunk received his B.S. in Computer Science from Michigan State University in 1984 and has worked as a business analyst, software developer, manager, and entrepreneur in the fields of education, government, and IT consulting. Joe is a Microsoft MVP, President of the Greater Lansing User Group for .Net, Board Member of the Lansing IT Council, Senior Consultant at A. J. Boggs & Company, and co-founder of Listen IT Solutions, LLC. Joe lives in Okemos, Michigan and enjoys the many events at the MSU Wharton Center for Performing Arts, speaking about technology at user groups and regional conferences, and family time with his wife and two daughters.

Credits

Acquisitions Editor
Paul Reese

Project Editor
Adaobi Obi Tulton

Technical Editor
Doug Parsons

Senior Production Editor
Debra Banninger

Copy Editors
Susan Christopherson
Kim Cofer

Editorial Director
Robyn B. Siesky

Editorial Manager
Mary Beth Wakefield

Production Manager
Tim Tate

Vice President and Executive Group Publisher
Richard Swadley

Vice President and Executive Publisher
Barry Pruett

Associate Publisher
Jim Minatel

Project Coordinator, Cover
Lynsey Stanford

Proofreader
Nancy Carrasco
Carrie Hunter, Word One

Indexer
Robert Swanson

Cover Image
PhotoDisc/Punchstock

Acknowledgments

The more I write the more I am indebted to the people who have helped me. These are my acknowledgment of thanks and gratitude for those people.

Thanks to Ray Navasarkian at DevExpress. Without Ray's creative insight, support, and drive this book could not have happened. Ray is by far one of the most driven and fun bosses I have ever had the pleasure of working for.

I would also like to thank Joe Kunk, Gary Short, Julian Bucknall, and Kevin White. The goal was to get the book done in time for PDC and without their extensive support and co-authorship I never would have made it. Joe did a tremendous job on the XtraReports parts, Gary helped with examples on XPO, and Julian pitched in on chapters, editing, and a sound understanding of the book writing and publishing business. Kevin had to listen to all of my whining, which in all likelihood was the worst job but the often most helpful. Thanks Kevin.

A special thanks to Adaobi Obi Tulton, Jim Minatel, and all of the fantastic and patient people at Wrox. This is my second time working with Adaobi and each time gets to be more rewarding.

Thanks to all of the developers, evangelists, and managers at DevExpress who provided timely and invaluable feedback, including Platon Fedorovsky, Roman Eremin, Mike "Falcon" Rozhdestvenskiy, Mehul Harry, Erika Day, Jeff Cosby, Mark Miller, Oliver Sturm, Gary Short, Kevin White, Julian Bucknall, Azret Botash, Emil Mesropian, Rachel Hawley, Richard Morris, Andrew Logachev, Dmitry Babayev, and Serge Seleznev. And, of course, thanks to all of the DevExpress designers and developers for creating a tremendous suite of products and software.

Thank you to Alex and Noah Kimmel. They are teenagers now and need less of my time, but every moment with them has been my greatest blessing.

As always I am the first beneficiary of this work. It has been an insightful education, and I am fortunate to have had the opportunity.

Contents

Contents

Contents

Part II: Data Sources, JavaScript, CSS, and Themes

Contents

Contents

Part III: Ajax, Charting, Reporting, and Cloud Computing

Chapter 11: Asynchronous Computing for ASP.NET   509

Chapter 12: Adding Charts and Graphs to Your Applications   531

Chapter 13: XtraReports For the Web   551

Introduction

I like writing because every book is a birth. Books are neat little packages that contain information that has been pulled out of mind stuff, written down, edited and re-edited, printed, and glued together. When I get my author copies there is always a sense of satisfaction at having been part of creating something. Then, I take a deep breath and wait to see what the readers think.

Components and controls are always just one part of application development. Developers have to get requirements, design solutions and databases, and assemble all of the various pieces and then refine the total effort. Writing books and software follow some of the same practices: define, design, implement, debug/edit, ship, and support. In either kind of implementation, whether book or software, sometimes requirements and features make it in and sometimes they don't.

This book was originally slated at 400 pages. There were so many more features that I wanted to cover that almost 200 additional pages were added. In truth, there were discussions we had internally about how we could have provided more samples and probably produced 1,000 more pages. DevExpress offers many rich products and this book really just focuses on the ASP.NET controls. (A WinForms book could easily cover its own 1,000 pages.)

Although many people participate in the process of a book, writing a book for the most part is about telling a story from one person's perspective. For this book I looked at all of the products DevExpress offers in the ASP.NET space and tried to cover every single one of them. The ASPxGridView is a widely used product and it got a lot of coverage, but the juicy products like ASPxScheduler, ASPxTreeList, ASPxHTMLEditor, ASPxPivotGrid, XtraCharts, XtraReports, and many more products got extensive coverage. Some of these products even got their own chapters. If you glance at the table of contents you will see that XPO, the ASPxCloudControl, and client-side controls are all covered. There are even sections on general ASP.NET topics like JavaScript, Themes and Skins, and cascading style sheets. Unfortunately, in 600 pages I couldn't cover everything and some samples that would have been good samples didn't make it. To that end this book will have a product support page where I (and others I suspect) will be adding updated information for new releases, additional samples, and samples based on your inquiries. As I am sure you have challenges I didn't think of, if you send inquiries to me at paulk@ devexpress.com I will work out a sample, and write a blog or an article as a supplement.

The real purpose of this book is to provide our very important customers with another resource that will help them build great software. Every effort is made to make your development experience intuitive, productive, and fun. However, our products are feature rich and we understand that sometimes it helps to have someone point you in the right direction or provide you with a little guidance. This book is one additional bit of that guidance. If you need more than what is between these pages, just ask.

The first beneficiary of a book is the author. Even authors gain tremendous insight as part of the process of writing. One not so obvious insight is that our dozens of developers can turn out dot releases faster than I can write about all of them. This book was produced against versions 8.3 to 9.1. Just as I finished writing, 9.2 was released and 9.3 will be done by the time you are holding this finished book. As soon as I finish my final edits to the draft, I will be working diligently to create new examples, write about what is new, and updating material in the form of blogs and articles so that information — on 9.2 and 9.3 — will be available in conjunction with this book.

Introduction

Many people helped this book get published, and I couldn't have done it without their help. Ownership of the story is mine, and any mistakes are my responsibility. The objective was and is to provide more support and a better customer experience. The real heroes are our developers, and I hope I did some justice to their great efforts.

Part I: Grids, Editors, Navigation, and Controls

Programming with the ASPxGridView

This year is the tenth anniversary of my *VB Today* column for Codeguru.com and Developer.com. (My first article was published in *PC World* in 1992.) In that time, during which I've written hundreds of articles, readers have written to me more about two subjects than any other: keyboard hooking and grid controls.

Low-level keyboard hooks are cool. I started using them with DOS interrupts and C++ in the early 1990s. Grids of data, however, have the more practical and compelling everyday usefulness.

For years now, customers have asked me to make grids do things that they originally did not seem designed to do, including doing complex relationship modeling with grid nesting and performing real-time calculations with solutions that are more like Rube Goldberg machines than algorithms. Although crafting these solutions — sometimes against my better judgment — with nested user controls and hand-written asynchronous callbacks from scratch has been fun, I'm pleased to pass the baton off to the ASPxGridView.

The ASPxGridView is designed to support nesting, the power of Ajax callbacks, tuned performance for small and huge data sets, sorting, grouping, creating summaries, working with themes and skins, and much more. This chapter and the next chapter explore the ASPxGridView. I created the TotalFlight database for the samples used in these chapters because I wanted large amounts of data, but you can easily use Northwind or any other database that has a great deal of data to run the samples. (I used Red Gate Software's SQL Data Generator 1 to populate the TotalFlight database.)

Understanding How Ajax Delivers Real Performance to the ASPxGridView

A lot of conventional wisdom floats around, including the idea that to get high performance from your Web applications, you need to limit the amount of data you return to the client. Generally, limiting returned data required that each programmer limit possible query results or invent some mechanism for micromanaging high-data-prone controls such as grids. Then, things changed — and they seemed to change pretty quickly even for Internet time. Ajax had arrived.

Now called Ajax (in mixed case), the term *AJAX* (all uppercase) was coined in 2005. Originally, AJAX was an acronym for Asynchronous JavaScript and XML. AJAX was a derivative of capabilities created in the 1990s, including Internet Explorer's IFrame and Java Applets, and is based on the ActiveX object `XMLHttpRequest`, or remote scripting for browsers that don't support `XMLHttpRequest`. The term AJAX brought asynchronous callbacks to the general programming community's attention, and AJAX made controls such as the `UpdatePanel` accessible to all developers. (These later developments actually happened in 2005 and 2006.) Originally dubbed AJAX for JavaScript, XML, or asynchronous calls, it is now simply referred to as Ajax.

What Does Ajax Do for Web Developers?

Web forms have a life cycle. (Refer to "Appendix A: Understanding How Web Applications Differ from Windows Applications" for more on page life cycles.) When a page is posted back from the client to the server, it goes through the entire life cycle. This life cycle includes rerendering the page, which in turn causes the very visible page flicker users experience. Many times, much of what the user experiences is the result of static content and minor changes based on their interactions with the page; what they pay for with a postback is the re-creation of everything.

Ajax uses callbacks. A callback sends data back to the server, but only the relevant response is returned through the browser. Ajax plumbing literally used to require — as late as 2005 — programmers to inject dynamic JavaScript, wire up event handlers, and manually parse and stuff text returned into the client Web page with more JavaScript. (There are dozens of JavaScript examples throughout the book.) The benefit of employing all this specialized knowledge is that users had a better experience because they paid for data refreshes only when something actually changed on a page. Also, pages seemed to update magically.

You can still use wired-up Ajax with injected script if you want, but it is more error prone and requires great JavaScript authoring and debugging skills. With DevExpress controls and the `ASPxGridView`, you get the benefit of Ajax without the hassle.

ASPxGridView and Ajax

On top of all the features in the `ASPxGridView`, including sorting, grouping, filtering, and summaries, the `ASPxGridView` does three very important things that help you get the highest performance: It uses the database server instead of client-side script to manage data; it manages the client `VIEWSTATE` block itself by using a smart caching engine rather than sending tons of VIEWSTATE to the client; and it is built using Ajax internally. The UpdatePanel is supported — by setting EnableCallbacks to false — but the UpdatePanel is not required.

> Microsoft shipped the UpdatePanel in late 2005 (or 2006). Any control can get some Ajax support with the UpdatePanel.

To demonstrate the ASPxGridView, you can follow the examples in this chapter and the next to build the TotalFlight sample shown in Figure 1-1, which includes a 1,000,000-row result set.

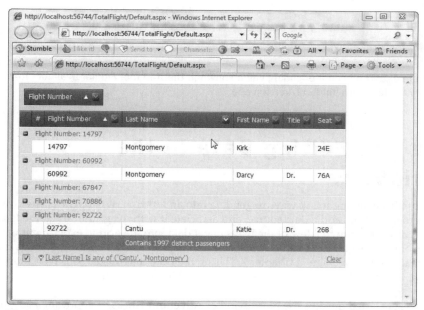

Figure 1-1: You can complete the TotalFlight passenger manifest sample by working through the samples in this chapter and in Chapter 2.

Another feature of the ASPxGridView is the EnableCallbackCompression property. IIS supports compression — a general approach — whereas the ASPxGridView will support compression for the grid if IIS compression is not enabled, a refinement from the general in IIS to the specific compression in the ASPxGridView. (Refer to the Appendix A section "Upgrading to IIS 7" for information on enabling IIS compression.) If you set ASPxGridView.EnableCallbackCompression to true, the grid checks to see whether the Accept-Encoding request header contains gzip or deflate — if content encoding is supported by the browser — and ASPxCallback compresses the result if supported. You can check the Accept-Encoding value by using a free tool such as Fiddler (see Figure 1-2) or exploring the Page.Request.ServerVariables["HTTP_ACCEPT_ENCODING"] value in Visual Studio debug mode.

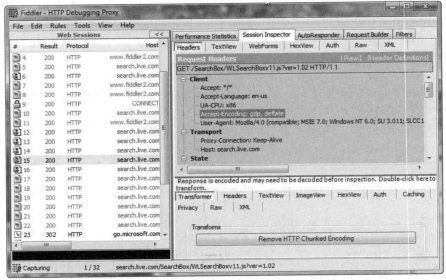

Figure 1-2: The Accept-Encoding value shown in the free tool Fiddler available from www.fiddler2.com/fiddler2/version.asp.

Binding and Editing Data in the ASPxGridView

You can choose from among many ways to get data into an `ASPxGridView`. The easiest way is to use declarative programming, add a data source, and associate it with the grid through the IDE. In this section, you can walk through a few of the ways to get data into the grid to experiment with the functionality of the `ASPxGridView`. (Because persistent objects and the `XpoDataSource` is a DevExpress product, it gets its own coverage in Chapter 7, "Using the Data that Makes Sense for Your Problem.") An exploration of editing column definitions is also included in this section.

If you want to get started quickly, use Northwind or AdventureWorks. If you want a large quantity of data, download the TotalFlight database from the Wrox code download site at `www.wrox.com`.

Creating a New Data Source from the Task Menu

To create a new data source — assuming that you have added an `ASPxGridView` — right-click the Tasks menu at the upper-right corner of the grid (see Figure 1-3) and follow these steps:

1. Click the `ASPxGridView`' Tasks menu (see Figure 1-3).

2. Select Choose Data Source.

3. From the Choose Data Source drop-down list, select `<New data source>` to start the Data Source Configuration Wizard.

4. From the Where Will the Application Get Data From? list, select Database. This selection adds the default data source name SqlDataSource1.

5. Click OK.

6. In the Choose Your Data Connection, click the New Connection button.

7. In the Add Connection option, change the Data Source to Microsoft SQL Server (refer to Figure 1-4).

8. For the sever name, enter .\SQLEXPRESS.

9. Leave authentication to Windows mode.

10. In the Connect to a database option, select the TotalFlight database.

11. In the Add Connection dialog box, click Test Connection. If the connection works, click OK.

12. Click Next.

13. Use the default name for the "Save Your Connection String to the Application Configuration File" step. Click Next.

14. In the Configure the Select Statement, specify the PassengerManifest view.

15. For the Columns, select the * check box for a SELECT * query of the view.

16. Click Next.

17. Click the Test Query button.

18. Click Finish.

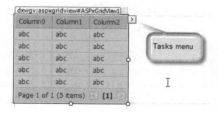

Figure 1-3: Click the tasks menu (indicated here), click Choose Data Source, and then click <New data source> to start the Data Source Configuration Wizard.

Figure 1-4: Configure the Add Connection dialog box as shown to add a connection string for TotalFlight to your web.config file.

After you finish using the wizard, a `SqlDataSource` is added to the Web page containing the `ASPxGridView`, the `ASPxGridView`'s `DataSourceID` property is set to the `SqlDataSource1` component, and the grid is updated to reflect the columns in the `PassengerManifest` view. If you look at the Source view of the Web page, the ASPX should look like Listing 1-1.

Listing 1-1: The ASPX after running through the new data source configuration wizard.

```
<%@ Page Language="C#" AutoEventWireup="true"  CodeFile="Default.aspx.cs"
Inherits="_Default"%>
<%@ Register assembly="DevExpress.Web.ASPxGridView.v8.3, Version=8.3.2.0,
Culture=neutral, PublicKeyToken=b88d1754d700e49a"
namespace="DevExpress.Web.ASPxGridView" tagprefix="dxwgv" %>
<%@ Register assembly="DevExpress.Web.ASPxEditors.v8.3, Version=8.3.2.0,
Culture=neutral, PublicKeyToken=b88d1754d700e49a"
namespace="DevExpress.Web.ASPxEditors" tagprefix="dxe" %>
<%@ Register assembly="DevExpress.Xpo.v8.3, Version=8.3.2.0, Culture=neutral,
PublicKeyToken=b88d1754d700e49a" namespace="DevExpress.Xpo" tagprefix="dxxpo"
%>

<%@ Register assembly="DevExpress.Web.ASPxGridView.v8.3, Version=8.3.4.0,
```

```
Culture=neutral, PublicKeyToken=b88d1754d700e49a"
namespace="DevExpress.Web.ASPxGridView" tagprefix="dxwgv" %>
<%@ Register assembly="DevExpress.Web.ASPxEditors.v8.3, Version=8.3.4.0,
Culture=neutral, PublicKeyToken=b88d1754d700e49a"
namespace="DevExpress.Web.ASPxEditors" tagprefix="dxe" %>

<!DOCTYPE html PUBLIC "-//W3C//DTD XHTML 1.0 Transitional//EN"
"http://www.w3.org/TR/xhtml1/DTD/xhtml1-transitional.dtd">

<html xmlns="http://www.w3.org/1999/xhtml">
<head runat="server">
    <title></title>
</head>
<body>
    <form id="form1" runat="server">
    <div>

      <dxwgv:ASPxGridView ID="ASPxGridView1" runat="server"
        AutoGenerateColumns="False" DataSourceID="SqlDataSource1">
        <Columns>
          <dxwgv:GridViewDataTextColumn FieldName="FlightNumber" VisibleIndex="0">
          </dxwgv:GridViewDataTextColumn>
          <dxwgv:GridViewDataTextColumn FieldName="LastName" VisibleIndex="1">
          </dxwgv:GridViewDataTextColumn>
          <dxwgv:GridViewDataTextColumn FieldName="FirstName" VisibleIndex="2">
          </dxwgv:GridViewDataTextColumn>
          <dxwgv:GridViewDataTextColumn FieldName="Title" VisibleIndex="3">
          </dxwgv:GridViewDataTextColumn>
          <dxwgv:GridViewDataTextColumn FieldName="Seat" VisibleIndex="4">
          </dxwgv:GridViewDataTextColumn>
        </Columns>
      </dxwgv:ASPxGridView>
      <asp:SqlDataSource ID="SqlDataSource1" runat="server"
        ConnectionString="<%$ ConnectionStrings:TotalFlightConnectionString
%>"
        SelectCommand="SELECT * FROM [PassengerManifest]"></asp:SqlDataSource>

    </div>
    </form>
</body>
</html>
```

The top of Listing 1-1 are the Page and assembly registration statements. The ASPXGridView is defined in the <div> tag section with the DataSourceID and columns specified. Note the definition of the SqlDataSource and the reference to the connection string and the select command. With the wizard and the declarative style approach, you can get a page up and running without writing a single line of ADO.NET code.

The `<%$ %>` tag is called an ASP.NET expression. ASP.NET expressions are used declaratively to set control properties at runtime based on connection strings, application settings, and configuration and resource file information.

To test the demo, click Debug ⇨ Start Debugging. The page will take several seconds to show up because the database contains a million rows in the `PassengerManifest` view. The page loads in about 20 seconds on my multiprocessor, 3GB, Windows Vista box running the Cassini server and SQLExpress 2005. These are pretty good results for everything running on a workstation; your results may vary but should improve in a deployment environment. (See Figure 1-5.)

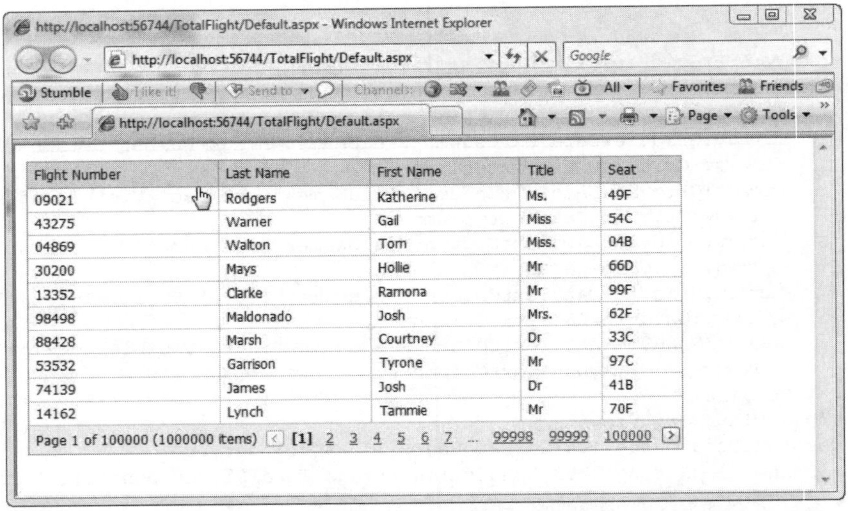

Figure 1-5: A million rows of data using the lightweight Cassini Web server, SQL Express, all running on a Windows Vista workstation.

I am not advocating that you routinely have million-row result sets, because 20 seconds is a long time in Internet time. (Anything more than a second is a long time in Internet time.) I am telling you that you can return many rows in the `ASPxGridView` if necessary, and the results will improve based on the deployment infrastructure.

If you need to modify the data source, you can select Configure Data Source from the Tasks menu. If the underlying schema changes, selecting Refresh Schema from the Tasks menu will update the columns in the grid relative to the current schema.

As a practical matter, begin building your applications with the amount and kind of information you need. Don't worry about matters such as speed too early on. You can always add hardware, tune, and write data-limiting queries after some careful profiling. It is worth stipulating performance characteristics in your requirements and keeping an eye on performance relative to these characteristics.

Editing Column Information

Among the several task menu items you can click, one is the Column item. From there, you can open the columns Editor Form. The Columns dialog box (see Figure 1-6) provides precise control over the ASPxGridView columns collection and each column's properties and sub-properties. You can use the Columns dialog box to add and remove bound and unbound columns, change the order of columns, and change just about every imaginable property associated with each column. For example, to start the grid with the data sorted by Flight Number, select the Flight Number column, expand the Data property, and change the SortOrder subproperty from None to Ascending.

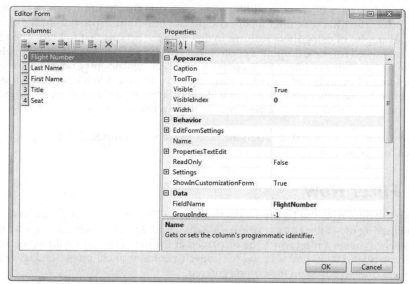

Figure 1-6: The columns Editor Form for managing column properties in the ASPxGridView.

Chapter 2, "Advanced ASPxGridView Computing," provides examples of defining unbound columns, and the section "Managing the Grid's Appearance," later in this chapter, tells more about using properties, including column properties. For more on sorting, refer to the "Grouping and Sorting Data" section, also later in this chapter.

Filtering Data

Filtering data is a critical aspect of programming, especially for controls such as the ASPxGridView, which is capable of showing large amounts of data. Customers don't want to scroll manually or page through large data sets. Customers want to put in some search criteria. Programmers, of course, are capable of handling filter queries entered through a control such as a TextBox and then filtering the data on a postback with an updated SQL query, LINQ, the Sort method of collections or by writing searching and sorting features manually. Of course, this isn't an efficient use of a programmer's time, either.

With the ASPxGridView, extensive support already exists for a variety of filtering. The ASPxGridView supports filtering through a filter row and filter menu, a header filter button (which is a drop-down list), or the filter control. The filter row, filter menu, and header filter button provide straightforward filtering. (I've included examples of using these features in this the sub-sections that follow). The ASPxGridView also supports advanced filtering through a control that supports a variety of Boolean-chained predicates, columns in the result set, every imaginable operator, and type-centric entry fields for the operand. In short, the filter control permits end users to build very complex filters in a visual and intuitive way, and these filters can be added programmatically as well. For the most part, however, the ASPxGridView offers an advanced filter that can be enabled and disabled without your writing a stitch of code.

You can start by working your way through the filter row and then through filtering options, including using the filter control and programmatic filtering at startup.

Using the Filter Row

You can enable the filter row (see Figure 1-7) in two ways. Click the ASPxGridView Task menu and select Enable Filtering or set the ASPXGridView's Settings.ShowFilterRow property to true. Either of these approaches causes a filter row to be displayed at the top of the grid with a TextBox for each column. Enter the filter data in the TextBox for a specific column or columns (see Figure 1-8), and the ASPxGridView is filtered based on the criteria entered.

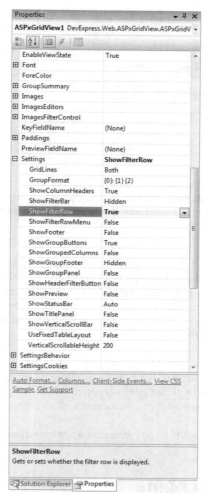

Figure 1-7: Click the Task menu and select Enable Filtering or set Settings.ShowFilterRow to true to display the ASPxGridView's filter row.

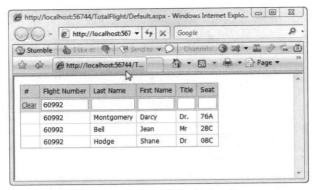

Figure 1-8: Enter criteria for the desired column or columns in the filter row, and the result set is filtered by the data.

In the example shown in Figure 1-8, the data is filtered by FlightNumber 60992. A minor limitation of the filter row is that it is displayed at the top of the grid and can't be repositioned, for example, at the bottom of the grid. A slightly more limiting factor is that the filter row fields do not permit operators. For example, you can enter a value to filter on, such as 60992 (for the FlightNumber), but you can't enter an operator with the value, such as >60990. To include operators, you need to include the filter row menu or turn on the filter control feature.

The filter row supports implicit-like — filters that use LIKE in a SQL WHERE clause — filters by using a wildcard (%, for SQL Server). For example, entering H% in the LastName column would return LastName LIKE H%, or all last names beginning with H. If a user is accustomed to seeing the * character as a wildcard, the ASPxGridView automatically switches * to %.

To clear the filter row items, click the Clear link that appears when filter data is present (refer to Figure 1-8).

Using the Filter Row Menu

A valid reason to use the filter row is that every user will understand the concept of entering the desired data. Some users may struggle with the concept of predicate calculus — building Boolean statements — that include operators and operands. Some users may understand simple filter values and the concept of applying operators such as the greater than operator (>) to these values. To provide filter values and operators, set the ASPxGridView.Settings.ShowFilterMenu to true. (See Figure 1-9.)

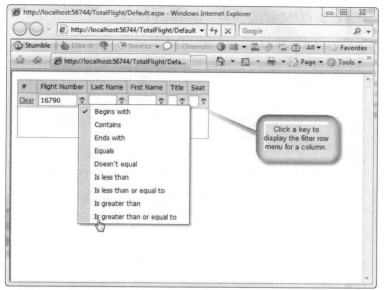

Figure 1-9: The filter row menu permits you to select an operator to apply to the filter value for each column.

The filter menu is a drop-down list that provides plain-text values that act as operators (behavior controllers) on the filter data. For example, selecting Is greater than — plain text that average users will understand — applies the > (greater than operator) on the filter data. As a programmer, you understand FlightNumber > 16790, what the user experiences as text, *is greater than* the value entered.

As a programmer, you can decide in advance the level of control the user will experience, or you can make this a configurable item and allow the user to indicate an experience level and enable or disable features accordingly.

Another final factor to consider is that the FilterRow and FilterRowMenu treat all filters as And operations. Advanced users will know the difference between And, Or, Not, Not And, and Not Or and may want more precise control over the filtering logic. You can offer these users advanced control, again without writing code, by turning on the filter control feature of the ASPxGridView (see the upcoming section "Defining Dynamic Predicates with the Filter Bar").

> The use of And to join filter row predicates is obviously visible when you use the XpoDataSource (see Chapter 7, "Using the Data that Makes Sense for Your Problem") in ServerMode and watch the queries sent to SQL with the SQL Server Profiler.

Filtering with the Header Filter Button

The Header Filter Button (see Figure 1-10) is a very easy filter for end users to use. Setting `ASPxGridView.Settings.ShowHeaderFilterButton` to `true`, places a button next to the column header. The user clicks the button, and a list of actual values from the result set is displayed in the drop-down list. Scroll to the desired value, and the grid is automatically filtered using Ajax.

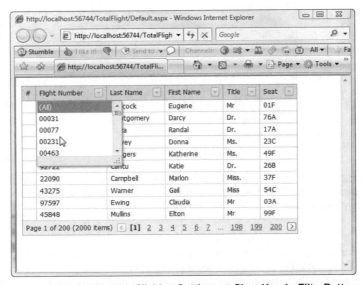

Figure 1-10: Setting the Clicking Settings ⇨ ShowHeaderFilterButton property to true displays a button next to the column name (in the ASPxGridView) permitting the user to filter by actual values in the result set.

How Do They Do That?

Properties that are displayed in the Properties window get there when a control author adds the `BrowsableAttribute(true)` attribute to a custom control. You can use the same technique for custom controls that you write.

Defining Dynamic Predicates with the Filter Bar

If you look in the Toolbox DX.*n.n*: Data tab, you see the `ASPxFilterControl`. An `ASPxFilterControl` is built into the `ASPxGridView`. To enable the advanced filter control, select `ASPxGridView.Settings.ShowFilterBar` and set it to `Visible` (see Figure 1-11). (The Filter Bar is set to `Hidden` by default.)

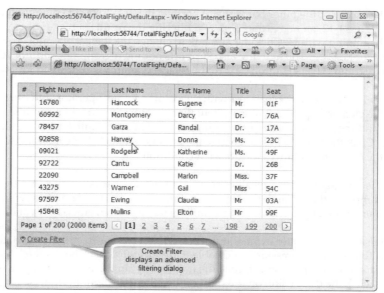

Figure 1-11: The Create Filter link (shown) displays a dialog box
(see Figure 1-12) that supports more advanced filter building.

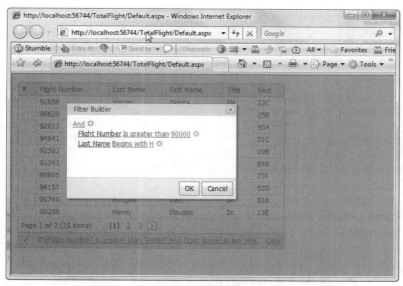

Figure 1-12: The filter control lets you add predicates and pick
columns, operators, and operands (that is, build filters from lists and
drop-down lists).

The power and flexibility of the Filter Bar is that it permits the user to build compound search predicates. For example, in Figure 1-12, an `And` group is shown filtering the result set by `FlightNumber > 90000 And LastName` beginning with H. Click the `And` link to change the logical operator. You can choose from `And`, `Or`, `Not And`, or `Not Or`. The `And` link also supports adding a group or condition, or removing all the conditions in a group. The (+) button next to the logical operator is shorthand for adding a condition.

The condition breaks down as a Boolean test with the column name, operator, and operand. Click the link for each of the elements to modify the element. For example, if you add a condition, the first column, Equals, and the `<enter a value>` prompt are added by default. Click the column name to change columns. Click the `Equals` link to change the operator, and click the operand to enter a test value. Clicking the (x) button removes the adjacent condition.

The filter control is designed to dynamically add a data-type appropriate control for the operand on the right side. For example, if the column is a `datetime` value, a `Calendar` date picker will be rendered for the value field. Using type-appropriate controls inhibits the user from entering invalid values.

When you are finished adding filter expressions, click OK. The `ASPxGridView` is updated to reflect the filter expression. To keep the expression but disable it, deselect the check box at the left of the filter expression. To redisplay the filter control, click the link (or key) in the Filter Bar. If you want to clear all filter expressions, click the `Clear` link on the right of the Filter Bar (bottom right; see Figure 1-13).

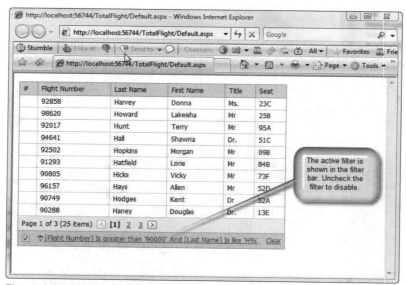

Figure 1-13: The active filter is shown in plain text in the Filter Bar and can be cleared (click the Clear link) or disabled by deselecting the check box.

You can combine filter features, too. For example, if you show the Header Filter Button and the Filter Bar, you can create a filter in the Filter Bar and then further refine your search by selecting a value from the list of items displayed in the Header Filter drop-down list. The effect of combining a filter in the Filter Bar and picking from the Header Filter is to have additional conditions displayed in the Filter Bar. For example, adding the condition `[Flight Number] Is greater than '40000'` in the Filter Bar and picking Adams (in my test database) adds the condition [Last Name] Equals 'Adams' to the filter expression in the Filter Bar. (Refer to Figure 1-14 to see ASPxGridView elements.)

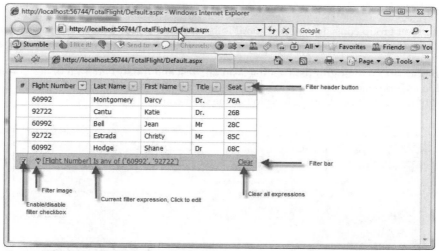

Figure 1-14: The ASPxGridView filtering elements.

Filtering with a Logical Or

Suppose you want to find a couple of specific flight numbers. You can use the Filter Bar to create expressions that use Or logic. For example, to find passengers on flight 60992 or 92722, follow these steps.

1. Clear the existing filter if one is present.

2. Click the Create Filter link in the Filter Bar.

3. Click the default And operator and select Or.

4. Click the Or link and click Add Condition from the menu (or click the [+] button). Now you should have two conditions.

5. Now you should have two conditions that both read
   Flight Number Equals <enter a value>.

6. Click the first <enter a value> link and change the value to 60992.

7. Repeat Step 6 and set the value to 92722.

8. Click OK.

The ASPxGridView shows only flights matching the two test values. (If you have modified the database or generated your own test data, pick two other flight numbers.)

> You can drag the filter control when it is visible, which permits you to see the visible grid results.

The result of the numbered steps is to create a straightforward WHERE clause with two predicates connected by an Or test.

Adding Condition Groups

A filter condition group consists of all the conditions combined using the same logical operator. For example, if the logical operator is Or, all the conditions under the Or are combined using the Or operator.

Figure 1-15 shows two filter groups: The first is an And test and the second is an Or test. (Your application may need to include some instruction to end-users about experimenting with the filter control or an explicit set of instructions describing how to use the filter control.)

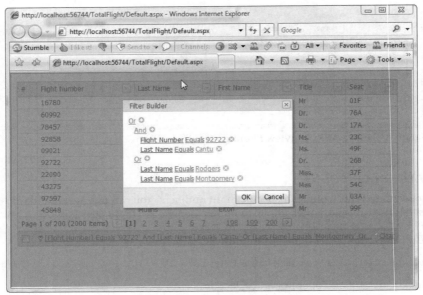

Figure 1-15: The topmost Or means that all the groups are combined by Or and the inner group is combined by And.

Say that Flight Number Equals 92722 is predicate A; Last Name Equals Cantu is predicate B; Last Name Equals Rodgers is predicate C; and Last Name Equals Montgomery is predicate D. The first subgroup uses And, so it is read as A and B. The second subgroup uses Or and is read C or D. With the outer Or, the whole expression is (A and B) OR (C or D). When you click OK, the subgroup C or D uses Or, which is redundant with the outer Or, so the second subgroup's Or is superfluous and removed (but the Or operation is still applied). Expanded, the whole expression is as follows:

```
[Flight Number] Equals '92722' And [Last Name] Equals 'Cantu' Or [Last Name]
Equals 'Rodgers' Or [Last Name] Equals 'Montgomery'
```

As a result of the expression, if Cantu is on Flight 92722, a row will be returned, and any flights with Rodgers or Montgomery will also be returned.

If you click OK on the Filter Builder, redisplaying it, the Or for Last Name Equals Rodgers and Last Name Equals Montgomery is implicitly inherited from the outer Or and won't be displayed in the Filter Builder (see Figure 1-16).

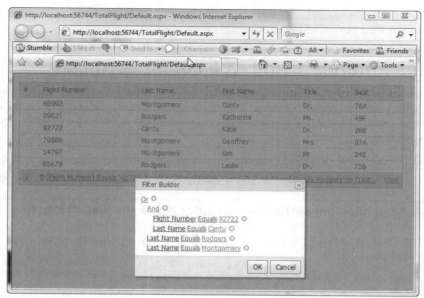

Figure 1-16: You can think of subgroups "inheriting" the logical operator of the outer group if the operators are identical; the result is that the logical operator is not redisplayed.

A nice customization to the Filter Builder (and ASPxFilterControl) *would be the ability to drag and drop and thereby rearrange filter predicates. DevExpress puts strong emphasis on receiving, considering, and addressing customer feedback, so if you think dragging and dropping predicates (or any other feature) would be cool, give us a shout at* www.devexpress.com. *Tell them Paul sent you.*

Filtering the Grid Programmatically

You have probably noticed by now that the ASPxGridView.Settings.ShowFilterBar options are Auto, Visible, or Hidden. That's because the filter capability is always enabled. Consequently, you can always apply a filter via the ASPxGridView.FilterExpression programmatically (as well as by applying SQL Server query filters).

To programmatically add a filter, use the actual column name FlightNumber instead of Flight Number, SQL operators such as > instead of Is greater than, and column data type values with the appropriate discriminator (for example, use the single quotation mark for string fields). Following are two programmatic expressions; the first returns flight numbers > 40000 and the second returns flights for Cantu.

```
ASPxGridView1.FilterExpression = "FlightNumber > 40000";
ASPxGridView1.FilterExpression = "LastName = 'Cantu'";
```

If properly defined programmtically, the filters will be converted to the user-friendly form and displayed in the Filter Bar (if visible). If the filters are improperly defined, the expression will be ignored. Properly defined expressions will always be applied even if the Filter Bar is hidden.

To disable the filter programmatically, set `ASPxGridView.FilterEnabled` to `false`. This programmtic option will be reflected in a visible Filter Bar.

Configuring Filtering Using web.config Settings

Applying a broader set of skills, you can perform tasks such as make the Filter Bar settings an external web.config setting without requiring a change in code, recompilation, and redeployment. You can accomplish this goal by adding a key to the `appSettings` section of the web.config file and using an ASP.NET expression.

Listing 1-2 shows the application setting in the `<configuration>` section of the web.config file, and Listing 1-3 shows the ASP.NET expression in the .ASPX. (Listing 1-3 is elided to keep the listing short.)

Listing 1-2: An application setting for the Filter Bar in the web.config file.

```
<?xml version="1.0"?>
<! —
    Note: As an alternative to hand editing this file, you can use the
    web admin tool to configure settings for your application. Use
    the Website->Asp.Net Configuration option in Visual Studio.
    A full list of settings and comments can be found in
    machine.config.comments, usually located in
    \Windows\Microsoft.Net\Framework\v2.x\Config.
  — >
<configuration>
  <appSettings>
    <add key="ShowFilterBar" value="Hidden"/>
  </appSettings>
</configuration>
```

Listing 1-3: The elided .aspx page showing the placement of the ShowFilterBar option and the ASP.NET expression.

```
<body>
    <form id="form1" runat="server">
    <div>

      <dxwgv:ASPxGridView ID="ASPxGridView1" runat="server"
        AutoGenerateColumns="False" DataSourceID="SqlDataSource1">
        <Columns>
          <dxwgv:GridViewCommandColumn VisibleIndex="0">
            <ClearFilterButton Visible="True">
            </ClearFilterButton>
          </dxwgv:GridViewCommandColumn>
          <dxwgv:GridViewDataTextColumn FieldName="FlightNumber" VisibleIndex="1">
          </dxwgv:GridViewDataTextColumn>
          <dxwgv:GridViewDataTextColumn FieldName="LastName" VisibleIndex="2">
          </dxwgv:GridViewDataTextColumn>
          <dxwgv:GridViewDataTextColumn FieldName="FirstName" VisibleIndex="3">
          </dxwgv:GridViewDataTextColumn>
```

```
      <dxwgv:GridViewDataTextColumn FieldName="Title" VisibleIndex="4">
      </dxwgv:GridViewDataTextColumn>
      <dxwgv:GridViewDataTextColumn FieldName="Seat" VisibleIndex="5">
      </dxwgv:GridViewDataTextColumn>
  </Columns>
      <Settings ShowHeaderFilterButton="True" ShowFilterBar="<%$
AppSettings:ShowFilterBar %>" />
    </dxwgv:ASPxGridView>
  ...
```

Grouping and Sorting Data

The ASPxGridView has many "wow" factors. In addition to filtering and sorting, another wow factor is the grouping capability built into the ASPxGridView. In this section, you explore sorting and grouping. (Custom sorting, which is also supported, is covered in Chapter 2, "Advanced ASPxGridView Computing.")

Sorting is enabled by default via the ASPxGridView.SettingsBehavior.AllowSort property. Click a column header and the grid is sorted in ascending order. Click the same column a second time and the grid is sorted in descending order. Hold the Shift key and click a second column header, and the grid is sorted on multiple columns. To implement custom sorting, refer to Chapter 2.

Grouping is supported through a property setting, too. By default, the group panel is hidden. Select ASPxGridView.Settings.ShowGroupPanel and set it to true, and a group panel is displayed at runtime (see Figure 1-17). All the end user has to do is click a column and drag the column header to the group panel, and the data will be grouped by that column (see Figure 1-18).

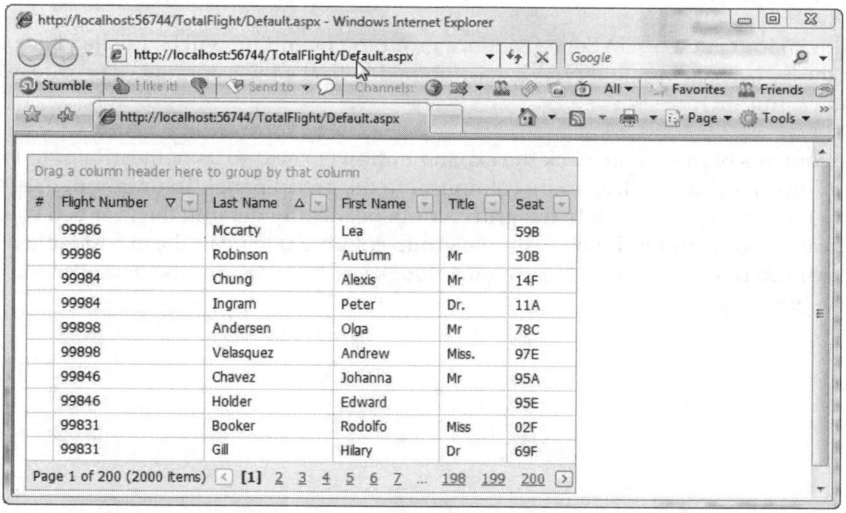

Figure 1-17: Show the group panel, and users can drag and drop columns to the group panel to group on that column.

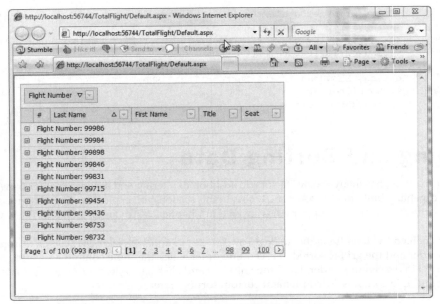

Figure 1-18: The grid grouped at runtime by Flight Number.

Users will find this powerful feature very useful, and you get grouping without writing any code. (The drag and drop grouping is very intuitive, and you are encouraged to brag to your customers a bit.)

If you use the XpoDataSource in ServerMode, a grouping operation will be pushed back to the server and run on the SQL Server as a query. When combined with the incorporated Ajax callback, the grouping feature is quick and slick.

To view the contents of the group, click the expand button (+) next to its name. (Refer to Figure 1-18.) To group by additional columns, drag more columns into the group panel. To ungroup, drag the column from the group panel back to the grid column header. By default, the grouped column does not appear in the expanded group. If you want the group column(s) to be in the expandable region, change ASPxGridView.Settings.ShowGroupedColumns from false (the default) to true. (See Figure 1-19.)

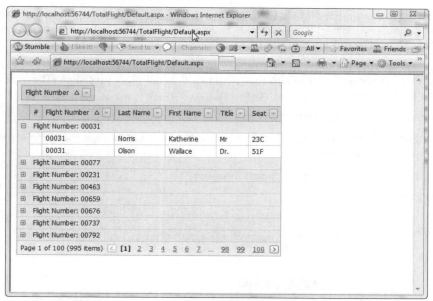

Figure 1-19: The grouped column values can be displayed in the expandable group region by changing Settings.ShowGroupedColumns to true.

Creating and Using Summary Values

The summary feature of the ASPxGridView supports adding ASPxSummaryItems to the grid and displaying these values in the summary footer. Traditionally, summaries were something I thought of as being on reports, and with the default Visual Studio Web controls, you and I would have to devise a separate mechanism for displaying summary values. The ASPxGridView has extensive built-in summary capabilities, many of which can be used without writing code. The ASPxGridView also supports creating custom summary values with event handlers. All summary values can be displayed in the footer of the grid with the summary value and some descriptive text.

To demonstrate summary values, I created a new view. The view is named PricedPassengerManifest and includes a PricePaid column in the grid view. The examples in this section demonstrate no-code summaries as well as custom summaries.

> Note that the LegManifestID was used in the PricedPassengerManifest view because unique keys aid in extracting specific rows from the ASPxGridView.

Calculating Summary Values

The easiest way to create a summary value is to show the footer (ASPxGridView.Settings .ShowFooter = true) and use the TotalSummary property to define the summary. For example, to display the average price per leg of a passenger ticket, click the Edit — ellipses (...) — button next to ASPxGridView.TotalSummary to display the total summary Editor Form. (See Figure 1-20.) Follow the numbered instructions using Figure 1-20 as a guide to define and display the average price per leg.

1. With the total summary Editor Form displayed, click the Add an Item button (top left of the `TotalSummary` toolbar). This step adds an `ASPxSummaryItem` to the `ASPxGridView` `.TotalSummary` collection property.

2. In the Properties window set the `DisplayFormat` to `Average Price: {0:2c}` to display the text and the average price as currency with two-decimal-place precision. (The `DisplayFormat` uses the same formatting characters as `string.Format`.)

3. For the `FieldName` property, select `PricePaid`.

4. For the `ShowInGroupFooterCo` property, select `PricePaid` to align the summary value with the `PricePaid` column.

5. For the `SummaryType` property, select `Average`.

6. Click OK.

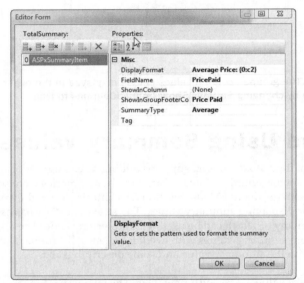

Figure 1-20: Fill out the total summary Editor Form as shown to create a summary for the average price paid per leg.

To test the summary, run the Web application (with Default2.aspx, or whatever the name of the Web page containing the `ASPxGridView` with summary is defined on, as the startup page). (See Figure 1-21.)

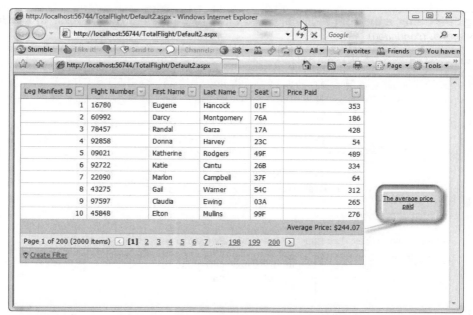

Figure 1-21: The average price paid is calculated and displayed without any code being written.

Calculating Custom Summaries

Programmers fall into a couple of camps when it comes to writing code. Some programmers prefer that the tools do as much as possible, and code is written when required. Some programmers prefer to write their own code. If I am trying to get a project done, I prefer to write only what is required, and only once.

The ASPxGridView supports creating a custom summary when one of the default options — Sum, Min, Max, Count, or Average — won't suffice. To create a custom summary, select Custom in the SummaryType (or indicate the type as SummaryItemType.Custom if adding the ASPxSummaryItem programmatically). Then, all you need to do is define a CustomSummaryCalculate event handler for the grid.

The revised code-behind for Default.aspx (the original page) demonstrates how to add an ASPXSummaryItem programmatically and uses a LINQ query in the CustomSummaryCalculate event handler to figure out how many passengers are distinct (see Listing 1-4).

Listing 1-4: Using a custom summary and LINQ to calculate the number of distinct passengers.

```
using System;
using System.Collections.Generic;
using System.Linq;
using System.Web;
using System.Web.UI;
```

Continued

Listing 1-4: Using a custom summary and LINQ to calculate the number of distinct passengers. *(continued)*

```csharp
using System.Web.UI.WebControls;
using DevExpress.Web.ASPxEditors;
using DevExpress.Web.ASPxGridView;
using DevExpress.Data;
using System.Collections;
using System.Data;

public partial class _Default: System.Web.UI.Page
{

  protected void Page_Load(object sender, EventArgs e)
  {
    if (!IsPostBack)
    {
      ASPxSummaryItem lastName = new ASPxSummaryItem();
      lastName.FieldName = "LastName";lastName.ShowInColumn = "LastName";
      lastName.SummaryType = SummaryItemType.Custom;
      ASPxGridView1.TotalSummary.Add(lastName);
    }

  }
  protected void ASPxGridView1_CustomSummaryCalculate(
    object sender, CustomSummaryEventArgs e)
  {
    if (e.SummaryProcess == CustomSummaryProcess.Finalize)
    {
      IEnumerable en =
        SqlDataSource1.Select(DataSourceSelectArguments.Empty);

      // figure out distinct number of passengers by first
      // and last name using LINQ with composite key
      var result = from DataRowView item in en
                   group item by
                   new
                   {
                     LastName = item.Row[1],
                     FirstName = item.Row[2] } into groups
                   select groups;
      e.TotalValue =
        string.Format("Contains {0} distinct passengers", result.Count());
    }
  }
}
```

The `Page_Load` method adds an `ASPxSummaryItem` to the `ASPxGridView` dynamically. The settings are the same as those set in the Editor Form (refer to Figure 1-20) and indicate that the summary is a Custom summary and will appear under the `LastName` column in the footer.

> It is worth noting that `CustomSummaryCalculate` is called once for `Start`, once for `Finalize`, and once for each item in the result set, so this event can be labor intensive for large datasets.

The `CustomSummaryCalculate` method can be generated from the `ASPxGridView` Properties window events view. The `CustomSummaryEventArgs` has a `SummaryProcess` value indicating the point in the summary calculation the event is in. There are three values: `Start`, `Calculate`, and `Finalize`. In the example, the only processing that occurs is when the summary process is ready to finish.

In the code listing, the data is returned as an instance of `IEnumerable` from the `SqlDataSource` `.Select` method. After you have `Ienumerable`, you can iterate over the data to perform calculations. You can, of course, process the enumerable collection any way you want, but `LINQ` is handy here. (For a complete guide to `LINQ`, refer to my book *LINQ Unleashed for C#*, published by Sams in 2008.)

The `LINQ` query is understood to mean *read each item in the collection grouping by last name and first name*, and the results are set in the `CustomSummaryEventArgs.Total` property.

> With `LINQ`, the `from` clause is the first to aid with IntelliSense. In the simplest sense, `LINQ` is like reverse polish notation SQL. Roughly.

Although `LINQ` is beyond the scope of this book, here is an interpretation of the `LINQ` query:

❑   `var result` is an anonymous type collection (usually) depending on the right-hand side query.

❑   `from DataRowView item in en` defines the the range (named `item` and typed as a `DataRowView`) from the source `en`.

❑   `group item by` is a group by clause.

❑   After the group by is `new{ }` when used this way, this is called a composite key for the group; use a composite key to group by multiple properties.

❑   The select statement is last.

`LINQ` is pretty advanced technology, and whole books, including mine and Charlie Calvert's *Essential Linq* (Addison-Wesley, 2009) are devoted to helping you master `LINQ`. The `result` variable contains a collection of the grouped composite key. Because it's a collection, you can ask (with code) about items such as the count.

After the `Finalize` step runs, the value you put in `CustomSummaryEventArgs.Total` is displayed in the `ASPxGridView` footer.

Calculating Total Custom Summaries

Suppose you want to enable multiple-row selection to determine, for example, how much an individual customer spent. You can accomplish this by again using a custom summary, enabling multiple-row selection, and processing each row to display the sum of the price paid. Follow these steps to display the sum of the price paid based on the rows selected in the `ASPxGridView`. (See Figure 1-22.)

1. Using Default2.aspx (the page using the `PricedPassengerManifest` view), select the `ASPxGridView` and enable multiple-row selections by setting `ASPxGridView` `.SettingsBehavior.AllowMultiSelection = true`.

2. Add an `ASPxSummaryItem` to the `Page_Load` method, as shown in Listing 1-5.

3. Define the `CustomSummaryCalculate` event as shown in Listing 1-5 (to initialize a total value, and add `PricePaid` based on the `CustomSummaryProcess.Calculate` state).

4. Add a server-side `SelectionChanged` event to re-bind the `ASPxGridView` (again, see Listing 1-5).

5. Switch to the page design view and click the `ClientSideEvents` property to display the ASPxGridView Client-Side Events Editor (shown in Figure 1-23).

6. Add the code `ASPxGridView1.PerformCallback();` to initiate an Ajax callback. Optionally add the `debugger;` statement to facilitate JavaScript debugging. (You will need to enable script debugging from the browser's Tools ⇨ Options menu item.)

7. Run the code.

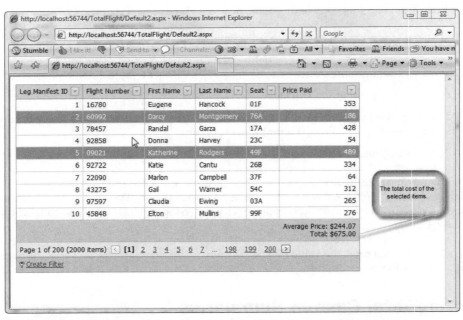

Figure 1-22: The average price paid and the total price based on the selection.

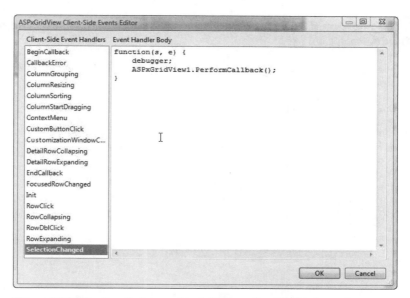

Figure 1-23: The JavaScript used to initiate a client callback on the selection changed with the debugger; call to aid in JavaScript debugging.

Listing 1-5: The additional ASPxSummaryItem that sums all the selected rows PricePaid fields.

```
using System;
using System.Collections.Generic;
using System.Linq;
using System.Web;
using System.Web.UI;
using System.Web.UI.WebControls;
using DevExpress.Web.ASPxGridView;
using DevExpress.Data;

public partial class Default2: System.Web.UI.Page
{
    protected void Page_Load(object sender, EventArgs e)
    {
      if (!IsPostBack)
      {
        ASPxSummaryItem totalSelected = new ASPxSummaryItem();
        totalSelected.DisplayFormat = "Total: {0:c2}";
        totalSelected.FieldName = "PricePaid";
        totalSelected.ShowInColumn = "PricePaid";
        totalSelected.SummaryType = SummaryItemType.Custom;
        ASPxGridView1.TotalSummary.Add(totalSelected);
      }
    }

    private decimal total = 0;
```

Continued

Listing 1-5: The additional ASPxSummaryItem that sums all the selected rows PricePaid fields. *(continued)*

```
protected void  ASPxGridView1_CustomSummaryCalculate(object sender,
  CustomSummaryEventArgs e)
{
  // initialize on start
  switch (e.SummaryProcess)
  {
    case CustomSummaryProcess.Start:
      total = 0M;
      break;
    case CustomSummaryProcess.Calculate:
      // a unique key is needed here, so LegID was used in the view
      if (ASPxGridView1.Selection.IsRowSelectedByKey(
        e.GetValue(ASPxGridView1.KeyFieldName)))
  e.TotalValue = (decimal)e.TotalValue +
          Convert.ToDecimal(e.FieldValue);
      break;
  }
}
protected void ASPxGridView1_SelectionChanged(object sender, EventArgs e)
{
  ASPxGridView1.DataBind();
}
}
```

Page_Load dynamically adds an ASPxSummaryItem. (Note that you can add multiple summary items per column.) The CustomSummaryCalculate event handler initializes the e.totalValue Property on CustomSummartProcess.Start. On CustomSummary.Calculate, the key field — LegManifestID — is used to determine whether a row is selected. (IsRowSelectedByKey requires a unique key.) If the row is selected, the e.FieldValue specified by ASPxSummaryItem.FieldName is added to e.totalValue. Finally, the server-side SelectionChanged event makes sure the grid is data bound.

You get the formatted output because of the ASPxSummaryItem.DisplayFormat value — Total: {0:c2} — set during initialization of the ASPxSummaryItem in the Page_Load method.

By combining techniques such as the ASPxGridView's custom summary feature with Ajax, JavaScript, and LINQ, you can create a wide variety of useful summary information, all displayable in the ASPxGridView footer while benefitting from the performance characteristics of Ajax (and LINQ, if you use LINQ).

Managing the Grid's Appearance

The power of the ASPxGridView is represented in a number of useful ways. The ASPxGridView incorporates Ajax for performance and ServerMode with the XpoDataSource. The grid also readily supports sorting, filtering, and summarizing with relatively little or no code. All these elements combine to give you the performance you need to provide the "wow" factor and utility that customers are coming to expect. (More features of the ASPxGridView, such as master-detail nesting, are covered in Chapter 2, "Advanced ASPxGridView Computing.")

The ASPxGridView also supports extensive support for CSS, themes, skins, and JavaScript. For example, click the ASPxGridView's Task menu and select Auto Format. In the AutoFormat dialog box, pick the Plastic Blue theme and then click OK. The grid is automatically updated to reflect the colors for the selected theme (see Figure 1-24). (For more on using themes, CSS, and JavaScript, see Chapter 10, "Using Themes, CSS, and JavaScript for Customizations and Enhancements.")

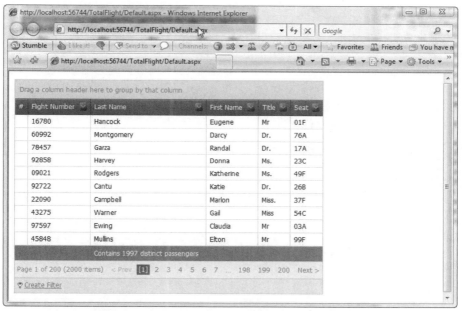

Figure 1-24: The Plastic Blue theme reflected in the ASPxGridView.

When you select an AutoFormat theme, an App_Themes folder is added to your project, and all the images and the Cascading Style Sheet (.css) that the theme is composed of are added to your project. Using pre-existing themes is a quick way to get a professional looking result quickly.

To complete the page, add a page title and some graphics; also, use some color to create the look you like. These elements require little or no programming but a lot of imagination.

Summary

The ASPxGridView is demonstrably one of the most advanced controls in any category. The ASPxGridView, as demonstrated in this chapter, supports automatic sorting, multiple ways to filter data (including a filter control), summary rows, and ServerMode with the XpoDataSource (see Chapter 6). The grid has Ajax support built in, so you get the benefit of the most advanced Web programming capability available and your customers get support. All of this technology is managed by DevExpress's programmers.

In Chapter 2, you can explore more features of the ASPxGridView, including master-detail nesting, custom sorting, binding to collections, client-side events, exporting, callback compression, using unbound columns, storing user settings with cookies, and much more.

Advanced ASPxGridView Computing

The one thing that I've learned from programming in multiple languages is that tools have one of the biggest impacts on productivity. My dad put it much more simply: "A craftsman is known by his tools."

A tool such as assembler that supports working with very small atoms of code requires a lot of effort to build up a toolset. On the other end of the spectrum, tools such as the ASPxGridView simply depend on you learning how to "turn" features on. Rather than roll your own search feature, use the built-in filter capabilities, for example. In this chapter, you continue your exploration of the ASPxGridView by reading about updating data, using collections as data sources, defining master-detail views, handling callback errors, exporting grid data, and much more.

The examples in this chapter continue using the TotalFlight database where it makes sense to do so; however, some sections, such as the section about grid templates ("Defining Template Regions"), use the Northwind database to demonstrate how to display images directly from a database.

Storing Changes

In Chapter 1, you explore some of the grid features related to reading data, including filtering, grouping, and using summary values, but reading data is only half of the picture. For applications, once a user gets the data they want, they often want to change it. The ASPxGridView supports using the grid to change the data and saving those changes back to the database.

The underlying operations for changing data are delete, update, and insert. The ASPxGridView has built-in metaphors for updating, deleting, and inserting data. Again, it is a matter of enabling these features of the grid.

You can enable write operations from the `ASPxGridView`'s Task menu by selecting Enable Editing, Enable Inserting, and Enable Deleting. When you select the write options from the Smart tags Edit, New, and Delete, links are added to the `ASPxGridView` for each row in the result set. Clicking these links in the grid is the first step in initiating the associated write action.

Implementing Write Behaviors Declaratively

There are two styles of programming in .NET: imperative programming and declarative programming. Imperative programming is when control flow and logic — the *how* — is combined with an objective — the *what*. For example, when applied to ADO.NET, imperative programming includes a connection object, optional transaction objects, using clauses, commands, SQL, and some more ADO.NET plumbing, depending on the goal. The newer kid on the block is declarative programming. Declarative programming leaves out control flow and logic — the *how* — and simply attempts to include the *what*. Declarative code manifests itself in a couple of ways. For instance, a SQL statement in the .ASPX is declarative — it instructs that a query should occur, but how it is to occur is left up to the agents of the declarative engine. (LINQ technology is declarative. LINQ permits you to query objects, data, and XML, but it indicates *what* to obtain in a result set, not *how*.)

Old timers like me may mistrust declarative programming a bit (just as we might mistrust text messaging and digital cable). The reason for this is that one gets used to control. However, control comes at a price. To have control over flow and logic requires quite a bit of additional effort. Consider saving the effort needed for imperative-style programming for things that aren't easily managed by declarative capabilities, where you get a bang for your buck (or unless you mistrust digital cable).

The quickest way to get declarative write procedures associated with your data source is to configure them when you configure your data source. To add update, insert, and delete behaviors to a `SqlDataSource` and enable write behaviors for the `ASPxGridView`, follow these steps:

1. Add a `PassengerMaintenance.aspx` page to the TotalFlight project.

2. Add an `ASPxGridView` to the `PassengerMaintenance.aspx` page.

3. Click the Smart tag and choose Choose Data Source ➪ <New data source>.

4. On the Configure the Select Statement step of the Configure Data Source Wizard (see Figure 2-1), select all of the columns and click the Advanced button.

5. In the Advanced SQL Generation Options dialog box, select Generate INSERT, UPDATE, and DELETE statements.

6. Click Next.

7. Click Finish.

8. In the Smart tag, select Enable Editing, Enable Inserting, and Enable Deleting for the grid.

After you complete the numbered steps, the `ASPxGridView` will contain Edit, New, and Delete links to initiate these behaviors, and the ASPX will contain `DeleteCommand`, `InsertCommand`, `SelectCommand`, and `UpdateCommand` attributes for the `SqlDataSource` (see Listing 2-1). The parameters will be added to the `SqlDataSource` within relevant tags; for example, the necessary delete parameters will be defined within a `<DeleteParameters>` tag.

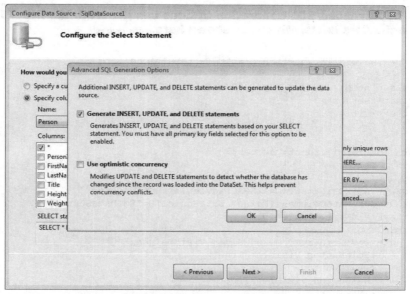

Figure 2-1: Generating INSERT, UPDATE, and DELETE statements declaratively.

Listing 2-1: The Advanced SQL Generation Options can generate the INSERT, UPDATE, and DELETE behaviors declaratively, as shown here.

```
<%@ Page Language="C#" AutoEventWireup="true"
CodeFile="PassengerMaintenance.aspx.cs"
  Inherits="PassengerMaintenance" %>

<%@ Register assembly="DevExpress.Web.ASPxGridView.v8.3,
Version=8.3.4.0, Culture=neutral,
PublicKeyToken=b88d1754d700e49a"
  namespace="DevExpress.Web.ASPxGridView"
  tagprefix="dxwgv" %>
<%@ Register assembly="DevExpress.Web.ASPxEditors.v8.3,
Version=8.3.4.0, Culture=neutral,
PublicKeyToken=b88d1754d700e49a"
 namespace="DevExpress.Web.ASPxEditors" tagprefix="dxe" %>

<!DOCTYPE html PUBLIC "-//W3C//DTD XHTML 1.0 Transitional//EN"
```

Continued

Listing 2-1: The Advanced SQL Generation Options can generate the INSERT, UPDATE, and DELETE behaviors declaratively, as shown here. *(continued)*

```
"http://www.w3.org/TR/xhtml1/DTD/xhtml1-transitional.dtd">

<html xmlns="http://www.w3.org/1999/xhtml">
<head runat="server">
    <title></title>
</head>
<body>
    <form id="form1" runat="server">
    <div>

      <dxwgv:ASPxGridView ID="ASPxGridView1" runat="server"
        AutoGenerateColumns="False" DataSourceID="SqlDataSource1"
        KeyFieldName="PersonID">
        <Columns>
          <dxwgv:GridViewCommandColumn VisibleIndex="0">
            <EditButton Visible="True">
            </EditButton>
            <NewButton Visible="True">
            </NewButton>
            <DeleteButton Visible="True">
            </DeleteButton>
          </dxwgv:GridViewCommandColumn>
          <dxwgv:GridViewDataTextColumn FieldName="PersonID" ReadOnly="True"
            VisibleIndex="1">
            <EditFormSettings Visible="False" />
          </dxwgv:GridViewDataTextColumn>
          <dxwgv:GridViewDataTextColumn FieldName="FirstName" VisibleIndex="2">
          </dxwgv:GridViewDataTextColumn>
          <dxwgv:GridViewDataTextColumn FieldName="LastName" VisibleIndex="3">
          </dxwgv:GridViewDataTextColumn>
          <dxwgv:GridViewDataTextColumn FieldName="Title" VisibleIndex="4">
          </dxwgv:GridViewDataTextColumn>
          <dxwgv:GridViewDataTextColumn FieldName="Height" VisibleIndex="5">
          </dxwgv:GridViewDataTextColumn>
          <dxwgv:GridViewDataTextColumn FieldName="Weight" VisibleIndex="6">
          </dxwgv:GridViewDataTextColumn>
          <dxwgv:GridViewDataTextColumn
            FieldName="SeatPreference" VisibleIndex="7">
          </dxwgv:GridViewDataTextColumn>
          <dxwgv:GridViewDataTextColumn FieldName="OriginCity" VisibleIndex="8">
          </dxwgv:GridViewDataTextColumn>
          <dxwgv:GridViewDataTextColumn FieldName="OriginState" VisibleIndex="9">
          </dxwgv:GridViewDataTextColumn>
          <dxwgv:GridViewDataTextColumn
            FieldName="DestinationCity" VisibleIndex="10">
          </dxwgv:GridViewDataTextColumn>
          <dxwgv:GridViewDataTextColumn
```

```
          FieldName="DestinationState" VisibleIndex="11">
      </dxwgv:GridViewDataTextColumn>
      <dxwgv:GridViewDataTextColumn FieldName="Address1" VisibleIndex="12">
      </dxwgv:GridViewDataTextColumn>
      <dxwgv:GridViewDataTextColumn FieldName="Address2" VisibleIndex="13">
      </dxwgv:GridViewDataTextColumn>
      <dxwgv:GridViewDataTextColumn FieldName="City" VisibleIndex="14">
      </dxwgv:GridViewDataTextColumn>
      <dxwgv:GridViewDataTextColumn FieldName="State" VisibleIndex="15">
      </dxwgv:GridViewDataTextColumn>
      <dxwgv:GridViewDataTextColumn FieldName="PostalCode" VisibleIndex="16">
      </dxwgv:GridViewDataTextColumn>
    </Columns>
</dxwgv:ASPxGridView>
<asp:SqlDataSource ID="SqlDataSource1" runat="server"
  ConnectionString="<%$ ConnectionStrings:TotalFlightConnectionString %>"
  DeleteCommand="DELETE FROM [Person] WHERE [PersonID] = @PersonID"
  InsertCommand="INSERT INTO [Person] ([FirstName], [LastName],
  [Title], [Height], [Weight], [SeatPreference], [OriginCity],
  [OriginState], [DestinationCity], [DestinationState],
  [Address1], [Address2], [City], [State], [PostalCode])
  VALUES (@FirstName, @LastName, @Title, @Height,
  @Weight, @SeatPreference, @OriginCity,
  @OriginState, @DestinationCity, @DestinationState,
  @Address1, @Address2, @City, @State, @PostalCode)"
  SelectCommand="SELECT * FROM [Person]"
  UpdateCommand="UPDATE [Person] SET [FirstName] = @FirstName,
  [LastName] = @LastName, [Title] = @Title,
  [Height] = @Height, [Weight] = @Weight, [SeatPreference] =
  @SeatPreference, [OriginCity] = @OriginCity,
  [OriginState] = @OriginState, [DestinationCity] =
  @DestinationCity, [DestinationState] = @DestinationState,
  [Address1] = @Address1, [Address2] = @Address2,
  [City] = @City, [State] = @State, [PostalCode] =
  @PostalCode WHERE [PersonID] = @PersonID">
  <DeleteParameters>
    <asp:Parameter Name="PersonID" Type="Int32" />
  </DeleteParameters>
  <UpdateParameters>
    <asp:Parameter Name="FirstName" Type="String" />
    <asp:Parameter Name="LastName" Type="String" />
    <asp:Parameter Name="Title" Type="String" />
    <asp:Parameter Name="Height" Type="String" />
    <asp:Parameter Name="Weight" Type="Int32" />
    <asp:Parameter Name="SeatPreference" Type="String" />
    <asp:Parameter Name="OriginCity" Type="String" />
    <asp:Parameter Name="OriginState" Type="String" />
    <asp:Parameter Name="DestinationCity" Type="String" />
    <asp:Parameter Name="DestinationState" Type="String" />
    <asp:Parameter Name="Address1" Type="String" />
    <asp:Parameter Name="Address2" Type="String" />
    <asp:Parameter Name="City" Type="String" />
    <asp:Parameter Name="State" Type="String" />
```

Continued

Listing 2-1: The Advanced SQL Generation Options can generate the INSERT, UPDATE, and DELETE behaviors declaratively, as shown here. *(continued)*

```
                <asp:Parameter Name="PostalCode" Type="String" />
                <asp:Parameter Name="PersonID" Type="Int32" />
            </UpdateParameters>
            <InsertParameters>
                <asp:Parameter Name="FirstName" Type="String" />
                <asp:Parameter Name="LastName" Type="String" />
                <asp:Parameter Name="Title" Type="String" />
                <asp:Parameter Name="Height" Type="String" />
                <asp:Parameter Name="Weight" Type="Int32" />
                <asp:Parameter Name="SeatPreference" Type="String" />
                <asp:Parameter Name="OriginCity" Type="String" />
                <asp:Parameter Name="OriginState" Type="String" />
                <asp:Parameter Name="DestinationCity" Type="String" />
                <asp:Parameter Name="DestinationState" Type="String" />
                <asp:Parameter Name="Address1" Type="String" />
                <asp:Parameter Name="Address2" Type="String" />
                <asp:Parameter Name="City" Type="String" />
                <asp:Parameter Name="State" Type="String" />
                <asp:Parameter Name="PostalCode" Type="String" />
            </InsertParameters>
        </asp:SqlDataSource>

    </div>
    </form>
</body>
</html>
```

Run the `PassengerMaintenance.aspx` page to verify that all of the CRUD (Create, Read, Update, and Delete) behaviors are supported without writing code. (You can run the SQL Profiler to see the application sending SQL to the database server.)

> *Using the declarative SQL does not reveal schema and SQL information to the client computer. The declarative SQL and parameters are not served to the client.*

When you click the Edit or New buttons, the `ASPxGridView` displays a user-friendly edit form style input region by default (see Figure 2-2) for entering new or modifying existing values for the row. The editing style can be changed by modifying the SettingsEditing.Mode property of the `ASPxGridView`. By default, Mode is `EditFormAndDisplayRow`. To change editing to an editing style similar to the `GridView`, change SettingsEditing.Mode to Inline.

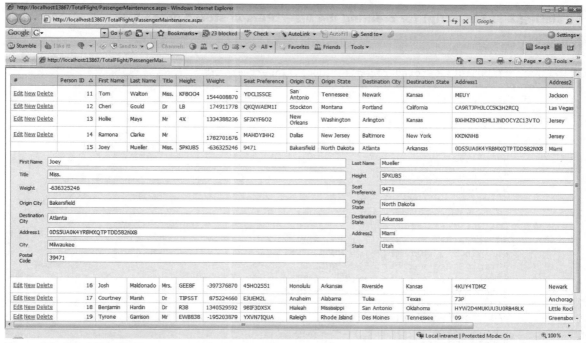

Figure 2-2: The ASPxGridView uses a dialog box style region for entering new or modifying existing field values.

Using Stored Procedures for Declarative Writes

You have the option of using stored procedures in place of literal SQL. To use stored procedures, define the stored procedure (or procedures), change the relevant command attribute to the name of the stored procedure, add a command type attribute, and initialize it with `StoredProcedure`. Listings 2-2, 2-3, and 2-4 contain examples of stored procedures for delete, insert, and update respectively.

Listing 2-2: Stored procedure script for deleting a person.

```
USE [TotalFlight]
GO
/****** Object:  StoredProcedure [dbo].[DeletePerson]
Script Date: 03/24/2009 16:32:59 ******/
SET ANSI_NULLS ON
GO
SET QUOTED_IDENTIFIER ON
GO
CREATE PROCEDURE [dbo].[DeletePerson]
     @PersonID int
AS
BEGIN
     DELETE FROM Person WHERE PersonID = @PersonID
END
```

Listing 2-3: SQL script for creating the InsertPerson stored procedure.

```sql
USE [TotalFlight]
GO
/****** Object:  StoredProcedure [dbo].[InsertPerson]
Script Date: 03/24/2009 16:36:22 ******/
SET ANSI_NULLS ON
GO
SET QUOTED_IDENTIFIER ON
GO
CREATE PROCEDURE [dbo].[InsertPerson]
    @PersonID int,
    @FirstName varchar(25),
    @LastName varchar(25),
    @Title varchar(50) = NULL,
    @Height varchar(8) = NULL,
    @Weight int = NULL,
    @SeatPreference varchar(10) = NULL,
    @OriginCity varchar(25) = NULL,
    @OriginState varchar(25) = NULL,
    @DestinationCity varchar(25) = NULL,
    @DestinationState varchar(25) = NULL,
    @Address1 varchar(30),
    @Address2 varchar(30) = NULL,
    @City varchar(30),
    @State varchar(25),
    @PostalCode varchar(50)
AS
BEGIN
    INSERT INTO Person
    (
        FirstName,
        LastName,
        Title,
        Height,
        Weight,
        SeatPreference,
        OriginCity,
        OriginState,
        DestinationCity,
        DestinationState,
        Address1,
        Address2,
        City,
        [State],
        PostalCode
    )
    VALUES
    (
```

```
        @FirstName,
        @LastName,
        @Title,
        @Height,
        @Weight,
        @SeatPreference,
        @OriginCity,
        @OriginState,
        @DestinationCity,
        @DestinationState,
        @Address1,
        @Address2,
        @City,
        @State,
        @PostalCode
    )

END
```

Listing 2-4: The SQL script for creating the UpdatePerson stored procedure.

```
USE [TotalFlight]
GO
/****** Object:  StoredProcedure [dbo].[UpdatePerson]
Script Date: 03/24/2009 16:46:13 ******/
SET ANSI_NULLS ON
GO
SET QUOTED_IDENTIFIER ON
GO
CREATE PROCEDURE [dbo].[UpdatePerson]
    @PersonID int,
    @FirstName varchar(25),
    @LastName varchar(25),
    @Title varchar(50) = NULL,
    @Height varchar(8) = NULL,
    @Weight int = NULL,
    @SeatPreference varchar(10) = NULL,
    @OriginCity varchar(25) = NULL,
    @OriginState varchar(25) = NULL,
    @DestinationCity varchar(25) = NULL,
    @DestinationState varchar(25) = NULL,
    @Address1 varchar(30),
    @Address2 varchar(30) = NULL,
    @City varchar(30),
    @State varchar(25),
    @PostalCode varchar(50)
AS
```

Continued

Listing 2-4: The SQL script for creating the UpdatePerson stored procedure. *(continued)*

```
BEGIN
    UPDATE
        Person
    SET
        FirstName = @FirstName,
        LastName = @LastName,
        Title = @Title,
        Height = @Height,
        Weight = @Weight,
        SeatPreference = @SeatPreference,
        OriginCity = @OriginCity,
        OriginState = @OriginState,
        DestinationCity = @DestinationCity,
        DestinationState = @DestinationState,
        Address1 = @Address1,
        Address2 = @Address2,
        City = @City,
        State = @State,
        PostalCode = @PostalCode
    WHERE PersonID = @PersonID
END
```

To use the `DeletePerson` stored procedure, for example, modify the .ASPX for the `PassengerMaintenance.aspx` page and change the `DeleteCommand` attribute of the `SqlDataSource` from

```
DeleteCommand="DELETE FROM [Person] WHERE [PersonID] = @PersonID"
```

to

```
DeleteCommand="DeletePerson"
```

and add the `DeleteCommandType` attribute after the `DeleteCommand` attribute

```
DeleteCommandType="StoredProcedure"
```

You can modify the ASPX directly in the .aspx page or you can use the Properties window. To specify the `DeleteCommand` and `DeleteCommandType` using the Properties window, select the `SqlDataSource`, open the Properties window, change the `DeleteCommandType` to `StoredProcedure`, and click the ellipsis for the `DeleteQuery` property. The latter step opens Command and Parameter Editor (see Figure 2-3). Modify the query in the command window or click the Query Builder button to display the Query Builder dialog box (see Figure 2-4).

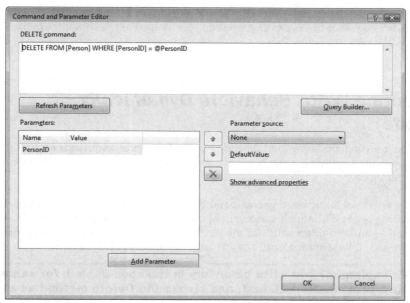

Figure 2-3: Use the Command and Parameter Editor to simplify defined queries or specifying stored procedures for the SqlDataSource.

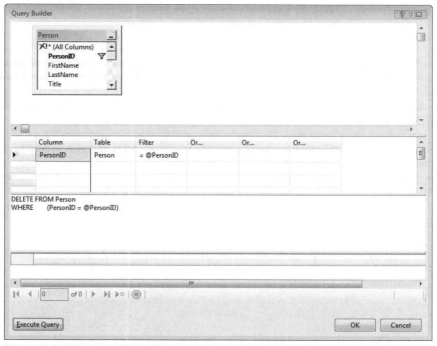

Figure 2-4: The Query Builder facilitates designing and testing queries for a data source.

If you want to get the parameter — in the example, the parameter is PersonID — from an alternative source such as a cookie or QueryString, you can specify the Parameter source in the Command and Parameter Editor (refer to Figure 2-3).

Implementing Write Behaviors Dynamically (with Code)

If you enable inserting, updating, and deleting but don't provide commands for these operations, a dialog box pops up displaying a message indicating that the SqlDataSource requires commands for the indicated operations.

You have the option of implementing command behavior programmatically. To implement the delete, insert, or update behavior, define the relevant operation's event handler Row*xxxxxxx* — for example, RowDeleting — and provide a value for the SqlDataSource's *xxxxxx*Command property. Listing 2-5 demonstrates an implementation of an ASPxGridView's RowDeleting event.

Listing 2-5: Implement grid write behaviors in the code-behind; for example, define RowDeleting, provide the SQL text, and invoke the Delete method as shown.

```
protected void ASPxGridView1_RowDeleting(object sender,
  DevExpress.Web.Data.ASPxDataDeletingEventArgs e)
{
  SqlDataSource1.DeleteCommand =
    "DELETE FROM Person WHERE PersonID = " + e.Values[0];
}
```

The ASPxDataDeletingEventArgs parameter contains information about the row for which the operation was invoked. For example, click the Delete link on a row and the primary key — PersonID for the PersonMaintenace.aspx page — will be passed in the ASPxDataDeletingEventArgs in the Values collection. Use the event arguments to build the correct command statement (as shown in Listing 2-5).

The ASPxDataDeletingEventArgs.Keys property (an OrderedDictionary) contains the list of parameter names for the event, and the Values property (also an OrderedDictionary) contains the parameter values for the event. Use the Keys and Values properties to assemble the command.

Enabling Callback Compression

The ASPxGridView has two properties: EnableCallbacks and EnableCallbackCompression. When EnableCallbacksTo is true, Encoding EnableCallbackCompression can be set to true. Enabling callback compression enables callback results for the grid to be sent compressed for compression-enabled browsers, improving performance by making better use of available bandwidth.

> *You can use a tool such as Fiddler to examine HTTP traffic and explore header values such as* Accept-Encoding, *and to see the compressed data moving between client and server. To use Fiddler with the Cassini Web server, replace* localhost *with* ipv4.fiddler. *For example, so that Fiddler can pick up the* TotalFlight/PassengerMaintenance.aspx *page, use the following URL:* http://ipv4.fiddler:port_number/TotalFlight/PassengerMaintenance.aspx. *(Make sure that the Fiddler application is running before you enter the URL.)*

By default, compression is disabled. When enabled, the ASPxCallback checks whether the client browser is compression-enabled by checking the Accept-Encoding header property for the gzip or deflate values. Don't enable compression if IIS HTTP compression is enabled.

Catching Callback Errors Using an ASPxHttpHandlerModule

An early challenge with asynchronous callbacks is that the callback is transparent to the user. If an error occurred, the Web application will appear to hang inexplicably. The reason for this is that a response to a Web page from a callback is rendered in script, not via the page's render behavior. Thus, if an error occurs during the normal course of operations, the results are unlikely to make it back to the client for rendering and the page render doesn't happen, resulting in an application that hangs. To solve this problem, the IHttpModule interface was introduced.

> *Another way that an "inexplicable" error can occur is if you deploy a Web site in debug mode and a* Debug.Assert *statement is hit. Unless interact with desktop is enabled for the Web server, the Web application will appear to hang while an Assertion Failed dialog box is waiting for a server operator to respond to the Abort, Retry, or Ignore buttons in the dialog box.*

If your Web application appears to be correct but hangs, search for and comment out all `Asserts`, *or select Allow service to interact with desktop for the IIS Admin Service. (See Figure 2-5.)*

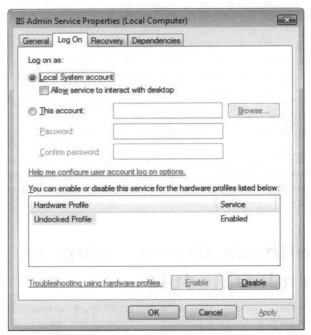

Figure 2-5: Select Allow service to interact with desktop to help debug arbitrary Web application hangs.

The `IHttpModule` was introduced to support implementing a custom HTTP module that will be called on every request, including Ajax requests. What the module does on the call is up to the module implementer.

DevExpress includes Ajax by default in the Web controls, and to ensure that you can handle errors (which are bound to happen occasionally) with grace, the `ASPxHttpHandlerModule` was implemented on top of the `IHttpModule`. The `ASPxHttpHandlerModule` is called for every postback or callback.

If a callback error occurs, the ASPxHttpHandlerModule can display the error associated with the control that caused the error or redirect to an error page configured in the web.config file.

Displaying Callback Errors

Without the ASPxHttpHandlerModule, a callback error will cause your application to appear to hang. In Listing 2-6, an arbitrary error for testing purposes was added to the PassengerMaintenance.aspx page. The error throws an exception on Page_Load. With no ASPxHttpHandlerModule, the application will appear to hang; as demonstrated in Figure 2-6, the ASPxGridView will show the Loading message indefinitely when the exception in Page_Load occurs.

Listing 2-6: An arbitrary exception is thrown to demonstrate the ASPxHttpHandlerModule (which is not present in the version of PersonMaintenance .aspx shown).

```
using System;
using System.Collections.Generic;
using System.Linq;
using System.Web;
using System.Web.UI;
using System.Web.UI.WebControls;
using System.Diagnostics;

public partial class PassengerMaintenance : System.Web.UI.Page
{
    protected void Page_Load(object sender, EventArgs e)
    {
      // comment out after we test our handler
      if (IsCallback)
      {
        throw new Exception("Test ASPxHttpHandlerModule");
      }
    }
}
```

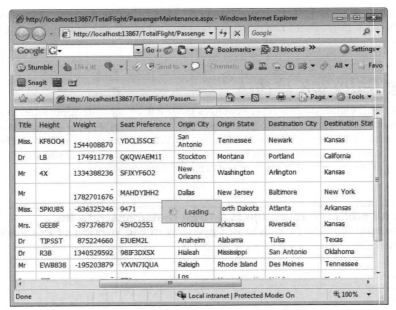

Figure 2-6: Without an ASPxHttpHandlerModule, a callback error will cause an application to appear to hang indefinitely (detectable by the never-ending Loading animated image).

The check for `IsCallback` is intended to throw the exception only when `Page_Load` is executed due to a callback. When you are debugging, the debugging will break on an exception that occurs during a callback, but whether you are debugging or not, the client will appear to hang (as depicted by Figure 2-6).

To make the error detectable by the client, add an `ASPxHttpHandlerModule`. For example, to add the handler from the `PersonMaintenance.aspx` page, click the `ASPxGridView`'s Smart tag and click Add an ASPxHttpHandlerModule to Web.Config (see Figure 2-7). The Smart tag item will modify the Web .Config, adding an `<httpModules>` tag and an `<add>` item for the `DevExpress.Web.ASPxClasses` `.ASPxHttpHandlerModule` (see Listing 2-7).

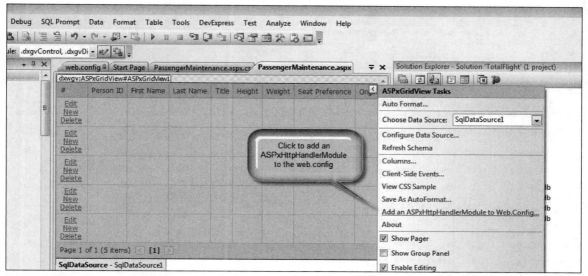

Figure 2-7: Choose Add an ASPxHttpHandlerModule to the web.config from the Smart tag to add callback handling to your Web application.

Listing 2-7: Clicking Add an ASPxHttpHandlerModule to web.config to add callback error handling to your Web application; the web.config will be modified with an \<httpModules\> section similar to the one shown.

```
<httpModules>
    <add name="ScriptModule" type="System.Web.Handlers.ScriptModule,
    System.Web.Extensions, Version=3.5.0.0, Culture=neutral,
    PublicKeyToken=31BF3856AD364E35" />
    <add type="DevExpress.Web.ASPxClasses.ASPxHttpHandlerModule,
    DevExpress.Web.v8.3, Version=8.3.4.0, Culture=neutral,
    PublicKeyToken=b88d1754d700e49a"
    name="ASPxHttpHandlerModule" />
</httpModules>
```

After you add the ASPxHttpHandlerModule, the callback error (which was coded intentionally for testing purposes) is presented to the client (as a pop-up associated with the ASPxGridView, see Figure 2-8) and the application continues to run.

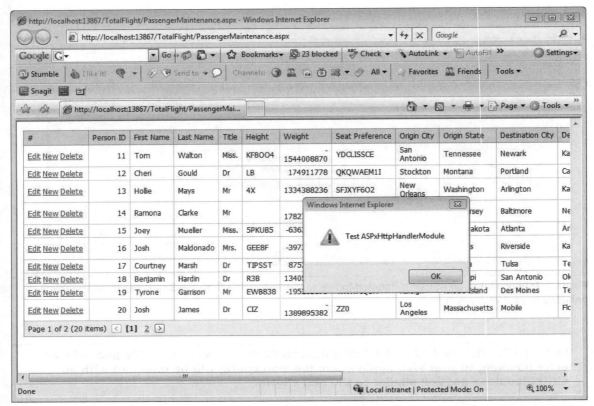

Figure 2-8: After the ASPxHttpHandlerModule is added to the web.config, the user is notified when a callback error has occurred.

Of course, notifying a client that an error has occurred is not the same thing as handling the error, but the basic idea in error handling is to let an application continue if it can so that the user can try something else or shut down gracefully. (The test code, as is, will obviously never run correctly.) In the event of real application errors, a good error-handling and logging strategy will help you track and resolve them.

Redirecting Callback Errors to a Specific Web Error Page

If you want to use an error page for a consolidated approach to error handling, you can add an <appSettings> entry for the DXCallbackErrorRedirectUrl key and provide the URL of the error-handling page. Listing 2-8 shows the <appSettings> section added to the <configuration> section of the web.config. As configured when a callback error occurs, the application will be redirected to ErrorPage.aspx.

Listing 2-8: Configure callback error redirection by adding the DXCallbackErrorRedirectUrl to the <appSettings> section of the web.config.

```
<configuration>
  <appSettings>
    <add key="DXCallbackErrorRedirectUrl" value="ErrorPage.aspx"/>
  </appSettings>
</configuration>
```

Users don't really need and generally don't want to know about the inner workings of a Web application. For the error page, you can put some basic boilerplate information about an error's occurring, trying again, or contacting the help desk (something like "We are sorry you are experiencing an error, but something has gone terribly wrong. Try hitting the Back button and trying again. Whatever you do, don't call the help desk because we outsourced customer service to Mars and they speak no known Earth language.").

Logging Errors in Application_Error Event

If you want to log the exceptions in a general location, you can use the Global.asax Application_Error and write the error information on its way to a general error page (specified in the DXCallbackErrorRedirectUrl). If you wait until the handling process reaches the callback error-handling page, the exception will have already been cleared.

Rather than repeat information, I refer you to the section in Appendix A called "Programming Application-Level Events." That section demonstrates how to code the Global.asax Application_Error and write to the EventLog; it also includes a subsection on coding an application installer to create an event source.

Implementing an Error Logging IHttpModule

You can implement a custom IHttpModule by implementing the interface and registering the custom module in the <httpModules> section the same way that the ASpxHttpHandlerModule is registered. To implement a custom IhttpModule that logs application errors, follow these steps:

1. Add a class file to the App_Code section of a Web application. (For the demo, I used CustomHttpHandler for the class filename.)

2. Inherit from IHttpModule and implement the Init and Dispose method. (For this example, only Init is needed; refer to Listing 2-9.)

3. In the Init method, attach an event handler to the HttpApplication.Error event. (An instance of the HttpApplication object representing your application is passed to the Init method.)

4. In the event handler, the object sender parameter is an instance of the exception that represents the error. Write the error message to the event log.

5. Add the registration <Add> tag to the <httpModules> section of the web.config. (Refer to Listing 2-10.)

6. Rebuild the application and test the error handler by throwing a test exception.

> For more on an existing general exception handler, refer to the MSDN link `http://msdn.microsoft.com/en-us/library/aa479332.aspx`, which introduces the ELMAH (Error Logging Modules and Handler) topic.

Listing 2-9: The code that implements CustomHttpHandler, an exception-logging module.

```csharp
using System;
using System.Collections.Generic;
using System.Linq;
using System.Web;
using System.Configuration;
using System.Diagnostics;

public class CustomHttpHandler : IHttpModule
{
    public CustomHttpHandler()
    {

    }

  public string ModuleName
  {
      get {return "CustomHttpHandler"; }
  }

  void context_Error(object sender, EventArgs e)
  {
    HttpApplication application = (HttpApplication)sender;
    HttpContext context = application.Context;

    Exception exception = context.Server.GetLastError();
    EventLog.WriteEntry("Application",
      GetMessage(context.Server.GetLastError()));
  }

    private string GetMessage(Exception exception)
  {
    if (exception == null) return "nothing";
    if (exception.InnerException != null)
      return exception.InnerException.Message;
    else
      return exception.Message;
  }
#region IHttpModule Members

  public void  Dispose()
  {
  }

  public void  Init(HttpApplication context)
```

```
    {
        context.Error += new EventHandler(context_Error);
    }
#endregion
}
```

Listing 2-10: The <httpModules> for TotalFlight containing the CustomHttpModule registration.

```
<httpModules>
        <add name="ScriptModule" type="System.Web.Handlers.ScriptModule,
        System.Web.Extensions, Version=3.5.0.0, Culture=neutral,
        PublicKeyToken=31BF3856AD364E35" />
        <add type="DevExpress.Web.ASPxClasses.ASPxHttpHandlerModule,
        DevExpress.Web.v8.3, Version=8.3.4.0, Culture=neutral,
        PublicKeyToken=b88d1754d700e49a"
        name="ASPxHttpHandlerModule" />
        <add type="CustomHttpHandler" name="CustomHttpHandler" />
        </httpModules>
```

The key functionality here is the `context_Error` event handler. `Context_Error` is a standard `EventHandler`; you just have to know that object sender is an instance of the `Exception` object. To glean more information from the `IhttpModule`, use the debugger to step through it. Notice that in the example, `GetMessage` returns the `InnerException.Message` if there is an `InnerException`.

To make the sample more robust, add a `try...catch` block around the code in the event that `GetLastError` returns null or to catch general problems. For more information on using the `EventLog`, see "Programming Application-Level Events" in Appendix A.

Binding the ASPxGridView to an ArrayList or Collection

Many programmers use custom objects. I am often one of them. Although DevExpress's eXpress Persistent Objects (XPO) and technologies such as LINQ to SQL are great technologies, and custom objects require more up-front work, I generally prefer (and, out of habit, use) custom objects for enterprise applications. The simplest reason for this preference is that historically, custom objects are always available, they always work, and customers don't always want to buy other-party code. (Generally, eschewing other-party code ends up being penny wise and pound foolish, but some projects and some customers demand custom code.) No worries: The `ASPxGridView` works great with `ArrayLists` or the better choice of generic `Lists`.

Where custom objects shine is when you have to use composite entities. It is seldom always the case that all an application needs are one-to-one entities mapped directly to tables. (In fact, a class library of only entity objects is often considered a weak database-composed system.) A more likely scenario is that you will have entities, boundary, and controller classes as well as composite entities derived from columns from multiple tables. In the latter case, using something like XPO or LINQ to SQL results in read-only entities derived from a view. Unfortunately, views are not writable by their very nature. The solution is to be fearless and use XPO or LINQ to SQL (of course, we'd like you to consider XPO) when you are working with simple entities and switch to custom objects for composited entities. This is because there is no reason you cannot update a database based on changes to composited entities in custom code; you are writing the behavior so that you can make the composited entities write to separate tables as part of a transaction.

In the following subsections, you can explore binding an ArrayList and a generic collection to the ASPxGridView.

Binding an ArrayList to an ASPxGridView

You can bind an ArrayList to an ASPxGridView. All you need is an ArrayList with some data or objects; then, assign the ArrayList to the ASPxGridView's DataSource property and call DataBind (see Listing 2-11). The grid will provide columns and column names, and paging and filtering are supported.

Listing 2-11: Binding an ArrayList to an ASPxGridView.

```
using System;
using System.Collections.Generic;
using System.Collections;
using System.Linq;
using System.Web;
using System.Web.UI;
using System.Web.UI.WebControls;
using BusinessObjects;

public partial class DefineAirports : System.Web.UI.Page
{
  private ArrayList airports = new ArrayList();

  protected void Page_Load(object sender, EventArgs e)
  {
    InitializeAirports();
    ASPxGridView1.DataSource = airports;
    ASPxGridView1.DataBind();
  }

  private void InitializeAirports()
  {
    airports.Add(new Airport(1, "KADG", "Adrian",
      "Lenawee County Airport"));
    airports.Add(new Airport(2, "35D", "Allegan",
      "Padgham Field Airport"));
    airports.Add(new Airport(3, "KAMN", "Alma",
      "Gratiot Community Airport"));
    airports.Add(new Airport(4, "KAPN", "Alpena",
      "Alpena County Regional Airport"));
    airports.Add(new Airport(5, "53M", "Alpena",
      "Silver City Airpark"));
    airports.Add(new Airport(6, "KARB", "Ann Arbor",
      "Ann Arbor Municipal Airport"));
```

```
        airports.Add(new Airport(7, "Y93", "Atlanta",
          "Atlanta Municipal Airport"));
        airports.Add(new Airport(8, "39G", "Avoca",
          "Avoca Airport"));
        airports.Add(new Airport(9, "07D", "Avoca",
          "Tackaberry Airport"));
        airports.Add(new Airport(10, "KBAX", "Bad Axe",
          "Huron County Memorial Airport"));
    }
}
```

The data were borrowed from www.airnav.com, which contains detailed information about airports. The Airport class contains fields such as AirportID, City, Identifier, and Name. As you can see from Listing 2-11, the airport objects are simply stored in the ArrayList and bound to the ASPxGridView.

The key here is that although you can do a thing, it is not always the right thing to do. At this point in the evolution of .NET, there are few times, if any, that I would use an ArrayList. If you are using custom objects, use a generic List. Another disadvantage in using the ArrayList is that the ASPxGridView is going to behave in a read-only manner. (Figure 2-9 shows the data with an applied filter in the ASPxGridView.)

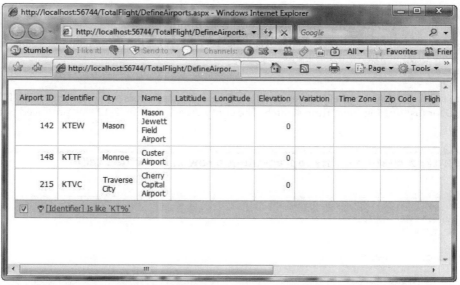

Figure 2-9: The ArrayList of Airport objects bound to an ASPxGridView and filtered.

Where the caveat to eschew the `ArrayList` is concerned, I would go so far as to even take the time to replace legacy code that used an `ArrayList` with a generic `List<T>` in all circumstances.

Binding a Generic Collection to an ASPxGridView

The steps for binding a generic collection to an `ASPxGridView` are identical for binding an `ArrayList` to an `ASPxGridView` — get some data and put it in a `List<T>`, assign the list to the `ASPxGridView` `.DataSource`, and call `DataBind`. Basically, a `List<T>` is just a much better mousetrap, a much better way to keep a collection of stuff.

Because showing the `DataSource` and `DataBind` statements isn't useful, I focus on some new skills. The subsections demonstrate how to define a custom entity and a custom collection, initialize the collection using ADO.NET, and incorporate unit test projects into your Web application. The chapter includes code that demonstrates how to bind the collection of objects. (It is worth noting that the custom type, collection, and ADO.NET perform exactly the same function as eXpress Persistent Objects (XPO), so if your entities are as lightweight as the example entities are, use XPO.)

Defining Custom Entities and Collections

An entity is a class that generally represents a table in a database. These are very basic kinds of classes; entity classes are the easiest to identify and build in any application. The best piece of advice I can give you about entities is that you do not need to define entity classes for every table. Be selective if you are rolling your own entities; define only those that you absolutely will be using in code.

> If you elect to roll your own custom entities, strongly consider `CodeRush`. `CodeRush` is a meta-programming tool that will help you produce code about ten times faster than if you type each element manually.

There are several ways to come by an entity, including code generators you or others write, LINQ to SQL, XPO, or just writing them from scratch. The entity class in Listing 2-12 was produced with `CodeRush`.

Listing 2-12: A custom entity representing a row in the Cities table.

```
using System;
using System.Collections.Generic;
using System.Linq;
using System.Web;

namespace BusinessObjects
{
  public class City
  {
    public City()
    {
    }

    /// <summary>
    /// Initializes a new instance of the City class.
```

```
/// </summary>
/// <param name="hubID"></param>
/// <param name="city"></param>
/// <param name="state"></param>
/// <param name="country"></param>
public City(int hubID, string city, string state, string country)
{
  this.hubID = hubID;
  this.cityName = city;
  this.state = state;
  this.country = country;
}

private int hubID;
public int HubID
{
  get { return hubID; }
}

private string cityName;
public string CityName
{
  get { return cityName; }
  set { cityName = value; }
}

private string state;
public string State
{
  get { return state; }
  set { state = value; }
}

private string country = "USA";
public string Country
{
  get { return country; }
  set { country = value; }
}
  }
}
```

City is a plain-vanilla entity class that maps one-to-one with a row in the TotalFlight Cities table. (The only saving grace for having a custom entity that is this basic is that CodeRush wrote most of the code for me.)

Next, add a class to the project and name the class CityList. Define CityList to inherit from List<City>. Using inheritance here is optional. You could just use List<City> directly in the code. Inheritance is a strategy to consider in case you want to add more behaviors — read "business rules" — to the generic collection. Listing 2-13 contains a definition of the CityList class.

Listing 2-13: Inheritance is used to provide a place to add business rules to the collection, as well as to serve as a good receptacle for adding extension methods.

```csharp
using System;
using System.Collections.Generic;
using System.Linq;
using System.Web;

namespace BusinessObjects
{

  public class CityList : List<City>
  {
    public CityList() { }

    private void AddCity(
      int hubID, string city,
      string state, string country)
    {
      this.Add(new City(hubID, city, state, country));
    }
  }
}
```

Notice that `CityList` in this case simply adds a convenience method for adding new items. Remember that `List<T>` has many useful capabilities already, including adding, removing, and finding items, as well as sorting items in the collection.

On a final note, notice that `City` and `CityList` are defined in a separate namespace, `BusinessObjects`. These classes are also defined in a `Class Library` rather than in the `App_Code` folder of the Web project. The reasons for composing your application in chunks has to do with compartmentalization, separation of responsibilities, limiting dependencies, facilitating unit testing, and, to some extent, promoting reuse. My projects are routinely compartmentalized into separate projects for the reasons stated. For instance, it's hard to unit test entities, business rules, and ADO.NET plumbing if these are sitting inside your Web project.

Initializing Custom Collections

The following code demonstrates plain-vanilla ADO.NET code to initialize a custom collection (see Listing 2-14). If you are very comfortable with ADO.NET, you can skim the code for useful bits and skip to the next section, "Using Test Projects."

Listing 2-14: Plain-vanilla ADO.NET code to read a collection of objects.

```csharp
using System;
using System.Collections.Generic;
using System.Linq;
using System.Web;
using System.Data.SqlClient;
using System.Configuration;

namespace BusinessObjects
```

```
{
  public class CityHelper
  {

    public static CityList GetCities()
    {
      string connectionString =
        ConfigurationManager.ConnectionStrings[
        "TotalFlightConnectionString"].ConnectionString;

      using(SqlConnection connection = new SqlConnection(connectionString))
      {
        connection.Open();
        SqlCommand command =
         new SqlCommand("SELECT * FROM CITIES", connection);
        SqlDataReader reader = command.ExecuteReader();

        return ReadCities(reader);
      }
    }

    private static CityList ReadCities(SqlDataReader reader)
    {
      if (reader == null)
        throw new NullReferenceException();

      CityList list = new CityList();
      while (reader.Read())
      {
        list.Add(ReadCity(reader));
      }
      return list;
    }

    private static City ReadCity(SqlDataReader reader)
    {
      int hubid = SafeRead<int>("HubID", reader, -1);
      string city = SafeRead<string>("City", reader, "");
      string state = SafeRead<string>("State", reader, "");
      string country = SafeRead<string>("Country", reader, "USA");
      return new City(hubid, city, state, country);
    }

    private static T SafeRead<T>(string fieldname,
      SqlDataReader reader, T defaultValue)
    {
      object o = reader[fieldname];
      return o == null || o == System.DBNull.Value ?
        defaultValue : (T)Convert.ChangeType(o, typeof(T));
    }
  }
}
```

The preceding code simply reads the entire `Cities` table. (If a table will likely change infrequently, it is a good candidate to cache objects like these. Refer to the section in Appendix A called "Programming Application-level Events" for more information on caching in the Global.asax.) Very little of this code is directly reusable except for `SafeRead`, which is field-helper reader. If you have to write code like this because XPO or LINQ to SQL is not an option, check out my article "The Only Data Access Layer You'll Ever Need" at www.developer.com/net/vb/article.php/3650241 for more information on making a generally reusable data access layer. That article describes how to extract the changing bits such as the field reader without rewriting all the general ADO.NET plumbing. As a preferable choice, consider using eXpress Persistent Objects (XPO).

Now that you have an entity type, a collection, and a means of populating the collection, a great next step is to write a unit test.

Using Test Projects

A popular approach to development is test-driven development known as TDD. The basic idea behind TTD is to write the tests first and then write just enough code to pass the test. I use a variation on TDD. Instead of pure TDD, consider writing code such as the entity, collection, and reader and then immediately writing a test to verify that everything compiles and reads and populates the collection as desired. Pure TDD is okay, but writing the code first and the tests immediately after is easier, and the results are approximately the same. Where one might run into trouble is by writing too much production code and deferring tests until later or not writing them at all.

The test for the `CityList` is straightforward: Call the `CityHelper.GetCities()` method and see whether you get valid data. Listing 2-15 contains a lot of `TestProject` boilerplate code and the `ReadAllCitiesTest` (at the end of the listing).

Listing 2-15: Write some production code and back it with tests; because you are writing the tests against code, writing the tests is very easy.

```
using System;
using System.Text;
using System.Collections.Generic;
using System.Linq;
using Microsoft.VisualStudio.TestTools.UnitTesting;
using BusinessObjects;

namespace TestProject1
{
  [TestClass]
  public class CityTests
  {
    public CityTests()
    {
    }

    private TestContext testContextInstance;

    public TestContext TestContext
    {
      get
      {
```

```
        return testContextInstance;
      }
      set
      {
        testContextInstance = value;
      }
    }

    #region Additional test attributes

  #endregion

    [TestMethod]
    public void ReadAllCitiesTest()
    {
      CityList list = CityHelper.GetCities();
      //Dumper.Dump<City>(list, Console.Out);
      Dumper.LinqDump<City>(list, Console.Out);
    }
  }
}
```

Notice that there are two methods shown for dumping an object's state. Dumper methods are invaluable for viewing an object's state during testing and debugging. .NET shipped an `ObjectDumper` with LINQ, and you are welcome to use that existing code or experiment with the two object dumpers, described in the next two subsections.

Implementing an Object Dumper Using Reflection

In my 1996 book, *Using C++ , Special Edition* (Que), I referred to testing code as scaffolding. None of the editors understood what was meant. Scaffolding is now called unit testing, which was popularized by JUnit and NUnit and is a mainstream part of development now incorporated into Visual Studio.

The first object dumper — commented out in Listing 2-15 — uses reflection to display all the properties and objects of a collection. Reflection can be a little slow for production code, but speed doesn't count at all in testing code. The Reflection dumper code is shown in Listing 2-16.

Listing 2-16: An object state dumper implemented using Reflection.

```
using System;
using System.Collections.Generic;
using System.Linq;
using System.Text;
using System.Reflection;
using System.IO;

namespace BusinessObjects
{
  public class Dumper
  {

    public static void Dump(object o, TextWriter writer)
    {
```

Continued

```
        string mask = "{0} : {1}";
        PropertyInfo[] properties = o.GetType().GetProperties();
        foreach(PropertyInfo p in properties)
        {
          try
          {
            writer.WriteLine(mask, p.Name,
              p.GetValue(o, null));
          }
          catch
          {
            writer.WriteLine(mask, p.Name, "unk.");
          }
        }
      }

      public static void Dump<T>(IEnumerable<T> list, TextWriter writer)
      {
        foreach(T o in list)
        {
          Dump(o, writer);
        }
      }
    }
  }
```

The `Dump` method is overloaded. If you call it with anything that implements `IEnumerable<T>`, the `Dump` version that reflects a collection is called. For items in the collection, `Dump(object o, TextWriter writer)` is called. (You could also implement `Dump(object o, TextWriter writer)` using generics such as `Dump<T>(T o, TextWriter writer)`). A perfect `TextWriter` to call the `Dump` method with is `Console.Out`. When you are writing unit tests, `Console.Out` is redirected to the IDE.

To see how Visual Studio (and NUnit) redirects `Console.Out`, check out my article "Redirect I/O to a TexBoxWriter in .NET at `www.codeguru.com/columns/vb/print.php/c11777`. If you want to try a `Dump` method with LINQ, read the next subsection.

For Fun: Implementing an Object Dumper with LINQ

LINQ is especially good at iterating against collections (and producing an enumerable collection result). Of course, you can just use LINQ to iterate over a collection and perform some behavior, ignoring the results. In Listing 2-17, `Dump` is rewritten as `LinqDump`. `LinqDump` was added by me to the `Dumper` class in Listing 2-16, shown previously.

Listing 2-17: Dumping an object's state using LINQ and multiple from clauses.

```
public static void LinqDump<T>(IEnumerable<T> list, TextWriter writer)
{
  string mask = "{0} : {1}";

  var results = from obj in list
                let properties = typeof(T).GetProperties()
                from prop in properties
                select
                   prop.GetValue(obj, null) != null ?
                   string.Format(mask, prop.Name, prop.GetValue(obj, null)) :
                   string.Format(mask, prop.Name, "unk.");

  Array.ForEach(results.ToArray(), s => writer.WriteLine(s));
}
```

Note that in the LINQ version shown in Listing 2-17, the results are indeed used to send the property dump to the `TextWriter`.

Although LINQ is beyond the scope of this book, in general you can learn more about LINQ by reading my book *LINQ Unleashed for C#* (Sam, 2008) or Charlie Calvert and Dinesh Kulkarni's *Essential LINQ* (Addison-Wesley, 2009), but to tide you over here is a brief explanation of the query.

The first from statement is like a `foreach` over the list. The local `obj` is called a *range variable*. A second range, `properties`, is initialized using the `let` clause. The second `from` clause defines a range variable `prop`, representing a single `PropertyInfo` object. The `select` clause uses the ternary operator to test to see whether a value exists for a given property and object pair, and that result is used to initialize an anonymous type containing a simple string, which in turn contains the property name and value.

`Array.ForEach` is a shorthand version of the `foreach` statement. The funny-looking bit, `s => writer.WriteLine(s)`, is called a Lambda expression. Lambda expressions are condensed anonymous methods, and the `=>` is the "goes to" operator (or what I like to call the *gosinta*). If you combine LINQ with Parallel Fx (and PLINQ), you can easily convert the preceding code to employ multithreaded parallelism. (Refer to my article "Parallel LINQ" in the January 2009 edition of *Dr. Dobbs Journal* ; the article was republished on the Dr. Dobbs Portal at www.ddj.com/windows/212700663.)

Binding a Custom Collection to an ASPxGridView

To use the `CityList` in a Web page, call `CityHelper.GetCities()`, assign the result to an `ASPxGridView`'s `DataSource` property, and call `ASPxGridView.DataBind()`. To improve performance, you could place the result from `CityHelpler.GetCities` in Session or store it in the application cache. Refer to Listing 2-18 for the code.

Listing 2-18: Databinding with the custom collection and using Session.

```
using System;
using System.Collections.Generic;
using System.Linq;
using System.Web;
using System.Web.UI;
using System.Web.UI.WebControls;
using BusinessObjects;

public partial class ViewCities : System.Web.UI.Page
{
  private CityList cities = null;
  private static readonly string CITIES = "CITIES";
  protected void Page_Load(object sender, EventArgs e)
  {
    cities = (CityList)Session[CITIES];
    if (cities == null)
    {
      cities = CityHelper.GetCities();
      Session[CITIES] = cities;
    }

    ASPxGridView1.DataSource = cities;
    ASPxGridView1.DataBind();
  }
}
```

> Suppose you click an `ASPxGridView` column to sort on that column and then you hold the Shift key and click another column to sort on a secondary column. You can clear column sorts by holding the Ctrl key and reclicking a column header for a previously sorted column.

Using Unbound Columns

Use unbound columns for data that doesn't automatically reside in your data source. The obvious example that comes to mind is calculated fields or data that you have to look up.

The example shows a `List<T>`, where `T` is an instance of a class named `Stock` that is bound to the grid. Stock prices are fluid, so storing the stock price would make sense only for historical purposes. The `Stock` class has the company name and stock symbol. Each time the grid is bound, the stock asking price is retrieved from Yahoo! Finance and inserted in the unbound `CurrentPrice` column, and the data and time are stored in the unbound `QuoteDateTime` column. To set up the example in Listing 2-19, complete the numbered steps to support the code.

1. Add an ASPxGridView to a Web form.

2. Click the Smart Tags and select columns.

3. Using Figure 2-10 as a guide, add a CompanyName and Symbol column, leaving the Data .UnboundType field as Decimal.

4. Add a CurrentPrice and QuoteDateTime and change the Data.UnboundType to decimal and DateTime, respectively.

5. Close the Editor Form.

6. In the IDE, select the grid and switch the Properties window to the Event view and create a handler for the CustomUnboundColumnData event.

7. Implement code to define values for each unbound column.

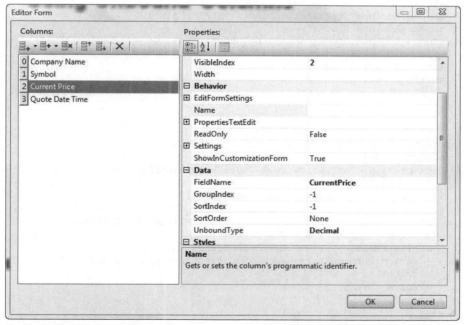

Figure 2-10: Use the Columns Editor Form to define the unbound grid columns as shown.

Listing 2-19: Code that uses a WebClient call to get stock quotes from Yahoo! Finance and populate unbound columns.

```csharp
using System;
using System.Collections.Generic;
using System.Linq;
using System.Web;
using System.Web.UI;
using System.Web.UI.WebControls;
using System.Net;

public partial class _Default : System.Web.UI.Page
{
    protected void Page_Load(object sender, EventArgs e)
    {
      List<Stock> stocks = new List<Stock>();
      stocks.Add(new Stock("Dell", "DELL"));
      stocks.Add(new Stock("Microsoft", "MSFT"));
      stocks.Add(new Stock("Google", "GOOG"));
      stocks.Add(new Stock("American International Group, Inc", "AIG"));

      ASPxGridView1.DataSource = stocks;
      ASPxGridView1.DataBind();

    }


    protected void ASPxGridView1_CustomUnboundColumnData(
      object sender,
      DevExpress.Web.ASPxGridView.ASPxGridViewColumnDataEventArgs e)
    {
      if (e.Column.FieldName == "CurrentPrice")
      {
        string symbol = (string)e.GetListSourceFieldValue("Symbol");
        WebClient client = new WebClient();
        string result = client.DownloadString(
          string.Format("http://download.finance.yahoo.com/d/?s={0}&f=a",
          symbol));
        e.Value = result;
      }
      else
        e.Value = DateTime.Now.ToString();


    }
}


public class Stock
```

```
{
   /// <summary>
   /// Initializes a new instance of the Stock class.
   /// </summary>
   /// <param name="companyName"></param>
   /// <param name="symbol"></param>
   public Stock(string companyName, string symbol)
   {
     this.companyName = companyName;
     this.symbol = symbol;
   }

   private string companyName;
   public string CompanyName
   {
     get { return companyName; }
     set { companyName = value; }
   }

   private string symbol;
   public string Symbol
   {
     get { return symbol; }
     set { symbol = value; }
   }
}
```

In the preceding code listing, the Stock class represents an entity and is self-explanatory. The Page_ Load populates a List<Stock> with some (currently depressed) stock values and binds the list to the ASPxGridView. The CustomUnboundColumnData event handler is called once for each row and each unbound column. In the example, the event handler is called twice for each row. If the ASPxGridViewColumnDataEventArgs represents the unbound CurrentPrice, the row's symbol is retrieved and a call is made to Yahoo! Finance to obtain the asking price, and the result is assigned to the ASPxGridViewColumnDataEventArgs.Value property, ultimately ending up in the right grid row and column.

If you bound the grid to a data source, the CustomUnboundColumnData event handler would still be coded in the same way.

Implementing a Custom Sort

DevExpress is continuously providing online content in the form of blogs, videos, step-by-step examples, and even Twitter posts (called *tweets*); follow @DevExpress to stay on top of the team's Twitter posts). A good place to watch videos about DevExpress products is http://tv.devexpress.com.

For example, the inspiration for this section can be found at `http://tv.devexpress.com/ASPxGridView09.movie`.

By default, sorting is enabled and no code is required. The default sort is one based on the data type in ascending or descending order, depending on the number of times you click a column header. If you want to sort based on some other criteria, implement a `CustomSortColumn` event handler for the `ASPxGridView`. For example, string columns are sorted alphabetically. In the aforementioned video, sorting by string length is implemented using a custom sort. To demonstrate sorting, I arbitrarily picked sorting stock symbols by the exchange the stock is listed on. (It is a stretch as far as examples go, but it demonstrates the custom sort capability.)

1. Click the Smart tag and select `Columns` to display the column Editor Form.

2. Select the `Symbol` column and change the Settings.SortMode property to `Custom`. (See Figure 2-11.)

3. Implement a `CustomColumnSort` event handler for the `ASPxGridView`.

4. In the event handler, compare `CustomColumnSortEventArgs.FieldName` to `Symbol`.

5. Implement the custom sorting behavior. (See Listing 2-20.)

6. Set the `CustomColumnSortEventArgs.Handled` property to true.

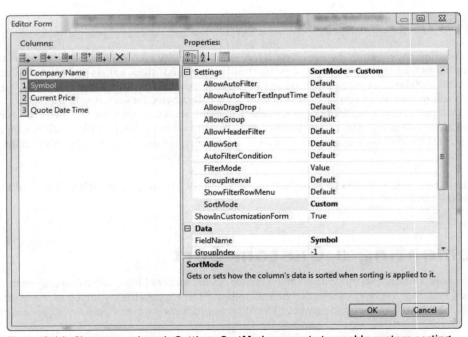

Figure 2-11: Change a column's Settings SortMode property to enable custom sorting on a particular column.

Listing 2-20: A custom sort that sorts the symbols by the exchange the stock is listed on.

```
protected void ASPxGridView1_CustomColumnSort(
     object sender,
     DevExpress.Web.ASPxGridView.CustomColumnSortEventArgs e)
{
  const string mask = "http://download.finance.yahoo.com/d/?s={0}&f=x";
  WebClient client = new WebClient();
  if(e.Column.FieldName == "Symbol")
  {
    string result1 = client.DownloadString(
      string.Format(mask, e.Value1.ToString()));
    string result2 = client.DownloadString(
      string.Format(mask, e.Value2.ToString()));

    e.Result = result1.CompareTo(result2);
e.Handled = true; // remember to set handled to true
    }
}
```

Castle Brands, Inc (ROX) was added to the stock list in the example so that a symbol on the American Stock Exchange was included in the result set. AIG is on NYSE; MSFT, DELL, and GOOG are all on NASDAQ. Thus, clicking the symbol will result in the stocks being sorted by AMEX, NASDAQ, and NYSE based on the search criteria in ascending order and NYSE, NASDAQ, and AMEX in descending order.

> To start the application with a pre-indicated sort order change the `Data.SortOrder` property from None to Ascending or Descending as desired in the columns Editor Form.

The Yahoo! Finance query `?s={0}&f=x` represents a query where the substitution string (`{0}`) is replaced with the symbol and *x* represents a request for the exchange name.

Exporting Grid Data

A lot of code has upper-bounds limitations. Run a SQL Query with millions of rows or a report based on gigabytes of data, or sort a collection with terabytes of data, and most code and many machines will come crawling to a halt. That's why it doesn't bug me that the ASPxGridViewExporter has some limitations. It is just a fact at present that millions of rows of data will cause an OutOfMemoryException for the ASPxGridViewExporter. Also, the exporter cannot export template content, detailed grid data, or hidden columns, and you can't export data during a callback. Over time, some of these limitations may be resolved.

For now, as with many upper-bound types of problems, you may have to roll your own solution if you have to export hundreds of thousands or millions of rows. At this time, the ASPxGridViewExporter is based on the XtraPrinting engine, and it attempts to read all the data into memory before streaming out the exported data. Clearly, reading all the data into memory is going to eventually exceed physical and virtual memory when there are too many rows and columns.

The subsections that follow demonstrate how to export the data in an `ASPxGridView` into the supported output formats and how to render just the selected rows in a grid.

Exporting ASPxGridView Data to PDF, RTF, CSV, and XLS

To export ASPxGridView data associate an `ASPxGridViewExporter` with the grid by setting the `ASpxGridViewExporter.GridViewID` to the `ASPxGridView` that contains the data you want to export. Then, it is just a matter of choosing from one of the supported output forms — PDF, RTF, CSV, or XLS. (PDF is Adobe's Portable Document Format. RTF is Rich Text Format, basically a text document with formatting metadata. CSV represents a text file with comma-separated values, and XLS refers to Microsoft Excel documents.)

To send the grid data to a document using one of the aforementioned formats, invoke the Write*xxx* for that format. For example, to export a text document with comma-separated values, call `ASPxGridViewExporter.WriteCsv`. Pass in an instance of a class that inherits from `System.IO.Stream` to the `Write` method. The stream argument represents the output target. For instance, if you want to export a grid's data to a CSV file, initialize a `FileStream` object with the file path.

Listing 2-21 contains a very simple Web form with an `ASPxGridView`, a `SqlDataSource`, an `ASPxGridViewExporter`, and a button. The `ASPxGridView`'s `DataSourceID` is associated with the `SqlDataSource`. The `ASPxGridViewExporter`'s `GridViewID` is associated with the `ASPxGridView`, and the button contains the code in Listing 2-21.

Listing 2-21: Exporting an ASPxGridView's data with an ASpxGridViewExporter.

```
using System;
using System.Collections.Generic;
using System.Linq;
using System.Web;
using System.Web.UI;
using System.Web.UI.WebControls;
using System.IO;
using System.ComponentModel;
using DevExpress.Web.ASPxGridView;

public partial class ExportPassengers : System.Web.UI.Page
{
  protected void ASPxButton1_Click(object sender, EventArgs e)
  {
    string filename = Server.MapPath("/TotalFlight") + "\\Passengers.csv";

    using (FileStream stream =
      new FileStream(filename, FileMode.CreateNew))
```

```
      {
        ASPxGridViewExporter1.WriteCsv(stream);
      }
    }
  }
```

The key in the sample is to use `Server.MapPath` if you want to write to a virtual Web address that may change when you deploy. It's also important to keep in mind that newer versions of Windows operating systems may not provide file write access by default.

There are a couple of other practical things to think about. If this code may be run multiple times, you may want to delete exiting exported files. Also, keep in mind that if a client computer is going to export data, the sample in Listing 2-21 writes to the Web server. It is unlikely that the end user will have permission on the Web server. To work around this challenge, you could let the user specify the filename and then update a dynamic link on the Web page to permit the user to download his or her exported data. The following fragment can be added to the end of the `Click` event handler in Listing 2-21 to make the exported file available to the client:

```
//Add this code to make the exported file available on the client
HyperLink link = new HyperLink();
link.NavigateUrl = "/TotalFlight/Passengers.csv";
link.Text = "Exported File";
Page.Controls.Add(link);
```

If you want to export just the selected rows, select Enable Selection on the `ASPxGridView` *Smart tag menu. Doing so adds a column of check boxes to the grid. Rows with checkmarks are selected rows. Change the* `ASPxGridViewExporter.ExportedRowType` *from All to Selected. Now when you export the grid data, only checked rows will be exported.*

If you just want to send the data directly to the client without creating an intermediate file, call the `ASPxGridViewExporter.WriteCsvToResponse()` method, replacing the `WriteCsv` call and the lines to add the preceding hyperlink. Calling `WritexxxToResponse` means you don't have to add a dynamic link to the Web form, worry about preexisting export files, or manage export clutter on your server.

Adding Export Detail with the RenderBrick Event

If you want to export the data differently from how it appears in the `ASPxGridView`, you can provide a handler for the `ASPxGridViewExporter.RenderBrick` event. The code in Listing 2-22 demonstrates how to add a `RenderBrick` event handler; also, in that handler you select the `GridViewRowType`, column, and `FieldName` for a specific field and add a border to that field. (The code in the listing can be added to Listing 2-21.) In the example, the output is exported to an Excel document and sent to the client directly.

`ASPxGridViewExportRenderingEventArgs` contains, among other things, a `BrickStyle` property. The `BrickStyle` property has subproperties for setting fonts, foreground and background color, width, padding, and text alignment. You can experiment with the other subproperties using the code in Listing 2-22 to achieve the desired visual output. Figure 2-12 shows the output from the code in Listing 2-22.

Listing 2-22: Add the following code (or code like it) to adorn elements of the exported data with customizations such as color.

```
protected void ASPxButton4_Click(object sender, EventArgs e)
{
    ASPxGridViewExporter1.ExportedRowType =
        DevExpress.Web.ASPxGridView.Export.GridViewExportedRowType.All;
    ASPxGridViewExporter1.RenderBrick +=
        new DevExpress.Web.ASPxGridView
        .Export.ASPxGridViewExportRenderingEventHandler(
        ASPxGridViewExporter1_RenderBrick);
    ASPxGridViewExporter1.WriteXlsToResponse();
}

void ASPxGridViewExporter1_RenderBrick(object sender,
    DevExpress.Web.ASPxGridView.Export.ASPxGridViewExportRenderingEventArgs e)
{
    if (GridViewRowType.Data == e.RowType
        && e.Column != null && e.Column.FieldName == "LastName")
        e.BrickStyle.BackColor = System.Drawing.Color.Silver;
}
```

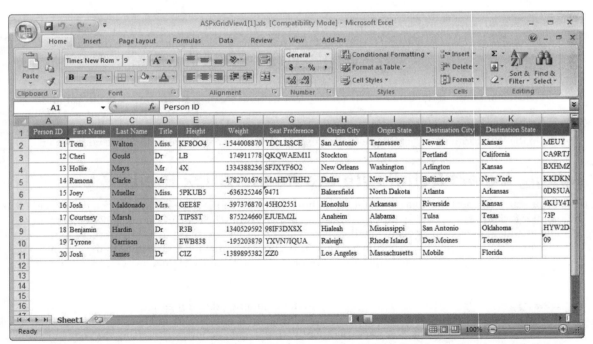

Figure 2-12: The code in Listing 2-22 uses the RenderBrick event to add a silver background color to the LastName as the data is being exported to an MS Excel spreadsheet.

Implementing Your Own Exporter

For everyday uses, I would encourage you to use the components and controls such as the ASPxGridViewExporter rather than write your own code. Generally, specialized code is going to provide you with a flexible and powerful solution and save you time. However, using controls such as the ASPxGridViewExporter doesn't stop you from rolling your own code — for instance, if you have a very large result set. For those instances, you can roll your own code. Generally, writing your own code entails more work with less flexibility unless you put hundreds of hours into building in the additional flexibility.

Assume, for example, that you occasionally need to export a million rows of data — although such scenarios should be carefully evaluated for the practical necessity. You can do so by implementing a custom exporter. Listing 2-23 uses a SqlDataReader and basic formatting to export approximately 1,000,000 rows in the TotalFlight database to a simple CSV text file. The reason the following code works — and it works pretty quickly — is that it reads one row at a time. The drawback is a loss of flexibility, including the flexibility to format the data for multiple output sources.

Listing 2-23 contains a very basic, no-frills CSV exporter that works pretty quickly on my laptop — taking about 20 seconds — with about a million rows of data. Based on the implementation, the grid's column headers and data are exported because the SqlDataSource's SELECT statement is used to derive the output data.

Listiing 2-23: This code uses a SqlDataReader to export the grid data based on the grid's data source SELECT statement.

```
using System;
using System.Collections.Generic;
using System.Linq;
using System.Web;
using System.Data.SqlClient;
using System.IO;
using System.Text;
using System.Data;

public class CustomCsvExporter
{

  private string[] columnHeaderNames;
  public string[] ColumnHeaderNames
  {
    get { return columnHeaderNames; }
    set { columnHeaderNames = value; }
  }


  private string connectionString;
  public string ConnectionString
  {
      get {      return connectionString; }
      set { connectionString = value;      }
```

Continued

Listing 2-23: This code uses a SqlDataReader to export the grid data based on the grid's data source SELECT statement. *(continued)*

```
    }

    private string selectStatement;
    public string SelectStatement
    {
        get {      return selectStatement; }
        set { selectStatement = value;      }
    }

    public CustomCsvExporter(string[] columnHeaderNames,
      string connectionString, string selectStatement)
    {
      this.ColumnHeaderNames = columnHeaderNames;
      this.connectionString = connectionString;
      this.selectStatement = selectStatement;
    }

    public void WriteToCsv(TextWriter stream)
    {
      if (stream == null)
        throw new NullReferenceException();

      WriteHeaders(stream);
      WriteData(stream);
    }

    private void WriteData(TextWriter stream)
    {
      using(SqlConnection connection = new SqlConnection(connectionString))
      {
        connection.Open();
        SqlCommand command = new SqlCommand(selectStatement, connection);
        SqlDataReader reader =
          command.ExecuteReader(CommandBehavior.SequentialAccess);
        while (reader.Read())
        {
          WriteRow(stream, reader);
        }
      }
    }

    private void WriteRow(TextWriter stream, SqlDataReader reader)
    {
      for (int i = 0; i < reader.FieldCount; i++)
      {
        object data = reader[i];
        if (data != null && data != System.DBNull.Value)
          stream.Write(data.ToString());
        if (i < reader.FieldCount - 1)
          stream.Write(", ");
      }
```

```
      stream.Write(Environment.NewLine);
    }

    private void WriteHeaders(TextWriter stream)
    {
      if(columnHeaderNames == null || columnHeaderNames.Length == 0) return;
      for(int i=0; i<columnHeaderNames.Length; i++)
      {
        stream.Write(columnHeaderNames[i]);
        if(i<columnHeaderNames.Length-1)
          stream.Write(", ");

      }
      stream.Write(Environment.NewLine);
    }
}
```

To use the CustomCsvExporter, pass in the grid column headers, SELECT statement, and connection string. When you call WriteCsv, pass in the TextWriter — the target — to write to. Listing 2-24 demonstrates a function that shows how to use the CustomCsvExporter.

Listing 2-24: An example demonstrating how to write the CustomCsvExporter.

```
protected void  ASPxButton3_Click(object sender, EventArgs e)
{
  string filename = Server.MapPath("/TotalFlight") + "\\Passengers.csv";
  var names = from GridViewColumn column in ASPxGridView1.Columns
              select column.ToString();

  CustomCsvExporter exporter = new CustomCsvExporter(names.ToArray(),
    SqlDataSource1.ConnectionString, SqlDataSource1.SelectCommand);

  using (TextWriter writer = new StreamWriter(filename))
  {
    exporter.WriteToCsv(writer);
  }
}
```

In Listing 2-24, LINQ is used to conveniently select the column headers. You could also get the schema using ADO.NET (which is not demonstrated). The CustomCsvExporter is initialized with the column names, SqlDataSource's ConnectionString and SelectCommand. Finally, a using construct is used to ensure that the TextWriter is finalized, and consequently the stream is closed.

> **Prioritizing Customer Needs**
>
> I could find only a few thread queries in which customers asked about exporting very large amounts of data. Consequently, supporting large datasets is probably prioritized based on customer demand. However, I do know that at DevExpress, there is a lot of emphasis on what our customers need. If you need support for large data exports or any other kind of product support, sound off. Our customers are very important to us and we are listening.

Using Master and Detail Grids

I have written several articles and created a few videos on using custom `UserControls` to create a nesting effect in ASP.NET. I know that many programmers are using this feature because I get a lot of feedback on those articles. Thankfully, for the cost of the `ASPxGridView`, DevExpress has solved this problem for you, and it requires almost no code on your part — if you use the `ASPxGridView`.

To implement a nested Master Detail view with the `ASPxGridView`, follow these steps (the ASP.NET code is provided after the numbered steps):

1. You will need at least two related tables representing the master data set and the detail data set. (Let's use Northwind's Orders and Order Details for the sake of familiarity so that you can focus on the mechanics of configuring the master and detail sources.)

2. You will need two data sources, one for each grid.

3. Add an `ASPxGridView` and a data source for that grid in the usual way; associating the grid and data source using the Smart tags menu is the easiest way.

4. Repeat Step 3, temporarily placing the second grid containing the detail data on the same page as the master grid. (See Figure 2-13.)

5. For the second data source, use the Configure Data Source Wizard in the Configure the Select Statement step and click the WHERE button to configure a `WHERE` clause based on the `OrderID`.

6. In the Add WHERE Clause dialog box (see Figure 2-14), configure the `WHERE` clause to get the `OrderID` from a Session variable.

7. From the master grid's Smart tags menu, choose Edit Template and pick the `DetailRow` template (see Figure 2-15).

8. Drag the detail grid into the `DetailRow` template for the master grid (again, see Figure 2-15).

9. For the `SettingsDetail` property for the detail grid (using the Properties window) change the `IsDetailGrid` property to true.

10. For the `SettingsDetail` property for the master grid, change `ShowDetailRow` to true (which will result in a column containing `[+]`, an expansion button to the master grid).

11. Add a `BeforePerformDataSelect` event handler for the detail grid and assign the master grid's primary key to the `Session["OrderID"]` Session variable slot. (See Listing 2-25.)

12. Run the example. (See Listing 2-26 for the ASP.NET that is created from completing the numbered steps.)

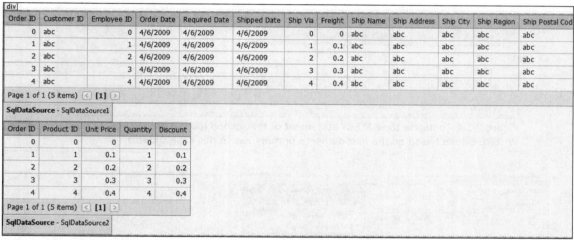

Order ID	Customer ID	Employee ID	Order Date	Required Date	Shipped Date	Ship Via	Freight	Ship Name	Ship Address	Ship City	Ship Region	Ship Postal Cod
0	abc	0	4/6/2009	4/6/2009	4/6/2009	0	0	abc	abc	abc	abc	abc
1	abc	1	4/6/2009	4/6/2009	4/6/2009	1	0.1	abc	abc	abc	abc	abc
2	abc	2	4/6/2009	4/6/2009	4/6/2009	2	0.2	abc	abc	abc	abc	abc
3	abc	3	4/6/2009	4/6/2009	4/6/2009	3	0.3	abc	abc	abc	abc	abc
4	abc	4	4/6/2009	4/6/2009	4/6/2009	4	0.4	abc	abc	abc	abc	abc

Page 1 of 1 (5 items) [<] **[1]** [>]

SqlDataSource - SqlDataSource1

Order ID	Product ID	Unit Price	Quantity	Discount
0	0	0	0	0
1	1	0.1	1	0.1
2	2	0.2	2	0.2
3	3	0.3	3	0.3
4	4	0.4	4	0.4

Page 1 of 1 (5 items) [<] **[1]** [>]

SqlDataSource - SqlDataSource2

Figure 2-13: Begin creating the master-detail page by adding two ASPxGridViews and two SqlDataSources to a Web form as if you were creating a form with two separate grids.

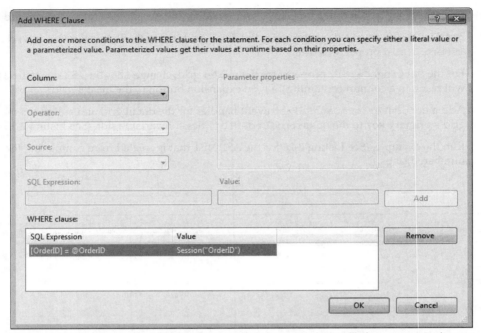

Figure 2-14: Configure the SELECT statement of the second (detail) data source to have a WHERE clause based on the first dataset's primary key, in this case OrderID.

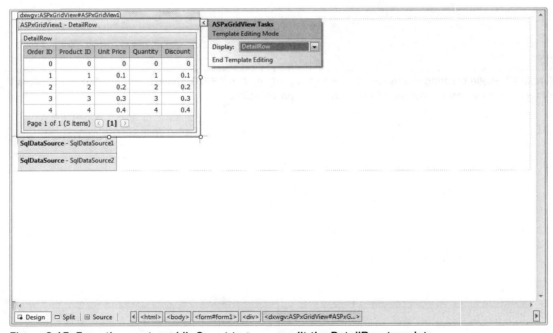

Figure 2-15: From the master grid's Smart tag menu, edit the DetailRow template.

Listing 2-25: Correlate the detail data with the master detail storing the selected row in the Session variable.

```
using System;
using System.Collections.Generic;
using System.Linq;
using System.Web;
using System.Web.UI;
using System.Web.UI.WebControls;
using DevExpress.Web.ASPxGridView;

public partial class _Default : System.Web.UI.Page
{
  protected void Page_Load(object sender, EventArgs e)
  {

  }

  protected void ASPxGridView2_BeforePerformDataSelect(
    object sender, EventArgs e)
  {
    Session["OrderID"] = ((ASPxGridView)sender).GetMasterRowKeyValue();
  }
}
```

Listing 2-26: The ASP for the master–detail view as described in the numbered listing that precedes the code listings.

```
<%@ Page Language="C#" AutoEventWireup="true"
  CodeFile="Default.aspx.cs" Inherits="_Default" %>

<%@ Register assembly="DevExpress.Web.ASPxGridView.v8.3,
Version=8.3.4.0, Culture=neutral, ⤸
  PublicKeyToken=b88d1754d700e49a"
  namespace="DevExpress.Web.ASPxGridView" tagprefix="dxwgv" %>
<%@ Register assembly="DevExpress.Web.ASPxEditors.v8.3,
Version=8.3.4.0, Culture=neutral,⤸
  PublicKeyToken=b88d1754d700e49a"
  namespace="DevExpress.Web.ASPxEditors" tagprefix="dxe" %>

<!DOCTYPE html PUBLIC "-//W3C//DTD XHTML 1.0 Transitional//EN"
  "http://www.w3.org/TR/xhtml1/DTD/xhtml1-transitional.dtd">

<html xmlns="http://www.w3.org/1999/xhtml">
<head runat="server">
    <title></title>
</head>
<body>
    <form id="form1" runat="server">
    <div>

      <dxwgv:ASPxGridView ID="ASPxGridView1" runat="server"
        AutoGenerateColumns="False" DataSourceID="SqlDataSource1"
```

Continued

Listing 2-26: The ASP for the master–detail view as described in the numbered listing that precedes the code listings. *(continued)*

```
KeyFieldName="OrderID">
<Templates>
  <DetailRow>
    <dxwgv:ASPxGridView ID="ASPxGridView2" runat="server"
      AutoGenerateColumns="False" DataSourceID="SqlDataSource2"
      KeyFieldName="OrderID"
      onbeforeperformdataselect="ASPxGridView2_BeforePerformDataSelect">
      <Columns>
        <dxwgv:GridViewDataTextColumn FieldName="OrderID" ReadOnly="True"
          VisibleIndex="0">
        </dxwgv:GridViewDataTextColumn>
        <dxwgv:GridViewDataTextColumn FieldName="ProductID" ReadOnly="True"
          VisibleIndex="1">
        </dxwgv:GridViewDataTextColumn>
        <dxwgv:GridViewDataTextColumn
          FieldName="UnitPrice" VisibleIndex="2">
        </dxwgv:GridViewDataTextColumn>
        <dxwgv:GridViewDataTextColumn
          FieldName="Quantity" VisibleIndex="3">
        </dxwgv:GridViewDataTextColumn>
        <dxwgv:GridViewDataTextColumn
          FieldName="Discount" VisibleIndex="4">
        </dxwgv:GridViewDataTextColumn>
      </Columns>
      <SettingsDetail IsDetailGrid="True" />
    </dxwgv:ASPxGridView>
  </DetailRow>
</Templates>
<Columns>
  <dxwgv:GridViewDataTextColumn FieldName="OrderID" ReadOnly="True"
    VisibleIndex="0">
    <EditFormSettings Visible="False" />
  </dxwgv:GridViewDataTextColumn>
  <dxwgv:GridViewDataTextColumn FieldName="CustomerID" VisibleIndex="1">
  </dxwgv:GridViewDataTextColumn>
  <dxwgv:GridViewDataTextColumn FieldName="EmployeeID" VisibleIndex="2">
  </dxwgv:GridViewDataTextColumn>
  <dxwgv:GridViewDataDateColumn FieldName="OrderDate" VisibleIndex="3">
  </dxwgv:GridViewDataDateColumn>
  <dxwgv:GridViewDataDateColumn FieldName="RequiredDate" VisibleIndex="4">
  </dxwgv:GridViewDataDateColumn>
  <dxwgv:GridViewDataDateColumn FieldName="ShippedDate" VisibleIndex="5">
  </dxwgv:GridViewDataDateColumn>
```

```
               <dxwgv:GridViewDataTextColumn FieldName="ShipVia" VisibleIndex="6">
               </dxwgv:GridViewDataTextColumn>
               <dxwgv:GridViewDataTextColumn FieldName="Freight" VisibleIndex="7">
               </dxwgv:GridViewDataTextColumn>
               <dxwgv:GridViewDataTextColumn FieldName="ShipName" VisibleIndex="8">
               </dxwgv:GridViewDataTextColumn>
               <dxwgv:GridViewDataTextColumn FieldName="ShipAddress" VisibleIndex="9">
               </dxwgv:GridViewDataTextColumn>
               <dxwgv:GridViewDataTextColumn FieldName="ShipCity" VisibleIndex="10">
               </dxwgv:GridViewDataTextColumn>
               <dxwgv:GridViewDataTextColumn FieldName="ShipRegion" VisibleIndex="11">
               </dxwgv:GridViewDataTextColumn>
               <dxwgv:GridViewDataTextColumn
                  FieldName="ShipPostalCode" VisibleIndex="12">
               </dxwgv:GridViewDataTextColumn>
               <dxwgv:GridViewDataTextColumn FieldName="ShipCountry" VisibleIndex="13">
               </dxwgv:GridViewDataTextColumn>
            </Columns>
            <SettingsDetail ShowDetailRow="True" />
         </dxwgv:ASPxGridView>
         <asp:SqlDataSource ID="SqlDataSource1" runat="server"
            ConnectionString="<%$ ConnectionStrings:NorthwindConnectionString %>"
            SelectCommand="SELECT * FROM [Orders]"></asp:SqlDataSource>
         <asp:SqlDataSource ID="SqlDataSource2" runat="server"
            ConnectionString="<%$ ConnectionStrings:NorthwindConnectionString %>"
            SelectCommand="SELECT * FROM [Order Details] WHERE (([OrderID] = @OrderID)">
            <SelectParameters>
               <asp:SessionParameter Name="OrderID"
                  SessionField="OrderID" Type="Int32" />
            </SelectParameters>
         </asp:SqlDataSource>

      </div>
      </form>
   </body>
   </html>
```

An example of the results is shown in Figure 2-16 with a detail row expanded. There aren't a lot of steps to set up the master-detail relationship, but they are somewhat intricate. If you get stuck, you can find supporting sources for the example, including this book's Web site, an article on Devsource.com at www.devsource.com/c/a/Add-Ons/MasterDetail-Nested-Grids-ASPxGridView/, and a video at http://tv.devexpress.com. (Also, of course you can write to me at paulk@devexpress.com if you need some additional clarification. The ASP.NET code is provided for completeness.

The key to defining the master-detail relationship with grids is to add the detail grid to the master grid's template detail row and to correlate the master and detail data with the primary and foreign keys. If you want to make the master or detail grid modifiable, use the Advanced button of the Configure Data Source Wizard's Configure the Select statement step, generate the INSERT, UPDATE, and DELETE methods, and enable the various updating options from the Smart tags menu (see Figure 2-17). Then check this chapter's earlier section "Storing Changes."

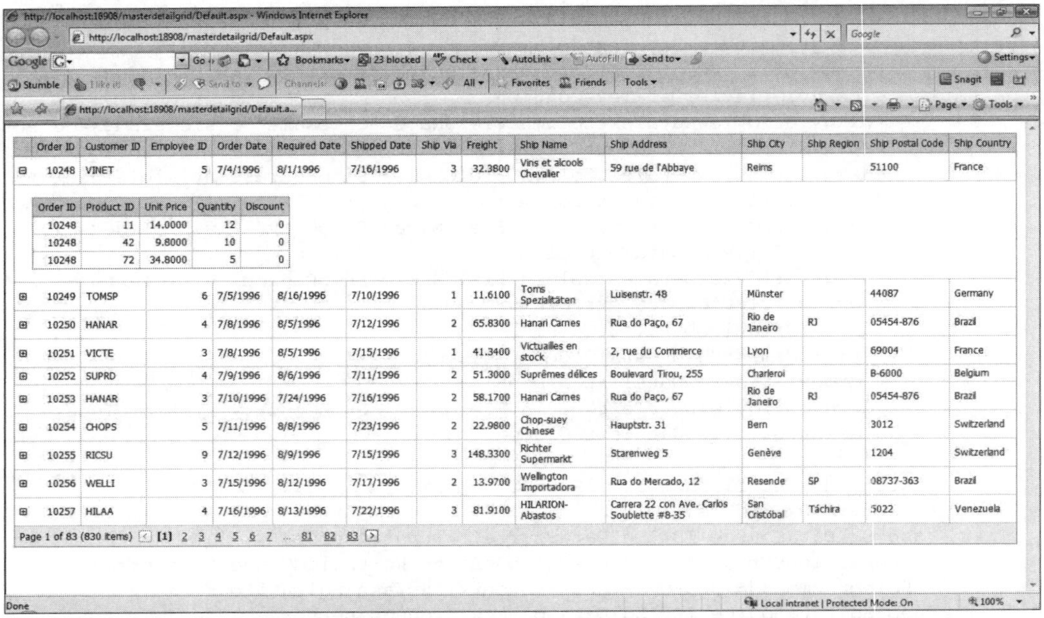

Figure 2-16: After editing the DetailRow template from the master grid's Smart tag menu, drag the detail grid into the master grid's template region.

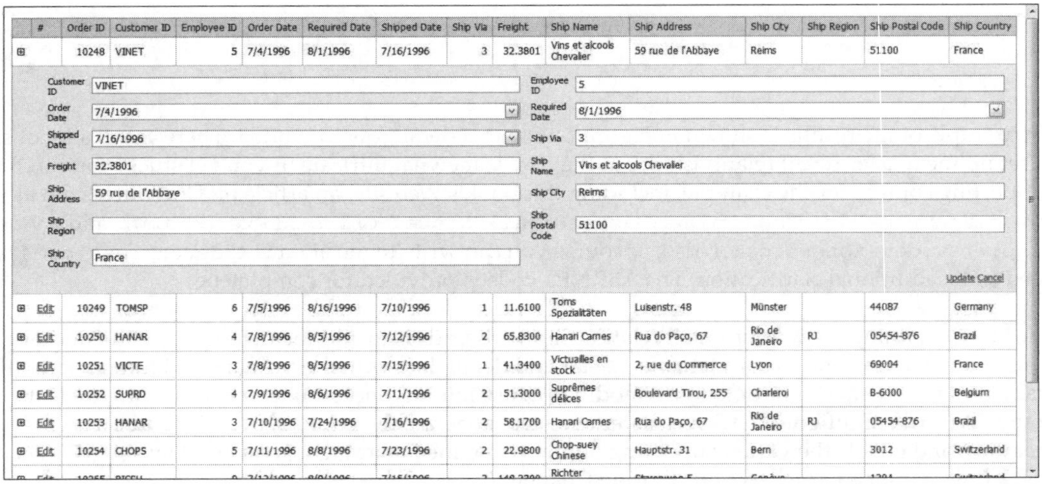

Figure 2-17: Updating data in master detail grids is a matter of generating the correct SQL using the Data Source Configuration Wizard and enabling the various write operations from the Smart tags menu.

Saving User Customizations with Cookies

DevExpress controls support permitting users to personalize sites as desired, and those settings are stored in cookies (if enabled on the browser). To enable storing grid changes, set `ASPxGridView`
`.SettingsCookies.Enabled` to true (see Figure 2-18), and changes made to the grid are stored in cookies and retrieved in later Sessions. For example, if cookies are enabled in the application and the browser and the user changes pages, when they return to the site they will start off on the prior page.

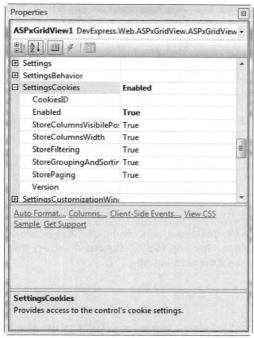

Figure 2-18: Enable cookies with SettingsCookies .Enabled = true to store user customizations and settings such as the current grid page.

To enable cookies on the Internet Explorer 8 browser, choose Tools ➾ Options, navigate to the Privacy tab, and click the Advanced button. The Advanced Privacy Settings dialog box contains the Cookies section. As you can see, First-party and Third-party cookies are on my browser (see Figure 2-19). Notice that the SettingsCookies property contains subproperties that indicate which settings you want to permit to be stored, including the CookieID, StoreColumnsVisiblePosition, StoreColumnsWidth, StoreFiltering, StoreGroupingAndSorting, StorePaging, and the Version.

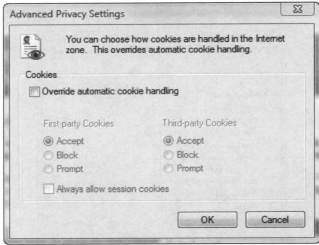

Figure 2-19: Cookie settings can be changed in Internet Explorer 8 by choosing Tools ➾ Options ➾ Privacy (tab) and clicking the Advanced button.

If you are interested in viewing the cookie being set, you can return to a tool such as Fiddler (see Figure 2-20) and examine the header information for the running Web application, or you can try to plow your way through the myriad of stumbling blocks set up by Windows and look for the specific cookie file in the file system.

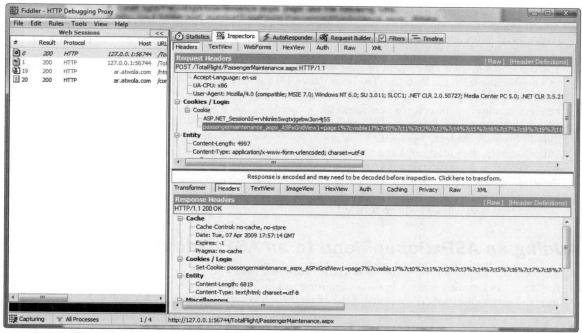

Figure 2-20: Fiddler2 showing the cookie being set in the header request.

Programming Client-Side Events

The behavior of Ajax is such that specific elements and of your page will be updated without the familiar page flicker of a postback. The result is that your client Web application will have some of the familiar features of a thick client Windows application. Rich behavior is generally what users want and what programmers want to offer. The way we used to offer rich client behavior in Web applications was with JavaScript. With Ajax, you may find yourself writing JavaScript code less often.

JavaScript is a language in its own right. JavaScript feels a bit like the C programming language to me. JavaScript has its own syntax, supports some object-oriented concepts, and has its own object model. All this means that JavaScript is a study in its own right if you want to use it to its full potential. To do small jobs, you can dabble in JavaScript. If you want to learn JavaScript in depth, check out *Professional JavaScript for Web Developers*, 2nd Edition, by Nicholas Zakas (Wrox, 2004).

You can always add a `<script>` tag to your ASP/HTML manually, but DevExpress controls such as the `ASPxGridView` have a `ClientSideEvents` property with subproperties that are pluggable points for JavaScript. Click one of the `ClientSideEvents` subproperties and a Client-Side Events Editor is displayed. This editor is a lightweight script editor. The `ClientSideEvents` class is a base class that contains information for available client-side events for particular objects. The `ClientSideEvents` class's job is to hook your JavaScript functions onto the corresponding client-side events.

You can find a lot of good content on `www.devexpress.com`, and some of the inspiration for sections in this book come from the Web site. The book examples are variations of the Web examples, extending them into additional territory. The inspiration for this sample — a context menu for `ASPxGridView` headers that invoke the column sort behavior — can be found at `http://tv.devexpress.com/ASPxGridViewContextMenuForColumn.movie`. The Web site example demonstrates how to replace the default browser context menu with a custom `ASPxPopupMenu` for the `ASPxGridView`'s headers. Unfortunately, the video stops at actually implementing the menu click behavior. I thought the example was interesting, so the example in this section demonstrates how to associate the `ASPxPopupMenu` with the grid, replacing the default context menu with a custom menu. The actual behaviors are implemented, too. In addition to completing the example, this section provides a tip that will help you explore JavaScript in new ways as you go forward.

Adding an ASPxPopupMenu to an ASPxGridView

The default column sorting behavior is to click a column once and the sort order is set — by default the first time to ascending order. Click a second time and the sort order switches to descending, and a third time the sort is disabled. The totality of the example in this section adds a context menu to just an `ASPxGridView`'s headers and lets the user select the desired sort operation — ascending, descending, or no sort.

To create the header context menu behavior, add an `ASPxPopupMenu` to a Web page with an `ASPxGridView` on it. (For our purposes, the example is contained on the `PassengerMaintenance.aspx` page.) To complete configuring the `ASPxPopupMenu`, finish the steps below:

1. Set the `ASPxPopupMenu`'s `ClientInstanceName` to `columnHeaderMenu`. (The name is case sensitive.) The `ClientInstanceName` is the name you will use to refer to the control in JavaScript.

2. Click the `ASPxPopupMenu`'s Items property and add the three menu items — Sort Ascending, Sort Descending, and Clear Sort. (See Figure 2-21.) The left button under the Items section adds new menu items.

3. Check to make sure that the `ASPxPopupMenuPopupAction` is `RightMouseClick`.

> You can access the `ASPxPopupMenu` **Items from the** `ASPxPopMenu's` **Smart tags item, too.**

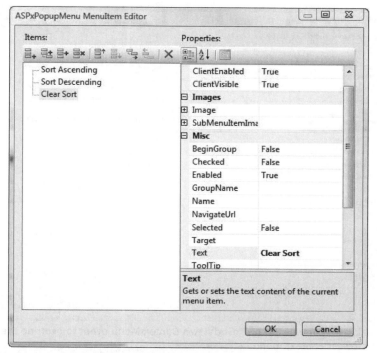

Figure 2-21: Use the ASPxPopupMenuEditor to manage the menu items that appear in the control.

You can explore the MenuItem properties and the ASPxPopupMenu properties to tweak the menu's appearance, including adding styles, tweaking opacity, and adding a check mark next to a menu item. For more on DevExpress navigation, menu, and pop-up controls, refer to Chapter 4, "Adding SiteMaps, Navigation, and Popup Dialogs."

Implementing the ASPxPopupMenu Behavior

The next stop is to add the code to pop up the new context menu in the column header that is right-clicked. This is where script and client-side events come into play. You can invoke the Client-Side Events Editor from a control's Smart tag or from the ClientSideEvents property.

When a user right-clicks the grid, the default browser menu is displayed. This behavior can be overridden by implementing the ContextMenu client-side event. The behavior implemented in the listing is such that when the user right-clicks, the code checks to see whether the object clicked is a 'header'. If it is, the code stores the column index and has the pop-up menu display at the current mouse position. (See Figure 2-22.) Listing 2-27 implements the client-side ContextMenu event for the ASPxGridView.

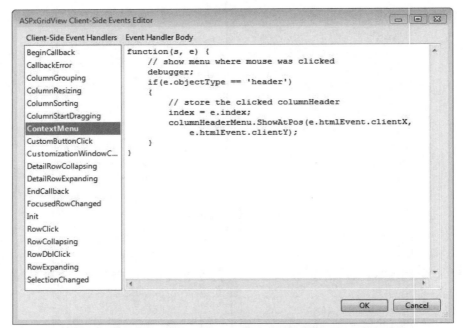

Figure 2-22: Implement the ASPxGridView's ContextMenu event to override the default browser context menu behavior.

Listing 2-27: The following code checks to see whether the event argument's objectType is a header, stores the column index, and shows the pop-up menu.

```
function(s, e) {
     // show menu where mouse was clicked
     // debugger;
     if(e.objectType == 'header')
     {
          // store the clicked columnHeader
          index = e.index;
          columnHeaderMenu.ShowAtPos(e.htmlEvent.clientX,
               e.htmlEvent.clientY);
     }
}
```

From the user's perspective, the obvious choice is to click one of the menu items. To support the stated behavior of the menu, implement the ASPxPopupMenu's client-side ItemClick event and call the grid's SortBy method from the client (see Figure 2-23). Listing 2-28 demonstrates an implementation that invokes the grid's sort behavior from the client.

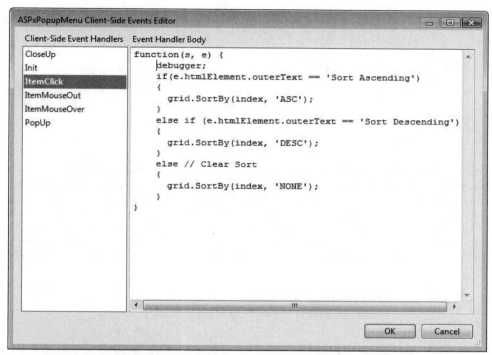

Figure 2-23: Implement the ASPxPopupMenu's ItemClick event to respond to client-side menu clicks.

Listing 2-28: Invoke the grid's sort behavior from the pop-up menu's ItemClick event.

```
function(s, e) {
  debugger;
  if(e.htmlElement.outerText == 'Sort Ascending')
  {
    grid.SortBy(index, 'ASC');
  }
  else if (e.htmlElement.outerText == 'Sort Descending')
  {
    grid.SortBy(index, 'DESC');
  }
  else // Clear Sort
  {
    grid.SortBy(index, 'NONE');
  }
}
```

The code in Listing 2-28 checks the menu's text, matching the menu name to the desired behavior. The variable 'grid' is actually the ASPxGridView.ClientInstanceName set to make it easy to find the grid object on the client. The SortBy method is callable from the client, and the index variable was added to a script block manually and saved in the ContextMenu event. The index variable tells SortBy which column to sort on, and the literal strings indicate the sort operation. As you might expect, all this information takes a little work to discover. The next subsection addresses JavaScript discovery in general. Here is the snippet defining the index variable used by the client-side event in listing 2-28.

```
. . .
</head><script type="text/javascript">
  var index;
</script>
<body>
. . .
```

A client-side event is implemented in such a way as to support all popular browsers without your needing to literally check browser brands and versions. The DevExpress Web site shows the popular browser supported, but I didn't see Google Chrome, so I thought I'd test general browser support. Figures 2-24 and 2-25 show that the context menu behavior is running equally well in Internet Explorer 8 and Google Chrome.

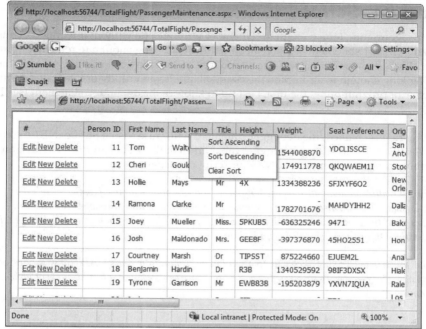

Figure 2-24: The new context menu running in IE8.

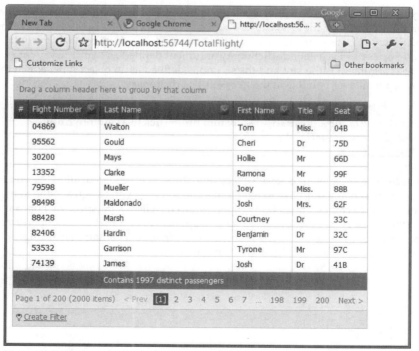

Figure 2-25: The new context menu is running just as well in Google Chrome.

Debugging JavaScript

I have been programming long enough to remember writing code without integrated debuggers (using make files and `printf` statements). I have been writing code long enough to remember programming interrupt 0x24 handlers for hard errors because exception handling didn't exist. All of us have been programming long enough to appreciate the essential quality and utility of integrated debugging. If you do any JavaScript programming, the first, best tip to know is the `debugger` statement (see Listings 2-27 and 2-28).

If script debugging is enabled, the debugger statement will cause Visual Studio .NET to break at that point in the JavaScript, and all the debugging capabilities of the Visual Studio .NET IDE are available to help you debug or figure out how to solve your script challenges.

> *JavaScript is really a general all-purpose language. You can obviously use JavaScript in Web applications, but you can also use it as a command-line programming language. You can run JavaScript (`.js`) files from the command line with the `wscript.exe` utility, and you can debug script with the Visual studio IDE or the Microsoft Script Editor.*

> *Check out my article "Talking Web Clients with JavaScript and the Speech API" at www.codeguru .com/vb/vb_internet/webservices/print.php/c13965 for a fun example of JavaScript programming.*

Using Custom Script Properties

Sometimes you want server information available to the client. The `CustomJSProperties` event is available but not exclusive to the `ASPxGridView`. The `CustomJSProperties` event's second argument for the `ASPxGridView` is `ASPxGridViewClientJSPropertiesEventArgs`, which contains a Properties subproperty. `Properties` is a generic dictionary argument defined as `Dictionary<string, object>`. The first generic argument is the key, and the second is defined as an object type, which means you can stuff pretty much whatever you like in the `Properties` dictionary.

> **Use a `cp` prefix for `ASPxGridView` custom properties to avoid rewriting `ASPxGridView` predefined properties.**

The `CustomJSProperties` event is raised every time the grid is rendered, allowing you to pass whatever information you would like to pass to the client. When you assign a value to the `Properties` dictionary, this value becomes a bona fide property from the client's perspective. For example, if you add `cpSample` to the `Properties` dictionary, `cpSample` appears to be a first-class property as far as the client is concerned. (See Figure 2-26.) The following code fragment contains an example of the `CustomJSProperties` event that adds a property called `cpSample`:

```
protected void ASPxGridView1_CustomJSProperties(object sender,
    DevExpress.Web.ASPxGridView.ASPxGridViewClientJSPropertiesEventArgs e)
{
  e.Properties["cpSample"] = "This is a test property";
}
```

Assume again that the client views the `ASPxGridView` as an object named `grid`. From the client's perspective, `cpSample` can then be accessed on the client as `grid.cpSample`.

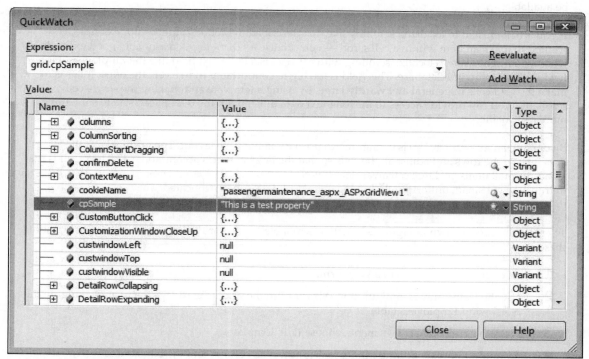

Figure 2-26: CustomJSProperties become bona fide, first-class properties as far as the client browser is concerned (as shown).

The value of the `CustomJSProperties` event is what you decide to put in the `Properties` dictionary that will add meaning and value to the client. The help documentation for the `CustomJSProperties` event (search "CustomJSProperties event") demonstrates how to put the `ASPxGridView`'s `PageIndex` in the `Properties` dictionary and display that value in an alert dialog box after a button click.

Enabling Horizontal Scrolling

Horizontal scrolling can be simulated by using a `<div>` tag and setting the style overflow property scroll, which will let the div scroll horizontally and vertically. (See Mehul Harry's demonstration video at `http://tv.devexpress.com/ASPxGridViewHorizontalScroll.movie`.) Since the release of the `ASPxGridView` version 9.1, horizontal scrolling has been integrated into the grid.

To enable horizontal scrolling, change the `ASPxGridView`'s `Settings.ShowHorizontalScrollbar` to true. If the grid's horizontal width exceeds the display width, the horizontal scrollbar and scrolling will be available.

If you are interested in localized scrolling like that described in Mehul's video — for example, you wanted to make an item within a cell scroll — you can use a `<div>` tag. A reasonably good example of when you might want to localize scrolling with a `<div>` is a large text field like the Employees' Notes field in the Northwind database. This field is too big to comfortably fit in a cell; the effect it has is to make the grid cells in general awkwardly large. By using a template and making the single cell scrollable, you can provide access to the long text data but contain the overall cell size to something more reasonable.

By default, an `ASPxGridView` is configured to use a dynamic table layout. The grid looks at the largest data item in the rows and adjust all the cells so that the largest item is accommodated. The result is that adjacent small items get large cell areas, too. If you set `ASPxGridViewSettings.UseFixedTableLayout` to true, you get small, uniform cells, but big chunks of data appear truncated. The trick is to enable `UseFixedTableLayout` and then use a template and `<div>` for the cells with large amounts of data.

To create the effect shown in Figure 2-27 with a scrollable `<div>` for the Employees' Notes field, follow these steps:

1. Add an `ASPxGridView` to a Web form.

2. Use the Data Source Configuration Wizard from the grid's Smart tags menu and configure the Northwind Employees table.

3. From the grid's Smart tags menu, choose Edit Templates.

4. From the Template Editing Mode, select the `Notes` column and the `DataItemTemplate`.

5. Place a `<div>` tag in the template and an `ASPxLabel` inside the `<div>` tag. (See Listing 2-29.)

6. Set the `<div>` tag's style to
   `style="overflow:scroll; height:60px; vertical-align:top; width: 100%; margin: 0 0 0 0".`

7. Set the `ASPxLabel`'s `Text` attribute to `<%# Eval("Notes") %>`, which will bind the label to the row's `Notes` field.

8. Using the columns editor (from the Smart tags menu), modify the `Notes` column's Width property to 100px. (You may have to experiment with the various width and height properties to get the cell look you desire)

9. Finally, set the `ASPxGridView`'s `Settings-UseFixedTableLayout="true"`. (You can change this attribute in the ASP.NET or by using the Properties window.)

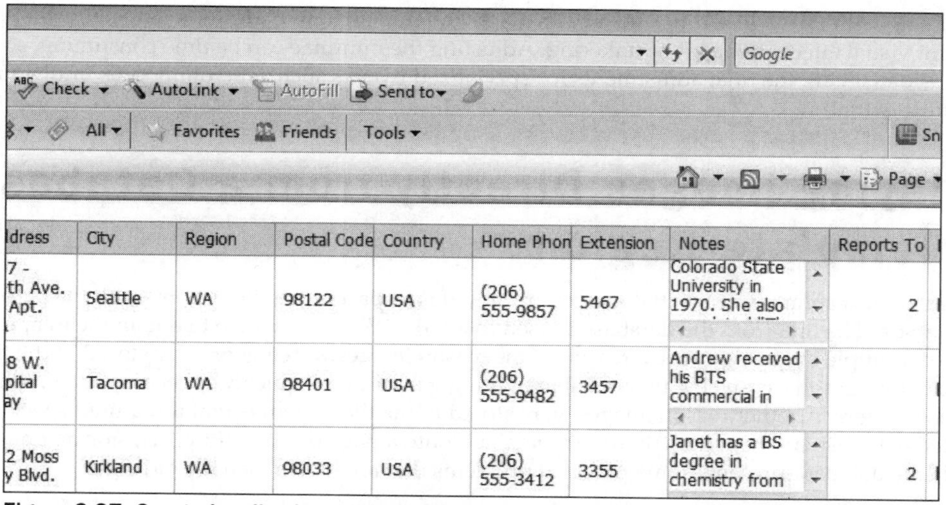

Figure 2-27: Create localized scrolling by using a template field and a <div> tag with the overflow style set to scroll.

Scrolling is more or less automatic. The scrollbars will be enabled when the content of the <div> exceeds the <div>'s bounds. Therefore, if you forget to adjust (usually shrink) the cell containing the grid, you will just see disabled scrollbars. Listing 2-29 shows you approximately what the GridViewDataTextColumn will need to contain to create the scrollable region.

Listing 2-29: The key to creating a scrolling cell is to add a template and use a <div> tag with the overflow style set to scroll (as shown).

```
<dxwgv:GridViewDataTextColumn FieldName="Notes" VisibleIndex="14" Width="100px">
  <DataItemTemplate>
    <div style="overflow:scroll; height:60px;
vertical-align:top; width:100%; margin:0 0 0 0">
      <dxe:ASPxLabel runat="server" Text='<%# Eval("Notes") %>'>
      </dxe:ASPxLabel>
    </div>
  </DataItemTemplate>
  <CellStyle VerticalAlign="Top">
    <Paddings Padding="0px" />
  </CellStyle>
</dxwgv:GridViewDataTextColumn>
```

Playing with the style settings for width, height, alignment, and padding will usually get you the right visual effect after a bit of tinkering. Adjusting the minutiae can be time consuming, so consider saving the final adjustments for specialized tweaks such as scrolling cells until you have a little extra time.

Displaying Images Directly from a Database in a Template Region

One of the most common ways that images are stored is as part of the file system, with the path stored in the database. The link from the database is used to tell the Web page where to obtain the image. This was done for a couple of quasi-practical reasons. One reason images were historically stored in the file system is that graphics can clog up a database with gigabytes very quickly, exceeding the limitations of database servers. Another reason images were stored in the file system is that it required specialized knowledge to display them directly from a database onto a page or grid. However, storing images outside the database presents some practical problems that are worse than the old cure.

One problem with external storage of images is that moving the images will break the Web application or at least require an update to the paths in the database. Another problem is that externally stored images may require access security that differs from database access, which sometimes means that images might be vulnerable in ways different from your database vulnerabilities. Another problem is versioning. If your system updates those images, and those images are stored externally, how do you track the revisions, old, and current images? Finally, when the database is backed up, your externally stored images are not backed up with the database. For these reasons, I prefer storing images in the database and displaying them from the database. Back up the database and the images get backed up, too.

If you know the trick for display from a database, then direct database retrieval and display is not a problem. The next section demonstrates how to display images from a database using the "trick," but the section after that shows you that when you are using the ASPxGridView, you don't need to know the trick. The ASPxGridView can, with very little effort, display images from a database. If you are pressed for time, skip the next subsection, "Displaying Images from a Database Manually," and go on to "Displaying Images from a Database in the ASPxGridView."

Displaying Images from a Database Manually

Probably the most glaring problem here is that images in the twenty-first century aren't treated like first-class data citizens and aren't displayable as any other native data type is. (Database providers, are you listening?) Luckily, a few clever people have worked out how to display images that are stored in a database.

Of course, some solutions store paths and refer to the paths with an image control. Some solutions store images, write them to file, and set the dynamic path, although doing so can cause concurrency issues. And then there are a couple of variations on storing the image and rendering it to the HttpResponse stream. Mehul Harry offers a solution at http://tv.devexpress.com/ASPxBinaryImageIntro .movie that passes the unique key as part of the query path on the URL and requeries the database for the image. The part that writes the image to the response stream can be handled with a UserControl or IHttpHandler. I already demonstrated how to render an image from a database using the query path and UserControl in "Rendering Images in ASP.NET Directly from Your Database" at www.codeguru .com/columns/vb/article.php/c14061, so in this example I use an IHttpHandler.

The solution is shown in Figure 2-28 as a UML model (created with Sparx Systems Enterprise Architect 7.0). In case you aren't really comfortable with UML, here is a brief explanation of the diagram:

❑ A Web Page has an ASPxGridView and SqlDataSource. (The ASPxGridView is shown as a separate class to permit visual elaboration, but the grid is just an attribute of the page, just as the SqlDataSource is.) The line with the diamond means aggregation or a "has-a" relationship.

❑ The ASPxGridView has GridViewDataTextColumn(s). The one that contains the Photo data contains a DataItemTemplate.

❑ The DataItemTemplate (for the Photo) has a UserControl called PhotoControl.

❑ PhotoControl has three relevant attributes: EmployeeID, Photo, and an HtmlImage (implied using an <img> tag).

❑ The PhotoControl's EmployeeID and Photo property are set declaratively in the DataItemTemplate column.

❑ PhotoControl has an association with the HttpApplication; PhotoControl stuffs the Photo bytes in the application cache (not depicted, but implied).

❑ The PhotoControl's HtmlImage — the <img> tag — has a Src property that is set to the URL for the Handler.ashx file containing the Handler class.

❑ The Handler class implements the IHttpHandler interface.

❑ IHttpHandler requires a ProcessRequest method.

❑ The EmployeeID is passed to the IHttpHandler as a QueryString.

Figure 2-28 depicts a class diagram. Class diagrams are good, in general, at displaying a static view of parts of a system. Class diagrams aren't really useful for showing dynamic behavior, but Figure 2-28 does give you an idea of what is involved in assembling the elements for displaying images out of a database. The basic behavior is as follows: The grid contains a template, and the template contains a user control. For each row, the EmployeeID and Photo are assigned to the UserControl's properties. The UserControl caches — as opposed to requerying — the Photo and implicitly loads the Handler.ashx through an <img>'s Src attribute, passing the EmployeeID to the Handler.ashx. The handler, in turn, grabs the Photo from the cache and adds it to the HttpResponse stream.

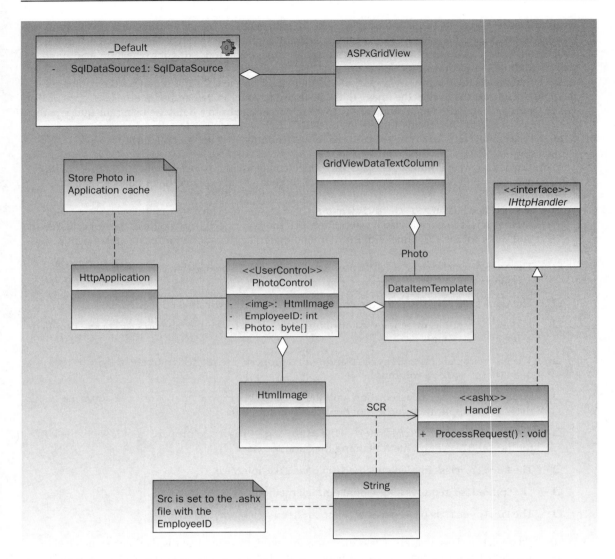

Figure 2-28: A very detailed UML that depicts the relationships used to load an image from a database to an ASPxGridView.

Listing 2-30 contains the ASP for the Default.aspx page. There is no code-behind for the default page; it just contains the ASPxGridView and SqlDataSource. Listing 2-31 contains the ASP.NET for the PhotoControl.ascx file, and Listing 2-32 contains the code-behind. Listing 2-33 does the actual work by loading the image for display.

Listing 2-30: The ASP.NET for the page containing the ASPxGridView and DataItemTemplate and the SqlDataSource.

```
<%@ Page Language="C#" AutoEventWireup="true"
  CodeFile="Default.aspx.cs" Inherits="_Default" %>
<%@ Register assembly="DevExpress.Web.ASPxGridView.v9.1,
Version=9.1.2.0, Culture=neutral,
PublicKeyToken=b88d1754d700e49a"
  namespace="DevExpress.Web.ASPxGridView" tagprefix="dxwgv" %>
<%@ Register assembly="DevExpress.Web.ASPxEditors.v9.1,
Version=9.1.2.0, Culture=neutral,
  PublicKeyToken=b88d1754d700e49a"
  namespace="DevExpress.Web.ASPxEditors" tagprefix="dxe" %>

<%@ Register src="PhotoControl.ascx" tagname="PhotoControl" tagprefix="uc1" %>

<!DOCTYPE html PUBLIC "-//W3C//DTD XHTML 1.0 Transitional//EN"
"http://www.w3.org/TR/xhtml1/DTD/xhtml1-transitional.dtd">

<html xmlns="http://www.w3.org/1999/xhtml">
<head runat="server">
    <title></title>
</head>
<body>
    <form id="form1" runat="server">
    <div>
      <dxwgv:ASPxGridView ID="ASPxGridView1" runat="server"
        AutoGenerateColumns="False" DataSourceID="SqlDataSource1"
        KeyFieldName="EmployeeID">
        <Columns>
          <dxwgv:GridViewDataTextColumn FieldName="EmployeeID" ReadOnly="True"
            VisibleIndex="0">
            <EditFormSettings Visible="False" />
          </dxwgv:GridViewDataTextColumn>
          <dxwgv:GridViewDataTextColumn FieldName="LastName" VisibleIndex="1">
          </dxwgv:GridViewDataTextColumn>
          <dxwgv:GridViewDataTextColumn FieldName="FirstName" VisibleIndex="2">
          </dxwgv:GridViewDataTextColumn>
          <dxwgv:GridViewDataTextColumn FieldName="Photo" VisibleIndex="3">
            <DataItemTemplate>
              <uc1:PhotoControl ID="PhotoControl1" runat="server"
EmployeeID='<%# Eval("EmployeeID") %>'
  Photo='<%# Eval("Photo") %>' />
            </DataItemTemplate>
          </dxwgv:GridViewDataTextColumn>
        </Columns>
      </dxwgv:ASPxGridView>
      <asp:SqlDataSource ID="SqlDataSource1" runat="server"
        ConnectionString="<%$ ConnectionStrings:NorthwindConnectionString %>"
        SelectCommand="SELECT [EmployeeID],
          [LastName], [FirstName], [Photo] FROM [Employees]">
      </asp:SqlDataSource>
    </div>
    </form>
</body>
</html>
```

Listing 2-31: Contains the ASP.NET for the PhotoControl; the key is that instead of an image for the Src property, an .ashx file is referred to.

```
<%@ Control Language="C#" AutoEventWireup="true" CodeFile="PhotoControl.ascx.cs"
Inherits="PhotoControl" %>
<img alt="" src="Handler.ashx?id=<%# EmployeeID %>" />
```

Listing 2-32: The code-behind for the PhotoControl.ascx file is rendered once for each row, receiving the EmployeeID and Photo.

```csharp
using System;
using System.Collections.Generic;
using System.Linq;
using System.Web;
using System.Web.UI;
using System.Web.UI.WebControls;
using System.Drawing;
using System.Drawing.Imaging;
using System.IO;

public partial class PhotoControl : System.Web.UI.UserControl
{
    protected void Page_Load(object sender, EventArgs e)
    {
    }

    protected void Page_Unload(object sender, EventArgs e)
    {
      Application[employeeID.ToString()] = photo;
    }

    private int employeeID = -1;
    public int EmployeeID
    {
      get { return employeeID; }
      set
      {
        employeeID = value;
      }
    }

    private byte[] photo = null;
    public byte[] Photo
    {
      get { return photo; }
      set
      {
        photo = value;
      }
    }
}
```

Listing 2-33: The .ashx file does the heavy lifting by putting the image's bytes into the HttpResponse stream.

```csharp
<%@ WebHandler Language="C#" Class="Handler" %>

using System;
using System.Web;

public class Handler : IHttpHandler {

    public void ProcessRequest (HttpContext context)
    {
      string id = context.Request.QueryString["id"];
      if (id == null) return;
      byte[] photo = (byte[])context.Application[id];
      System.Drawing.ImageConverter converter =
        new System.Drawing.ImageConverter();
      System.Drawing.Image image =
        (System.Drawing.Image)converter.ConvertFrom(photo);
      image.Save(context.Response.OutputStream,
        System.Drawing.Imaging.ImageFormat.Jpeg);
    }

    public bool IsReusable
    {
        get
        {
            return true;
        }
    }
}
```

Collectively, the solution in Listings 2-30 through 2-33 remind me of a Rube Goldberg device (see www .rubegoldberg.com). Rube Goldberg is most famous for cartoons that depict the most convoluted and ridiculous way to automate what seems like a trivial task. Goldberg's devices invariably seem to include boots, buckets, pulleys, and levers all working toward sharpening a pencil, washing a window, or teeing up golf balls. In short, displaying images from databases shouldn't require this much work.

Figure 2-29 shows employees from the Northwind database. In my version of the database, the Employee photographs are pixilated; this is not a by-product of the solution, as you will see in the next section (in which better images are used).

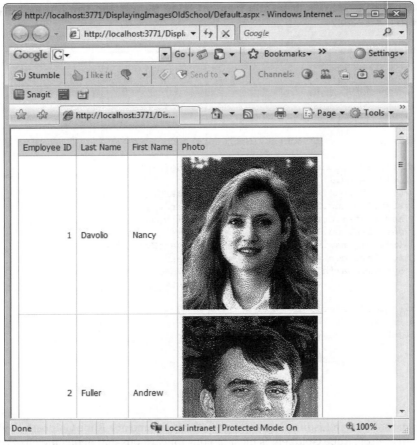

Figure 2-29: The (pixilated) images displayed directly, albeit painfully, from the Northwind database.

Displaying Images from a Database in the ASPxGridView

Since version 9.1 of the DevExpress Web controls, the ASPxGridView is capable of displaying images directly from the database. To make this work, you need only the ASPxGridView with a template column and an ASPxBinaryImage in the template column. (You don't need the UserControl, <img>, and IHttpHandler because the ASPxBinaryImage control knows how to load an image.)

I got tired of looking at the pixilated images in the Northwind database, so for this example I used the AdventureWorks `ProductPhoto` table.

To display an image using the `ASPxGridView` and `ASPxBinaryImage` control, follow these steps. (The code is provided after the steps.)

1. Add a Web page to your application.

2. Add an `ASPxGridView` to the Web page.

3. Use the Configure Data Source Wizard to configure a `SqlDataSource` for the `ASPxGridView`, selecting the AdventureWorks database and `ProductPhoto` table.

4. Pick whatever columns you like; just include the `LargePhoto` column.

5. Because AdventureWorks uses schema names other than `dbo` after you close the wizard, modify the `SELECT` statement's `FROM` clause to include the Production schema. Here is the modified declarative `SELECT` statement:

```
SELECT [ProductPhotoID], [LargePhoto], [LargePhotoFileName]
FROM [Production].[ProductPhoto]
```

6. The `LargePhoto` column won't be added by default because the grid can't figure out that a varbinary column is an image (yet). Use the Smart tags `Column` option to add a column for the `LargePhoto` column.

7. Set the `LargePhoto` column's `FieldName` to `LargePhoto`.

8. Close the columns editor.

9. From the Smart tags menu, choose Edit Templates and select the `DataItemTemplate` for the `LargePhoto` column.

10. Drag and drop an `ASPxBinaryImage` from the toolbox into the template region of the grid.

11. For the `Value` attribute of the `ASPxBinaryImage` use block script and `Eval` to bind the image to the LargePhoto column.

```
<dxe:ASPxBinaryImage ID="ASPxBinaryImage1" runat="server"
          Value='<%# Eval("LargePhoto") %>'></dxe:ASPxBinaryImage>
```

That's all there is to it: a template column with an ASPxBinaryImage. The entire ASP.NET listing for the preceding solution is provided in Listing 2-34. There is no code-behind for this example. The salient elements are depicted in a boldface font.

> **If you use newer databases that include schemas other than dbo, you may need to modify the FROM clauses to indicate the schema.**

Listing 2-34: An ASPxGridView with a template column containing an ASPxBinaryImage is all you need to load images directly from your database.

```
<%@ Page Language="C#" AutoEventWireup="true"
  CodeFile="Default3.aspx.cs" Inherits="Default3" %>

<%@ Register assembly="DevExpress.Web.ASPxGridView.v9.1,
Version=9.1.2.0, Culture=neutral,↵
  PublicKeyToken=b88d1754d700e49a"
  namespace="DevExpress.Web.ASPxGridView" tagprefix="dxwgv" %>
<%@ Register assembly="DevExpress.Web.ASPxEditors.v9.1, Version=9.1.2.0,
Culture=neutral, PublicKeyToken=b88d1754d700e49a"↵
  namespace="DevExpress.Web.ASPxEditors" tagprefix="dxe" %>

<!DOCTYPE html PUBLIC "-//W3C//DTD XHTML 1.0 Transitional//EN"
"http://www.w3.org/TR/xhtml1/DTD/xhtml1-transitional.dtd">

<html xmlns="http://www.w3.org/1999/xhtml">
<head runat="server">
    <title></title>
</head>
<body>
    <form id="form1" runat="server">
    <div>

    <dxwgv:ASPxGridView ID="ASPxGridView1" runat="server"
      DataSourceID="SqlDataSource1" AutoGenerateColumns="False"
      KeyFieldName="ProductPhotoID">
    <Columns>
      <dxwgv:GridViewDataTextColumn FieldName="ProductPhotoID" ReadOnly="True"
        VisibleIndex="0">
        <EditFormSettings Visible="False" />
      </dxwgv:GridViewDataTextColumn>
      <dxwgv:GridViewDataTextColumn
        FieldName="LargePhotoFileName" VisibleIndex="1">
      </dxwgv:GridViewDataTextColumn>
      <dxwgv:GridViewDataTextColumn FieldName="LargePhoto" VisibleIndex="2">
        <DataItemTemplate>
          <dxe:ASPxBinaryImage ID="ASPxBinaryImage1"
          runat="server" Value='<%# Eval("LargePhoto") %>'>
          </dxe:ASPxBinaryImage>
        </DataItemTemplate>
      </dxwgv:GridViewDataTextColumn>
    </Columns>
    </dxwgv:ASPxGridView>
    <asp:SqlDataSource ID="SqlDataSource1" runat="server"
    ConnectionString="<%$ ConnectionStrings:AdventureWorksConnectionString %>"

        SelectCommand="SELECT [ProductPhotoID], [LargePhoto],
    [LargePhotoFileName] FROM [Production].[ProductPhoto] ">
```

```
            </asp:SqlDataSource>

        </div>
        </form>
    </body>
    </html>
```

One objective of this book is to teach those of you who have purchased the DevExpress controls how to use them more effectively by showcasing existing and newer features. Another objective of this book is to provide you with ammunition that may help you convince your boss to spend a few hundred bucks to save thousands in unnecessary labor costs by illustrating how our controls can provide you with the results you want more simply and more quickly than if you had to plumb the Internet for every combination of published trick.

Summary

There is a lot of information in Chapter 1 and Chapter 2. After writing the two chapters, it is apparent to me that DevExpress's ASPxGridView control is rich enough in features that a whole book on this one control could be written. But that is not this book. After covering templates, editing, scripts, pop-up menus, horizontal scrolling, callback compression, using stored procedures, callback-error handlers, and much more, it is time to move on to the rest of the controls in this suite.

The examples in Chapter 1 and this chapter are designed to coexist with the many examples provided on the DevExpress Web site by supplementing those examples, providing variations, and introducing supporting material that will help you make the most of the ASPxGridView.

## 3

Using the ASPxTreeList, ASPxDataView, and ASPxNewsControl

Users have come to expect that data appear in anticipated ways based on the kinds of data. Rows of data are expected to be in grids or forms with some kind of navigation bar; something that looks like a file system is expected to be presented in trees; and so on. This is not to say that these visual metaphors are mandatory or one must not deviate from expected cues. In truth, if you can create something new and cool and your users will buy it, that's great. Most of the time, however, you have enough to do without dramatically trying to change what users expect.

Consider this example: Many of us have a ton of what is referred to as muscle memory invested in the old menu system of Microsoft Office tools. I am not sure who was clamoring for the ribbon style menus Office uses now, but for a while it caused me some personal consternation. Generally, people can become a little disoriented if things are moved around too much — like when my local mega-supermarket rearranges the shelves — or the expected visual cues aren't present. If you want to invent something new, you can assemble new visual metaphors from DevExpress controls. If you want to use existing metaphors — components and controls — in expected ways, you'll find them in this chapter, which demonstrates trees, lists, and the news controls.

Displaying Data in Tree Views

I am listening to *Bonedriven* by Bush with Mekon and *Phatty's Lunchbox* by Mekon as I write this. People always seem genuinely surprised when they find out I have seen *Rent* (three times) and like rap music (well, good rap). I am a 43-year-old Irish Catholic, but I get jazzed up by creative things, cool things, sexy things, and fun things. That hasn't changed since I was a little kid. Really digging into the DevExpress ASP.NET controls is like that for me. It's fun. The challenge for me is in trying to find something that will help or surprise you, or make using the DevExpress tools and controls more fun and more productive for you.

Trees are great data structures. I recall in college a two-hour test that required an implementation of a B-Tree (or it may have been a multiway tree). The professor was nice enough to tell me I got an A and was one of only three (out of 200) students who provided a functional solution. At the time, I think I hard-coded the solution to six levels, which was sufficient on a sliding scale for an A but, of course, of no real practical use. These days, for the most part, you and I don't even write these algorithms anymore. The task before us, some 20 years after my college years, is to figure out how to use existing data structures such as generic `Dictionary` classes or trees via the `ASPxTreeList` in new and useful ways.

This section provides several examples of the `ASPxTreeList` that include bound and unbound mode as well as virtual mode. Some new .NET technologies, such as LINQ, are rolled in to show you how you can combine everyday uses of new .NET technologies with our controls. DevExpress' ASP.NET controls will help you achieve a professional-looking result, and newer .NET capabilities such as LINQ and generics will add facility to your efforts.

Using the ASPxTreeList in Unbound Mode

Bound mode literally means that you will provide a value for the `DataSource` — `ArrayList`, results of a LINQ query, or an `XpoDataSource`, for example — and call `DataBind`. Unbound mode means you will write the lines of code that construct and shape the `ASPxTreeList` by creating `TreeListNodes`, which you do by appending them with the `ASPxTreeList.AppendNode` method.

When you work in unbound mode, you need to figure out a mechanism for the unique object key for each node and provide values that will be displayed in each of the columns. You have to define the columns, too. Unbound mode is about manual control, which necessarily means a little more work.

To try the demo — a simple file system explorer — in this section, create a new Web page and place an `ASPxTreeList` on the page. The subsections describe how to assemble the various elements to create a solution that looks like Figure 3-1. You might want a file system management tool for an administrative mode. For example, my personal Web site at `www.softconcepts.com` has graphics from my book covers. Adding new book covers or other images could be managed as basic file operations using an Explorer-style page without your having to log on to the physical Web server.

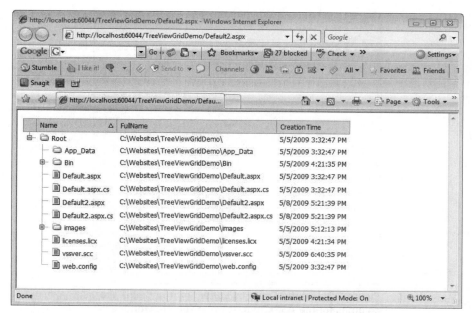

Figure 3-1: Create a file system explorer Web page using the ASPxTreeList in unbound mode.

Defining Columns

In bound mode, assign a collection or suitable data source to the ASPxTreeList; the control then figures out what columns to create. In unbound mode, you have to define the columns. The ASPxTreeList Smart tags menu and Properties window have a Columns menu item and property (respectively). Clicking either the Smart tags menu item or the Columns property opens the Columns property editor.

The Columns Editor Form works the same for the ASPxTreeList as it does for the ASPxGridView. On the left — see Figure 3-2 — is the list of Columns. The toolbar buttons perform the add, insert, move, and remove operations. The Properties view on the right side contains the properties for the selected column. Add Name, FullName, and CreationTime columns for the demo. Provide the FieldName property — again using Name, FullName, and CreationTime — for each of the columns. The other properties provide control over the appearance, behavior, data, and styles for the column. For example, you can use the Data ➪ SortOrder property to indicate that a column should be presorted.

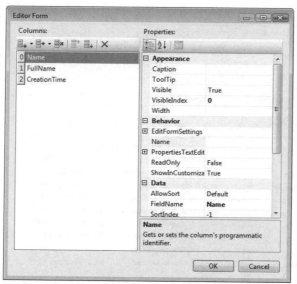

Figure 3-2: Use the Columns Editor Form to define the columns for the ASPxTreeList when you are working in unbound mode.

You can also specify columns in bound mode. For example, if you set `ASPxTreeList`
`.AutoGenerateColumns` to false and specify columns, only those columns will be assigned data in bound mode.

Adding TreeListNodes Programmatically

The `ASPxTreeList` fundamentally consists of nodes, and nodes can have child nodes. The class of each node is `TreeListNode`. Thus, constructing a tree is a matter of adding nodes at any level and then adding the child nodes for each node and repeating the process. As described, possible solutions are loops or recursion. To add a node, just call `ASPxTreeList.AppendNode`. The parent node is specified as an argument to `AppendMode`.

`AppendMode` returns a `TreeListNode`. To indicate columns for a node, treat the `TreeListNode` like an array and specify the field name you want to bind the data to as the index of the array. For instance, assigning a value to `TreeListNode["Name"]` actually assigns a value to the column whose `FieldName` property is Name. For the TreeListNode the indexer property calls the GetValue and SetValue methods, which assign values to specific fields, with the index string being the field name.

You can emulate this indexing capability in your classes by implementing a this *property, called an indexer. A* this *property — an indexer — is the property that is called when you refer to an object as if it were an array.*

The implementation of the code-behind for the demo shown in Figure 3-1 is provided in Listing 3-1.

Listing 3-1: The code-behind that recursively walks the part of the file system specified in the Page_Load event and shapes the ASPxTreeList to reflect the file system.

```
using System;
using System.Collections.Generic;
using System.Linq;
using System.Web;
using System.Web.UI;
using System.Web.UI.WebControls;
using System.IO;
using DevExpress.Web.ASPxTreeList;

public partial class Default2 : System.Web.UI.Page
{
    private static readonly string FOLDER_ICON = "~/images/folder.gif";
    private static readonly string FILE_ICON = "~/images/file.gif";
    private int key = 1;
    protected void Page_Load(object sender, EventArgs e)
    {
      CreateNodes(Server.MapPath("~/"), "Root", null);
    }

    private void CreateNodes(string path, string name, TreeListNode parent)
    {
      var files = Directory.GetFiles(path);
      var all = Directory.GetDirectories(path).Union(files);
      var infos = from file in all
                  let info = new FileInfo(file)
                  // filter out hidden files
                  where (info.Attributes
                    & FileAttributes.Hidden) != FileAttributes.Hidden
                  select info;

      FileInfo rootFileInfo = new FileInfo(path);
      TreeListNode root = ASPxTreeList1.AppendNode(key++, parent);
      root["IconName"] = FOLDER_ICON;
      root["Name"] = rootFileInfo.Name == "" ? "Root" : rootFileInfo.Name;
      root["FullName"] = rootFileInfo.FullName;
      root["CreationTime"] = rootFileInfo.CreationTime;

      foreach(FileInfo o in infos)
```

Continued

Listing 3-1: The code-behind that recursively walks the part of the file system specified in the Page_Load event and shapes the ASPxTreeList to reflect the file system. *(continued)*

```
        {
          if ((o.Attributes & FileAttributes.Directory) ==
            FileAttributes.Directory)
          {
            CreateNodes(o.FullName, o.Name, root);
          }
          else
          {
            TreeListNode node = ASPxTreeList1.AppendNode(key++, root);
            node["IconName"] = FILE_ICON;
            node["Name"] = o.Name;
            node["FullName"] = o.FullName;
            node["CreationTime"] = o.CreationTime;
          }
        }
      }
    }
  }
```

The code listing is straightforward. Page_Load indicates the starting node to create as the root of the Web site (represented by the ~/). Server.MapPath maps a virtual location (such as ~/) to a server physical path. CreateNodes is a recursive function that I defined. CreateNodes uses the Directory class's static method GetFiles to read all the files in the specified path. Directory.GetDirectories reads all the subfolders and returns an array of strings. The array of directory strings is unioned with the array of file strings.

The statement beginning with var infos is a LINQ query. The LINQ query uses a temporary range value — the let info = statement — to create a FileInfo object. The FileInfo object is used to filter out hidden files in the where clause, and the FileInfo object representing each of the files and directories is returned.

Next, the initial path — the parent directory — is added to the ASPxTreeList using the folder.gif graphic. After the parent directory is added, each FileInfo in infos is checked. If the FileInfo represents a Directory object, CreateNodes recurses; otherwise, if it's a file, the file is added to the ASPxTreeList as a child of the current node.

Tightening Up the Code with Refactor! Pro

The best way to manage your code as you go is to perform housekeeping as you go. Reusing code means fewer total lines of code and less debugging. To that end, DevExpress offers another tool, Refactor! Pro. You can tighten up CreateNodes with Refactor! Pro. Follow these steps to tighten up the code — producing the revision in Listing 3-2 — with Refactor! Pro:

1. Select all the code that creates the root TreeListNode starting with TreeListNode root to rootFileInfo["CreationTime"].

2. Right-click to display the context menu and click the Refactor! (Pro) menu item. (See Figure 3-3.)

3. Click Extract Method.

4. The extracted method will have the focus; change the name from GetRoot to CreateNode, and Refactor! Pro will rename the reference in the CreateNodes method too.

5. Double-click the `rootFileInfo` parameter and change it to info. Refactor! Pro will update references to this variable in the new method.

6. Using Refactor! Pro again, rename the local variable from `root` to `node`. Refactor! Pro will update all local variable references.

7. Add a method called `GetIcon` and pass in the `FileInfo` object. `GetIcon` returns the `FOLDER_ICON` or `FILE_ICON` depending on whether the `FileInfo` represents a folder or file.

8. Change the assignment to `node["Name"]` to determine whether Name is `""`. If Name is `""`, use "Root"; otherwise, use the `info.Name` property.

9. Change the code in the `else` condition to call `CreateNode`.

All the changes are shown in Listing 3-2. (The constants FOLDER_ICON and FILE_ICON were declared in Listing 3-1; the code in Listing 3-2 is a continuation of that code.)

Figure 3-3: Pick the Refactor! Pro context menu item and select Extract Method to refactor the code that adds and configures TreeListNode objects.

Listing 3-2: All the code related to the refactoring steps described in Steps 1 through 9.

```
private string GetIcon(FileInfo info)
{
    return (info.Attributes & FileAttributes.Directory) ==
      FileAttributes.Directory ? FOLDER_ICON : FILE_ICON;
}

private TreeListNode CreateNode(TreeListNode parent, FileInfo info)
{
  TreeListNode node = ASPxTreeList1.AppendNode(key++, parent);
  node["IconName"] = GetIcon(info);
  node["Name"] = info.Name == "" ? "Root" : info.Name;
  node["FullName"] = info.FullName;
  node["CreationTime"] = info.CreationTime;
  return node;
}

private void CreateNodes(string path, string name, TreeListNode parent)
{
  var files = Directory.GetFiles(path);
  var all = Directory.GetDirectories(path).Union(files);
  var infos = from file in all
              let info = new FileInfo(file)
              // filter out hidden files
              where (info.Attributes & FileAttributes.Hidden)
                != FileAttributes.Hidden
              select info;

  FileInfo rootFileInfo = new FileInfo(path);

  TreeListNode root = CreateNode(parent, rootFileInfo);

  foreach(FileInfo o in infos)
  {
    if ((o.Attributes
      & FileAttributes.Directory) == FileAttributes.Directory)
    {
      CreateNodes(o.FullName, o.Name, root);
    }
    else
    {
      CreateNode(root, o);
    }
  }
}
```

Replacing foreach with Array.ForEach

The last step in tightening up the code in Listings 3-1 and 3-2 is to replace the foreach loop with an Array.ForEach statement and a Lambda expression. This is an optional step, but having fewer lines of code generally costs less over time as well as promotes reuse and reduces debugging costs.

Refactor the `if` conditional test to determine whether the `FileInfo` is a directory, naming the extracted method `IsDirectory`. (You can replace the call in `CreateNode` to use this new method, too.) Rewrite the entire `for` loop as a call to `Array.ForEach`. The final changes with the `Array.ForEach` and Lambda expression are provided in Listing 3-3.

Listing 3-3: The use of the Array.ForEach statement with a Lambda expression.

```
private string GetIcon(FileInfo info)
{
  return IsDirectory(info) ? FOLDER_ICON : FILE_ICON;
}

private static bool IsDirectory(FileInfo info)
{
  return (info.Attributes
    & FileAttributes.Directory) == FileAttributes.Directory;
}

private TreeListNode CreateNode(TreeListNode parent, FileInfo info)
{
  TreeListNode node = ASPxTreeList1.AppendNode(key++, parent);
  node["IconName"] = GetIcon(info);
  node["Name"] = info.Name == "" ? "Root" : info.Name;
  node["FullName"] = info.FullName;
  node["CreationTime"] = info.CreationTime;
  return node;
}

private void CreateNodes(string path, string name, TreeListNode parent)
{
  var files = Directory.GetFiles(path);
  var all = Directory.GetDirectories(path).Union(files);
  var infos = from file in all
              let info = new FileInfo(file)
              // filter out hidden files
              where (info.Attributes
                & FileAttributes.Hidden) != FileAttributes.Hidden
              select info;

  FileInfo rootFileInfo = new FileInfo(path);

  TreeListNode root = CreateNode(parent, rootFileInfo);

  Array.ForEach(infos.ToArray(), i=>
    {
      if (IsDirectory(i))
        CreateNodes(i.FullName, i.Name, root);
      else
        CreateNode(root, i);
    });
}
```

A Lambda expression is quite simply a shorter version of the anonymous method. Lambda expressions are very compact (usually) and fit nicely into method calls, such as the call to `Array.ForEach`. Think of the argument on the left side of *goes to* (=>) as the method header and parameters and the right side as the method body.

Some people may wonder why it matters. It matters because shorter methods are easier to reuse and debug. It also matters because changes like the one shown promote further refinements. For example, you could download the parallel FX library extensions and parallelize the `Array.ForEach` with a call to `Parallel.ForEach`, and automatically use multiple threads for your loop operation.

The last change I would make in production is to move the LINQ query to a separate function. The reason I promote this approach is because I refactor methods to as close to singular operations or one line of code as possible. Very short methods are extremely easy to debug (at a glance, really) and short methods are the easiest to reuse. They're also easier to write unit tests for, and easier to reorchestrate into many variations. For example, in the final version of the code in Listing 3-3, each method can be visually inspected quickly and each method could be unit tested separately if a bug occurred. Simple, singular kinds of functions promote what I call intensity of focus. If too much is going on in a single function, it is distracting. Admittedly, some programmers don't like more, small methods, but during my twenty years' experience, time and again the long methods are the ones that have contained the most bugs and caused the most headaches. Refactoring as a principle clearly supports the notion that order and simplicity are desirable aspects of code.

Defining Template Columns

Considerable effort goes into producing Help documentation. The Help documentation for the `ASPxTreeList`'s `Templates` property states that "a template is a set of HTML elements and Web controls that define the layout of a particular element of a control." I think of templates in a pretty basic way. Everything ultimately is rendered as HTML. Even if you don't specify some controls for a particular part of your Web page, someone has. For example, if you don't specify a template for a grid, something is ultimately being used to render the text in browse mode and the text boxes in edit mode. As HTML, these might be `<input>` or `<span>` tags, but something is there. A template is sort of like agreeing that the default look is okay, but you'd prefer something that looks a little different.

When you use the default element layout as decided by the control programmer, you get the controls that the programmer chose and the default binding to those controls. When you specify a template, you are simply indicating that you want a different set of controls for that element, and you will be responsible for the binding. Binding is basically indicating that control X gets its data from property or function Y. A control generally has a parent control, and that parent control is getting its data from an object or some other source, such as a row of data. Binding generally indicates a field from a row or a property. However, binding can also use the field or property as input to a function call, and that input is used to return a calculated result. The upshot is that control designers make some basic guesses as to what some of you might want — which is the default output — and a template lets you express that something else is desired.

In our example, I chose to display a graphic that visually provides a cue to the user that indicates what a particular node is for. (See Figure 3-1.) You can define a custom view for an `ASPxTreeListDataCell` by selecting Edit Templates from the Smart tags menu for the `ASPxTreeList` and picking the `DataCell` template of the column containing the element you want to customize. In our example, pick the `Name` column and drop an `ASPxImage` and an `ASPxLabel`, in that order, in the template region. (See Figure 3-4.) Now when the `ASPxTreeList` is rendered, the image and label will be rendered instead of the default label-only view.

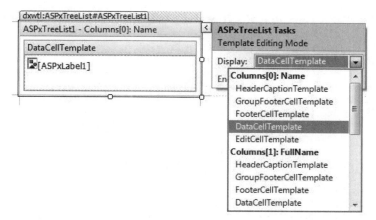

Figure 3-4: Pick the Name DataCell template to add an ASPxImage and ASPxLabel for the Name column instead of the default which displays just text.

The last step is for you to specify how the controls in the template get their data. The nature of an image control is to display graphics. The nature of a label control is to display text. To get data into your template, you need to add a binding statement for each control; the binding statement needs to provide the requisite kinds of data. For the ASPxImage, you need to provide a value for the ImageUrl property and for the ASPxLabel control, you need to provide a value for the text property. For the ASPxTreeList control, use a script block (<%# %>) and the Container.GetValue method call, passing in the name of the data value. (See Listing 3-4.)

Listing 3-4: The ASPX for the ASPxTreeList demo showing a basic file system browser.

```
<%@ Page Language="C#" AutoEventWireup="true" CodeFile="Default2.aspx.cs"
 Inherits="Default2" %>

<%@ Register assembly="DevExpress.Web.ASPxTreeList.v9.1, Version=9.1.2.0,
Culture=neutral, PublicKeyToken=b88d1754d700e49a"
 namespace="DevExpress.Web.ASPxTreeList" tagprefix="dxwtl" %>
<%@ Register assembly="DevExpress.Web.ASPxEditors.v9.1, Version=9.1.2.0,
Culture=neutral, PublicKeyToken=b88d1754d700e49a"
 namespace="DevExpress.Web.ASPxEditors" tagprefix="dxe" %>

<!DOCTYPE html PUBLIC "-//W3C//DTD XHTML 1.0 Transitional//EN"
 "http://www.w3.org/TR/xhtml1/DTD/xhtml1-transitional.dtd">

<html xmlns="http://www.w3.org/1999/xhtml">
<head runat="server">
    <title></title>
</head>
<body>
    <form id="form1" runat="server">
    <div>

        <dxwtl:ASPxTreeList ID="ASPxTreeList1" runat="server"
```

Continued

```
              AutoGenerateColumns="False">
              <Columns>
                <dxwtl:TreeListTextColumn FieldName="Name" VisibleIndex="0">
                  <DataCellTemplate>
                    <dxe:ASPxImage ID="ASPxImage1" runat="server"
                      ImageUrl='<%# Container.GetValue("IconName") %>'>
                    </dxe:ASPxImage>
                    <dxe:ASPxLabel ID="ASPxLabel1" runat="server"
                      Text='<%# Container.GetValue("Name") %>'>
                    </dxe:ASPxLabel>
                  </DataCellTemplate>
                </dxwtl:TreeListTextColumn>
                <dxwtl:TreeListTextColumn FieldName="FullName" VisibleIndex="1">
                </dxwtl:TreeListTextColumn>
                <dxwtl:TreeListTextColumn FieldName="CreationTime" VisibleIndex="2">
                </dxwtl:TreeListTextColumn>
              </Columns>
            </dxwtl:ASPxTreeList>

        </div>
        </form>
    </body>
    </html>
```

Recall from a previous section, "Adding TreeListNodes Programmatically," the discussion about the default indexer. IconName and Name were actually values that were set in the code-behind using the default indexer property of the TreeListNode. (See CreateNode in Listing 3-3.)

Creating a Windows Explorer-Style Web Page with Virtual Mode

The challenge with creating tree hierarchies with manual code is that the amount of data when created at one time can be prohibitively large. The problems are that processing large amounts of data adds wait time for the end user, most end users can't mentally process all the data at one time, and there are bandwidth considerations. A lot of data is going to take up a lot of unnecessary bandwidth. This means that the solution in a previous section, "Using the ASPxTreeList in Unbound Mode," is not wholly satisfactory if you intend to build a large tree. To address the large data set problem space, the ASPxTreeList supports virtual mode.

The ASPxTreeList is essentially a hierarchy of nodes. A node may be comprised of *n*-child nodes. When the user wants to drill down, she clicks the node (or child node) of interest. Virtual mode comes into play automatically when you implement two event handlers: VirtualModeCreateChildren and VirtualModeNodeCreating. VirtualModeCreateChildren is called when a node or child nodes need to be created, and VirtualModeNodeCreating is called when each node's details need to be filled in. The key is that the VirtualModeCreateChildren is called only when a node is expanded and needs to be populated. The result is that your tree appears to the end user to be fully populated without making the user pay for all the upfront processing and bandwidth.

To demonstrate virtual mode, the ASPX page in Listing 3-5 is almost identical to the ASPX in Listing 3-4. The differences are that the ASPX wires up the virtual mode events and the code-behind contains the implementation of the virtual mode events `VirtualModeCreateChildren` and `VirtualModeNodeCreating` (see Listing 3-5).

Listing 3-5: The ASPX for virtual mode includes wiring up the virtual mode event handlers VirtualModeCreateChildren and VirtualModeNodeCreating.

```
<%@ Page Language="C#" AutoEventWireup="true"  CodeFile="Default.aspx.cs"
 Inherits="_Default" %>
<%@ Register assembly="DevExpress.Web.ASPxTreeList.v9.1, Version=9.1.2.0,
Culture=neutral, PublicKeyToken=b88d1754d700e49a"
 namespace="DevExpress.Web.ASPxTreeList" tagprefix="dxwtl" %>
<%@ Register assembly="DevExpress.Web.ASPxEditors.v9.1, Version=9.1.2.0,
Culture=neutral, PublicKeyToken=b88d1754d700e49a"
 namespace="DevExpress.Web.ASPxEditors" tagprefix="dxe" %>

<!DOCTYPE html PUBLIC "-//W3C//DTD XHTML 1.0 Transitional//EN"
 "http://www.w3.org/TR/xhtml1/DTD/xhtml1-transitional.dtd">

<html xmlns="http://www.w3.org/1999/xhtml">
<head runat="server">
    <title></title>
</head>
<body>
    <form id="form1" runat="server">
    <div>
        <dxwtl:ASPxTreeList ID="ASPxTreeList1" runat="server"
          onvirtualmodecreatechildren=
            "ASPxTreeList1_VirtualModeCreateChildren"
          onvirtualmodenodecreating="ASPxTreeList1_VirtualModeNodeCreating"
          AutoGenerateColumns="False" EnableCallbackCompression="True">
          <Settings ShowColumnHeaders="False" />
            <SettingsBehavior ExpandCollapseAction="NodeDblClick" />
          <Templates>
            <DataCell>
              <dxe:ASPxImage ID="ASPxImage1" runat="server"
                ImageUrl='<%# Container.GetValue("IconName") %>'>
              </dxe:ASPxImage>
               <dxe:ASPxLabel ID="ASPxLabel1" runat="server"
                Text='<%# Container.GetValue("Name") %>'>
              </dxe:ASPxLabel>
            </DataCell>
          </Templates>
          <Columns>
            <dxwtl:TreeListTextColumn FieldName="Name" VisibleIndex="0">
            </dxwtl:TreeListTextColumn>
          </Columns>
        </dxwtl:ASPxTreeList>
    </div>
    </form>
</body>
</html>
```

When a user clicks to expand a node, an Ajax call to `VirtualModeCreateChildren` is made. `VirtualModeCreateChildren` creates all the nodes at the same level of abstraction. The first time `VirtualModeCreateChildren` is called, the `TreeListVirtualModeCreateChildrenEventArgs` `.NodeObject` property is null (unless the tree contains at least one item). In Listing 3-6, the `if`-conditional check — `if (e.NodeObject == null)` — ensures that the C:\ node will be created first. Nodes are added to the tree by adding them to the `TreeListVirtualModeCreateChildEventArgs.Children` property. The `Children` property is null by default and is defined as an `object` type, so you can assign the data type you need to the `Children` property.

Each subsequent call to `VirtualModeCreateChildren` examines `NodeObject`. `NodeObject` represents the expanded node. Because the demo builds a map of the file system, the nodes will be directories. The `else` condition reads the files and directories — see `GetFiles` — and uses those files to turn the file and directory names into `FileInfo` objects. All the `FileInfo` objects are added as children to the `TreeListVirtualModeCreateChildEventArgs.Children` property.

When an item is added to the `Children` property, the `VirtualModeNodeCreating` event is called for each item. Again because this example is adding file system items to the tree, the data being associated with each node is data from a `FileInfo` object. In `VirtualModeNodeCreating`, `GetNodeGuid` — a local method — is called to associate and reuse a unique `GUID` with each node. `IsLeaf` indicates whether a node will have other children; in this instance, directories are not leaf nodes and files are. `SetNodeValue` is called to associate values with field names. For example, the `DataCell` in the `Name` column contains an `ASPxImage` and `ASPxLabel`. The binding statements for the `ASPxImage.ImageUrl` and `ASPxLabel.Text` properties are received from the `IconName` and `Name` values, respectively. (Refer to Listing 3-6 for the code-behind implementation.)

Listing 3-6: The code-behind for the virtual mode file system explorer.

```
using System;
using System.Collections.Generic;
using System.Linq;
using System.Web;
using System.Web.UI;
using System.Web.UI.WebControls;
using System.IO;
using DevExpress.Web.ASPxTreeList;
using System.Security.Permissions;

public partial class _Default : System.Web.UI.Page
{
    private static readonly string FOLDER_ICON = "~/images/folder.gif";
    private static readonly string FILE_ICON = "~/images/file.gif";

    private static IEnumerable<FileInfo> GetFileInfoData(
      IEnumerable<string> files)
    {
      return from file in files
            let info = new FileInfo(file)
            where (info.Attributes
              & FileAttributes.Hidden) != FileAttributes.Hidden
            select info;
```

```
    }

    private static IEnumerable<string> GetFiles(string start)
    {
      return
        Directory.GetDirectories(start).Union(Directory.GetFiles(start));
    }

    private string GetIcon(FileInfo info)
    {
      return (info.Attributes
      & FileAttributes.Directory) == FileAttributes.Directory
      ? FOLDER_ICON : FILE_ICON;
    }

    protected void ASPxTreeList1_VirtualModeCreateChildren(
      object sender, TreeListVirtualModeCreateChildrenEventArgs e)
    {
      e.Children = new List<FileInfo>();

      if (e.NodeObject == null)
      {
        FileInfo info = new FileInfo("C:\\");
        e.Children.Add(info);
      }
      else
      {
        string path = e.NodeObject == null ? "C:\\"
          : e.NodeObject.ToString();

        if (!Directory.Exists(path)) return;

        try
        {
          var files = GetFiles(path);
          var infos = GetFileInfoData(files);
          e.Children = new List<FileInfo>();
          foreach (var info in infos)
          {
            e.Children.Add(info);
          }
        }
        catch { }
      }
    }

    protected void ASPxTreeList1_VirtualModeNodeCreating(
      object sender, TreeListVirtualModeNodeCreatingEventArgs e)
    {
      FileInfo info = (FileInfo)e.NodeObject;
      e.NodeKeyValue = GetNodeGuid(info.FullName);
```

Continued

Listing 3-6: The code-behind for the virtual mode file system explorer. *(continued)*

```
      e.IsLeaf = !Directory.Exists(info.FullName);

      if(info.FullName == "C:\\")
        e.SetNodeValue("Name", "C:\\");
      else
        e.SetNodeValue("Name", info.Name);

      e.SetNodeValue("IconName", GetIcon(info));
      e.SetNodeValue("NodePath", info.FullName);
    }

    // need a unique key, so GUID is used
    private Guid GetNodeGuid(string path)
    {
      if (!Map.ContainsKey(path))
        Map[path] = Guid.NewGuid();
      return Map[path];
    }

    private Dictionary<string, Guid> Map
    {
      get
      {
        const string key = "DX_PATH_GUID_MAP";
        if (Session[key] == null)
          Session[key] = new Dictionary<string, Guid>();
        return Session[key] as Dictionary<string, Guid>;
      }
    }
  }
```

Using a GUID with a generic Dictionary object is a technique borrowed from one of our Web demos. When you construct the tree manually, you need to associate a unique key with each node. GUIDs are useful here. The Map property is a generic Dictionary and it stores the path and a GUID in the Dictionary, and the Dictionary is stored in Session. You can just use this code verbatim in your code.

Binding (over Building) to a SqlDataSource

I have mentioned in previous books, articles, blog posts, and tweets that one of the reasons I write so much is that when I get a pretty good solution to something, it's worth sharing and posting. The Internet seems as good a place as any to store information I might need again or someone else might find useful.

Sitting on the Skyview Terrace at the Hilton Hotel, watching the sunset on beautiful Glendale, California, waiting to go home, I want to illustrate another point. Using someone else's code often results in arriving at a solution substantially faster and generally with a better outcome. To emphasize the point, I created a rough solution for generating a tree-like hierarchy from scratch without the aid of the Internet. (I couldn't get a connection 19 stories up outside the Hilton. Too bad, but that's another problem — lack of Internet ubiquity — that is way overdue for a solution.)

A clever data structure solution that is often employed is the self-referencing table. A self-referencing table is one that has foreign keys that refer to rows in the same table. For example, the AdventureWorks HumanResources.Employee table has an EmployeeID and a ManagerID. The ManagerID actually refers to rows in the HumanResources.Employee table, because basically an employee record is an employee record. The challenge is not designing a table with an extra key that refers to other rows in the same table; the problem is organizing the data in a way that reflects the relationships specified by the keys. This is because such a table is basically a tree that has been flattened into a single table. Exacerbating the problem is that the level of relationships can be an arbitrarily large number of levels deep.

You can find plenty of posts on the Internet about how to manage such data with SQL queries and code. Some of these posts work in a general way and other posts are a mess, further illustrating that the problem can be challenging. To illustrate, Listing 3-7 contains C# code that builds a tree hierarchy from the HumanResources.Employees table in AdventureWorks. The code is intentionally rough, and by the time I hacked it together, had dinner, and began writing this section of the book, I had spent about three hours — and I spent much of that time deciding on a class structure and data structure that I could live with even as a hack. Keep in mind that it took several hours, the code is contained in a console application (which by itself isn't very useful), and the solution employs recursion, which will fail for large data sets. Figure 3-5 shows the unremarkable output from Listing 3-7.

Listing 3-7: C# code that assembles the self-referencing AdventureWorks HumanResources.Employee table into a tree-like hierarchy and displays the results.

```csharp
using System;
using System.Collections.Generic;
using System.Linq;
using System.Text;
using System.Data.SqlClient;
using System.Collections;

namespace TreeTraversalDemo
{
  class Program
  {
    static void Main(string[] args)
    {
      List<Employee> all = new List<Employee>();
      all.Read();
      List<Employee> list = new List<Employee>();
      InsertAll(list, all);
      Print(list, 0);
      Console.ReadLine();
    }

    private static void Print(List<Employee> list, int tab)
    {
      string pad = new string(' ', tab);
      foreach (Employee e in list)
      {
        Console.WriteLine("{0}{1}", pad, e);
        Print(e.ManagedEmployees, tab + 2);
```

Continued

Listing 3-7: C# code that assembles the self-referencing AdventureWorks HumanResources.Employee table into a tree-like hierarchy and displays the results. *(continued)*

```csharp
      }
    }

    private static void InsertAll(List<Employee> list,
      List<Employee> employees)
    {
      foreach (Employee e in employees)
      {
        if (list.Count == 0 || e.ManagerID == null)
        {
          list.Add(e);
        }
        else
        {
          foreach (Employee manager in list)
            if (Insert(manager, e, 2))
              break;
        }
      }
    }

    private static bool Insert(Employee manager, Employee e, int tab)
    {
        if (manager.EmployeeID == e.ManagerID)
        {
          manager.ManagedEmployees.Add(e);
          e.Manager = manager;
          return true;
        }
        else
        {
          foreach (Employee m in manager.ManagedEmployees)
            if (Insert(m, e, tab))
              return true;
        }

        return false;
    }
  }

  public static class EmployeeReader
  {
    public static void Read(this List<Employee> employees)
    {
      string connectionString =
        @"Data Source=.\SQLEXPRESS; " +
         "Initial Catalog=AdventureWorks;Integrated Security=True";
      string sql =
        "select e.EmployeeID, e.ManagerID, e.Title, c.FirstName, " +
        "c.LastName, e.LoginID from HumanResources.Employee " +
        "e inner join Person.Contact c on " +
```

```
      "e.ContactID = c.ContactID " +
      "order by e.ManagerID";

   using (SqlConnection connection = new SqlConnection(connectionString))
   {
     connection.Open();
     SqlCommand command = new SqlCommand(sql, connection);
     SqlDataReader reader = command.ExecuteReader();
     while (reader.Read())
     {
       employees.Add(Read(reader));
     }
   }

 }

 private static Employee Read(SqlDataReader reader)
 {
   int employeeID = reader.GetInt32(0);
   int? managerID = reader[1] == System.DBNull.Value
     ? null : (int?)reader.GetInt32(1);
   string title = reader.GetString(2);
   string firstName = reader.GetString(3);
   string lastName = reader.GetString(4);
   string loginID = reader.GetString(5);
   return new Employee(employeeID, managerID, title, firstName,
     lastName, loginID);
 }
}

public class Employee
{
 /// <summary>
 /// Initializes a new instance of the Employee class.
 /// </summary>
 /// <param name="employeeID"></param>
 /// <param name="managerID"></param>
 /// <param name="title"></param>
 /// <param name="firstName"></param>
 /// <param name="lastName"></param>
 /// <param name="loginID"></param>
 public Employee(int employeeID, int? managerID,
   string title, string firstName, string lastName, string loginID)
 {
   this.employeeID = employeeID;
   this.managerID = managerID;
   this.title = title;
   this.firstName = firstName;
   this.lastName = lastName;
   this.loginID = loginID;
 }

 private int employeeID;
```

Continued

Listing 3-7: C# code that assembles the self-referencing AdventureWorks HumanResources.Employee table into a tree-like hierarchy and displays the results. *(continued)*

```csharp
public int EmployeeID
{
  get { return employeeID; }
  set { employeeID = value; }
}

private int? managerID;
public int? ManagerID
{
  get { return managerID; }
  set { managerID = value; }
}

private string title;
public string Title
{
  get { return title; }
  set { title = value; }
}

private string firstName;
public string FirstName
{
  get { return firstName; }
  set { firstName = value; }
}

private string lastName;
public string LastName
{
  get { return lastName; }
  set { lastName = value; }
}

private string loginID;
public string LoginID
{
  get { return loginID; }
  set { loginID = value; }
}

public override string ToString()
{
  string mask = "{0} {1} {2} {3} {4}";
  return string.Format(mask, managerID, employeeID,
    title, firstName, lastName);
}

private List<Employee> managedEmployees = new List<Employee>();
public List<Employee> ManagedEmployees
```

```
    {
      get { return managedEmployees; }
      set { managedEmployees = value; }
    }

    private Employee manager;
    public Employee Manager
    {
      get { return manager; }
      set { manager = value; }
    }
  }
}
```

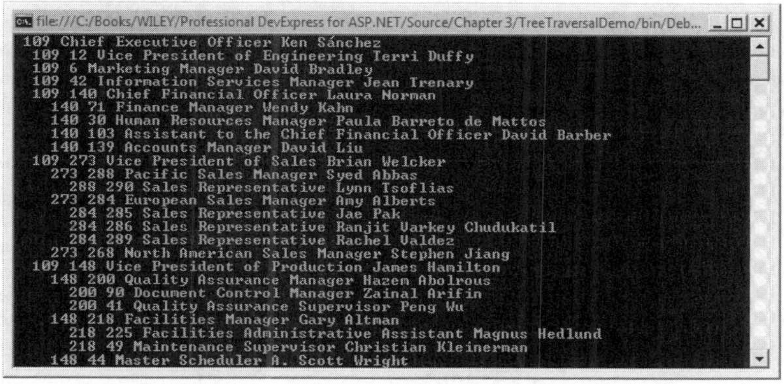

Figure 3-5: The output from Listing 3-7 visually approximates a tree hierarchy that reflects the self-referencing employee data.

The code in Listing 3-7 is intentionally unremarkable. Recreating tree hierarchies from scratch is seldom worth doing. The `Employee` class and ADO.NET code went very quickly, especially with `CodeRush` helping with the typing, because entities and ADO.NET code are code I write all the time.

The relationships between all employees are represented by a generic `List` of `Employee` objects, which saved quite a bit of time. The `ManagedEmployees` property of the `Employee` class is also a `List` of `Employee` objects. The rest of the code in the `Program` class is just trying to figure out which list or sublist to put `Employees` into.

This code has several problems , and many programmers will likely experience some of these (perhaps you have recently). Because the code is new and was written from scratch — that is, I own it — I am encouraged to try to perfect it with tinkering. You may have heard of the concept of "beautiful code." The code in Listing 3-7 is not beautiful, so the potential exists for tinkering because most programmers are conscientious about what the code looks like. Second, the `Insert` method uses recursion. Recursion can and ultimately usually does blow the stack, which again means that the code will need to be rewritten to eliminate recursion. Third, the code really can't be used as is because it just dumps the hierarchy to the Console. This means that the code is not flexible enough as is for general-purpose use. Finally, the output isn't pretty. (You can probably find more issues, but you get the point.) Figure 3-6 shows the same hierarchy displayed using the `ASPxTreeList`. The differences are stark. The results are pretty. It took me two minutes to create. The code (for the tree) is owned by DevExpress, so tinkering is out of the question. It required no code on my part to create because everything was done with the IDE designer tools. Also, the `ASPxTreeList` doesn't really care that the database data are sorted, which is something that was not tested in the solution in Listing 3-7. (Notice that the literal SQL in Listing 3-7 has an `order by` statement.)

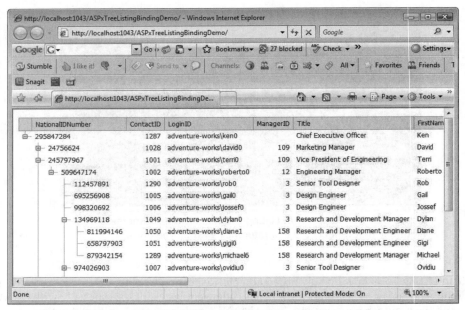

Figure 3-6: The no-code solution displaying the HumanResources.Employee hierarchy in an ASPxTreeList.

SQL 2005 supports schemas other than dbo. If you use a SQL Server 2005 database, you need to include the schema in the query — `SELECT * FROM HumanResources.Employee`, for example — or check the declarative SQL in the ASPX to ensure that the schema name is included.

This is worth pointing out because the Choose Data Source Wizard will display table names and generate SQL without the schema name. Another solution is to specify a custom SQL statement in the Configure the Select Statement step in the Choose Data Source Wizard.

To assemble the `ASPxTreeList` demo as shown in Figure 3-6, follow these steps:

1. On a Web page, add an `ASPxTreeList`.

2. From the `ASPxTreeList`'s Smart tags menu, select Choose Data Source.

3. You will need a data source with a hierarchy. A natural hierarchy is a self-referencing table (where foreign keys refer to other rows in the same table). Use the AdventureWorks `HumanResources.Employee` table.

4. In AdventureWorks, the `Employee` name information is actually stored in the `Contacts` table. Define a custom query to join on the `Person.Contact` table. (See Listing 3-8 for an example.)

5. Specify the `KeyFieldName` as `EmployeeID`.

6. Specify the `ParentFieldName` as `ManagerID`. (`ManagerID` really refers to an `EmployeeID` in the same table; that is, the employee that represents this employee's manager.)

When you define the custom query (see Listing 3-8), make sure to use the schema names. SQL Server 2005 permits schemas other than dbo, but you need to express them in the SQL. For example, in the Choose Data Source Wizard, if you select AdventureWorks, the wizard will show you `Employee` as a possible data source and write the `SELECT` statement as `SELECT * FROM [Employee]`. Unfortunately, this query won't work because dbo is the assumed schema. This dbo-assumed-schema problem is a known problem with the data source configuration wizard, not the `ASPxTreeList`.

Listing 3-8: Use schema names when you are using a SQL Server 2005 database such as AdventureWorks; otherwise, dbo is the assumed schema name.

```
SELECT HumanResources.Employee.EmployeeID,
HumanResources.Employee.NationalIDNumber, HumanResources.Employee.ContactID,
HumanResources.Employee.LoginID, HumanResources.Employee.ManagerID,
HumanResources.Employee.Title, HumanResources.Employee.BirthDate,
HumanResources.Employee.MaritalStatus, HumanResources.Employee.Gender,
HumanResources.Employee.HireDate, HumanResources.Employee.SalariedFlag,
HumanResources.Employee.VacationHours, HumanResources.Employee.SickLeaveHours,
HumanResources.Employee.CurrentFlag, HumanResources.Employee.rowguid,
HumanResources.Employee.ModifiedDate, Person.Contact.FirstName,
Person.Contact.MiddleName, Person.Contact.LastName FROM HumanResources.Employee
INNER JOIN Person.Contact ON HumanResources.Employee.ContactID =
Person.Contact.ContactID
```

Creating SQL like that shown in Listing 3-8 isn't hard because the Configure the Select Statement step of the Configure Data Source Wizard has an option to specify a custom SQL statement, which leads to a Define Custom Statements or Stored Procedure step. The latter step has a Query Builder button (see Figure 3-7). The query builder button will open a Query Builder (see Figure 3-8), which in turn will generate SQL for you based on a few selections.

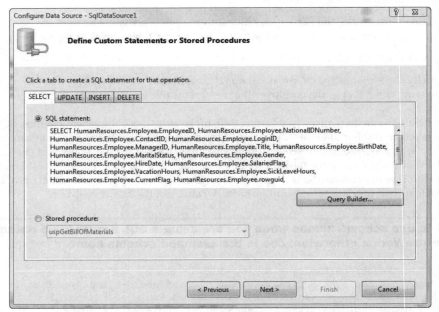

Figure 3-7: The Configure the Select Statement supports defining custom SQL statements that lead to the step shown; click Query Builder to visually define a query.

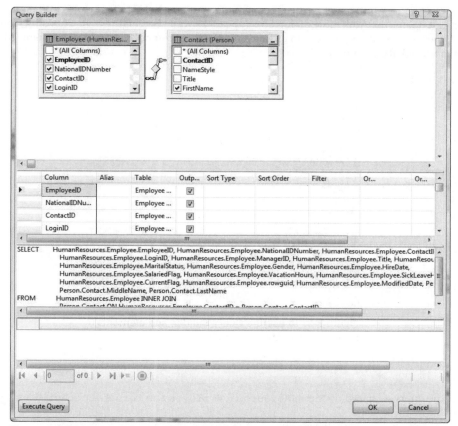

Figure 3-8: The Query Builder is basically the same Query Builder accessible through the Server Explorer in Visual Studio.

Defining a Query with the Query Builder

If you want to use a custom query when you configure a data source, select Specify a Custom SQL Statement or Stored Procedure in the Configure the Select Statement step of the Configure Data Source Wizard. When you click Next, the wizard will switch to the Define Custom Statements or Stored Procedures optional step. You can define a SQL statement or pick an existing stored procedure from a drop-down list.

To use a visual query builder, click the Query Builder button. (Refer to Figure 3-7.) When the Query Builder first opens, the Add Table dialog box appears as well. (See Figure 3-9). Choosing from Tables, Views, Functions, and Synonyms, add as many elements as you need. To add an element, click the element and click the Add button.

Figure 3-9: To use the Query Builder, add elements from the Add Table dialog box.

To build the query — based on `HumanResources.Employee` and `Person.Contact` — using the Query Builder, follow these steps:

1. When the Query Builder is first displayed, the Add Table dialog box (see Figure 3-9) is displayed as a modal dialog window. Add the `HumanResources.Employee` and `Person.Contact` tables by selecting each table in turn and clicking Add.

2. Close the Add Table dialog box.

3. The join on `ContactID` will be added for you.

4. At the top of the Query Builder, click each of the `Employee` table columns.

5. At the top of the Query Builder, select the `Title`, `FirstName`, `MiddleName`, and `LastName` columns for the `Contact` table.

6. Click Execute Query to make sure you get some data.

7. Click OK.

Use the Columns Editor Form to reposition the `FirstName`, `MiddleName`, *and* `LastName` *columns.*

It is worth noting that if you change the SQL statement, the `ASPxTreeList.ParentFieldName` property may be reset to an empty string. The indication that this has happened is that your tree hierarchy will be flattened out.

Paging (and Overlapping Control Features)

The `ASPxTreeList` supports paging. This is a no-code feature. To enable paging, change the `ASPxTreeList.SettingsPager.Mode` property from `ShowAllNodes` (the default) to `ShowPager`. If you want to adjust the page size, change the default value of 10 for the `SettingsPager.PageSize` property.

Many features, such as paging, overlap. Because the `ASPxTreeList` is a hybrid control with grid-like features, there is a Columns editor, which works the same way as the `ASPxGridView` Columns editor. From the `ASPxTreeList`'s Smart tags menu, you can add an `ASPxHttpHandlerModule` (see the section in Chapter 2 called "Catching Callback Errors Using an ASPxHttpHandlerModule"). The `ASPxTreeList` supports templates (see "Defining Template Columns," earlier in this chapter), and custom styles and much more. Features that are shared across controls are not repeated for each control. Use the Table of Contents and the Index to find where specific, shared features are covered.

If you interested in how to use the `ASPxTreeList` with the `ASPxSiteMapControl`, refer to Chapter 4, "Adding SiteMaps, Navigation, and Pop-Up Dialog Boxes."

Sorting Hierarchies of Data

Sorting is another feature that is built into the `ASPxTreeList`, as it is in the `ASPxGridView`. To enable sorting set the `ASPxTreeList.SettingsBehavior.Sort` property to true. With the headers visible, click any header to sort on that column. Use the Shift key to sort on additional columns. To clear sorting for a single column, hold the Ctrl key down and click the column header of the column for which you want sorting removed.

As a developer, all you need to do is enable sorting to permit your end users to sort on any number of columns in the `ASPxTreeList`. To support client-side sorting, use the `ASPxClientTreeList.SortBy` method. An example demonstrating how you might implement client-side sorting is demonstrated with the grid and an `ASPxPopupMenu` in Chapter 2 in the section "Implementing the ASPxPopupMenu Behavior."

Modifying ASPxTreeList Data

The nuts and bolts for modifying data in an `ASPxTreeList` are in place. By checking the Smart tags menu options for editing, inserting, and deleting — Enable Editing, Enable Inserting, and Enable Deleting — can be turned on. These settings add Edit, Insert, and Delete links to the `ASPxTreeList`. Click the Edit link and the `ASPxTreeList` is placed in Edit mode; also, the Update and Cancel links are visible. Click Update (or Cancel) and the related action is taken.

Like the grid's `SettingsEditing.Mode`, the `ASPxTreeList`'s `SettingsEditing.Mode` property will determine what edit mode will look like. The default `SettingsEditing.Mode` is `Inline`, which places simple controls in the node being edited. The `EditForm` and `EditFormAndDisplayNode` modes use an embedded Form — a basic template-styled appearance (see Figure 3-10) — for editing.

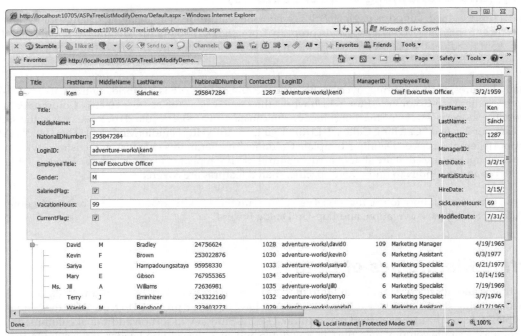

Figure 3-10: The ASPxTreeList with a node being edited with the SettingsEditing.Mode set to EditFormAndDisplayNode.

Again, as with the grid, the key to completing the edit behaviors is for you to define them. If the ASPxTreeList is showing data from a single source — such as one table — you can use the Choose Data Source Wizard's Advanced button in the Configure the Select Statement step and let the wizard write the CRUD — create, read, update, and delete — SQL for you. (See "Implementing Write Behaviors Declaratively" in Chapter 2.) An example of letting the wizard create the SQL is provided in Chapter 2. Continuing with the AdventureWorks example from the previous section "Defining a Query with the Query Builder," the next section looks at supporting updates when more than a single table is being edited in a node.

Editing When a Node Contains Multiple Tables

Recall that the ASPxTreeList from the earlier section "Defining a Query with the Query Builder" contains data from the AdventureWorks HumanResources.Employee and Person.Contact tables connected with a join. For all intents and purposes, this is equivalent to a view. A simple UPDATE SQL statement will not get the job of updating done. What is needed to update fields from multiple tables is a stored procedure and a transaction. The Choose Data Source Wizard supports specifying stored procedures, and stored procedures — T-SQL — supports transactions.

> *Inserting and deleting can be implemented the same way updating is demonstrated here: Add a stored procedure for each behavior and use a transaction.*

To build the ASPxTreeList and support updating as depicted in Figure 3-10, you can start with the sample from "Defining a Query with the Query Builder" section earlier in this chapter. Before you begin constructing the Web page, you need to define the stored procedure for updating columns from two tables.

Implementing an UPDATE Stored Procedure with T-SQL

Going forward with the example based on the AdventureWorks HumanResources.Employee and Person.Contact table joined on ContactID, you will need to implement a stored procedure that updates both tables involved. Generally, you want to modify multiple tables inside a transaction. Because the example will be using a stored procedure called declaratively, the transaction needs to be defined in T-SQL (as opposed to in code with ADO.NET).

You can use SQL Server Management Studio or Visual Studio to implement the stored procedure. To create the stored procedure in Visual Studio — shown in Listing 3-9 — follow these steps:

1. In Visual Studio, open the Server Explorer by choosing View] Server Explorer.

2. Expand the Data Connections node and expand the AdventureWorks connection.

3. Right-click Stored Procedures and click Add New Stored Procedure.

4. Add the stored procedure shown in Listing 3-9.

5. Press Ctrl+R to run the stored procedure (or right-click over the stored procedure and choose Execute).

Listing 3-9: UpdateEmployee updates columns in two tables wrapped in a transaction.

```
CREATE PROCEDURE dbo.UpdateEmployee
(
      @EmployeeID           int,
      @NationalIDNumber       nvarchar(15),
      @ContactID            int,
      @LoginID          nvarchar(256),
      @ManagerID            int,
      @EmployeeTitle        nvarchar(50),
      @BirthDate            datetime,
      @MaritalStatus        nchar(1),
      @Gender           nchar(1),
      @HireDate             datetime,
      @SalariedFlag       bit,
      @VacationHours        smallint,
      @SickLeaveHours       smallint,
      @CurrentFlag        bit,
      @ModifiedDate         datetime,
      @Title            nvarchar(8),
      @FirstName            nvarchar(50),
      @MiddleName             nvarchar(50),
      @LastName             nvarchar(50)
)
AS
BEGIN
    BEGIN TRY
        BEGIN TRANSACTION

        UPDATE HumanResources.Employee
        SET
            NationalIDNumber = @NationalIDNumber,
            LoginID = @LoginID,
            ManagerID = @ManagerID,
            Title = @EmployeeTitle,
            BirthDate = @BirthDate,
            MaritalStatus = @MaritalStatus,
            Gender = @Gender,
            HireDate = @HireDate,
            SalariedFlag = @SalariedFlag,
            VacationHours = @VacationHours,
            SickLeaveHours = @SickLeaveHours,
            CurrentFlag = @CurrentFlag,
            ModifiedDate = @ModifiedDate
        WHERE
            EmployeeID = @EmployeeID

        UPDATE Person.Contact
        SET
            Title = @Title,
            FirstName = @FirstName,
            MiddleName = @MiddleName,
            LastName = @LastName
        WHERE
```

```
                ContactID = @ContactID
            COMMIT TRANSACTION
      END TRY
      BEGIN CATCH
            ROLLBACK TRANSACTION
      END CATCH
END
```

If you are completely new to T-SQL and stored procedures, a good SQL primer will help. (Unfortunately, if I cover everything you need to know as a developer — such as basic SQL — this book will never get to press, but try *Beginning T-SQL with Microsoft SQL Server 2005 and 2008,* by Paul Turley and Dan Wood and published by Wrox.) In short, though, the stored procedure is two SQL UPDATEs wrapped in a transaction. The reason that defining the stored procedure first is helpful is that the Choose Data Source Wizard will list existing stored procedures, and the input parameters — appearing right after the stored procedure header — are used to generate declarative input parameters.

Constructing the Web Page with an Updatable ASPxTreeList

To construct the ASPxTreeList shown in Figure 3-10, you will need an ASPxTreeList configured for an edit mode and a SqlDataSource that selects from the AdventureWorks HumanResources.Employee and Person.Contact tables joined on ContactID and the UpdateEmployee stored procedure defined in the previous section.

Notice the @EmployeeTitle input parameter from Listing 3-9. This is an alias for HumanResources.Employee.Title. It will be helpful to alias the same column as EmployeeTitle in the SELECT statement to facilitate matching columns between the SELECT statement and the stored procedure that updates the data. To build the sample, follow these steps. (The code follows.)

1. Add an ASPxTreeList to a Web page.

2. From the Smart tags menu, choose Choose Data Source.

3. Choose New data source.

4. On the Configure the Select Statement step, select "Specify a custom SQL statement or stored procedure."

5. Click Next.

6. On the SELECT tab of the "Define Custom Statements or Stored Procedures" step, use the Query Builder or write the SQL statement as shown in Listing 3-10. (This step is where you can define your other CRUD behaviors.)

7. Click the UPDATE tab.

8. Click Stored Procedure.

9. Pick the UpdateEmployee procedure. (This step is why it is helpful to define your stored procedures before configuring data sources.)

10. Click Next.

11. Click Finish.

12. From the `ASPxTreeList`'s Smart tags menu, click Enable Editing.

13. In the Properties window (making sure that the `ASPxTreeList` is selected), change the `SettingsEditor.Mode` property to `EditFormAndDisplayMode`. (Refer to Listing 3-11 for the generated ASPX.)

Listing 3-10: The SELECT statement that joins Employee and Person on ContactID and aliases the Employee.Title column.

```
    SELECT Person.Contact.Title, Person.Contact.FirstName,
Person.Contact.MiddleName, Person.Contact.LastName,
HumanResources.Employee.EmployeeID, HumanResources.Employee.NationalIDNumber,
HumanResources.Employee.ContactID, HumanResources.Employee.LoginID,
HumanResources.Employee.ManagerID, HumanResources.Employee.Title AS
EmployeeTitle, HumanResources.Employee.BirthDate, HumanResources.Employee.Gender,
HumanResources.Employee.MaritalStatus, HumanResources.Employee.SalariedFlag,
HumanResources.Employee.HireDate, HumanResources.Employee.VacationHours,
HumanResources.Employee.SickLeaveHours, HumanResources.Employee.CurrentFlag,
HumanResources.Employee.ModifiedDate FROM HumanResources.Employee INNER JOIN
Person.Contact ON HumanResources.Employee.ContactID = Person.Contact.ContactID
```

Listing 3-11: The generated ASPX shows the ASPxTreeList and declarative SQL behaviors.

```
<%@ Page Language="C#" AutoEventWireup="true"  CodeFile="Default.aspx.cs"
 Inherits="_Default" %>

<%@ Register assembly="DevExpress.Web.ASPxTreeList.v9.1, Version=9.1.2.0,
Culture=neutral, PublicKeyToken=b88d1754d700e49a"
 namespace="DevExpress.Web.ASPxTreeList" tagprefix="dxwtl" %>
<%@ Register assembly="DevExpress.Web.ASPxEditors.v9.1, Version=9.1.2.0,
Culture=neutral, PublicKeyToken=b88d1754d700e49a"
 namespace="DevExpress.Web.ASPxEditors" tagprefix="dxe" %>

<!DOCTYPE html PUBLIC "-//W3C//DTD XHTML 1.0 Transitional//EN"
 "http://www.w3.org/TR/xhtml1/DTD/xhtml1-transitional.dtd">

<html xmlns="http://www.w3.org/1999/xhtml">
<head runat="server">
  <title></title>
</head>
<body>
  <form id="form1" runat="server">
  <div>

    <dxwtl:ASPxTreeList ID="ASPxTreeList1" runat="server"
      AutoGenerateColumns="False" DataSourceID="SqlDataSource1"
      KeyFieldName="EmployeeID" ParentFieldName="ManagerID">
      <SettingsEditing Mode="EditFormAndDisplayNode" />
```

```
    <Columns>
      <dxwtl:TreeListTextColumn FieldName="Title" VisibleIndex="0">
      </dxwtl:TreeListTextColumn>
      <dxwtl:TreeListTextColumn FieldName="FirstName" VisibleIndex="1">
      </dxwtl:TreeListTextColumn>
      <dxwtl:TreeListTextColumn FieldName="MiddleName" VisibleIndex="2">
      </dxwtl:TreeListTextColumn>
      <dxwtl:TreeListTextColumn FieldName="LastName" VisibleIndex="3">
      </dxwtl:TreeListTextColumn>
      <dxwtl:TreeListTextColumn FieldName="NationalIDNumber" VisibleIndex="4">
      </dxwtl:TreeListTextColumn>
      <dxwtl:TreeListTextColumn FieldName="ContactID" VisibleIndex="5">
      </dxwtl:TreeListTextColumn>
      <dxwtl:TreeListTextColumn FieldName="LoginID" VisibleIndex="6">
      </dxwtl:TreeListTextColumn>
      <dxwtl:TreeListTextColumn FieldName="ManagerID" VisibleIndex="7">
      </dxwtl:TreeListTextColumn>
      <dxwtl:TreeListTextColumn FieldName="EmployeeTitle" VisibleIndex="8">
      </dxwtl:TreeListTextColumn>
      <dxwtl:TreeListDateTimeColumn FieldName="BirthDate" VisibleIndex="9">
      </dxwtl:TreeListDateTimeColumn>
      <dxwtl:TreeListTextColumn FieldName="Gender" VisibleIndex="10">
      </dxwtl:TreeListTextColumn>
      <dxwtl:TreeListTextColumn FieldName="MaritalStatus" VisibleIndex="11">
      </dxwtl:TreeListTextColumn>
      <dxwtl:TreeListCheckColumn FieldName="SalariedFlag" VisibleIndex="12">
      </dxwtl:TreeListCheckColumn>
      <dxwtl:TreeListDateTimeColumn FieldName="HireDate" VisibleIndex="13">
      </dxwtl:TreeListDateTimeColumn>
      <dxwtl:TreeListTextColumn FieldName="VacationHours" VisibleIndex="14">
      </dxwtl:TreeListTextColumn>
      <dxwtl:TreeListTextColumn FieldName="SickLeaveHours" VisibleIndex="15">
      </dxwtl:TreeListTextColumn>
      <dxwtl:TreeListCheckColumn FieldName="CurrentFlag" VisibleIndex="16">
      </dxwtl:TreeListCheckColumn>
      <dxwtl:TreeListDateTimeColumn FieldName="ModifiedDate" VisibleIndex="17">
      </dxwtl:TreeListDateTimeColumn>
      <dxwtl:TreeListCommandColumn VisibleIndex="18">
        <EditButton Visible="True">
        </EditButton>
      </dxwtl:TreeListCommandColumn>
    </Columns>
  </dxwtl:ASPxTreeList>
  <asp:SqlDataSource ID="SqlDataSource1" runat="server"
    ConnectionString="<%$ ConnectionStrings:AdventureWorksConnectionString %>"
    SelectCommand="SELECT Person.Contact.Title, Person.Contact.FirstName,
Person.Contact.MiddleName, Person.Contact.LastName,
HumanResources.Employee.EmployeeID, HumanResources.Employee.NationalIDNumber,
HumanResources.Employee.ContactID, HumanResources.Employee.LoginID,
HumanResources.Employee.ManagerID, HumanResources.Employee.Title AS
EmployeeTitle, HumanResources.Employee.BirthDate, HumanResources.Employee.Gender,
HumanResources.Employee.MaritalStatus, HumanResources.Employee.SalariedFlag,
HumanResources.Employee.HireDate, HumanResources.Employee.VacationHours,
```

Continued

141

Listing 3-11: The generated ASPX shows the ASPxTreeList and declarative SQL behaviors. *(continued)*

```
HumanResources.Employee.SickLeaveHours, HumanResources.Employee.CurrentFlag,
HumanResources.Employee.ModifiedDate FROM HumanResources.Employee INNER JOIN
Person.Contact ON HumanResources.Employee.ContactID = Person.Contact.ContactID"
        UpdateCommand="UpdateEmployee" UpdateCommandType="StoredProcedure">
        <UpdateParameters>
          <asp:Parameter Name="EmployeeID" Type="Int32" />
          <asp:Parameter Name="NationalIDNumber" Type="String" />
          <asp:Parameter Name="ContactID" Type="Int32" />
          <asp:Parameter Name="LoginID" Type="String" />
          <asp:Parameter Name="ManagerID" Type="Int32" />
          <asp:Parameter Name="Title" Type="String" />
          <asp:Parameter Name="BirthDate" Type="DateTime" />
          <asp:Parameter Name="MaritalStatus" Type="String" />
          <asp:Parameter Name="Gender" Type="String" />
          <asp:Parameter Name="HireDate" Type="DateTime" />
          <asp:Parameter Name="SalariedFlag" Type="Boolean" />
          <asp:Parameter Name="VacationHours" Type="Int16" />
          <asp:Parameter Name="SickLeaveHours" Type="Int16" />
          <asp:Parameter Name="CurrentFlag" Type="Boolean" />
          <asp:Parameter Name="ModifiedDate" Type="DateTime" />
          <asp:Parameter Name="EmployeeTitle" Type="String" />
          <asp:Parameter Name="FirstName" Type="String" />
          <asp:Parameter Name="MiddleName" Type="String" />
          <asp:Parameter Name="LastName" Type="String" />
        </UpdateParameters>
      </asp:SqlDataSource>

    </div>
    </form>
  </body>
</html>
```

The example in this section uses a declarative approach to using the ASPxTreeList. Declarative development — in this case where the use of ADO.NET is implicit — takes some getting used to, but it is a pretty fast way to assemble all the elements and write less code. It is worth noting that the commands and parameters are not served to the client in plain text, which might be an objection one might have to programming declaratively.

What is important is that the ASPxTreeList supports editing data, even if the tree nodes are constructed from multiple sources. You just simply need to define all the write behaviors as well as the read behavior.

Defining a Custom Form Template

If you ran the example described in the previous section, "Editing When a Node Contains Multiple Tables" and its subsections, or looked at Figure 3-10, you will see that the DevExpress ASPxTreeList programmers take data type into account. For example, notice that the bit field SalariedFlag has a checkbox, and datetime fields employ a drop-down control that displays a Calendar. (See Figure 3-11.)

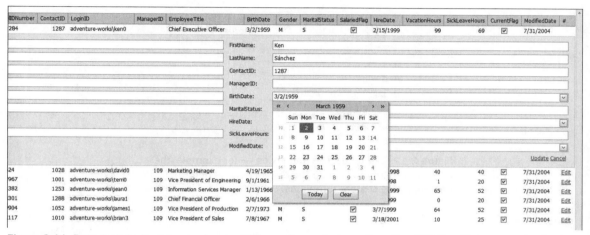

Figure 3-11: Data type is used to construct edit forms for controls such as the ASPxTreeList, so you don't have to create a template for control edit modes.

You can define custom templates for form editing mode by choosing Edit Templates from the Smart tag menu and picking the EditForm template, but before you do, experiment with the Columns properties and styles to see whether you can achieve the appearance you are going for. Defining templates for an entire Web site gives you a tremendous amount of control over the appearance of your application but takes an equally tremendous amount of time. Often, styles and properties can be used to achieve a desirable effect. For example, if you don't like the fact that field names are used for column headers and label text (in edit mode), change the Caption property of the column. For instance, putting First Name in the Caption property for the FirstName field will add the space for both the header in view mode and the label in edit mode. (See Figure 3-12.)

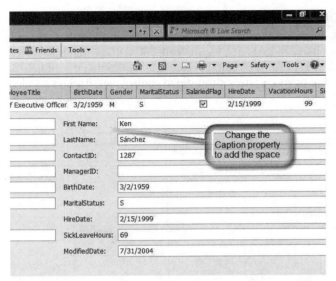

Figure 3-12: Use properties and styles — for example, the Caption property to change the display text — before implementing custom templates.

By simply defining a single control for the EditForm *template, you effectively will replace the default edit form behavior with your template. If the template is empty, the* ASPxTreeList *will generate the edit form for you. Your template will not be used in Inline mode.*

If you decide to implement a template, design the template as you would a form. Use controls such as the ASPxLabel control and modify the Text property and the ASPxTextBox control, and use the Smart tags Edit Bindings option to bind the control to a field. You will need to modify the template for every value that can be updated; you also will need to add the links for indicating that changes are to be saved or cancelled — the controls for the Update and Cancel behavior, for example.

Adding the Update and Cancel Command Controls to the Toolbox

It may seem a little awkward to talk about the Update and Cancel behaviors before talking about designing the template, but there is a reason for doing so.

When you define a custom template for the `ASPxTreeList`, you need to add the equivalent of the `Update` and `Cancel` link buttons. These are actually instances of the `ASPxTreeListTemplateReplacement` control. Unfortunately — and admittedly it might be a bit frustrating for you — this control is not even in the toolbox by default. You have to add it.

To add the `ASPxTreeListTemplateReplacement` control, follow these steps:

1. Open the Toolbox in Visual Studio.

2. Expand the DevExpress Data tab.

3. Right-click the Toolbox and click Choose Items.

4. In the Choose Toolbox Items dialog box, scroll to the `ASPxTreeListTemplateReplacement` control.

5. Select the `ASPxTreeListTemplateReplacement` control. (See Figure 3-13.)

6. Close the Choose Toolbox Items dialog box.

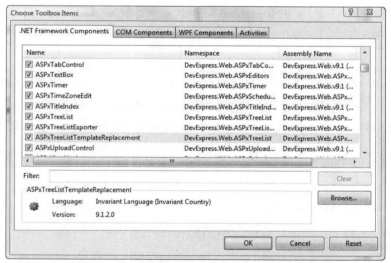

Figure 3-13: Use the Choose Toolbox Items dialog box to add the **ASPxTreeListTemplateReplacement** control to the toolbox.

Although the `ASPxTreeListTemplateReplacement` control is a little hidden and out of the way, having it makes properly configuring the `Update` and `Cancel` behavior for `ASPxTreeList` templates a two-step process. Read the next section to see how to configure the control.

Constructing a Custom Edit Template

Suppose you wanted to provide a custom template to support editing the AdventureWorks `Person` `.Contact` table's `Title`, `FirstName`, and `LastName` columns. Create a Web page with an `ASPxTreeList` and bind it to a `SqlDataSource` referring to the `Person.Contact` table. You will need to implement the `UPDATE` command, too.

> *The larger data set, including all the* `HumanResources.Employee` *and* `Person.Contact` *tables, was not used because after you know how to add one control to a template, you know how to add as many as you need; it just becomes a matter of time and patience.*

Follow these steps to define a template that supports editing a Contact's name information:

1. Add a Web page.

2. Add an `ASPxTreeList` to the Web page.

3. Click the Smart tags menu and choose Choose Data Source.

4. Using the wizard, configure the data source to refer to the AdventureWorks `Person.Contact` table.

5. When you are configuring the `SELECT` statement, select the `ContactID`, `Title`, `FirstName`, and `LastName` columns. (You need the primary key, `ContactID`, for updates to work.)

6. When you are configuring the `SELECT` statement, click the Advanced button.

7. In the Advanced SQL Generation Options dialog box, select Generate INSERT, UPDATE, and DELETE.

8. Complete the Data Source Configuration Wizard.

9. Click the `ASPxTreeList`'s Smart tags menu and click Edit Templates.

10. Select the `EditForm` template.

11. Drag and drop an `ASPxLabel` and `ASPxTextBox` for each of the `Title`, `FirstName`, and `LastName` columns.

12. For each of the `ASPxTextBox` controls, click the Smart tags menu and click Edit Bindings. Add the binding statement for the Text property; for example, enter **Bind("Title")** to establish a two-way bind to the `Title` column.

13. Click the Smart tags menu and click End Template Editing.

14. Click the `ASPxTreeList`'s Smart tags menu again and select Enable Editing.

15. Open the Properties window and change the `ASPxTreeList`'s `SettingsEditing.Mode` property to `EditFormAndDisplayNode`.

16. Drag and drop two `ASPxTreeListTemplateReplacement` controls into the `EditForm` template region.

17. Set the first `ASPxTreeListTemplateReplacement` control's `ReplacementType` to `UpdateButton` and the second one to `CancelButton`. (The finished result should look like Figure 3-14 and contain the ASPX content shown in Listing 3-12.)

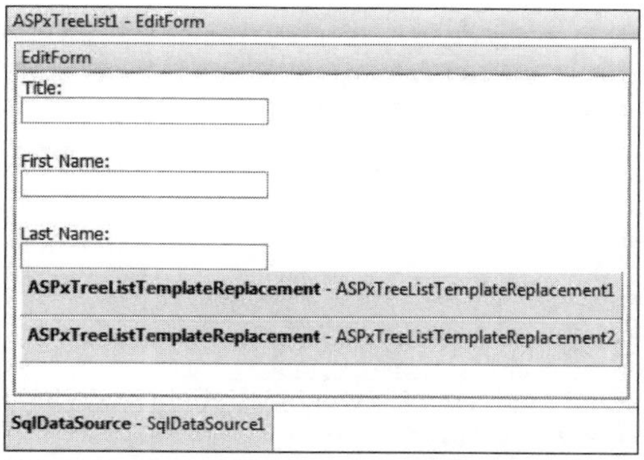

Figure 3-14: The completed EditForm template as described in the preceding text.

Listing 3-12: The ASPX showing the various CRUD commands and the EditForm template.

```
<%@ Page Language="C#" AutoEventWireup="true"  CodeFile="Default.aspx.cs"
 Inherits="_Default" %>

<%@ Register assembl="DevExpress.Web.ASPxTreeList.v9.1, Version=9.1.2.0,
Culture=neutral, PublicKeyToken=b88d1754d700e49a"
 namespace="DevExpress.Web.ASPxTreeList" tagprefix="dxwtl" %>
<%@ Register assembly="DevExpress.Web.ASPxEditors.v9.1, Version=9.1.2.0,
Culture=neutral, PublicKeyToken=b88d1754d700e49a"
 namespace="DevExpress.Web.ASPxEditors" tagprefix="dxe" %>

<!DOCTYPE html PUBLIC "-//W3C//DTD XHTML 1.0 Transitional//EN"
```

Continued

147

Listing 3-12: The ASPX showing the various CRUD commands and the EditForm template. *(continued)*

```
  "http://www.w3.org/TR/xhtml1/DTD/xhtml1-transitional.dtd">

<html xmlns="http://www.w3.org/1999/xhtml">
<head runat="server">
  <title></title>
</head>
<body>
  <form id="form1" runat="server">
  <div>

    <dxwtl:ASPxTreeList ID="ASPxTreeList1" runat="server"
      DataSourceID="SqlDataSource1" AutoGenerateColumns="False"
      KeyFieldName="ContactID" >
      <SettingsPager AlwaysShowPager="True" Mode="ShowPager" PageSize="4"
        ShowDefaultImages="False">
      </SettingsPager>
      <Templates>
        <EditForm>
          <dxe:ASPxLabel ID="ASPxLabel1" runat="server"
            Text="Title:"></dxe:ASPxLabel>
          <dxe:ASPxTextBox ID="ASPxTextBox1" runat="server" Width="170px"
            Text='<%# Bind("Title") %>'>
          </dxe:ASPxTextBox>
          <br />
          <dxe:ASPxLabel ID="ASPxLabel2" runat="server" Text="First Name:">
          </dxe:ASPxLabel>
          <dxe:ASPxTextBox ID="ASPxTextBox2" runat="server"
            Text='<%# Bind("FirstName") %>' Width="170px">
          </dxe:ASPxTextBox>
          <br />
          <dxe:ASPxLabel ID="ASPxLabel3" runat="server" Text="Last Name:">
          </dxe:ASPxLabel>
          <dxe:ASPxTextBox ID="ASPxTextBox3" runat="server"
            Text='<%# Bind("LastName") %>' Width="170px">
          </dxe:ASPxTextBox>
          <dxwtl:ASPxTreeListTemplateReplacement
            ID="ASPxTreeListTemplateReplacement1"
            runat="server" ReplacementType="UpdateButton" />
          <dxwtl:ASPxTreeListTemplateReplacement
            ID="ASPxTreeListTemplateReplacement2"
            runat="server" ReplacementType="CancelButton" />
           
        </EditForm>
      </Templates>
      <SettingsEditing Mode="EditFormAndDisplayNode" />
      <Columns>
        <dxwtl:TreeListTextColumn FieldName="Title" VisibleIndex="0">
        </dxwtl:TreeListTextColumn>
        <dxwtl:TreeListTextColumn FieldName="FirstName" VisibleIndex="1">
        </dxwtl:TreeListTextColumn>
        <dxwtl:TreeListTextColumn FieldName="LastName" VisibleIndex="2">
        </dxwtl:TreeListTextColumn>
```

```
            <dxwtl:TreeListCommandColumn VisibleIndex="3">
              <EditButton Visible="True">
              </EditButton>
            </dxwtl:TreeListCommandColumn>
          </Columns>
        </dxwtl:ASPxTreeList>
        <asp:SqlDataSource ID="SqlDataSource1" runat="server"
          ConnectionString="<%$ ConnectionStrings:AdventureWorksConnectionString %>"
          DeleteCommand="DELETE FROM [Person].[Contact] WHERE [ContactID] = @ContactID"
          InsertCommand="INSERT INTO [Person].[Contact] ([Title], [FirstName],
            [LastName]) VALUES (@Title, @FirstName, @LastName)"
          SelectCommand="SELECT TOP 10 [Title], [FirstName], [LastName],
            [ContactID] FROM [Person].[Contact]"
          UpdateCommand="UPDATE [Person].[Contact] SET [Title] = @Title,
            [FirstName] = @FirstName, [LastName] = @LastName WHERE
            [ContactID]=@ContactID">
          <DeleteParameters>
            <asp:Parameter Name="ContactID" Type="Int32" />
          </DeleteParameters>
          <UpdateParameters>
            <asp:Parameter Name="Title" Type="String" />
            <asp:Parameter Name="FirstName" Type="String" />
            <asp:Parameter Name="LastName" Type="String" />
            <asp:Parameter Name="ContactID" Type="Int32" />
          </UpdateParameters>
          <InsertParameters>
            <asp:Parameter Name="Title" Type="String" />
            <asp:Parameter Name="FirstName" Type="String" />
            <asp:Parameter Name="LastName" Type="String" />
          </InsertParameters>
        </asp:SqlDataSource>

      </div>
    </form>
  </body>
</html>
```

Run the example. When you click the Edit button next to a tree node, you should see the template as it appears at design time with controls for the Title, FirstName, and LastName columns and the Update and Cancel buttons. Note that the Update and Cancel behavior work correctly without your writing any code.

The ASPxTreeListTemplateReplacement controls are a little out of the way, but the alternative is to use a LinkButton, configure a couple of properties correctly, and write some event-handling code to complete the template. With the DevExpress ASPxTreeListTemplateReplacement control, all that plumbing is handled for you; you need only to figure out one time where it is stashed.

Editing ASPxTreeList Data Programmatically

The editing capability of the ASPxTreeList is supported through server-side code. Each of the edit behaviors has a server-side method that you can invoke on the ASPxTreeList to programmatically invoke the equivalent client-side operation. For example, StartEdit places the ASPxTreeList in edit mode; it's like clicking the Edit button. The ASPxTreeList supports server-side edits through the StartEdit, UpdateEdit, CancelEdit, StartEditNewNode, and DeleteNode methods.

To try programmatic edits, you need to invoke one of the edit behaviors, grab an instance of the control (or controls) containing data, modify the data, and end the edit. For example, if you want to change a node's value, call StartEdit, passing in the key value as a string for the node. The key is the primary key when the node is bound to a data set or whatever value you provided in unbound mode. To find a control in the EditForm template, call ASPxTreeList.FindEditFormTemplateControl, passing the control's name. Typecast the return type to the control type, modify the value by changing the control's value, and for edits, call UpdateEdit to save the changes. The fragment in Listing 3-13 changes the Title — which is bound to ASPxTextBox1 in Listing 3-12 — and saves the changes.

Listing 3-13: You can call server methods to manipulate the ASPxTreeList programmatically, as shown.

```
using System;
using System.Collections.Generic;
using System.Linq;
using System.Web;
using System.Web.UI;
using System.Web.UI.WebControls;
using DevExpress.Web.ASPxEditors;

public partial class _Default : System.Web.UI.Page
{
    protected void Page_Load(object sender, EventArgs e)
    {
        // programmatic edit
        ASPxTreeList1.StartEdit("1");
        ASPxTextBox textbox =
            (ASPxTextBox)ASPxTreeList1
                .FindEditFormTemplateControl("ASPxTextBox1");
        textbox.Text = "Herr";
        ASPxTreeList1.UpdateEdit();

    }
}
```

Exporting Data from an ASPxTreeList

From Listing 3-7 in the section "Binding (Over Building) to a SqlDataSource," earlier in this chapter, you saw that quite a bit of code is required to fabricate a tree from self-referencing data. Even using the generic List<T> class, building a basic tree takes longer. With the ASPxTreeList, you get advanced editing, sorting, custom templates, and the ability to tweak the appearance with properties and styles. Creating such a control from scratch could take one person hundreds or even thousands of hours to reproduce. In addition, , as does the ASPxGridView, the ASPxTreeList has an exporter. As you do with the ASPxGridView's exporter, if you point the ASPxTreeListExporter at an ASPxTreeList, then you get exported data capabilities, too.

Returning to the demo in Listing 3-11 from the earlier section "Constructing the Web Page with an Updatable ASPxTreeList" and combining that with what you learned in Chapter 2, "Exporting Grid Data," you can export the contents of an ASPxTreeList. To export the HumanResources.Employee and Person.Contact data from Listing 3-11, follow these steps:

1. Add an ASPxTreeListExporter control to the Web page. (Any page with an ASPxTreeList will do.)

2. Set the ASPxTreelistExporter.TreeListID property to the page's ASPxTreeList.

3. Add a button (or code to the Page_Load event) to call the desired write method. (See Listing 3-14.)

Listing 3-14: Basic code to send the contents of an ASPxTreeList in its present state — expanded state when the click event fires — to a .pdf file.

```
using System;
using System.Collections.Generic;
using System.Linq;
using System.Web;
using System.Web.UI;
using System.Web.UI.WebControls;
using System.IO;

public partial class _Default : System.Web.UI.Page
{
    protected void Page_Load(object sender, EventArgs e)
    {

    }
    protected void ASPxButton1_Click(object sender, EventArgs e)
    {
        string filename = Server.MapPath("~/") + "\\Employees.pdf";
        using(FileStream stream =
          new FileStream(filename, FileMode.CreateNew))
            ASPxTreeListExporter1.WritePdf(stream);
    }
}
```

The sample above is the code-behind for Listing 3-11. When I ran the example, I expanded the first node (the CEO node) and then clicked the ASPxButton1 control (see Figure 3-15). The other columns were too big to fit on one page, so they were printed on additional pages. What is worth noting is that the export occurred based on the current expanded state of the ASPxTreeList, and the output looks almost identical to the Web page on the client browser.

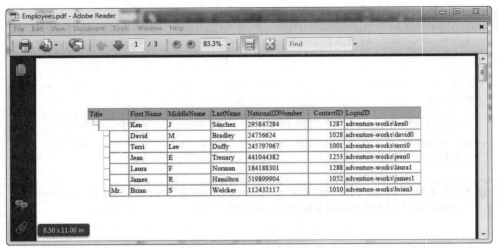

Figure 3-15: When you export an ASPxTreeList, it exports only the nodes that are visible to the client, not the entire tree; keep in mind that unexpanded nodes aren't actually sent to the client.

There are options in the `ASPxTreeListExporter`, such as `Settings.ExpandAllNodes` and `Settings.ExpandAllPages`, which will effectively retrieve and cause all data to be printed. The `ASPxTreeListExporter.Styles` property and subproperties can be used to experiment with the final appearance of the exported `ASPxTreeList`. (These features require no programming, just design-tie experimentation to get the output look-and-feel that you want your clients to experience.)

Introducing the ASPxDataView

The `ASPxDataView` is an ASP.NET Web control designed for data presentation in a specific number of columns and rows. The `ASPxDataView` supports binding, appearance customization, templates, Ajax, paging, and empty-row suppression.

The `ASPxDataView` supports search engine optimization (SEO) via the `PagerSettings.SEOFriendly` property. A known problem is that search engines ignore pager controls because they represent something that sends a post to your Web server rather than contain links to other pages. By setting the `PagerSettings.SEOFriendly` property to `SEOFriendlyMode.CrawlerOnly`, hyperlinks are rendered when a crawler is detected. Noncrawler visitors experience standard pager links. The result is that Web crawlers do a better job of indexing your site, and users experience the same great callback experience.

The `ASPxNewsControl` is an implementation of the `ASPxDataView`. The `ASPxNewsControl` is an `ASPxDataView` and `ASPxHeadline`. For a detailed example, refer to the next section, which displays news and product headlines in a Web page.

Because the ASPxDataView is a view control — editing is not supported — it is a relatively easy control to use. To experiment with the ASPxDataView control by itself (creating the results shown in Figure 3-16), use the AdventureWorks Production.Product, Production.ProductProductPhoto, and Production.ProductPhoto table. The ProductPhoto contains pictures of the bicycles for sale.

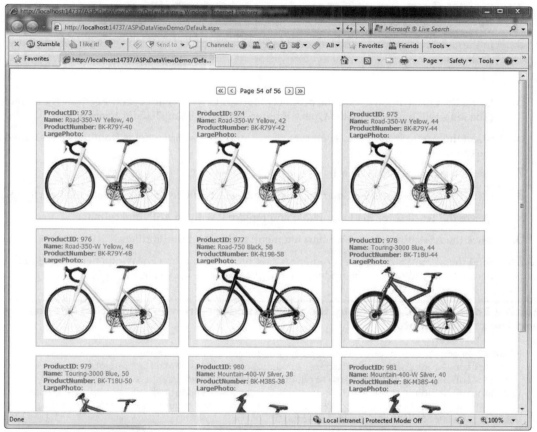

Figure 3-16: The ASPxDataView easily creates a view with a fixed number of columns and rows, including graphics, with a minimal amount of effort.

The basic page shown in Figure 3-16 employs several of the skills and techniques you have read about in this and the first couple of chapters, such as binding an image from a database and using the Query Builder to generate joins. Here are the steps you can follow to recreate the page using the `ASPxDataView`:

1. Place an `ASPxDataView` on a Web page.

2. From the `ASPxDataView`'s Smart tag menu, select Choose Data Source and configure the AdventureWorks database.

3. In the Configure the Select Statement step, choose Specify a Custom SQL Statement or Stored Procedure.

4. Click Next.

5. Using the Query Builder, add the product, `ProductProductPhoto`, and `ProductPhoto` tables. (The joins will be added by the Query Builder. Refer to Listing 3-15 for the SQL.)

6. Select the `ProductID`, `Name`, `ProductNumber`, and `LargePhoto` fields from the tables added to the query.

7. Finish the Data Source Wizard.

8. Click the `ASPxDataView`'s Smart tag menu and select Edit Templates, choose the ItemTemplate.

9. Delete the TextBox for the LargePhoto and replace it with an ASPxBinaryImage.

10. Click the ASPxBinaryImage's Smart tag menu and select Edit Bindings.

11. Bind the `ASPxBinaryImage.ContentBytes` property to the `LargePhoto` field. (Use `Eval` because the photo won't be updated in the `ASPxDataView`; see Figure 3-17.)

Listing 3-15: the SQL created by the Query Builder retrieves production information and the product photo.

```
SELECT Production.Product.ProductID, Production.Product.Name,
Production.Product.ProductNumber, Production.ProductPhoto.LargePhoto FROM
Production.Product INNER JOIN Production.ProductProductPhoto ON
Production.Product.ProductID = Production.ProductProductPhoto.ProductID INNER
JOIN Production.ProductPhoto ON Production.ProductProductPhoto.ProductPhotoID =
Production.ProductPhoto.ProductPhotoID
```

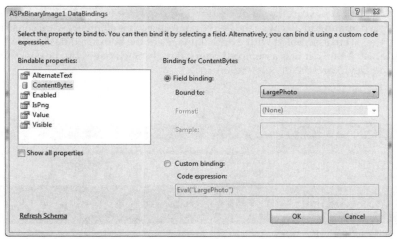

Figure 3-17: The ASPxDataView just needs one-way data binding via the Eval method because data isn't updated.

Run the sample. Some of the product images are unavailable. If you page through the result set, you will see some of the names of bicycles in the AdventureWorks database.

Displaying News and Product Headlines in a Web Page

Some Web sites are very simple like the one I used for my consulting business, www.softconcepts.com, which these days mostly displays general information and books I have written. Some Web sites are actually full-blown applications; others, such as www.devexpress.com, are a mixture of both, containing content and objective-based activities such as buying software. Most Web sites have one thing in common. Except the rare few I find with StumbleUpon that show a single picture or drawing, most Web sites display the content, news, or information that represents their reason for existing.

My Web site has a books I have authored or co-authored page (see Figure 3-18) and news about some of the things I am participating in. Because the books page and other elements were constructed several years ago, the pages were assembled with external images of the books, a database, user controls, custom code, and a DataList. That is, it was assembled painstakingly. Such pages can be constructed quite simply now using DevExpress's `ASPxNewsControl`.

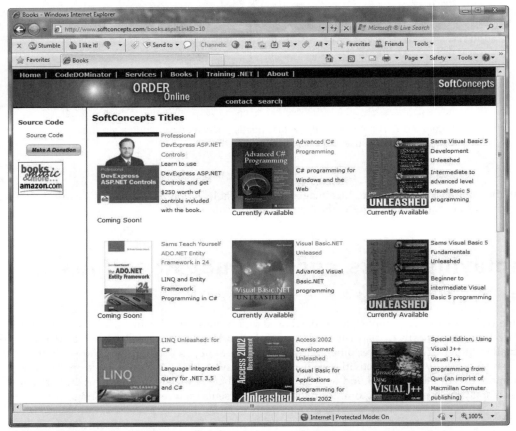

Figure 3-18: My original books page constructed manually from classes, user controls, a DataList, and external Web images.

The `ASPxNewsControl` is a combination of the `ASPxDataView` with an `ASPxHeadline`. Point it at a data source containing the content you want to display and in a couple of minutes — rather than several hours — you can produce a content page that shows a combination of graphics and text (or just text, if that's all you need). A reproduction of the book's page (shown in Figure 3-18) is demonstrated here using the `ASPxNewsControl`. The original source code, controls, and page used to produce the page shown in Figure 3-18 is not shown because the listings would add ten pages to this chapter unnecessarily. (Take my word for it.)

The `ASPxNewsControl` is sort of like the Staples' Easy Button or Amazon's One-Click for displaying content in a format that looks approximately like a news item in a paper or Web site. The basic configuration of an `ASPxNewsControl` can be accomplished by binding the `ASPxNewsControl` to a data source and setting a few properties. Generally, no code is required. The design of the control is based on common practices, especially as regards handling images. To date, I have seen many more applications that refer to images as external URLs, so the `ASPxNewsControl` is designed to expect the URL of an external image file to link to. The examples in this section demonstrate three ways to use the `ASPxNewsControl`: the no-code way, in which the database contains a URL for the image, and two ways to load the image directly from the database. The latter two approaches require a little code, but if you want to load the image form the database, you can do so.

Using the ASPxNewsControl to Display Information about Published Books

The noun News is a metaphor to convey the idea that the `ASPxNewsControl` is designed to display images and text, as you would expect in any news item, but the actual image and text can be whatever you want.

For the first sample program, you are not required to use any code. The sample is intended to approximately redesign the Books page shown in Figure 3-18, but any database table with string and image fields can be substituted if you like.

To create the revised version shown in Figure 3-19, I upsized my original Microsoft Access database to SQL Server 2005. Listing 3-16 shows the scripted CREATE TABLE command displaying the schema for the `Books` table. For the example, you are interested in the `ID`, `PublicationDate`, `Title`, `Description`, `Hyperlink`, and `CoverImageLink` columns. The `CoverImageLink` column contains relative path information to the book cover images, and the Hyperlink column contains a URL to the publisher's location or the book listing on Amazon.com.

Figure 3-19: A revised page showing published books, constructed using the ASPxNewsControl.

Listing 3-16: The CREATE TABLE script that contains information about the Books table schema.

```
USE [Books]
GO
/****** Object:  Table [dbo].[Books]    Script Date: 05/20/2009 18:15:18 ******/
SET ANSI_NULLS ON
GO
SET QUOTED_IDENTIFIER ON
GO
CREATE TABLE [dbo].[Books](
    [ID] [int] NOT NULL,
    [Title] [nvarchar](50) COLLATE SQL_Latin1_General_CP1_CI_AS NULL,
    [Author] [nvarchar](50) COLLATE SQL_Latin1_General_CP1_CI_AS NULL,
    [Publisher] [nvarchar](50) COLLATE SQL_Latin1_General_CP1_CI_AS NULL,
    [ISBN] [nvarchar](50) COLLATE SQL_Latin1_General_CP1_CI_AS NULL,
    [Description] [nvarchar](max) COLLATE SQL_Latin1_General_CP1_CI_AS NULL,
    [Hyperlink] [nvarchar](255) COLLATE SQL_Latin1_General_CP1_CI_AS NULL,
    [Tip] [nvarchar](50) COLLATE SQL_Latin1_General_CP1_CI_AS NULL,
    [Language] [nvarchar](50) COLLATE SQL_Latin1_General_CP1_CI_AS NULL,
    [PublicationDate] [datetime] NULL,
    [CoverImageLink] [nvarchar](255) COLLATE SQL_Latin1_General_CP1_CI_AS NULL,
    [BookImage] [image] NULL,
    [Visible] [bit] NOT NULL
) ON [PRIMARY] TEXTIMAGE_ON [PRIMARY]
```

The basic no-code configuration of the ASPxNewsControl begins by placing an ASPxNewsControl on a Web page and defining a data source. All the steps below describe how to configure the ASPxNewsControl to show the book cover, title, publication data, and a description. The book (or product) is loaded through a URL stored in the database. The title header is configured to be a click-through link to online purchase or publisher information, and the date and description are database fields. To create the sample, follow these steps:

1. Add an ASPxNewsControl to a Web page.

2. Click the Smart tags menu and click Choose Data Source.

3. Click New Data Source.

4. Select the Books connection.

5. When you get to the Configure the Select Statement step, select the Books table and ID, Title, Description, Hyperlink, PublicationDate, and CoverImageLink columns.

6. Click the ORDER BY on the same tab.

7. On the Add ORDER BY Clause, configure the Sort By column to be PublicationDate in descending order. (See Figure 3-20.)

8. Click OK.

9. Click Next.

10. Click Finish. (At this point, you haven't yet indicated how the selected columns are applied to the `ASPxNewsControl`.)

11. Open the Properties window.

12. Click the Categorized button at the top of the Properties window to organize the `ASPxNewsControl` properties by category.

13. In the Data category of the Properties window, set `DateField` to `PublicationDate`, `HeaderTextField` to `Title`, `ImageUrlField` to `CoverImageLink`, `NameField` to `ID`, `NavigateUrlField` to `Hyperlink`, and `TextField` to `Description`. (All these are selectable items available in drop-down lists in the Properties window.)

14. In the Misc category, choose ImageSettings and change the `ShowHeaderASLink` to `True` and the `Target` to `_blank`.

15. Run the sample.

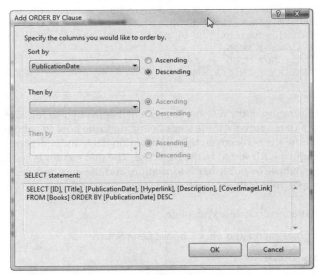

Figure 3-20: The Add ORDER BY Clause dialog box in the Configure Data Source Wizard facilitates designing queries with sort order specified.

When you run the sample, you will see the images and the pager. When you click the pager, the next group of images is retrieved with an Ajax call. It is annoying when you go to an actual News site and clicking the images in a photo story cause postbacks.

Clearly one of the objectives achieved by DevExpress controls is the ability to create great-looking, high-performing, Ajax-enabled applications very quickly without a lot of code. However, this is a book for programmers who like to write code, too. The next subsection kicks it up a notch by demonstrating how to get images out of a database.

Reading ASPxNewsControl Images from a Database

By design, the ASPxNewsControl uses a URL to incorporate an image into each item. With a little bit of ingenuity and a few extra lines of code, you can display the image in the ASPxNewsControl from a database. To do so, implement an IHttpHandler — which processes HTTP Web requests — and replace the ImageUrlField with a request to the IHttpHandler (.ashx) handler instead of a literal URL.

Detailed information on the IHttpHandler is provided in the MSDN help document and Chapter 2 in the section "Displaying Images from a Database Manually." Two variations demonstrating this approach for an ASPxNewsControl are provided here. The first approach uses a second SQL call to get the image, and the second uses the application cache. (The code for both approaches is provided in the following subsections, but the IHttpHandler information is in the aforementioned section of Chapter 2.)

Using an IHttpHandler to Read Images from the Database

The original approach that many developers used to load images was to replace an <img> tag's src attribute with the name of a Web page, and the Web page loaded the image and wrote the image bits to the HttpResponse stream. An IHttpHandler enables you to add bits to an HttpResponse stream with an IHttpHandler (.ashx) file instead of an .aspx (Web page) file.

Replacing an Image URL Field with an IHttpHandler Request

When you see a property such as ImageUrlField that is a string property, it is natural to place the path or relative path to an image — such as ~/books/images/LinqUnleashed.jpg — in the property. You can put a Web request there instead. An interesting way to do this is to construct the Web request with the SQL statement.

The following SQL statement queries all the fields from Books — see the schema in Listing 3-16 — and adds a derived column aliased as ImageID:

```
SELECT 'handler.ashx?ID='+Convert(varchar, [ID]) As ImageID, * FROM BOOKS ORDER BY
PublicationDate DESC
```

The preceding fragment includes an aliased field named `ImageID` that returns a string column that will look something like 'handler.ashx?ID=1', where the query parameter is the ID field of a row in the Books table. The call to convert changes the data type of ID so that it can be concatenated with the + operator to the first part of the query string. Simply set the `ASPxNewsControl.ImageUrlField` to the name of the derived field `ImageID`, and instead of the image's being loaded, the handler.ashx file will be requested. The next step is to implement the `handler.ashx` file.

Querying the Image and Writing It to the HttpResponse Stream

After you have effectively replaced the image URL with the `handler.ashx` request, you can add the `IHttpHandler` by choosing Website ⇨ Add New Item and selecting the Generic Handler item from the Add New Item dialog box that appears. Doing so adds an `.ashx` file to your project.

You can name the `.ashx` file anything you want; just keep the `.ashx` extension.

To complete the implementation, just provide code for the `IHttpHandler.ProcessRequest` method. Read the `ID` value from the `HttpRequest.QueryString`, use the `ID` to perform a SQL query for the associated image bits, and write those bits to the `HttpResponse`. More details for `.ashx` files are provided in Chapter 2, in the section "Displaying Images from a Database Manually." The code that implements the `ProcessRequest` is provided in Listing 3-17.

Listing 3-17: Using an IHttpHandler to query a database for an image, which in this example is the book cover for the sample.

```
<%@ WebHandler Language="C#" Class="Handler" %>
using System;
using System.Web;
using System.Data.SqlClient;
using System.Configuration;
using System.IO;
using System.Drawing;
using System.Drawing.Imaging;

public class Handler : IHttpHandler {

    public void ProcessRequest(HttpContext context)
    {
        int ID = Convert.ToInt32(context.Request.QueryString["ID"]);
        string connectionString =
            ConfigurationManager
            .ConnectionStrings["BooksConnectionString"].ConnectionString;
        string SQL = string.Format(
            "SELECT BookImage FROM Books WHERE ID = {0}", ID);
        using(SqlConnection connection = new SqlConnection(connectionString))
        {
            connection.Open();
```

```
            SqlCommand command = new SqlCommand(SQL, connection);
            SqlDataReader reader = command.ExecuteReader();
            if(reader.Read())
            {
                byte[] data = (byte[])Convert
                  .ChangeType(reader["BookImage"], typeof(byte[]));
                context.Response.ContentType = @"image\jpeg";
                context.Response.BinaryWrite(data);
            }
        }
    }
    public bool IsReusable {
        get {
            return false;
        }
    }
}
```

In Listing 3-17, the ID parameter is read from the QueryString through the `HttpContext` argument's `Response` property. Then, plain-vanilla ADO.NET is used to query the database. Finally, the image bytes are sent to the `HttpContext`'s `Response` property's `BinaryWrite` method.

The one drawback to this approach is that a second SQL request is made for each image; however, because the `ASPxNewsControl` uses Ajax by default, your end users will still have a good user experience.

Optimizing Database Reads with the Application Cache

If you want to read an image from a database but don't want to pay for a second SQL query for each image, you can shorten and revise the approach. Instead of reading the image separately, use the image already being read — implied by the `*--select all` fields — in the original SQL. You still need to build the `.ashx` handler request in the query string, so you can reuse the SQL statement from the prior section:

```
SELECT 'handler.ashx?ID='+Convert(varchar, [ID]) As ImageID, * FROM BOOKS ORDER BY
PublicationDate DESC
```

For this approach, the `IHttpHandler.ProcessRequest` method needs to be changed and you need one additional event handler.

Clearly, all fields are being read in the preceding SQL fragment. The key is to use the image read the first time, and when a particular image is read, place it in the application cache. Then, modify the `IHttpHandler` to grab the image from the application cache. The `ASPxNewsControl`'s `ItemDataBound` event is the perfect place to add the code to place the image in the application cache. Listing 3-18 demonstrates an implementation using `ItemDataBound`. Listing 3-19 shows the revised `IHttpHandler`, and Listing 3-20 shows the ASPX for the solution.

Listing 3-18: Store the available image in the application cache in the ItemDataBound event.

```
protected void ASPxNewsControl1_ItemDataBound(object source,
  DevExpress.Web.ASPxNewsControl.NewsItemEventArgs e)
{
  if(Application[e.Item.Name] == null)
    Application[e.Item.Name] =
      ((DataRowView)e.Item.DataItem).Row["BookImage"];
}
```

Listing 3-19: Use the ID query parameter to retrieve the image from the application cache.

```
<%@ WebHandler Language="C#" Class="Handler" %>
using System;
using System.Web;
using System.Data.SqlClient;
using System.Configuration;
using System.IO;
using System.Drawing;
using System.Drawing.Imaging;

public class Handler : IHttpHandler {

    public void ProcessRequest(HttpContext context)
    {
        string ID = context.Request.QueryString["ID"];
        if (ID == null) return;
        context.Response.ContentType = @"image\jpeg";
        context.Response.BinaryWrite((byte[])context.Application[ID]);
    }

    public bool IsReusable {
        get {
            return false;
        }
    }

}
```

Listing 3-20: The ASPX code for the Books sample, which uses the ASPxNewsControl.

```
<%@ Page Language="C#" AutoEventWireup="true"  CodeFile="Default.aspx.cs"
 Inherits="_Default" %>

<%@ Register assembly="DevExpress.Web.v9.1, Version=9.1.2.0,↵
Culture=neutral, PublicKeyToken=b88d1754d700e49a"
 namespace="DevExpress.Web.ASPxNewsControl" tagprefix="dxnc" %>

<%@ Register assembly="DevExpress.Web.ASPxGridView.v9.1, ↵
Version=9.1.2.0, Culture=neutral, PublicKeyToken=b88d1754d700e49a"
```

```
   namespace="DevExpress.Web.ASPxGridView" tagprefix="dxwgv" %>
<%@ Register assembly="DevExpress.Web.ASPxEditors.v9.1, ➥
Version=9.1.2.0, Culture=neutral, PublicKeyToken=b88d1754d700e49a"
 namespace="DevExpress.Web.ASPxEditors" tagprefix="dxe" %>

<!DOCTYPE html PUBLIC "-//W3C//DTD XHTML 1.0 Transitional//EN"
 "http://www.w3.org/TR/xhtml1/DTD/xhtml1-transitional.dtd">

<html xmlns="http://www.w3.org/1999/xhtml">
<head runat="server">
  <title></title>
</head>
<body>
  <form id="form1" runat="server">
  <div>

    <dxnc:ASPxNewsControl ID="ASPxNewsControl1" runat="server"
      CssFilePath="~/App_Themes/Aqua/{0}/styles.css" CssPostfix="Aqua"
      DataSourceID="SqlDataSource1" DateField="PublicationDate"
      EnableCallbackCompression="True" HeaderTextField="Title"
      ImageFolder="~/App_Themes/Aqua/{0}/" LoadingPanelText=""
      PagerAlign="Center"
      PagerPanelSpacing="0px" RowPerPage="4" TextField="Description"
      Width="400px" ImageUrlField="CoverImageLink" NameField="ID"
      onitemdatabound="ASPxNewsControl1_ItemDataBound"
      NavigateUrlField="Hyperlink">
      <Items>
        <dxnc:NewsItem Date="2009-09-01"
          HeaderText="Professional DevExpress ASP.NET Controls"

          Text="Learn to use DevExpress ASP.NET Controls and get $250➥
worth of controls included with the book."
          Name="21"
          NavigateUrl="http://www.wiley.com/WileyCDA/WileyTitle/➥
productCd-0470500832.html">
          <Image Url="handler.ashx?ID=21" />
        </dxnc:NewsItem>
        <dxnc:NewsItem Date="2009-08-31"
          HeaderText="Sams Teach Yourself ADO.NET Entity Framework in 24"
          Text="LINQ and Entity Framework Programming in C#" Name="23"
          NavigateUrl="http://www.amazon.com/➥
Teach-Yourself-ADO-NET-Entity-Framework/dp/0672330539">
          <Image Url="handler.ashx?ID=23" />
        </dxnc:NewsItem>
        <dxnc:NewsItem Date="2008-07-01" HeaderText="LINQ Unleashed: for C#"
          Text="Language integrated query for .NET 3.5 and C#" Name="20"
          NavigateUrl="http://www.amazon.com/LINQ-Unleashed-C-➥
Paul-Kimmel/dp/0672329832/ref=sr_1_1?ie=UTF8&amp;➥
s=books&amp;qid=1203016050&amp;sr=8-1">
          <Image Url="handler.ashx?ID=20" />
        </dxnc:NewsItem>
        <dxnc:NewsItem Date="2005-10-31" HeaderText="UML Demystified"
          Text="An easy, fast, and practical guide to UML" Name="19"
          NavigateUrl="http://www.amazon.com/exec/obidos/tg/➥
```

Continued

165

Listing 3-20: The ASPX code for the Books sample, which uses the ASPxNewsControl.
(continued)

```
detail/-/007226182X/qid=1121823742/sr=1-3/ref=sr_1_3/↵
002-2650943-1487215?v=glance&amp;s=books">
        <Image Url="handler.ashx?ID=19" />
      </dxnc:NewsItem>
    </Items>
    <ItemDateStyle Spacing="5px">
    </ItemDateStyle>
    <ItemSettings ShowHeaderAsLink="True" Target="_blank">
    </ItemSettings>
    <ItemLeftPanelStyle Spacing="25px">
    </ItemLeftPanelStyle>
    <LoadingPanelImage Url="~/App_Themes/Aqua/Web/Loading.gif" />
    <PagerSettings ShowDefaultImages="True">
      <AllButton Text="">
        <Image Height="19px" Width="27px" />
      </AllButton>
      <FirstPageButton Text="">
        <Image Height="19px" Width="23px" />
      </FirstPageButton>
      <LastPageButton Text="">
        <Image Height="19px" Width="23px" />
      </LastPageButton>
      <NextPageButton Text="">
        <Image Height="19px" Width="19px" />
      </NextPageButton>
      <PrevPageButton Text="">
        <Image Height="19px" Width="19px" />
      </PrevPageButton>
    </PagerSettings>
    <ItemRightPanelStyle Spacing="25px">
    </ItemRightPanelStyle>
    <ItemHeaderStyle Spacing="7px">
    </ItemHeaderStyle>
    <ItemImage Height="126px" Width="100px" />
  </dxnc:ASPxNewsControl>
  <asp:SqlDataSource ID="SqlDataSource2" runat="server"
    ConnectionString="<%$ ConnectionStrings:BooksConnectionString %>"
    SelectCommand="SELECT [ID], [Title], [PublicationDate], [Hyperlink],
      [Description], [CoverImageLink] FROM [Books] ORDER BY
      [PublicationDate] DESC">
  </asp:SqlDataSource>
  <asp:SqlDataSource ID="SqlDataSource1" runat="server"
    ConnectionString="<%$ ConnectionStrings:BooksConnectionString %>"
    SelectCommand="select 'handler.ashx?ID='+Convert(varchar, [ID]) As
      ImageID, * FROM BOOKS
      ORDER BY PublicationDate DESC" >
  </asp:SqlDataSource>

  </div>
  </form>
</body>
</html>
```

Note that both `SqlDataSource` components are shown in Listing 3-20. Both are present to facilitate your switching between various approaches for using the `ASPxNewsControl` — that is, with image URLs and `IHttpHandler` requests.

Of course, most code is a series of trade-offs and compromises. If your images are stored externally and links are in the database, provide that actual image URL. If your images are in the database, use an `IHttpHandler` and requery or store images in the application cache. A limitation of the approach shown in this section is that images can take up a lot of memory, and a lot of images can fill up your Web server's RAM pretty quickly. Using the application cache means that only one copy of a particular image exists for all users, but it's still a trade-off, and the approach you use will depend on your particular needs.

Summary

Many of the DevExpress controls have scores of properties and subproperties. Many of these require a simple decision: Do you need to change the default property value? If this book tried to simply list all the properties and describe what they are for, the book would end up being a dictionary that replicates what the extensive help documentation already contains. Instead, a few scenarios were picked, and then some techniques for doing something with the control that requires you to write some custom code were incorporated into the chapter. If you need a simple answer to what a particular property will do, I encourage you to check the help files, look at the samples online at www.devexpress.com, read our blogs, or watch a related video on http://tv.devexpress.com. If you need something that's not covered, then ask us.

In this chapter, I provided scenarios for using the `ASPxTreeList` in bound and unbound mode and using the virtual mode behavior. Extensive support also exists for tweaking the appearance or behavior of the control by experimenting with the many properties — and this is true of all the DevExpress controls. The `ASPxNewsControl`, which is an implementation of the `ASPxDataView`, was covered as well as a simple demonstration of the `ASPxDataView` itself.

On a final note: I used new core .NET technologies such as LINQ, Lambda expressions, or the `IHttpHandler` to show you how to blend a lot of the built-in capability of DevExpress controls that can be accessed without writing code with relatively new or established .NET features.

4

Adding SiteMaps, Navigation, and Pop-Up Dialog Boxes

Menus and navigation mechanisms are essential for providing easy access to the products and services offered by your Web application. Pop-up modal windows add focused dimensionality to your Web application. Other considerations include providing cues to areas of interest or places you'd like to guide the user and search engine optimization — making it easy for Web crawlers to lead others to your products and services.

This chapter covers menus, navigation controls, and pop-up dialog boxes as well as how to build a site map and use the DevExpress `ASPxCloudControl`. All these important supplemental elements will help you provide your users with a richer experience and help you guide them successfully around your Web application.

Implementing a Navigation Bar

About 20 years ago, an urban legend circulated that someone created a graphical DOS-based batch menu system and a local auto company paid $500,000 for it. Whether true or not, it was a great story at the time. I recall creating a graphical-based menu in DOS Basic version 7.1, which included drop down, clickable items. Customers were willing to pay for these items to be fabricated from scratch because they didn't exist as components at the time. (In fact, components as a product were an almost unheard-of concept.)

These days, customers want menus and navigability, and they are still willing to pay for them but not pay for the dozens of hours it might take to fabricate them from scratch. Customers expect menus and navigators for Windows applications and Web applications, even though it wasn't that long ago that you had to assemble menus for Web-based applications by carefully managing and placing `div` or `table` elements. With the `ASPxSiteMapControl` and `ASPxNavBar`, incorporating advanced navigation features, including optimizing for search engines, can be accomplished in minutes, and highly specialized navigability can be added in an hour or two.

The easiest use of the `ASPxNavBar` can be had by pointing the `ASPxNavbar` at an XML data source, and it's ready to go. More advanced uses are possible by defining templates, nesting controls, and using custom callbacks. This section demonstrates both ends of the `ASPxNavBar` spectrum.

Incorporating Basic Navigation Using an XML File

Navigation is based on a hierarchy of choices. These options generally focus on guiding the user through one, two, or more options homing in on a specific desired choice. In the simplest sense, a navigation bar is a vertical menu. It is quite natural to equate a progressing series of choices as a path. Menus, trees, directory structures, and XML files all can be conceptualized as containing or defining a series of paths. The path-like structure of an XML file makes it a suitable candidate for populating the choices of an `ASPxNavBar`.

In an online DevExpress example, the `ASPxNavBar` is used to show cameras by manufacturer. The navigation control's Groups are the individual manufacturers, and within each group is the list of cameras. Links to such a page might lead to production information about each camera and the eventual product support or sale of a camera. (The demo exists to illustrate data binding, but adding a shopping cart or product support page would be a natural addition.)

The camera information for the sample application is contained in an XML Web file. Even though you might not have an XML file available, you can readily produce such a file from a database with a query or by using LINQ. (Maintaining such an XML data source manually is not really practical but is, of course, an option.)

Returning to the book's sample from Chapter 3, you can use the ASPxNavBar to display product information — such as books for sale. One useful utility of the ASPxNavBar is the collapsible groups that permit you to cram a ton of information in the n-dimensional, infinite space of the Web (see Figure 4-1).

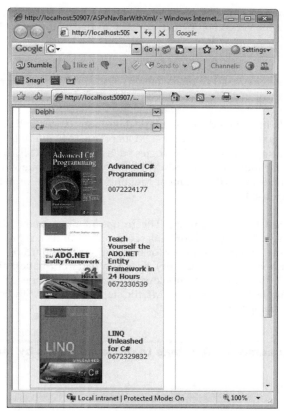

Figure 4-1: The ASPxNavBar's collapsing groups make it easy to maximize the available real estate on a Web page.

Three core elements are employed to create the effect shown in Figure 4-1: the ASPxNavBar; an XML file containing the navigator items; and one of the DevExpress skins. (The ASPxRoundPanel, also shown, was added for flair. For fans of *Office Space*, you know that flair counts.) How to skin an entire Web application using a theme is provided in Chapter 9, "Using Themes, CSS, and JavaScript for Customizations and Enhancements." Using the ASPxRoundPanel is explained in the next section, "Exploring the Boundaries of the ASPxNavBar." The two following sections describe how to create the XML file containing the data, how to associate that data with the ASPxNavBar using an XmlDataSource, and how to configure the ASPxNavBar.

Authoring an XML File

There is a lot more to XML (eXtensible Markup Language) technology than there is room to cover here. However, a basic XML file is a text file with an .xml extension and it has to be well formed and valid. Well formed means that if a start tag (< >) is present, an end tag (</>) is required. Validity means that the file conforms to some known schema. The root element — the first or outer tag — is preceded by an XML declaration element stating the version of XML in use. The XML declaration looks something like this:

```
<?xml version="1.0" encoding="UTF-8" ?>
```

After the XML declaration element, additional elements come in < > </> tag pairs. A tab has an element name and any number of attributes. Between the start and end element, there is generally some value.

There is a lot more to XML, including document type definitions (DTD) and schemas (XSD), XSLT (eXtensible Stylesheet Language Transformations), XQuery (an XML query language), and XPath (XML Path Language). You can also use newer technologies such as LINQ to XML to query XML documents. As already stated, a lot of technology surrounds XML, but you have enough information from the preceding paragraph to create an XML document containing the book information document to create the example shown in Figure 4-1.

The ASPxNavBar in Figure 4-1 contains groups. The groups are organized by language or technology — C#, VB.NET, UML, and so on. Each group contains several items and each item contains an image of the book's cover, the book's title, and ISBN number (or International Standard Book Number, a unique number assigned to published books worldwide). Based on that information, the hierarchy can be expressed as an outer tag by language or technology and an inner tag for each book. Listing 4-1 contains the XML used for the example. You can get an XML file started in Visual Studio by picking the XML File from the Add New Items dialog box.

Listing 4-1: An XML document using tags to organize books by language or technology and individual book.

```
<?xml version="1.0" encoding="utf-8" ?>
<Books>
  <Topic Text="Access">
    <Book NavigateUrl="javascript:void(1);" Title=
"Teach Yourself Microsoft Access 2000 Programming in 24 Hours"
 ISBN="0672316617" ImageUrl="~/Books/Images/Access2000.jpg" />
    <Book NavigateUrl="javascript:void(2);" Title=
"Teach Yourself Microsoft Access 2000 Programming in 24 Hours"
 ISBN="0672320983" ImageUrl="~/Books/Images/Access2002.jpg" />
    <Book NavigateUrl="javascript:void(3);" Title=
"Access 2002 Developerment Unleashed" ISBN="0672321203"
ImageUrl="~/Books/Images/AccessUnleashed.jpg" />
    </Topic>
  <Topic Text="Excel">
    <Book NavigateUrl="javascript:void(11);" Title=
"Excel 2003 VBA Programmer's Reference" ISBN="0764556606"
ImageUrl="~/Books/Images/ExcelVBA.jpg" />
    </Topic>
  <Topic Text="C++">
    <Book NavigateUrl="javascript:void(21);" Title=
"Special Edition, Using Borland C++ 5.0" ISBN="0789702843"
ImageUrl="~/Books/Images/bcpp5.jpg" />
    <Book NavigateUrl="javascript:void(22);" Title=
"Special Edition, Using Visual C++ 4.2" ISBN="9780789708939"
```

```
     ImageUrl="~/Books/Images/vcpp42.jpg" />
       </Topic>
    <Topic Text="Delphi">
       <Book NavigateUrl="javascript:void(31);" Title=
"Delphi 2 Database Applications" ISBN="0789704927"
 ImageUrl="~/Books/Images/bd2d.jpg" />
       <Book NavigateUrl="javascript:void(31);" Title=
"Building Delphi 6 Applications" ISBN="0072129956"
 ImageUrl="~/Books/Images/Delphi6.jpg" />
       </Topic>
    <Topic Text="C#">
       <Book NavigateUrl="javascript:void(41);" Title=
"Advanced C# Programming" ISBN="0072224177"
 ImageUrl="~/Books/Images/csharp_dev_guide.jpg" />
       <Book NavigateUrl="javascript:void(42);" Title=
"Teach Yourself the ADO.NET Entity ↵
 Framework in 24 Hours" ISBN="0672330539"
 ImageUrl="~/Books/Images/Entityframework.jpg" />
       <Book NavigateUrl="javascript:void(43);" Title=
"LINQ Unleashed for C#" ISBN="0672329832"
 ImageUrl="~/Books/Images/LinqUnleashed.jpg" />
       </Topic>
    <Topic Text="VB.NET">
        <Book NavigateUrl="javascript:void(51);" Title=
"Visual Basic .NET Power Coding" ISBN="0672324075"
 ImageUrl="~/Books/Images/powercoding.jpg" />
        <Book NavigateUrl="javascript:void(52);" Title=
"Visual Basic .NET Unleashed" ISBN="067232234X"
 ImageUrl="~/Books/Images/VBNETUnleashed.jpg" />
        <Book NavigateUrl="javascript:void(53);" Title=
"Visual Basic .NET Tips, Tutorials, and Code" ISBN=""
 ImageUrl="~/Books/Images/VBTips.jpg" />
       </Topic>
    <Topic Text="UML">
         <Book NavigateUrl="javascript:void(61);" Title="UML DeMystified"
 ISBN="007226182X" ImageUrl="~/Books/Images/umldemyst.jpg" />
       </Topic>
    <Topic Text="ASP.NET">
       <Book NavigateUrl="javascript:void(71);" Title=
"Professional DevExpress ASP.NET Controls" ISBN="9780470500835"
 ImageUrl="~/Books/Images/DevExpress.jpg" />
       </Topic>
    <Topic Text="J++">
         <Book NavigateUrl="javascript:void(81);" Title=
"Special Edition, Using Visual J++" ISBN="078970899X"
 ImageUrl="~/Books/Images/vjpp.jpg" />
       </Topic>
    <Topic Text="VB">
       <Book NavigateUrl="javascript:void(91);" Title=
"Visual Basic 5 Development Unleashed" ISBN="0672310724"
 ImageUrl="~/Books/Images/vb5du.jpg" />
         <Book NavigateUrl="javascript:void(92);" Title=
"Visual Basic 5 Fundamentals Unleashed" ISBN="0672310732"
```

Continued

Listing 4-1: An XML document using tags to organize books by language or technology and individual book. *(continued)*

```
          ImageUrl="~/Books/Images/vb5fu.jpg" />
            </Topic>
          <Topic Text=".NET General">
            <Book NavigateUrl="javascript:void(101);" Title=
      ".NET Mobile Application Development" ISBN="0764548506"
      ImageUrl="~/Books/Images/Wireless.jpg" />
          </Topic>
      </Books>

      <Books>
        <Topic Text="Access">
          <Book NavigateUrl="javascript:void(1);" Title=
      "Teach Yourself Microsoft Access 2000 Programming in 24 Hours"
      ISBN="0672316617" ImageUrl="~/Books/Images/Access2000.jpg" />
          <Book NavigateUrl="javascript:void(2);" Title=
      "Teach Yourself Microsoft Access 2000 Programming in 24 Hours"
      ISBN="0672320983" ImageUrl="~/Books/Images/Access2002.jpg" />
          <Book NavigateUrl="javascript:void(3);" Title=
      "Access 2002 Developerment Unleashed" ISBN="0672321203"
      ImageUrl="~/Books/Images/AccessUnleashed.jpg" />
        </Topic>
      </Books>
```

In Listing 4-1, Books is the root element. Note the end element at the bottom of the listing. Nested in Books are Topic tags. Topic has a single attribute ,"Text," which represents the language or technology, the Topic. Nested in Topic elements are Book elements. Book elements have three attributes: NavigateUrl, Title, ISBN, and ImageUrl. The NavigateUrl and ImageUrl are there to satisfy the needs of the ASPxNavBar. Title and ISBN were added by me to assign to ASPxLabel controls in the ASPxNavBar.

Notice the use of javascript:void(#) for the NavigateUrl. The javascript:void is a mechanism that prevents the browser from loading a new page or refreshing the current page. If you forget to pass a number to the void function, you will receive a javascript exception if the method is invoked: javascript:void(). Using javascript:void(#) acts like a placeholder until actual URLs are provided. In a real application you will use an actual URL for the NavigateUrl attribute.

You can create the XML file in Visual Studio or with any text or XML editor using manual techniques such as copy-paste-edit, but in a production environment or with large amounts of data, such an approach is impractical. A better approach might be to use technology such as LINQ to XML.

Creating an XML File Using Functional Construction and LINQ

LINQ, or Language INtegrated Query, is basically the ability to query a wide variety of data types using a unified query syntax. Historically, developers have used SQL for SQL databases, XPath for XML, custom code for objects, LDAP (Lightweight Directory Access Protocol) for directory services, and the list goes on. LINQ is ultimately an extensible query language for anything that needs querying. The objective for LINQ is that after you learn LINQ syntax, you can use LINQ to query any data source. The extensibility part means that LINQ is designed to grow into other data source spaces.

Out of the box, LINQ queries SQL, custom objects, and XML. Already, LINQ has been extended into places such as XSD (XML Schema Definition), SharePoint, and Active Directory.

Another capability of .NET is referred to as functional construction. Functional construction is the chaining of calls to XElement and XAttribute objects together to form an XML document. If you combine LINQ with functional construction, you literally query data from one source, such as a database, and send the output to an XML document.

Recall the Books database sample from Chapter 3. That sample database already contains all the data needed to recreate the ASPxNavBar, as shown in Figure 4-1. Rather than construct an XML document manually, you can use LINQ and functional construction to create the XML file. In the future then, as the data changes — as I publish more books or your customer adds routes to its airline — the XML file can be created automatically. In fact, there is no reason that you couldn't make this an administrative feature of a Web application. The code in Listing 4-2 reads the book data from the Books database (see Chapter 3) using plain-vanilla ADO.NET and then uses a LINQ query and functional construction to generate the XML file.

Listing 4-2: ADO.NET reads the Books table, and a LINQ query using functional construction assembles the XML output.

```
using System;
using System.Collections.Generic;
using System.Linq;
using System.Text;
using System.Data;
using System.Data.SqlClient;
using System.Xml.Linq;

namespace LINQAndFuncConstruction
{
  class Program
  {
    static void Main(string[] args)
    {
      DataTable allBooks = GetData();
      XElement doc =
      new XElement("Books",
        from book in allBooks.AsEnumerable()
        group book by book.Field<string>("Language") into g
        select
          new XElement("Topic",
            new XAttribute("Text", g.Key),
              from item in g
              let isbn = item.Field<string>("ISBN")
              select new XElement("Book",
              new XAttribute("NavigateUrl", "javascript:void(0);"),
              new XAttribute("Title", item.Field<string>("Title")),
              new XAttribute("ISBN", isbn == null ? "" : isbn),
              new XAttribute("ImageUrl", item.Field<string>("CoverImageLink"))
              ))));
      doc.Save("..\\..\\Books.xml");
      Console.WriteLine(doc);
      Console.ReadLine();
    }

    private static DataTable GetData()
```

Continued

Listing 4-2: ADO.NET reads the Books table, and a LINQ query using functional construction assembles the XML output. *(continued)*

```
  {
    string connectionString =
      @"Data Source=.\SQLEXPRESS;Initial Catalog=Books;" +
        "Integrated Security=True";
    DataTable data = new DataTable();
    using (SqlConnection connection = new SqlConnection(connectionString))
    {
      connection.Open();
      SqlCommand command =
        new SqlCommand("SELECT * FROM BOOKS", connection);
      SqlDataAdapter adapter = new SqlDataAdapter(command);
      adapter.Fill(data);
    }

    return data;
  }
 }
}
```

The GetData method returns a DataTable. This is plain ADO.NET. The interesting bit of code is the LINQ query in the Main method. The statement that declares and initializes the XElement demonstrates functional construction and LINQ together.

Functional construction uses XDocument, XElement, and XAttribute as the main elements, but the System.Xml.Linq namespaces has other XML types. Functional construction works by having constructors for items such as XElement take the element name and a parameter array of objects — params[] object. The additional arguments can be any number of chained-together calls to things such as XAttribute or nested XElement objects. In the listing, Books is the root element and the second argument is the results of the LINQ query beginning with `from book in allBooks.AsEnumerable`. The call to the extension method AsEnumerable returns an EnumerableRowCollection<DataRow>, which permits LINQ to work with the DataTable represented by allBooks.

The from clause defines the range variable, `book`. Range variables act like an iterator loop control variable. The second clause — group book by book.Field<string>("Language") into g — groups all the items in the LINQ query into a group by Language. Book.Field<T> is how you get data from a Data Table or DataSet used in a LINQ query. As with all LINQ queries, the `select` comes at the end. `Select` can be used to add the value of the range variable into the output or create a projection — a new anonymous type. In this instance, `select` is projecting a new `XElement "Topic"` with an `XAttribute "Text"`. The value of Text will be the value of the Language field for the group.

Nested in the XElement is an additional LINQ query. Beginning with the range variable item — the clause `from item in g` — the inner LINQ query is getting each of the book DataRows in each group. Finally, the inner `select` clause is projecting some more XML using more functional construction. The inner `select` is building the individual `Book` elements with the NavigateUrl, Title, ISBN, and ImageUrl, as shown in Listing 4-1.

On a final note, check out the use of the let clause in the inner LINQ query. The `let` keyword is used to define a range variable. In the example, some of the books are missing the ISBN number, so you can handle null with the inline ternary operator ?:, as demonstrated for the ISBN XAttribute.

Binding the XML Data to an ASPxNavBar

The `ASPxNavBar` is smart about how it binds to data. Configure it with an `XmlDataSource` pointing at an XML file and the `ASPxNavBar` will bind fields such as the NavigateUrl and ImageUrl. Other elements you want can easily be configured using a template and controls such as the `ASPxLabel`.

To use the .xml file in Listing 4-1 or the file generated by Listing 4-2, click the `ASPxNavBar`'s Smart tags menu and select New Data Source from the Choose Data Source option. When the Data Source Configuration Wizard is displayed, pick the XML File option as the data source and click OK. The Configure Data Source for the XmlDataSource is displayed (see Figure 4-2). Browse to the .xml file and provide the XPath expression.

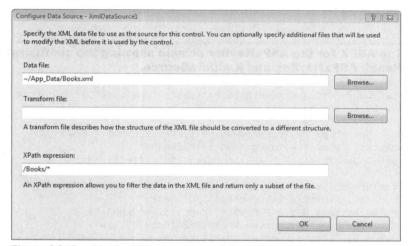

Figure 4-2: Provide the XML data file and the XPath expression as shown to configure the XmlDataSource for the Books example.

In a very simple sense, XPath expressions are like file system expressions. The XPath expression acts like a filter returning only the portion of the XML file desired. In the example, /Books/* means to filter (or return) everything under the Books element. The utility of XPath is that it supports more than just basic expressions. For example, adding a filter expression — [*pattern*] — to the XPath filter. A filter acts like a SQL WHERE clause, as demonstrated by the following XPath statement, which means for every element below Books, check to see whether there is a Text attribute that has the value 'Access'. The @ symbol means to check element attributes.

```
/Books/*[@Text='Access']
```

XPath is an entire technology in its own right, and an adequate tutorial is beyond the scope of this book. LINQ to XML is actually designed to complete in the XPath space. For more on LINQ to XML, see my book *LINQ Unleashed for C#*, from Sams. For a great tutorial on Xpath, try *XPath 2.0 Programmer's Reference* by Michael Kay (Wiley).

Configuring the ASPxNavBar

To complete the effect and get the sample to look like Figure 4-1, place the ASPxNavBar in an ASPxRoundPanel. Also, apply the Aqua schema from the Smart tags Auto Format dialog box.

The additional content is derived from a template and the XML file. In Figure 4-1, two ASPxLabel controls were added to the ASPxNavBar's ItemTextTemplate template. The Title uses a bold font and the ASPxLabel containing the ISBN does not. To achieve uniformity between the book cover graphics, the ASPxNavBar.ItemImage Height and Width subproperties are set to a uniform 140 by 11 pixels, respectively.

The data binding statements use block script and call Container.EvalDataItem("Title") for the Title and Container.EvalDataItem("ISBN") for the ISBN number. No code-behind is required for the sample. The ASPX is shown in Listing 4-3.

Listing 4-3: The ASPX for the ASPxNavBar sample showing the configuration of the ASPxRoundPanel, ASPxNavBar, and XmlDataSource.

```
<%@ Page Language="C#" AutoEventWireup="true"  CodeFile="Default.aspx.cs"
 Inherits="_Default"  %>

<%@ Register Assembly="DevExpress.Web.v9.1, Version=9.1.4.0,↵
 Culture=neutral, PublicKeyToken=b88d1754d700e49a"
    Namespace="DevExpress.Web.ASPxRoundPanel" TagPrefix="dxrp" %>

<%@ Register assembly="DevExpress.Web.v9.1, Version=9.1.4.0,↵
 Culture=neutral, PublicKeyToken=b88d1754d700e49a"
 namespace="DevExpress.Web.ASPxNavBar" tagprefix="dxnb" %>
<%@ Register assembly="DevExpress.Web.ASPxEditors.v9.1,↵
 Version=9.1.4.0, Culture=neutral, PublicKeyToken=b88d1754d700e49a"
 namespace="DevExpress.Web.ASPxEditors" tagprefix="dxe" %>

<!DOCTYPE html PUBLIC "-//W3C//DTD XHTML 1.0 Transitional//EN"
 "http://www.w3.org/TR/xhtml1/DTD/xhtml1-transitional.dtd">

<html xmlns="http://www.w3.org/1999/xhtml">
<head runat="server">
    <title></title>
</head>
<body>
    <form id="form1" runat="server">
    <div>
        <dxrp:ASPxRoundPanel ID="ASPxRoundPanel1"
        runat="server" EnableViewState="False" Width="200px" HeaderText="" >
        <PanelCollection >
        <dxrp:PanelContent runat="server">
        <dxnb:ASPxNavBar ID="ASPxNavBar1" runat="server"
          AllowSelectItem="True"
          AutoCollapse="True" DataSourceID="XmlDataSource1"
```

```
                    EnableViewState="False"
                      EncodeHtml="False">
                      <GroupHeaderStyle HorizontalAlign="Left">
                      </GroupHeaderStyle>
                      <ItemTextTemplate>
                          <dxe:ASPxLabel ID="ASPxLabel1" runat="server" Font-Bold="True"
                              Text='<%# Container.EvalDataItem("Title") %>'>
                          </dxe:ASPxLabel>
                          <br />
                          <dxe:ASPxLabel ID="ASPxLabel2" runat="server"
                              Text='<%# Container.EvalDataItem("ISBN") %>'>
                          </dxe:ASPxLabel>
                      </ItemTextTemplate>
                      <ItemStyle HorizontalAlign="Left" />
                      <ItemImage Height="140px" Width="111px" />
                  </dxnb:ASPxNavBar>
                  </dxrp:PanelContent>
                  </PanelCollection>
                  </dxrp:ASPxRoundPanel>

                  <asp:XmlDataSource ID="XmlDataSource1" runat="server"
                      DataFile="~/App_Data/Books.xml"
        XPath="/Books/*"></asp:XmlDataSource>

        </div>
        </form>
    </body>
    </html>
```

Exploring the Boundaries of the ASPxNavBar

The classic comparison between Windows and Web applications is that Windows applications feature rich clients and Web forms facilitate broad, easy deployment. The hallmark of good Web controls is that they make routine tasks easier and yield great-looking Web applications without a lot of wrangling. Great Web controls support creating a rich Windows-style feel to the application. To that end, the sample application in this section is basically a file system explorer like Windows Explorer. I chose to poke around the boundaries of the ASPxNavBar, like taking a new car out for a spin, rather than describe its general utility. However, if you separate the demo application's practicality from the features used, you have a good understanding of what might be possible in your Web applications.

The Web file system explorer demonstrates how to do the following: use groups; define ItemTextTemplate with nested controls; use the ASPxNavBar's ContentTemplate; add and bind controls in the ASPxNavBar manually; update across content boundaries using custom callbacks; add JavaScript JSProperties; enable animation; and write ClientSideEvents for the ASPxNavBar. The combined result yields a very dynamic, fluid, Windows-like application (see Figure 4-3).

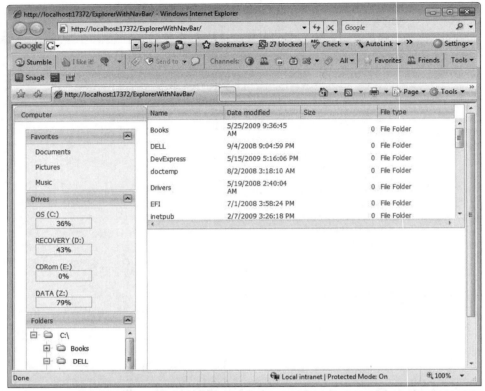

Figure 4-3: Click one region of the Web page — such as a folder — and related regions are updated with custom callbacks, behaving very much like a Windows application.

The application has four regions. The ASPxNavBar contains three groups. The Favorites group links to the current user's Documents, Pictures, and Music folders. The Drives group switches drives and updates the Folders group. The Folders group contains an ASPxTreeList. Click a folder in the ASPxTreeList, and the child files and folders for that parent folder are displayed in the ASPxGridView to the right. Paging and virtual paging are enabled for the ASpxGridView. Virtual paging is a relatively new feature. The following sections describe how to assemble the various elements.

Before you begin, it is worth noting that the general layout of the page is managed with the HTML `<table>` tag. Using a table or a cascading style sheet is still a pretty good way to manage page layout. The table has one row (<tr> tag) — and two cells (<td> tags).

Adding Groups to an ASPxNavBar

Because I like the look of rounded corners — after so many years of rectilinear shapes — the ASPxRoundPanel was added to the left cell and stretched to fill that cell. To recreate the navigator in the example (see Figure 4-3), an ASPxNavBar was added to the ASPxRoundPanel (see the upcoming "Using the ASPxRoundPanel" sidebar).

To add the groups, use the ASPxNavBar Group Editor, which is accessible from the Properties window or the Smart tags menu. To add the Favorites, Drives, and Folders groups, follow these steps (referring to Figure 4-4 as a guide):

1. Click the Groups property in the Properties window.

2. In the ASPxNavBar Groups Editor, click the Add an Item toolbar button three times to add three groups.

3. Change the `Text` property of each of the groups to Favorites, Drives, and Folders.

4. Click OK.

5. Change the ASPxRoundPanel's HeaderText property to Computer to be consistent with the results in Figure 4-3.

Figure 4-4: The ASPxNavBar Groups editor can be used to add navigation groups and set the properties for each group.

Using the ASPxRoundPanel

The ASPxRoundPanel at its essence is what it sounds like: a panel control with rounded corners. The ASPxRoundPanel has properties, which makes it similar to many of the DevExpress controls, and it includes a designer (see Figure 4-5) that facilitates adjusting the properties and previewing the results that are most germane to the essence of a rounded-corner panel control. The corner radius is probably the most important property.

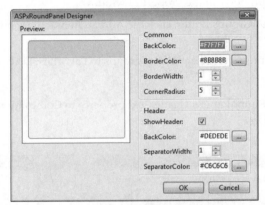

Figure 4-5: The ASPxRoundPanel Designer lets you visually preview the effect that property changes will have on the control.

Defining Templates and Nesting Controls in the ASPxNavBar

The ASPxNavBar in the demo has three groups. The first group, Favorites, uses standard group items. The second group, Drives, contains a nested ASPxLabel and ASPxProgressBar in the ItemTextTemplate, and the Folders group contains an ASPxTreeList. The next section explains the features of the ASPxNavBar that support using these various approaches for creating a feature-rich navigator.

Adding Group Items

The Favorites items are added at design time, and the associated links are configured at runtime based on the current user and stored as JSProperties. (See the next section, "Defining Custom JSProperties.")

The group items are added at design time using the ASPxNavBar Item Editor (see Figure 4-6). The item editor works like the group editor. Click the Add an Item button. To add the three favorites for the demo, click the Add an Item button three times and change the text property for each to Documents, Pictures, and Music, respectively.

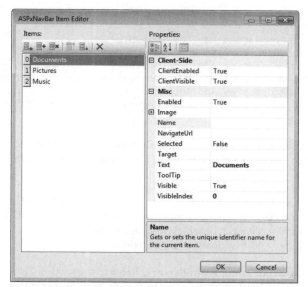

Figure 4-6: You can add items to an ASPxNavBar group using the ASPxNavBar Item Editor (shown).

Defining Custom JSProperties

When the user clicks one of the Favorites items, the navigator is designed to list the files and folders in that location for the current user. These folders — such as Documents, Pictures, and Music — are special folders and even have analogous properties in the .NET framework.

It is worth noting that this application is for demonstration purposes, and particularly for demonstration of JSProperties in this part. File system navigation based on the current user will work well using the Cassini server because it runs with user permissions. For IIS, the default behavior is to run with the ASP.NET user, and accessing user folders will raise an exception. In addition, if you request special folders on the file server, the folders returned are Web server folders, not the client's folders.

If you wanted a general-purpose file system to manage files on a client, you would need to authenticate the user and request file information on the client using script rather than doing so in the code-behind. Some parts of the file system would still be inaccessible by default.

To create custom JavaScript properties, the ASPxNavBar — as with other DevExpress controls — has a recent addition, the JSProperties property. JSProperties is defined as a Dictionary<string, object>. The first parameter is a key and the second is the value. When you add an item to the JSProperties collection, it becomes a full-fledged property on the client side for JavaScript programming purposes. The only requirement is that you use a cp prefix for the property name — a convention that DevExpress imposes to avoid conflict with existing properties. Add the following statements to the Page_Load to create dynamic equivalents for the Documents, Pictures, and Music items in Favorites.

```
protected void Page_Load(object sender, EventArgs e)
{
  ASPxNavBar1.JSProperties.Add("cpDocuments",
    Environment.GetFolderPath(Environment.SpecialFolder.MyDocuments));
  ASPxNavBar1.JSProperties.Add("cpPictures",
    Environment.GetFolderPath(Environment.SpecialFolder.MyPictures));
  ASPxNavBar1.JSProperties.Add("cpMusic",
    Environment.GetFolderPath(Environment.SpecialFolder.MyMusic));
}
```

The special `Environment` variable values, such as Environment.SpecialFolder.MyDocuments, actually resolve to the file system's documents folder based on the current user for the Cassini server and the ASPNET user for IIS.

Assume that you define a ClientInstanceName of NavBar for the ASPxNavBar. Then, on the client for script purposes, you can access the custom properties by writing NavBar.cpDocuments, NavBar.cpPictures, and NavBar.cpMusic, each of which resolves to the path for each of those locations — MyDocuments, MyPictures, and MyMusic — on the end user's file system.

The Favorites section still needs some script to work. Refer to the section "Updating Dependent Controls Asynchronously with the CustomCallback," later in this chapter, for the implementation of the script that supports these properties.

Getting User Information with JavaScript

I like to cover the bases so that you don't have to leave the book to go to Google too often. To that end, you can get information such as the current user and special folders in JavaScript. To do so, you need to enable unsigned ActiveX objects for your browser and use a browser that supports ActiveX objects such as IE 7 or IE 8. (Earlier versions of Internet Explorer support ActiveX objects, too.)

If you want to query the client's user, creating an instance of the WScript.Network object will let you obtain the user name:

```
var o = new ActiveXObject("WScript.Network");
alert(o.UserName);
```

and you can get information about the path to special folders with an instance of the WScript.Shell object:

```
var path = w.SpecialFolders("MyDocuments");
alert(path);
```

Defining an ItemTextTemplate

The next element of the solution is to configure the Drives group of the ASPxNavBar. The Drives group can be created by selecting Edit Templates from the ASPxNavBar's Smart tags menu and picking the ItemTextTemplate from the list of templates under Groups[1].

> Did you know that if you select the template title instead of a specific template type, the designer will show all templates? For example, selecting Edit Templates from the ASPxNavBar's Smart tags menu and clicking Groups[1], all templates, Content-Template, HeaderTemplate, HeaderTemplateCollapsed, ItemTemplate, and Item TextTemplate will all be visible in the designer.

To recreate the Drives group, add an ASPxLabel and ASPxProgressBar to the group's ItemTextTemplate (see Figure 4-7). Set the ASPxNavBar.EnableHotTrack to true and change the ASPxNavBar. ItemLinkMode to ContentBounds (in the Properties window) to make selection and hot tracking enclose both the ASPxLabel and ASPxProgressBar as you hover over each drive. The other options for IItemLinkMode are TextAndImage and TextOnly.

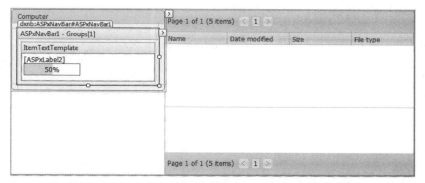

Figure 4-7: Add an ASPxLabel and ASPxProgressBar to the ItemTextTemplate to recreate the drive label and space available — represented visually by the progress bar — for the Drives group.

I felt that the code necessary to populate the ItemTextTemplate containing the drive information was a little clumsy. (Thanks to one of our developer, Platon Fedorovksy, for working out the kinks with me.) The code that populates the Drives group, showing each drive, is contained in Listing 4-4.

Listing 4-4: The code that populates the Drives group of the ASPxNavBar, including updating the ASPxProgressBar.

```
protected void Page_Init(object sender, EventArgs e)
{
  Initialize();
}

private void Initialize()
{
  DriveInfo[] drives = DriveInfo.GetDrives();
  if (ASPxNavBar1.Groups[1].Items.Count == 0)
```

Continued

Listing 4-4: The code that populates the Drives group of the ASPxNavBar, including updating the ASPxProgressBar. *(continued)*

```
      foreach (DriveInfo drive in drives)
        ASPxNavBar1.Groups[1].Items.Add();

  for (int i = 0; i < ASPxNavBar1.Groups[1].Items.Count; i++)
  {
    NavBarItem item = ASPxNavBar1.Groups[1].Items[i];
    ASPxLabel label = (ASPxLabel)item.FindControl("ASPxLabel2");
    ASPxProgressBar progressBar =
      (ASPxProgressBar)item.FindControl("ASPxProgressBar1");

    item.Text = drives[i].Name;
    label.Text = GetDriveLabel(drives[i]);
    progressBar.Value = GetValue(drives[i]);
  }

  private static string GetDriveLabel(DriveInfo drive)
  {
    const string mask = "{0} ({1})";
    try
    {
      return string.Format(mask,
        drive.VolumeLabel, drive.Name.Replace("\\", ""));
    }
    catch
    {
      return string.Format(mask,
        drive.DriveType.ToString(), drive.Name.Replace("\\", ""));
    }
  }

  private static int GetValue(DriveInfo drive)
  {
    try
    {
      return (int)((float)(drive.TotalSize - drive.TotalFreeSpace) /
            (float)drive.TotalSize * 100);
    }
    catch
    {
      return 0;
    }
  }
}
```

The Page_Init method calls Initialize, which populates the Drives group. Initialize uses System.IO and the DriveInfo class to get the drives. This method will return mapped drives and CD/DVD drives, too. The if-conditional actually adds a new item for each drive. (This is the awkward part. It would seem intuitive that you could add the items and initialize the template controls in the same loop, but I tried that and it doesn't work.) After each group item has been created, the template controls exist, and the second loop finds the actual group item control and fills in the detail information.

GetDriveLabel and GetValue update the ASPxLabel and ASPxProgressBar, respectively. The ASPxProgressBar uses the default Minimum of 0 and default Maximum of 100. The GetValue method calculates free space as a percentage of the TotalSize and TotalFreeSpace.

When you click one of the drives, the ASPXTreeList in the last group — Folders — and the ASPxGridView are updated using a custom callback. Refer to the upcoming section "Updating Dependent Controls Asynchronously with the CustomCallback."

Nesting Controls in a ContentTemplate

In the previous section, the ItemTextTemplate was used to define a template for each group item. The ContentTemplate is used to define a template for the entire group region. Borrowing from the example in Chapter 3, an ASPXTreeList containing folders for the selected drive was added to the Folders group's ContentTemplate region.

In an effort to use all available space to constrain the physical real estate used by the grid, yet allow for an arbitrarily large number of possible folders, a `<div>` tag was placed in the ContentTemplate and the ASPxTreeList was placed inside the `<div>` tag. The `<div>` tag was defined for a specific size with the overflow style set to auto, which turns on scroll bars for the `<div>` as needed.

```
<div style="width:190px;height:250px;overflow:auto;">
```

The ASPxTreeList is designed like the example in Chapter 3. An ASPXImage and ASPxLabel were added to the DataCell template. The ASPxImage is populated by binding the ImageUrl to Container. GetValue("IconName"), and the ASPxLabel's Text property is bound by a call to Container. GetValue("Name"). The actual binding is accomplished by using the virtual mode feature of the ASPxTreeList. (See the section in Chapter 3 called "Creating a Windows Explorer-Style Web Page with Virtual Mode.") The code to populate the ASPxTreeList is almost identical to the example in Chapter 3, so I don't reproduce it here.

There is a difference between this example and the example in Chapter 3. In this example, when the user clicks a drive, the folder is updated to reflect the drive. When the user clicks an item in the tree, the ASPxGridView is updated to show the child files and folders. That is, selecting an item in the ASPxTreeList updates the ASPxGridView. The entire listing for the ASPX and code-behind for the sample is contained in the next section, "Updating Dependent Controls Asynchronouusly with the CustomCallbacks."

I wanted the sample Web application to store the expanded state of the ASPxTreeList, so that when I switched focus between drives the ASPxTreeList state was maintained. You can enable this feature by changing the ASPxTreeList.SettingsCookies.StreExpandedNodes to true. Storing the expanded state requires that Ajax be turned on. Unfortunately, if Ajax is on for the ASPxTreeList, changes to the ASPxTreeList cannot be used to update the ASPxGridView. If Ajax is enabled — ASPxTreeList EnableCallbacks is false — you use an UpdatePanel to change the ASPxGridView when a new node in the tree list is selected, but then the cookie's behavior storing the ASPxTreeList states will not be updated. What to do? The solution is to leave Ajax on for the ASPxTreeList and to not use an UpdatePanel but use custom callbacks instead.

Updating Dependent Controls Asynchronously with the CustomCallback

Ajax is designed to avoid the appearance of a callback and update just parts of a page. Basically, by design, the calling control is the one that is updated. If you use an UpdatePanel — one of the Ajax controls that comes with Windows — you can implement a trigger so that an event on a control triggers a callback and an update on a second or third control in the UpdatePanel. Updating based on a trigger in a control in an UpdatePanel to a control not in the panel, referred to as cross-UpdatePanel updating, is a bit trickier (see the note in this section).

> You can perform cross-content updates by calling UpdatePanel.Update() from the event handler of an initiating control to a second UpdatePanel. You can also implement cross-UpdatePanel updates by setting UpdatePanel.UpdateMode to false, ChildrenAsTriggers to false, and calling the ScriptManager's RegisterAsyncPostBackControl method. You can find a detailed explanation of this approach at www.asp.net/Learn/ajax/tutorial-02-cs.aspx. A simpler approach is to use a CustomCallback, which avoids the need to use UpdatePanels at all.

The sample application performs three cross-content updates. Click an item in the Favorites group and the ASPxGridView is updated to show files and folders in the selected location. Click a drive from the Drives group and the ASPxTreeList in the Folders group is updated to reflect folders for that drive. Click a folder in the ASPxTreeList and the ASPxGridView (see Figure 4-3) is updated to list child files and folders. This means that you need to implement code to support these three events.

Making JavaScript Easier with the ClientInstanceName

A common problem I occasionally encounter is finding a control by its client name in JavaScript, especially when the control is deeply nested or its UniqueID, ClientID, and the value for the ID property are vastly different. A solution DevExpress has incorporated to address this problem is the ClientInstanceName. Set the ClientInstanceName property of a DevExpress control and that is the name you will use in script on the client.

> Set **ASPxNavBar.EnableClientSideAPI** to true if you want to manipulate the ASPxNavBar on the client side. The **EnableClientSideAPI** property is common in DevExpress control.

For the sample in this section, you will be working with the `ASPxGridView` and `ASPxTreeList` in script. The `ClientInstanceName` name for the `ASPxGridView` was set to Grid, and the `ClientInstanceName` for the `ASPxTreeList` was set to `TreeList`.

It is worth noting that in addition to the `ClientInstanceName`, client-side controls are represented by a different actual class. For example, on the client side, the `ASPxNavBar` becomes an instance of the `ASPxClientNavBar`. The client-side instances are represented by a different class and hence have a different object model. It is worth exploring the client instance of DevExpress controls, especially if you will be writing a lot of script.

Programming ClientSideEvents to Initiate a CustomCallback

I introduced client-side events in Chapter 2, in the section "Programming Client-Side Events. To reiterate, DevExpress Web controls a ClientSideEvents property. This property lists the client-events added for a control and provides an editor that supports writing the implementation of the event in the Visual Studio IDE. (An instance of the client-side event editor for the ASPxGridView was shown in Figure 2-22.) For the introductory coverage of client-side events, refer to Chapter 2.

In this section, you use client-side events to initiate a CustomCallback. A CustomCallback is an event handler that you implement in code-behind and initiate by calling PerformCallback from the client. The callback uses Ajax and is therefore asynchronous and updates parts of your Web page without the apparent full postback. The benefit here is that you can respond to a client-side event from one part of a Web page and perform an asynchronous call to update something else, effectively replacing the need for an UpdatePanel and simplifying cross-content updates with Ajax.

In the Web file system explorer sample — the complete listing is provided in 4-11 — there are three places where a change in one part of the ASPxNavBar updates another part of the page: Clicking an item in the ASPxTreeList updates the ASPxGridView; clicking one of the favorites updates the ASPxGridView; and clicking one of the drives updates the drive and folders listed in the ASPxTreeList. This is where the JSProperties is used, too, and because the client-side events are changing only either the ASPxTreeList or the ASPxGridView, you can handle the client's initiation behavior with two client-side events.

The first client-side event handles the FocusedNodeChanged for the ASPxTreeList. The code just calls `Grid.PerformCallback('')`. PerformCallback actually raises the CustomCallback, so you need to define the CustomCallback event handler in code-behind for the ASPxGridView. Listing 4-5 shows how the client-side event is stored as a string property (and attached to the event later as script at runtime), and Listing 4-6 shows the implementation of CustomCallback handler and the associated helper methods and properties. (Grid is the ClientInstanceName defined in the ASPxGridView's properties.)

Listing 4-5: Client-side events are stored as string properties for a control and are rendered at runtime as script.

```
<ClientSideEvents FocusedNodeChanged="function(s, e) {
  Grid.PerformCallback('');}" />
```

Listing 4-6: The CustomCallback event handler and the helper methods that update the grid when the ASPxTreeList FocusedNodeChanged event is fired on the client.

```
private static readonly string SELECTED_PATH = "SelectedPath";

protected void ASPxGridView1_CustomCallback(object sender,
  DevExpress.Web.ASPxGridView.ASPxGridViewCustomCallbackEventArgs e)
{
  if (e.Parameters != "")
    if (Directory.Exists(e.Parameters))
      SelectedPath = e.Parameters;
  UpdateGrid(SelectedPath);
}

public string SelectedPath
{
  get
  {
    if (Session[SELECTED_PATH] == null)
      Session[SELECTED_PATH] = "C:\\";

    return (string)Session[SELECTED_PATH];
  }
  set { Session[SELECTED_PATH] = value; }
}

private void UpdateGrid(string path)
{
  var files = Directory.GetDirectories(path).Union(Directory.GetFiles(path));

  var infos = from file in files
    let info = new FileInfo(file)
    let isDirectory = (info.Attributes & FileAttributes.Directory)
      == FileAttributes.Directory
    where (info.Attributes
      & FileAttributes.Hidden) != FileAttributes.Hidden
    select new
    {
      Name = info.Name,
      LastWriteTime = info.LastWriteTime,
      Length = isDirectory == false ? info.Length : 0,
      FileType = isDirectory ? "File Folder" : "File"
    };

  ASPxGridView1.DataSource = infos;
  ASPxGridView1.DataBind();

}
```

In the example, when ASPxTreeList.FocusedNodeChanged is fired on the client, Grid.PerformCallback is called. The CustomCallback method is invoked asynchronously. CustomCallback checks for an empty e.Parameters argument. It is empty in the call — Grid.PerformCallback — in this instance, so UpdateGrid is called with the current value stored in the SelectedPath property, a wrapper for a Session variable. UpdateGrid just uses a LINQ query more or less from Chapter 3's "Adding TreeListNodes Programmatically" section and creates an enumerable collection of the projected type. The projected type is the new type defined and initialized by the select new part of the query. (For in-depth coverage of LINQ, try my book *LINQ Unleashed for C#* from Sams or *Professional LINQ* from Wiley by Scott Klein, but a very similar query is listed in Chapter 3 and explained there.)

As you might have guessed, the ASPxGridView has columns defined that match the types in the projection — Name, LastWriteTime, Length, and FileType.

The next client-side event handles the ASPxNavBar ItemClick event. If the item clicked is one of the Favorites items, the Grid is updated. If not one of the Favorites then the only other items are drive-items and the ASPxTreeList is updated to show the drive letters. If the grid is to be updated, the CustomCallback from Listing 4-6 is reused. If the tree list is to be updated, a CustomCallback for the ASPxTreeList is invoked asynchronously. Listing 4-7 contains the ClientSideEvents tag and the string value of the ItemClick event as it will appear in the ASPX. Listing 4-8 contains the CustomCallback for the ASPxTreeList.

Listing 4-7: The ItemClick ClientSideEvent will be rendered as script at runtime.

```
<ClientSideEvents ItemClick="function(s,e){
  try
  {
    //debugger;
    if(s.GetSelectedItem().GetText()=='Documents')
      Grid.PerformCallback(s.cpDocuments);
    else if(s.GetSelectedItem().GetText()=='Pictures')
      Grid.PerformCallback(s.cpPictures);
    else if(s.GetSelectedItem().GetText()=='Music')
      Grid.PerformCallback(s.cpMusic);
    else
      TreeList.PerformCallback(s.GetSelectedItem().GetText());
  }
  catch(oException)
  {
    alert(oException);
  }
}" />
```

Listing 4-7 demonstrates how to use the debugger; statement. If you need to debug the script, simply uncomment the debugger; statement. Listing 4-7 also demonstrates the proper syntax for exception handling in JavaScript and the use of the custom JSProperties, defined earlier, in the section "Defining Custom JSProperties."

If you will be supporting multiple languages in your solution then the value of GetSe-lectedItem().GetText() might change. An alternate solution for Listing 4-7 is to set the ASpxNavBarItem.Name property and rewrite the if conditional tests to check the name property. (Note that name is lower case on the client-side.)

```
try
{
  //debugger;
  var item = s.GetSelectedItem();
  if(item.name=='Documents')
    Grid.PerformCallback(s.cpDocuments);
  else if(item.name=='Pictures')
   Grid.PerformCallback(s.cpPictures);
  else if(item.name=='Music')
   Grid.PerformCallback(s.cpMusic);
  else
    TreeList.PerformCallback(item.name);
}
catch(oException)
{
  alert(oException);
}
```

Thanks to Roman R. from DevExpress for providing this alternate solution.

Listing 4-8: TheCustomCallback that handles TreeList.PerformCallback from Listing 4-7.

```
protected void ASPxTreeList1_CustomCallback(object sender,
  TreeListCustomCallbackEventArgs e)
{
  SelectedDrive = ASPxNavBar1.SelectedItem.Text;
  ASPxTreeList tree =
    (ASPxTreeList)ASPxNavBar1.Groups[2].FindControl("ASPxTreeList1");
  tree.RefreshVirtualTree();
}
```

Remember that Grid.PerformCallback (from Listing 4-7) is handled by the method already defined in Listing 4-6. If TreeList.PerformCallback is called from the client, the event handler in Listing 4-8 responds.

The actual ASPxTreeList is defined as a ContentTemplate item in the ASPxNavBar, so you can cast the sender to the ASPxTreeList or use FindControl, as demonstrated in Listing 4-8. The actual selected item is simply requested from the ASPxNavBar itself.

Set ASPxGridView.Settings.VerticalScrollBarStyle to Virtual to enable virtual paging. Virtual paging means that paging happens if you use the vertical scroll bar to scroll past the top or bottom item shown in the grid.

Before you see the entire listings (Listing 4-9 for the ASPX and Listing 4-10 for all the code-behind), there is an additional refinement worth mentioning. The ASPxGridView has paging enabled and Settings. VerticalScrollBarStyle set to Virtual. With this setting, the ASPxGridView uses virtual paging. Virtual paging means that if you keep scrolling down or up with the vertical scroll bar, the the grid will page up or down, as the case may be, when it reaches the top or bottom of the list of items shown.

Listing 4-9: The complete ASPX listing for the Web file system explorer.

```
<%@ Page Language="C#" AutoEventWireup="true"  CodeFile="Default.aspx.cs"
 Inherits="_Default" StyleSheetTheme="Aqua" %>

<%@ Register assembly="DevExpress.Web.v9.1, Version=9.1.4.0,
 Culture=neutral, PublicKeyToken=b88d1754d700e49a"
 namespace="DevExpress.Web.ASPxRoundPanel" tagprefix="dxrp" %>
<%@ Register assembly="DevExpress.Web.v9.1, Version=9.1.4.0,
 Culture=neutral, PublicKeyToken=b88d1754d700e49a"
 namespace="DevExpress.Web.ASPxPanel" tagprefix="dxp" %>
<%@ Register assembly="DevExpress.Web.v9.1, Version=9.1.4.0,
 Culture=neutral, PublicKeyToken=b88d1754d700e49a"
 namespace="DevExpress.Web.ASPxNavBar" tagprefix="dxnb" %>

<%@ Register assembly="DevExpress.Web.ASPxTreeList.v9.1,
 Version=9.1.4.0, Culture=neutral, PublicKeyToken=b88d1754d700e49a"
 namespace="DevExpress.Web.ASPxTreeList" tagprefix="dxwtl" %>
<%@ Register assembly="DevExpress.Web.ASPxEditors.v9.1,
 Version=9.1.4.0, Culture=neutral, PublicKeyToken=b88d1754d700e49a"
 namespace="DevExpress.Web.ASPxEditors" tagprefix="dxe" %>
<%@ Register assembly="DevExpress.Web.ASPxGridView.v9.1,
 Version=9.1.4.0, Culture=neutral, PublicKeyToken=b88d1754d700e49a"
 namespace="DevExpress.Web.ASPxGridView" tagprefix="dxwgv" %>


<!DOCTYPE html PUBLIC "-//W3C//DTD XHTML 1.0 Transitional//EN"
 "http://www.w3.org/TR/xhtml1/DTD/xhtml1-transitional.dtd">

<html xmlns="http://www.w3.org/1999/xhtml">
<head id="Head1" runat="server">
  <title></title>
</head>

<body style="padding: 0px; margin: 0px;">
  <form id="form1" runat="server">
  <div style="padding: 0px; margin: 0px; width:100%; height:100%;">

  <table style="padding:0px;margin:0px;border-style:solid;
border-width:thin;height:98%;width:100%;"
      align="left" cellpadding="0" cellspacing="0" >
    <tr>
    <td align="left" valign="top"
style="width:200px;height:100%;position:fixed;">
    <dxrp:ASPxRoundPanel ID="ASPxRoundPanel1" runat="server"
HeaderText="Computer"
```

Continued

Listing 4-9: The complete ASPX listing for the Web file system explorer. *(continued)*

```
              Width="200px">
              <PanelCollection>
<dxp:PanelContent ID="PanelContent1" runat="server">
  <div id="RoundPanelDiv" style="height:98%;width:98%;">
    <dxnb:ASPxNavBar ID="ASPxNavBar1" runat="server"
        AllowSelectItem="True"
        style="margin-top: 0px" EnableClientSideAPI="True"
        >
      <Groups>
        <dxnb:NavBarGroup Text="Favorites">
          <Items>
            <dxnb:NavBarItem Text="Documents">
            </dxnb:NavBarItem>
            <dxnb:NavBarItem Text="Pictures">
            </dxnb:NavBarItem>
            <dxnb:NavBarItem Text="Music">
            </dxnb:NavBarItem>
          </Items>
        </dxnb:NavBarGroup>
        <dxnb:NavBarGroup Text="Drives">
          <ItemTextTemplate>
            <dxe:ASPxLabel ID="ASPxLabel2" runat="server">
            </dxe:ASPxLabel>
            <dxe:ASPxProgressBar ID="ASPxProgressBar1" runat="server" Height="20px"
              Position="50" Width="100px">
            </dxe:ASPxProgressBar>
          </ItemTextTemplate>
        </dxnb:NavBarGroup>
        <dxnb:NavBarGroup Text="Folders" >
          <ContentTemplate>
            <div style="width:190px;height:250px;overflow:auto;">
            <dxwtl:ASPxTreeList ID="ASPxTreeList1" runat="server"
              AutoGenerateColumns="False"
              EnableCallbackCompression="True" Height="100%"

OnVirtualModeCreateChildren="ASPxTreeList1_VirtualModeCreateChildren"
              OnVirtualModeNodeCreating="ASPxTreeList1_VirtualModeNodeCreating"↵
 Width="100%"
              SettingsBehavior-AllowFocusedNode="true"
              SettingsBehavior-FocusNodeOnExpandButtonClick="false"
              SettingsBehavior-ProcessSelectionChangedOnServer="true"
              onfocusednodechanged="ASPxTreeList1_FocusedNodeChanged"
              ClientInstanceName="TreeList"
 oncustomcallback="ASPxTreeList1_CustomCallback"
              >
            <Columns>
              <dxwtl:TreeListTextColumn FieldName="Name" VisibleIndex="0">
              </dxwtl:TreeListTextColumn>
            </Columns>
            <Images ImageFolder="~/App_Themes/Aqua/{0}/">
              <CollapsedButton Height="15px"
```

```
                        Url="~/App_Themes/Aqua/TreeList/CollapsedButton.png"
Width="15px" />
                <ExpandedButton Height="15px"
                    Url="~/App_Themes/Aqua/TreeList/ExpandedButton.png" Width="15px" />
                <SortAscending Height="5px"
Url="~/App_Themes/Aqua/TreeList/SortAsc.png"
                    Width="7px" />
                <SortDescending Height="5px"
Url="~/App_Themes/Aqua/TreeList/SortDesc.png"
                    Width="7px" />
                <CustomizationWindowClose Height="16px" Width="17px" />
            </Images>
            <SettingsText LoadingPanelText="" />
            <SettingsLoadingPanel Text="" />
            <SettingsPager>
              <AllButton>
                <Image Height="19px" Width="27px" />
              </AllButton>
              <FirstPageButton>
                <Image Height="19px" Width="23px" />
              </FirstPageButton>
              <LastPageButton>
                <Image Height="19px" Width="23px" />
              </LastPageButton>
              <NextPageButton>
                <Image Height="19px" Width="19px" />
              </NextPageButton>
              <PrevPageButton>
                <Image Height="19px" Width="19px" />
              </PrevPageButton>
            </SettingsPager>
            <Settings ShowColumnHeaders="False" />
            <SettingsBehavior AllowSort="False" AutoExpandAllNodes="False"
              ExpandCollapseAction="NodeClick"
              ProcessFocusedNodeChangedOnServer="False"
              FocusNodeOnLoad="False" />
            <ClientSideEvents FocusedNodeChanged="function(s, e) {
      Grid.PerformCallback('');
}"
/>
            <SettingsCookies CookiesID="TreeList" Enabled="true"
              StoreExpandedNodes="true" />
            <Templates>
              <DataCell>
                  <dxe:ASPxImage ID="ASPxImage1" runat="server"
                    ImageUrl='<%# Container.GetValue("IconName") %>'>
                  </dxe:ASPxImage>
                   <dxe:ASPxLabel ID="ASPxLabel1" runat="server"
                    Text='<%# Container.GetValue("Name") %>'
                    >
                  </dxe:ASPxLabel>
              </DataCell>
            </Templates>
```

Continued

Listing 4-9: The complete ASPX listing for the Web file system explorer. *(continued)*

```
            </dxwtl:ASPxTreeList>
            </div>
          </ContentTemplate>
        </dxnb:NavBarGroup>
      </Groups>
      <ClientSideEvents ItemClick="function(s,e){
        try
        {
          //debugger;
          if(s.GetSelectedItem().GetText()=='Documents')
            Grid.PerformCallback(s.cpDocuments);
          else if(s.GetSelectedItem().GetText()=='Pictures')
            Grid.PerformCallback(s.cpPictures);
          else if(s.GetSelectedItem().GetText()=='Music')
            Grid.PerformCallback(s.cpMusic);
          else
            TreeList.PerformCallback(s.GetSelectedItem().GetText());
        }
        catch(oException)
        {
          alert(oException);
        }

      }" />
    </dxnb:ASPxNavBar>
    </div>
</dxp:PanelContent>
</PanelCollection>
      </dxrp:ASPxRoundPanel>
      </td>
      <td style="width:100%; height: 100%;" align="left" valign="top" >
        <dxwgv:ASPxGridView ID="ASPXGridView1" runat="server"
          style="height:100%" AutoGenerateColumns="False" ClientInstanceName="Grid"
          oncustomcallback="ASPxGridView1_CustomCallback" Width="100%" >
          <SettingsPager PageSize="25" Position="TopAndBottom">
          </SettingsPager>
          <Columns>
            <dxwgv:GridViewDataTextColumn Caption="Name"
              FieldName="Name" VisibleIndex="0">
            </dxwgv:GridViewDataTextColumn>
            <dxwgv:GridViewDataTextColumn Caption="Date modified"
              FieldName="LastWriteTime"
              VisibleIndex="1">
            </dxwgv:GridViewDataTextColumn>
            <dxwgv:GridViewDataTextColumn Caption="Size" FieldName="Length"
              VisibleIndex="2">
            </dxwgv:GridViewDataTextColumn>
            <dxwgv:GridViewDataTextColumn Caption="File type"
              FieldName="FileType"
```

```
                VisibleIndex="3">
             </dxwgv:GridViewDataTextColumn>
          </Columns>
          <Settings ShowHorizontalScrollBar="True" GridLines="None"
             ShowVerticalScrollBar="True" VerticalScrollBarStyle="Virtual" />
        </dxwgv:ASPxGridView>
     </td>
     </tr>
   </table>
   </div>
   <script type="text/javascript">
   RoundPanelDiv.style.height = document.documentElement.clientHeight - 80 + "px";
//   debugger;
//   var o = new ActiveXObject("WScript.Network");
//   var w = new ActiveXObject("WScript.Shell");
//   var path = w.SpecialFolders("MyDocuments");
//   alert(o.UserName);
//   alert(path);

</script>
   </form>
   </body>
</html>
```

Listing 4-10: The complete code-behind listing for the Web file system explorer.

```csharp
using System;
using System.Collections.Generic;
using System.Linq;
using System.Web;
using System.Web.UI;
using System.Web.UI.WebControls;
using System.IO;
using DevExpress.Web.ASPxTreeList;
using DevExpress.Web.ASPxNavBar;
using DevExpress.Web.ASPxEditors;
using System.Diagnostics;

public partial class _Default : System.Web.UI.Page
{
  private static readonly string FOLDER_ICON = "~/images/folder.gif";
  private static readonly string FILE_ICON = "~/images/file.gif";
  private static readonly string SELECTED_DRIVE = "SelectedDrive";
  private static readonly string SELECTED_PATH = "SelectedPath";

  protected void Page_Load(object sender, EventArgs e)
  {
  ASPxNavBar1.JSProperties.Add("cpDocuments",
    Environment.GetFolderPath(Environment.SpecialFolder.MyDocuments));
  ASPxNavBar1.JSProperties.Add("cpPictures",
    Environment.GetFolderPath(Environment.SpecialFolder.MyPictures));
```

Continued

Listing 4-10: The complete code-behind listing for the Web file system explorer.
(continued)

```
ASPxNavBar1.JSProperties.Add("cpMusic",
  Environment.GetFolderPath(Environment.SpecialFolder.MyMusic));
}

protected void Page_Init(object sender, EventArgs e)
{
Initialize();
UpdateGrid(SelectedPath);
}


public string SelectedPath
{
get
{
  if (Session[SELECTED_PATH] == null)
  Session[SELECTED_PATH] = "C:\\";

  return (string)Session[SELECTED_PATH];
}
set { Session[SELECTED_PATH] = value; }
}

public string SelectedDrive
{
get
{
  if (Session[SELECTED_DRIVE] == null)
  Session[SELECTED_DRIVE] = "C:\\";

  return (string)Session[SELECTED_DRIVE];
}
set { Session[SELECTED_DRIVE] = value; }
}

private static string GetDriveLabel(DriveInfo drive)
{
const string mask = "{0} ({1})";
try
{
  return string.Format(mask,
  drive.VolumeLabel, drive.Name.Replace("\\", ""));
}
catch
{
  return string.Format(mask,
  drive.DriveType.ToString(), drive.Name.Replace("\\", ""));
}
}

private static int GetValue(DriveInfo drive)
```

```
      {
      try
      {
        return (int)((float)(drive.TotalSize - drive.TotalFreeSpace) /
            (float)drive.TotalSize * 100);
      }
      catch
      {
        return 0;
      }
      }


      //Thanks to Platon for help-add to ack.
      private void Initialize()
      {
      DriveInfo[] drives = DriveInfo.GetDrives();
      if (ASPxNavBar1.Groups[1].Items.Count == 0)
        foreach (DriveInfo drive in drives)
        ASPxNavBar1.Groups[1].Items.Add();

      for (int i = 0; i < ASPxNavBar1.Groups[1].Items.Count; i++)
      {
        NavBarItem item = ASPxNavBar1.Groups[1].Items[i];
        ASPxLabel label = (ASPxLabel)item.FindControl("ASPxLabel2");
        ASPxProgressBar progressBar =
          (ASPxProgressBar)item.FindControl("ASPxProgressBar1");

        item.Text = drives[i].Name;
        label.Text = GetDriveLabel(drives[i]);
        progressBar.Value = GetValue(drives[i]);

      }
      }


#region ASPxTreeList Code
   private static IEnumerable<FileInfo> GetFileInfoData(IEnumerable<string> files)
   {
   return from file in files
      let info = new FileInfo(file)
      where (info.Attributes
      & FileAttributes.Hidden) != FileAttributes.Hidden
      select info;
   }

   private static IEnumerable<string> GetDirectories(string start)
   {
   return
      Directory.GetDirectories(start);
   }

   private string GetIcon(FileInfo info)
```

Continued

Listing 4-10: The complete code-behind listing for the Web file system explorer.
(continued)

```csharp
{
return (info.Attributes & FileAttributes.Directory) == FileAttributes.Directory
  ? FOLDER_ICON : FILE_ICON;
}

protected void ASPxTreeList1_VirtualModeCreateChildren(object sender,
  TreeListVirtualModeCreateChildrenEventArgs e)
{
((ASPxTreeList)sender).SettingsBehavior.AutoExpandAllNodes = false;
e.Children = new List<FileInfo>();

if (e.NodeObject == null)
{
  FileInfo info = new FileInfo(SelectedDrive);
  e.Children.Add(info);
}
else
{
  string path = e.NodeObject == null ? SelectedDrive
  : e.NodeObject.ToString();

  if (!Directory.Exists(path)) return;

  try
  {
  var files = GetDirectories(path);
  var infos = GetFileInfoData(files);
  e.Children = new List<FileInfo>();
  foreach (var info in infos)
  {
    e.Children.Add(info);
  }
  }
  catch { }
}
}

protected void ASPxTreeList1_VirtualModeNodeCreating(object sender,
  TreeListVirtualModeNodeCreatingEventArgs e)
{
FileInfo info = (FileInfo)e.NodeObject;
e.NodeKeyValue = GetNodeGuid(info.FullName);
e.IsLeaf = !Directory.Exists(info.FullName);

if(info.FullName == SelectedDrive)
  e.SetNodeValue("Name", SelectedDrive);
else
  e.SetNodeValue("Name", info.Name);

e.SetNodeValue("IconName", GetIcon(info));
e.SetNodeValue("NodePath", info.FullName);
```

```
  }

  // need a unique key, so GUID is used
  private Guid GetNodeGuid(string path)
  {
  if (!Map.ContainsKey(path))
    Map[path] = Guid.NewGuid();
  return Map[path];
  }

  private Dictionary<string, Guid> Map
  {
  get
  {
    const string key = "DX_PATH_GUID_MAP";
    if (Session[key] == null)
    Session[key] = new Dictionary<string, Guid>();
    return Session[key] as Dictionary<string, Guid>;
  }
  }

#endregion

  protected void ASPxTreeList1_FocusedNodeChanged(object sender, EventArgs e)
  {
  try
  {
    string path = ((ASPxTreeList)sender).FocusedNode["NodePath"].ToString();
    SelectedPath = path;
  }
  catch { }
  }

  private void UpdateGrid(string path)
  {
  var files = Directory.GetDirectories(path).Union(Directory.GetFiles(path));

  var infos = from file in files
        let info = new FileInfo(file)
        let isDirectory = (info.Attributes & FileAttributes.Directory)
          == FileAttributes.Directory
        where (info.Attributes
        & FileAttributes.Hidden) != FileAttributes.Hidden
        select new
        {
          Name = info.Name,
          LastWriteTime = info.LastWriteTime,
          Length = isDirectory == false ? info.Length : 0,
          FileType = isDirectory ? "File Folder" : "File"
        };

  ASPxGridView1.DataSource = infos;
  ASPxGridView1.DataBind();

  }
```

Continued

Listing 4-10: The complete code-behind listing for the Web file system explorer.
(continued)

```
    protected void ASPxNavBar1_ExpandedChanging(object source,
    NavBarGroupCancelEventArgs e)
    {
    Initialize();
    }
    protected void ASPxGridView1_CustomCallback(object sender,
     DevExpress.Web.ASPxGridView.ASPxGridViewCustomCallbackEventArgs e)
    {
    if (e.Parameters != "")
      if (Directory.Exists(e.Parameters))
      SelectedPath = e.Parameters;
    UpdateGrid(SelectedPath);
    }

    protected void ASPxTreeList1_CustomCallback(object sender,
    TreeListCustomCallbackEventArgs e)
    {
    SelectedDrive = ASPxNavBar1.SelectedItem.Text;
    ASPxTreeList tree =
      (ASPxTreeList)ASPxNavBar1.Groups[2].FindControl(
        "ASPxTreeList1");
    tree.RefreshVirtualTree();
    }
  }
```

Enabling animation

Animation used in moderation can add liveliness and visual interest for your users. A lot of blinking or fidgeting, animated GIFs can be overwhelming, but animation where it makes sense and seems natural can work in your favor by adding a little bit of dynamic appeal.

If you have `AutoPostBack` set to false and the `ASPxNavBar.EnableAnimation` set to true, the `ASPxNavBar` uses an animation effect when you expand and collapse groups. If `EnableCallbacks` is true, the animation effect is not used the first time a collapsed group is expanded. Animation was not used with the explorer demo, but you can turn it on to experiment with animation.

Improving the appearance with a theme

Cascading style sheets (.css files) can be used to enhance the appearance of controls and pages, manage layout, and even run code — for example, defining a behavior that loads an ActiveXObject to include gradient shading. CSS is an underlying technology that is used to apply themes and skins to Web pages or whole sites.

If you ever need help with a specific DevExpress control or component, click Get Support from that item's Smart tags menu to navigate to the Support Center Search Results page on the DevExpress Web site. You can use that site location to search the knowledgebase for existing support center questions and solutions.

You can apply existing themes to individual controls, such as the Smart Tag Auto Format feature of the ASPxNavrBar, or to an entire site by modifying the `web.config` file. The Aqua format was applied as skin in the `web.config` file for the explorer demo. For more information on using CSS, themes, and skin, refer to Chapter 9, "Using Themes, CSS, and JavaScript for Customizations and Enhancements." To apply the Aqua skin to the explorer demo as shown previously in Figure 4-1 (for the Books demo), copy all the files under the Aqua folder — stored by default in the C:\Program Files\DevExpress 2009.1\ Components\Demos\Data\App_Themes folder — and modify the `<pages>` tag in the `web.config` file to by adding the theme attribute as shown:

```
<pages theme="Aqua">
```

You can remove all the individual autoformat style tags from the ASPX after you have added the theme attribute to the `<pages>` tag. When you switch to using a Web site skin, the runtime view will reflect the styles defined by the skin but the design time view will not.

Facilitating Social Networking with the ASPxCloudControl

My friend Joe Kunk is a huge fan of computing in the cloud. Joe's kind of cloud computing means using some external resource with which you can scale as you go using a pay-grow approach. A favorite topic of his is cloud computing with Amazon.com's resources. The ASPxCloudControl is not that kind of control.

The ASPxCloudControl has more to do with what is called Web 2.0, which emphasizes the social networking aspects of the Internet through Facebook, Twitter, MySpace, LinkedIn, and tags. I first heard of Web 2.0 and the concept of tags from Reb Rebholz at Microsoft. Rob referred to tags as creating a *tagsonomy* — a play on taxonomy or classification. The basic idea is that keyword tags help create links between related topics. For example, DevExpress's community server implementation supports tags for the Evangelist blog posts, with the aim of helping customers find topics of interest. The ASPxCloudControl is a social networking control.

The ASPxCloudControl enables you to incorporate a navigation and data analysis UI into your ASP.NET project. The control organizes and arranges hyperlinks within an area of interest, indicating their importance by font weight, size, and color. The ASPxCloudControl can be used in bound or unbound mode, and customizable text, rank count, and sizes can vary linearly or logarithmically. By default, links are displayed in the order they appear in the data source or can be arranged alphabetically.

I write a lot of articles. In fact, I have had my VB Today column at www.codeguru.com/columns/VB/ for ten years now. In that time, I have written hundreds of articles. The sample program for this part uses Microsoft Indexing Service at the ASPxCloudControl to list articles and list (and font-weight) them by rank and title. The use of the Indexing Service is not required, and you can easily substitute any other data source for the query results returned by the Indexing Service query.

Configuring Microsoft Indexing Service

Microsoft Indexing Service (MSIDXS) is not installed by default. Indexing Service is cool because you can index your file system, associate the file system to the MSIDXS with a SQL stored procedure, and then use SQL to query the indexed catalogs.

> *Microsoft Indexing Service (MSIDXS) is not required for the ASPxCloudControl. Using the indexing service just makes for a more compelling demonstration of the cloud control and perhaps teaches you a few new generally useful and leverageable skills.*

To use the MSIDXS service, you need to

❑ Install the Microsoft Indexing Service

❑ Create a catalog and indexed directory

❑ Link the file system and indexing service to SQL Server using a stored procedure

❑ Query the indexing service

After installing and configuring the indexing service, the sample program queries the indexing service and binds the results to an ASPxCloudControl yielding a basic Web site query subsystem. (It's like having your own tiny Google service.) Here are the steps for installing the Microsoft Indexing Service:

1. Click Start ➪ Control Panel.

2. For Vista, find the Programs and Features applet (or the equivalent for other versions of Windows).

3. In the Tasks pane of Control Panel window, Programs and Features view, click Turn Windows Features On or Off.

4. In the Turn Windows Features On or Off dialog box that appears, scroll to Indexing Service and select the box next to it (see Figure 4-8).

5. Click OK. (The service may take a couple of minutes to finish installing.)

6. From the Control Panel, choose Administrative Tools ➪ Services, making sure that the Indexing Service is installed and started (see Figure 4-9).

Figure 4-8: Install the Windows Indexing
Service from the Turn Windows Features On
or Off dialog box.

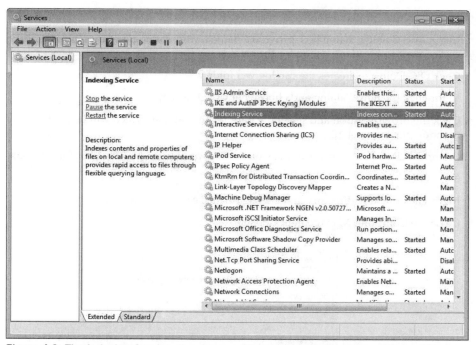

Figure 4-9: The Indexing Service shows up as Start with a Startup Type of Automatic in
the Services console.

When the Index service is installed and running, you need to create a catalog and define a directory to index.

Defining a Catalog and Directory, and Building the Index

In the sample application, you index the directory (or directories) containing the content that you want users to be able to query. For the sample application, this consists of the folder containing the articles. The Indexing Service can be accessed through the Computer Management console. To run the Computer Management Console, click Start, and in the Start Search input (on Vista), enter **compmgmt.msc**. Then press Enter.

> You can press Windows key+R to open the Run dialog box and enter commands (such as `compmgmt.msc`) there, too.

To define the catalog and the directory and then start the indexing process for the Articles folder, follow these steps:

1. In the Computer Management dialog box, expand the Services and Applications tab.

2. Right-click the Indexing Service and choose New ⇨ Add Catalog.

3. In the Add Catalog dialog box, provide a name for the catalog. For the example, use ARTICLES and browse to a folder location for the catalog.

4. Click OK. Doing so creates the catalog.wci folder.

5. Right-click the new Catalog and choose New ⇨ Directory.

6. Click the Browse button and select the path for the catalog, which will be the location of the files to index (see Figure 4-10).

7. Provide a UNC (Universal Naming Convention) alias (using ARTICLES) for the alias.

8. Click OK.

9. Right-click the new directory and choose All Tasks ⇨ Rescan (Full).

10. Close the Computer Management Console.

Figure 4-10: Define a directory and alias for the ARTICLES folder to tell the Indexing Service what to index.

After you have started the scan, you can query the files in the indexed folder. To query the files with SQL Server, you need to associate the Indexing Service with the FileSystem object and the indexed folder.

Linking the Indexing Service to the FileSystem Via SQL Server

Two stored procedures are useful for adding and dropping linked servers such as the Microsoft Indexing Service. These are sp_addlinkedserver and sp_dropserver. To add the FileSystem to the Microsoft Indexing Service, execute the follow command in the Microsoft SQL Server Management Studio or a Visual Studio query:

```
EXEC sp_addlinkedserver FileSystem, 'Index Server', 'MSIDXS', 'ARTICLES'
```

If you decide to associate another location to the FileSystem, you can drop an existing link with

```
EXEC sp_dropserver FileSystem
```

The preceding stored procedures are installed with SQL server (and SQL Server Express). You can look up their parameters and definitions online on MSDN or in the Visual Studio Help.

Querying the Indexing Service

To test the running Indexing Service and your indexed location, you can run a query right in Visual Studio. The command can be written along these lines:

```
SELECT RANK, FILENAME, VPATH, CHARACTERIZATION
FROM
    OPENQUERY(FileSystem, 'SELECT RANK, FileName,  VPath, Characterization
    FROM SCOPE() WHERE FREETEXT( ''LINQ'') > 0 ORDER BY RANK DESC') AS temp
```

In short, the query is using the Indexing Service to scan the files associated with the FileSystem object, but a lot is going on in this query. I will walk you through the various query elements, working from the inside out.

The FREETEXT predicate uses the full-text query engine to separate text into individual words based on word-breaking rules such as whitespace, generates inflectional forms of the word referred to as stemming, and identifies a list of expansions and replacements. Think of FREETEXT as performing a full-text search of each column.

The Scope() function defines the scope of the query. With no parameters, Scope() means the whole directory in this instance. Scope is one of those functions that seems pitifully underrepresented, but you can read about the Indexing Service and Scope() at http://idunno.org/articles/278.aspx.

The inner SELECT is the query sent to the Indexing Service; OPENQUERY is the function that forwards the inner SELECT to the linked MSIDXS server. The outer SELECT is the SQL query that returns the columns that are passed back from the Indexing Service. You can also query the Indexing Service directly by establishing an OLEDB connection directly to the Indexing Service and using the inner SELECT only. (Refer to the aforementioned article for more examples of the Indexing Service.)

The query in this section returns a FileName and Rank, which are data items ideally suited for displaying in an ASPxCloudControl.

Configuring the ASPxCloudControl

The demo uses an `ASPxRoundPanel` with a nested `ASPxTextBox` and `ASPxButton` to initiate the search, and the search results are bound to an `ASPxCloudControl`. (Refer to Figure 4-11.) Listing 4-11 contains the ASPX for the sample, and Listing 4-12 contains the code-behind.

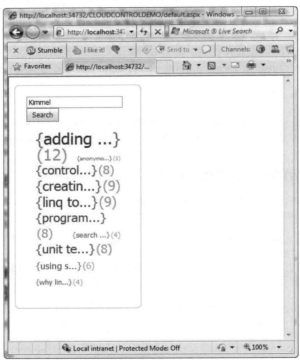

Figure 4-11: An ASPxRoundPanel with a search feature that binds the results of a search via Microsoft's Indexing Service to an ASPxCloudControl.

Listing 4-11: The ASPX for the sample application that uses Microsoft's Indexing Service and the ASPxCloudControl.

```
<%@ Page Language="C#" AutoEventWireup="true"
  CodeFile="Default.aspx.cs" Inherits="_Default" %>

<%@ Register Assembly="DevExpress.Web.ASPxEditors.v9.1,↵
  Version=9.1.4.0, Culture=neutral, PublicKeyToken=b88d1754d700e49a"
    Namespace="DevExpress.Web.ASPxEditors" TagPrefix="dxe" %>

<%@ Register assembly="DevExpress.Web.v9.1, Version=9.1.4.0,↵
```

```
  Culture=neutral, PublicKeyToken=b88d1754d700e49a"
  namespace="DevExpress.Web.ASPxRoundPanel" tagprefix="dxrp" %>
<%@ Register assembly="DevExpress.Web.v9.1, Version=9.1.4.0,↵
  Culture=neutral, PublicKeyToken=b88d1754d700e49a"
  namespace="DevExpress.Web.ASPxPanel" tagprefix="dxp" %>
<%@ Register assembly="DevExpress.Web.v9.1, Version=9.1.4.0,↵
  Culture=neutral, PublicKeyToken=b88d1754d700e49a"
  namespace="DevExpress.Web.ASPxCloudControl" tagprefix="dxcc" %>

<!DOCTYPE html PUBLIC "-//W3C//DTD XHTML 1.0 Transitional//EN"
"http://www.w3.org/TR/xhtml1/DTD/xhtml1-transitional.dtd">

<html xmlns="http://www.w3.org/1999/xhtml">
<head runat="server">
    <title></title>
</head>
<body>
    <form id="form1" runat="server">
    <div>
      <dxrp:ASPxRoundPanel ID="ASPxRoundPanel1" runat="server" Width="200px"
          HeaderText="" ShowHeader="False">
        <PanelCollection>
<dxp:PanelContent runat="server">
    <dxe:ASPxTextBox ID="ASPxTextBox1" runat="server" Width="170px">
    </dxe:ASPxTextBox>
    <dxe:ASPxButton ID="ASPxButton1" runat="server" Text="Search"
        OnClick="ASPxButton1_Click">
    </dxe:ASPxButton>


  <dxcc:ASPxCloudControl ID="ASPxCloudControl1" runat="server" ItemBeginText="{"
        ItemEndText="}" NameField="FileName" NavigateUrlField="FileName"
        NavigateUrlFormatString="~/Articles/{0}" Scale="Linear" ShowValues="True"
        Target="_blank" TextField="ShortName" ValueField="Rank"
        OnItemDataBound="ASPxCloudControl1_ItemDataBound">
    <rankproperties>
      <dxcc:RankProperties />
        <dxcc:RankProperties />
        <dxcc:RankProperties />
        <dxcc:RankProperties />
        <dxcc:RankProperties />
        <dxcc:RankProperties />
        <dxcc:RankProperties />
    </rankproperties>
  </dxcc:ASPxCloudControl>
          </dxp:PanelContent>
</PanelCollection>
      </dxrp:ASPxRoundPanel>

    </div>
    </form>
</body>
</html>
```

Listing 4-12: The code-behind accepts the input from the ASPxTextBox, performs the search, and binds the results to the ASPxCloudControl.

```csharp
using System;
using System.Collections.Generic;
using System.Linq;
using System.Web;
using System.Web.UI;
using System.Web.UI.WebControls;
using System.Data.SqlClient;
using System.Data;

public partial class _Default : System.Web.UI.Page
{
    protected void Page_Load(object sender, EventArgs e)
    {
      if(!IsPostBack)
        LoadData("LINQ");
    }

    private void LoadData(string criteria)
    {
      string connectionString ConnectionString=
        @"Data Source=FRANKLIN\SQLEXPRESS; " +
          "Initial Catalog=master;Integrated Security=True";
      string sql =
        "SELECT Rank, FileName, SUBSTRING(FILENAME, 0, 8) " +
        "'...' AS ShortName, " +
        "Characterization FROM OPENQUERY(FileSystem, " +
        "'SELECT RANK, FileName, VPath, Characterization " +
        "FROM SCOPE() WHERE FREETEXT( ''{0}'') " +
        "ORDER BY RANK DESC') AS Temp";
      sql = string.Format(sql, criteria);

      using (SqlConnection connection = new SqlConnection(connectionString))
      {

        connection.Open();
        SqlCommand command = new SqlCommand(sql, connection);
        DataTable table = new DataTable();
        SqlDataAdapter adapter = new SqlDataAdapter(command);
        adapter.Fill(table);
        ASPxCloudControl1.DataSource = table;
        ASPxCloudControl1.DataBind();
      }
    }
    protected void ASPxCloudControl1_ItemDataBound(object source,
      DevExpress.Web.ASPxCloudControl.CloudControlItemEventArgs e)
    {
      e.Item.ToolTip = e.Item.NavigateUrl;
    }

    protected void ASPxButton1_Click(object sender, EventArgs e)
```

```
      {
        if (ASPxTextBox1.Text == "") return;
        LoadData(ASPxTextBox1.Text);
      }
  }
```

Setting the ASPxCloudControl properties

As with all of the DevExpress controls, the ASPxCloudControl has dozens of properties. In my experience, the default settings are always a pretty good start, and the Devexpress.com web and integrated help site do a great job of cataloging detailed information about all the properties. The key to getting data in the ASPxCloudControl is to define the properties that describe where the data comes from.

For the example, ItemBeginText and ItemEndText are set to { and }, respectively, which brackets each cloud item. The NameField is used to provide a unique identifier for each value in the result set. The NavigateUrlField describes the field that contains navigation information; when combined with the NavigateUrlFormatString — -~/Articles/{0} in the example — a URL is defined for the item. By clicking the item in the ASPxCloudControl, the control redirects to that URL. For the example, this means that you open a document containing the selected search item. The Scale property defines the algorithm that normalizes item weights. The two available values are Linear and Logarithm. The Scale property is used to establish the font sizes for items; for the example, this is based on the RANK. I used Target=_blank, which opens a new Web page for the selected item. The display value is the TextField. The derived ShortName field is used for the display text. The ValueField sets the weight. For the example, the ValueField is set to RANK, which is the rank value assigned by the Indexing Service based on the query.

> **For MS Office Documents (Office 2007), you can set the title by clicking the Office Button, choosing Prepare ⇨ Properties, and setting the title. The title can be read using Indexing Service with the DOCTITLE column.**

Finally, the OnItemDataBound event handler is defined. OnItemDataBound (see Listing 4-12) assigns ToolTip to the NavigateUrl, which is the same as the document's complete filename. (See the Tip for how to use the DOCTITLE field of the Indexing Service with MS Office documents.)

Examining the Supporting C# code

Because you linked the Indexing Service with SQL Server, the C# code-behind is plain-vanilla ADO.NET. When the user clicks the Search button, the LoadData method is called, passing the search criteria to LoadData. LoadData builds a SQL string with the nested indexing Service query to SQL Server, which in turn runs the query against the linked MSIDXS service. (Refer to the earlier subsection "Querying the Indexing Service" for more information on OPENQUERY, FREETEXT, and Scope().)

This section is not meant to be a comprehensive presentation of T-SQL, FREETEXT, OPENQUERY, and the Indexing Service. Sources for those materials are abundant. However, if you are unfamiliar with any of these topics, I encourage further exploration. For more on T-SQL, see *Beginning T-SQL with Microsoft*

SQL Server 2005 and 2008 by Paul Turley and Dan Wood (Wrox, 2008). Unfortunately, there don't seem to be any really good titles focused on Indexing Service, but there are bits and pieces all over the Web.

Creating a Sitemap with XML and the ASPxSiteMapControl

One of the Web legends is Alexa Internet. Alexa Internet was named in homage to the famous Library of Alexandria. Started as a California company, one of Alexa's cool features was that it archived the Internet with web crawls every month or so. Alexa was started in 1996 and purchased by Amazon.com in 1999. Sometime since, the "Wayback Machine" was started in 1996 and purchased by Amazon.com more recently, it ended up on www.archive.org.

Plumbing the depths of the Wayback Machine, I was able to find a Web presence for my consulting company as far back as December 1997 — although it goes back to 1995. I quickly noticed a couple of things, in addition to the fact that my Web site and many others were hideous in the 1990s and that my Web site is due for an update: The site map I fabricated was labor intensive.

In the mid-1990s until the last few years, site maps were cobbled together by <div> tags or <html> tags and URLs to other locations on the site. XML didn't really exist until 1997 or 1998 and probably wasn't very mainstream for a few more years after that. My Web site's map was fabricated from <html> tags and a database that contained the link names and the URLs. The difficulty with such a map is that it is labor intensive and doesn't support much flexibility in terms of layout without a lot of additional, manual recoding. In truth, a site map is generally not much more than the names you'd like to use to refer to links and the URLs for those links. Spending a lot of time manually coding these elements isn't a good use of time. This is where the ASPxSiteMapControl and XML come into play.

XML is great at containing easy-to-manage text content in a meaningful, self-describing format, making it ideal for hierarchies of names and links. The ASPxSiteMapControl is great at referencing that data and displaying it in a wide variety of layouts with an equally wide variety of ways to format the appearance, all with little or no coding. So, rather than have an abundance of SQL skills, a database, HTML programming skills, and lot of hard-coded layout information, you can use the ASPxSiteMapControl and a text editor and set a couple of properties for a quick-and-easy site map.

Another useful feature of the `ASPxSiteMapControl` is the ability to point at an empty sitemap file and use the site map editor to visually design the site map (and the `.sitemap` file) at design time, selecting existing elements from your Web application. Combine the ability to optionally use database data, manually bind site map items, change the layout with properties, and use templates to create customizable map nodes, and the ASPxSiteMapControl offers the most flexibility with the least amount of effort.

Binding an ASPxSiteMapControl to an Existing .sitemap File

A site map file is an XML file. By convention, the `.sitemap` extension is used. You can add a `.sitemap` file to a Web site project from the Add New Items dialog box. The .sitemap file will be stubbed out with a siteMap root node, a siteMapNode, and nested siteMapNode elements. The siteMapNode elements contain `url` and `title` attributes (see Listing 4-13), which are string values, showing you how to manually define the XML content for a site map.

Listing 4-13: The Add New Items Site Map applet adds an XML .sitemap file to your project with stubbed nodes, demonstrating the desired format for sitemap content.

```xml
<?xml version="1.0" encoding="utf-8"?>
<siteMap xmlns="http://schemas.microsoft.com/AspNet/SiteMap-File-1.0">
  <siteMapNode url="" title="">
    <siteMapNode url="" title="" />
    <siteMapNode url="" title="" />
  </siteMapNode>
</siteMap>
```

Assume that you have a Web site with content laid out using the following file structure:

```
~/SiteMapDemo/
~/SiteMapDemo/Default.aspx
  ~/SiteMapDemo/About/
    ~/SiteMapDemo/About/About.aspx
    ~/SiteMapDemo/About/ContactInformation.aspx
  ~/SiteMapDemo/Products/
    ~/SiteMapDemo/Products/Products.aspx
  ~/SiteMapDemo/Publications/
    ~/SiteMapDemo/Publications/Publications.aspx
  ~/SiteMapDemo/Services/
    ~/SiteMapDemo/Services/Services.aspx
  ~/SiteMapDemo/Training/
    ~/SiteMapDemo/Training/Training.aspx
```

You can manually modify the `.sitemap` file to describe the site's file locations, as shown in Listing 4-14.

Listing 4-14: A .sitemap file manually created by modifying the nodes and node attributes to reflect the site's structure.

```xml
<?xml version="1.0" encoding="utf-8"?>
<siteMap xmlns="http://schemas.microsoft.com/AspNet/SiteMap-File-1.0">
  <siteMapNode url="" title="Web Site">
    <siteMapNode url="~/About/" title="About">
      <siteMapNode url="~/About/About.aspx" title="About.aspx" />
      <siteMapNode url="~/About/Contactinformation.aspx"
        title="Contactinformation.aspx" />
    </siteMapNode>
    <siteMapNode url="~/Default.aspx" title="Default.aspx" />
    <siteMapNode url="~/Products/" title="Products">
      <siteMapNode url="~/Products/Products.aspx" title="Products.aspx" />
    </siteMapNode>
    <siteMapNode url="~/Publications/" title="Publications">
      <siteMapNode url="~/Publications/Publications.aspx"
        title="Publications.aspx" />
    </siteMapNode>
```

Continued

```
<siteMapNode url="~/Services/" title="Services">
  <siteMapNode url="~/Services/Services.aspx" title="Services.aspx" />
</siteMapNode>
<siteMapNode url="~/Training/" title="Training">
  <siteMapNode url="~/Training/Training.aspx" title="Training.aspx" />
</siteMapNode>
    </siteMapNode>
  </siteMap>
```

Bind the `.sitemap` control to an ASPxSiteMapControl and the design time view with site map in Listing 4-14, and the default property settings, appears as shown in Figure 4-12. Of course, the whole point of using components and controls is to make your life easier, which means letting the ASPxSiteMapControl build the .sitemap for you.

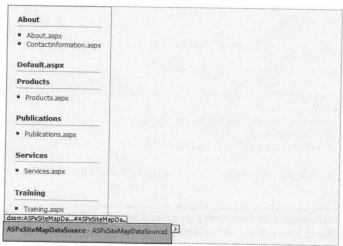

Figure 4-12: Bind the .sitemap file to an ASPxSiteMapControl using the default property settings and the .sitemap in Listing 4-14, and you get a functional site map.

Building a Sitemap Based on the Current Structure of Your Site

One of my favorite features of any control is when the control can do labor-intensive work for me based on reasonable assumptions and the least amount of work. After all, a site map is basically a navigator pointing to pages on your Web site.

The least labor-intensive way to build a site map with the ASPxSiteMapControl is to build your site first and then let the site map editor retrieve the site structure and infer the map based on the actual layout of the site. The site map editor is fully customizable, so if you don't like the titles, for example, inferred from the pages themselves, use the editor to change the titles. To create a `.sitemap` file based on the site structure defined in the preceding section and bind the map to the ASPxSiteMapControl, follow these steps:

1. Add an ASPxSiteMapControl to a Web page.

2. On the ASPxSiteMapControl's Smart tags menu, choose Choose Data Source ⇨ <New data source . . . >.

3. In the Choose Data Source dropdown select the ASPxSiteMapDataSource item.

4. Click OK.

5. Click the Smart tag on the ASPxSiteMapDataSource.

6. In the Smart tags menu, select Create New SiteMap.

7. In the [SiteMap] Editing dialog box, click the Retrieve Site Structure button (see Figure 4-13).

8. Click each of the items and modify the Description and Title properties as desired.

9. If you want to add items, use the toolbar buttons at the top of the same dialog box. (These buttons are similar to every like editor discussed in the book so far; the buttons add, remove, and organize the arrangement of buttons.)

10. Click OK when you are finished.

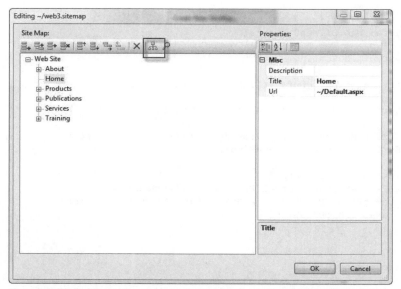

Figure 4-13: Retrieve the site map structure from the site itself using the editor (shown) and the Retrieve Site Structure toolbar button.

If you want to customize the appearance of the sitemap nodes, define a template by placing additional controls and binding statements in the NodeTemplate or NodeTextTemplate. If you want to change the appearance, use the Smart tags Auto Format feature or apply a theme to the site. If you want a sitemap that looks like links, perhaps to display as a page footer, change the ASPxSiteMapControl.ColumnCount property to reflect the number of columns desired. If you want to create group categories, set Categorized to true, and each top-level node will serve as a category name.

All these configuration options can be set at design time or programmatically if desired. You also have the option of adding items with code.

Building a Site Map Dynamically

Suppose that you want to support a user's ability to add content dynamically or update the site map based on user permissions. In this instance, you could dynamically create the site map in unbound mode at runtime based on some requirements-based criteria. The code in Listing 4-15 demonstrates the elements necessary to populate the ASPxSiteMapControl in unbound mode with code (with criteria to be provided by you). The code in Listing 4-15 demonstrates the mechanics of building a rudimentary site map programmatically. The path is shown in a SiteMapPath control.

Listing 4-15: Building a site map dynamically using the UnboundSiteMapProvider.

```
using System;
using System.Collections.Generic;
using System.Linq;
using System.Web;
using System.Web.UI;
using System.Web.UI.WebControls;
using DevExpress.Web.ASPxSiteMapControl;
using System.Web.Hosting;

public partial class _Default : System.Web.UI.Page
{
    protected void Page_Load(object sender, EventArgs e)
    {
      ASPxSiteMapDataSource1.Provider = CreateUnboundSiteMapProvider();
      ASPxSiteMapControl1.DataBind();

      SiteMapNode currentNode =
       ASPxSiteMapDataSource1.Provider.CurrentNode;
      SiteMapPath1.Provider = ASPxSiteMapDataSource1.Provider;
      SiteMapPath1.DataBind();
    }


    public string RootPath
    {
      get { return Request.AppRelativeCurrentExecutionFilePath; }
    }

    private UnboundSiteMapProvider CreateUnboundSiteMapProvider()
    {
```

```
.....UnboundSiteMapProvider provider =
      new UnboundSiteMapProvider(RootPath, "Directories");
    VirtualDirectory root =
      HostingEnvironment.VirtualPathProvider.GetDirectory(
        HostingEnvironment.ApplicationVirtualPath +
        "/SiteMap/Directories");
    BuildSiteMap(root, provider.RootNode);
    return provider;
  }

  private void BuildSiteMap(VirtualDirectory parentDirectory,
    SiteMapNode parent)
  {
    UnboundSiteMapProvider provider =
      parent.Provider as UnboundSiteMapProvider;
    foreach (VirtualDirectory dir in parentDirectory.Directories)
    {
      string url = RootPath + "?id=" +
        dir.VirtualPath.Replace(
          HostingEnvironment.ApplicationVirtualPath, string.Empty);
      SiteMapNode node = provider.CreateNode(
        url.Replace(" ", "%20"), dir.Name);
      BuildSiteMap(dir, node);
      provider.AddSiteMapNode(node, parent);
    }
  }
}
```

The code looks a little more complicated than it is. Essentially, the code is walking the Web site directory structure and creating SiteMaNode objects. Most of what the code is doing is replacing site-hosting environment paths to virtual paths and using BuildsiteMap to recurse into child directories.

The sample folders for this example were borrowed from the demos that are installed with your Develop Express controls. By default, the samples are installed at C:\Program Files\DevExpress 2009.1\ Components\Demos. The code is a slightly modified and simpler version of the SiteMap demo for unbound mode at C:\Program Files\DevExpress 2009.1\Components\Demos\ASPxperience\ ASPxperienceDemos\SiteMap\UnboundMode.aspx.

Each time Page_Load is called, the site map is rebuilt into this example; thus, if you were to add dynamic content, this code would pick up new folders. (You could cache the UnboundSiteMapProvider in Session to eliminate the site map rebuild for every postback.) Page_Load also updates the visible SiteMapPath control.

CreateUnboundSiteMapProvider creates an instance of the UnboundSiteMapProvider, starting with the site root and recursing into child folders by calling BuildSiteMap. BuildSiteMap initializes a child node for each subdirectory, replacing spaces with the URL-acceptable %20 character and recursing into the child directories. The URL for each node is given the form ~/UnboundSiteMapDemo/Default .aspx?id=*directory_name*, where directory_name is the name of the folder associated with that node. (This is a little different from the demo in the preceding section, which actually is a link to a specific file.)

Finally, you set the ASPxSiteMapDataSource.StartFromCurrentNode to true and ShowStartingNode = true. Doing so causes the ASPxSiteMapControl to display the child nodes relative to the currently selected node.

To complete the visual appearance, an ASPxRoundPanel is wrapped around the ASPxSiteMapControl, and the ASPxSiteMapControl.MaximumDisplayLevels is set to 3. Refer to Figure 4-14 for the completed result and to Listing 4-16 for the ASPX (which shows you detailed attribute and property settings).

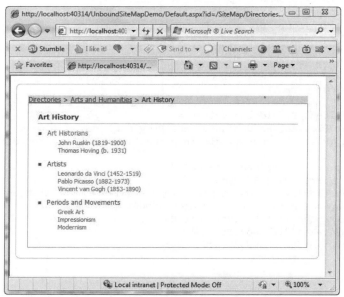

Figure 4-14: The dynamically populated ASPxSiteMapControl (see Listings 4-15 and 4-16 for the code-behind and ASPX) inside an ASPxRoundPanel.

Listing 4-16: The ASPX for the ASPxSiteMapControl demo shown in Figure 4-14.

```
<%@ Page Language="C#" AutoEventWireup="true"  CodeFile="Default.aspx.cs"
 Inherits="_Default" Theme="Aqua" StyleSheetTheme="" %>

<%@ Register Assembly="DevExpress.Web.v9.1, Version=9.1.4.0,
 Culture=neutral, PublicKeyToken=b88d1754d700e49a"
    Namespace="DevExpress.Web.ASPxRoundPanel" TagPrefix="dxrp" %>

<%@ Register assembly="DevExpress.Web.v9.1, Version=9.1.4.0,
 Culture=neutral, PublicKeyToken=b88d1754d700e49a"
 namespace="DevExpress.Web.ASPxSiteMapControl" tagprefix="dxsm" %>

<!DOCTYPE html PUBLIC "-//W3C//DTD XHTML 1.0 Transitional//EN"
 "http://www.w3.org/TR/xhtml1/DTD/xhtml1-transitional.dtd">

<html xmlns="http://www.w3.org/1999/xhtml">
```

```
<head runat="server">
    <title></title>
</head>
<body>
    <form id="form1" runat="server">
    <div>
        <dxrp:ASPxRoundPanel ID="ASPxRoundPanel1" runat="server" Width="100%"
            ShowHeader="False">
        <PanelCollection>
         <dxrp:PanelContent ID="PanelContent1" runat="server">
            <asp:SiteMapPath ID="SiteMapPath1" runat="server"
              BackColor="#E0E0FF"
              Width="100%">
            </asp:SiteMapPath>
            <dxsm:ASPxSiteMapControl ID="ASPxSiteMapControl1" runat="server"
                DataSourceID="ASPxSiteMapDataSource1"
                MaximumDisplayLevels="3" Width="100%">
            </dxsm:ASPxSiteMapControl>
            <dxsm:ASPxSiteMapDataSource ID="ASPxSiteMapDataSource1"
              runat="server"
              StartFromCurrentNode="True" ShowStartingNode="true"/>
         </dxrp:PanelContent>
         </PanelCollection>
         </dxrp:ASPxRoundPanel>

    </div>
    </form>
</body>
</html>
```

Using Modal Dialogs in ASP.NET

A modeless window is one that permits the user to switch between it and other modeless windows. A modal window, also called a dialog window, is one that demands attention until it is closed, putting an application in a linear mode. Statefulness is when an application is actively connected to its executing code. The Web is a modeless, stateless environment by default. A modal dialog is more generally a WinForms application concept. A modal window (also called a dialog or pop-up) is more of an afterthought for the Web. For that reason, using pop-up dialogs in a Web application can be challenging.

JavaScript supports dialog windows and pop-ups, and there are a few ways that programmers have simulated pop-ups with <div> and <table> tags, but each requires a lot of script or fine-tuning of HTML and script. As mentioned, you can use a <div> or <html> tag to overlay a Web page. You can also write script that calls window.ShowModalDialog(), window.createPopup(), or window.show() to display a dialog or pop-up in your Web applications. The problem with any of these approaches is that you have to spend too much time on plumbing to make them work effectively and correctly, and you usually have to write some JavaScript. (The JavaScript has to be downloaded to the client machine, which can make your Web application a little more sluggish, too.) Another complication is that the intent of a dialog is to elicit some input and return that data back to the calling form. Coordinating user input between dialogs requires extra coordination: Either you have to return the results to more script or you have to pass the data using Session state. Again, this is a lot of extra work that generally doesn't work toward solving your business problem, nor does it promote building applications quickly.

The Web has many resources (Google or bing on topics such as "javascript popup dialog"), so it's not worth reproducing all of them here. However, to contrast the significant labor involved with using script versus the ASPxPopupControl there is a brief sample in the next section. The next section shows the interplay between ASPX, JavaScript, and Popups followed by samples using the ASPxPopupControl.

Blending showModalDialog with JavaScript and the ASPxCallbackPanel

A general pattern for modal dialogs is to use them as composite controls for inputting and validating data on the client and returning that data to the caller. Another pattern is to use the dialog to perform an action and return a success or failure value. For example, you can define a login dialog so that when it is displayed, the user enters his or her credentials and the dialog authenticates the credentials and returns the authentication results to the caller. An alternative implementation pattern is that the login dialog is displayed, the user enters his or her credentials, the credentials are returned, and the caller authenticates the credentials. Both implementation styles work. I call the first style implementation style 1 and the second implementation style 2.

For implementation style 1, the business code is not in the modal dialog; it's in the calling page. I like this style when I want to make a form that is generally reusable. For example, if you want to change the authentication code used, you can reuse the Login Web page because there is no authentication code in it. Implementation style 2 means that the business logic is in the dialog and the caller gets a simple return result that indicates success or failure. Both implementation styles work. When using modal dialogs in ASP.NET, the only significant difference between implementation style 1 and 2 is how much data the dialog returns.

The sample in this section represents a login dialog. The sample uses implementation style 1; the login page returns the user-entered data from the dialog. The only thing the dialog does is use a RequiredFieldValidator to check that there is a username and password if the user clicks OK; it then sets up the return values through a client-side click event handler.

Using a RequiredFieldValidator

Any Web page will work to demonstrate the plumbing and mechanics of a modal dialog. I picked a Login Web page because it is familiar. The login form shown in Figure 4-15 is assembled from an ASPxRoundPanel containing an <html> table and the typical controls — two ASPxLabel controls, two ASPxTextBox controls, and two ASPxButton controls. A RequiredFieldValidator is associated with each of the ASPxTextBox controls and each RequiredFieldValidator.ControlToValidate property. In addition to making sure that the ControlToValidate — one of the ASPxTextBox controls — contains data, an ErrorMessage is set for each validator and the SetFocusOnError property is set to true.

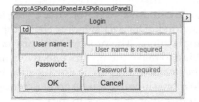

Figure 4-15: The login form will be displayed as a modal dialog, and it will return the user-entered username and password values.

The more interesting use of the validator controls has to do with their client-side behavior. The login form will be called through JavaScript — window.showModalDialog — and the user name and password will be returned through JavaScript. The minor challenge here is that when the user clicks OK, the OK button's client event handler will close the (login) dialog before the validator validates its associated controls. The client-side event handler for the OK button demonstrates how to force the validation.

Implementing the OK Behavior

The login form has an OK and a Cancel button. The OK button's AutoPostBack property is set to false. Because the user-entered data is returned through JavaScript, having the login form post back to the server isn't necessary. (In fact, if the login form does post back to the server, a second instance of the login form is opened, which is an undesirable side effect.)

For the OK button, an ASPxButton was used. Implement the ASPxButton's client-side click event using the Client-Side Events Editor. The code for the OK button's Click event is provided in Listing 4-17.

Listing 4-17: The client-side click event for the ASPxButton providing the OK behavior.

```
function(s, e) {
  debugger;
  if(typeof(Page_ClientValidate)=='function')
    if(Page_ClientValidate())
    {
      var returnValue = new Object();
      returnValue.UserName = UserName.GetText();
      returnValue.Password = Password.GetText();
      window.returnValue = returnValue;
      window.close();
    }
}
```

> Using JavaScript Object Notation (JSON) you can rewrite the lines that initialize the returnValue and assign the UserName and Password in Listing 4-17 to
>
> ```
> var returnValue = {'UserName':UserName.GetText(),
>                    'Password':Password.GetText()};
> ```
>
> Thanks to Roman R. for this tip too.

An interesting property of JavaScript is that the classes support dynamic properties. Simply by having a value assigned to returnValue.UserName (in Listing 4-17), returnValue dynamically has a UserName property.

The debugger; statement is added as a habit to facilitate debugging script. You can comment debugger; statements out when you are finished testing your script. The if(typeof(Page_ClientValidate) == 'function') is a technique used to determine whether a name exists in script and, in this case, to determine whether the name is a function. The next statement invokes the method Page_ClientValidate(). Page_ClientValidate updates all the validators and returns true if the page is valid and false if not. If the page is not valid, the login form is not closed and the RequiredFieldValidator controls are updated to reflect the invalid state. If the page is valid, the remaining lines of code are run. The var returnValue = new Object() instantiates a new object. Each ASPxTextBox is given a ClientInstanceName — UserName and Password, respectively — and the GetText method obtains the Text value and assigns it to the returnValue object. Finally, returnValue is assigned to window.returnValue and the (login) window is closed.

Implementing the Cancel Behavior

The ASPxButton assigned the Cancel behavior is provided with a client-side Click event. Again, use the ASPxButton Client-Side Events Editor to define the click event. All the click event has to do is call window.close(). Keep in mind that JavaScript is case sensitive. Listing 4-18 contains the ASPX for the login form, which includes the string that represents the Click event handler that will be rendered at runtime.

Listing 4-18: The ASPX for the login form, which will be used as a modal dialog.

```
<%@ Page Language="C#" AutoEventWireup="true" CodeFile="Popup.aspx.cs"
 Inherits="Popup" %>

<%@ Register assembly="DevExpress.Web.v9.1, Version=9.1.4.0,↵
 Culture=neutral, PublicKeyToken=b88d1754d700e49a"
 namespace="DevExpress.Web.ASPxRoundPanel" tagprefix="dxrp" %>
<%@ Register assembly="DevExpress.Web.v9.1, Version=9.1.4.0,↵
 Culture=neutral, PublicKeyToken=b88d1754d700e49a"
 namespace="DevExpress.Web.ASPxPanel" tagprefix="dxp" %>
<%@ Register assembly="DevExpress.Web.ASPxEditors.v9.1,↵
 Version=9.1.4.0, Culture=neutral, PublicKeyToken=b88d1754d700e49a"
 namespace="DevExpress.Web.ASPxEditors" tagprefix="dxe" %>

<!DOCTYPE html PUBLIC "-//W3C//DTD XHTML 1.0 Transitional//EN"
 "http://www.w3.org/TR/xhtml1/DTD/xhtml1-transitional.dtd">

<html xmlns="http://www.w3.org/1999/xhtml">
<head runat="server">
    <title></title>
</head>
<body>
  <form id="form1" runat="server">
  <div align="center" style="margin: 20px; vertical-align: middle; height: 100%;">

  <dxrp:ASPxRoundPanel ID="ASPxRoundPanel1" runat="server" HeaderText="Login"
    Height="100%" Width="300px">
    <PanelCollection>
    <dxp:PanelContent runat="server">
    <table width="100%">
      <tr>
      <td>
      <dxe:ASPxLabel ID="ASPxLabel1" runat="server" Text="User name:"
        AssociatedControlID="ASPxTextBoxUserName">
```

```
      </dxe:ASPxLabel>
      </td>
      <td>
      <dxe:ASPxTextBox ID="ASPxTextBoxUserName" runat="server" Height="16px"
        Width="150px" ClientInstanceName="UserName">
      </dxe:ASPxTextBox>
      <asp:RequiredFieldValidator ID="RequiredFieldValidator2" runat="server"
       ControlToValidate="ASPxTextBoxUserName" ErrorMessage="User name is required"
       SetFocusOnError="True"></asp:RequiredFieldValidator>
      </td>
      </tr>
      <tr>
      <td>
      <dxe:ASPxLabel ID="ASPxLabel2" runat="server" Text="Password:"
        AssociatedControlID="ASPxTextBoxPassword">
      </dxe:ASPxLabel>
      </td>
      <td>
      <dxe:ASPxTextBox ID="ASPxTextBoxPassword" runat="server" Height="16px"
      Password="True" Width="150px" ClientInstanceName="Password">
      </dxe:ASPxTextBox>
      <asp:RequiredFieldValidator ID="RequiredFieldValidator1" runat="server"
      ControlToValidate="ASPxTextBoxPassword" ErrorMessage="Password is required"
      SetFocusOnError="True"></asp:RequiredFieldValidator>
      </td>
      </tr>
      <tr>
      <td align="right">
      <dxe:ASPxButton ID="ASPxButton1" runat="server" Text="OK" Width="100px"
        AutoPostBack="False" Native="True" UseSubmitBehavior="False"
          >
        <ClientSideEvents Click="function(s, e) {
  debugger;
  if(typeof(Page_ClientValidate)==='function')
  if(Page_ClientValidate())
  {
    var returnValue = new Object();
    returnValue.UserName = UserName.GetText();
    returnValue.Password = Password.GetText();
    window.returnValue = returnValue;
    window.close();
  }
}" />
      </dxe:ASPxButton>
      </td>
      <td align="left">
      <dxe:ASPxButton ID="ASPxButton2" runat="server" Text="Cancel"
        Width="100px" AutoPostBack="False" Native="True"
      UseSubmitBehavior="False" CausesValidation="False"
          >
          <ClientSideEvents Click="function(s, e) {
      window.close();
```

Continued

Listing 4-18: The ASPX for the login form, which will be used as a modal dialog.
(continued)

```
    }" />

            </dxe:ASPxButton>
            </td>
            </tr>
          </table>
          </dxp:PanelContent>
          </PanelCollection>
        </dxrp:ASPxRoundPanel>

        </div>
        </form>
      </body>
      </html>
```

A quick glance at the ASPX reveals that a dialog form is designed exactly the same way as a Web page that will not be used as a dialog. What makes the login form act like a dialog is in the way that it is invoked.

Displaying a Modal Dialog with showModalDialogs

The remaining constituent elements are to show the login form as a modal dialog and to respond to the user input. The login form can be displayed as a pop-up in JavaScript using window.showModalDialog. The showModalDialog method of the window object requires a URL for the form to display and accepts two optional arguments: vArguments, and sFeatures. The vArguments parameter represents any variant input argument that you want to send to the pop-up, and sFeatures is a semicolon delimited string describing the optional window ornaments. The call to show the login form — named popup.aspx — use for the sample is as follows:

```
var results = window.showModalDialog('popup.aspx', "",
  "dialogwidth:350px;dialogHeight:180px;resizable:false;status:false; ");
```

The first argument is the name of the page that will be displayed as a modal dialog. No input arguments were sent, as represented by the empty input string, and the self-describing arguments used include the dialog width, height, resizable (a Boolean indicating if the dialog is resizable or not), and status. (More arguments are available. You can read about these in the MSDN help at ms-help://MS.VSCC.v90/ MS.MSDNQTR.v90.en/dhtml/workshop/author/dhtml/reference/methods/showmodaldialog. htm.) The resizable value of false means that the dialog is fixed, and a status of false means that the dialog will have no status bar. The results at runtime look like Figure 4-16.

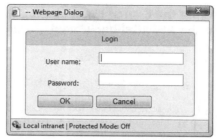

Figure 4-16: The login form (popup.aspx) at runtime with the feature arguments used in the code snippet.

Sending User Input to the Server Using the ASPxCallbackPanel

To complete the sample, an ASPxCallbackPanel is used. When the modal login dialog returns, the results are evaluated. If the user entered data and clicked OK, the user-entered information is sent to the calling page's code-behind using the ASPxCallbackPanel's ClientInstanceName CallbackPanel and the PerformCallback method. (Refer to the "Programming ClientSideEvents to Initiate a CustomCallback" section, earlier in this chapter.) An ASPxLabel inside the ASPxCallbackPanel is updated to display the user-entered data. In an actual application, you will want to use the information to authenticate the username and password. The ASPX for the calling form is shown in Listing 4-19 and the simple code-behind is shown in Listing 4-20.

Listing 4-19: The ASPX showing the calling for, including the showModalDialog call and the PerformCallback call to the ASPxCallbackPanel.

```
<%@ Page Language="C#" AutoEventWireup="true"  CodeFile="Default.aspx.cs"
 Inherits="_Default" %>

<%@ Register assembly="DevExpress.Web.v9.1, Version=9.1.4.0,⏎
 Culture=neutral, PublicKeyToken=b88d1754d700e49a"
 namespace="DevExpress.Web.ASPxCallback" tagprefix="dxcb" %>

<%@ Register assembly="DevExpress.Web.ASPxEditors.v9.1,⏎
 Version=9.1.4.0, Culture=neutral, PublicKeyToken=b88d1754d700e49a"
 namespace="DevExpress.Web.ASPxEditors" tagprefix="dxe" %>
<%@ Register assembly="DevExpress.Web.v9.1, Version=9.1.4.0,⏎
 Culture=neutral, PublicKeyToken=b88d1754d700e49a"
 namespace="DevExpress.Web.ASPxCallbackPanel" tagprefix="dxcp" %>
<%@ Register assembly="DevExpress.Web.v9.1, Version=9.1.4.0,⏎
 Culture=neutral, PublicKeyToken=b88d1754d700e49a"
 namespace="DevExpress.Web.ASPxPanel" tagprefix="dxp" %>

<!DOCTYPE html PUBLIC "-//W3C//DTD XHTML 1.0 Transitional//EN"
 "http://www.w3.org/TR/xhtml1/DTD/xhtml1-transitional.dtd">

<html xmlns="http://www.w3.org/1999/xhtml">
<head runat="server">
```

Continued

225

Listing 4-19: The ASPX showing the calling for, including the showModalDialog call and the PerformCallback call to the ASPxCallbackPanel. *(continued)*

```
    <title></title>

    <script language="javascript" type="text/javascript">
      function Button1_onclick() {
        var results = window.showModalDialog('popup.aspx', "",
"dialogwidth:350px;dialogHeight:180px;resizable:false;status:false;");
        //debugger;
        if (results != null) {
          //alert(results.UserName + ' ' + results.Password);
          CallbackPanel.PerformCallback('User=' + results.UserName +
          ',Password=' + results.Password);
        }
      }
    </script>
</head>
<body>
  <form id="form1" runat="server">
  <div>

    <input id="Button1" type="button" value="button"
      onclick="return Button1_onclick()" /><dxcp:ASPxCallbackPanel
      ID="ASPxCallbackPanel1" runat="server"
      ClientInstanceName="CallbackPanel"
      oncallback="ASPxCallbackPanel1_Callback" Width="200px">
      <PanelCollection>
        <dxp:PanelContent runat="server">
          <dxe:ASPxLabel ID="ASPxLabel1" runat="server">
          </dxe:ASPxLabel>
        </dxp:PanelContent>
      </PanelCollection>
    </dxcp:ASPxCallbackPanel>
  </div>
  </form>
</body>
</html>
```

Listing 4-20: The code-behind that updates the ASPxLabel contained in the ASPxCallbackPanel.

```
using System;
using System.Collections.Generic;
using System.Linq;
using System.Web;
using System.Web.UI;
using System.Web.UI.WebControls;

public partial class _Default : System.Web.UI.Page
{
    protected void Page_Load(object sender, EventArgs e)
```

```
        {

        }

        protected void ASPxCallbackPanel1_Callback(object source,
          DevExpress.Web.ASPxClasses.CallbackEventArgsBase e)
        {
          ASPxLabel1.Text = e.Parameter;
        }
    }
```

It is worth mentioning that the password is being passed around in the clear. In practice, you will want to use some form of encryption if you are passing sensitive data around. You could use simple encryption or an HTTPS connection as a couple of options for helping secure sensitive data.

Implementing a Modal Login Window with the ASPxPopupControl

A simpler and cleaner option for displaying and using modal dialogs is to use the ASPxPopupControl. One of the features of the ASPxPopupControl is to design the view of the pop-up on its hosting page in the template regions provided. In this example, you still have to design what the pop-up will look like, but the appearance, placement, and behavior of the pop-up are managed through ASPxPopupControl properties at design time.

To design the popup to have the same inner appearance as the example in the previous section, add the ASPxLabel, ASPxTextBox, ASPxButton, and RequiredFieldValidators inside an <html> table, as described in the previous section. All these elements are placed in the PopupControlContentControl section of the ASPxPopupControl (see the before and after pictures in Figures 4-17 and 4-18).

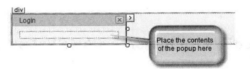

Figure 4-17: The ASPxPopupControl before the controls are added.

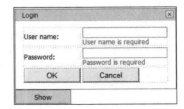

Figure 4-18: Place the content to be displayed in the ASPxPopupControl in the PopupControlContentControl as shown.

227

The key to getting the pop-up appearance is to set the ASPxPopupControl.Modal property to true. The ASPxPopupControl's CloseAction was set to CloseButton; PopupHorizontalAlign was set to WindowsCenter; PopupVerticalAlign was set to WindowCenter; ClientInstanceName was set to Popup; the HeaderText was changed to Login; AllowDragging was set to true; and EnableAnimation and EnableViewState were both set to false. The runtime appearance after the changes, when the pop-up is displayed, looks like Figure 4-19.

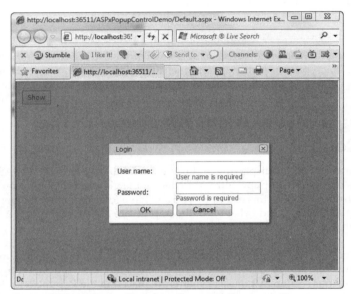

Figure 4-19: With the Modal setting and alignment, the pop-up looks and feels like an independent modal dialog.

Replacing the RequiredFieldValidators with ASPxTextBox ValidationSettings

Listing 4-18 — using the JavaScript showModalDialog method — uses the RequiredFieldValidator to make sure that the username and password TextBox controls don't contain empty strings. The ASPxTextBox controls already contain a ValidationSettings property with subproperties that perform the same functions of the RequiredFieldValidators and other validators like the RegularExpressionValidator.

To replace the .NET RequiredFieldValidators with ValidationSettings, remove the RequriedFieldValidator for each of the username and password TextBox controls. (Listed alphabetically, the ValidationSettings are near the bottom of the properties window.) To reproduce the same behavior as the example in Listing 4-18 for each of the TextBox controls, modify the validation settings as follows:

❑ Change ValidationSettings.EnableCustomValidation to true.

❑ Define a ValidationGroup. Use 'entryGroup' as the value. A ValidationGroup will let you manipulate controls as a group using the ASPxClientEdit object (refer to the section "Using the ASPxClientEdit Object," later in this chapter).

- ❏ Change ValidationSettings.SetFocusOnError to true.

- ❏ Change ValidationSettings.ErrorDisplayMode to Text

- ❏ Change ValidationSettings.ErrorTextPosition to "Bottom".

- ❏ Change ValidationSettings.CausesValidation to true.

- ❏ Change ValidationSettings.RequiredField.IsRequried to true.

- ❏ Change the ValidationSettings.RequriedField.ErrorText to reflect the text you'd like displayed, such as "user name required."

Finally, if the controls on the ASPxPopupControl post back to the server, the validation information will be reset. To stop the postback, don't define any server side events for the pop-up controls, and change the AutoPostBack property to false.

Defining a ValidationGroup

The ValidationSettings.ValidationGroup property is a string. Defining a validation group using the same string for a collection of controls permits you to manipulate them as a group. (Refer to the section "Using the ASPxClientEdit Object," later in this chapter, for the complete listing for this section and to see how the validation group is used to initialize the pop-up controls with a single line of code.

Specifying a Required Field

A required field is a field into which you want to ensure that the user enters data. For a login, it makes sense to require that the user provide the actual username and password. To make a Web application seem more responsive, it helps if these kinds of simple validations happen before the page is posted back. A common use for such validation is to make sure that a TextBox is not empty.

There are all kinds of light-weight validation that can and should happen on the client: "has data"; "data meets a basic input format"; "data falls within a desirable range"; and that "data is of the right type." You can use the .NET Validation controls RequiredFieldValidator, RangeValidation, RegularExpressionValidator, CompareValidator, CustomValidator, ValidationSummary, or DynamicValidator or you can use the integrated validation built into controls such as the ASPxTextBox.

The login pop-up simply uses the required capability of the `ASPxTextBox.ValidationSettings` property, but you could just as easily provide a regular express. For example, if you wanted to make the username an e-mail address, you could provide a regular expression that matches the signature of an e-mail address. For example, adding

```
\b[A-Z0-9._%+-]+@[A-Z0-9.-]+\.[A-Z]{2,4}\b
```

`ValidationSettings.RegularExpression.ValidationExpression` to the ASPxTextBox for the username client-side validation would use the Regular Expression extensions in .NET to make sure that the format of the string matches the regular expression.

A great feature of the ValidationSettings.RegularExpression.ValidationExpression property is the built-in picklist of regular expressions. The canned regular expression for Internet e-mail addresses is \w+([-+.']\w+)*@\w+([-.]\w+)*\.\w+([-.]\w+)*.

As with any code — and regular expressions represent code — not all expressions are created equal. In addition to keeping a lot of different books on a given subject on hand (on a wide variety of subjects, such as Regular Expressions), you should consider consulting some good online resources for building Regular Expressions. Try www.fileformat.info/tool/regex.htm *for an online Regular Expression tool.*

A regular expression language is a complete language in its own right. For more information on regular expressions, check out *Beginning Regular Expressions (Programmer to Programmer)*, by Andrew Watt (Wrox). A pocket-sized edition I keep on hand is *Sams Teach Yourself Regular Expressions in 10 Minutes*, by Ben Forta (Sams).

Coding the Client-Side Events for the Popup

There are three client-side events for the example. Each was defined using the ClientSideEvents (editor) property of the related control. ASPxPopupControl.Popup was defined to clear the login controls, and Click was defined for each of the ASPxButtons.

ClientSideEvents are stored as string properties in the IDE and dynamically injected using the client event objects and the AddHandler. Recall that each control has a client-side version; for example, the ASPxButton is represented on the client as an ASPxClientButton and the events like Click are public event properties. Click is defined as an instance of the ASPxClientProcessingModeEventHandler. Click has defined methods, including AddHandler and RemoveHandler.

The code for the Popup event clears the login controls by the ValidationSettings.ValidationGroup name. The code for the Cancel button hides the pop-up, and the code for the OK button forces the validators to run. If the pop-up is valid, the control is hidden on OK, too. Here are the three script versions of the Popup and Click methods:

```
function(s, e) {
  ASPxClientEdit.ClearGroup('controlGroup');
}

function(s, e) {
  debugger;
  if(ASPxClientEdit.ValidateGroup('controlGroup'))
    Popup.Hide();

}
function(s, e) {
  //debugger;
  Popup.Hide();
}
```

> **Remember to enable browser debugging if you are going to debug your script. Refer to the section in Chapter 1 called "Calculating Total Custom Summaries" for step-by-step instructions for enabling script debugging in Internet Explorer.**

No name is provided because these are added like anonymous methods — unnamed functions — with the AddHandler script function. A good strategy is to add the debugger; statement when you are writing these script functions. The debugger; statement will permit you to easily step into your script code at runtime and debug the code. Adding the debugger; statement will also let you explore properties of the client-side version of controls such as the ASPxTextBox.

Using the ASPxClientEdit Object

The ASPxClientEdit object is the base object for all objects that support editing. In the Popup and Click events (see the preceding section), this object is used to manipulate all the controls — the two ASPxTextBox controls — on the client that have user-entered data. The Popup event clears the controls defined as being part of the controlGroup and the OK button's Click event instructs all validators in the same group to validate. Effectively, if any of the controls' associated validators are invalid, the pop-up is not closed. (Refer to the help documentation on ASPxClientEdit for more information on this class.)

There is no code-behind for the ASPxPopupControl sample in this section. The complete ASPX listing is provided in Listing 4-21.

Listing 4-21: The complete ASPX listing for the ASPxPopupControl sample described in this section.

```
<%@ Page Language="C#" AutoEventWireup="true"  CodeFile="Default.aspx.cs"
 Inherits="_Default" %>

<%@ Register assembly="DevExpress.Web.v9.1, Version=9.1.4.0,↩
 Culture=neutral, PublicKeyToken=b88d1754d700e49a"
 namespace="DevExpress.Web.ASPxPopupControl" tagprefix="dxpc" %>
<%@ Register assembly="DevExpress.Web.ASPxEditors.v9.1,↩
 Version=9.1.4.0, Culture=neutral, PublicKeyToken=b88d1754d700e49a"
 namespace="DevExpress.Web.ASPxEditors" tagprefix="dxe" %>

<!DOCTYPE html PUBLIC "-//W3C//DTD XHTML 1.0 Transitional//EN"
 "http://www.w3.org/TR/xhtml1/DTD/xhtml1-transitional.dtd">

<html xmlns="http://www.w3.org/1999/xhtml">
<head runat="server">
  <title></title>
</head>
<body>
  <form id="form1" runat="server">
  <div>

    <dxpc:ASPxPopupControl ID="Login" runat="server" ClientInstanceName="Popup"
      HeaderText="Login" Modal="True" AllowDragging="True"
      CloseAction="CloseButton" EnableAnimation="False" EnableViewState="False"
      PopupHorizontalAlign="WindowCenter" PopupVerticalAlign="WindowCenter">
      <ClientSideEvents PopUp="function(s, e) {
      ASPxClientEdit.ClearGroup('controlGroup');
}" />
      <ContentCollection>
<dxpc:PopupControlContentControl runat="server">
```

Continued

Listing 4-21: The complete ASPX listing for the ASPxPopupControl sample described in this section. *(continued)*

```
<table width="100%">
  <tr>
    <td>
      <dxe:ASPxLabel ID="ASPxLabel1" runat="server"
        AssociatedControlID="ASPxTextBoxUserName" Text="User name:">
      </dxe:ASPxLabel>
    </td>
    <td>
      <dxe:ASPxTextBox ID="ASPxTextBoxUserName" runat="server"
        ClientInstanceName="UserName" Height="16px" Width="150px">
        <ValidationSettings ErrorDisplayMode="Text" ErrorTextPosition="Bottom"
          ValidationGroup="controlGroup" EnableCustomValidation="True"
SetFocusOnError="True">
          <RegularExpression ErrorText="Login required" />
          <RequiredField ErrorText="User name required" IsRequired="True" />
        </ValidationSettings>
      </dxe:ASPxTextBox>
    </td>
  </tr>
  <tr>
    <td>
      <dxe:ASPxLabel ID="ASPxLabel2" runat="server"
        AssociatedControlID="ASPxTextBoxPassword" Text="Password:">
      </dxe:ASPxLabel>
    </td>
    <td>
      <dxe:ASPxTextBox ID="ASPxTextBoxPassword" runat="server"
        ClientInstanceName="Password" Height="19px" Password="True"
          Width="150px">
        <ValidationSettings ErrorDisplayMode="Text"
          ErrorTextPosition="Bottom"
          ValidationGroup="controlGroup" EnableCustomValidation="True"
            SetFocusOnError="True">
          <RegularExpression ErrorText="Login required" />
          <RequiredField ErrorText="Password required" IsRequired="True" />
        </ValidationSettings>
      </dxe:ASPxTextBox>
    </td>
  </tr>
  <tr>
    <td align="right">
      <dxe:ASPxButton ID="ASPxButton1" runat="server" AutoPostBack="False"
        Text="OK" Width="100px">
        <ClientSideEvents Click="function(s, e) {
debugger;
    if(ASPxClientEdit.ValidateGroup('controlGroup'))
        Popup.Hide();

}" />
      </dxe:ASPxButton>
    </td>
    <td align="left">
```

```
          <dxe:ASPxButton ID="ASPxButton2" runat="server" AutoPostBack="False"
            Text="Cancel"
            Width="100px">
            <ClientSideEvents Click="function(s, e) {
        //debugger;
        Popup.Hide();
}" />
          </dxe:ASPxButton>
        </td>
      </tr>
    </table>
          </dxpc:PopupControlContentControl>
</ContentCollection>
    </dxpc:ASPxPopupControl>

  </div>
  <dxe:ASPxButton ID="ASPxButton3" runat="server" Text="Show"
    AutoPostBack="False" UseSubmitBehavior="False">
    <clientsideevents click="function(s, e) {
      Popup.Show();
      UserName.Focus();
}" />
  </dxe:ASPxButton>
  </form>
</body>
</html>
```

Summary

Spending a couple of hundred hours writing a chapter this large is like giving birth (to a very large-headed child). I am not complaining, because I feel fortunate to get to write as part of how I make my living, nor am I trying to be gratuitously graphic. (Relieved, yes.) The point is that as large as this chapter is, to actually finish it, decisions have to be made. Unfortunately, some things make it in the chapter but many more do not, and it's always a little bittersweet to close out a chapter for those reasons.

Every Thursday, an evangelist meeting takes place at DevExpress, and a common theme is what do the customers (you) want and need. As promised, this chapter covered the ASPxPopupControl, ASPxNavBar, ASPxCloudControl, and the ASPxSiteMapControl. I also threw in a lot of supporting ASP.NET material and an example that demonstrates how to use the Microsoft Indexing Service, the ASPxCallbackPanel, RequiredFieldValidator and regular expressions, modal dialogs, and some more JavaScript examples. I hope you get out of it some of what you want and some of what you need.

## 5

Implementing a Menu and Tabbed Controls

Although I generally have a little of the Irish gift of blarney, I don't always have a suitable story for opening a chapter on technical subjects. In the absence of a story, I'd like to share with you my three favorite Web-application sites: I like Dell.com, Amazon.com, and FedEx.com. I order at least one computer a year, and Dell.com makes it pretty easy to customize a computer, arrange payment — even apply for credit — and schedule shipping. Amazon.com is the site I use most frequently. I go to the local mall — the Meridian Mall in Okemos — about twice a year. Everything else comes from the local grocery store or Amazon.com. Finally, one of my favorite movie lines is "you know you have made it when the FedEx guy shows up at your door." I can't remember the movie, but I love the line. What do all these sites have in common? Menus.

Menus help you figure out what the options are. Can you imagine walking into an Italian restaurant and finding that it had no menu? I love gnocchi with marinara, spaghetti Fruitti de Mare, and spaghetti Bolognese, but I would have never discovered Boquerones — white Spanish anchovies — in olive oil with pepper flakes without a menu. Menus tell you what is available, what is possible. In a good restaurant, you can order items that aren't on the menu. With software, however, it is difficult to support ordering beyond the menu, which makes menus essential.

This chapter demonstrates the `ASPxMenu`, `ASPxPopupMenu`, `ASPxTabControl`, and the `ASPxPageControl`. Collectively, these controls help you provide your users with a rich application experience and ease of access to features provided by your Web application.

Building Menus with the ASPxMenu

A menu isn't supposed to be rocket science. Describe a hierarchy of items and associate an action with each item. A menu can be made a little smarter by defining inter-dependencies between items. For example, you can disable menus for nonadministrative users or enable a File ⇨ Save only after a File ⇨ Open, but one of the biggest challenges in defining a menu is simply the act of organizing and naming menu items.

The `ASPxMenu` makes defining a basic menu very easy. You can use the `ASPxSiteMapDataSource` as described in Chapter 4's section "Building a Sitemap Based on the Current Structure of Your Site" and construct a menu that more or less supports menu-based site navigation. This is a useful feature, for sure, but the `ASPxMenu` supports constructing several popular metaphors besides a basic menu. The examples in the section demonstrate how to use the `ASPxSiteMapDataSource` as well as add graphics and tooltips to your menus; how to implement a tabbed menu; and how to emulate a toolbar with the `ASPxMenu`.

Defining Menu Items

If the `ASPxMenu` is not assigned to a data source, the Smart tags menu for the `ASPxMenu` will display the Items property. The Items property opens the `ASPxMenu` MenuItem Editor (see Figure 5-1). The MenuItem Editor supports adding menus statically at design time and defining the properties for each MenuItem.

Figure 5-1: Use the ASPxMenu MenuItem Editor to define menus at design time.

For example, to add a static menu at design time, click the Add an Item toolbar button — at the top left of the MenuItem Editor — and supply the `Text` property, the `NavigateUrl`, the `Target`, a `ToolTip`, and an `Image.Url`. The `Text` property is the string that will be displayed, representing the MenuItem at runtime. The `NavigateUrl` is where the application will be redirected when the MenuItem is clicked. The `Target` can be `_blank`, `_parent`, `_search`, `_self`, `_top`, or the literal name of a window or frame. For example, setting `Target` to `_blank` means that a new instance of the browser will be used when the `MenuItem` is clicked. ToolTip represents the text that will be displayed when the mouse hovers over the `MenuItem`, and the `Image.Url` property defines a link for the `MenuItem`'s image if one is desired.

The Target options are a general HTML feature that you may have used before with an `<a>` tag's href attribute. These options behave as follows:

❑ You can express the name of a window or frame to display the contents of the link in.

❑ `_blank` loads the linked document into a new window.

❑ `_parent` loads the linked document into the immediate parent of the link.

❑ `_search` loads the linked document into the browser search pane (since IE 5).

❑ `_self` loads the linked document into the active window.

❑ `_top` loads the linked document into the top most window.

MenuItems also support defining a group — `GroupName` — `Visible`, `Selected`, and `Enabled` properties. `Selected` is a Boolean that indicates whether the `MenuItem` is selected; `Visible` indicates whether the `MenuItem` is visible; and `Enabled` turns the `MenuItem` off or on. The `GroupName` property lets you arrange the MenuItems into logical groups. (Refer to the section "Emulating a Toolbar with the `ASPxMenu`," much later in this chapter, for more on using the `GroupName` property.)

Binding to an ASPxSiteMapDataSource and XML File

XML by nature is self-describing and supports hierarchies. Because the `ASPxSiteMapDataSource` is designed to refer to an XML file, using a specific schema — `http://schemas.microsoft.com/AspNet/SiteMap-File-1.0`. Using an XML file containing correct schema is a great way to define your menu for your application. The `ASPxMenu` has an Items property that is defined as a `MenuItemCollection`. When you're using a .sitemap file, the menu items will automatically map to a `<siteMapNode>`. The url attribute will map to the NavigateUrl, the siteMapNode's title attribute will map to the `MenuItem.Text` property, the siteMapNode's ImageUrl attribute will map to the `MenuItem.Image.Url` property, and the siteMapNode's description property will map to the MenuItem's `ToolTip` property. Listing 5-1 shows a .sitemap file that can be associated with an `ASPxSiteMapDataSource` and through the data source to an `ASPxMenu`. The results are a menu that has flag images of countries of the world, and the links map to a Wikipedia page for that country.

Listing 5-1: A .sitemap file that that defines a menu hierarchy of continents and countries by continent.

```xml
<?xml version="1.0" encoding="utf-8"?>
<siteMap xmlns="http://schemas.microsoft.com/AspNet/SiteMap-File-1.0">
  <siteMapNode url="javascript:void(1);" title="Countries of the World">
    <siteMapNode url="javascript:void(2);" title="North America">
      <siteMapNode url=http://en.wikipedia.org/wiki/United_states
        title="United States" ImageUrl="~/Flags/en-US.gif"
        description="Wiki of U.S."/>
      <siteMapNode url=http://en.wikipedia.org/wiki/Canada
        title="Canada" ImageUrl="~/Flags/en-CA.gif" />
      <siteMapNode url="http://en.wikipedia.org/wiki/Mexico" title="Mexico"
        ImageUrl="~/Flags/es-MX.gif" />
      <siteMapNode url=http://en.wikipedia.org/wiki/Antigua_and_Barbuda
        title="Antigua and Barbuda" ImageUrl="" />
      <siteMapNode url=http://en.wikipedia.org/wiki/The_Bahamas
        title="The Bahamas" ImageUrl="~/Flags/en-CB.gif" />
      <siteMapNode url=http://en.wikipedia.org/wiki/Barbados
        title="Barbados" ImageUrl="" />
      <siteMapNode url=http://en.wikipedia.org/wiki/Belize
        title="Belize" ImageUrl="~/Flags/en-BZ.gif" />
      <siteMapNode url=http://en.wikipedia.org/wiki/Costa_Rica
        title="Costa Rica" ImageUrl="~/Flags/th-TH.gif" />
      <siteMapNode url=http://en.wikipedia.org/wiki/Cuba
        title="Cuba" ImageUrl="~/Flags/es-PR.gif" />
      <siteMapNode url=http://en.wikipedia.org/wiki/Dominica
        title="Dominica" ImageUrl="" />
      <siteMapNode url=http://en.wikipedia.org/wiki/Dominican_Republic
        title="Dominican Republic" ImageUrl="~/Flags/es-DO.gif" />
      <siteMapNode url=http://en.wikipedia.org/wiki/El_Salvador
        title="El Salvador" ImageUrl="~/Flags/es-SV.gif" />
      <siteMapNode url=http://en.wikipedia.org/wiki/Greenland
        title="Greenland" ImageUrl="" />
      <siteMapNode url=http://en.wikipedia.org/wiki/Grenada
        title="Grenada" ImageUrl="" />
      <siteMapNode url=http://en.wikipedia.org/wiki/Guatemala
        title="Guatemala" ImageUrl="~/Flags/es-GT.gif" />
      <siteMapNode url=http://en.wikipedia.org/wiki/Haiti
        title="Haiti" ImageUrl="~/Flags/de-LI.gif" />
      <siteMapNode url=http://en.wikipedia.org/wiki/Honduras
        title="Honduras" ImageUrl="~/Flags/es-HN.gif" />
      <siteMapNode url=http://en.wikipedia.org/wiki/Jamaica
        title="Jamaica" ImageUrl="~/Flags/en-JM.gif" />
      <siteMapNode url=http://en.wikipedia.org/wiki/Nicaragua
        title="Nicaragua" ImageUrl="~/Flags/es-NI.gif" />
      <siteMapNode url="http://en.wikipedia.org/wiki/Panama"
        title="Panama" ImageUrl="~/Flags/es-PA.gif" />
      <siteMapNode url=http://en.wikipedia.org/wiki/Saint_kitts_and_nevis
        title="Saint Kitts and Nevis" ImageUrl="" />
      <siteMapNode url=http://en.wikipedia.org/wiki/Saint_Lucia
        title="Saint Lucia" ImageUrl="" />
      <siteMapNode url="http://en.wikipedia.org/wiki/Saint Vincent and the
Grenadines" title="Saint Vincent and the Grenadines"
```

```
                ImageUrl="~/Flags/es-MX.gif" />
            <siteMapNode url=http://en.wikipedia.org/wiki/Trinidad and Tobago
              title="Trinidad and Tobago" ImageUrl="~/Flags/en-TT.gif" />
          </siteMapNode>
          <siteMapNode url="javascript:void(4);" title="South America">
            <siteMapNode url=http://en.wikipedia.org/wiki/Argentina
              title="Argentina" ImageUrl="~/Flags/es-AR.gif" />
            <siteMapNode url="http://en.wikipedia.org/wiki/Bolivia" title="Bolivia"
              ImageUrl="~/Flags/es-BO.gif" />
            <siteMapNode url="http://en.wikipedia.org/wiki/Brazil" title="Brazil"
              ImageUrl="~/Flags/pt-BR.gif" />
            <siteMapNode url="http://en.wikipedia.org/wiki/Chile" title="Chile"
              ImageUrl="~/Flags/es-CL.gif" />
            <siteMapNode url=http://en.wikipedia.org/wiki/Colombia
              title="Colombia" ImageUrl="~/Flags/es-CO.gif" />
            <siteMapNode url="http://en.wikipedia.org/wiki/Ecuador" title="Ecuador"
              ImageUrl="~/Flags/es-EC.gif" />
            <siteMapNode url=http://en.wikipedia.org/wiki/French_Guiana
              title="French Guiana" ImageUrl="" />
            <siteMapNode url="http://en.wikipedia.org/wiki/Guyana" title="Guyana"
              ImageUrl="" />
            <siteMapNode url=http://en.wikipedia.org/wiki/Paraguay
              title="Paraguay" ImageUrl="~/Flags/es-PY.gif" />
            <siteMapNode url="http://en.wikipedia.org/wiki/Peru" title="Peru"
              ImageUrl="~/Flags/es-PE.gif" />
            <siteMapNode url=http://en.wikipedia.org/wiki/Suriname
              title="Suriname" ImageUrl="" />
            <siteMapNode url=http://en.wikipedia.org/wiki/Uruguay
              title="Uruguay" ImageUrl="~/Flags/es-UY.gif" />
            <siteMapNode url=http://en.wikipedia.org/wiki/Venezuela
              title="Venezuela" ImageUrl="~/Flags/es-VE.gif" />
          </siteMapNode>
          <siteMapNode url="javascript:void(5);" title="Africa">
          </siteMapNode>
          <siteMapNode url="javascript:void(6);" title="Europe">

          </siteMapNode>
          <siteMapNode url="javascript:void(7);" title="Asia">

          </siteMapNode>
          <siteMapNode url="javascript:void(8);" title="Antartica">

          </siteMapNode>
          <siteMapNode url="javascript:void(9);" title="Australia">

          </siteMapNode>
        </siteMapNode>
      </siteMap>
```

Using the Choose Data Source option of the ASPxMenu's Smart tags, you can associate the preceding .sitemap file with the ASPxMenu through an ASPxSiteMapDataSource. The results will look like the menu shown in Figure 5-2.

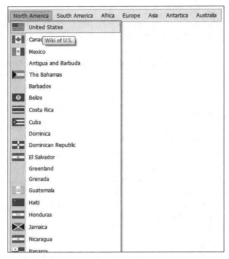

Figure 5-2: The .sitemap in Listing 5-1
bound to the ASPxMenu through an
ASPxSiteMapDataSource.

ShowSubMenuShadow is true by default (see Figure 5-2). You can turn off this 3D
effect by setting this property to false.

The default orientation shown in Figure 5.2 is Horizontal. You can display the menu horizontally by
setting the ASPxMenu.Orientation property to Vertical. Among other effects are the
ShowSubMenuShadow, SkinID, padding, and separator information. Some of these property settings are
demonstrated in the other sections of this part (on the ASPxMenu).

Exploring ASPxMenu Features

The ASPxMenu is mostly a visual control. You define hierarchical links manually or with an XML (or
.sitemap) file, and the rest is about the property settings that define how the menu will appear to the end
user. There are features such as Auto Formatting, themes, and skins that are common with other
DevExpress controls, and there are features that are unique to menus.

Defining Menu Separators

The ASPxMenu defines an AutoSeparators property. The AutoSeparators property adds a separator
between menu items. The settings are None (the default), All, and RootOnly. All places a separator
between every menu and submenu item. The RootOnly setting places a separator between only top-
level menu items. The default menu separator is a thin, gray line (see Figure 5-3), appearing vertically
between root level menus and horizontally between submenus if the ASPxMenuOrientation option is
Horizontal. If the ASPxMenuOrientation is Vertical, all menu separators are horizontal gray lines by
default.

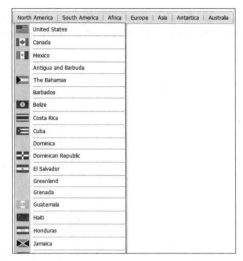

Figure 5-3: The default menu separator (shown between menu items) is configurable but shows up as a thin, dark-gray line by default.

The `ASPxMenu` also supports a `SeparatorBackgroundImage` composite property, a `SeparatorColor` property, `SeparatorHeight`, `SeparatorPaddings`, and a `SeparatorWidth` property. The `SeparatorHeight` and `SeparatorWidth` properties literally adjust with the vertical and horizontal thickness of the separator. The `SeparatorPaddings` property lets you specify the amount of padding around the top, left, bottom, and right of the separator. The `SeparatorColor` sets the color of the padding, letting you change it from the default dark gray to any color you like, and the `SeparatorBackgroundImage` property lets you specify a separator image other than the default gray line. You could place any image you'd like between MenuItems, but most users are likely to expect a variation on the solid gray line. The `SeparatorBackgroundImage` has the subproperties `HorizontalPosition`, `ImageUrl`, `Repeat`, and `VerticalPosition`.

Adding Menu Tooltips

A tooltip is text that pops up whenever the mouse hovers over a control. If you are defining MenuItems manually, you can also set the `ToolTip` property — which is a string property — manually. By default, if you bind to an `XmlSiteMapDataSource`, the siteMapNode description attribute will be treated as the ToolTip value. (In fact, url, title, and description are loaded before the `ASPxMenu` gets the data, and these values will be used for the `NavigateUrl`, `Text`, and `ToolTip` properties of each MenuItem, respectively.) However, if you use an XML file or other data source, you can specify the field containing the tooltip by providing a value for the `ASPxMenu.ToolTipField` property. The partial XML file in Listing 5-2 can be mapped to an `ASPxMenu` using an `XmlDataSource`. Notice how the attributes precisely match the properties of the `ASPxMenu` properties.

Listing 5-2: An XML file can be mapped to an ASPxMenu using an XmlDataSource; with an XML file, map the attribute names to the ASPxMenu properties.

```xml
<?xml version="1.0" encoding="utf-8" ?>
<mainmenu>
  <item Text="Countries of the World">
    <item NavigateUrl="javascript:void(2);" Text="North America">
      <item NavigateUrl=http://en.wikipedia.org/wiki/United_States
        Text="United States"
        ImageUrl="~/Flags/en-US.gif" ToolTip="Wiki of U.S."
        MyField="Alternate Tip"/>
      <item NavigateUrl=http://en.wikipedia.org/wiki/Canada
        Text="Canada" ImageUrl="~/Flags/en-CA.gif" />
      <item NavigateUrl=http://en.wikipedia.org/wiki/Mexico
        Text="Mexico" ImageUrl="~/Flags/es-MX.gif" />
      <item NavigateUrl=http://en.wikipedia.org/wiki/Antigua_and_Barbuda
        Text="Antigua and Barbuda" ImageUrl="" />
      <item NavigateUrl=http://en.wikipedia.org/wiki/The_Bahamas
        Text="The Bahamas" ImageUrl="~/Flags/en-CB.gif" />
      <item NavigateUrl=http://en.wikipedia.org/wiki/Barbados
        Text="Barbados" ImageUrl="" />
      <item NavigateUrl=http://en.wikipedia.org/wiki/Belize
        Text="Belize" ImageUrl="~/Flags/en-BZ.gif" />
      <item NavigateUrl=http://en.wikipedia.org/wiki/Costa_Rica
        Text="Costa Rica" ImageUrl="~/Flags/th-TH.gif" />
      <item NavigateUrl=http://en.wikipedia.org/wiki/Cuba
        Text="Cuba" ImageUrl="~/Flags/es-PR.gif" />
      <item NavigateUrl=http://en.wikipedia.org/wiki/Dominica
        Text="Dominica" ImageUrl="" />
      ...
```

Notice that in Listing 5-1, the `siteMapNode` attributes in the XML file map the properties of an `ASPxSiteMapDataSource`'s node properties — url, title, and description. After they are loaded into the `ASPxSiteMapDataSource`, the XML attributes are mapped to the `ASPxMenu` MenuItem properties `NavigateUrl`, `Text`, and `ToolTip`. If you elect to use an XML file and XmlDataSource and you want to take advantage of automatic binding, define XML file attributes to match the MenuItem properties: NavigateUrl, Text, and ImageUrl. (Manual mapping is supported too.) If the XML file for the XmlDataSource contains a ToolTip attribute, that is used for the ToolTip. If there is an alternative attribute and that attribute's name is specified for the `ASPxMenu.ToolTipField`, that alternative attribute is used for all MenuItems. The `<item>` tag for the United States has a ToolTip attribute with the value `Wiki of U.S.` This value will be used unless `ASPxMenu.ToolTipField` is set to `MyField`. You can also set it to the `Text` attribute, making the ToolTip and the MenuItem text the same value.

Specifying Display Delay

The `ASPxMenu` has the `AppearAfter` and `DisappearAfter` properties. When a user hovers the mouse cursor over a MenuItem, if there is a submenu, it is displayed after the interval specified in the `AppearAfter` setting and disappears after the `DisappearAfter` interval unless the user clicks it. `AppearAfter` and `DisappearAfter` are integer properties, and the intervals are expressed as milliseconds. The default value for `AppearAfter` is 300 milliseconds, or about ⅓ of a second, and 500 milliseconds for `DisappearAfter`.

When combined with the `EnableAnimation` property, which is true by default, the `ASPxMenu` has a neat animated, slightly delayed sliding effect.

Using MenuItem Hot Tracking and Opacity

`EnableHotTrack` is true by default. Hot tracking means that as a mouse passes over a MenuItem, a bordered gray box is overlaid on the MenuItem, showing you that the MenuItem has the focus. This is a kinder, gentler property but is especially useful if you have more closely spaced items than usual, such as with a toolbar-style menu configuration.

Opacity is –1 (or disabled) by default. You can set this property between –1 and 100. Lower values mean that the menu will appear less visible, and higher values mean it will be more visible. A setting of 100 means that the menu will be opaque so that the user can't see through it. (The value –1 also means that the menu will be opaque.) The closer to 0 the setting is, the more transparent the menu will be.

Defining Menu Items with Code

You can add MenuItems to an `ASPxMenu` with code. The `ASPxMenu.Items` property is a `MenuItemCollection`. The Items property has seven Add methods. Add with no parameters returns the added MenuItem, and you can populate the MenuItem properties with lines of code. The second Add method accepts a MenuItem argument, and the remaining five overloaded methods accept the core properties of a MenuItem in varying detail, beginning with the menu text, name, imageUrl, navigateUrl, and target. Listing 5-3 contains a line of code that adds a MenuItem containing the text, name, an empty string for the imageUrl, and the navigateUrl.

Listing 5-3: A Page_Load method that dynamically adds a MenuItem.

```
using System;
using System.Collections.Generic;
using System.Linq;
using System.Web;
using System.Web.UI;
using System.Web.UI.WebControls;

public partial class _Default : System.Web.UI.Page
{
    protected void Page_Load(object sender, EventArgs e)
    {
      ASPxMenu1.Items.Add("File", "FileMenu", "", "~/Default2.aspx");
    }
}
```

Defining Menu Templates

Generally, people think of menus as being text (and graphics). The user clicks the menu item and something happens. In a Web page, that something is commonly a redirection to another Web page. However, the `ASPxMenu`, which supports the features you'd expect in a menu control, supports templates, too. Therefore, you can also think of the `ASPxMenu` as a kind of drop-down or slide-out window you can design to contain any controls.

The ASPxMenu itself supports an Itemtemplate, ItemTextTemplate, a RootItemTemplate, RootItemTextTemplate, and SubMenuTemplate. The MenuItems support SubMenuTemplate, Template, and TextTemplate. For the MenuItem element, the SubMenuTemplate element defines what a MenuItem's child menu will look like — what controls it will contain. The Template element is used to place the controls for a MenuItem, and the TextTemplate replaces the text contents of an individual MenuItem. The TextTemplate can also contain controls. The example shown in Figure 5-4 (with the code shown in Listing 5-4 and Listing 5-5) lets you dynamically experiment with the properties of an ASPxMenu by actually displaying those properties in template MenuItems.

Figure 5-4: The ASPxMenu with several TextTemplate definitions that contain ASPxLabels, ASPxTextBoxes, ASPxButtons, ASPxComboBoxes, and an ASPxSpinEdit control.

Listing 5-4: The code-behind for the ASPxMenu as configured in Figure 5-4.

```csharp
using System;
using System.Collections.Generic;
using System.Linq;
using System.Web;
using System.Web.UI;
using System.Web.UI.WebControls;
using DevExpress.Web.ASPxMenu;
using DevExpress.Web.ASPxEditors;

public partial class _Default : System.Web.UI.Page
{
    protected void Page_Load(object sender, EventArgs e)
```

```
    {
      ASPxComboBox control =
      (ASPxComboBox)ASPxMenu1.Items[0].Items[2]

  .FindControl("ASPxComboBox1");
      control.Value = ASPxMenu1.AutoSeparators.ToString();
    }

    protected void ASPxComboBox1_ValueChanged(object sender, EventArgs e)
    {
      try
      {
        ASPxMenu1.AutoSeparators =
          (AutoSeparatorMode)Enum.Parse(typeof(AutoSeparatorMode),
            ((ASPxComboBox)sender).Text);
      }
      catch { }
    }
    protected void ASPxCallbackPanel1_Callback(object source,
      DevExpress.Web.ASPxClasses.CallbackEventArgsBase e)
    {
      ASPxMenu1.Opacity = Convert.ToInt32(e.Parameter);
    }

    protected void ASPxCheckBox2_CheckedChanged(object sender, EventArgs e)
    {
      ASPxMenu1.EnableHotTrack = ((ASPxCheckBox)sender).Checked;
    }
}
```

Listing 5-5: The ASPX for the ASPxMenu example shown in Figure 5-4.

```
<%@ Page Language="C#" AutoEventWireup="true"
  CodeFile="Default.aspx.cs" Inherits="_Default" %>

<%@ Register Assembly="DevExpress.Web.v9.1, Version=9.1.4.0,↩
  Culture=neutral, PublicKeyToken=b88d1754d700e49a"
  Namespace="DevExpress.Web.ASPxCallbackPanel" TagPrefix="dxcp" %>

<%@ Register assembly="DevExpress.Web.v9.1, Version=9.1.4.0,↩
  Culture=neutral, PublicKeyToken=b88d1754d700e49a"
  namespace="DevExpress.Web.ASPxMenu" tagprefix="dxm" %>
<%@ Register assembly="DevExpress.Web.v9.1, Version=9.1.4.0,↩
  Culture=neutral, PublicKeyToken=b88d1754d700e49a"
  namespace="DevExpress.Web.ASPxRoundPanel" tagprefix="dxrp" %>
<%@ Register assembly="DevExpress.Web.v9.1, Version=9.1.4.0,↩
```

Continued

245

Listing 5-5: The ASPX for the ASPxMenu example shown in Figure 5-4. *(continued)*

```
        Culture=neutral, PublicKeyToken=b88d1754d700e49a"
        namespace="DevExpress.Web.ASPxPanel" tagprefix="dxp" %>

<%@ Register assembly="DevExpress.Web.ASPxEditors.v9.1,↩
    Version=9.1.4.0, Culture=neutral, PublicKeyToken=b88d1754d700e49a"
    namespace="DevExpress.Web.ASPxEditors" tagprefix="dxe" %>

<%@ Register assembly="DevExpress.Web.v9.1, Version=9.1.4.0,↩
    Culture=neutral, PublicKeyToken=b88d1754d700e49a"
    namespace="DevExpress.Web.ASPxCallback" tagprefix="dxcb" %>

<!DOCTYPE html PUBLIC "-//W3C//DTD XHTML 1.0 Transitional//EN"
 "http://www.w3.org/TR/xhtml1/DTD/xhtml1-transitional.dtd">

<html xmlns="http://www.w3.org/1999/xhtml">
<head runat="server">
  <title></title>
</head>

<body>
  <form id="form1" runat="server">
  <div>
    <dxrp:ASPxRoundPanel ID="ASPxRoundPanel1" runat="server" HeaderText=""
    ShowHeader="False" Width="200px">
    <PanelCollection>
<dxp:PanelContent runat="server">
<dxcp:ASPxCallbackPanel ID="ASPxCallbackPanel1" runat="server" Width="200px"
  OnCallback="ASPxCallbackPanel1_Callback" ClientInstanceName="CallbackPanel" >
<PanelCollection>
<dxp:PanelContent>
<dxm:ASPxMenu ID="ASPxMenu1" runat="server"
ClientInstanceName="Menu" EnableClientSideAPI="True" GutterWidth="0px"
BorderBetweenItemAndSubMenu="HideRootOnly" AutoSeparators="None"
>
<Items>
  <dxm:MenuItem Text="Menu Options">
  <Items>
    <dxm:MenuItem Text="AppearAfter" BeginGroup="true">
    <TextTemplate>
    <dxe:ASPxLabel ID="ASPxLabel1" runat="server"
      Text="<%# Container.Item.Text %>" >
    </dxe:ASPxLabel>
    <table>
    <tr>
    <td>
    <dxe:ASPxTextBox ID="AppearAfterTextBox" runat="server"
      Width="170px" ClientInstanceName="AppearAfterTextBox"
      EnableClientSideAPI="true" AutoPostBack="false">
    <ClientSideEvents Init="function(s, e){
      AppearAfterTextBox.SetValue(Menu.appearAfter+''); }" />
    </dxe:ASPxTextBox>
```

```
</td>
<td>
<dxe:ASPxButton ID="ASPxButton1" runat="server"
  Text="Apply" AutoPostBack="false">
<ClientSideEvents Click="function(s, e)
  {debugger; Menu.appearAfter =
    parseInt(AppearAfterTextBox.GetValue());
  ASPxClientMenuBase.GetMenuCollection().HideAll();
  return false; }" />
</dxe:ASPxButton>
</td>
</tr>
</table>
</TextTemplate>
</dxm:MenuItem>
<dxm:MenuItem Text="DisappearAfter">
<TextTemplate>
<dxe:ASPxLabel ID="ASPxLabel1" runat="server"
  Text="<%# Container.Item.Text %>" >
</dxe:ASPxLabel>
<table>
<tr>
<td>
<dxe:ASPxTextBox ID="DisappearAfterTextBox" runat="server"
  Width="170px" ClientInstanceName="DisappearAfterTextBox"
  EnableClientSideAPI="true" AutoPostBack="false">
<ClientSideEvents Init="function(s, e){
  DisappearAfterTextBox.SetValue(Menu.disappearAfter+''); }" />
</dxe:ASPxTextBox>
</td>
<td>
<dxe:ASPxButton ID="ASPxButton1" runat="server"
  Text="Apply" AutoPostBack="false">
<ClientSideEvents Click="function(s, e)
  {debugger; Menu.disappearAfter =
  parseInt(DisappearAfterTextBox.GetValue());
  ASPxClientMenuBase.GetMenuCollection().HideAll();
  return false; }" />
</dxe:ASPxButton>
</td>
</tr>
</table>
</TextTemplate>
</dxm:MenuItem>
<dxm:MenuItem Text="AutoSeparators" BeginGroup="true">
<TextTemplate>
<table>
<tr>
<td>
  <dxe:ASPxLabel ID="ASPxLabel2" runat="server"
    Text="<%# Container.Item.Text %>">
  </dxe:ASPxLabel>
</td>
```

Continued

Listing 5-5: The ASPX for the ASPxMenu example shown in Figure 5-4. *(continued)*

```
      </tr>
      <tr>
      <td>
        <dxe:ASPxComboBox ID="ASPxComboBox1" runat="server"
        ClientInstanceName="SeparatorComboBox" EnableClientSideAPI="True"
        ValueType="System.String" AutoPostBack="True"
        onvaluechanged="ASPxComboBox1_ValueChanged">
        <Items>
          <dxe:ListEditItem Text="All" Value="All" />
          <dxe:ListEditItem Text="RootOnly" Value="RootOnly" />
          <dxe:ListEditItem Text="None" Value="None" />
        </Items>
        </dxe:ASPxComboBox>
      </td>
      </tr>
      </table>
      </TextTemplate>
      </dxm:MenuItem>
      <dxm:MenuItem Text="Opacity">
      <TextTemplate>
      <dxe:ASPxLabel ID="ASPxLabel1" runat="server"
        Text="<%# Container.Item.Text %>" >
      </dxe:ASPxLabel>
      <table>
      <tr>
      <td>
      <dxe:ASPxSpinEdit ID="ASPxSpinEdit1" runat="server" Height="21px"
        Number="<%# Container.Item.Menu.Opacity %>" MinValue="-1"
        MaxValue="100" ClientInstanceName="Opacity">
        <ClientSideEvents ValueChanged="function(s,e){
        CallbackPanel.PerformCallback(s.GetText());
        return false;
        }" />
      </dxe:ASPxSpinEdit>
      </td>
      </tr>
      </table>
      </TextTemplate>
      </dxm:MenuItem>
      <dxm:MenuItem Text="EnableAnimation" BeginGroup="true">
      <TextTemplate>
        <dxe:ASPxCheckBox ID="ASPxCheckBox1" runat="server"
          Text="<%# Container.Item.Text %>"
         Checked="<%# Container.Item.Menu.EnableAnimation %>"
         ClientInstanceName="EnableAnimationCheckBox"
        >
        <ClientSideEvents CheckedChanged="function(s,e){
         debugger;
         Menu.enableAnimation = EnableAnimationCheckBox.GetChecked();
         ASPxClientMenuBase.GetMenuCollection().HideAll();

        }" />
```

```
        </dxe:ASPxCheckBox>
      </TextTemplate>
      </dxm:MenuItem>
      <dxm:MenuItem Text="EnableHotTrack">
        <TextTemplate>
        <dxe:ASPxCheckBox ID="ASPxCheckBox2" runat="server"
          Text="<%# Container.Item.Text %>"
         Checked="<%# Container.Item.Menu.EnableHotTrack %>"
          TextAlign="Right"
         ClientInstanceName="EnableHotTrackCheckBox"
          oncheckedchanged="ASPxCheckBox2_CheckedChanged" AutoPostBack="True"
         >
          <ClientSideEvents CheckedChanged="function(s,e){
          ASPxClientMenuBase.GetMenuCollection().HideAll();
        }" />
        </dxe:ASPxCheckBox>
      </TextTemplate>
      </dxm:MenuItem>
    </Items>
      </dxm:MenuItem>
   </Items>
   </dxm:ASPxMenu>
   </dxp:PanelContent>
   </PanelCollection>
   </dxcp:ASPxCallbackPanel>
        </dxp:PanelContent>
</PanelCollection>
    </dxrp:ASPxRoundPanel>

  </div>
  </form>
</body>
</html>
```

Each of the following subsections disects some element of the code-behind and ASPX that you may find useful, or it describes a technique I used to make managing nested templates and ClientSideEvent code a little easier. There are a lot of techniques in this code. Some of the code is similar to earlier ASPX, JavaScript, and DevExpress-related solutions in earlier chapters, so the subsection explanations are to the point.

Using the ASPxRoundPanel

The ASPxRoundPanel has its own design time editor and simply adds rounded corners to a panel. This can be done in a lot of ways manually. For example, you can overlay a panel with custom graphics of rounded corners, or you can also use GDI+ and perform custom drawing of rounded rectangles and then render the rectangle to the response stream. The designer is a WinForms window, so the designer draws a rounded rectangle using GDI+. If you use the designer to create custom corners then these are rendered and added to your Web project as .png (image) files. If you are curious about how things are built, download Red-Gate's Reflector and decompile the code, unless you have access to the source. DevExpress provides you with the source code for its controls. The source code for the ASPxRoundPanel, for example, can be found at C:\Program Files\DevExpress 2009.1\Components\ Sources\DevExpress.Web\ASPxRoundPanel (substituting the version information for your version). The ASPxRoundPanel designer class is RoundPanelDesignerForm which inherits from EditFormBase.

Adding a CallbackPanel

Some controls, such as the `ASPxGridView`, support a `CustomCallback`. You write `PerformCallback` in JavaScript, and the `CustomCallback` for the control is called on the server. The `ASPxMenu` does not support `CustomCallbacks` yet, so if you need a callback, use the `ASPxCallbackPanel`. Call `PerformCallback` from JavaScript and handle the server-side code in the `ASPxCallbackPanel`'s Callback event handler.

Place the `ASPxMenu` in the `ASPxCallbackPanel`. When a client event fires on the `ASPxMenu` and you want to perform an Ajax call, call the `ASPxCallbackPanel`'s `PerformCallback` method. In the example (see Figure 5-4), when the `ASPxSpinEdit`'s value is changed, the `ClientSideEventValueChanged` is invoked. `ValueChanged` gets the `ASPxSpinEdit`'s value represented by the script argument s and the call to `GetText()`. The text value is sent to the `ASPxCallbackPanel`'s Callback event handler on the server (see Listing 5-6) and the `ASPxMenu`'s `Opacity` is adjusted in the code-behind (see Listing 5-7).

Listing 5-6: The settings for the ASPxSpinEdit control that adjusts the ASPxMenu's Opacity is based on using an Ajax call through the ASPxCallbackPanel.

```
<dxe:ASPxSpinEdit runat="server" Height="21px"
Number="<%# Container.Item.Menu.Opacity %>" MinValue="-1"
MaxValue="100" ClientInstanceName="Opacity">
<ClientSideEvents ValueChanged="function(s,e){
CallbackPanel.PerformCallback(s.GetText());
return false;
}" />
</dxe:ASPxSpinEdit>
```

Listing 5-7: The ASPxCallbackPanel's Callback event handler.

```
protected void ASPxCallbackPanel1_Callback(object source,
  DevExpress.Web.ASPxClasses.CallbackEventArgsBase e)
{
  ASPxMenu1.Opacity = Convert.ToInt32(e.Parameter);
}
```

Here is another aspect of Listing 5-6 that I like. Notice the `Number` attribute of the `ASPxSpinEdit`. Knowing that the thing containing the `ASPxSpinEdit` in this instance is a `MenuItemTemplateContainer`, you can look up the properties and, with a little detective work, figure out that there is an Item property, which is a MenuItem. Looking up the MenuItem class you can see that a MenuItem has a property — Menu — which is the parent `ASPxMenu`. You can use this knowledge to bind the Number property to the parent Menu's `Opacity` property.

It isn't always easy figuring out where things are in relationship hierarchies. Hierarchies and composite objects are two types of elements that make object-oriented programming languages and frameworks a bit challenging. However, as challenging as they can be to use, creating the frameworks is much more challenging. Books such as this one, articles, and blogs can help you figure out how to access various features much faster than detective work can, but doing so takes a lot of reading and browsing on the Web.

Defining the ClientInstanceName or Not

DevExpress controls support the ClientInstanceName. Setting this property helps you work with the client version of controls in script without wrestling with getElementById. You can provide a client instance name or, if you just want to refer to the calling control in a ClientSideEvent, use the s argument, which is the calling object reference (refer to Listing 5-7). No ClientInstanceName was provided for the ASPxSpinEdit, so its value was retrieved through the s argument of the client-side event handler.

Adjusting the ASPxMenu's Gutter Width

The gutter width is a gray space along the margin of a menu. This value is set by changing the Gutterwidth property in Figure 5-4 and Listing 5-5 (which appears earlier in the chapter), you can see that the GutterWidth is set 0 pixels. Figure 5-5 shows the same solution, as it would appear if you changed the SubmenuStyle's GutterWidth attribute set to 50 pixels expressed as 50px.

> The GutterWidth property is only applied to vertical menus.

Figure 5-5: You can add visible margin to a submenu by adjusting the ASPxMenu's GutterWidth property.

Adding Separators between Groups of MenuItems

The `AutoSeparators` lets you specify `None`, `All`, or `RootOnly`. `RootOnly` means only root menu items will have a separator. `All` means that every MenuItem will have a separator. However, if you want to create logical groups, you can use a MenuItem's `BeginGroup` property, as was done for the `AutoSeparators` MenuItem (see Listing 5-8). A separator — the default gray line — will be placed before the MenuItem, visually creating a new group.

Listing 5-8: The property/attribute of a MenuItem places a separator before that MenuItem, creating a visual group, as shown in the elided listing.

```
<Items>
 <dxm:MenuItem Text="AppearAfter" BeginGroup="true">
 <TextTemplate>
 <dxe:ASPxLabel ID="ASPxLabel 1" runat="server"
     Text="<%# Container.Item.Text %>" >
 </dxe:ASPxLabel>
 <table>
...
```

Using an HTML<table> to Manage Template Layout

Many of you have probably already used an HTML `<table>` to manage layout. Some of you have probably read the various debates on div/table versus CSS to manage layouts. For those of you who haven't, you can use a div or table to help manage the layout of a template (or a page or `UserControl`, for that matter). I use a `<table>` out of habit. One thing I like about using an HTML table for layout is that it is easy to type from scratch — `<table><tr><td></td></tr></table>` gives you a one-cell table — and by turning on borders and adding an obvious border color, you can make sure that the layout is correct. Generally, though, you need one approach or the other to facilitate managing where your controls end up.

The code in Listing 5-9, which is an excerpt from Listing 5-5, uses an HTML table with one row — `<tr></tr>` — and two cells — `<td></td>` — to arrange the side-by-side layout of the `ASPxTextBox` and `ASPxButton` for the `AppearAfter` MenuItem. If you set the border to 4, the table is very visible even in this black-and-white book (see Figure 5-6).

Listing 5-9: Use an HTML table to easily manage layout for template controls, as demonstrated here with a single-row, double-cell table around the ASPxTextBox and ASPxButton.

```
<dxm:MenuItem Text="AppearAfter" BeginGroup="true">
<TextTemplate>
<dxe:ASPxLabel ID="ASPxLabel1" runat="server"
  Text="<%# Container.Item.Text %>" >
</dxe:ASPxLabel>
```

```
<table>
<tr>
<td>
<dxe:ASPxTextBox ID="AppearAfterTextBox" runat="server"
  Width="170px" ClientInstanceName="AppearAfterTextBox"
  EnableClientSideAPI="true" AutoPostBack="false">
<ClientSideEvents Init="function(s, e){
  AppearAfterTextBox.SetValue(Menu.appearAfter+''); }" />
</dxe:ASPxTextBox>
</td>
<td>
<dxe:ASPxButton ID="ASPxButton1" runat="server"
  Text="Apply" AutoPostBack="false">
<ClientSideEvents Click="function(s, e) {debugger;
  Menu.appearAfter = parseInt(AppearAfterTextBox.GetValue());
  ASPxClientMenuBase.GetMenuCollection().HideAll();
  return false; }" />
</dxe:ASPxButton>
</td>
</tr>
</table>
</TextTemplate>
</dxm:MenuItem>
```

Figure 5-6: Setting the border attribute of a table makes visualizing the table layout easy at design time.

Converting a Number to a String in JavaScript

In Listing 5-9 the `ClientSideName` for the `ASPxTextBox` used to set the appear-delay is named `AppearAfterTextBox`. The Menu's `appearAfter` attribute is a number. The `ASPxClientTextBox` is expecting a string. You can easily convert a number to a string in JavaScript by appending an empty string to the number, as shown in Listing 5-9 (and the following fragment).

```
function(s, e){
        AppearAfterTextBox.SetValue(Menu.appearAfter+''); }
```

In this particular instance, you can leave the + '' bit off. The script seems to manage setting the `ASPxTextBox` just fine from the menu.appearAfter numeric property. Numeric types in JavaScript also support the `toString()` method. (JavaScript is case sensitive.)

Converting a String to a Number

If you want to literally convert a string to a number, you can call the parseInt JavaScript function, passing in the string to convert. (There are other parseXXX functions that you can find in the help or online pretty easily with blinq.com. (A good book on JavaScript, such as *Professional JavaScript for Web Developers* by Nicholas C. Zakas [Wrox] is a better idea, though.) The following fragment from Listing 5-9 shows parseInt in use:

```
Menu.appearAfter = parseInt(AppearAfterTextBox.GetValue());
```

As with the technique in the preceding section, this fragment seems to work fine without the call to parseInt. JavaScript is a loosely typed language as well as a language in its own right. One of my copies of a JavaScript has a detailed table of information describing a wide assortment of automatic data type conversions.

Closing All Menus with JavaScript

If you look at the code in Listing 5-5, you see a ASPxxClientMenuBase.GetMenuCollection().HideAll() script statement. ASPxClientMenuBase is the client-side base class for the ASPxMenu. GetMenuCollection is a static method in that type. In the snippet that follows, this line of code is closing all the menus, which is a useful task to perform after the user has finished manipulating the templatized controls.

```
ASPxClientMenuBase.GetMenuCollection().HideAll();
```

When the user clicks a MenuItem, by default the MenuItem closes on its way to performing its task. As a user manipulates template controls, it isn't going to be clear to the ASPxMenu which action signifies that the operation is complete. The HideAll method in script takes care of that for you.

Converting Strings to Enum Types

A common challenge is to display meaningful options to end users. A common complement to using meaningful text is to define meaningful types. One such meaningful data type is an enumeration. Enumerations limit the list of permissible choices. For instance, instead of some meaningless integers for ASPxMenu.AutoSeparator, three values of an enumerated type are available — All, RootOnly, and None. Displaying these values is often done as radio buttons or text. If you display possible enum values as radio buttons, you can convert their index to an enumerated value. If you display them as text, as demonstrated by the ASPxComboBox in Listing 5-5 (and shown here as a fragment), you can convert them to a value from their loosely associated enumerated type.

```
<dxe:ASPxComboBox ID="ASPxComboBox1" runat="server"
ClientInstanceName="SeparatorComboBox" EnableClientSideAPI="True"
ValueType="System.String" AutoPostBack="True"
onvaluechanged="ASPxComboBox1_ValueChanged">
<Items>
  <dxe:ListEditItem Text="All" Value="All" />
  <dxe:ListEditItem Text="RootOnly" Value="RootOnly" />
  <dxe:ListEditItem Text="None" Value="None" />
</Items>
</dxe:ASPxComboBox>
```

The preceding fragment of code adds three ListEditItems to the ASPxComboBox and invokes a server-side ValueChanged event handler when the user makes a change to the combobox. The server-side fragment (shown next) demonstrates how to perform the conversion from string to enum.

```
protected void ASPxComboBox1_ValueChanged(object sender, EventArgs e)
{
  try
  {
    ASPxMenu1.AutoSeparators = (AutoSeparatorMode)Enum.Parse(
      typeof(AutoSeparatorMode),
      ((ASPxComboBox)sender).Text);
  }
  catch { }
}
```

The static method Enum.Parse accepts a type argument of the target enum type and a string representing the name of the enum value, and converts the string to one of the enum values. Because Enum is a static method, it returns an object that must be cast to the target type.

Check out the help documentation on the Enum class for more information on methods such as GetNames, getName, Format, and IsDefined. For example, Format converts an enumerated type to its equivalent string representation.

Creating Templates Quickly

If you look at the tiny default space (see Figure 5-7) available in the designer for template regions, you see that it doesn't look as though they were made to permit dragging and dropping a lot of controls in there. The visual implication is that a template is intended to be simple or contain just one or two controls. Template regions are resizable and can be as complex as you want them to be. To resize a template region, click it and grab the size grips (see Figure 5-8).

Figure 5-7: By default, some template regions are so small — as demonstrated by the dotted interior box — that it doesn't look as though you can drag and drop a lot of controls in there; template regions are resizable at design time.

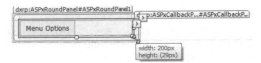

Figure 5-8: Template regions are resizable at design time. Make a region bigger to give yourself some design room.

> A good tip is to create some basic HTML tables with a couple of variations of rows and cells and store these in the ToolBox. Defining these elements isn't hard, but every little bit of canned code, even canned HTML, makes your job a little easier.

A better technique for creating templates is to copy and paste the ASPX rather than use the designer. When you have an existing template, especially if it is similar to what you need for a second or third template, switch to the source view in the Visual Studio Designer and cut and paste the template text. This approach takes care of things such as similarities in HTML tables used for layout, attribute settings, labels, and buttons. Of course, if the template regions are dissimilar, you will have to create each region individually. Another alternative to designing in the template region directly is to design in a `UserControl` and drop the `UserControl` in the template region. With a `UserControl`, you have easily accessible ASPX for other uses, but binding and accessing subcontrols takes a little extra effort.

A third approach is to use a `MasterPage`. A `MasterPage` page can be added from the Add New Item dialog. A master page will have a .master extension. Design the `MasterPage` with features you would like to share in common across multiple pages. Then, after you have defined the `MasterPage`, and you want to add new pages (Web Forms), pick the Web form template and check Select Master Page. When you click Add, the Select a Master Page dialog will appear and you can pick the `MasterPage` to base your new page on.

Implementing a Tabbed Menu

There are some clever programmers at DevExpress and some folks who are creative and clever about using our controls in interesting ways. One of the demos on the DevExpress Web site that I like is how, with a little nudging, the ASPxMenu can be made to look like a tabbed menu.

The example in this section borrows from this book's table of contents to create a tab menu. The example incorporates tweaks to some additional properties of the ASPxMenu — such as specifying a RootItemTextTemplate, RootItemSubMenuOffset, and SubMenuStyle — and using a Cascading Style Sheet to specify images to create the tabbed appearance and filters for a gradient background. The XML file for the sample is provided in Listing 5-10, producing the results shown in Figure 5-9.

Listing 5-10: The XML file used to produce the tabbed effect shown in Figure 5-9.

```xml
<?xml version="1.0" encoding="utf-8"?>
<mainmenu>
  <item Text="Professional DevExp ASP.NET Controls" Selected="True">
  <item Text="Front Matter">
    <item Text="Author Biography" />
    <item Text="Dedication" />
    <item Text="Acknowledgements" />
    <item Text="About DevExpress, Inc" />
  </item>
  <item Text="Table of Contents">
    <item Text="Chapter 1: Programming with the ASPxGridView" />
    <item Text="Chapter 2: Advanced ASPxGridView Computing" />
    <item Text="Chapter 3: Using the ASPxTreeList, ASPxDataView,↵
      and ASPxNewsControl" />
    <item Text="Chapter 4: Adding SiteMaps, Navigation,↵
      and Popup Dialogs" />
    <item Text="Chapter 5: Implementing a Menu and Tabbed Controls" />
    <item Text="Chapter 6: Managing Scheduled Items, Browsing Data,↵
      and Spell Checking" />
    <item Text="Chapter 7: Using the Data that Makes Sense for↵
      Your Problem " />
    <item Text="Chapter 8: Data Mining with OLAP" />
    <item Text="Chapter 9: Using the HTML Editor Suite" />
    <item Text="Chapter 10: Using Themes, CSS, and JavaScript for↵
      Customizations and Enhancements" />
    <item Text="Chapter 11: Asynchronous Computing for ASP.NET" />
    <item Text="Chapter 12: Adding Charts and Graphs to Your Applications" />
    <item Text="Chapter 13: Defining and Printing Reports" />
    <item Text="Appendix A: Understanding How Web Applications↵
Differ from Windows Applications" />
```

Continued

Listing 5-10: The XML file used to produce the tabbed effect shown in Figure 5-9. *(continued)*

```
        </item>
        </item>
        <item Text="Chapter 1" Tooltip="Programming with the ASPxGridView"></item>
        <item Text="Chapter 2" ToolTip="Advanced ASPxGridView Computing"></item>
        <item Text="Chapter 3" ToolTip="Using the ASPxTreeList, ASPxDataView,
and ASPxNewsControl"></item>
        <item Text="Chapter 4" ToolTip="Adding SiteMaps, Navigation, and
Popup Dialogs"></item>
        <item Text="Chapter 5" ToolTip="Implementing a Menu and Tabbed Controls"></item>
        <item Text="Chapter 6" ToolTip="Managing Scheduled Items,
Browsing Data, and Spell Checking"></item>
        <item Text="Chapter 7" ToolTip="Using the Data that Makes Sense
for Your Problem "></item>
        <item Text="Chapter 8" ToolTip="Data Mining with OLAP"></item>
        <item Text="Chapter 9" ToolTip="Using the HTML Editor Suite"></item>
        <item Text="Chapter 10" ToolTip="Using Themes, CSS, and JavaScript
for Customizations and Enhancements"></item>
        <item Text="Chapter 11" ToolTip="Asynchronous Computing for ASP.NET"></item>
        <item Text="Chapter 12" ToolTip="Adding Charts and Graphs to
Your Applications"></item>
        <item Text="Chapter 13" ToolTip="Defining and Printing Reports"></item>
        <item Text="Appendix A" ToolTip="Understanding How Web
Applications Differ from Windows Applications"></item>
    </mainmenu>
```

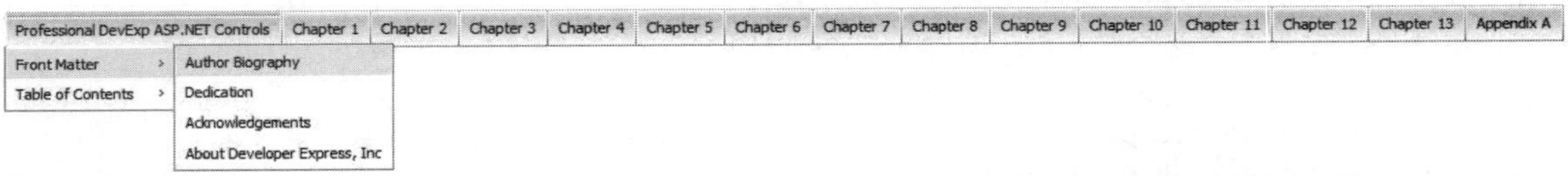

Figure 5-9: You can make an ASPxMenu look like a tabbed menu (shown) with some adjustments to the style attribute and a few small graphics.

Associate the .xml file in Listing 5-10 to the ASPxMenu using the Choose Data Source option from the ASPxMenu's Smart tags menu. In the Choose Data Source Wizard, choose the XmlDataSource, browse for the .xml file, and specify /mainmenu/item as the XPath expression when configuring the

XmlDataSource. (There are several examples demonstrating how to use and configure a data source using the Configure Data Source Wizard, hence the very brief explanation here.)

> If you adjust the .xml file containing the menu items, refresh the schema from the ASPxMenu's Smart tags menu. If you change the .xml file without refreshing the ASPxMenu's inferred schema information, you will get a 403 Forbidden error when you run the Web application.

Defining the RootItemTemplate

The tabbed appearance is totally created by style information applied to the ASPxMenu. For example, the RootItemTemplate is defined as a <div> tag containing a <table>. The table contains an ASPxLabel, which is bound to the text of the root menu item, and the style is applied with a CSS class. (More on classes in a minute.) Here is the fragment for the Root ItemTemplate:

```
<RootItemTextTemplate>
  <div>
    <table cellpadding="0" cellspacing="0" border="0">
      <tr>
        <th class="WhiteBorderRight"><dxe:ASPxLabel ID="lblText" runat="server"
          EnableTheming="False" EnableDefaultAppearance="False"
          Text='<%# Eval("Text") %>' />
        </th>
      </tr>
    </table>
  </div>
</RootItemTextTemplate>
```

Notice that the root item's text value is displayed in the <th> (table header) tag. Previously, I mentioned <tr> and <td> tags as defining rows and cells to look much like spreadsheet. The optional <th> tag defines a header cell for a table.

The <th> attribute class means that the attribute tag will apply the style information defined by a class named WhiteBorderRight. In the following section, I talk about CSS.

Enhancing Visual Appearance with a Cascading Style Sheet

Cascading Style Sheets (CSS) is another technology in its own right. Whole books have been written on CSS. For more information on the standard definition of CSS, you can read the World Wide Web consortium's (W3C) definition of CSS at www.w3.org/Style/CSS/. For a more user-friendly read, check out *Beginning CSS: Cascading Style Sheets for Web Design* by Richard York (Wrox). However, a little general knowledge of CSS, as presented here, can go a long way, too.

Style information can be applied inline for each element of your ASPX (or HTML) by modifying the style attribute. Style information can also be applied at the page level with a <link> tag. Assuming that you have a .css file in your project in a folder named CSS (a convention that you can adopt or not), you can link the style sheet to your page with the following <link> tag inside the <head> tag shown in position in the ASPX, as follows:

```
<!DOCTYPE html PUBLIC "-//W3C//DTD XHTML 1.0 Transitional//EN"
 "http://www.w3.org/TR/xhtml1/DTD/xhtml1-transitional.dtd">

<html xmlns="http://www.w3.org/1999/xhtml">
<head runat="server">
    <title></title>
    <link rel="Stylesheet" href="~/CSS/TabbedMenu.css" type="text/css" />
</head>
```

With the stylesheet, the sample looks like Figure 5-9, shown previously. Without the stylesheet, the sample looks like Figure 5.10. Clearly, a lot of information is being applied by the stylesheet.

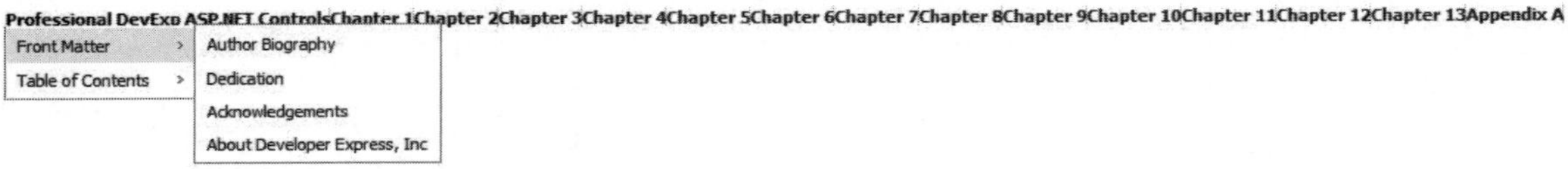

Figure 5-10: Without the stylesheet used for the example, the ASPxMenu appears quite plain.

The fragment of HTML above contains a lot of often-overlooked information. The <!DOCTYPE> tag defines the document type definition (DTD), which indicates that this document will use formatting XHTML 1.0 rules defined by the W3 organization. You can look up more about this DTD at www.w3 .org/TR/xhtml1/. The XHTML 1.0 definition includes rules, such as that attributes need to be in lowerclass letters. The <link> tag includes the rel, href, and type attributes. The rel attribute establishes that the relationship between the linked document and this document is a stylesheet relationship. The href attribute sets the destination URL for the related document, and the type attribute describes the contents of the document. The Cascading Style Sheet for the document that is for the sample is shown in Listing 5-11.

Listing 5-11: The CSS document that creates the appearance shown in Figure 5-9.

```
.TabbedMenuTableSide {
    width: 1px;
    height: 28px;
    background-image: url('../Images/LeftSideSeparators.gif');
    overflow: hidden;
}
.TabbedMenu .rootItem table {
    background-image: url('../Images/ItemBackground.gif');
}
.TabbedMenu_other .rootItem table
{
  filter: progid:DXImageTransform.Microsoft.Gradient(
    GradientType=0, StartColorStr='white', EndColorStr=#F4F7FC);
  background-color: #3366FF;
}
.TabbedMenu_other .rootItemHover table {
  filter: progid:DXImageTransform.Microsoft.Gradient(
    GradientType=0, StartColorStr='white', EndColorStr='#3366FF');
}
.TabbedMenu .rootItemHover table {
    background-image: url('../Images/ItemBackgroundHover.gif');
}
.TabbedMenu .rootItemSelected table {
    background-image: url('../Images/ItemBackgroundSelected.gif');
}
.TabbedMenu .rootItem div,
.TabbedMenu .rootItemHover div,
.TabbedMenu .rootItemSelected div {
    padding: 0px;
    margin: 0px;
}
.TabbedMenu .rootItem div {
    height: 26px;
    border-top: solid 1px #D8D8D8;
    border-bottom: Solid 1px #A3A3A3;
}
.TabbedMenuSideBorders {
    border-bottom: Solid 1px #A3A3A3;
}
.TabbedMenu .rootItemHover div,
.TabbedMenu .rootItemSelected div {
    height: 27px;
    border-top: none;
}
.TabbedMenu .rootItem table,
.TabbedMenu .rootItemHover table,
.TabbedMenu .rootItemSelected table {
    border-collapse: collapse;
    border-width: 0px;
    margin-left: 1px;
    margin-right: 1px;
```

Continued

Listing 5-11: The CSS document that creates the appearance shown in Figure 5-9.
(continued)

```
        background-repeat: repeat-x;
        background-position: top;
}
.TabbedMenu .rootItem th,
.TabbedMenu .rootItemHover th,
.TabbedMenu .rootItemSelected th {
        padding: 7px;
            padding-top: 6px;
            white-space: nowrap;
        font-weight: normal;
}
.TabbedMenu .rootItemHover th,
.TabbedMenu .rootItemSelected th {
        padding-top: 7px;
}
.TabbedMenu .WhiteBorderRight { border-right: solid 1px White; }
.TabbedMenu .rootItemSelected div {
        border-bottom: 0px;
}
```

The salient elements of the CSS document use CSS language but contain the same elements you define when you use the style editor in Visual Studio (see Figure 5-11) or the newer CSS designer in Visual Studio (see Figure 5-12). You can manage the CSS document itself from the CSS Document Outline window (when the CSS document is open in Visual Studio; see Figure 5-13). The CSS Outline window makes navigating around a CSS document easier.

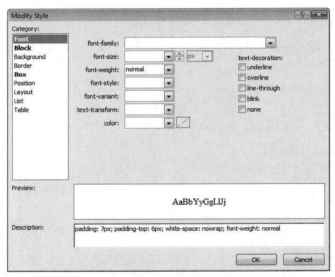

Figure 5-11: The Modify Style dialog box is accessed by selecting the style property of an element in the Properties window.

Figure 5-12: The CSS style designer in Visual Studio.

Figure 5-13: The CSS document Outline window visible when a CSS document is loaded in Visual Studio.

Without trying to give you a comprehensive explanation, which would take hundreds of pages, I summarize by saying that the CSS document contains Elements, Classes, Element IDs, and @ Blocks. Classes are represented by elements with a period preceding the class name in the CSS document. For example, `.TabbedMenuTableSide` defines a class. A class contains a block of style attribute information such as width, height, and background-image. The `.TabbedMenuTableSide` class is shown here:

```
.TabbedMenuTableSide {
    width: 1px;
    height: 28px;
    background-image: url('../Images/LeftSideSeparators.gif');
    overflow: hidden;
}
```

The preceding style means that anything adorned with `.TabbedMenuTableSide` would have the styles applied, including the background-image referenced by the url() function. A more complex style element such as the following:

```
.TabbedMenu .rootItem div,
.TabbedMenu .rootItemHover div,
.TabbedMenu .rootItemSelected div {
    padding: 0px;
    margin: 0px;
}
```

means that all the `<div>` tags in the `.TabbedMenu` elements containing `.rootItem`, `.rootItemHover`, and `.rootItemHoverSelected` will have padding and margins of 0 pixels.

Stylesheets can quickly get complex because styles are inherited, style elements can be applied to all the downstream items, and styles can be limited to specific elements such as specifying that only the `<div>` tags within `.rootItem` elements within `.Tabbedmenu` elements get a specific set of style information. After you have figured out what to apply a style to, then between the {} for the class, you are specifying suitable values for the attributes of interest, such as padding, margin, or `background-image`.

> **Use a cascading style sheet to ensure that styles are applied uniformly across your Web site and to keep the locus of change to one place.**

As mentioned, you can apply individual styles for single controls, define classes within each document (ASPX page), or use a Cascading Style Sheet. Ultimately, developers prefer style sheets because a lot of inline tags clutter your document (referred to as *tag soup*), but if you use a `.css` document, you can reskin (change the appearance of) an entire Web site simply by changing the referenced `.css` document or changing the style in one location. (Web pages that often have varying appearances for similar kinds of things such as labels suffer from the problem of tag soup because the styles were added inline and weren't uniformly changed.)

Using a Background Image to Create a Gradient Effect

One neat trick for creating visual effects is to create a small image slice. These images can be repeated as a `background-image` for a control and to change the control from a mono-colored control to a stunningly visual control. For example, the `.TabbedMenu.rootItemHover` definition adds the ItemBackgroundHover.gif for `<table>` tags (see Listing 5-11). Here is the tag taken from Listing 5-11.

```
.TabbedMenu .rootItemHover table {
  background-image: url('../Images/ItemBackgroundHover.gif');
}
```

The url function accepts the relative path of an image and loads that image at runtime. The `ItemBackgroundImage` was painted with a gradient shade of gray with a blue stripe along the top, and the image is repeated to fill the background.

Using Images to Shape the ASPxMenu's Appearance

You can create border effects by setting the border style and applying it to tables, or you can use the same background-image style with the `url` function and load an image. For example, the WhiteBorderRight element defines border-right as a solid, 1-pixel, white border:

```
.TabbedMenu .WhiteBorderRight {border-right: solid 1px White; }
```

which is applied to the a `<th>` tag of a `<table>` defined in the `RootItemTextTemplate` of the ASPxMenu. `TabbedMenuTableSide` loads `background-image` with the `url` function.

```
.TabbedMenuTableSide {
    width: 1px;
    height: 28px;
    background-image: url('../Images/LeftSideSeparators.gif');
    overflow: hidden;
}
```

Creating a Gradient Effect with a DXImageTransform

As an alternative to drawing and capturing images and loading them as the background, you can use a filter in CSS and perform gradient shading with an ActiveX object. The `.TabbedMenu_other` and `.rootItem` element for `<table>` tags loads the `DXImageTransform`. A `GradientType` of 0 means that a vertical shading will be applied, and 1 means that a horizontal shading will be applied. The `StartColorStr` indicates the starting gradient shade, and `EndColorStr` indicates the ending color. You can specify the colors as the name of the color or an RGB (red-green-blue)-encoded color number.

```
.TabbedMenu_other .rootItem table
{
  filter: progid:DXImageTransform.Microsoft.Gradient(
   GradientType=0, StartColorStr='white', EndColorStr=#F4F7FC);
  background-color: #3366FF;
}
```

Listing 5-12 includes all the code for the tabbed menu example. You can explore the ASPX, modify the ASPX definition, and tweak the CSS document to experiment with the effect the changes will have on the appearance of the ASPxMenu.

Listing 5-12: The ASPX that in conjunction with the CSS in Listing 5-10 creates the tabbed menu as shown in Figure 5-9.

```
<%@ Page Language="C#" AutoEventWireup="true"
  CodeFile="Default.aspx.cs" Inherits="_Default" %>
<%@ Register Assembly="DevExpress.Web.v9.1, Version=9.1.4.0,
 Culture=neutral, PublicKeyToken=b88d1754d700e49a"
 Namespace="DevExpress.Web.ASPxMenu" TagPrefix="dxm" %>
<%@ Register Assembly="DevExpress.Web.v9.1, Version=9.1.4.0,
 Culture=neutral, PublicKeyToken=b88d1754d700e49a"
 Namespace="DevExpress.Web.ASPxRoundPanel" TagPrefix="dxrp" %>
<%@ Register Assembly="DevExpress.Web.ASPxEditors.v9.1,
 Version=9.1.4.0, Culture=neutral, PublicKeyToken=b88d1754d700e49a"
 Namespace="DevExpress.Web.ASPxEditors" TagPrefix="dxe" %>

<!DOCTYPE html PUBLIC "-//W3C//DTD XHTML 1.0 Transitional//EN"
 "http://www.w3.org/TR/xhtml1/DTD/xhtml1-transitional.dtd">

<html xmlns="http://www.w3.org/1999/xhtml">
<head runat="server">
    <title></title>
    <link rel="Stylesheet" href="~/CSS/TabbedMenu.css" type="text/css" />
</head>
<body>
    <form id="form1" runat="server">
<div>
<dxm:ASPxMenu EnableTheming="False" ID="ASPxMenu1"
 CssClass="TabbedMenu" runat="server" AppearAfter="0"
 DataSourceID="XmlDataSource1" ItemSpacing="0px" SeparatorHeight="28px"
 SeparatorWidth="1px" ShowSubMenuShadow="False"
 BorderBetweenItemAndSubMenu="HideRootOnly"
 Font-Names="Tahoma" Font-Size="8pt" Font-Underline="False"
 ForeColor="Black" AutoPostBack="True" SyncSelectionMode="None"
 EnableDefaultAppearance="False" ClientInstanceName="tabbedMenu"
 AllowSelectItem="True" SelectParentItem="True">
    <ItemStyle CssClass="rootItem" Wrap="False">
        <BackgroundImage ImageUrl="~/Images/RootItemSeparator.gif"
Repeat="NoRepeat" HorizontalPosition="right" />
        <Paddings Padding="0px" />
        <HoverStyle CssClass="rootItemHover">
        </HoverStyle>
        <SelectedStyle CssClass="rootItemSelected">
        </SelectedStyle>
    </ItemStyle>
    <Paddings Padding="0px" />
    <Border BorderStyle="None" />
```

```
        <RootItemSubMenuOffset X="-1" Y="-2" FirstItemX="-1"
FirstItemY="-2" LastItemX="-1"
            LastItemY="-2" />
        <SubMenuStyle GutterWidth="0px" ItemSpacing="0px"
BackColor="White" CssClass="TabbedMenu">
            <Paddings Padding="1px" />
            <Border BorderColor="#919191" BorderStyle="Solid" BorderWidth="1px" />
        </SubMenuStyle>
        <SubMenuItemStyle Wrap="False">
            <HoverStyle BackColor="#EDEDED">
                <Border BorderWidth="0px" />
            </HoverStyle>
            <Paddings Padding="5px" PaddingLeft="7px" PaddingRight="7px" />
        </SubMenuItemStyle>
        <VerticalPopOutImage Height="5px" Url="~/Images/ItemArrow.gif" Width="4px" />
        <ItemSubMenuOffset X="-1" Y="-2" FirstItemY="-3" LastItemY="-2" />
        <LinkStyle Color="Black">
            <Font Underline="False"></Font>
        </LinkStyle>
        <RootItemTextTemplate>
            <div><table cellpadding="0" cellspacing="0" border="0"><tr>
<th class="WhiteBorderRight"><dxe:ASPxLabel ID="lblText"
 runat="server" EnableTheming="False" EnableDefaultAppearance="False"
Text='<%# Eval("Text") %>' /></th></tr></table></div>
        </RootItemTextTemplate>
</dxm:ASPxMenu>
        <asp:XmlDataSource ID="XmlDataSource1" runat="server"
          DataFile="~/App_Data/Menu.xml" XPath="/mainmenu/item"></asp:XmlDataSource>
        </div>
        </form>
    </body>
</html>
```

Notice that in Listing 5-12 I used the `<link>` tag to load the CSS stylesheet. No code-behind is necessary for the example as defined. However, the code in Listing 5-13 demonstrates how you can use code to insert the <link> tag and associate the stylesheet programmatically with the HtmlLink class.

Listing 5-13: You can specify the link tag in the ASPX or define it with code, as demonstrated in the example.

```
using System;
using System.Collections.Generic;
using System.Linq;
using System.Web;
using System.Web.UI;
using System.Web.UI.WebControls;
using System.Web.UI.HtmlControls;

public partial class _Default : System.Web.UI.Page
{
    protected void Page_Load(object sender, EventArgs e)
    {
```

Continued

Listing 5-13: You can specify the link tag in the ASPX or define it with code, as demonstrated in the example. *(continued)*

```
      RegisterCSSLink("~/CSS/TabbedMenu.css");
  }

  private void RegisterCSSLink(string url)
  {
    HtmlLink link = new HtmlLink();
    Page.Header.Controls.Add(link);
    link.EnableViewState = false;
    link.Attributes.Add("type", "text/css");
    link.Attributes.Add("rel", "stylesheet");
    link.Href = url;
  }
}
```

Emulating a Toolbar with the ASPxMenu

The previous section demonstrates how you can create a tabbed effect using a stylesheet, some background images, and property tweaks. You can use the same approach, with graphics for the menu items, and recreate Windows-style toolbars. The online demo at http://demos.devexpress.com/ASPxperienceDemos/Menu/Toolbars.aspx shows how to emulate Office 2003, Office 2007 (the ribbon-style menu), and Windows XP toolbars.

You can quickly whip up a great-looking toolbar with the ASPxMenu (see Figure 5-14) by using the basic menu, some good-looking icons or graphics, and the ASPxMenu Editor to add menu items and define their properties. To create a toolbar similar to the one shown in Figure 5-14, try these steps:

1. Add an ASPxRoundPanel to a Web page and set its ContentPadding property to 0px.

2. Add an ASPxMenu to the ASPxRoundPanel.

3. From the ASPxMenu's Smart tags menu, choose Items to open the ASPxMenu MenuItem Editor.

4. For each tool button you would like to have, click the Add an Item button in the editor.

5. Expand the MenuItem's Image property and browse to the URL of the button image for that MenuItem.

6. Set the MenuItem's Text property to an empty string.

7. If you want the separator to create a visual group, set the BeginGroup property to true.

8. For the Search feature, choose Edit Templates from the Smart tags menu and select the Template for the MenuItem that is to contain the ASPxLabel and ASPxTextBox.

9. Finally, code whatever events you want for each item.

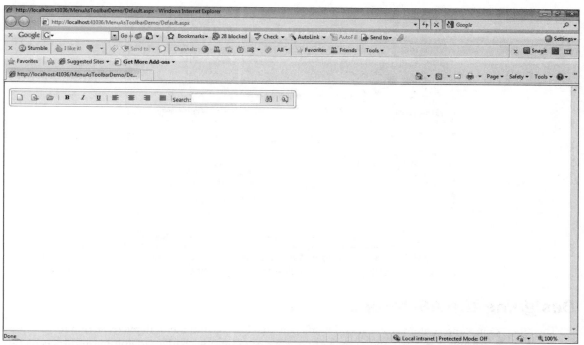

Figure 5-14: You can quickly make a mockup of polished toolbars with professional icons, graphics, and the ASPxMenu.

Incorporating Pop-Up Menus into Your Web Application

Chapter 2 demonstrates how to associate an ASPxPopupMenu with the column headers of an ASPxGridView (see the section "Adding an ASPxPopupMenu to an ASPxGridView"). As can other controls, the ASPxPopupMenu can be configured with templates to change from the default menu (and optional graphic) to using other controls such as an ASPxSpinEdit. It's a matter of figuring out what you want the menu item to do. To build on your knowledge of the ASPxPopupMenu and ASP.NET in general, the example (shown in Figure 5-15) uses the Microsoft Speech API and converts text to speech. This example also shows you how to use the ASPxPopuMenuTextTemplate, add a menu image, and write basic, object-oriented JavaScript.

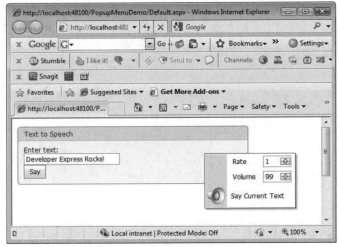

Figure 5-15: The ASPxPopupMenu is configured with template and control settings in a client-side JavaScript object.

Designing the ASPxPopupMenu

The `ASPxPopupMenu` contains three menu items. The first and second menu items (referring to Figure 5-15) use an `ASPxLabel` and `ASPxSpinEdit` for representing changes to volume and speech rate. The third is just a regular menu item that has the `Image.ImageUrl` set (showing the little speaker icon). All the controls are placed inside an `ASPxRoundPanel`, and the `ASPxPopupMenu`'s `PopupElementID` is set to the `ASPxRoundPanel`. The behavior for each menu item is coded as a client-side event. Listing 5-14 shows the HTML/ASPX for the GUI design.

Listing 5-14: A partial listing for the example in Figure 5-15 showing the implementation of the ASPxPopupMenu and menu templates.

```
<body>
    <form id="form1" runat="server">
  <div>

    <dxm:ASPxPopupMenu ID="ASPxPopupMenu1" runat="server">
    </dxm:ASPxPopupMenu>

  </div>
  <dxrp:ASPxRoundPanel ID="ASPxRoundPanel1" runat="server"
    HeaderText="Text to Speech" Height="316px" Width="409px">
    <PanelCollection>
<dxp:PanelContent runat="server">
  <dxe:ASPxLabel ID="ASPxLabel1" runat="server" Text="Enter text:">
  </dxe:ASPxLabel>
  <dxe:ASPxTextBox ID="ASPxTextBox1" runat="server" ClientInstanceName="TextBox"
  Width="170px">
  </dxe:ASPxTextBox>
  <dxm:ASPxPopupMenu ID="ASPxPopupMenu2" runat="server"
```

```
       PopupElementID="ASPxRoundPanel1">
       <Items>
         <dxm:MenuItem Text="Rate">
         <TextTemplate>
         <table>
         <tr><td width="50%" align="left">
           <dxe:ASPxLabel ID="ASPxLabel2" runat="server"
Text="<%# Container.Item.Text %>">
           </dxe:ASPxLabel></td>
           <td width="50%" align="right">
           <dxe:ASPxSpinEdit ID="ASPxSpinEdit1" runat="server" Height="21px"
           MaxValue="100" MinValue="1" Number="3" Width="50px">
           <ClientSideEvents ValueChanged="function(s,e){
             if(configuration != null)
             {
             configuration.Rate = s.GetValue();
             }
             ASPxClientMenuBase.GetMenuCollection().HideAll();
           }" />
           </dxe:ASPxSpinEdit>
         </td></tr>
         </table>
         </TextTemplate>
         </dxm:MenuItem>
         <dxm:MenuItem Text="Volume">
         <TextTemplate>
         <table>
         <tr><td width="50%" align="left">
           <dxe:ASPxLabel ID="ASPxLabel2" runat="server"
Text="<%# Container.Item.Text %>">
           </dxe:ASPxLabel>
           </td>
           <td width="50%" align="right">
           <dxe:ASPxSpinEdit ID="ASPxSpinEdit1" runat="server" Height="21px"
           MaxValue="100" MinValue="1" Number="75" Width="50px">
           <ClientSideEvents ValueChanged="function(s,e){
             if(configuration != null)
             {
             //debugger;
             configuration.Volume = s.GetValue();
             }
             ASPxClientMenuBase.GetMenuCollection().HideAll();
           }" />
           </dxe:ASPxSpinEdit>
           </td>
           </tr>
           </table>
         </TextTemplate>
         </dxm:MenuItem>
         <dxm:MenuItem Text="Say Current Text">
         <Image Url="~/Images/pcdrsound.ico" />
         </dxm:MenuItem>
       </Items>
```

Continued

271

Listing 5-14: A partial listing for the example in Figure 5-15 showing the implementation of the ASPxPopupMenu and menu templates. *(continued)*

```
          <ClientSideEvents ItemClick="function(s,e){
            if(e.htmlElement.outerText == 'Say Current Text')
            {
            SayIt();
            }}" />
          </dxm:ASPxPopupMenu>
          <dxe:ASPxButton ID="ASPxButton1" runat="server" Text="Say" AutoPostBack="False">
          <ClientSideEvents Click="function(s,e){
          SayIt();
          }" />
          </dxe:ASPxButton>
            </dxp:PanelContent>
      </PanelCollection>
        </dxrp:ASPxRoundPanel>
        </form>
      </body>
```

The ASPX is consistent with code already displayed in this chapter a couple of times. Here is a quick review of the Rate MenuItem; you can check earlier sections for more details on additional aspects of the listing if you need to.

Each ASPxPopupMenu item is represented by a MenuItem element. The appearance of the Rate MenuItem is established by the <TextTemplate> element. The TextTemplate uses an HTML <table> to manage the specific layout, and the table contains two cells. The first cell contains an ASPxLabel, and the Text attribute is bound to the MenuItem's Text element. The second cell contains an ASPxSpinEdit. The ASPxSpinEdit has one ClientSideEvent handler defined for the ValueChanged event. When the user changes the ASPxSpinEdit value, the code represented by the text, which is added dynamically as script, looks to see whether something called configuration is initialized. It then sets the Rate property of the configuration object (more on this in a minute). Next, the ASPxPopupMenu is hidden using ASPxClientMenuBase.GetMenuCollection().HideAll().

The Volume MenuItem is designed the same way, and the Say Current Text MenuItem calls the SayIt() method. The next two sections describe how all these elements work in concert.

Implementing the JavaScript Class

JavaScript is an object-based language. This means that you can define classes and use them in your JavaScript. Using a class lets you define more advanced ways of storing state in script than having a bunch of disparate variables and functions would.

A JavaScript class is defined initially just like a function. The biggest difference is that you can add nested functions and properties and access those through instances of the script object. Listing 5-15 contains the definition of the Configuration class used for the sample.

Listing 5-15: A JavaScript class uses function syntax but can contain nested properties and functions, as shown here.

```
<script type="text/javascript">
  function Configuration() {
    this.Rate = rate;
    this.Volume = volume;
    this.Voice = voice;
    this.Initialize = initialize;
    var rate, volume, voice;

    function initialize() {
      //debugger;
      this.Volume = 75;
      this.Rate = 3;
      var obj = new ActiveXObject("SAPI.SpVoice");
      var voices = obj.GetVoices();
      if (voices.count > 0)
        this.Voice = voices[0];
    }
  }

  var configuration = new Configuration();
  configuration.Initialize();
```

The function `Configuration` demonstrates an example of a JavaScript class. `Configuration` defines the fields rate, volume, and voice. Properties are created when you assign fields to names using the `this` reference. By convention, the lowercase fields are assigned to i-capped word properties with the same name as their associated field. The function `initialize` demonstrates how to nest functions. The final two lines show how to create an instance of the class `Configuration` and call its `Initialize` method. Note also that the function initialize is assigned to an i-capped `Initialize`.

In the listing, when `Initialize` is called, default values for Volume and Rate are defined and an instance of the `ActiveXObject` "SAPI.SpVoice" is created. (You need to enable ActiveX for the Web browser to be able to load the Speech API object. ActiveX is a Microsoft Internet Explorer feature and has no bearing on how JavaScript classes are defined.) Finally, the Voice property is set to the first voice available in the Speech API.

Coding the Client-Side Behaviors

All the `ASPxPopupMenu` events interact with the `Configuration` object, which stores the Speech API settings except the Say Current Text `ASPxPopupMenu` menuItem and the `ASPxButton`. The button and the last MenuItem call the SayIt JavaScript function. Listing 5-16 shows the implementation of `SayIt`, and Listing 5-17 shows the complete ASPX for the sample program.

Listing 5-16: The implementation of SayIt uses the Speech API represented by the ActiveXObject and plays the text in the ASPxTextBox on your PCs speaker.

```
function SayIt() {
  //debugger;
  var SpeechObject = new ActiveXObject("SAPI.SpVoice");
  if (configuration != null) {
    SpeechObject.Rate = configuration.Rate;
    SpeechObject.Volume = configuration.Volume;
    if (configuration.Voice != null)
      SpeechObject.Voice = configuration.Voice;
  }
  SpeechObject.Speak(TextBox.GetText());
}
```

Listing 5-17: The complete listing of the ASPX for the demo.

```
<%@ Page Language="C#" AutoEventWireup="true"
  CodeFile="Default.aspx.cs" Inherits="_Default" %>

<%@ Register assembly="DevExpress.Web.v9.1, Version=9.1.4.0,
 Culture=neutral, PublicKeyToken=b88d1754d700e49a"
 namespace="DevExpress.Web.ASPxMenu" tagprefix="dxm" %>
<%@ Register assembly="DevExpress.Web.v9.1, Version=9.1.4.0,
 Culture=neutral, PublicKeyToken=b88d1754d700e49a"
 namespace="DevExpress.Web.ASPxRoundPanel" tagprefix="dxrp" %>
<%@ Register assembly="DevExpress.Web.v9.1, Version=9.1.4.0,
 Culture=neutral, PublicKeyToken=b88d1754d700e49a"
 namespace="DevExpress.Web.ASPxPanel" tagprefix="dxp" %>
<%@ Register assembly="DevExpress.Web.ASPxEditors.v9.1,
 Version=9.1.4.0, Culture=neutral, PublicKeyToken=b88d1754d700e49a"
 namespace="DevExpress.Web.ASPxEditors" tagprefix="dxe" %>

<!DOCTYPE html PUBLIC "-//W3C//DTD XHTML 1.0 Transitional//EN"
 "http://www.w3.org/TR/xhtml1/DTD/xhtml1-transitional.dtd">

<html xmlns="http://www.w3.org/1999/xhtml">
<head runat="server">
    <title></title>
</head>
<script type="text/javascript">
  function Configuration() {
    this.Rate = rate;
    this.Volume = volume;
    this.Voice = voice;
    this.Initialize = initialize;
    var rate, volume, voice;

    function initialize() {
      //debugger;
      this.Volume = 75;
      this.Rate = 3;
      var obj = new ActiveXObject("SAPI.SpVoice");
```

```
            var voices = obj.GetVoices();
            if (voices.count > 0)
              this.Voice = voices[0];
        }
    }

    var configuration = new Configuration();
    configuration.Initialize();

    function SayIt() {
      //debugger;
      var SpeechObject = new ActiveXObject("SAPI.SpVoice");
      if (configuration != null) {
        SpeechObject.Rate = configuration.Rate;
        SpeechObject.Volume = configuration.Volume;
        if (configuration.Voice != null)
          SpeechObject.Voice = configuration.Voice;
      }
      SpeechObject.Speak(TextBox.GetText());
    }

</script>
<body>
    <form id="form1" runat="server">
    <div>

        <dxm:ASPxPopupMenu ID="ASPxPopupMenu1" runat="server">
        </dxm:ASPxPopupMenu>

    </div>
    <dxrp:ASPxRoundPanel ID="ASPxRoundPanel1" runat="server"
      HeaderText="Text to Speech" Height="316px" Width="409px">
      <PanelCollection>
<dxp:PanelContent runat="server">
  <dxe:ASPxLabel ID="ASPxLabel1" runat="server" Text="Enter text:">
  </dxe:ASPxLabel>
  <dxe:ASPxTextBox ID="ASPxTextBox1" runat="server" ClientInstanceName="TextBox"
    Width="170px">
  </dxe:ASPxTextBox>
  <dxm:ASPxPopupMenu ID="ASPxPopupMenu2" runat="server"
    PopupElementID="ASPxRoundPanel1">
    <Items>
      <dxm:MenuItem Text="Rate">
        <TextTemplate>
        <table>
        <tr><td width="50%" align="left">
          <dxe:ASPxLabel ID="ASPxLabel2" runat="server"
 Text="<%# Container.Item.Text %>">
          </dxe:ASPxLabel></td>
          <td width="50%" align="right">
          <dxe:ASPxSpinEdit ID="ASPxSpinEdit1" runat="server" Height="21px"
            MaxValue="100" MinValue="1" Number="3" Width="50px">
            <ClientSideEvents ValueChanged="function(s,e){
```

Continued

275

Listing 5-17: The complete listing of the ASPX for the demo. *(continued)*

```
            if(configuration != null)
            {
              configuration.Rate = s.GetValue();
            }
            ASPxClientMenuBase.GetMenuCollection().HideAll();
          }" />
          </dxe:ASPxSpinEdit>
      </td></tr>
      </table>
      </TextTemplate>
    </dxm:MenuItem>
    <dxm:MenuItem Text="Volume">
      <TextTemplate>
      <table>
      <tr><td width="50%" align="left">
        <dxe:ASPxLabel ID="ASPxLabel2" runat="server"
Text="<%# Container.Item.Text %>">
        </dxe:ASPxLabel>
        </td>
        <td width="50%" align="right">
        <dxe:ASPxSpinEdit ID="ASPxSpinEdit1" runat="server" Height="21px"
          MaxValue="100" MinValue="1" Number="75" Width="50px">
          <ClientSideEvents ValueChanged="function(s,e){
            if(configuration != null)
            {
              //debugger;
              configuration.Volume = s.GetValue();
            }
            ASPxClientMenuBase.GetMenuCollection().HideAll();
          }" />
          </dxe:ASPxSpinEdit>
          </td>
          </tr>
          </table>
      </TextTemplate>
    </dxm:MenuItem>
    <dxm:MenuItem Text="Say Current Text">
      <Image Url="~/Images/pcdrsound.ico" />
    </dxm:MenuItem>
  </Items>
  <ClientSideEvents ItemClick="function(s,e){
    if(e.htmlElement.outerText == 'Say Current Text')
    {
      SayIt();
    }}" />
</dxm:ASPxPopupMenu>
<dxe:ASPxButton ID="ASPxButton1" runat="server" Text="Say" AutoPostBack="False">
<ClientSideEvents Click="function(s,e){
  SayIt();
  }" />
</dxe:ASPxButton>
      </dxp:PanelContent>
```

```
    </PanelCollection>
        </dxrp:ASPxRoundPanel>
        </form>
    </body>
    </html>
```

The JavaScript function SayIt creates an instance of the `SAPI.SpVoiceActiveXObject` and initializes it from the `configuration` object converting the text in the `ASPxTextBox` (who's `ClientInstanceName` is `TextBox`) to speech.

By combining JavaScript, templates, and controls, you can create some interesting solutions. Using JavaScript classes as shown in the demo means that you can initialize and use composite objects, which will help you better manage and reuse your JavaScript just as it helps you manage and better use your C# code.

Creating Tabbed Views

Two controls support tab-style navigation in the ASPxperience Suite. One is the `ASPxTabControl`, which just has tabs that are designed to be used as a visual navigation aid. The other control is the `ASPxPageControl`, which combines the tabs with content templates. If you want the tabbed look, use the `ASPxTabControl` by itself and define the content to navigate to when the tab is clicked. If you want the tabs and content, use the `ASPxPageControl` and define the content in tab pages.

The ASPX controls share many features in common. For example, they all support client-side events, Ajax, and customized appearance with templates. Rather than repeat in every section the parts that each control has in common, I use the demos to try to touch on some of the core common features, such as client-side events, as well as features that are unique to a particular control.

This section has two demos. The first demo shows you how to customize the appearance of the tabs themselves, and you can apply that technique to the `ASPxTabControl` and `ASPxPageControl`. The second demo shows you how to use the `ASPxPageControl` to associate content with the tabs and use a vertical alignment for the tabs themselves.

Customizing the Appearance of Tabs

Earlier in the chapter, I talk about how you can use repeated background images to customize the appearance of the `ASPxMenu`. In that sample — in the section "Implementing a Tabbed Menu" — the `ASPxMenu` was visually manipulated to change the appearance of tabs of a menu to make the root menu items look like tabs. You can employ a similar technique to change the appearance of the tab controls. By default, the `ASPxTabControl` (and `ASPxPageControl`) tabs are pretty generic looking (see Figure 5-16). By defining templates for the `TabTemplate` and `ActiveTabTemplate`, and with the use of a couple of clever images, you can dramatically change the appearance of the tabs for the `ASPxTabControl` and `ASPxPageControl` (see Figure 5-17).

Figure 5-16: The default appearance of the ASPxTabControl at design time.

Figure 5-17: By defining the TabTemplate and ActiveTabTemplate, you can alter and even improve the appearance of the ASPxTabControl (and the ASPxPageControl).

To create the rounded tabs shown in Figure 5-17, you need a rounded corner graphic for each corner of the tab, and a thin image for the filler in between. Use an `ASPxImage` for each of the tab corners and set the cell background-image for the filler in between. You use an HTML table to position the three cells — containing the two corners and the filler — adjacent to each other. The templates (see Listing 5-18) for the `TabTemplate` and `ActiveTabTemplate` are the same; only the URLs to the images to change the appearance differs for active versus non-active tabs.

Listing 5-18: By laying out three table cells with ASPxImages and a background-image, you can easily change the appearance of the tabs.

```
<%@ Page Language="C#" AutoEventWireup="true"
  CodeFile="Default.aspx.cs" Inherits="_Default" %>

<%@ Register Assembly="DevExpress.Web.ASPxEditors.v9.1,↵
 Version=9.1.4.0, Culture=neutral, PublicKeyToken=b88d1754d700e49a"
 Namespace="DevExpress.Web.ASPxEditors" TagPrefix="dxe" %>

<%@ Register Assembly="DevExpress.Web.v9.1, Version=9.1.4.0,↵
 Culture=neutral, PublicKeyToken=b88d1754d700e49a"
 Namespace="DevExpress.Web.ASPxTabControl" TagPrefix="dxtc" %>

<!DOCTYPE html PUBLIC "-//W3C//DTD XHTML 1.0 Transitional//EN"
 "http://www.w3.org/TR/xhtml1/DTD/xhtml1-transitional.dtd">

<html xmlns="http://www.w3.org/1999/xhtml">
<head runat="server">
  <title></title>
</head>
<body>
  <form id="form1" runat="server">
  <div>
    <dxtc:ASPxTabControl ID="ASPxTabControl1" runat="server" ActiveTabIndex="2"
    BackColor="Transparent" EnableDefaultAppearance="False" TabSpacing="0px">
    <TabTemplate>
    <table border="0" cellpadding="0" cellspacing="0">
    <tr>
      <td><asp:Image ID="Image2" runat="server"
GenerateEmptyAlternateText="true"
```

```
        ImageUrl="Images/UnSelectedLeft.gif"/></td>
            <td style="white-space: nowrap;↩
    background-image:url(Images/UnSelectedCenter.gif);">
            <dxe:ASPxLabel ID="Label1" runat="server"
    Text="<%# Container.Tab.Text %>"
    Font-Names="Tahoma" ForeColor="#333333" Font-Size="8pt" /></td>
            <td><asp:Image ID="Image5" runat="server" GenerateEmptyAlternateText="true"
    ImageUrl="Images/UnSelectedRight.gif"/></td>
        </tr>
        </table>
        </TabTemplate>
        <ActiveTabTemplate>
        <table border="0" cellpadding="0" cellspacing="0">
        <tr>
            <td><asp:Image ID="Image2" runat="server"
    GenerateEmptyAlternateText="true"
    ImageUrl="Images/SelectedLeft.gif"/></td>
            <td style="white-space: nowrap;↩
    background-image:url(Images/SelectedCenter.gif);">
            <dxe:ASPxLabel ID="Label1" runat="server"
    Text="<%# Container.Tab.Text %>"
    Font-Names="Tahoma" ForeColor="#333333" Font-Size="8pt" /></td>
            <td><asp:Image ID="Image5" runat="server"
    GenerateEmptyAlternateText="true"
    ImageUrl="Images/SelectedRight.gif"/></td>
            <td>
        </tr>
        </table>
        </ActiveTabTemplate>
        <Tabs>
            <dxtc:Tab Text="Lamborghini">
            </dxtc:Tab>
            <dxtc:Tab Text="Astin Martin">
            </dxtc:Tab>
            <dxtc:Tab Text="Mercedes">
            </dxtc:Tab>
        </Tabs>
        </dxtc:ASPxTabControl>
    </div>
    </form>
  </body>
  </html>
```

Both the TabTemplate and the ActiveTabTemplate have the same contents, except for the actual images that each template item refers to. For this reason, I describe only the code for the TabTemplate.

The TabTemplate contains an HTML table with no border, no cellpadding, and no cellspacing. (If these are nonzero, you will have gaps in the image effect.) The table has one row (<tr>) and three cells (<td>). The first and third cells contain asp image controls. The first cell's ImageUrl refers to the left corner, and the third cell's ImageUrl refers to the graphics for the right corner. The middle cell's image is set using the style attribute background-image, and the actual graphic is loaded by calling the url function. The middle cell also contains an ASPxLabel, which is bound to the tab's Text property. (To use this code for an ASPxPageControl, change the Text binding from Container.Tab.Text to Container.TabPage. Text.) Choose a font and color you like. The appearance is dictated by the actual images referred to.

> The HTML `<img>` tag requires an alt attribute even if it's an empty string. Because Web controls ultimately generate HTML, some value for the alt attribute is required. `GenerateEmptyAlternateText`=true is one means of providing the alt text for an image.

The tabs in Figure 5-17 are rounded because the template graphics are rounded. Change the graphics and the tab appearance changes as well. That's all there is to it.

Using the ASPxPageControl

The `ASPxPageControl` is basically an `ASPxTabControl` with content. An important point here is that although all the tabs are present at runtime, only the active tab in the `ASPxPageControl` has its content loaded and sent to the client. You determine the content by defining the `<ContentCollection>` for each `<TabPage>` of the `ASPxPageControl`. If you want each tab to appear to change as though the content were already present on the client, set `ASPxPageControl.EnableCallBack` to true. To change the tabs — for example, to display them on the left or right instead of top or bottom — set the `TabPosition` to `Right` or `Left`, as the case may be. The ASPX in Listing 5-19 creates the Web page containing the `ASPxPageControl` (shown in Figure 5-18 at runtime).

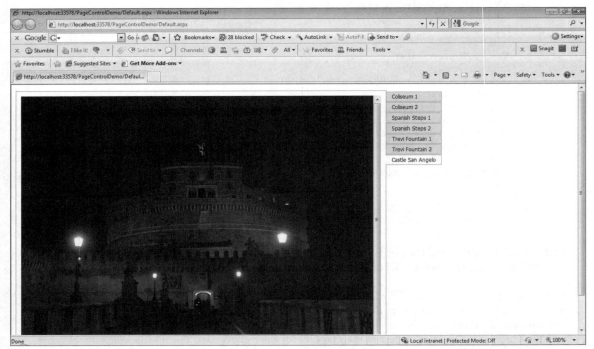

Figure 5-18: Castle San Angelo in Rome, just a couple of blocks away from St. Peters, shown here at night with the ASPxPageControl tabs shown on the right.

Listing 5-19: Define the <TabPage><ContentCollection> to describe what will be rendered when a tab becomes active.

```
<%@ Page Language="C#" AutoEventWireup="true"  CodeFile="Default.aspx.cs"
 Inherits="_Default" %>

<%@ Register assembly="DevExpress.Web.v9.1, Version=9.1.4.0,↵
 Culture=neutral, PublicKeyToken=b88d1754d700e49a"
 namespace="DevExpress.Web.ASPxTabControl" tagprefix="dxtc" %>
<%@ Register assembly="DevExpress.Web.v9.1, Version=9.1.4.0,↵
 Culture=neutral, PublicKeyToken=b88d1754d700e49a"
 namespace="DevExpress.Web.ASPxClasses" tagprefix="dxw" %>
<%@ Register assembly="DevExpress.Web.ASPxEditors.v9.1,↵
 Version=9.1.4.0, Culture=neutral, PublicKeyToken=b88d1754d700e49a"
 namespace="DevExpress.Web.ASPxEditors" tagprefix="dxe" %>

<!DOCTYPE html PUBLIC "-//W3C//DTD XHTML 1.0 Transitional//EN"
 "http://www.w3.org/TR/xhtml1/DTD/xhtml1-transitional.dtd">

<html xmlns="http://www.w3.org/1999/xhtml">
<head runat="server">
  <title></title>
</head>
<body>
  <form id="form1" runat="server">
  <div>
    <dxtc:ASPxPageControl ID="ASPxPageControl1" runat="server" ActiveTabIndex="0"
    EnableCallBacks="True" EnableViewState="False" TabPosition="Right">
    <TabPages>
      <dxtc:TabPage Text="Coliseum 1">
      <ContentCollection>
        <dxw:ContentControl runat="server">
        <div style="overflow:scroll;height:600px;width:800px;" >
        <dxe:ASPxImage ID="ASPxImage1" runat="server"
ImageUrl="~/Images/Coliseum1.JPG"
        Width="100%" Height="100%" ClientInstanceName="PageControl">
        </dxe:ASPxImage>
        </div>
        </dxw:ContentControl>
      </ContentCollection>
      </dxtc:TabPage>
      <dxtc:TabPage Text="Coliseum 2">
      <ContentCollection>
        <dxw:ContentControl runat="server">
        <div style="overflow:scroll;height:600px;width:800px;" >
        <dxe:ASPxImage ID="ASPxImage2" runat="server"
ImageUrl="~/Images/Coliseum2.JPG" Width="100%" Height="100%">
        </dxe:ASPxImage>
        </div>
        </dxw:ContentControl>
      </ContentCollection>
      </dxtc:TabPage>
      <dxtc:TabPage Text="Spanish Steps 1">
```

Continued

Listing 5-19: Define the <TabPage><ContentCollection> to describe what will be rendered when a tab becomes active. *(continued)*

```
        <ContentCollection>
          <dxw:ContentControl runat="server">
          <div style="overflow:scroll;height:600px;width:800px;" >
          <dxe:ASPxImage ID="ASPxImage3" runat="server"
ImageUrl="~/Images/Spanish Steps 1.JPG"
Width="100%" Height="100%">
          </dxe:ASPxImage>
          </div>
          </dxw:ContentControl>
        </ContentCollection>
      </dxtc:TabPage>
      <dxtc:TabPage Text="Spanish Steps 2">
        <ContentCollection>
          <dxw:ContentControl runat="server">
          <div style="overflow:scroll;height:600px;width:800px;" >
          <dxe:ASPxImage ID="ASPxImage4" runat="server"
ImageUrl="~/Images/Spanish Steps 2.JPG"
Width="100%" Height="100%">
          </dxe:ASPxImage>
          </div>
          </dxw:ContentControl>
        </ContentCollection>
      </dxtc:TabPage>
      <dxtc:TabPage Text="Trevi Fountain 1">
        <ContentCollection>
          <dxw:ContentControl runat="server">
          <div style="overflow:scroll;height:600px;width:800px;" >
          <dxe:ASPxImage ID="ASPxImage5" runat="server"
ImageUrl="~/Images/Trevi Fountain 1.JPG"
Width="100%" Height="100%">
          </dxe:ASPxImage>
          </div>
          </dxw:ContentControl>
        </ContentCollection>
      </dxtc:TabPage>
      <dxtc:TabPage Text="Trevi Fountain 2">
        <ContentCollection>
          <dxw:ContentControl runat="server">
          <div style="overflow:scroll;height:600px;width:800px;" >
          <dxe:ASPxImage ID="ASPxImage6" runat="server"
ImageUrl="~/Images/Trevi Fountain 2.JPG"
Width="100%" Height="100%">
          </dxe:ASPxImage>
          </div>
          </dxw:ContentControl>
        </ContentCollection>
      </dxtc:TabPage>
      <dxtc:TabPage Text="Castle San Angelo">
        <ContentCollection>
          <dxw:ContentControl runat="server">
          <div style="overflow:scroll;height:600px;width:800px;" >
```

```
        <dxe:ASPxImage ID="ASPxImage7" runat="server"
ImageUrl="~/Images/Castle San Angelo 1.JPG"
Width="100%" Height="100%">
        </dxe:ASPxImage>
        </div>
        </dxw:ContentControl>
    </ContentCollection>
    </dxtc:TabPage>
  </TabPages>
  </dxtc:ASPxPageControl>

</div>
</form>
</body>
</html>
```

The pages in the ASPxPageControl are listed in the TabPages element. Each page is represented by a TabPage element. Each TabPage element contains a ContentCollection, which in turn contains a ContentControl element. You can build these elements using the ASPxPageControl Tab Editor (see Figure 5-19), which is accessible from the ASPxPageControl's Smart tags tab Pages menu item, or you can define them directly in the ASPX. Each tab page in the demo contains a <div> and an ASPxImage, but the individual pages can vary as much as you like.

Figure 5-19: Use the ASPxPageControl's Tab Editor
(shown) or modify the ASPX to directly define tab
page content.

Summary

Menus, pop-up menus, and tab controls used to be a bit challenging, time consuming, and tedious to implement in Web applications. They used to require a lot of careful HTML coding to get right. With the DevExpress `ASPxMenu`, `ASPxPopupControl`, and `ASPxPageControl`, covered in this chapter, you can incorporate these rich client elements with ease. With a little bit of ingenuity, you can even recreate the appearance of rich controls, such as tool strips.

This chapter also introduced some additional uses of the `CallbackPanel` and object-oriented JavaScript. With rich controls, your starting point is substantially farther along than if you tried to reproduce some of these controls — such as pop-up context menus — from scratch, but sometimes using JavaScript helps provide a richer user experience.

## 6

Managing Scheduled Items and Using Gauges

This chapter introduces and demonstrates the ASPxScheduler and ASPxGaugeControl. The ASPxScheduler is a suite of elements that offers a fully operational calendaring subsystem. With the ASPxScheduler, you can let your users define resources and add appointment elements, define recurring appointments with reminders, and use the canned search, export, and import features. The ASPxGaugeControl contains dozens of predefined gauges that you can use to visually represent values, or you can design your own custom gauges with the Visual Gauge Control Designer.

Supporting ASP.NET and .NET framework topics are incorporated into the samples in this chapter. By trying the examples in this chapter, you can learn about using extension methods, querying XML with LINQ to XML, implementing a custom data source, and inheriting from BindingList<T>. You also explore several additional examples of client-side JavaScript.

Scheduling Calendar Events

The ASPxScheduler is an Outlook-style control that supports creating Web subsystems that need to store appointments or events at some point in time. The ASPxScheduler has built-in support for editing calendar events, creating recurring events, reminders, and search functionality. (These elements are added as user controls to your project when you add the ASPxScheduler.)

The ASPxScheduler has built-in support that permits the end user to switch between a Day, Work Week, Week, Month, or Timeline views. You don't need to write any code; the various views are available out of the box. Figure 6-1 highlights some of the built-in features, including those mentioned, of the ASPxScheduler control.

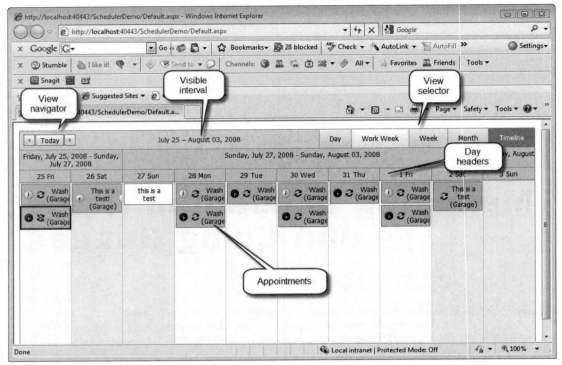

Figure 6-1: Some of the visible features — based on property settings — of the ASPxScheduler out of the box.

The ASPxScheduler control separates presentation — drawing the GUI — from persistence — storing the data. The ASPxScheduler itself knows nothing about the data layer; rather, it has a Storage property that is an instance of ASPxSchedulerStorage. The Storage property holds and manages the appointments (and resources) for the scheduler. The actual underlying data store is normalized into two separate entities: Appointments and Resources. Appointments contain information about the calendar item and recurrence information, if the appointment is a recurring appointment. The Resources item contains information about the resource associated with the appointment. For example, if you used the ASPxScheduler to create a project planner, a resource would be the person assigned to implement an item in the project plan. If you created a dental appointment planner, resources might be dentists or hygienists. The basic idea behind splitting resources and appointments is that one resource may be assigned to multiple appointments, which is basically similar to the motivation for database normalization.

Navigation between appointments in the ASPxScheduler can be accomplished with stand-alone controls or the controls hosted in the main scheduler, such as the view navigator (see Figure 6-1).

Appointment editing can be done by editing appointment items in place or by using one of the user control editing forms added to the project with the ASPxScheduler. The editing features are added to your project, and editing is coordinated between the in-place editor or editor user controls automatically. A templating mechanism supports letting you customize the appearance of the editing forms.

The ASPxScheduler performs its function, as involved as that is, out of the box without a lot of code on your end. The biggest challenge for general use is to map your objects or data tables representing Appointments and Resources to the Appointment and Resource field names that the ASPxScheduler uses. For example, the ASPxScheduler thinks of the time and date that the appointment begins as the StartDate. If your table uses BeginDate to represent the same thing, you will need to map your entity's properties to the ASPxScheduler's fields. The good news is that there is a mapping wizard that does a pretty good job guessing at the mapping relationships. Figure 6-2 describes the schema, if you will, of the ASPxScheduler's appointment fields, and Figure 6-3 shows the schema of the resource fields. The closer your entity fields match these fields in name and type (although it isn't necessary for the names to match), the easier it will be to map between the ASPxScheduler and your data entities.

Field Name	Data Type	Description
UniqueID	AutoNumber	Required, Indexed (No Duplicates)
Type	Number	Not required, Not indexed
StartDate	Date/Time	Not required, Indexed (Duplicates OK)
EndDate	Date/Time	Not required, Indexed (Duplicates OK)
AllDay	Yes/No	Not indexed
Subject	Text	Not required, Not indexed, Size = 100
Location	Text	Not required, Not indexed, Size = 50
Description	Memo	Not required, Not indexed
Status	Number	Not required, Not indexed
Label	Number	Not required, Indexed (Duplicates OK)
ResourceID	Number	Not required, Indexed (Duplicates OK)
RecurrenceInfo	Memo	Not required, Not indexed
ReminderInfo	Memo	Not required, Not indexed
CustomField1	Memo	Not required, Not indexed

Figure 6-2: The world as the ASPxScheduler Appointment views it.

Field Name	Data Type	Description
UniqueID	AutoNumber	Required, Indexed (No Duplicates)
ResourceID	Number	Required, Indexed (No Duplicates)
ResourceName	Text	Not required, Not indexed, Size = 50
Color	Number	Not required, Not indexed
Image	OLE Object	Not required
CustomField1	Memo	Not required, Not indexed

Figure 6-3: The world as the ASPxScheduler views Resources.

The `ASPxScheduler` is customizable by applying styles, changing the default editing forms, setting or unsetting properties, and modifying the Labels and Statuses values. You can also use database tables as the data repository, or use custom objects and a `BindingList` to store and manage appointments. The subsections in this part of the chapter show you how to take advantage of some of these features.

Data Binding an AccessDataSource to the ASPxScheduler

Picking one database provider over any other is more about showing the diversity of support than it is an endorsement of any one database technology. Although I haven't used Microsoft Access as a database in a Web application other than for a Web site, there are classes of applications (and budgets) for which Microsoft Access might be a perfect choice. (However, you can easily substitute the sample in the section with a SQL Server database by upsizing from Access to SQL Server. One way to do this is described in my blog post at `http://community.devexpress.com/blogs/paulk/archive/2009/05/20/upsizing-an-ms-access-2007-database-to-sql-server.aspx`.)

Having said that, I want to also point out that the sample in this part uses the CarsDB.mdb Microsoft Access database that ships with the samples when you download and install the ASPxperience Suite from DevExpress. The sample application itself is original to this text. The sample demonstrates how to pair tables in an Access database to the Appointments and Resources stores for the `ASPxScheduler` and construct the relatively minor bit of code that facilitates inserting new items into the `ASPxScheduler`.

Reviewing the CarsDB.mdb Database Tables

The demo for this section contains a database that stores information about cars to be washed, included the time, location, and specific car to wash. (I like to think of this demo as a mobile car-washing service. Apparently, there is at least one in Michigan (at `www.spotlessdetailing.com`; for $25, the company will come to you.) The CarsDB.mdb MS Access database contains two tables that are of interest for the demo. The Cars table contains information about specific cars to be washed. This table represents the resources in this instance, so they will need to be mapped to the `ASPxScheduler`'s Resources. The CarsScheduling table represents the appointment information describing which car is to be washed, as well as where and when. The schema for the Cars table is provided in Table 6-1, and the schema for the CarsScheduling table is provided in Table 6-2.

Table 6-1: The Table Structure for the Cars Table.

Name	Type
ID	Long Integer
Trademark	Text
Model	Text
HP	Integer
Liter	Double
Cyl	Byte

When you have finished assigning a data source to the Appointments data, you need to use the Appointments Mapping Wizard (available from the Smart tags menu; refer to Figure 6-4). The mappings dialog does a pretty good job initially at guessing the mappings between the data source properties and the ASPxScheduler fields when the dialog box is first displayed. You can choose the Clear button to clear the default mappings, click Generate to regenerate mappings, and manually adjust the mappings by selecting an alternate source from the right side of the mappings columns (see Figure 6-5).

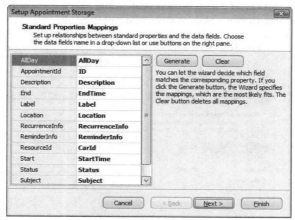

Figure 6-4: The Mappings Wizard displays the Standard Properties Mappings dialog box, which assists you in mapping your data source's properties for the ASPxScheduler's fields.

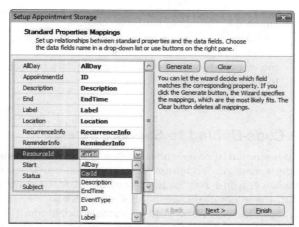

Figure 6-5: You can manually adjust the mappings by selecting an alternate available field from the drop-down list of the Standard Properties Mappings dialog box.

After you define the standard mappings, you can click Next to define custom mappings or click Finish to complete the mapping step. There are no custom mappings for this sample.

After you have finished mapping the Appointments data to the ASPxScheduler, you can map the Resources data source. The ASPxScheduler will operate without a Resources data source, but the only resource option available will be the default (Any) choice.

Mapping the Resources Data Source

The Resources data source and mappings are configured in the same way. The biggest difference is that you don't need to generate the UPDATE, INSERT, and DELETE statements for the Resources data source. The Resources data is a read-only data source. To complete configuring the mapping of the CarsDB.mdb Cars table to the resources storage map set the ASPxStorage.Caption to Cars.Model, set the ASPxResourceStorage.Image to Cars.Picture, and set the ASPxResourceStorage. ResourceId to Cars.ID. The Standard Properties Mappings for the Resources data source is shown in Figure 6-6.

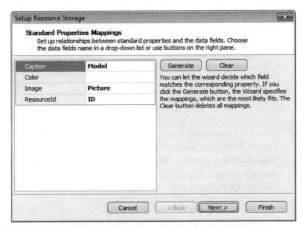

Figure 6-6: This figure illustrates how the ASPxScheduler's fields do not have to precisely map by name of number of elements to the data source; the wizard assists you in mapping your data sources to the ASPxScheduler.

Implementing the Code-Behind to Support Inserts

There isn't a tremendous amount of code-behind needed to implement the insert behavior. The user interface already supports managing appointments (or time cell items) because User Controls and pop-up menus are added when you add the scheduler. The only basic code you need to add is code to set a unique AppointmentId. The minor challenge in this instance is that the AppointmentId is mapped to the CarsScheduling.ID field, which is an auto-incremented identifier. That means that it is created by the database on insert. The events in Listing 6-1 are coordinated to read the last inserted @@IDENTITY and use that value to update the ASPxScheduler's AppointmentId, in effect, to coordinate the value set by the database with the ASPxScheduler's identifier.

Listing 6-1: The events in the listing read the auto-incremented ID set by the database and store it in an inserted Appointment's AppointmentId.

```
using System;
using System.Collections.Generic;
using System.Linq;
using System.Web;
using System.Web.UI;
using System.Web.UI.WebControls;
using System.Data.OleDb;
using DevExpress.XtraScheduler;
using DevExpress.Web.ASPxScheduler;

public partial class _Default : System.Web.UI.Page
{
  private int lastInsertedAppointmentId;
  protected void Page_Load(object sender, EventArgs e)
  {

  }
  protected void ASPxScheduler1_AppointmentRowInserted(object sender,
    DevExpress.Web.ASPxScheduler.ASPxSchedulerDataInsertedEventArgs e)
  {
    e.KeyFieldValue = this.lastInsertedAppointmentId;
  }
  protected void ASPxScheduler1_AppointmentRowInserting(object sender,
    DevExpress.Web.ASPxScheduler.ASPxSchedulerDataInsertingEventArgs e)
  {
    e.NewValues.Remove("ID");
  }
  protected void AccessDataSource1_Inserted(object sender,
    SqlDataSourceStatusEventArgs e)
  {
    OleDbConnection connection = (OleDbConnection)e.Command.Connection;
    using (OleDbCommand cmd =
      new OleDbCommand("SELECT @@IDENTITY", connection))
    {
      this.lastInsertedAppointmentId = (int)cmd.ExecuteScalar();
    }
  }

  protected void ASPxScheduler1_AppointmentsInserted(object sender,
    DevExpress.XtraScheduler.PersistentObjectsEventArgs e)
  {
    int count = e.Objects.Count;
    System.Diagnostics.Debug.Assert(count == 1);
    Appointment apt = (Appointment)e.Objects[0];
    ASPxSchedulerStorage storage = (ASPxSchedulerStorage)sender;
    storage.SetAppointmentId(apt, lastInsertedAppointmentId);
  }
}
```

The event handlers `ASPxScheduler.AppointmentRowInserting`, `AccessDataSource.Inserting`, `ASPxScheduler.AppointmentRowInserted`, and `ASPxScheduler.AppointmentsInserted` are added through the Events view of the Properties window. The events are called in the order listed in the preceding sentence.

`AppointmentRowInserting` removes the value for the ID column, if one is set. `AccessDataSource.Inserted` uses the event argument's `Command.Connection` to obtain the underlying OleDbConnection to the AccessDataSource and query the identity assigned to the last row. This value is stored in the page's local field `lastInsertedAppointmentId`. Next, the `AppointmentRowInserted` event is called and the identity is stored in the `ASPxSchedulerDataInsertedEventArgs.KeyFieldValue` argument. Finally, the `AppointmentsInserted` event is used to set the `AppointmentId`, also using the locally stored `lastInsertedAppointmentId`.

With the addition of the code for coordinating an auto-incremented database identity with the in-memory `AppointmentId`, all the CRUD behaviors of the ASPxScheduler are supported. Figure 6-7 shows the default user control displayed as a pop-up, supporting the creation (or editability) of an Appointment.

Figure 6-7: The default Appointment editor that makes up part of the ASPxScheduler suite.

The `ASPxScheduler` has a runtime context menu for the ASPxScheduler and appointment items too. The appointment items menu has options for opening an appointment (Open), editing a recurring appointment (Edit Series), restoring the default state (Restore Default State), changing how the appointment is reflected (Show Time As, with default options of Free, Tentative, Busy, or Out of Office), labeling the appointment (Label As), and deleting an appointment (Delete). If you click over a time cell area in the `ASPxScheduler`, an additional set of options for managing the time cell item is displayed to the end user; these options include adding new, recurring, and all-day appointments; searching;

changing the default view; and setting the appointment increments (see Figure 6-8). Behaviors and user controls for managing these capabilities are also added to your project at design time when you add the `ASPxScheduler`.

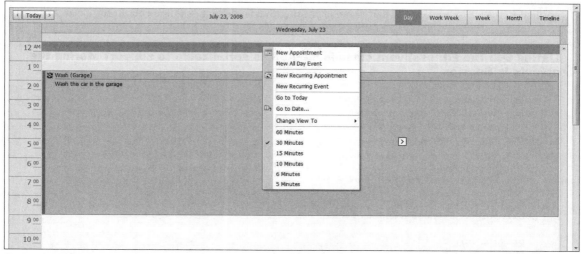

Figure 6-8: When you click over an open region in the ASPxScheduler, numerous menu items (shown) for managing the scheduler are displayed.

Using the Scheduler in List Bound Mode

Some developers use data binding to databases and some use data binding to custom controls. DevExpress controls support both models of implementation. In the previous section, binding to an AccessDataSource was demonstrated. You could just as easily have used a SqlDataSource. If you bind to database, the entities are implicit; they are table entities. If you bind to custom objects, the biggest two differences are that you have to write the entities and implement the basic behaviors of an object data source or use XPO. (XPO will write entities for you. If you want to hand-craft entities, CodeRush is a great tool for speeding that process along.)

East Lansing has one of the nicest athletic facilities I have experienced in the country. (I have lived in a lot of places, and I am sure there are many cool places to go, but if you get a chance, visit the Michigan Athletic Club in East Lansing.) The demo in this section creates a schedule demo for scheduling fitness activities. The sample uses an ObjectDataSource, custom entities, a `BindingList<T>`, and an implementation of a custom DataSource. In this sample, you learn how to populate the Resources storage and define the mappings programmatically.

Defining the Custom Entity Class

I am light years past the point where I will be writing code without CodeRush. I write code pretty fast, but I write code substantially faster with CodeRush than without. CodeRush is a meta-programming tool that is extensible and will shorten the number of key strokes it takes to codify most or all of the common code elements such as classes, fields, properties, methods, events, and interfaces. Also, if there is some code pattern that you use that isn't in CodeRush already, you can define the pattern very quickly.

The custom entity for the fitness scheduler is defined as the `FitnessEvent` class and is provided in Listing 6-2. Because `FitnessEvent` is used in a Web application, the `SerializableAttribute` is applied to the class, but besides that, there is nothing that is distinct or unique about the class.

Listing 6-2: The FitnessEvent class is marked as serializable to support storing the objects in Session.

```
using System;
using System.Collections.Generic;
using System.Collections;
using System.ComponentModel;
using System.Linq;
using System.Web;
using System.Runtime.Serialization;

[Serializable]
public class FitnessEvent
{
  private object id;
  public object Id
  {
    get
    {
      return id;
    }
    set { id = value; }
  }

  private DateTime startTime;
  public DateTime StartTime
  {
    get { return startTime; }
    set { startTime = value; }
  }

  private DateTime endTime;
  public DateTime EndTime
  {
    get { return endTime; }
    set { endTime = value; }
  }

  private string subject;
  public string Subject
  {
    get {  return subject; }
    set { subject = value;  }
  }

  private int status;
```

```
public int Status
{
  get {  return status; }
  set { status = value;  }
}

private string description;
public string Description
{
  get {  return description; }
  set { description = value;  }
}

private long label;
public long Label
{
  get {  return label; }
  set { label = value;  }
}

private string location;
public string Location
{
  get {  return location; }
  set { location = value;  }
}

private bool allDay;
public bool AllDay
{
  get {  return allDay; }
  set { allDay = value;  }
}

private int eventType;
public int EventType
{
  get {  return eventType; }
  set { eventType = value;  }
}

private string recurrenceInfo;
public string RecurrenceInfo
{
  get {  return recurrenceInfo; }
  set { recurrenceInfo = value;  }
}

private string reminderInfo;
public string ReminderInfo
{
```

Continued

Listing 6-2: The FitnessEvent class is marked as serializable to support storing the objects in Session. *(continued)*

```
      get   { return reminderInfo; }
      set
      {
        reminderInfo = value;
      }
    }

    private object ownerId;
    public object OwnerId
    {
      get   { return ownerId; }
      set
      {
        ownerId = value;
      }
    }

    private double price;
    public double Price
    {
      get   { return price; }
      set
      {
        price = value;
      }
    }

    private string contactInfo;
    public string ContactInfo
    {
      get   { return contactInfo; }
      set
      {
        contactInfo = value;
      }
    }

    public FitnessEvent()
    {
    }
  }
```

Because FitnessEvent is a new class, I can elect to name the properties pretty consistently with the Appointment fields. However, the Mapping facility in the ASPxScheduler does not make doing this a necessity. Ultimately, the mapping feature means that you can use existing classes without renaming the entity property names. (Refer to the subsection "Programmatically Defining the Appointment Mappings," later in this chapter, for more information.)

Implementing the BindingList<T> class

The generic class `BindingList<T>` is a generic collection that is specifically suited for data binding. The difference between `List<T>` and `BindingList<T>` is that `BindingList<T>` contains additional methods for adding, inserting, and removing elements from the collection, which is consistent with operations associated with data binding behaviors.

Listing 6-3 contains the implementation of the `BindingList<T>` generalization `FitnessEventList`. `FitnessEventList` is also serializable (it has the `SerializableAttribute` applied) to promote Session caching and has two additional methods added — `AddRange` and `GetEventIndex` — to simplify its use with the `ASPxScheduler`.

Listing 6-3: The BindingList<T> class FitnessEventList represents the custom collection of FitnesssEvent objects.

```
using System;
using System.Collections.Generic;
using System.Linq;
using System.Web;
using System.ComponentModel;

[Serializable]
public class FitnessEventList : BindingList<FitnessEvent>
{
  public void AddRange(FitnessEventList events)
  {
    Array.ForEach(events.ToArray(), e=>this.Add(e));
  }

  public int GetEventIndex(object eventId)
  {
    for(int i=0; i< Count; i++)
      if(this[i].Id == eventId)
        return i;
    return -1;
  }
}
```

The `FitnessEventList` is only somewhat distinct in that it uses the Array.ForEach method and the Lambda expression `e=>this.Add(e)` to add each element from an existing collection of `FitnessEvent` objects. You could just as easily use a `for` loop if you are unfamiliar with Lambda expressions or use `Parallel.ForEach` if you have downloaded and installed the Parallel extensions for .NET.

To reiterate, a Lambda expression is a more condensed version of anonymous methods. The function header and parameters are represented by the left-side argument followed by the goes to operator (=>), and the method body is represented by the right-side argument. Lambda expressions are based notationally on the mathematics of the same name and were adopted for .NET because their consolidated nature more easily fit syntactically into things like extension methods and LINQ statements.

Implementing the Custom Data Source

The ObjectDataSource component works with a custom data source. The ObjectDataSource has stubs for invoking CRUD (CREATE, READ, UPDATE, and DELETE) behaviors. The purpose of the custom data source is to implement those behaviors and associate the actual methods with the custom methods for providing CRUD relative to your custom collections and entities. This is a lot easier than it may sound.

Listing 6-4 provides an implementation of the custom data source FitnessEventDataSource. The sole purpose of FitnessEventDataSource is to provide an implementation of the insert, select, delete, and update behaviors that will be called from by the ObjectDataSource and in turn manipulate the underlying object — a FitnessEventList, in this demo.

Listing 6-4: A custom data source can be associated with an ObjectDataSource; the ObjectDataSource's CRUD behaviors will invoke the mapped insert, update, delete, and select methods of the custom data source.

```
using System;
using System.Collections.Generic;
using System.Collections;
using System.Linq;
using System.Web;

public class FitnessEventDataSource
{
  public FitnessEventDataSource(FitnessEventList events)
  {
    if (events == null)
      DevExpress.XtraScheduler.Native
        .Exceptions.ThrowArgumentNullException("events");
    this.events = events;
  }

  /// <summary>
  /// Initializes a new instance of the FitnessEventDataSource class.
  /// </summary>
  public FitnessEventDataSource()
    : this(new FitnessEventList())
  {

  }

  private FitnessEventList events;
  public FitnessEventList Events
  {
    get {  return events; }
    set { events = value;  }
  }

    #region ObjectDataSource methods
  public void InsertMethodHandler(FitnessEvent fitnessEvent)
  {
    Events.Add(fitnessEvent);
```

```
        }

        public void DeleteMethodHandler(FitnessEvent fitnessEvent)
        {
          int eventIndex = Events.GetEventIndex(fitnessEvent.Id);
          if (eventIndex >= 0)
            Events.RemoveAt(eventIndex);
        }
        public void UpdateMethodHandler(FitnessEvent fitnessEvent)
        {
          int eventIndex = Events.GetEventIndex(fitnessEvent.Id);
          if (eventIndex >= 0)
          {
            Events.RemoveAt(eventIndex);
            Events.Insert(eventIndex, fitnessEvent);
          }
        }
        public IEnumerable SelectMethodHandler()
        {
          FitnessEventList result = new FitnessEventList();
          result.AddRange(Events);
          return result;
        }
        #endregion
      }
```

The key to understanding the custom data source is that the actual data, in this case a FitnessEventList, is associated with the custom data source — FitnessEventDataSource — through the constructor call. When one of the CRUD behaviors is invoked, the relevant operation is performed on the list. For example, suppose that an ASPxScheduler is mapped to an ObjectDataSource. Next, suppose that the underlying custom data source object is associated with the FitnessEventDataSource through the ObjectDataSource's TypeName. Then you are correct in concluding that an insert operation on the ASPxScheduler daisy-chains its way through the ObjectDataSource.Insertmethod, which in turn invokes FitnessEventDataSource. InsertMethodHandler, which in turn calls FitnessEventList.Add.

For new users, all this abstraction makes using object-oriented techniques a bit more challenging, but abstraction exists for a reason. A lot of abstraction exists to promote reuse. For instance, separating data sources from controls means that the data source code can be used with other controls. And, of course, if the data source code hadn't been separated from the Microsoft controls, it would be impossible for other party providers to use those controls or provide data sources for those controls. The challenge, then, in producing classes (which includes controls and components) and frameworks is striking a balance between abstraction and simplicity. A single class can be easier to use than several classes strung together working in concert, but separating classes by layers of abstraction can promote varied orchestration and reuse. Balancing these concerns represents just some of the challenges framework designers, tools creators, and everyday programmers face.

Defining and Associating the Custom Data Source with an ObjectDataSource

The example in this section performs the data binding programmatically. To kick off the sample, add an ASPxScheduler to a Web page and add an ObjectDataSource from the Toolbox — instead of from the Smart tags menu — to the Web page.

To configure the `ObjectDataSource`, click its Smart tags menu and follow these steps:

1. In the Configure Data Source dialog box, choose the FitnessEventDataSource business object.

2. Click Next.

3. In the Define Data Methods for the SELECT tab, choose the SelectMethodHandler (see Figure 6-9) defined in the FitnessEventDataSource.

4. In the UPDATE tab, select the UpdateMethodHandler.

5. In the INSERT tab, select the InsertMethodHandler.

6. In the DELETE tab, select the DeleteMethodHandler.

7. Click Finish.

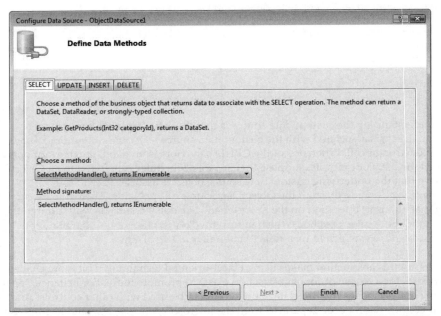

Figure 6-9: Pick the custom data source methods that provide the SELECT, UPDATE, INSERT, and DELETE behaviors, respectively.

In the background, the wizard also sets the `ObjectDataSource`'s `DataObjectTypeName` to `FitnessEvent`. The ASPX for the sample is provided in Listing 6-5. The code shows that the `ObjectDataSource`'s `TypeName` is set (by the wizard) to FitnessEventDataSource, the `DataObjectTypeName` is set to `FitnessEvent`, and the CRUD methods were set during the wizard configuration process.

Listing 6-5: The ASPX for the demo shows that the ObjectDataSource was configured by the wizard to determine the underlying type that will be manipulated by the ObjectDataSource.

```
<%@ Page Language="C#" AutoEventWireup="true"  CodeFile="Default.aspx.cs"
 Inherits="_Default" %>
<%@ Register assembly="DevExpress.Web.ASPxScheduler.v9.1,↵
 Version=9.1.4.0, Culture=neutral, PublicKeyToken=b88d1754d700e49a"
 namespace="DevExpress.Web.ASPxScheduler" tagprefix="dxwschs" %>
<%@ Register assembly="DevExpress.XtraScheduler.v9.1.Core,↵
 Version=9.1.4.0, Culture=neutral, PublicKeyToken=b88d1754d700e49a"
 namespace="DevExpress.XtraScheduler" tagprefix="dxschsc" %>

<!DOCTYPE html PUBLIC "-//W3C//DTD XHTML 1.0 Transitional//EN"
 "http://www.w3.org/TR/xhtml1/DTD/xhtml1-transitional.dtd">

<html xmlns="http://www.w3.org/1999/xhtml">
<head runat="server">
  <title></title>
</head>
<body>
  <form id="form1" runat="server">
  <div>
  <dxwschs:ASPxScheduler ID="ASPxScheduler1" runat="server"
OnAppointmentInserting="ASPxScheduler1_AppointmentInserting">
    <Views>
      <DayView>
        <TimeRulers>
          <dxschsc:TimeRuler />
        </TimeRulers>
      </DayView>
      <WorkWeekView>
        <TimeRulers>
          <dxschsc:TimeRuler />
        </TimeRulers>
      </WorkWeekView>
      <TimelineView />
    </Views>
    <Storage EnableReminders="false"></Storage>
  </dxwschs:ASPxScheduler>
    <asp:ObjectDataSource ID="ObjectDataSource1" runat="server"
    DataObjectTypeName="FitnessEvent" DeleteMethod="DeleteMethodHandler"
    InsertMethod="InsertMethodHandler" SelectMethod="SelectMethodHandler"
    TypeName="FitnessEventDataSource" UpdateMethod="UpdateMethodHandler"
    onobjectcreated="ObjectDataSource1_ObjectCreated">
    </asp:ObjectDataSource>

  </div>
  </form>
</body>
</html>
```

You can go ahead and create a stub for the `ObjectDataSource.ObjectCreated` events and the `ASPxScheduler.AppointmentInserting` events. The `ObjectCreated` event is used to associate an actual `FitnessEventDataSource` with the FitnessEventList stored in Session, and the `AppointmentInserting` event is used to set a unique identifier for the Appointment object. (Refer to the upcoming section "Completing the Code-Behind" for the implementation of these events.)

Programmatically Defining the Appointment Mappings

When you configure the `ASPxScheduler` with the ObjectDataSource, the Mappings Wizards menu item is not displayed in the Smart tags menu. You will need to write a few lines of code to correlate the properties in your custom classes with the Appointments fields. The Appointments fields remain consistent, so it's always a matter of matching the source data's properties to the Appointments fields.

The `FitnessEvent` properties were intentionally defined to closely match the Appointments' fields. Keep in mind that it is the ASPxSchedulerStorage object represented by the ASPxScheduler's Storage property that manages the Appointments, Resources, and mappings for the `ASPxScheduler`. Listing 6-6 contains a property that surfaces the `ASPxSchedulerStorage` property and a locally defined `SetupMappings` method that correlates (by assignment using the equals operator) the `FitnessEvent` properties on the right with the Appointment fields on the left.

Listing 6-6: Programmatically define the mappings between the data source and the Appointment field mappings.

```
ASPxSchedulerStorage Storage { get { return ASPxScheduler1.Storage; } }

private void SetupMappings()
{
  ASPxAppointmentMappingInfo mappings = Storage.Appointments.Mappings;
  Storage.BeginUpdate();
  try
  {
    mappings.AllDay = "AllDay";
    mappings.AppointmentId = "Id";
    mappings.Description = "Description";
    mappings.End = "EndTime";
    mappings.Label = "Label";
    mappings.Location = "Location";
    mappings.RecurrenceInfo = "RecurrenceInfo";
    mappings.ReminderInfo = "ReminderInfo";
    mappings.ResourceId = "OwnerId";
    mappings.Start = "StartTime";
    mappings.Status = "Status";
    mappings.Subject = "Subject";
    mappings.Type = "EventType";
  }
  finally
  {
    Storage.EndUpdate();
  }
}
```

The local mappings variable is actually the ASPxScheduler1.Storage.Appointments.Mappings property. BeginUpdate prevents the control from being updated until EndUpdate is called. The use of the try...finally block ensures that EndUpdate is eventually called.

Programmatically Specifying the Resources

In the AccessDataSource example in the opening sample of the chapter, both of the Appointments and Resources properties of the ASPxScheduler were bound to a data source. In the example in this section, the Appointments property is bound to an ObjectDataSource, and to change it up, the Resources data is added with code. To add basic resources, you need a unique identifier and a caption value. For a fitness calendar, the key value can be a sequential integer. A useful caption would be a name representing a fitness instructor.

The FillResources method in Listing 6-7 demonstrates how you can use something as simple as an array of strings and an incremented integer to populate the Resources data. (Of course, you can use a table or XML file to populate the resources, too.)

Listing 6-7: In this sample, the ASPxScheduler Resources are populated from a string array and the ID is an incremented integer.

```
public static string[] Users = new string[] { "Peter Dolan", "Ryan Fischer",
  "Andrew Miller", "Tom Hamlett", "Jerry Campbell", "Carl Lucas",
  "Mark Hamilton", "Steve Lee" };

    public static void FillResources(ASPxSchedulerStorage storage, int count)
    {
      ResourceCollection resources = storage.Resources.Items;
      storage.BeginUpdate();
      try
      {
        int c = Math.Min(count, Users.Length);
        for (int i = 1; i <= c; i++)
          resources.Add(new Resource(i, Users[i - 1]));
      }
      finally
      {
        storage.EndUpdate();
      }
    }
```

In Listing 6-7, the ASPxSchedulerStorage object is passed into FillResources. In Listing 6-6, the local Storage property was used. Whether you elect to use the property or pass in a reference to the property is a stylistic choice. I've shown you both styles. I generally prefer to declare and use fields and properties and keep the argument list short. Some people may prefer to pass in all the arguments that a method needs to make it obvious where a value is coming from. Again, it's a matter of style. In contrast, I pass in all the arguments only when declaring a static method.

Completing the Code-Behind

With many Web pages, the data for the page is stored in Session. A reasonable strategy is to declare a method or property returning the type of data stored in Session, and the property setter and getter manage putting the page data into and getting (and type casting) the data out of the Session object.

Listing 6-8 contains the complete listing for the sample application. GetFitnessEvents is the method that manages the Session object. GenerateFitnessEventList is the method that in a real-world application would reconstitute the business objects from whatever persistence store it resided in; in the sample, starting with an empty list is sufficient. The AppointmentInserting event handler is used just as it was used in the data-bound sample in the chapter opener: AppointmentInserting inserts a value for the AppointmentId. Because an object's hash code is *not* guaranteed to be unique, using an object's own hash code is not guaranteed to satisfy the uniqueness requirement. (Generally acceptable ways to generate unique values is to use a GUID or a table column that is incremented after each request read.) Finally, the ObjectDataSource's ObjectCreated event handler creates a specific instance of the custom data source — FitnessEventDataSource — and initializes it with the FitnessEventList object stored in the Session object.

Listing 6-8: The code-behind for the List Bound Mode of the ASPxScheduler.

```
using System;
using System.Collections.Generic;
using System.Linq;
using System.Web;
using System.Web.UI;
using System.Web.UI.WebControls;
using DevExpress.Web.ASPxScheduler;
using DevExpress.XtraScheduler;
using DevExpress.Data;
using System.Diagnostics;


public partial class _Default : System.Web.UI.Page
{
  protected void Page_Load(object sender, EventArgs e)
  {
    SetupMappings();
    FillResources(Storage, 5);
    ASPxScheduler1.AppointmentDataSource = ObjectDataSource1;
    ASPxScheduler1.DataBind();
  }

  public static string[] Users = new string[] { "Peter Dolan",
    "Ryan Fischer", "Andrew Miller", "Tom Hamlett",
    "Jerry Campbell", "Carl Lucas", "Mark Hamilton", "Steve Lee" };

  public static void FillResources(ASPxSchedulerStorage storage, int count)
  {
    ResourceCollection resources = storage.Resources.Items;
    storage.BeginUpdate();
    try
    {
```

```
      int c = Math.Min(count, Users.Length);
      for (int i = 1; i <= c; i++)
        resources.Add(new Resource(i, Users[i - 1]));
    }
    finally
    {
    storage.EndUpdate();
    }
  }


ASPxSchedulerStorage Storage { get { return ASPxScheduler1.Storage; } }

private void SetupMappings()
{
  ASPxAppointmentMappingInfo mappings = Storage.Appointments.Mappings;
  Storage.BeginUpdate();
  try
  {
    mappings.AllDay = "AllDay";
    mappings.AppointmentId = "Id";
    mappings.Description = "Description";
    mappings.End = "EndTime";
    mappings.Label = "Label";
    mappings.Location = "Location";
    mappings.RecurrenceInfo = "RecurrenceInfo";
    mappings.ReminderInfo = "ReminderInfo";
    mappings.ResourceId = "OwnerId";
    mappings.Start = "StartTime";
    mappings.Status = "Status";
    mappings.Subject = "Subject";
    mappings.Type = "EventType";
  }
  finally
  {
    Storage.EndUpdate();
  }
}


protected void ObjectDataSource1_ObjectCreated(object sender,
  ObjectDataSourceEventArgs e)
{
  e.ObjectInstance = new FitnessEventDataSource(GetFitnessEvents());

}

private FitnessEventList GetFitnessEvents()
{
  FitnessEventList events =
    Session["ListBoundModeObjects"] as FitnessEventList;
  if (events == null)
  {
```

Continued

Listing 6-8: The code-behind for the List Bound Mode of the ASPxScheduler. *(continued)*

```
      events = GenerateFitnessEventList();
      Session["ListBoundModeObjects"] = events;
    }
    return events;
}

private FitnessEventList GenerateFitnessEventList()
{
  return new FitnessEventList();
}

protected void ASPxScheduler1_AppointmentInserting(object sender,
  PersistentObjectCancelEventArgs e)
{
  ASPxSchedulerStorage storage = (ASPxSchedulerStorage)sender;
  Appointment appointment = (Appointment)e.Object;
  storage.SetAppointmentId( appointment, "a" + appointment.GetHashCode());
}
}
```

The obvious subsystem missing from the sample programming is a persistence store. Even when you use custom objects, the data is persisted somewhere. In Listing 6-8, GenerateFitnessEventList represents the stub function, in which a call can be placed to reconstitute the FitnessEvent objects from a persistence store. Probably the most common way to persist data, even if you are using custom objects, is a database. The difference is when you are using custom objects and a database there needs to be code that reads from the database and builds the custom object instances.

Exploring View Types

When I was writing the code for a custom calendar, writing code to display overlapping events and create an aesthetically pleasant user interface comprised a significant part of the effort. The ASPxScheduler already supports overlapping and simultaneous events, and painting time cell items that occur on the same date and time are managed by the ASPxScheduler. On top of that, the ASPxScheduler supports multiple kinds of views. By changing the enumerated property value ActiveViewType, you can change the default view.

ActiveViewType is defined as a SchedulerViewType. Supported view types are Day, Month, TimeLine, Week, and WorkWeek. You can change the ActiveViewType at design time in the Properties window or at runtime with code. For example, if you set the ActiveViewType to Day, you will be presented with all the appointments for a single day. By changing the time scales (by right-clicking over the calendar's appointments area) you can show time cell items at intervals of 6, 10, 15, 30, or 60 minutes.

The Day view shows appointments for a single day. The Week view shows all the appointments in a week. The WorkWeek view shows just the working days for the selected week. (To specify which days are regarded as work days, you can manipulate the ASPxScheduler.WorkDays collection.) The Month view shows all the days in the selected month, and the TimeLine view displays appointments as horizontal bars along the time scales.

Changing Work Days

Sometimes you have to put in *crunch* days — that is, work on what are considered nontraditional work days in order to meet a deadline.

The `ASPxScheduler` has a `WorkDays` property. You can programmatically manipulate the `WorkDays` property, a `WorkDaysCollection`, to change the days that are considered working days. By default, `WorkDays` are Monday to Friday, and the work days affect the days shown when the `ActiveViewType` is `SchedulerViewType.WorkWeek`. To add Saturday as a work day in the `WorkWeek` view (see Figure 6-10), add the following line of code to the `Page_Load` event:

```
ASPxScheduler1.WorkDays.Add(WeekDays.Saturday);
```

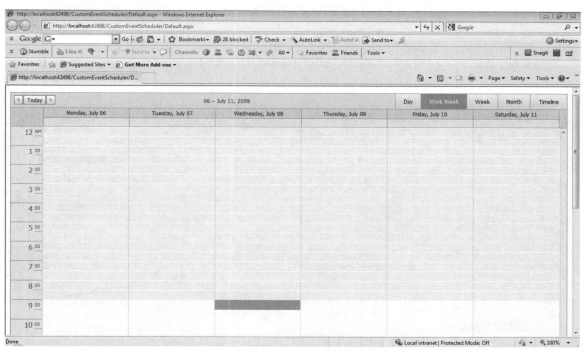

Figure 6-10: Adding WeekDays.Saturday to the WorkDays collection causes Saturday to appear when the ASPxScheduler is in WorkWeek mode.

Modifying the Holidays Collection

There are all kinds of sneaky forms of taxation in the U.S. Businesses are taxed on business income, employees are taxed on wages, people are taxed on purchases, tobacco, alcohol, toll bridges, and the list goes on and on. While new and inventive forms of taxing businesses and people seem to abound, there seem to be very few occasions for increasing or extending benefits such as employee holidays. However, in case your end users have occasion for adding to (or, tragically, deleting from) the number of nonwork holidays, the `ASPxScheduler` has built-in support standing by.

To add a holiday to the `ASPxScheduler`, call the `AddHoliday` method of the `ASPxScheduler`. `WorkDays` property, specifying the `DateTime` value and caption for the holiday. The following statement schedules my birthday in 2010 as a holiday. Here is the statement that inserts the holiday into the `WorkDays` collection:

```
ASPxScheduler1.WorkDays.AddHoliday(new DateTime(2009, 2, 12),
    "Paul's Birthday");
```

More than likely, you will be adding prescheduled holidays to the `ASPxScheduler`, and you can use code similar to the preceding statement to do so.

Using the ASPxDateNavigator

You can add an `ASPxDateNavigator` control to a Web page with an `ASPxScheduler` and use the `ASPxDateNavigator` to coordinate the selected `ASPxScheduler` date. To designate the `ASPxScheduler` that the `ASPxDateNavigator` will manipulate, set the `ASPxDateScheduler`'s `MasterSourceID` to the name of the `ASPxScheduler`. When you change the date on the `ASPxDateNavigator`, the `ASPxScheduler`'s date will reflect the navigator date (see Figure 6-11).

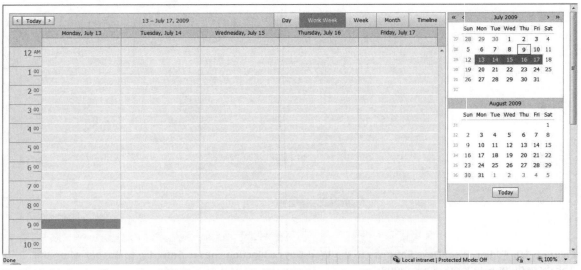

Figure 6-11: In the figure, the ASPxScheduler is in WorkWeek mode. Clicking a date in the ASPxDateNavigator sets the date in the ASPxScheduler.

When you click a date in the `ASPxDateNavigator`, it moves the `ASPxScheduler` to include the selected date, and the `ASPxDateNavigator` has dates selected that reflect the active view mode of the `ASPxScheduler`. For example, (referring to Figure 6-11), if the `ASPxScheduler` is in `WorkWeek` mode, clicking July 15, 2009 moves the `ASPxScheduler` to show the selected date, and it updates the `ASPxDateNavigator` to reflect all the selected work days in that week.

Figure 6-12 illustrates some additional features of the ASPxDateNavigator. The figure includes a description of the scroll buttons, the meaning of the numbers in the left column, and the cues to dates that contain appointments or have special associations, such as holidays.

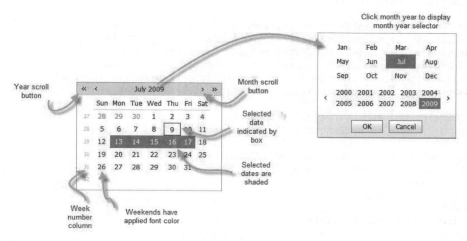

Figure 6-12: Features of the ASPxDateNavigator.

Displaying Multiple Months

The ASPxDateNavigator has basic properties that can be manipulated programmatically or in the Properties window at design time. The ASPxDateNavigator also contains a property named Properties. Properties contains the subproperty settings that are particular to the presentation of the dates and layout of the calendar items in the ASPxDateNavigator. Many of the subproperties of Properties include styles for the elements described in Figure 6-12. Of the many properties, the Rows and Columns subproperties can be set to show multiple months. For example, if you want to show two successive months in a vertical layout (see Figure 6-11), set the Properties.Rows to 2.

Most of the properties are self-explanatory and can be experimented with at design time. For example, the DayNameFormat is set to Short by default. This setting shows the abbreviated days of the week in the column header; other possible settings are Full, FirstLetter, FirstTwoLetters, and Shortest. If you want to hide the day headers altogether, set Properties.ShowDayHeaders to false. You can use the sample application DateNavigatorDemo to experiment with other property settings. (The code for the DateNavigatorDemo is basically the same as the code in Listing 6-1 with the addition of an ASPxDateNavigator, whose MasterSourceID is set to ASPxScheduler1.) Listing 6-9 contains the ASPX for the DateNavigatorDemo.

Listing 6-9: The ASPX for the DateNavigatorDemo; the code-behind is identical to the code in Listing 6-1.

```
<%@ Page Language="C#" AutoEventWireup="true"  CodeFile="Default.aspx.cs"
 Inherits="_Default" %>

<%@ Register assembly="DevExpress.Web.ASPxScheduler.v9.1,
 Version=9.1.4.0, Culture=neutral, PublicKeyToken=b88d1754d700e49a"
 namespace="DevExpress.Web.ASPxScheduler" tagprefix="dxwschs" %>
<%@ Register assembly="DevExpress.XtraScheduler.v9.1.Core,
 Version=9.1.4.0, Culture=neutral, PublicKeyToken=b88d1754d700e49a"
 namespace="DevExpress.XtraScheduler" tagprefix="dxschsc" %>

<!DOCTYPE html PUBLIC "-//W3C//DTD XHTML 1.0 Transitional//EN"
 "http://www.w3.org/TR/xhtml1/DTD/xhtml1-transitional.dtd">

<html xmlns="http://www.w3.org/1999/xhtml">
<head runat="server">
  <title></title>
</head>
<body>
  <form id="form1" runat="server">
  <div>
  <table>
    <tr>
    <td>
    <dxwschs:ASPxScheduler ID="ASPxScheduler1" runat="server"
      AppointmentDataSourceID="AccessDataSource1"
      onappointmentrowinserted="ASPxScheduler1_AppointmentRowInserted"
      onappointmentrowinserting="ASPxScheduler1_AppointmentRowInserting"
      onappointmentsinserted="ASPxScheduler1_AppointmentsInserted"
      ResourceDataSourceID="AccessDataSource2" Start="2009-07-08">
      <Storage>
      <Resources>
        <Mappings Caption="Model" ResourceId="ID" />
      </Resources>
      </Storage>
<Views>
<DayView><TimeRulers>
<dxschsc:TimeRuler></dxschsc:TimeRuler>
</TimeRulers>
</DayView>

<WorkWeekView><TimeRulers>
<dxschsc:TimeRuler></dxschsc:TimeRuler>
</TimeRulers>
</WorkWeekView>
</Views>
```

```
</dxwschs:ASPxScheduler>
<asp:AccessDataSource ID="AccessDataSource2" runat="server"
  DataFile="~/App_Data/CarsDB.mdb"
  SelectCommand="SELECT [ID], [Model] FROM [Cars]"></asp:AccessDataSource>
<asp:AccessDataSource ID="AccessDataSource1" runat="server"
  DataFile="~/App_Data/CarsDB.mdb"
  DeleteCommand="DELETE FROM [CarScheduling] WHERE [ID] = ?"
  InsertCommand="INSERT INTO [CarScheduling] ([CarId], [Status],
[Subject], [Description], [Label], [StartTime], [EndTime], [Location],
[AllDay], [EventType], [RecurrenceInfo], [ReminderInfo]) VALUES (?, ?, ?, ?,
?, ?, ?, ?, ?, ?, ?, ?)"
    oninserted="AccessDataSource1_Inserted"
  SelectCommand="SELECT [ID], [CarId], [Status], [Subject],
[Description], [Label], [StartTime], [EndTime], [Location], [AllDay],
[EventType], [RecurrenceInfo], [ReminderInfo] FROM [CarScheduling]"
  UpdateCommand="UPDATE [CarScheduling] SET [CarId] = ?, [Status] = ?,
[Subject] = ?, [Description] = ?, [Label] = ?, [StartTime] = ?, [EndTime] =
?, [Location] = ?, [AllDay] = ?, [EventType] = ?, [RecurrenceInfo] = ?,
[ReminderInfo] = ? WHERE [ID] = ?">
  <DeleteParameters>
  <asp:Parameter Name="ID" Type="Int32" />
  </DeleteParameters>
  <UpdateParameters>
  <asp:Parameter Name="CarId" Type="Int32" />
  <asp:Parameter Name="Status" Type="Int32" />
  <asp:Parameter Name="Subject" Type="String" />
  <asp:Parameter Name="Description" Type="String" />
  <asp:Parameter Name="Label" Type="Int32" />
  <asp:Parameter Name="StartTime" Type="DateTime" />
  <asp:Parameter Name="EndTime" Type="DateTime" />
  <asp:Parameter Name="Location" Type="String" />
  <asp:Parameter Name="AllDay" Type="Boolean" />
  <asp:Parameter Name="EventType" Type="Int32" />
  <asp:Parameter Name="RecurrenceInfo" Type="String" />
  <asp:Parameter Name="ReminderInfo" Type="String" />
  <asp:Parameter Name="ID" Type="Int32" />
  </UpdateParameters>
  <InsertParameters>
  <asp:Parameter Name="ID" Type="Int32" />
  <asp:Parameter Name="CarId" Type="Int32" />
  <asp:Parameter Name="Status" Type="Int32" />
  <asp:Parameter Name="Subject" Type="String" />
  <asp:Parameter Name="Description" Type="String" />
  <asp:Parameter Name="Label" Type="Int32" />
  <asp:Parameter Name="StartTime" Type="DateTime" />
  <asp:Parameter Name="EndTime" Type="DateTime" />
  <asp:Parameter Name="Location" Type="String" />
  <asp:Parameter Name="AllDay" Type="Boolean" />
  <asp:Parameter Name="EventType" Type="Int32" />
  <asp:Parameter Name="RecurrenceInfo" Type="String" />
  <asp:Parameter Name="ReminderInfo" Type="String" />
```

Continued

313

Listing 6-9: The ASPX for the DateNavigatorDemo; the code-behind is identical to the code in Listing 6-1. *(continued)*

```
        </InsertParameters>
      </asp:AccessDataSource>
      </td>
      <td valign="top">
      <dxwschs:ASPxDateNavigator ID="ASPxDateNavigator1" runat="server"
        MasterControlID="ASPxScheduler1">
        <Properties Rows="2">
        </Properties>
      </dxwschs:ASPxDateNavigator>
      </td>
      </tr>
    </table>
    </div>
    </form>
  </body>
</html>
```

Changing the Active View with Client-Side Script

The ASPxScheduler supports a ClientInstanceName and, as a client-side equivalent, the ASPxClientScheduler. You can use the client function capabilities to implement client-side events. For instance, if you set the ASPxScheduler's Options.ShowViewSelector = false, hiding the ASPxScheduler's view selector, you could make view selection available through a menu option and client-side script.

The example in this section uses the CarsDB.mdb database for the scheduler's appointments and adds an ASPxMenu to the Web page containing the ASPxScheduler. The ASPxMenu has a View root menu and Day View Week View, Work Week View, Month View, and Timeline View menu items. Clicking any one of the menu items invokes the ItemClick client-side event. The client-side event uses an array and the menu item's index to obtain the view name and sets the active view from a client-side call (see Listing 6-10).

Listing 6-10: Add this element to the ASPxMenu to set the active view type from a client-side menu event.

```
<ClientSideEvents ItemClick="function(s, e) {
  debugger;
  var items = new Array('Day', 'Week', 'WorkWeek',
    'Month', 'Timeline');
  Scheduler.SetActiveViewType(items[e.item.index]);
}" />
```

Keep in mind that the ClientSideEvents property has a built-in script editor that emits script as a string (see Listing 6-10) and binds the event at runtime.

All the code for this demo can be found in the SchedulerClientScriptDemo project.

In the preceding code, the `debugger` statement can be removed after the script has been tested. The Array implicitly associates each of the view types with an index that coincides with the `ASPxMenu`'s placement of each menu item. The event argument `e` contains the clicked item, which in turn has the menu item's index. The `index` property is used to index the `Array` items, and the `ASPxScheduler`'s `ClientInstanceName` is used to invoke the `SetActiveViewType` method. (A series of if-condition tests could be used to implement the same behavior; I like the Array usage for its brevity.)

Grouping Schedule Events with the ASPxResourceNavigator

The `ASPxResourceNavigator` is a stand-alone control that can be associated with the `ASPxScheduler` through its `MasterControlID` (a string); it is also embedded in the `ASPxScheduler`. If you set `ASPxScheduler.GroupType` to `Date` or `Resource` and the `ASPxScheduler.ResourceNavigator. Visibility` is anything but `Never`, the `ASPxResourceNavigator` will be displayed in the `ASPxScheduler` (see Figure 6-13) and the schedule items will be grouped by Date or Resource depending on your selection.

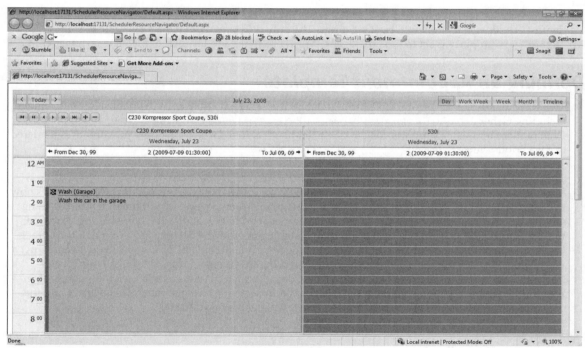

Figure 6-13: The ASPxScheduler with GroupType set to Resource divides the scheduler appointment region by resource groups.

The sample is showing two resources at a time, which is managed by the `ASPxScheduler` `.Views.`*viewtype*`.ResourcesPerPage` property. For example, setting `ASPxScheduler.Views` `.DayView.ResourcesPerPage = 2` will split the DayView in half, showing two of the resources at a time. The `ASPxResourceNavigator` extracted in Figure 6-14 supports navigation through resources. For instance, if `ResourcesPerPage` is set to 2, when the user clicks the Next (the single right-arrow) navigator button, the next two resources for the current date will be displayed and the appointments for those resources will be displayed while the date remains unchanged.

Current Resources

First, Previous Page, Previous, Next, Next Page, Last. Increase visible resource count, Decrease visible count

Figure 6-14: The ASPxResourceNavigator buttons change the view to show schedule items based on the selected resource or resources.

The `SchedulerResourceNavigator` sample uses the CarsDB.mdb database and is basically the same demo — code-wise — shown in earlier listings. The only difference is that the `ASPxScheduler` `.GroupType` property is set to `Resource`, and `ResourcesPerPage` for each of the view types is set to 2.

Defining an Appointment Template

The `ASPxScheduler` is customizable through templates. There are dozens of definable template regions, including General, `DayView`, `WorkWeekView`, `WeekView`, `MonthView`, and `TimelineView` templates. Each of these templates supports customizable template regions for defining how the content is rendered in the various views.

There is an online sample (at `http://demos.devexpress.com/ASPxSchedulerDemos/Templates/` `AppointmentTemplate.aspx`, and it is installed with your DevExpress controls) that demonstrates how to create a custom template. That sample meticulously constructs several appointment templates using an HTML `<table>` adding graphics for rounded corners and background filters for shading. A reason for using an HTML table in this instance is that the table can easily be designed to expand and contract to fill the size of the time cell area. In this section, the SchedulerTemplateDemo shows how to construct a `VerticalAppointmentTemplate` for the DayView using the `ASPxRoundPanel` and a UserControl. (Refer to Figure 6-15 for the results.) Using a UserControl for templates is a little easier than designing the template in the region provided in the designer because you get independent design space and the convenience of separating the code-behind for the template in its own file.

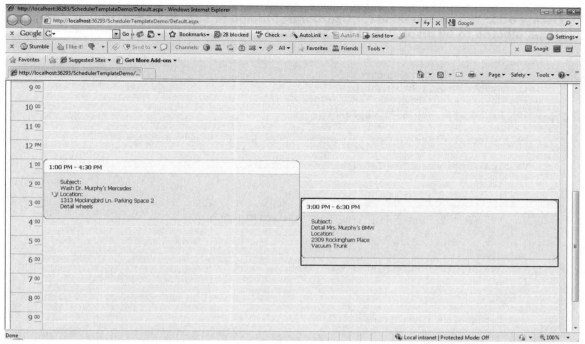

Figure 6-15: The VerticalAppointmentTemplate designed using an ASPxRoundPanel, shown in the DayView for the ASPxScheduler.

Implementing the UserControl Template

If a template contains just a few controls with some simple binding statements, you can easily define the template in the template designer region of a control right in the Web page. If a template needs some code and has quite a few controls, I find using a separate UserControl easier.

Templates for the ASPxScheduler generally will have to bind data to the controls you place in the template, render images associated with the appointment, and display customized information such as header text. The code in Listing 6-11 contains the code-behind that manipulates a label for the Subject, Location, and Description of a template and placeholder HTML <table> for the appointment's images. The ASPX in Listing 6-12 shows the orchestration and placement of the aforementioned elements all nested inside an ASPxRoundPanel.

Listing 6-11: The code-behind for UserControl-template sets the appointment data items elected to be displayed in the template.

```
using System;
using System.Web.UI.WebControls;
using System.Web.UI.HtmlControls;
using DevExpress.Web.ASPxScheduler.Drawing;
using DevExpress.Web.ASPxScheduler;

public partial class DayAppointment : System.Web.UI.UserControl
{
  VerticalAppointmentTemplateContainer Container
  {
    get
    {
      return (VerticalAppointmentTemplateContainer)Parent;
    }
  }

  VerticalAppointmentTemplateItems Items
  {
    get
    {
      return Container.Items;
    }
  }

  protected void Page_Load(object sender, EventArgs e)
  {
    ASPxRoundPanel1.HeaderText = GetHeaderText();
    Subject.Text = Container.AppointmentViewInfo.Appointment.Subject;
    Location.Text = Container.AppointmentViewInfo.Appointment.Location;
    Description.Text = Container.AppointmentViewInfo.Appointment.Description;

    LayoutAppointmentImages();
  }

  private string GetHeaderText()
  {
    string start =
      Container.AppointmentViewInfo.AppointmentInterval
      Start.ToShortTimeString();
    string end =
Container.AppointmentViewInfo.Appointment.End.ToShortTimeString();
    return String.Format("{0} - {1}", start, end);
  }

  private void LayoutAppointmentImages()
  {
    int count = Items.Images.Count;
    for (int i = 0; i < count; i++)
    {
      HtmlTableRow row = new HtmlTableRow();
```

```
        HtmlTableCell cell = new HtmlTableCell();
        AddImage(cell, Items.Images[i]);
        row.Cells.Add(cell);
        imageContainer.Rows.Add(row);
      }
    }

    private void AddImage(HtmlTableCell targetCell,
      AppointmentImageItem imageItem)
    {
      Image image = new Image();
      imageItem.ImageProperties.AssignToControl(image, false);
      targetCell.Controls.Add(image);
    }
  }
```

Listing 6-12: The ASPX that defines the layout of the UserControl.

```
<%@ Control Language="C#" AutoEventWireup="true"
 CodeFile="DayAppointment.ascx.cs" Inherits="DayAppointment" %>
<%@ Register assembly="DevExpress.Web.v9.1, Version=9.1.4.0,↵
 Culture=neutral, PublicKeyToken=b88d1754d700e49a"
 namespace="DevExpress.Web.ASPxRoundPanel" tagprefix="dxrp" %>
<%@ Register assembly="DevExpress.Web.v9.1, Version=9.1.4.0,↵
 Culture=neutral, PublicKeyToken=b88d1754d700e49a"
 namespace="DevExpress.Web.ASPxPanel" tagprefix="dxp" %>
<%@ Register assembly="DevExpress.Web.ASPxEditors.v9.1,↵
 Version=9.1.4.0, Culture=neutral, PublicKeyToken=b88d1754d700e49a"
 namespace="DevExpress.Web.ASPxEditors" tagprefix="dxe" %>
<dxrp:ASPxRoundPanel ID="ASPxRoundPanel1" runat="server" Width="100%" Height="100%"
  BackColor="#EBF2F4" CssFilePath="~/App_Themes/Glass/{0}/styles.css"
  CssPostfix="Glass"
  style="filter: alpha(opacity=80)"
  >
  <BottomRightCorner Height="10px"
  Url="~/Images/ASPxRoundPanel/1867795062/BottomRightCorner.png"
  Width="10px" />
  <ContentPaddings PaddingBottom="10px" PaddingLeft="4px" PaddingTop="10px" />
  <NoHeaderTopRightCorner Height="10px"
  Url="~/Images/ASPxRoundPanel/1867795062/NoHeaderTopRightCorner.png"
  Width="10px" />
  <HeaderRightEdge>
  <BackgroundImage
 ImageUrl="~/Images/ASPxRoundPanel/1867795062/HeaderRightEdge.png"
    VerticalPosition="bottom" HorizontalPosition="right" Repeat="NoRepeat" />
  </HeaderRightEdge>
  <Border BorderColor="#7EACB1" BorderStyle="Solid" BorderWidth="1px" />
  <HeaderLeftEdge>
  <BackgroundImage ImageUrl="~/Images/ASPxRoundPanel/1867795062/HeaderLeftEdge.png"
    Repeat="NoRepeat" VerticalPosition="bottom" HorizontalPosition="left" />
  </HeaderLeftEdge>
```

Continued

319

Listing 6-12: The ASPX that defines the layout of the UserControl. *(continued)*

```
                    <HeaderStyle BackColor="White" Height="23px">
                    <Paddings PaddingBottom="0px" PaddingLeft="2px" PaddingTop="0px" />
                    <BorderLeft BorderStyle="None" />
                    <BorderRight BorderStyle="None" />
                    <BorderBottom BorderStyle="None" />
                    </HeaderStyle>
                    <TopRightCorner Height="10px"
                      Url="~/Images/ASPxRoundPanel/1867795062/TopRightCorner.png"
                    Width="10px" />
                    <HeaderContent>
                    <BackgroundImage ImageUrl="~/Images/ASPxRoundPanel/1867795062/HeaderContent.png"
                      Repeat="RepeatX" VerticalPosition="bottom" HorizontalPosition="left" />
                    </HeaderContent>
                    <NoHeaderTopEdge BackColor="#EBF2F4">
                    </NoHeaderTopEdge>
                    <NoHeaderTopLeftCorner Height="10px"
                    Url="~/Images/ASPxRoundPanel/1867795062/NoHeaderTopLeftCorner.png"
                    Width="10px" />
                    <PanelCollection>
            <dxp:PanelContent runat="server">
                    <table>
                    <tr>
                      <td>
                      <table id="imageContainer" runat="server" cellpadding="1"
                        cellspacing="0" style="text-align: center">
                        <tr>
                        <td></td>
                        </tr>
                      </table>
                      </td>
                      <td>
                      <div>
                      Subject:
                      </div>
                      <div>
                      <dxe:ASPxLabel ID="Subject" runat="server" Text="ASPxLabel">
                      </dxe:ASPxLabel>
                      </div>
                      <div>
                      Location:
                      </div>
                      <div>
                      <dxe:ASPxLabel ID="Location" runat="server" Text="ASPxLabel">
                      </dxe:ASPxLabel>
                      </div>
                      <div>
                      <dxe:ASPxLabel ID="Description" runat="server" Text="ASPxLabel">
                      </dxe:ASPxLabel>
                      </div>
                      </td>
                    </tr>
                  </table>
```

```
      </dxp:PanelContent>
   </PanelCollection>
     <TopLeftCorner Height="10px"
       Url="~/Images/ASPxRoundPanel/1867795062/TopLeftCorner.png"
     Width="10px" />
     <BottomLeftCorner Height="10px"
     Url="~/Images/ASPxRoundPanel/1867795062/BottomLeftCorner.png" Width="10px" />
   </dxrp:ASPxRoundPanel>
```

The ASPX is generated by actions in the designer. Of note for the ASPX are the literal graphic elements — image URLs — for the ASPXRoundPanel. I manipulated the ASPxRoundPanel using the ASPxRoundPanel's Smart tags designer, which caused those elements to be added. The other noteworthy fragment in the ASPX are the two HTML table elements added. The table element with the id imageContaineris used as a placeholder for dynamic insertion of the appointment-relevant images, and the other table element is used to simplify managing the layout of the ASPxLabel controls that display the appointment text.

> In the book Blink: The Power of Thinking Without Thinking, by Malcolm Gladwell, one section of the book talks about how people mind read — not quite literally — by examining facial expressions. We detect anger, jealousy, happiness, and the truth of what someone is saying by genuine reflected facial expressions. Gladwell talks about the research that went into naming each element of expressions. By providing names for things, experts can more precisely describe the meaning of something. In Gladwell's example, names are given for each element of a facial expression. Software developers do the same thing; names are provided to convey a more precise meaning.

> When I write surfacing when referring to a constituent property, it literally means adding a property or method for a nested element that flattens out access to that element. For example, in Listing 6-11, the Container.Items property is flattened out as Items, reducing the amount of typing needed to access Container.Items. Surfacing is also useful if you want constituent properties to appear from the outside — by users, in this case of the UserControl — as first-class members of the containing class itself.

The interesting code is contained in Listing 6-11. The VerticalAppointTemplateContainer surfaces the UserControl's parent container, providing easier access to template control containing this UserControl. The VerticalAppointmentTemplateItems surfaces the Container.Items property. In the example, surfacing the Items sub-property only makes it easier for you to access Container.Items in the UserControl. If you made the member public, Container.Items would be accessible outside the UserControl, too.

The Page_Load event calls GetHeaderText to fill in the ASPxRoundPanel's HeaderText, and each of the Subject, Location, and Description ASPxLabels is populated from the Appointment object associated with each instance of the UserControl. Finally, LayoutAppointmentImages is called to render relevant images, such as reminder icons, associated with the Appointment.

The method GetHeaderText formats the Appointment's Start and End time. This string value is displayed in the ASPxRoundPanel's header (see Figure 6-15).

LayoutAppointmentImages is a micro HTML renderer. For each image associated with an Appointment, a new HtmlTableRow and HtmlTableCell are added to the placeholder (<table>) imageContainer and painted in that cell by AddImage. Finally, AddImage creates an image and renders it in the newly created table cell.

321

Incorporating the Template in the ASPxScheduler's DayView

To use the template UserControl for a specific ASPxScheduler template region, you can drag and drop it into that template region or you can add the @Register element to the Web page that will use the UserControl and add the template tag manually. The complete Web page for this sample is basically the same ASPxScheduler example with the CarsDB.mdb file listed and referenced several times through this chapter, so the complete ASPX and code-behind listing are not relisted here. Instead, @Register statement is provided as well as the fragment that shows the declaration of the template region for the ASPxScheduler's DayView.

```
<%@ Register Src="~/UserControls/DayAppointment.ascx"
  TagName="DayAppointment" TagPrefix="va" %>
```

Add the @Register tag to the top section of the Web page after the @Page directive. The Src defines the relative path to the UserControl. The TagName is the name used to reference the control in the ASPX, and the TagPrefix is used as part of the tag name to distinguish between elements that may have the same TagName. Here is the fragment that shows how to incorporate the UserControl into the template region:

```
<Views>
<DayView ><TimeRulers>
<dxschsc:TimeRuler></dxschsc:TimeRuler>
</TimeRulers>
<Templates>
 <VerticalAppointmentTemplate>
   <va:DayAppointment runat="server"/>
 </VerticalAppointmentTemplate>
</Templates>
</DayView>
```

The basic DayView displays appointment items vertically. Other view templates have variations of the <VerticalAppointmentTemplate> tag. When you define other kinds of templates for the other views, the biggest difference will be the actual name of the template tag. If you drag and drop UserControl into the template at design time, the designer will take care of the @Register statement, including the TagName, TagPrefix, and Src, and properly define the ASPX for the template region's ASPX for you.

Exporting and Importing a Calendar

You can export and import the appointments in an ASPxScheduler using the iCalendarExporter and iCalendarImporter classes. The basic solution for exporting is to initialize an iCalendarExporter with the ASPxSchedulerStorage object and send the data to a stream object. For example, to write the appointment data to a file, call iCalendarExporter.Export, passing an instance of a FileStream object to the Export method. You could invoke the export (or import) behavior with a postback through a menu or button or an asynchronous callback using the ASPxCallback.

The `ASPxScheduler` also has predefined commands that can be called with the `RaiseCallback` method. The syntax for `RaiseCallback` is <command identifier>|<command delimited parameters>. (Refer to the help documentation `ms-help://MS.VSCC.v90/MS.VSIPCC.v90/DevExpress.NETv9.1/DevExpress.ASPxScheduler/CustomDocument5462.htm` for detailed information on the `ASPxScheduler` Callback Commands.) For instance, to initiate an asynchronous export, add an `ASPxButton` and in the client-side Click event, call `ASPxScheduler.RaiseCallback`, passing `EXPORTAPT|` in the `RaiseCallback` method. I used a `ClientInstanceName` of `Scheduler`. Listing 6-13 shows the `ASPxButton`'s `ClientSideEvents` attribute with the definition of the JavaScript that invokes the callback.

Listing 6-13: The ClientSideEvents attribute that contains the definition of the JavaScript that initiates the asynchronous callback.

```
<dxe:ASPxButton ID="ASPxButton1" runat="server" Text="Export Calendar">
<ClientSideEvents Click="function(s, e) {
    debugger;
    Scheduler.RaiseCallback('EXPORTAPT|');
}" />
</dxe:ASPxButton>
```

When `RaiseCallback` is called, the `ASPxScheduler`'s `BeforeExecuteCallbackCommand` event is called. The `SchedulerCallbackCommandEventArgs` has a `CommandId` property. When you invoke `RaiseCallback` with `EXPORTAPT|`, the `CommandId` will be `EXPORTAPT` (without the |). When `EXPORTAPT` is the command, you can initiate the export behavior.

The `SchedulerCallbackCommand` is the base class for all scheduler callback commands. By assigning a custom `SchedulerCallbackCommand` class to the `SchedulerCallbackCommandEventArgs.Command`, the callback behavior will be rerouted from the default `ASPxScheduler` behavior for that command (or a given command) and routed to your custom `SchedulerCallbackCommand`. By implementing custom subclasses of `SchedulerCallbackCommand`, you can effectively replace intrinsic `ASPxScheduler` behavior with new behaviors. Listing 6-14 contains the implementation of the `BeforeExecuteCallbackCommand` event handler for the page containing the `ASPxScheduler`, and Listing 6-15 contains the separate `SchedulerCallbackCommand` subclass.

Listing 6-14: The BeforeExecuteCallbackCommand event replaces the behavior for EXPORTAPT command with the custom ExportAppointmentCallbackCommand.

```
protected void ASPxScheduler1_BeforeExecuteCallbackCommand(
  object sender, SchedulerCallbackCommandEventArgs e)
  {
    if (e.CommandId == "EXPORTAPT")
    {
      ExportAppointmentCallbackCommand command =
        new ExportAppointmentCallbackCommand((ASPxScheduler)sender);
      command.Path = Server.MapPath("~/");
      e.Command = command;
    }
  }
```

Listing 6-15: This code contains the custom SchedulerCallbackCommand class that provides export-to-file behavior.

```
public class ExportAppointmentCallbackCommand : SchedulerCallbackCommand
{
    public ExportAppointmentCallbackCommand(ASPxScheduler control)
        : base(control)
    {
    }

    public override string Id { get { return "EXPORTAPT"; } }

    private string path;
    public string Path
    {
        get { return path; }
        set { path = value; }
    }

    protected override void ParseParameters(string parameters)
    {
    }

    protected override void ExecuteCore()
    {
        ExportCalendar();
    }

    private void ExportCalendar()
    {
        iCalendarExporter exporter =
            new iCalendarExporter(Control.Storage);
        FileStream stream =
            new FileStream(path + "Calendar.ics", FileMode.CreateNew);
        exporter.Export(stream);
    }
}
```

After the `BeforeExecuteCallbackCommand` event fires, the `ASPxScheduler` command behavior will be invoked. Because the default behavior was replaced with the `ExportAppointmentCallbackCommand`, it is the `ExportAppointmentCallbackCommand`-defined behavior that will be initiated. The `ExecuteCore` behavior method is invoked. In the `ExportAppointmentCallbackCommand.ExecuteCore` method invokes `ExportCalendar`. `ExportCalendar` creates an instance of `iCalendarExporter`, initializing it with the `ASPxSchedulerStorage` object and a `FileStream` object. The `FileStream` is passed to the `iCalendarExporter.Export` method, resulting in the contents of the `ASPxScheduler` being written to a file.

If you double-click the exported .ics file in Windows Explorer, the contents will be opened. (By default, ics files are associated with Microsoft Outlook. Figure 6-16 shows how the `ASPxScheduler`'s contents — running on my machine — look in Microsoft Outlook 2007.)

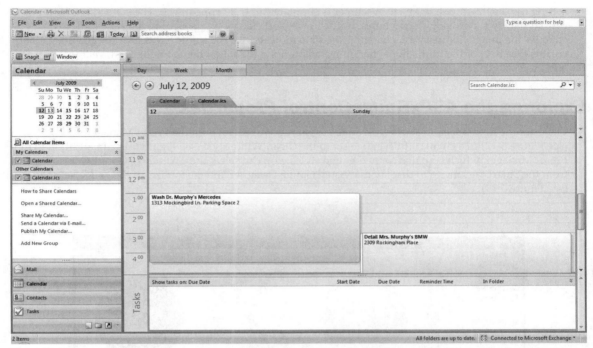

Figure 6-16: The Calendar.ics opened (by double-clicking the .ics file) in Microsoft Outlook, showing the exported appointments from the ASPxScheduler demo (SchedulerTemplateDemo).

The .ics file format is a file extension used to designate a file containing calendaring and scheduling information associated with the iCalendar format.

Using the ASPxGaugeControl

I was leaving Yoga class at the Michigan Athletic Club one night at about 8:15 p.m., and parked next to my car was a beautiful Maserati GranTurismo, black with red interior trim. I didn't gawk too much because I didn't want to exhibit such obvious car envy, but the Maserati GranTurismo — I think it was the S type — is about as sexy an automobile as I have seen. (Check out `www.maserati.com` to see pictures of the Maserati models.) I didn't check out the interior of the Maserati — the gawking thing again — but I imagine that the Pininfarina finish on the interior is as cool as the exterior.

As far as I know, Pininfarina had nothing to do with the design of our `ASPxGaugeControl`, but the developers who worked on the `ASPxGaugeControl` went to a lot of trouble to incorporate flexibility and variety, and they produced some pretty sweet-looking gauges. The `ASPxGaugeControl` can be configured to display circular, linear, digital, and state indicator gauges. For the circular and linear gauges, you can specify attributes such as the scale, range bar and marker features, state indicators, labels, and ranges. For digital gauges, you can specify the digit count and display mode. For example, setting the display mode to fourteen segments simulates an LCD appearance. The state indicator mode displays arrows, currency, flags, smiles, traffic lights, and electric lights. Setting the state indicator changes the image; for instance, changing the state indicator for the traffic lights changes the image that creates the effect of the traffic light changing states among the following: no lights, red, yellow, and green.

Exploring the ASPxGaugeControl Properties

The example in this section starts with an `ASPxGaugeControl` set with the Preset Manager (see Figure 6-17) to a circular (full) gauge set to the Clean White style (see Figure 6-18). In addition to the Preset Manager, which contains canned gauge styles, you can select the Customize Gauge Control item from the Smart tags menu to display the Visual Gauge Designer and customize all the gauge settings (see Figure 6-19).

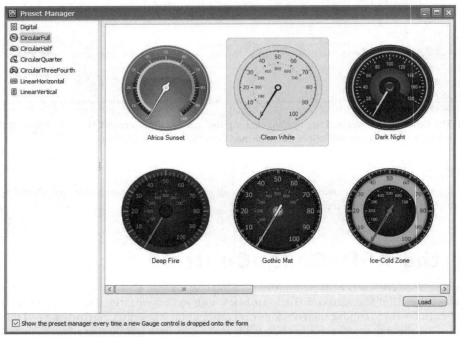

Figure 6-17: The Preset Manager (accessible from the ASPxGaugeControl's Smart tags menu) lets you quickly and easily choose from the available gauge types and styles within those types.

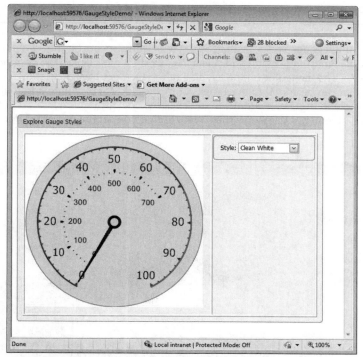

Figure 6-18: The sample application is designed to let you choose a style, and all the properties that create the style's appearance are applied to the ASPxGaugeControl.

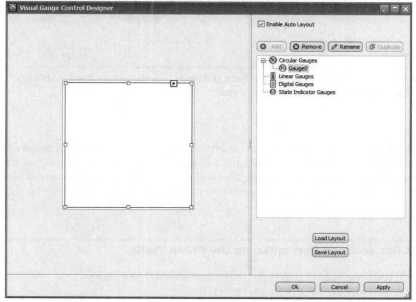

Figure 6-19: The Visual Gauge Control Designer is a comprehensive designer that facilitates designing every element of a gauge from the ground up.

When you use one of the gauge styles, a small Smart tags icon appears on the gauge (refer to Figure 6-19). Click the Smart tags menu and select Run Designer to display the designer for that gauge type (see Figure 6-20). The navigator on the left side of the Element Designer (shown in Figure 6-20) contains elements that can be added to the gauge. Click the Add (+) button to add that element to the gauge you are assembling. For example, if you click the Background Layers Add (+) button, the Background Layers – Element Designer is displayed, letting you set the properties for that element.

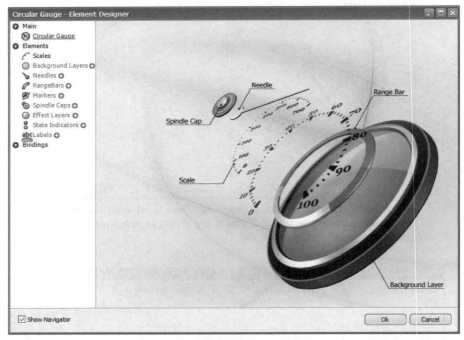

Figure 6-20: The (Circular Gauge) Element Designer is accessed by the Smart tags menu item after a gauge has been selected.

After you painstakingly select and set every element of your custom gauge, you can save the layout (refer to Figure 6-19) to an XML file. The XML file will contain all the details of designer configuration settings. Listing 6-16 contains the XML listing for all of the property settings that make up the Clean White style, clearly illustrating the extensive possibilities available for creating custom gauge appearances.

Listing 6-16: The settings that make up the Clean White.

```
<XtraSerializer version="1.0" application="IGaugeContainer">
  <property name="AutoLayout">true</property>
  <property name="SizeEx">@3,Width=350@3,Height=350</property>
  <property name="Items" iskey="true" value="5">
```

```xml
<property name="Item1" isnull="true" iskey="true">
  <property name="ParentCollectionName">Gauges</property>
  <property name="Name">cGauge1</property>
  <property name="TypeNameEx">CircularGauge</property>
  <property name="Bounds">@1,X=6@1,Y=6@3,Width=338@3,Height=338</property>
  <property name="ParentName" />
  <property name="ProportionalStretch">true</property>
</property>
<property name="Item2" isnull="true" iskey="true">
  <property name="MajorTickCount">11</property>
  <property name="MajorTickmark" isnull="true" iskey="true">
    <property name="ShowFirst">true</property>
    <property name="ShowTick">true</property>
    <property name="ShapeType">Circular_Style11_4</property>
    <property name="ShapeOffset">-5</property>
    <property name="ShapeScale">0.6, 0.8</property>
    <property name="ShowLast">true</property>
    <property name="ShowText">true</property>
    <property name="FormatString">{0:F0}</property>
    <property name="TextOrientation">LeftToRight</property>
    <property name="AllowTickOverlap">false</property>
    <property name="TextOffset">-17</property>
  </property>
  <property name="Ranges" iskey="true" value="0" />
  <property name="Labels" iskey="true" value="0" />
  <property name="MaxValue">100</property>
  <property name="MinValue">0</property>
  <property name="MinorTickCount">4</property>
  <property name="MinorTickmark" isnull="true" iskey="true">
    <property name="ShowFirst">true</property>
    <property name="ShapeOffset">-2.5</property>
    <property name="ShapeScale">0.6, 1</property>
    <property name="ShowTick">true</property>
    <property name="ShowLast">true</property>
    <property name="ShapeType">Circular_Style11_3</property>
  </property>
  <property name="BoundElementName" isnull="true" />
  <property name="ParentCollectionName">Scales</property>
  <property name="Name">scale1</property>
  <property name="TypeNameEx">ArcScaleComponent</property>
  <property name="Shader" isnull="true" iskey="true">
    <property name="TypeTag">Empty</property>
  </property>
  <property name="Enabled" isnull="true" iskey="true" />
  <property name="ParentName">cGauge1</property>
  <property name="ZOrder">0</property>
  <property name="EndAngle">60</property>
  <property name="AppearanceMajorTickmark" isnull="true" iskey="true">
    <property name="BorderWidth">0</property>
    <property name="ContentBrush" isnull="true" iskey="true" />
    <property name="BorderBrush" isnull="true" iskey="true" />
  </property>
  <property name="AppearanceTickmarkTextBackground" isnull="true" iskey="true">
```

Continued

Listing 6-16: The settings that make up the Clean White. *(continued)*

```xml
      <property name="BorderWidth">0</property>
      <property name="ContentBrush" isnull="true" iskey="true" />
      <property name="BorderBrush" isnull="true" iskey="true" />
    </property>
    <property name="Center">125, 125</property>
    <property name="AppearanceScale" isnull="true" iskey="true">
      <property name="Width">0</property>
      <property name="Brush" isnull="true" iskey="true" />
    </property>
    <property name="AppearanceMinorTickmark" isnull="true" iskey="true">
      <property name="BorderWidth">0</property>
      <property name="ContentBrush" isnull="true" iskey="true" />
      <property name="BorderBrush" isnull="true" iskey="true" />
    </property>
    <property name="Appearance" isnull="true" iskey="true">
      <property name="Width">0</property>
      <property name="Brush" isnull="true" iskey="true" />
    </property>
    <property name="RadiusY">107</property>
    <property name="StartAngle">-240</property>
    <property name="RadiusX">107</property>
    <property name="AppearanceTickmarkText" isnull="true" iskey="true">
      <property name="Format" isnull="true" iskey="true">
        <property name="Trimming">Character</property>
        <property name="FormatFlags">NoClip</property>
        <property name="Alignment">Center</property>
        <property name="LineAlignment">Center</property>
      </property>
      <property name="TextBrush" isnull="true" iskey="true">
        <property name="Color">Black</property>
      </property>
      <property name="Font">Tahoma, 12pt</property>
      <property name="Spacing">0, 0, 0, 0</property>
    </property>
    <property name="Value">0</property>
  </property>
  <property name="Item3" isnull="true" iskey="true">
    <property name="MajorTickCount">8</property>
    <property name="MajorTickmark" isnull="true" iskey="true">
      <property name="ShowFirst">true</property>
      <property name="ShowTick">true</property>
      <property name="ShapeType">Circular_Style11_2</property>
      <property name="ShapeOffset">0</property>
      <property name="ShapeScale">1, 1</property>
      <property name="ShowLast">true</property>
      <property name="ShowText">true</property>
      <property name="FormatString">{0:F0}</property>
      <property name="TextOrientation">LeftToRight</property>
      <property name="AllowTickOverlap">false</property>
      <property name="TextOffset">-15</property>
    </property>
    <property name="Ranges" iskey="true" value="0" />
```

```xml
<property name="Labels" iskey="true" value="0" />
<property name="MaxValue">700</property>
<property name="MinValue">0</property>
<property name="MinorTickCount">4</property>
<property name="MinorTickmark" isnull="true" iskey="true">
  <property name="ShowFirst">true</property>
  <property name="ShapeOffset">0</property>
  <property name="ShapeScale">1, 1</property>
  <property name="ShowTick">true</property>
  <property name="ShowLast">true</property>
  <property name="ShapeType">Circular_Style11_1</property>
</property>
<property name="BoundElementName" isnull="true" />
<property name="ParentCollectionName">Scales</property>
<property name="Name">scale2</property>
<property name="TypeNameEx">ArcScaleComponent</property>
<property name="Shader" isnull="true" iskey="true">
  <property name="TypeTag">Empty</property>
</property>
<property name="Enabled" isnull="true" iskey="true" />
<property name="ParentName">cGauge1</property>
<property name="ZOrder">-1</property>
<property name="EndAngle">-30</property>
<property name="AppearanceMajorTickmark" isnull="true" iskey="true">
  <property name="BorderWidth">0</property>
  <property name="ContentBrush" isnull="true" iskey="true" />
  <property name="BorderBrush" isnull="true" iskey="true" />
</property>
<property name="AppearanceTickmarkTextBackground" isnull="true" iskey="true">
  <property name="BorderWidth">0</property>
  <property name="ContentBrush" isnull="true" iskey="true" />
  <property name="BorderBrush" isnull="true" iskey="true" />
</property>
<property name="Center">125, 125</property>
<property name="AppearanceScale" isnull="true" iskey="true">
  <property name="Width">0</property>
  <property name="Brush" isnull="true" iskey="true" />
</property>
<property name="AppearanceMinorTickmark" isnull="true" iskey="true">
  <property name="BorderWidth">0</property>
  <property name="ContentBrush" isnull="true" iskey="true" />
  <property name="BorderBrush" isnull="true" iskey="true" />
</property>
<property name="Appearance" isnull="true" iskey="true">
  <property name="Width">0</property>
  <property name="Brush" isnull="true" iskey="true" />
</property>
<property name="RadiusY">70</property>
<property name="StartAngle">-240</property>
<property name="RadiusX">70</property>
<property name="AppearanceTickmarkText" isnull="true" iskey="true">
  <property name="Format" isnull="true" iskey="true">
    <property name="Trimming">Character</property>
    <property name="FormatFlags">NoClip</property>
```

Continued

Listing 6-16: The settings that make up the Clean White. *(continued)*

```xml
        <property name="Alignment">Center</property>
        <property name="LineAlignment">Center</property>
      </property>
      <property name="TextBrush" isnull="true" iskey="true">
        <property name="Color">Black</property>
      </property>
      <property name="Font">Microsoft Sans Serif, 8pt, style=Bold</property>
      <property name="Spacing">0, 0, 0, 0</property>
    </property>
    <property name="Value">0</property>
  </property>
  <property name="Item4" isnull="true" iskey="true">
    <property name="BoundElementName">scale1</property>
    <property name="Shader" isnull="true" iskey="true">
      <property name="TypeTag">Empty</property>
    </property>
    <property name="Enabled" isnull="true" iskey="true" />
    <property name="Name">bg1</property>
    <property name="ParentCollectionName">BackgroundLayers</property>
    <property name="ParentName">cGauge1</property>
    <property name="TypeNameEx">ArcScaleBackgroundLayerComponent</property>
    <property name="ShapeType">CircularFull_Style11</property>
    <property name="Size">@3,Width=250@3,Height=250</property>
    <property name="ZOrder">1000</property>
    <property name="ScaleCenterPos">0.5, 0.5</property>
  </property>
  <property name="Item5" isnull="true" iskey="true">
    <property name="BoundElementName">scale1</property>
    <property name="Shader" isnull="true" iskey="true">
      <property name="TypeTag">Empty</property>
    </property>
    <property name="Enabled" isnull="true" iskey="true" />
    <property name="Name">needle1</property>
    <property name="ParentCollectionName">Needles</property>
    <property name="ParentName">cGauge1</property>
    <property name="TypeNameEx">ArcScaleNeedleComponent</property>
    <property name="ShapeType">CircularFull_Style11</property>
    <property name="ZOrder">-50</property>
    <property name="EndOffset">5</property>
    <property name="StartOffset">-9.5</property>
  </property>
  </property>
</XtraSerializer>
```

Many existing gauge styles are available in the Preset Manager. You can pick from one of those already defined or design a custom gauge. Designing a custom gauge is a matter of extensive experimentation and taste.

Dynamically Applying Gauge Styles

The sample application shown in Figure 6-18 demonstrates how to load and apply all those property settings from a saved XML layout file. The sample is comprised of three parts: the ASPX, the code-behind, and the saved layout (XML) files representing the layout files for the preset circular gauge styles.

> The XML preset layouts are available with the demo applications downloaded with your copy of ASPxperience.

Assembling the Sample GUI

The sample application is comprised of an ASPxRoundPanel containing a table with two cells. The cell on the left has an ASPxCallbackPanel containing the ASPxGaugeControl. The ASPxCallbackPanel exists to provide that nice Ajax feeling when a new style is applied. The cell on the right contains an ASPxRoundPanel. The ASPxRoundPanel contains a table with two cells. The left cell contains an ASPxLabel, and the right panel contains an ASPxComboBox. The behavior is designed so that when the user picks a style from the combo box, an Ajax call is made to apply the named style to the ASPxGaugeControl.

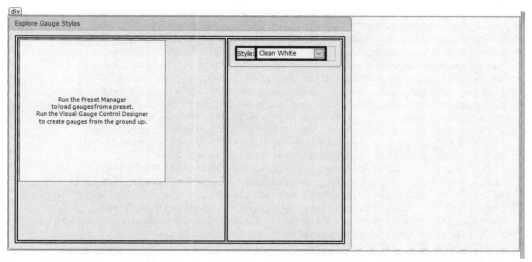

Figure 6-21: The design-time designer view of the GUI, clearly showing the HTML elements (with the borders made visible for illustration purposes).

The only code for the client side is the `SelectedIndexChanged` event for the `ASPxComboBox`. `SelectedIndexChanged` obtains the value associated with the selected combo box item and uses the `ASPxCallbackPanel`'s `ClientInstanceName`, `CallbackPanel`, to call PerformCallback, passing in a preformatted string containing the selected style. Listing 6-17 contains the ASPX for the sample.

Listing 6-17: The ASPX for the sample showing all the elements of the solution.

```
<%@ Page Language="C#" AutoEventWireup="true"
  CodeFile="Default.aspx.cs" Inherits="_Default" %>

<%@ Register Assembly="DevExpress.Web.v9.1, Version=9.1.4.0,↵
  Culture=neutral, PublicKeyToken=b88d1754d700e49a"
  Namespace="DevExpress.Web.ASPxCallbackPanel" TagPrefix="dxcp" %>

<%@ Register assembly="DevExpress.Web.v9.1, Version=9.1.4.0,↵
  Culture=neutral, PublicKeyToken=b88d1754d700e49a"
  namespace="DevExpress.Web.ASPxRoundPanel" tagprefix="dxrp" %>
<%@ Register assembly="DevExpress.Web.v9.1, Version=9.1.4.0,↵
  Culture=neutral, PublicKeyToken=b88d1754d700e49a"
  namespace="DevExpress.Web.ASPxPanel" tagprefix="dxp" %>

<%@ Register assembly="DevExpress.Web.ASPxGauges.v9.1,↵
  Version=9.1.4.0, Culture=neutral, PublicKeyToken=b88d1754d700e49a"
  namespace="DevExpress.Web.ASPxGauges" tagprefix="dxg" %>
<%@ Register assembly="DevExpress.Web.ASPxGauges.v9.1,↵
  Version=9.1.4.0, Culture=neutral, PublicKeyToken=b88d1754d700e49a"
  namespace="DevExpress.Web.ASPxGauges.Gauges" tagprefix="dxg" %>
<%@ Register assembly="DevExpress.Web.ASPxGauges.v9.1,↵
  Version=9.1.4.0, Culture=neutral, PublicKeyToken=b88d1754d700e49a"
  namespace="DevExpress.Web.ASPxGauges.Gauges.Linear" tagprefix="dxg" %>
<%@ Register assembly="DevExpress.Web.ASPxGauges.v9.1,↵
  Version=9.1.4.0, Culture=neutral, PublicKeyToken=b88d1754d700e49a"
  namespace="DevExpress.Web.ASPxGauges.Gauges.Circular" tagprefix="dxg" %>
<%@ Register assembly="DevExpress.Web.ASPxGauges.v9.1,↵
  Version=9.1.4.0, Culture=neutral, PublicKeyToken=b88d1754d700e49a"
  namespace="DevExpress.Web.ASPxGauges.Gauges.State" tagprefix="dxg" %>
<%@ Register assembly="DevExpress.Web.ASPxGauges.v9.1,↵
  Version=9.1.4.0, Culture=neutral, PublicKeyToken=b88d1754d700e49a"
  namespace="DevExpress.Web.ASPxGauges.Gauges.Digital" tagprefix="dxg" %>
<%@ Register assembly="DevExpress.Web.ASPxEditors.v9.1,↵
  Version=9.1.4.0, Culture=neutral, PublicKeyToken=b88d1754d700e49a"
  namespace="DevExpress.Web.ASPxEditors" tagprefix="dxe" %>

<!DOCTYPE html PUBLIC "-//W3C//DTD XHTML 1.0 Transitional//EN"
  "http://www.w3.org/TR/xhtml1/DTD/xhtml1-transitional.dtd">

<html xmlns="http://www.w3.org/1999/xhtml">
<head runat="server">
    <title></title>
</head>
<body>
  <form id="form1" runat="server">
  <div>
```

```
<dxrp:ASPxRoundPanel ID="ASPxRoundPanel1" runat="server"
HeaderText="Explore Gauge Styles" Height="378px" Width="452px">
<PanelCollection>
<dxp:PanelContent runat="server">
<table width="100%">
  <tr>
  <td style="height:100%; width:50%">
  <dxcp:ASPxCallbackPanel ID="ASPxCallbackPanel1" runat="server"
  ClientInstanceName="CallbackPanel"
  HideContentOnCallback="False" Width="364px"
  BackColor="Transparent" Height="364px" ShowLoadingPanel="True"
    OnCallback="ASPxCallbackPanel1_Callback">
  <PanelCollection>
  <dxp:PanelContent>
  <dxg:ASPxGaugeControl ID="ASPxGaugeControl1" runat="server" BackColor="White"
    Height="260px" Width="260px" DefaultValue="0">
    <Gauges>
    <dxg:CircularGauge Bounds="0, 0, 260, 260" Name="cGauge1">
      <backgroundlayers>
      <dxg:ArcScaleBackgroundLayerComponent Name="bg1" ScaleID="scale1"
        ShapeType="CircularFull_Style11" ZOrder="1000" />
      </backgroundlayers>
      <needles>
      <dxg:ArcScaleNeedleComponent EndOffset="5" Name="needle1"
        ScaleID="scale1"
        ShapeType="CircularFull_Style11" StartOffset="-9.5" ZOrder="-50" />
      </needles>
      <scales>
      <dxg:ArcScaleComponent AppearanceTickmarkText-Font="Tahoma, 12pt"
        AppearanceTickmarkText-TextBrush="&lt;BrushObject⏎
Type=&quot;Solid&quot; Data=&quot;Color:Black&quot;/&gt;"
        Center="125, 125" EndAngle="60"
        MajorTickmark-FormatString="{0:F0}"
        MajorTickmark-ShapeOffset="-5"
        MajorTickmark-ShapeScale="0.6, 0.8"
        MajorTickmark-ShapeType="Circular_Style11_4"
        MajorTickmark-TextOffset="-17"
        MajorTickmark-TextOrientation="LeftToRight" MaxValue="100"
        MinorTickCount="4"
        MinorTickmark-ShapeOffset="-2.5"
        MinorTickmark-ShapeScale="0.6, 1"
        MinorTickmark-ShapeType="Circular_Style11_3"
        Name="scale1" RadiusX="107"
        RadiusY="107" StartAngle="-240">
      </dxg:ArcScaleComponent>
      <dxg:ArcScaleComponent AppearanceTickmarkText-Font=
        "Microsoft Sans Serif, 8pt, style=Bold"
        AppearanceTickmarkText-TextBrush="&lt;BrushObject⏎
Type=&quot;Solid&quot; Data=&quot;Color:Black&quot;/&gt;"
        Center="125, 125" EndAngle="-30" MajorTickCount="8"
        MajorTickmark-FormatString="{0:F0}"
        MajorTickmark-ShapeType="Circular_Style11_2"
        MajorTickmark-TextOffset="-15"
```

Continued

Listing 6-17: The ASPX for the sample showing all the elements of the solution.
(continued)

```
               MajorTickmark-TextOrientation="LeftToRight"
               MaxValue="700" MinorTickCount="4"
               MinorTickmark-ShapeType="Circular_Style11_1"
               Name="scale2" RadiusX="70"
               RadiusY="70" StartAngle="-240" ZOrder="-1">
          </dxg:ArcScaleComponent>
          </scales>
        </dxg:CircularGauge>
        </Gauges>
    </dxg:ASPxGaugeControl>
    </dxp:PanelContent>
    </PanelCollection>
    </dxcp:ASPxCallbackPanel>
    </td>
    <td style="height:100%; width:50%" valign="top">
    <dxrp:ASPxRoundPanel ID="ASPxRoundPanel2" runat="server" ShowHeader="False"
      Width="200px">
      <PanelCollection>
      <dxp:PanelContent runat="server">
      <table cellpadding="0" cellspacing="0">
      <tr>
      <td >
        <dxe:ASPxLabel ID="ASPxLabel1" runat="server" Text="Style: ">
        </dxe:ASPxLabel>
      </td>
      <td >
        <dxe:ASPxComboBox ID="ASPxComboBox1" runat="server"
         SelectedIndex="1" ValueType="System.String" Width="120px">
         <ClientSideEvents SelectedIndexChanged="function(s, e) {
        var stylePath = s.GetValue();
        CallbackPanel.PerformCallback('Style=' + stylePath);
        }" />
        <Items>
          <dxe:ListEditItem Text="Africa Sunset" Value="AfricaSunset.xml" />
          <dxe:ListEditItem Text="Clean White" Value="CleanWhite.xml" />
          <dxe:ListEditItem Text="Dark Night" Value="DarkNight.xml" />
          <dxe:ListEditItem Text="Deep Fire" Value="DeepFire.xml" />
          <dxe:ListEditItem Text="Gothic Mat" Value="GothicMat.xml" />
          <dxe:ListEditItem Text="Ice Cold Zone" Value="IceColdZone.xml" />
          <dxe:ListEditItem Text="Mechanical" Value="Mechanical.xml" />
          <dxe:ListEditItem Text="Pure Dark" Value="PureDark.xml" />
          <dxe:ListEditItem Text="Shining Dark" Value="ShiningDark.xml" />
          <dxe:ListEditItem Text="Silver Blur" Value="SilverBlur.xml" />
          <dxe:ListEditItem Text="White" Value="Style1NoName.xml" />
          <dxe:ListEditItem Text="Sport Car" Value="Style12NoName.xml" />
          <dxe:ListEditItem Text="Military" Value="Style13NoName.xml" />
          <dxe:ListEditItem Text="Retro" Value="Style14NoName.xml" />
          <dxe:ListEditItem Text="Disco" Value="Style15NoName.xml" />
        </Items>
      </dxe:ASPxComboBox>
      </td>
      </tr>
      </table>
```

```
        </dxp:PanelContent>
        </PanelCollection>
      </dxrp:ASPxRoundPanel>
      </td>
      </tr>
    </table>
    </dxp:PanelContent>
    </PanelCollection>
    </dxrp:ASPxRoundPanel>
  </div>
  </form>
</body>
</html>
```

Implementing the Code-Behind

There are three supporting elements for the sample. The code-behind for the Web page contains the `Page_Load` and `Callback` event handler (see Listing 6-18); the `CallbackParameterParser` class has a static method, `TryParse`, that parses the style expression (see Listing 6-19) passed from the client; and the `StyleChangedHandler` class processes the property change (see Listing 6-20).

Listing 6-18: The Web page code-behind handles the Page Load and Callback events.

```csharp
using System;
using System.Collections.Generic;
using System.Linq;
using System.Web;
using System.Web.UI;
using System.Web.UI.WebControls;
using DevExpress.XtraGauges.Base;
using DevExpress.Web.ASPxClasses;
using DevExpress.Web.ASPxGauges;


public partial class _Default : System.Web.UI.Page
{
  protected void Page_Load(object sender, EventArgs e)
  {
    if (!IsCallback)
    {
    ((IGaugeContainer)ASPxGaugeControl1).ForceClearOnRestore = true;
    ((IGaugeContainer)ASPxGaugeControl1)
      .RestoreLayoutFromXml(MapPath("~/Styles/"
      + (string)ASPxComboBox1.Value));
    }

  }

  protected void ASPxCallbackPanel1_Callback(object source,
  DevExpress.Web.ASPxClasses.CallbackEventArgsBase e)
```

Continued

Listing 6-18: The Web page code-behind handles the Page Load and Callback events.
(continued)

```
    {
      string propertyName = string.Empty;
      string propertyValue = string.Empty;
      if (CallbackParameterParser.TryParse(e,
        out propertyName, out propertyValue))
      {
        new StyleChangedHandler(this, ASPxGaugeControl1)
          .ProcessPropertyChanged(propertyName, propertyValue);
      }
    }
  }
```

Listing 6-19: The CallbackParameterParser parses the style-expression sent from the client.

```
using System;
using System.Collections.Generic;
using System.Linq;
using System.Web;
using System.Text.RegularExpressions;
using DevExpress.Web.ASPxClasses;

public static class CallbackParameterParser
{
  public static bool TryParse(CallbackEventArgsBase e,
    out string propertyName, out string propertyValue)
  {
    string pattern = "(?<propName>.*?)\\s*=\\s*(?<propValue>.*?)$";
    MatchCollection matches = Regex.Matches(e.Parameter, pattern);
    propertyName = propertyValue = null;
    if (matches.Count > 0)
    {
      propertyName = matches[0].Groups["propName"].Value;
      propertyValue = matches[0].Groups["propValue"].Value;
    }
    return propertyName != null;
  }
}
```

Listing 6-20: The StyleChangedHandler is the work horse behind the Callback event.

```
using System;
using System.Collections.Generic;
using System.Linq;
using System.Web;
using DevExpress.XtraGauges.Presets.PresetManager;
using DevExpress.Web.ASPxGauges;
using DevExpress.XtraGauges.Base;
```

```
using System.Web.UI;

public class StyleChangedHandler : BasePropertyChangedHandler
{
  IGaugeContainer gaugeContainerCore;
  Page pageCore;
  public StyleChangedHandler(Page page, IGaugeContainer container)
  {
    this.gaugeContainerCore = container;
    this.pageCore = page;
  }

  protected override void CreateActions()
  {
    Actions.Add("Style", OnStyleChanged);
  }

  protected Page Page
  {
    get { return pageCore; }
  }

  protected IGaugeContainer GaugeContainer
  {
    get { return gaugeContainerCore; }
  }

  void OnStyleChanged(string stylePath)
  {
    GaugeContainer.ForceClearOnRestore = true;
    GaugeContainer.RestoreLayoutFromXml(
      Page.MapPath("~/Styles/" + stylePath));
  }
}
```

Exploring the Page_Load and Callback Handlers

The ASPxGaugeControl implements the IGaugeContainer. IGaugeContainer declares many members, including the ForceClearOnRestore property and the RestoreLayoutFromXml method. The Page_Load event handler in Listing 6-18 sets ForceClearOnRestore to true and calls RestoreLayoutFromXml using the currently selected style from the ASPxComboBox to restore the selected style to the ASPxGaugeControl. With the IsCallback check, the selected style will be restored on a callback but in this instance not a postback — for example, if the user clicks the Refresh button.

The ASPxCallbackPanel1_Callback event handler coordinates processing the Ajax callback from the CallbackPanel. The incoming argument is the string sent from the client-side SelectedIndexChanged event (see Listing 6-17) for the ASPxComboBox. The incoming string will contain the literal value 'Style=' and the value of the selected style. The Callback event handler uses the static method TryParse defined in the CallbackParameterParse class. The propertyName — which will be Style — and the propertyValue — which will be the selected style — will be returned as out parameters from TryParse and used as input parameters for ProcessPropertyChanged.

Reviewing the MatchCollection in the CallbackParameterParser

The `CallbackParameterParser` class is a static class that ships with the ASPxperience samples written by one of DevExpress's programmers. The class has one static method `TryParse` that accepts a `CallbackEventArgsBase` argument and two out arguments. A return value of true indicates that the parse succeeded and the out arguments have valid data.

`TryParse` uses the `System.Text.RegularExpressions` namespace, the `MatchCollection`, and a regular expression represented by the local variable pattern. The Regular Expression language is its own language, and entire books have been written about the subject. (For a book on Regular Expressions, refer to *Beginning Regular Expressions* by Andrew Watt, from Wrox.)

> *You can use Regular Expressions in Visual Studio in the Find and Replace dialog box (choose View ⇨ Quick Find) to devise more advanced searches. For more information, refer to my article in VB Today on Codeguru.com at* `www.codeguru.com/columns/vb/article.php/c14977/`.

The basic idea behind regular expressions is that you use a very terse set of matching language values in a string expression, and the engine compares the pattern to the some text. You can write pattern matching expressions, such as the expression `\w+([-+.']\w+)*@\w+([-.]\w+)*\.\w+([-.]\w+)*` that matches Internet e-mail addresses from the note in the section "Specifying a Required Field" in Chapter 4, or you can write expressions that return a collection of matches such as the pattern in Listing 6-19: `(?<propName>.*?)\\s*=\\s*(?<propValue>.*?)$`.

The `Regex.Matches` static method returns all the matches named in the pattern string found in the search string represented by `e.Parameter`. The regular expression represented by the local variable pattern is decomposed as follows:

❑   () is a grouping construct that captures that matched subexpression.

❑   (?<name>*subexpression*) is a named grouping construct matching *subexpression* and storing it in the named group between the < and > characters.

❑   *? is referred to as a lazy quantifier, telling the Regular Expression engine to search the minimum number of repetitions first.

❑   . matches any character except \n (the new line).

❑   * means match the preceding element zero or more times.

❑   = as used is the literal equal symbol.

❑   \s (lowercase *s*) matches any whitespace character. (The double slash is used to indicate that the \ is literal in this string rather than an escape character; you can also use a single slash and precede the string with the @ symbol).

❑   * following the \s means that there can be zero or more whitespace characters in that position.

❑ $ matches the position at the end of the input string.

What you probably know instinctively from the whole of the code is that the Regular Expression in Listing 6-19 matches strings that look like *name=value*, as in `Style=GothicMat.xml`. The left side of the equal symbol will be stored in a group referred to by propName, and the right side value will be stored in the group referred to by propValue. Given an input value of `Style=GothicMat.xml`, `matches[0].Groups["propName"].Value` will be Style and `matches[0].Groups["propValue"].Value` will be GothicMat.xml.

Unfortunately, just as it would be impossible to master C# from a small smattering of code, it is equally impossible to master Regular Expressions from a couple of expressions. I recommend picking up at least one book on Regular Expressions or finding a great source or tool for helping you generate Regular Expressions on the fly.

Exploring the StyleChangedHandler

Events are an implementation of the Observer design pattern. When an event handler is wired to an event, it is the equivalent of saying "when x happens, respond with y behavior." The reason that events are so powerful is that event x is distinct from behavior y and the behavior can be changed at runtime or stacked. This means that event x can be responded to with behavior y, y1, y2, and so on, all on a single event; or behavior y can be replaced with behavior z simply by assigning a new behavior.

The StyleChangedHandler in Listing 6-20 encapsulates a behavior. When the Callback event is fired, a new behavior instance — StyleChangedHandler — is created and the method ProcessPropertyChanged is called. The StyleChangedHandler class overrides CreateActions and dynamically adds the OnStyleChanged event effectively, causing ProcessPropertyChanged to fire the StyleChangedHandler.OnStyleChanged event, which in this case simply clears the existing layout and restores the layout represented by propertyValue.

One could simplify some of the code presented here by flattening the regular expression behavior code in CallbackParameterParser and using the code in OnStyleChanged more directly, but I present it as is for a couple of reasons. The first is that CallbackParameterParser and StyleChangedHandler are examples in the DevExpress distributed sample code, so it will help you to understand it. The second reason is that this style of code is based on well-documented patterns and ultimately leads to powerful and flexible code that clearly delineates responsibilities of the client, facilitating reuse.

Data Binding Gauges

As demonstrated in the preceding section, the ASPxGaugeControl has extensive support for implementing a variety of gauge styles from the Preset Manager or the Visual Gauge Control Designer. You can check out the Smart tags menu to see these options. What is conspicuously absent is a Data Source Configuration Wizard option. There is no default wizard for binding a data source to an instance of the ASPxGaugeControl. You can use data binding with the ASPxGaugeControl, but you have to know that the option is available, and you configure data binding manually.

The example in this section borrows heavily from the online ASPxGaugeDemos DataBinding.aspx page. The solution shows two needles on a gauge, using the gauge as a means of comparing the attributes of Car objects. The code in the book is distinct from the example. In addition to describing how all the elements work collaboratively, the sample in the book varies in that it uses LINQ for XML to read the Cars.xml rather than use the System.Xml.XPath elements. The result is that the code for loading the XML Cars elements is much more concise.

Listing 6-21 contains the ASPX for the GaugeDataBound sample. All the elements are present, including the OnDataBinding attribute, which you have to add manually in the ASPX. There is no property access via the designer (that is, the Properties window) to this event. You just need to know that OnDataBinding is a valid attribute of the ArcScaleComponent element and add it manually, as shown, to each of the `ArcScaleComponent` elements. (The `OnDataBinding` attribute — and event — is shown in bold font in the listing and is the last attribute of the two `ArcScaleComponent` elements.)

Listing 6-21: The ASPX for the sample application, which dynamically adjusts the gauge.

```
<%@ Page Language="C#" AutoEventWireup="true"  CodeFile="Default.aspx.cs"
  Inherits="_Default" %>
<%@ Register Assembly="DevExpress.Web.v9.1, Version=9.1.4.0,↵
  Culture=neutral, PublicKeyToken=b88d1754d700e49a"
  Namespace="DevExpress.Web.ASPxCallbackPanel" TagPrefix="dxcp" %>
<%@ Register Assembly="DevExpress.Web.ASPxEditors.v9.1,↵
  Version=9.1.4.0, Culture=neutral, PublicKeyToken=b88d1754d700e49a"
  Namespace="DevExpress.Web.ASPxEditors" TagPrefix="dxe" %>
<%@ Register assembly="DevExpress.Web.ASPxGauges.v9.1,↵
Version=9.1.4.0, Culture=neutral, PublicKeyToken=b88d1754d700e49a"
 namespace="DevExpress.Web.ASPxGauges" tagprefix="dxg" %>
<%@ Register assembly="DevExpress.Web.ASPxGauges.v9.1,↵
 Version=9.1.4.0, Culture=neutral, PublicKeyToken=b88d1754d700e49a"
 namespace="DevExpress.Web.ASPxGauges.Gauges" tagprefix="dxg" %>
<%@ Register assembly="DevExpress.Web.ASPxGauges.v9.1,↵
 Version=9.1.4.0, Culture=neutral, PublicKeyToken=b88d1754d700e49a"
 namespace="DevExpress.Web.ASPxGauges.Gauges.Linear" tagprefix="dxg" %>
<%@ Register assembly="DevExpress.Web.ASPxGauges.v9.1,↵
 Version=9.1.4.0, Culture=neutral, PublicKeyToken=b88d1754d700e49a"
 namespace="DevExpress.Web.ASPxGauges.Gauges.Circular" tagprefix="dxg" %>
<%@ Register assembly="DevExpress.Web.ASPxGauges.v9.1,↵
 Version=9.1.4.0, Culture=neutral, PublicKeyToken=b88d1754d700e49a"
 namespace="DevExpress.Web.ASPxGauges.Gauges.State" tagprefix="dxg" %>
<%@ Register assembly="DevExpress.Web.ASPxGauges.v9.1,↵
 Version=9.1.4.0, Culture=neutral, PublicKeyToken=b88d1754d700e49a"
 namespace="DevExpress.Web.ASPxGauges.Gauges.Digital" tagprefix="dxg" %>
<%@ Register assembly="DevExpress.Web.v9.1, Version=9.1.4.0,↵
 Culture=neutral, PublicKeyToken=b88d1754d700e49a"
 namespace="DevExpress.Web.ASPxRoundPanel" tagprefix="dxrp" %>
<%@ Register assembly="DevExpress.Web.v9.1, Version=9.1.4.0,↵
 Culture=neutral, PublicKeyToken=b88d1754d700e49a"
 namespace="DevExpress.Web.ASPxPanel" tagprefix="dxp" %>

<!DOCTYPE html PUBLIC "-//W3C//DTD XHTML 1.0 Transitional//EN"
"http://www.w3.org/TR/xhtml1/DTD/xhtml1-transitional.dtd">

<html xmlns="http://www.w3.org/1999/xhtml">
<head runat="server">
  <title></title>
</head>
<body>
  <form id="form1" runat="server">
  <div>
    <table>
    <tr>
    <td>
    <dxcp:ASPxCallbackPanel ID="ASPxCallbackPanel1" runat="server" Width="200px"
```

```
        oncallback="ASPxCallbackPanel1_Callback">
<PanelCollection>
<dxp:PanelContent runat="server">
<dxg:ASPxGaugeControl ID="ASPxGaugeControl1" runat="server" BackColor="White"
DefaultValue="50" Height="260px" Width="260px"
>
<Gauges>
  <dxg:CircularGauge Bounds="0, 0, 260, 260" Name="cGauge1">
  <Labels>
    <dxg:LabelComponent AppearanceText-Font="Tahoma, 10pt, style=Bold"
    Text="HP" Name="criteria" Position="125, 125"
    ZOrder="-25"></dxg:LabelComponent>
    <dxg:LabelComponent
      Text="<color=Silver>First Car       <color=Blue>Second Car"
      AllowHTMLString="True" Name="circularGauge1_Label2"
      Position="125, 225" Size="200, 25">
    </dxg:LabelComponent>
  </Labels>
  <BackgroundLayers>
    <dxg:ArcScaleBackgroundLayerComponent Name="bg1" ScaleCenterPos="0.5, 0.72"
    ScaleID="scale1" ShapeType="CircularHalf_Style2" Size="244, 170"
    ZOrder="1000" />
  </BackgroundLayers>
  <Needles>
    <dxg:ArcScaleNeedleComponent EndOffset="-6"
    Name="needle1" ScaleID="scale1"
    Shader='<ShaderObject Type="Style"
    Data="Colors[Style1:Black;Style2:Silver]" />'
    ShapeType="CircularFull_Style2" StartOffset="9" ZOrder="-50" />
    <dxg:ArcScaleNeedleComponent EndOffset="-6"
    Name="needle2" ScaleID="scale2"
    Shader='<ShaderObject Type="Style"
    Data="Colors[Style1:Black;Style2:Blue]" />'
    ShapeType="CircularFull_Style2" StartOffset="9"
    ZOrder="-50" Color="Green"/>
  </Needles>
  <SpindleCaps>
    <dxg:ArcScaleSpindleCapComponent Name="cap1" ScaleID="scale1"
    ShapeType="CircularFull_Style2" Size="24, 24" ZOrder="-100" />
  </SpindleCaps>
  <Scales>
    <dxg:ArcScaleComponent AppearanceTickmarkText-Font=
    "Arial Narrow, 11pt, style=Bold"
    AppearanceTickmarkText-TextBrush="&lt;BrushObject↵
Type=&quot;Solid&quot; Data=&quot;Color:#C0C0FF&quot;/&gt;"
    Center="125, 165" EndAngle="0" MajorTickCount="7"
    MajorTickmark-FormatString="{0:F0}" MajorTickmark-ShapeOffset="-9"
MajorTickmark-ShapeType="Circular_Style2_2"
    MajorTickmark-TextOffset="-22"
MajorTickmark-TextOrientation="LeftToRight"
    MaxValue="100" MinorTickCount="4"
MinorTickmark-ShapeType="Circular_Style2_1"
    MinValue="10" Name="scale1" RadiusX="91" RadiusY="91" StartAngle="-180"
```

Continued

Listing 6-21: The ASPX for the sample application, which dynamically adjusts the gauge. *(continued)*

```
            Value="80" MajorTickmark-AllowTickOverlap="True"
            OnDataBinding="OnScale1DataBinding">
          </dxg:ArcScaleComponent>
          <dxg:ArcScaleComponent AppearanceTickmarkText-Font=
"Arial Narrow, 11pt, style=Bold"
            AppearanceTickmarkText-TextBrush="&lt;BrushObject↵
Type=&quot;Solid&quot; Data=&quot;Color:#C0C0FF&quot;/&gt;"
            Center="125, 165" EndAngle="0" MajorTickCount="7"
            MajorTickmark-FormatString="{0:F0}"
  MajorTickmark-ShapeOffset="-9"
  MajorTickmark-ShapeType="Circular_Style2_2"
            MajorTickmark-TextOffset="-22" MajorTickmark-TextOrientation="LeftToRight"
            MaxValue="100" MinorTickCount="4"
  MinorTickmark-ShapeType="Circular_Style2_1"
            MinValue="10" Name="scale2" RadiusX="91" RadiusY="91" StartAngle="-180"
            Value="40" MajorTickmark-AllowTickOverlap="True"
            OnDataBinding="OnScale2DataBinding">
          </dxg:ArcScaleComponent>
        </Scales>
        </dxg:CircularGauge>
      </Gauges>
      </dxg:ASPxGaugeControl>
      </dxp:PanelContent>
      </PanelCollection>
      </dxcp:ASPxCallbackPanel>
      </td>
      <td valign="top">
      <dxrp:ASPxRoundPanel ID="ASPxRoundPanel1" runat="server"
        BackColor="Transparent" ShowHeader="False" Width="200px">
        <PanelCollection>
        <dxp:PanelContent runat="server">
        <table>
        <tr><td>
        <dxe:ASPxLabel ID="ASPxLabel1" runat="server" Text="First Car:">

        </dxe:ASPxLabel>
        </td><td>
        <dxe:ASPxComboBox ID="firstCar" runat="server" ValueType="System.Int32">
          <ClientSideEvents ValueChanged="function(s, e) {
          var id = s.GetValue();
          ASPxCallbackPanel1.PerformCallback('ID=' + id);
        }" />
        </dxe:ASPxComboBox>
        </td></tr>
        <tr><td><dxe:ASPxLabel ID="ASPxLabel2" runat="server" Text="Second Car:">
        </dxe:ASPxLabel></td>
        <td><dxe:ASPxComboBox ID="secondCar" runat="server" ValueType="System.Int32">
        <ClientSideEvents ValueChanged="function(s, e) {
          var id = s.GetValue();
          ASPxCallbackPanel1.PerformCallback('ID=' + id);
        }" />
        </dxe:ASPxComboBox></td></tr>
```

```
      <tr><td><dxe:ASPxLabel ID="ASPxLabel3" runat="server"
Text="Comparison Criteria:">
        </dxe:ASPxLabel></td>
        <td><dxe:ASPxComboBox ID="criteria" runat="server" SelectedIndex="0">
         <ClientSideEvents ValueChanged="function(s, e) {
           var criteria = s.GetValue();
           ASPxCallbackPanel1.PerformCallback('Criteria=' + criteria);
         }" />
         <Items>
          <dxe:ListEditItem Text="HP" Value="HP" />
          <dxe:ListEditItem Text="Cylinders" Value="Cylinders" />
          <dxe:ListEditItem Text="Liter" Value="Liter" />
          <dxe:ListEditItem Text="MPG City" Value="MPG City" />
          <dxe:ListEditItem Text="MPG Highway" Value="MPG Highway" />
         </Items>
        </dxe:ASPxComboBox></td></tr>
        </table>
        </dxp:PanelContent>
        </PanelCollection>
      </dxrp:ASPxRoundPanel>

      </td>
      </tr>
      </table>
    </div>
    </form>
  </body>
  </html>
```

Adding Labels

You can access the many advanced nested properties of an ASPxGaugeControl through the Gauges property Properties window, which will display the Gauges Editor. In the Gauges Editor, you will see the properties for each Gauge, such as the Labels property. However, if you click the nested properties, you get a warning that "Editing this Collection via the Collection Editor is strikingly not recommended. Please use the Visual Designer instead. Do you still want to edit the collection via the Collection Editor?" If you selected the Labels collection and click Yes to the warning, the Labels Editor is displayed. For this control, it is best to use the Visual Designer, as the warning suggests.

To use the Visual Designer and add a Label, click the ASPxGaugeControl's Smart tags menu and select Customize Gauge Control. In the Visual Gauge Control Designer, click the gauge's Smart tags menu and select Add Label. Perform this operation two times. Click the Rename button and rename the first label "criteria" (see Figure 6-22). Click the criteria Label's Smart tags menu and select Run Designer. Adjust the criteria Label to be roughly in the center of the gauge (using Figure 6-23 as a guide). Set the default text to HP (stands for horse power). Repeat the process for the second label and use the Position property to display the label underneath the gauge, setting the text property to <color=Silver>First Car<color=Blue>Second Car.

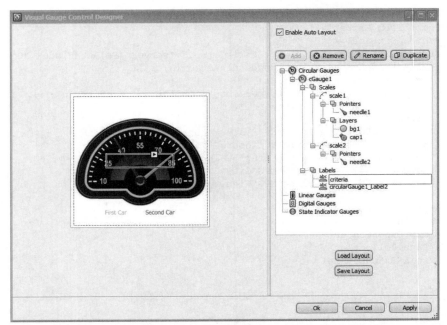

Figure 6-22: The Visual Gauge Control Designer is a rich designer that lets you adjust every aspect of a gauge.

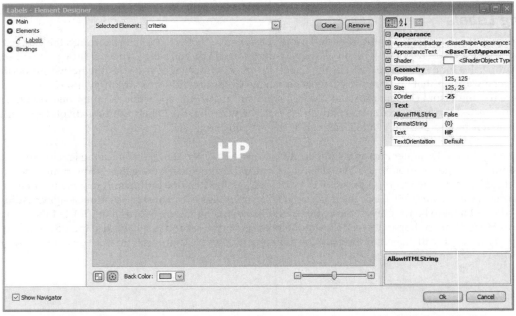

Figure 6-23: Set the Position property of the Label named criteria to position this Label in the center of the gauge control.

The embedded <color=*value*> tags actually embed color information with the Text property of the Label. This approach lets you use multiple colors for a single Label. The Labels as defined become a nested element of the indicated gauge. Listing 6-21 shows the Labels as defined in context; they are extracted in the following snippet for review.

```
<Labels>
  <dxg:LabelComponent AppearanceText-Font="Tahoma, 10pt, style=Bold"
    Text="HP" Name="criteria" Position="125, 125" ZOrder="-25">
  </dxg:LabelComponent>
  <dxg:LabelComponent Text="<color=Silver>First Car <color=Blue>Second Car"
    AllowHTMLString="True" Name="circularGauge1_Label2" Position="125, 225"
    Size="200, 25">
  </dxg:LabelComponent>
</Labels>
```

Adding Gauge Needles

The gauge indicators are instances of the `ArcScaleNeedleComponent` in the `<Needles>` element of a specific gauge. You can use the Smarts tags menu of a gauge in the Visual Gauge Control Designer to add additional needles — by choosing the Add Needle option — or you can simply copy an existing needle element and paste it into the `<Needles>` element. Using either approach, you can add as many needles as you want your gauge to have.

Individual needles are selectable elements in the Visual Gauge Control Designer and can be modified in the Needles — Element Designer (see Figure 6-24). Because there are only three things different about the two needles — the `ScaleID`, the `Name`, and the `Shader` attribute — it is easier to copy and paste the second needle in the ASPX in this instance. Here is the definition of the Needles element from Listing 6-21:

```
<Needles>
  <dxg:ArcScaleNeedleComponent EndOffset="-6" Name="needle1" ScaleID="scale1"
    Shader='<ShaderObject Type="Style"
    Data="Colors[Style1:Black;Style2:Silver]" />'
    ShapeType="CircularFull_Style2" StartOffset="9" ZOrder="-50" />
  <dxg:ArcScaleNeedleComponent EndOffset="-6" Name="needle2" ScaleID="scale2"
    Shader='<ShaderObject Type="Style" Data="Colors[Style1:Black;Style2:Blue]" />'
    ShapeType="CircularFull_Style2" StartOffset="9" ZOrder="-50" Color="Green"/>
</Needles>
```

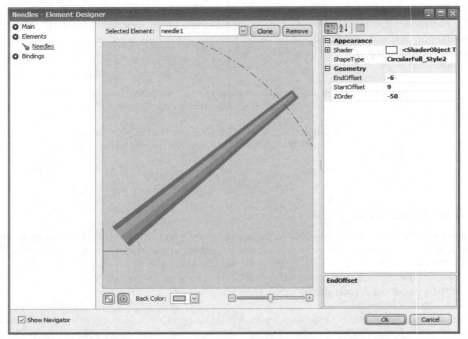

Figure 6-24: Click a needle in the Visual Gauge Control Designer and select Run Designer from the needle's Smart tags menu.

Associating Needles with ArcScaleNeedleComponents

Needles are associated with Scales — a specific `ArcScaleComponent` — through the `ArcScaleNeedleComponent`'s `ScaleID`. If you create a needle in the Visual Gauge Control Designer, the `ScaleID` will be automatically associated with the scale that the needle is added to. If you create the needle with the copy-and-paste approach, you need to manually set the `ArcScaleNeedleComponent`'s `ScaleID`. In the example, needle1's `ScaleID` is scale1 and needle2's `ScaleID` is scale2. The Scales element from Listing 6-21 is as follows:

```
<Scales>
  <dxg:ArcScaleComponent AppearanceTickmarkText-Font="Arial Narrow, 11pt,
  style=Bold"
    AppearanceTickmarkText-TextBrush="&lt;BrushObject Type=&quot;Solid&quot;
    Data=&quot;Color:#C0C0FF&quot;/&gt;"
    Center="125, 165" EndAngle="0" MajorTickCount="7"
    MajorTickmark-FormatString="{0:F0}" MajorTickmark-ShapeOffset="-9"
    MajorTickmark-ShapeType="Circular_Style2_2"
    MajorTickmark-TextOffset="-22" MajorTickmark-TextOrientation="LeftToRight"
    MaxValue="100" MinorTickCount="4" MinorTickmark-ShapeType="Circular_Style2_1"
    MinValue="10" Name="scale1" RadiusX="91" RadiusY="91" StartAngle="-180"
    Value="80" MajorTickmark-AllowTickOverlap="True"
    OnDataBinding="OnScale1DataBinding">
  </dxg:ArcScaleComponent>
  <dxg:ArcScaleComponent AppearanceTickmarkText-Font="Arial Narrow, 11pt,
```

```
        style=Bold"
        AppearanceTickmarkText-TextBrush="&lt;BrushObject
        Type=&quot;Solid&quot; Data=&quot;Color:#C0C0FF&quot;/&gt;"
        Center="125, 165" EndAngle="0" MajorTickCount="7"
        MajorTickmark-FormatString="{0:F0}" MajorTickmark-ShapeOffset="-9"
        MajorTickmark-ShapeType="Circular_Style2_2"
        MajorTickmark-TextOffset="-22" MajorTickmark-TextOrientation="LeftToRight"
        MaxValue="100" MinorTickCount="4" MinorTickmark-ShapeType="Circular_Style2_1"
        MinValue="10" Name="scale2" RadiusX="91" RadiusY="91" StartAngle="-180"
        Value="40" MajorTickmark-AllowTickOverlap="True"
        OnDataBinding="OnScale2DataBinding">
    </dxg:ArcScaleComponent>
  </Scales>
```

The `ArcScaleComponent` represents all those elements that make up the interior view of the gauge, including major and minor tick marks, and it is the nested component in an `ASPxGaugeControl` that holds the `OnDataBinding` statements. When `ASPxGaugeControl.DataBind` is called, the methods associated with the `OnDataBinding` attribute for the `ArcScaleComponent` will be called.

Specifying (Needle) Shaders

The `ASPxGaugeControl` is one of the more challenging controls to use. Almost every aspect is customizable. The `ASPxGaugeControl` has individualized designers for all the nested components, and some elements, such as `OnDataBinding` for the `ArcScaleComponent`, require that you know they exist — they don't jump out at you from the Visual Studio Properties window.

The `ArcScaleNeedleComponent`'s `Shader` attribute is another one of those elements that is tucked away and has some not-so-obvious or easy-to-find capabilities. If you look at Figure 6-24, you will see the Shader property in the Needles — Element Designer dialog. What will not be so obvious is when you use something like the `StyleShader`. The `Shader` attribute is going to build a complex-looking `ShaderObject` element assigned as a string — as shown excerpted from Listing 6-21 here:

```
Shader='<ShaderObject Type="Style" Data="Colors[Style1:Black;Style2:Blue]" />'
```

The attribute will actually be assigned a string that is a `ShaderObject` attribute, containing its own child attributes, which in turn look a bit challenging. In this example, the Data attribute with the value `Colors[Style1:Black;Style2:Blue]` defines the needle outline — Style1 — as being rendered in a black color and the needle fill color — Style2 — as being rendered in Blue.

A lot of information is packed into that one property. When you see the `Shader` element in the ASPX, it looks pretty complicated. The fact that the designer is packing a lot of information into tiny spaces is one of the reasons the IDE encourages you to use the Visual Gauge Control Designer instead of the plain-vanilla collections editor provided by default in Visual Studio.

Adding DataBinding to the ArcScaleComponent

The `OnDataBinding` event is defined as an `EventHandler` type. This means that the two arguments are `object sender` and `EventArgs e`. To add an `OnDataBinding` attribute to the ArcScaleComponent, add it manually in the ASPX and assign it the name of a method in the code-behind that provides the behavior.

Add an `OnDataBinding` attribute for each of the `ArcScaleComponent` elements. The event handlers for scale1 and scale2 are shown here. The actual behavior is provided in the UpdateScale method. Refer to the upcoming subsection "Dynamically Updating the Scale" for a description of the code that updates the gauge scales and the complete code listing for the code-behind.

```
protected void OnScale1DataBinding(object sender, EventArgs e)
{
  UpdateScale((ArcScale)sender, Convert.ToInt32(firstCar.Value),
    Convert.ToString(criteria.Value));
}

protected void OnScale2DataBinding(object sender, EventArgs e)
{
  UpdateScale((ArcScale)sender, Convert.ToInt32(secondCar.Value),
    Convert.ToString(criteria.Value));
}
```

Defining the Custom Data Type

Basic entity classes have fields, properties, and a constructor. They are unremarkable in their construction but useful in the data that they contain. The Car class is designed (and shown here in Listing 6-22) to mirror the desired elements of the Cars.xml data.

Listing 6-22: Instances of the Car class will be initialized from Cars.xml.

```
using System;
using System.Collections.Generic;
using System.Linq;
using System.Web;

public class Car
{
  private string name;
  public string Name
  {
    get {  return name; }
    set { name = value;   }
  }

  private int id;
  public int Id
  {
    get {  return id; }
    set { id = value;   }
  }

  private int cylinder;
  public int Cylinder
  {
    get {  return cylinder; }
    set { cylinder = value;   }
  }
```

```csharp
    private float hp;
    public float Hp
    {
      get {  return hp; }
      set { hp = value;  }
    }

    private float litre;
    public float Litre
    {
      get {  return litre; }
      set { litre = value;  }
    }

    private float mpgCity;
    public float MpgCity
    {
      get {  return mpgCity; }
      set { mpgCity = value;  }
    }

    private float mpgHighway;
    public float MpgHighway
    {
      get {  return mpgHighway; }
      set { mpgHighway = value;  }
    }

    /// <summary>
    /// Initializes a new instance of the Car class.
    /// </summary>
    /// <param name="name"></param>
    /// <param name="id"></param>
    /// <param name="cylinder"></param>
    /// <param name="hp"></param>
    /// <param name="litre"></param>
    /// <param name="mpgCity"></param>
    /// <param name="mpgHighway"></param>
    public Car(string name, int id, int cylinder,
      float hp, float litre, float mpgCity, float mpgHighway)
    {
        this.name = name;
        this.id = id;
        this.cylinder = cylinder;
        this.hp = hp;
        this.litre = litre;
        this.mpgCity = mpgCity;
        this.mpgHighway = mpgHighway;
    }
}
```

Implementing Custom Extension Methods

The use of extension methods is a technology that was added to .NET to support adding methods to classes without inheritance. In essence, you can define new behaviors for existing classes, and those behaviors are used as though they were actual members of the extended class.

Extension methods are inordinately valuable for new technologies like LINQ and Lambda Expressions because they permit framework developers to add all the necessary behaviors to IEnumerable<T>, *for instance, without completely rewriting* IEnumerable<T> *and potentially breaking a whole lot of customer code. (Check out my book LINQ Unleashed for C# from Sams for more on extension methods.)*

To define an extension method, define a static class and add static methods. The first argument takes the this modifier, and the type of the argument identifies the type extended. For example, Listing 6-23 shows two extension methods, GetCarByID and GetCarProperty. GetCarByID's first argument is List<Car>. This means that GetCarByID extends the type List<Car>, and you would call the method using member-of syntax. Assume a local variable List<Car> cars and invoke the method by calling cars.GetCarByID(*id*), passing in the id argument. The argument modified by the keyword this is the object that calls the method, and the second, third, or fourth arguments, and so on, are passed in the method parameters.

Listing 6-23: The CarExtension class defines extension methods for the Car class.

```
using System;
using System.Collections.Generic;
using System.Linq;
using System.Web;
using System.Runtime.CompilerServices;

public static class CarExtension
{
  public static Car GetCarByID(this List<Car> cars, int id)
  {
    var result = cars.Where(car=>car.Id == id);
    if(result != null)
      return result.First();
    return null;
  }

  public static object GetCarProperty(this Car car, string propertyName)
  {
    switch(propertyName)
    {
      case "Cylinders": return car.Cylinder;
      case "HP": return car.Hp;
      case "Liter": return car.Litre;
      case "MPG City": return car.MpgCity;
      case "MPG Highway": return car.MpgHighway;
      default: return car.Name;
    }
  }
}
```

GetCarByID searches the list of cars using the Where extension method and a Lambda Expression — car=>car.Id == id — to find the indicated Car object, and the First extension method to convert the collection returned by Where to the first item in the collection. GetCarProperty is used to convert the scale on the gauge to the selected car property.

Reading the XML Data with LINQ for XML

The Cars.xml contains schema information and Cars elements; see Listing 6-24 for an excerpt from the Cars.xml file. Each Cars element contains the subelements that define the persisted state of each Cars element. The Car entity as defined in Listing 6-23 (shown previously) maps only the ID, Model, Liter, Cyl, MPG_x0020_City, and MPG_x0020_Highway values.

Listing 6-24: An excerpt from the Cars.xml file shows the elements that make up persisted car data. (The Description, Icon, and Picture value were removed to shorten the listing.)

```
<Cars>
  <ID>1</ID>
  <Trademark>Mercedes-Benz</Trademark>
  <Model>SL500 Roadster</Model>
  <HP>302</HP>
  <Liter>4.966</Liter>
  <Cyl>8</Cyl>
  <Transmiss_x0020_Speed_x0020_Count>5</Transmiss_x0020_Speed_x0020_Count>
  <Transmiss_x0020_Automatic>Yes</Transmiss_x0020_Automatic>
  <MPG_x0020_City>16</MPG_x0020_City>
  <MPG_x0020_Highway>23</MPG_x0020_Highway>
  <Category>SPORTS</Category>
  <Description>
</Description>
  <Hyperlink>http://www.mercedes.com</Hyperlink>
  <Icon></Icon>
  <Picture></Picture>
  <Price>83800</Price>
  <Delivery_x0020_Date>2002-07-24T07:15:00.0000000</Delivery_x0020_Date>
  <Is_x0020_In_x0020_Stock>true</Is_x0020_In_x0020_Stock>
</Cars>
```

Listing 6-25 shows how you can quickly and easily read XML data using the System.Xml.Linq .XDocument object. Call XDocument.Load to load the XML data file, and all the data can be loaded into a collection of anonymous objects, or in the example in Listing 6-25, to a specific type.

Listing 6-25: Reading the XML file with LINQ for XML.

```
private List<Car> LoadCars()
{
    XDocument xml = XDocument.Load(Server.MapPath("App_Data\\Cars.xml"));
    var cars = from car in xml.Elements("NewDataSet").Elements("Cars")
        select new Car(
        car.Element("Model").Value,
        Convert.ToInt32(car.Element("ID").Value),
        Convert.ToInt32(car.Element("Cyl").Value),
        Convert.ToSingle(car.Element("HP").Value),
        Convert.ToSingle(car.Element("Liter").Value),
        Convert.ToSingle(car.Element("MPG_x0020_City").Value),
        Convert.ToSingle(car.Element("MPG_x0020_Highway").Value));

    float maxLitre = cars.Max<Car>(c=>c.Litre);
    float maxMpgCity = cars.Max<Car>(c=>c.MpgCity);
    float maxMpgHighway = cars.Max<Car>(c=>c.MpgHighway);
    float maxHp = cars.Max<Car>(c=>c.Hp);
    float maxCylinder = cars.Max<Car>(c=>c.Cylinder);

    carPropertyLimits = new Car("Limit", -1,
        (int) CorrectLimit(maxCylinder), CorrectLimit(maxHp),
        CorrectLimit(maxLitre), CorrectLimit(maxMpgCity),
        CorrectLimit(maxMpgHighway));

    return cars.ToList<Car>();
}
```

The LINQ query iterates over each `Cars` element and projects the desired subelements into instances of the `Car` class. After the LINQ query, the Max extension method is called with a Lambda Expression to find the maximal value of each property. These max values are stored in a local field `carPropertyLimits`. The maximal values are used to ensure that both ArcScales have the same max value.

Dynamically Updating the Scale

When any of the `ASPxComboBox objects` representing the first car, second car, or comparison criteria is changed, the client-side event `ValueChanged` is called. `ValueChanged` calls `ASPxCallbackPanel1.PerformCallback`, passing in the criteria. The `ASPxCallbackPanel.Callback` event handler is called asynchronously. If the Criteria `ASPxComboBox` was the invoking component, the criteria label is updated to display the new criteria. No matter which `ASPxComboBox` initiates the callback, the `ASPxGaugeControl.DataBind` method is called (see Listing 26).

When `DataBind` is called, the `DataBinding` events are called for each of the `ArcScaleComponent` objects. Each of those events uses the UpdateScale method. The `UpdateScale` method determines which car is selected for a given `ASPxComboBox` and gets the `Car` object from the `GetCarByID` extension method. Then, `UpdateScale` sets the minimum and maximum values for the `ArcScaleComponent` and sets the value for the selected criteria for that `Car`. For example, if the selected criteria is 'HP,' then the ArcScale's maximum limit is set from the `carPropertyLimits` object, the minimum scale value is set from the simple ternary operator test, and the value is set based on the selected criteria.

Listing 6-26: The code-behind for the sample program.

```
using System;
using System.Collections.Generic;
using System.Linq;
using System.Web;
using System.Web.UI;
using System.Web.UI.WebControls;
using System.Xml;
using System.Xml.Linq;
using System.Diagnostics;
using DevExpress.XtraGauges.Core.Model;
using DevExpress.Web.ASPxEditors;
using DevExpress.Web.ASPxGauges.Base;

public partial class _Default : System.Web.UI.Page
{
  protected void Page_Load(object sender, EventArgs e)
  {
    if (!IsPostBack)
    {
      if (Cars.Count > 0)
      {
        foreach (Car car in Cars)
        {
          firstCar.Items.Add(new ListEditItem(car.Name, car.Id));
          secondCar.Items.Add(new ListEditItem(car.Name, car.Id));
        }
        firstCar.Text = Cars[0].Name;
        secondCar.Text = Cars[1].Name;
      }
      ASPxGaugeControl1.DataBind();
    }
  }

  private Car carPropertyLimits = null;
  private List<Car> cars;
  public List<Car> Cars
  {
    get { return cars == null ? cars = LoadCars() : cars; }
  }

  private List<Car> LoadCars()
  {
    XDocument xml = XDocument.Load(Server.MapPath("App_Data\\Cars.xml"));
    var cars = from car in xml.Elements("NewDataSet").Elements("Cars")
               select new Car(
                 car.Element("Model").Value,
                 Convert.ToInt32(car.Element("ID").Value),
                 Convert.ToInt32(car.Element("Cyl").Value),
                 Convert.ToSingle(car.Element("HP").Value),
                 Convert.ToSingle(car.Element("Liter").Value),
                 Convert.ToSingle(car.Element("MPG_x0020_City").Value),
```

Continued

Listing 6-26: The code-behind for the sample program. *(continued)*

```
                    Convert.ToSingle(car.Element("MPG_x0020_Highway").Value));

    float maxLitre = cars.Max<Car>(c=>c.Litre);
    float maxMpgCity = cars.Max<Car>(c=>c.MpgCity);
    float maxMpgHighway = cars.Max<Car>(c=>c.MpgHighway);
    float maxHp = cars.Max<Car>(c=>c.Hp);
    float maxCylinder = cars.Max<Car>(c=>c.Cylinder);

    carPropertyLimits = new Car("Limit", -1,
      (int) CorrectLimit(maxCylinder), CorrectLimit(maxHp),
      CorrectLimit(maxLitre), CorrectLimit(maxMpgCity),
      CorrectLimit(maxMpgHighway));

    return cars.ToList<Car>();
}

private float CorrectLimit(float limit)
{
  int[] limits = new int[] { 7, 12, 36, 360 };
  for (int i = 0; i < limits.Length; i++)
  {
    if (limit < limits[i]) return limits[i];
  }
  return limit;
}


protected void OnScale1DataBinding(object sender, EventArgs e)
{
  UpdateScale((ArcScale)sender, Convert.ToInt32(firstCar.Value),
    Convert.ToString(criteria.Value));
}

protected void OnScale2DataBinding(object sender, EventArgs e)
{
  UpdateScale((ArcScale)sender, Convert.ToInt32(secondCar.Value),
    Convert.ToString(criteria.Value));
}

private void UpdateScale(ArcScale scale, int id, string criteria)
{
  if (Cars.Count > 0 && id < Cars.Count)
  {
    Car car = cars.GetCarByID(id);
    float maxValue = Convert.ToSingle(
      carPropertyLimits.GetCarProperty(criteria));
    scale.MaxValue = maxValue;
    scale.MinValue = (maxValue == 7) ? 1 : 0;
    scale.Value = Convert.ToSingle(car.GetCarProperty(criteria));
  }
}
```

```
    protected void ASPxCallbackPanel1_Callback(object source,
      DevExpress.Web.ASPxClasses.CallbackEventArgsBase e)
{
    string propertyName = string.Empty;
    string propertyValue = string.Empty;
    if (CallbackParameterParser.TryParse(e, out propertyName,
      out propertyValue))
    {
      if (propertyName == "Criteria")
      {
        ((ICircularGauge)ASPxGaugeControl1.Gauges[0])
          .Labels["criteria"].Text = propertyValue;
      }
    }
    ASPxGaugeControl1.DataBind();
  }
}
```

The ASPxGaugeControl is a way of visually representing data values using a graphic that will be familiar and have an intuitive meaning for most users. In its essence, an ASPxGaugeControl is a graphic element that has an indicator that represents a value between some minimum and maximum value that you set. The significant difference between the ASPxGaugeControl and any basic gauge is that the Visual Gauge Control Designer lets you visually and intricately design and manage all the elements of a gauge.

Summary

The ASPxScheduler and ASPxGaugeControl are rich controls with their own diverse set of properties and designers. The ASPxScheduler is really a suite of elements that is closer to an application than a control. When you add an ASPxScheduler, several UserControls are added to the project. The UserControls facilitate managing recurring appointments, finding existing appointments, appointment editors, and reminder forms. If you provide the data source representing appointments and resources, you essentially have a running calendar/scheduling application ready to go.

The ASPxGaugeControl has dozens of predefined gauges that were created and stored as XML with the Visual Gauge Control Designer. You can choose from any of these preset gauges or you can use the designer to create your own gauge.

Part II: Data Sources, JavaScript, CSS, and Themes

7

Using the Data That Makes
Sense for Your Solution

An interesting quote published in "Build Blazing Fast Windows and ASP.NET Applications with DevExpress LINQ-Enabled Grid Controls" on `http://aspalliance.com` reads: "No matter how well one designs a data controller, it will never do its job well if one fails to recognize that database specific operations ought to be executed on the database server. No matter how ingenious the algorithms — no matter how brilliant the technology . . . if the grid is forced to manage data itself, you can bet that a large dataset will eventually bring the server or the Windows Smart Client to its knees and make the application totally unusable." Published by DevExpress, this quote represents DevExpress's interests to some extent, but there is an important underlying idea as well. Managing databases and data is still hard, there is no current trend on a single technology, and in fact the opposite of that is true: There are more ways to connect to your data than ever before.

Having been a code slinger for 20 years now, I have seen a lot of history. Data technologies have improved, but now we have many more choices: LINQ for SQL, nHibernate, ADO.NET, eXpress Persistent Objects (DevExpress's XPO), to name a few. During much of the last decade, developers (or technologists or managers) picked a database technology, and if they were .NET programmers, they generally settled on a provider — elements of the .NET framework, such as OleDB — that provided them access to their data. Then, developers generally bifurcated into one or the other camps: the roll-your-own camp, with the database technology buried under a tier, or the read-data-and-bind-to-controls camp. With more vendors jumping on the database-technology-providing bandwagon, there are naturally many more choices. [LINQ (for SQL and Entities] are among my favorites.)

Throughout this book, I have introduced or demonstrated LINQ, SQL, Access, and Object data sources. In this chapter, I'd like to showcase DevExpress's XPO. XPO, eXpress Persistent Objects, is DevExpress's foray into database technology and has some unique features that make it database-flavor independent. It also has some features that are similar to technologies such as LINQ, but distinct in capabilities that XPO offers. With XPO, you can generate persistent classes and objects from an existing database. (This is a feature similar to LINQ to SQL.) With XPO, you can generate a database from classes, and XPO incorporates the UnitOfWork pattern, which makes it possible for you to manage transactions — multistepped changes to data — transparently to the underlying database. With XPO you can change the underlying database used for any one of the supported databases without making code changes. This multi-provider support is referred to as agnosticism. With XPO in ServerMode you can push common tasks such as managing large amounts of data back to the database server itself, yielding blazing speed and higher performance as well as making better use of your hardware infrastructure.

Database agnosticism is important and XPO supports it, but it is hard to demonstrate in the context of a book. If you are implementing a solution that may need to change or support a variety of database vendor's products, then XPO will let you do so without code changes. XPO supports MS Access, MS SQL Server, Oracle, PostgreSql, Firebird, PervavsiveSQL, VistaDB, SQL Anywhere, Advantage, DB2, and Sybase. Database agnosticism is an important reason to choose XPO, and multi-vendor support is there if you need it. This chapter includes samples that demonstrate using XPO for persistent classes to generate a database, enterprise transaction patterns using the UnitOfWork, ServerMode, and using XPO as a traditional object mapping tool. Collectively, these capabilities of XPO make it a very compelling choice for managing your data.

Using an XpoDataSource

The most basic use of the `XpoDataSource` is to associate the `XpoDataSource` component with a control in your GUI and associating persistent classes with the `XpoDataSource`. The persistent classes approximately match some aspect of your database schema, and the `XpoDataSource` — the code that provides the behavior — uses the entity classes to figure out what to read from the data store and populate instances of the entity classes.

> *According to Booch in* Object-Oriented Analysis and Design With Applications, 3rd Edition *(Addison Wesley, page 45),* an entity abstraction is *"an object that represents a useful model of a problem domain or solution domain entity." Commonly the term is used to refer to classes that map to aspects of a database schema. In XPO vernacular, database entities are called persistent classes. In the rest of this chapter the two terms can be thought of interchangeably. For technical clarity where relative to XPO, persistent classes will be used.*

All these elements sound a little more complicated than they actually are. For instance, when you are ready for your persistent classes, you can add a persistent class from the Add New Items dialog box in Visual Studio, and the DevExpress Object Relational Mapper (wizard) will visually guide you through the creation of the persistent classes, including all the elements that assist in the mapping process.

The sample in this section associates an `XpoDataSource` with a persistent class mapped to the `AdventureWorks.Production.Product` table and displays the products in an `ASPxTitleIndex`. A description of each element of the sample is provided in the subsections.

Using the DevExpress' Object Relational Mapping Capability

The basic job of any object relational mapping tool is to map a class to an element in a database. The basic process of mapping a class to a database table can be accomplished by reading a schema and generating a class. You can use simple string substitution to generate a class or use the CodeDOM tools in the .NET framework and write a full-blown generator. A common element in any ORM mapping tool, in addition to mapping class members to database elements, is the presence of helper attributes. Helper attributes often provide additional cues such as the actual name of a table element associated with a property, data type, and data size. When you take all these often very necessary items — mapping classes to tables, code-generating classes and attributes — with an ability to work with table-mapped functions and views, writing a production-worthy ORM can be a big chore. Although writing code generators and basic ORM tools can be fun to explore, assuming that you have time, luckily you don't have to write an ORM tool. DevExpress has included an ORM tool with the XPO technology. You just have to tap into it.

The Add New Items dialog box in Visual Studio contains those seemingly simple icons that describe different kinds of items you can add to a Visual Studio project. Click the Class template, and a code file is added to your project. Click another item, and something else happens. Underneath it all are things like the `IDTExtensibility2` interface, `EnvDTE`, and the wizard technologies. Visual Studio is a fully extensible environment, which means, in a nutshell, that something as simple as a template in the Add New Items dialog box can kick off a complex process that ultimately saves you a lot of work.

To use DevExpress' Object Relational Mapping tool and add a persistent class that is mapped to the `AdventureWorks.Production.Product` table, follow these steps:

1. In your Web project click the Website | Add New Item menu.

2. From the list of templates, select the Persistent Classes *version.x* item (see Figure 7-1), name the class file **Products.cs**, and click Add.

3. Click Yes in response to the message about adding the code to the App_Code folder.

4. Select the Persistent Classes template item to start the ORM tool, which then brings up the Generating Persistent Classes for an Existing Database dialog box.

5. In the dialog box, enter a Server Name — either your database server or .\SQLExpress, for SQL Server Express.

6. For the Database, select AdventureWorks (refer to Figure 7-2).

7. Click Next.

8. Deselect all the tables except for Production.Product, and make sure that all the columns for the Product table are selected (see Figure 7-3).

9. Click Finish to let the wizard generate the class representing the selected table and finish running.

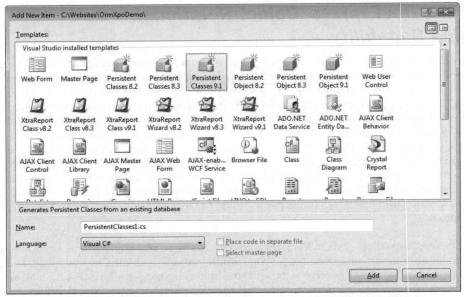

Figure 7-1: Select the Persistent Classes template to run the DevExpress Object Relational Mapping Wizard.

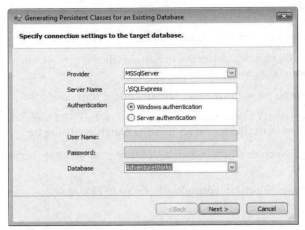

Figure 7-2: Specify the database server and database name in Step 1 of the ORM Wizard.

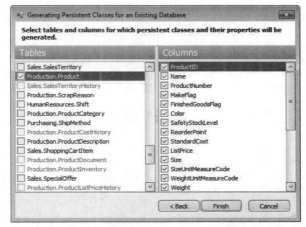

Figure 7-3: Specify the table(s) and column(s) for which you want classes generated.

When pointed at the AdventureWorks.Production.Product table, the DevExpress ORM Wizard generates the `Production_Product` table, as shown in Listing 7-1.

Listing 7-1: The generated persistent class generated by the XPO ORM tool.

```
using System;
using DevExpress.Xpo;
namespace AdventureWorks {

  [Persistent("Production.Product")]
  public class Production_Product : XPLiteObject {
    int fProductID;
    [Key(true)]
    public int ProductID {
      get { return fProductID; }
      set { SetPropertyValue<int>("ProductID",
        ref fProductID, value); }
    }
    string fName;
    [Size(50)]
    public string Name {
      get { return fName; }
      set { SetPropertyValue<string>("Name", ref fName, value); }
    }
    string fProductNumber;
    [Size(25)]
    public string ProductNumber {
      get { return fProductNumber; }
      set { SetPropertyValue<string>("ProductNumber",
```

Continued

Listing 7-1: The generated persistent class generated by the XPO ORM tool. *(continued)*

```
        ref fProductNumber, value); }
}
bool fMakeFlag;
public bool MakeFlag {
  get { return fMakeFlag; }
  set { SetPropertyValue<bool>("MakeFlag",
    ref fMakeFlag, value); }
}
bool fFinishedGoodsFlag;
public bool FinishedGoodsFlag {
  get { return fFinishedGoodsFlag; }
  set { SetPropertyValue<bool>("FinishedGoodsFlag",
    ref fFinishedGoodsFlag, value); }
}
string fColor;
[Size(15)]
public string Color {
  get { return fColor; }
  set { SetPropertyValue<string>("Color", ref fColor, value); }
}
short fSafetyStockLevel;
public short SafetyStockLevel {
  get { return fSafetyStockLevel; }
  set { SetPropertyValue<short>("SafetyStockLevel",
    ref fSafetyStockLevel, value); }
}
short fReorderPoint;
public short ReorderPoint {
  get { return fReorderPoint; }
  set { SetPropertyValue<short>("ReorderPoint",
    ref fReorderPoint, value); }
}
decimal fStandardCost;
public decimal StandardCost {
  get { return fStandardCost; }
  set { SetPropertyValue<decimal>("StandardCost",
    ref fStandardCost, value); }
}
decimal fListPrice;
public decimal ListPrice {
  get { return fListPrice; }
  set { SetPropertyValue<decimal>("ListPrice",
    ref fListPrice, value); }
}
string fSize;
[Size(5)]
public string Size {
```

```
    get { return fSize; }
    set { SetPropertyValue<string>("Size", ref fSize, value); }
  }
  string fSizeUnitMeasureCode;
  [Size(3)]
  public string SizeUnitMeasureCode {
    get { return fSizeUnitMeasureCode; }
    set { SetPropertyValue<string>("SizeUnitMeasureCode",
      ref fSizeUnitMeasureCode, value); }
  }
  string fWeightUnitMeasureCode;
  [Size(3)]
  public string WeightUnitMeasureCode {
    get { return fWeightUnitMeasureCode; }
    set { SetPropertyValue<string>("WeightUnitMeasureCode",
      ref fWeightUnitMeasureCode, value); }
  }
  decimal fWeight;
  public decimal Weight {
    get { return fWeight; }
    set { SetPropertyValue<decimal>("Weight", ref fWeight, value); }
  }
  int fDaysToManufacture;
  public int DaysToManufacture {
    get { return fDaysToManufacture; }
    set { SetPropertyValue<int>("DaysToManufacture",
      ref fDaysToManufacture, value); }
  }
  string fProductLine;
  [Size(2)]
  public string ProductLine {
    get { return fProductLine; }
    set { SetPropertyValue<string>("ProductLine",
      ref fProductLine, value); }
  }
  string fClass;
  [Size(2)]
  public string Class {
    get { return fClass; }
    set { SetPropertyValue<string>("Class", ref fClass, value); }
  }
  string fStyle;
  [Size(2)]
  public string Style {
    get { return fStyle; }
    set { SetPropertyValue<string>("Style", ref fStyle, value); }
  }
  int fProductSubcategoryID;
  public int ProductSubcategoryID {
    get { return fProductSubcategoryID; }
```

Continued

367

Listing 7-1: The generated persistent class generated by the XPO ORM tool. *(continued)*

```
                set { SetPropertyValue<int>("ProductSubcategoryID",
                  ref fProductSubcategoryID, value); }
            }
            int fProductModelID;
            public int ProductModelID {
              get { return fProductModelID; }
              set { SetPropertyValue<int>("ProductModelID",
                ref fProductModelID, value); }
            }
            DateTime fSellStartDate;
            public DateTime SellStartDate {
              get { return fSellStartDate; }
              set { SetPropertyValue<DateTime>("SellStartDate",
                ref fSellStartDate, value); }
            }
            DateTime fSellEndDate;
            public DateTime SellEndDate {
              get { return fSellEndDate; }
              set { SetPropertyValue<DateTime>("SellEndDate", ref fSellEndDate, value); }
            }
            DateTime fDiscontinuedDate;
            public DateTime DiscontinuedDate {
              get { return fDiscontinuedDate; }
              set { SetPropertyValue<DateTime>("DiscontinuedDate",
                ref fDiscontinuedDate, value); }
            }
            Guid frowguid;
            public Guid rowguid {
              get { return frowguid; }
              set { SetPropertyValue<Guid>("rowguid", ref frowguid, value); }
            }
            DateTime fModifiedDate;
            public DateTime ModifiedDate {
              get { return fModifiedDate; }
              set { SetPropertyValue<DateTime>("ModifiedDate",
                ref fModifiedDate, value); }
            }
            public Production_Product(Session session) : base(session) { }
            public Production_Product() : base(Session.DefaultSession) { }
            public override void AfterConstruction() { base.AfterConstruction(); }
          }
        }
```

Exploring generated code is worth doing, especially if you may want to reproduce something similar, but manually. (See the upcoming subsection "Using a View with (XPO) Persistent Objects" for just such a scenario.) The generated code references the `DevExpress.Xpo` namespace. The generated namespace maps to the database instance name. Notice that the class name reflects the database schema and table name, and that the Persistent attribute actually contains the *schema.table* name. These are mapping elements that establish the reference to the underlying associations.

Note that, in Listing 7-1, the fields are associated with properties, and attributes are applied to the properties. XPO needs to perform updates in many instances; therefore, a unique key identified by the Key attribute is needed. If the property name precisely matches the underlying table column name, no mapping attribute is needed. The property name is used. Changed data needs to be tracked, which is why a helper method — `SetPropertyValue` — is used for writes.

For database string types, a `SizeAttribute` can be applied to indicate the maximum length of the string, and there are attributes for names, associations, type information, and display aliases. The XPO ORM engine will automatically add these elements as needed. For example, to map a table field named Format to a property named `FormatString`, apply the `PersistentAttribute` and the MapTo argument indicating the name of the underlying table field.

Persistent classes inherit from `XPLiteObject`, and the child classes introduce constructors that accept a Session object or call the base class constructor with the `DefaultSession` and an `AfterConstruction` method.

The `XPLiteObject` base class already contains methods for saving, deleting, and reloading persistent objects, as well as properties for determining the state that a persistent object is in. For example, the `IsDeleted` property in the `XPLiteObject` — which in turn is inherited from `DevExpress.Xpo` `.PersistentBase` — is used to determine whether an object has been marked as deleted.

Using the ASPxTitleIndex with an XpoDataSource

When you have the persistent classes, you need to associate the class-type with an `XpoDataSource` via the `XpoDataSource`'s `TypeName` property. The `ASPxTitleIndex` is a neat Web control that takes the heavy lifting out of creating a navigable index page. If you provide the data and set the `TextField` property, the `ASPxTitleIndex` control will display a search filter, index group headers, and add the clickable items (see Figure 7-4). Add a `NavigateUrlField` and click the text (represented by the column assigned to the `TextField` property), and navigability is built into the `ASPxTitleIndex`.

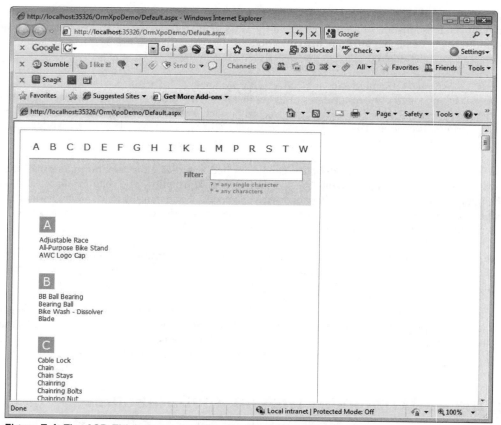

Figure 7-4: The ASPxTitleIndex automatically organizes and groups items based on the data read through the TextField property, and the Filter feature is built-in.

To recreate the sample with the ASPxTitleIndex, you need to add an XpoDataSource to the Web page containing the ASPxTitleIndex. The XpoDataSource's TypeName property needs to refer to the generated persistent class, and a little bit of plumbing needs to be defined so that the XpoDataSource knows where and how to get its data and work with Session. The code in Listing 7-2 contains the startup code. The very little bit of code in Listing 7-3 contains the very limited code-behind for the Web page, and the following instructions walk you through the steps needed to assemble the various bits and pieces:

1. To your project containing the Production_Product persistent class, add or use the default Web page.

2. Add an ASPxTitleIndex from the Navigation & Layout tab of the Toolbox to the Web page.

3. Associate an XpoDataSource to the ASPxTitleIndex from the ASPxTitleIndex's smart tags menu's Choose Data Source option. (You can select the XpoDataSource from the Choose a Data Source Type step of the wizard; it is probably the last data source in the list of types.)

4. Click OK.

5. In the Properties window, select the `AdventureWorks.Production_Product` class for the `XpoDataSource`'s `TypeName`.

6. For the `ASPxTitleIndex`, select the Name field (from the `Production_Product` class) for the `TextField` property.

7. Finally, implement the `Page_Init` method for the Web page's code-behind (see Listing 7-3).

8. Add a Global.asax file from the Add New Items dialog box in Visual Studio and code the Application_Start event as shown in Listing 7-2.

Listing 7-2: Add an Application_Start event to the Global.asax file (that you have to add to the project) to wire the database to the XPO plumbing.

```
<%@ Application Language="C#" %>

<script runat="server">

   void Application_Start(object sender, EventArgs e)
   {
     string connectionString =
        DevExpress.Xpo.DB.MSSqlConnectionProvider
        .GetConnectionString(@".\SQLExpress",
        "AdventureWorks");

     DevExpress.Xpo.Metadata.XPDictionary dictionary =
     new DevExpress.Xpo.Metadata.ReflectionDictionary();

     DevExpress.Xpo.DB.IDataStore store =
     DevExpress.Xpo.XpoDefault.GetConnectionProvider(connectionString,
     DevExpress.Xpo.DB.AutoCreateOption.SchemaAlreadyExists);

     dictionary.GetDataStoreSchema(
        typeof(AdventureWorks.Production_Product).Assembly);
     DevExpress.Xpo.XpoDefault.DataLayer =
        new DevExpress.Xpo.ThreadSafeDataLayer(dictionary, store);
     DevExpress.Xpo.XpoDefault.Session = null;

   }

   void Application_End(object sender, EventArgs e)
   {
     //  Code that runs on application shutdown
   }

   void Application_Error(object sender, EventArgs e)
   {
     // Code that runs when an unhandled error occurs
   }

   void Session_Start(object sender, EventArgs e)
   {
```

Continued

Listing 7-2: Add an Application_Start event to the Global.asax file (that you have to add to the project) to wire the database to the XPO plumbing. *(continued)*

```
        // Code that runs when a new session is started
    }

    void Session_End(object sender, EventArgs e)
    {
        // Code that runs when a session ends.
        // Note: The Session_End event is raised only when the sessionstate mode
        // is set to InProc in the Web.config file. If session
        // mode is set to StateServer
        // or SQLServer, the event is not raised.
    }

</script>
```

Listing 7-3: Add a Page_Init event handler to assign a DevExpress.Xpox.Session object to the XpoDataSource.Session property.

```
using System;
using System.Collections.Generic;
using System.Linq;
using System.Web;
using System.Web.UI;
using System.Web.UI.WebControls;

public partial class _Default : System.Web.UI.Page
{
    protected void Page_Load(object sender, EventArgs e)
    {

    }

    protected void Page_Init(object sender, EventArgs e)
    {
        XpoDataSource1.Session = new DevExpress.Xpo.Session();
    }
}
```

The DevExpress.Xpo.Session component exists to help load and save persistent objects. It is distinct from the Session object in Web pages. The Application_Start method contains plumbing that is almost boilerplate. (You can drag and drop it into the Toolbox for future use.) The only code you need to change each time is the argument passed to the GetConnectionString method indicating the database information and the typeof operator in the dictionary.GetDataStoreSchema method. Change the arguments to reflect the actual database and the type of your persistent class.

The Application_Start method acquires a connection string to the database and creates an XPDictionary. The connection string is used to create an instance of an IDataStore from XpoDafault.GetConnectionProvider. The dictionary is used to read the data store schema for the indicated type, a ThreadSafeDataLayer is associated with the dictionary and data store, and the XpoDefault.Session is set to null. Again, it's boilerplate. Keep a copy handy in the Toolbox, perhaps with your own comments that remind you of what you need to change.

With a half-dozen lines of boilerplate code and a single statement in the `Page_Init` method, the `XpoDataSource` will coordinate everything else.

The `ASPxTitleIndex` is highly configurable, as are all the other controls you have read about. You can assign auto-formatting to change the appearance of the control. You can add client-side events for programmatic customizations, add Tooltips, and tweak just about every imaginable aspect of the `ASPxTitleIndex`'s appearance. For more demos on the `ASPxTitleIndex`, including filtering and grouping demos, refer to the ASPxperienceDemos for the `ASPxTitleIndex` at `http://demos .devexpress.com/ASPxperienceDemos/`.

Using a View with (XPO) Persistent Objects

When you selected Persistent Classes from the Add New Item dialog box in the previous section, you may (or may not) have noticed that there were no views or table-valued functions listed in the wizard (refer to Figure 7-3). This doesn't mean you can't use these elements. You just need to manually define the persistent class yourself (which if you use CodeRush then this only takes a few minutes). If, for instance, you want to use XPO with a view, base the class on the view items. If the view doesn't have a single field that represents a unique key, you contrive uniqueness in the code, employing a technique included in this subsection.

Defining a Persistent Class Based on a View

The sample in this section is similar to the opening chapter sample. The AdventureWorks database Production.Product table is used to populate an `ASPxTitleIndex`. The version of the sample in this section uses a SQL Server view "Current Product List" based on the Production.Product table. Because the `ASPxTitleIndex` is read-only, using a view is a little better fit. You can create the SQL Server view with the SQL Create View statement provided in Listing 7-4.

Listing 7-4: The view was created with Visual Studio's built-in designer, but you can run the following script against the AdventureWorks database to recreate the view.

```
USE [AdventureWorks]
GO
/****** Object:  View [dbo].[Current Product List]
    Script Date: 07/25/2009 15:58:34 ******/
SET ANSI_NULLS ON
GO
SET QUOTED_IDENTIFIER ON
GO
CREATE VIEW [dbo].[Current Product List]
AS
SELECT DISTINCT ProductID, Name
FROM             Production.Product
```

To create the persistent class that represents the view results (ProductID and Name), add a Persistent Object item — not a Persistent Classes item — from the Add New Items dialog box, naming the file ProductView. You can use the Web sample from the opening chapter sample or add it to any Web project. Follow these steps to recreate the sample using the Current Product List view:

1. After you have added the template item Persistent Object, manually change the base type from XPObject to XPLiteObject because XPObject defines its own unique ID but the Product table already has one — ProductID.

2. Add properties for ProductID and Name.

3. Add the Key and Persistent attributes to the ProductID property.

4. Add the Persistent attribute to the Name property.

5. Add the Persistent attribute to the ProductView class, passing the name of the SQL Server View "Current Product List" to the attribute (see Listing 7-5).

6. Add a Global.asax file.

7. Add the boilerplate code (refer to Listing 7-2) to the Application_Start event, changing the GetDataStoreSchema argument to typeof(ProductView) — the name of your persistent class.

8. Add an ASPxTitleIndex to a Web page.

9. Use the Smart tags Choose Data Source menu item for the ASPxTitleIndex and add an XpoDataSource.

10. Set the XpoDataSource's TypeName to ProductView. (The ASPX is provided in Listing 7-6.)

Listing 7-5: The persistent class based on a SQL Server view.

```
using System;
using DevExpress.Xpo;

[Persistent("Current Product List")]
public class ProductView : XPLiteObject
{
  private int productID;
  [Key, Persistent]
  public int ProductID
  {
    get { return productID; }
    set { productID = value; }
  }

  private string name;
  [Persistent("Name")]
  public string Name
  {
    get { return name; }
    set { name = value; }
  }

  public ProductView() : base() {
  // This constructor is used when an
  // object is loaded from a persistent storage.
  // Do not place any code here.
```

```
    }

    public ProductView(Session session) : base(session) {
    // This constructor is used when an
    // object is loaded from a persistent storage.
    // Do not place any code here.
    }

    public override void AfterConstruction() {
      base.AfterConstruction();
    // Place here your initialization code.
    }
}
```

Listing 7-6: The ASPX that shows the relationships and property settings for the ASPxTitleIndex and XpoDataSource.

```
<%@ Page Language="C#" AutoEventWireup="true"
  CodeFile="Default.aspx.cs" Inherits="_Default" %>

<%@ Register assembly="DevExpress.Web.v9.1, Version=9.1.4.0,↩
 Culture=neutral, PublicKeyToken=b88d1754d700e49a"
 namespace="DevExpress.Web.ASPxTitleIndex" tagprefix="dxti" %>

<%@ Register assembly="DevExpress.Xpo.v9.1, Version=9.1.4.0,↩
 Culture=neutral, PublicKeyToken=b88d1754d700e49a" namespace="DevExpress.Xpo"
 tagprefix="dxxpo" %>

<!DOCTYPE html PUBLIC "-//W3C//DTD XHTML 1.0 Transitional//EN"
  "http://www.w3.org/TR/xhtml1/DTD/xhtml1-transitional.dtd">

<html xmlns="http://www.w3.org/1999/xhtml">
<head runat="server">
  <title></title>
</head>
<body>
  <form id="form1" runat="server">
  <div>

    <dxti:ASPxTitleIndex ID="ASPxTitleIndex1" runat="server"
    DataSourceID="XpoDataSource1" TextField="Name">
    </dxti:ASPxTitleIndex>

    <dxxpo:XpoDataSource ID="XpoDataSource1" runat="server"
      TypeName="ProductView">
    </dxxpo:XpoDataSource>

  </div>
  </form>
</body>
</html>
```

Specifying XpoDataSource Criteria

XpoDataSources have a couple of interesting properties, including `Criteria` and `CriteriaCollection`. `XpoDataSource.Criteria` permits you to define a logical filter expression(s) using the Simple tab or Advanced tab (see Figure 7-5). The Simple tab provides an expression-builder that works just like the filter builder does for the ASPxGridView described in Chapter 1; refer to the section "Filtering Data" in Chapter 1. The Advanced tab has a free-form editor that lets you type the filter expression yourself.

Figure 7-5: The Simple filter builder for the XpoDataSource.

In Figure 7-5, the `Criteria [ProductID] < 325` causes the XpoDataSource to return only rows that match the criteria. A cool feature of the Criteria (filter builder) dialog box is that if you use the Simple tab to construct the expression, the Advanced tab is updated to reflect the expression, and vice versa.

The Parameter Collection Editor dialog box (see Figure 7-6) supports expressing criteria that can be originated from a variety of sources, including a Cookie, Control, Form, Profile, QueryString, and Session. (Click the Show Advanced Properties link to display and modify the Parameter Collection properties, such as by changing the name of the parameter.)

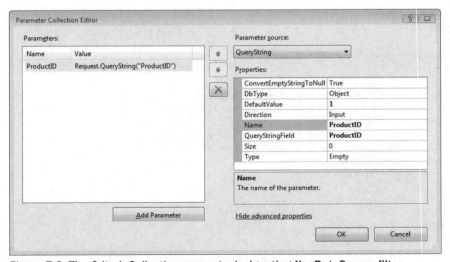

Figure 7-6: The CriteriaCollection supports designating XpoDataSource filter criteria from a variety of sources, such as the QueryString.

When you add criteria, a `Criteria` attribute is added to the `XpoDataSource` and the value of the attribute is stored as a string. When you add items to the `CriteriaCollection` using the Parameter Collection Editor (see Figure 7-6), a `<CriteriaParameters>` sub-element is added to the `XpoDataSource` element and the parameter types are listed as child elements of the `CriteriaParameters` element. The following code snippet shows the `Criteria` attribute and `<CriteriaParameters>` element based on the settings reflected in Figures 7-5 and 7-6:

```
<dxxpo:XpoDataSource ID="XpoDataSource1" runat="server" TypeName="ProductView"
   Criteria="[ProductID] &lt; 325">
   <CriteriaParameters>
     <asp:QueryStringParameter DefaultValue="1" Name="ProductID"
        QueryStringField="ProductID" />
   </CriteriaParameters>
</dxxpo:XpoDataSource>
```

Contriving a Unique ID for Views

The `XpoDataSource` requires a unique identifier. The unique identifier is used to precisely distinguish one object from the next. Sometimes views don't have a distinct identifier; there may in fact be keys from multiple sources. If you want to use a view and there is no single unique identifier, you can contrive a key based on multiple fields.

For simplicity's sake, assume that `ProductID` is not a unique key — maybe it's indexed but not unique. Then, if you want to define an XPO persistent class based on the view Current Product List, place the fields from the view in a struct and attribute them with the `PersistentAttribute` class. Define a class that inherits from `XPLiteObject` and attribute the class with the `PersistentAttribute`, passing in the view name as a string to the attribute. To the new class, define a private field whose type is the struct type, and indicate that the field is the Key and it is Persistent (using attributes). Finally, along with the two constructors and the `AfterConstruction` method, define two read-only properties named `ProductID` and `Name` that return their underlying values from the associated values in the struct type. Listing 7-7 shows a struct that represents the key and a class that uses that struct as its key.

Listing 7-7: Contriving a unique key based on a struct that contains multiple persistent fields, if a unique key is unavailable in a view.

```
using System;
using DevExpress.Xpo;

public struct ProductViewKey
{
  [Persistent("ProductID")]
  public int ProductID;
  [Persistent("Name")]
  public string Name;
}

[Persistent("Current Product List")]
public class ProductView2 : XPLiteObject
{
```

Continued

Listing 7-7: Contriving a unique key based on a struct that contains multiple persistent fields, if a unique key is unavailable in a view. *(continued)*

```
    [Key, Persistent]
    private ProductViewKey Key;
    public int ProductID { get { return Key.ProductID; } }
    public string Name { get { return Key.Name; } }
    public ProductView2(Session session) : base(session) { }
    public ProductView2() : base(Session.DefaultSession) { }
    public override void AfterConstruction() { base.AfterConstruction(); }
}
```

Two persistent classes mapped to the same table or view in a project will cause a runtime exception (and there is really no need for this situation to occur). If you want to use the `ProductView` class defined in Listing 7-5 (shown previously) for the sample, comment out the code in ProductView2. If you want to try the code in `ProductView2`, comment out the code in productView. Remember to change the `typeof` operator in the call to `GetDataStoreSchema` in the `Application_Start` method depending on which of the persistent classes (based on "Current Product List") you want to try.

Enabling ServerMode for High Performance Applications

A big problem with large to enterprise applications is that they contain huge amounts of data. Sometimes the data set is so large that special third-party software is needed just to perform routine operations such as sorting the data. I worked on a state Medicaid project that had data in the petabytes. (A petabyte is 1,000 terabytes, or 1,000,000 gigabytes.) Although you can buy a terabyte hard drive for around $100, a petabyte is still a huge amount of data.

So if working with large amounts of data can require third-party, specialized (and often expensive) software for routine tasks, imagine the performance hit a Web application can take when trying to manage data in something like a grid. The difficulty of large data sets in Web clients is caused by a couple of things. A first and obvious challenge will be Internet speed and bandwidth. The amount of data that can be returned to a client in any reasonable amount of time — in Internet time, reasonable is about half a second — is still finite. Another problem is that when a developer creates a Web page with a lot of data and the user tries to sort a grid column, for example, the sort operation often happens in the Web server's memory unless the developer intentionally requeries the database. Of course, requerying the database means that the applications pay a database hit, the developer has to write a lot of plumbing code, and performance suffers because the Session data is useless. Now imagine that 100 or 1,000 users all want to sort large data sets based on different column values, and the sort happens in the Web server. The result is that the Web server slows to a crawl and users give up. In this scenario, all this happens while the other server, usually a database server, is sitting there doing nothing because all the data is in Session on the Web server.

In short, in everyday scenarios in which developers are building a Web application with a lot of data, there is a good chance that the developer will write custom sorting, paging, grouping, searching, or caching routines to manage the data, or worse, write custom code to push all those operations to the database server. However, the XpoDataSource can already handle large amounts of data and already knows how to push data operations back to the database server, if ServerMode is set to true.

If you set the `XpoDataSource.ServerMode` property to true, the XPO technology uses its internal database engine and rewrites paging, grouping, filtering (searching), and sorting operations back to the database server. `XpoDataSource.ServerMode = true` essentially offloads memory-intensive operations from the Web server and moves them to the database server by rewriting common tasks such as queries. The database is there waiting for work, and common database tasks perform substantially better on a database server designed for the purpose than custom code does.

You can see how the `XpoDataSource` rewrites data operations by opening the SQL Server Profiler and tracing queries sent to the SQL Server instance. To view the `XpoDataSource` server mode (`XpoDataSource.ServerMode = true`) behavior, you can use the XpoWithView sample project and set `XpoDataSource.ServerMode` to true. You need to have the SQL Server Profiler installed on your workstation to follow these steps, which walk you through starting a trace:

1. If you're using Microsoft SQL Server Management Studio (not the Express version), choose Tools ⇨ SQL Server Profiler. (If SQL Server Management Studio is not running, in Windows, choose Start ⇨ All Programs ⇨ Microsoft SQL Server 2005 ⇨ Performance Tools ⇨ SQL Server Profiler.)

2. In SQL Server Profiler, click File ⇨ New Trace to start a new trace.

3. Connect to the server instance containing the database you want to profile. The Trace Properties will be displayed.

4. In the Trace Properties dialog box (see Figure 7-7), you can specify a Name and other information on the General tab, and choose from a large selection of Events to trace on the Events Selection tab. By default, all events are selected.

5. Click Run to start tracing.

6. Run the sample Web application and you will see every query sent to the SQL Server instance (see Figure 7-8).

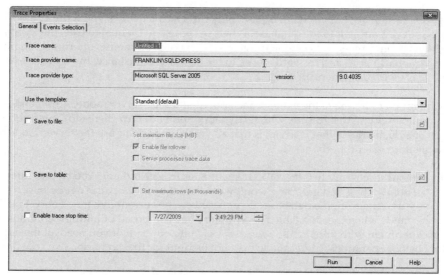

Figure 7-7: Define Trace properties and make event selections; then Click Run to start tracing.

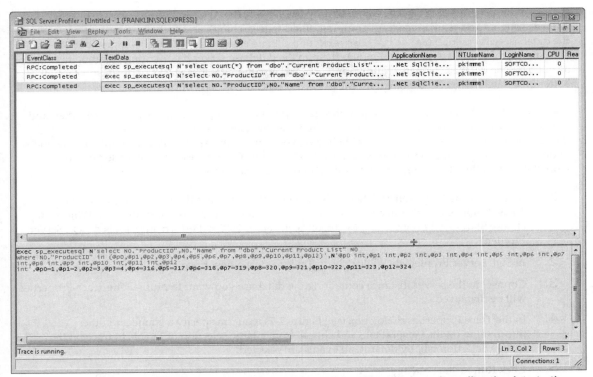

Figure 7-8: The XPO ServerMode engine is writing queries based on the criteria and sending the data to the SQL Server database, as shown in the SQL Server Profiler trace window.

When the `XpoDataSource.ServerMode` is false, only the specific queries you write or associate with your `XpoDataSource` are sent to the database. When `ServerMode` is equal to true, the `XpoDataSource` working with its behind-the-scenes engine turns operations such as paging, filtering, grouping, and sorting into dynamic queries and forwards those to the SQL Server instance. In Figure 7-8, XPO wrote the selected query with the generic in clause.

It is not my intention to trivialize the value of the `XpoDataSource` server mode. A tremendous amount of work went into building this feature, with its dynamic ability to turn client-side interactions into database server-side queries. What is trivial is that all you have to do to use the server mode feature is change a single `Boolean` property.

There are limitations imposed when the `XpoDataSource` is in server mode. You cannot filter and sort by display text. Custom sorting and grouping won't work because the `XpoDataSource` in server mode brings back only the data from the database server based on the current dynamic query. Finally, you can't use server mode when the data table has a primary key composed of multiple columns. If you have a lot of data, experiment with `XpoDataSource.ServerMode = true`. If you need all the data in the result set for custom operations, server mode may not be right for that scenario.

Generating a Database Dynamically with XPO

Gary Short, a DevExpress Technical Evangelist, wrote the sample in this part of the chapter. The sample sends queries to Twitter to sniff for tweets containing *devexpress*, *CodeRush*, *XAF*, or *XPO*. (You could easily just replace the keywords to tailor the sample for your purposes.) Information about discovered tweets is extracted from the XML returned from the Twitter query, and stored in a database. The coolest part of this demo is that XPO will create the database automagically using XPO, XPObjects, and UnitOfWork.

> *The term* automagically *is a play on the third of Arthur C. Clarke's three laws: "Any sufficiently advanced technology is indistinguishable from magic." Clarke was a British science fiction author, inventor, and futurist most famous for writing* 2001: A Space Odyssey.

The sample is explained in the six subsections remaining. Each section is a partial decomposition describing the useful or interesting elements of the sample that will help you understand how the sample works or provide you with useful skills for other solutions. Without further ado, let's continue.

Requesting a Connection String from the Database Server

There are a lot of ways to create a connection string. You can create a connection string by creating a text file with a `.udl` extension in Windows Explorer, double-clicking it, and using the Data Links Properties Editor to visually define a database connection. If the database is visible in Visual Studio's Server Explorer under the Data Connections node, you can copy a connection string out of the Visual Studio Properties window. Another neat way to obtain a connection is demonstrated in the XPODemo project; you can pass the server and database name to `MSSqlConnectionProvider.GetConnectionString` and let the MSSqlConnectionProvider class return a connection string for you. Here is the snippet from the sample:

```
MSSqlConnectionProvider.GetConnectionString(".\\SQLEXPRESS", "Tweets");
```

In the snippet, the database server is the localhost SQLEXPRESS instance represented by `".\\ SQLEXPRESS"` and the database name is `"Tweets"`.

Defining the Tweet Class

XPO works with persistent classes. This is true whether you are defining persistent classes that map to existing tables or persistent classes that will be used to create a database and tables. If you are defining persistent classes for an existing table, use `XPLiteObject` as the persistent base class. If you are defining persistent classes for tables and a database will be generated by XPO, define the persistent class that inherits from `XPObject` and define the property set methods to call the `XPObject` `.SetPropertyValue` method, passing a string indicating the property name, a `ref` argument for the underlying field, and the value parameter with the new value. `SetPropertyValue` will set the underlying field value and perform housekeeping and plumbing such as change tracking. Listing 7-8 provides Gary's implementation of the Tweet class.

Listing 7-8: The XPObject child class that defines a Tweet entity.

```csharp
using System;
using System.Collections.Generic;
using System.Linq;
using System.Web;
using DevExpress.Xpo;

public class Tweet: XPObject
{
    public Tweet(Session session)
        : base(session)
    { }

    private string url;

    [Size(256)]
    public string Url
    {
        get
        {
            return url;
        }
        set
        {
            SetPropertyValue("Url", ref url, value);
        }
    }

    private string author;

    [Size(256)]
    public string Author
    {
        get
        {
            return author;
        }
        set
        {
            SetPropertyValue("Author", ref author, value);
        }
    }
    private string content;
    [Size(256)]
    public string Content
    {
```

```
        get
        {
            return content;
        }
        set
        {
            SetPropertyValue("Content", ref content, value);
        }
    }
}
```

Implicit in the definition of the Tweet class is the primary key. When you use an XPObject, XPO manages the primary key. XPObject has a property Oid that contains the primary key. When the table is generated, it has a primary key defined as an integer and named OID. The Oid property is accessible through XPObject by type base.Oid. (Using base and the member of operator [.] is optional.)

In the sample, because the property names match the table field names, the persistent attribute is not required. In the example, the Size attribute is used as a guide to help XPO generate the table field lengths.

Creating a Database Dynamically with XPO

In the XPODemo example, the database is not predefined. Instead, there is a helper class named DataArchiver. DataArchiver is defined by the caller invoking the static method DataArchiver.Archive. The first thing that Archive does is call the static method SetSqlServerDatabase.

```
private static void SetSqlServerDatabase()
{
  string connectionString =
    MSSqlConnectionProvider.GetConnectionString(".\\SQLEXPRESS", "Tweets");

  XpoDefault.DataLayer =
    XpoDefault.GetDataLayer(connectionString, AutoCreateOption.DatabaseAndSchema);
}
```

The first thing that SetSqlServerDatabase does is ask the MSSqlConnectionProvider to get the connection string. The next thing the method does is to auto-create the database if it doesn't exist. The static method XpoDefault.GetDataLayer with the AutoCreateOption.DatabaseAndSchema creates or updates the database schema for any persistent objects currently defined in the project. For the example, this is the Tweet table that mirrors the Tweet class and a table named XPObjectType that contains information about what is in the database, including the TypeName and AssemblyName. The XPObjectType table is managed by XPO. (The complete listing for DataArchiver is provided at the end of the chapter.)

The concept of refactoring has been around a while. The basic idea is that refactoring helps you improve the design of existing code. One of the refactorings is Inline Temporary. Inline Temporary means that local variables such as connectionString in `SetSqlServerDatabase` mostly just clutter code. In practice, it is preferable to simply place the right side of temporary where the temporary variable is used. Applying the refactoring Inline Temporary in the `SetSqlServerDatabase` yields the following code:

```
private static void SetSqlServerDatabase()
{
  XpoDefault.DataLayer =
     XpoDefault.GetDataLayer(MSSqlConnectionProvider
     .GetConnectionString(
          ".\\SQLEXPRESS", "Tweets"), AutoCreateOption
          .DatabaseAndSchema);
}
```

Writing the refactored code is a stylistic choice, but understanding the principles of refactoring will help you write better code in general.

Querying Twitter

A neat feature of Gary Short's sample is that he shows you how you can query Twitter with a URL query. For example, if you wanted to find Tweets about DevExpress, you could enter the following query in the address bar of your browser:

```
http://search.twitter.com/search.atom?lang=en&q=deveexpress
```

Twitter will respond with links containing the relevant matching part of the query string.

In the sample application, this query string is used in the `ArchiveKeyword` method to load the results as an instance of a `System.Xml.Linq.XDocument` (an aspect of the LINQ for XML capability of .NET). Here is the statement demonstrating how the query string is sent to Twitter in code:

```
XDocument searchXML = XDocument.Load(
   @"http://search.twitter.com/search.atom?lang=en&q=" + keyword);
```

In the fragment, the query string is passed to `XDocument.Load`, returning the results as an `XDocument` object that is queryable using LINQ for XML.

Extracting the Tweet Data with LINQ for XML

The next step in the sample is to parse the salient elements — the properties represented by the `Tweet` class — of the XML document to create an instance of the `Tweet` object in preparation for storing the Tweet data in the Tweets.Tweet table. Listing 7-9 shows the `ArchiveKeyword` method.

Listing 7-9: The implementation of the DataArchiver.ArchiveKeyword method.

```
private static void ArchiveKeyword(string keyword, ref UnitOfWork uow)
{
  //GS - Pull back the search results from search.twitter.com
  XDocument searchXML =
    XDocument.Load(
    @"http://search.twitter.com/search.atom?lang=en&q=" + keyword);

  //GS - Add in the Atom namespace
  XNamespace xmlns = "http://www.w3.org/2005/Atom";

  //GS - From the 'entry' element in the feed pull
  //out url, content and author
  var results = from entry in searchXML.Descendants(xmlns + "entry")
    select new
    {
      Url = entry.Element(xmlns + "link").Attribute("href").Value,
      Content = entry.Element(xmlns + "title").Value,
      Author = entry.Element(xmlns + "author")
        .Element(xmlns + "name").Value
    };

  //GS - Iterate over the results and create new Tweet objects...
  foreach (var result in results)
  {
    //GS - If the tweet as been archived already then skip it.
    if (TweetAlreadyArchived(result.Url))
      continue;

    Tweet tweet = new Tweet(uow);
    tweet.Url = result.Url;
    tweet.Content = result.Content;
    tweet.Author = result.Author;
  }
}
```

Listing 7-9 contains Gary Short's original comments. Here is some additional technical information elaborating on elements of the framework used and Gary's solution. The first statement returns Tweets based on the search keyword. The second statement defines an XML namespace for the XDocument. The results local variable is the result of the LINQ for XML query of the returned XML document. The LINQ for XML select clause is employing function construction to dynamically create a class that contains a URL, Content, and Author properties. The results variable will be an instance of IEnumerable<T>, where T is a project of a type containing URL, Content, and Author information. Finally, results is checked in a for each loop to see whether the specified URL already exists in the database by calling TweetAlreadyArchived (see Listing 7-10 in the next subsection). If not, the Tweet object is created and associated with an instance of UnitOfWork (passed into ArchiveKeyword.) The remaining aspect of the sample is to look at how UnitOfWork is used in conjunction with the DataArchiver class.

Using UnitOfWork to Update the Database

DevExpress's UnitOfWork class was designed internally based on the UnitOfWork design pattern as specified by Martin Fowler (*Patterns of Enterprise Application Architecture*, Addison Wesley, page 184). UnitOfWork supports writing code that makes multiple changes together — similarly to how a transaction works — and commits all the changes together. The database is hidden behind the UnitOfWork object, so you write code focusing on adding, updating, and removing persistent objects, and the UnitOfWork class coordinates all the changes to update the underlying data store. Here is Listing 7-10 containing all of the DataArchiver code.

Listing 7-10: The DataArchiver class uses XPO's UnitOfWork class to coordinate updating the Tweets database with all instances of matching keywords.

```
using System;
using System.Collections.Generic;
using System.Linq;
using System.Web;
using System.ComponentModel;
using System.Xml.Linq;
using DevExpress.Xpo;
using DevExpress.Xpo.DB;
using DevExpress.Data.Filtering;

/// <summary>
/// Summary description for DataLoader
/// </summary>
public class DataArchiver
{
  public static void Archive()
  {
    //The number one feature of the UnitOfWork is that it can be
    //passed around various functions and it will 'remember' creates,
    //updates and deletes to objects from those various functions so
    //that the developer doesn't have to track them himself. This function
    //demonstrates this functionality.

    //GS - Tell XPO which database to use
    SetSqlServerDatabase();

    //GS - Archive a few important keywords, building up the
    //objects in the UnitOfWork which we pass around.
    UnitOfWork uow = new UnitOfWork();
    ArchiveKeyword("devexpress", uow);
    ArchiveKeyword("CodeRush", uow);
    ArchiveKeyword("XAF", uow);
    ArchiveKeyword("XPO", uow);

    // GS - Commit the outstanding changes that the UnitOfWork knows about.
    // That is all we have to do to have our
```

```
    // changes persisted to the database.
    uow.CommitChanges();

    //GS - A tidy programmer is a happy programmer :-)
    uow.Dispose();
}

private static bool TweetAlreadyArchived(string url)
{
    Tweet target;

    //GS - Within the context of a UnitOfWork...
    using (UnitOfWork uow = new UnitOfWork())
    {
        //GS - Specify a criteria based on a given url...
        CriteriaOperator criteria =
            new BinaryOperator("Url", url, BinaryOperatorType.Equal);

        //GS - And retrieve the object matching that criteria.
        target = uow.FindObject<Tweet>(criteria);
    }

    //GS - Answer whether or not we found that object
    return target != null;
}

private static void SetSqlServerDatabase()
{
    string connectionString =
        MSSqlConnectionProvider.GetConnectionString(
        ".\\SQLEXPRESS", "Tweets");

    XpoDefault.DataLayer =
        XpoDefault.GetDataLayer(connectionString,
        AutoCreateOption.DatabaseAndSchema);
}

private static void ArchiveKeyword(string keyword, UnitOfWork uow)
{
    //GS - Pull back the search results from search.twitter.com
    XDocument searchXML =
        XDocument.Load(
        @"http://search.twitter.com/search.atom?lang=en&q=" + keyword);

    //GS - Add in the Atom namespace
    XNamespace xmlns = "http://www.w3.org/2005/Atom";

    //GS - From the 'entry' element in the feed pull
    //out url, content and author
    var results = from entry in searchXML.Descendants(xmlns + "entry")
        select new
        {
            Url = entry.Element(xmlns + "link").Attribute("href").Value,
```

Continued

387

Listing 7-10: The DataArchiver class uses XPO's UnitOfWork class to coordinate updating the Tweets database with all instances of matching keywords. *(continued)*

```
          Content = entry.Element(xmlns + "title").Value,
          Author = entry.Element(xmlns + "author").Element(xmlns + "name").Value
       };

       //GS - Iterate over the results and create new Tweet objects...
       foreach (var result in results)
       {
          //GS - If the tweet as been archived already then skip it.
          if (TweetAlreadyArchived(result.Url))
            continue;

          Tweet tweet = new Tweet(uow);
          tweet.Url = result.Url;
          tweet.Content = result.Content;
          tweet.Author = result.Author;
       }
    }
 }
```

To use the `DataArchiver` just call `DataArchiver.Archive`. `Archive` establishes the target database with the call to `SetSqlServerDatabase`. Next, a `UnitOfWork` object is created. Notice that because you are using `UnitOfWork`, the ADO.NET plumbing usually needed is not necessary. (`UnitOfWork` manages the database plumbing from here on out.) For each keyword, call `ArchiveKeyWord`, passing in the `UnitOfWork` instance. (The only change you might make to Gary's code is to employ the using clause or a `try...catch...except...finally` block to manage the `UnitOfWork` object. When all the work encapsulated in `UnitOfWork` has been completed, call `UnitOfWork.CommitChanges`. `CommitChanges` will make all the database changes that are necessary. Finally, dispose of the `UnitOfWork` object (`uow`).

If you decided to employ the using statement, `CommitChanges` would be the last statement in the using block, and `Dispose` is called implicitly at the end of the using block because `UnitOfWork` implements `IDisposable`. (An `IDisposable` object's `Dispose` method is automatically called at the end of a using block.)

`UnitOfWork` is also demonstrated in the method `TweetAlreadyArchived`. (In that method, the using block technique is demonstrated.) `TweetAlreadyArchived` accepts a URL parameter and creates a `BinaryOperator` object to determine whether the underlying data store contains that URL already.

That's all there is to it. In Gary's example, about 100 lines of code do everything — with XPO — from creating the database and table to searching and updating the underlying database with very little explicit ADO.NET code.

Summary

A year ago when someone asked about DevExpress, I automatically thought of a great company with smart developers who produced really professional-looking windows and Web controls, and CodeRush. DevExpress does offer these benefits to customers, but it provides much more as well. DevExpress also offers great infrastructure tools, such as XPO, XAF (an application framework that, unfortunately, didn't make it in this book), Refactor! Pro, and now Silverlight tools. DevExpress also offers its customers a commitment to innovative solutions and a tremendous amount of online content to help you do a better job at a wide variety of challenges you face as developers.

XPO is the acronym given for DevExpress's foray into the database framework solutions. XPO is database agnostic, allowing you to switch database providers without code changes. As do some other solutions, XPO lets you define persistent classes and use custom objects against your database. Perhaps in contrast to a lot of other database framework solutions, XPO also offers the ability to create the persistence layer from custom classes. It also contains the `UnitOfWork` class for a simplified transaction style of design and development that hides a lot of ADO.NET plumbing and the `XpoDataSource` for high-volume, server-mode database needs.

8

Implementing Data Solutions with the ASPxPivotGrid

I took the whole family to Washington D.C. for a vacation in 2001. We had an itinerary that included staying at the wonderful Watergate hotel in a suite on the Potomac side; touring the White House; seeing Mozart's *Marriage of Figaro* at the Kennedy Center, and visiting several of the museums in the Smithsonian complex. We were able to do everything except go to the Kennedy Center; Mozart was sold out. The opera was replaced with a trip on the Metro to see the Ringling Brothers. (I think the kids enjoyed that more, anyway.)

I recall that at the Smithsonian Natural Museum of American History we saw the Fonz's jacket (played by Henry Winkler on Happy Days), the Howdy Doody puppet, and an Altair MITS. The Altair was a blue box with lights. My recollection of this nascent period of the microcomputer industry is that the Altair was the first complete microcomputer kit, and it was the first microcomputer to have Microsoft software, a version of BASIC. The early version of BASIC made the lights blink, and the user had to interpret the meaning of the lights. I recall that microcomputers didn't seem to hit the mainstream consciousness until computers with monitors and keyboards existed and Lotus 1-2-3 started flying off the shelves. This interval spanned roughly 1975 to 1985 (or a little later).

Lotus 1-2-3 was the brainchild of Mitch Kapor and Jonathan Sachs. Lotus 1-2-3 was a spreadsheet application and was instrumental in helping microcomputers make business sense to everyday companies. (I know some of this firsthand because I started working with computers as part of my job around the same time period.) What is interesting about spreadsheets is that they permit users to arrange all kinds of data in rows and columns and explore the meaning of that data based on row and column intersections, generally referred to as cells. By performing mathematical operations, lookups, and logical operations, users can garner meaning from data.

Twenty-five years later, businesses still want to mine data, create intersections between rows and columns, and compute or convey meaning based on the data. An ability to slice, dice, and rearrange the data by an end user, and doing so over an Internet connection, makes this capability as compelling, if not more so, as it was when Kapor and Sachs helped cause the microcomputer explosion.

Data compiled into these clumps of rows, columns, and meaning are synonymously referred to as OLAP (online analytical processing) cubes, multidimensional cubes, or hypercubes. An ability to dynamically manipulate and slice and dice data using OLAP or relational data, by developers and end users, is supported by DevExpress's ASPxPivotGrid. The ASPxPivotGrid is a very rich Web control, and this chapter shows you how to use the ASPxPivotGrid with an OLAP cube, relational data, and as a data source for DevExpress's XtraChart control.

Transforming Relational Data into an ASPxPivotGrid

In some scenarios, developers can use OLE Automation to interact with an application such as Microsoft Excel, which in turn supports creating PivotTables. The challenge is that out-of-process applications such as Excel are much harder to integrate into Web solutions, and because of perceived or real security concerns, many companies are reluctant to put client applications on servers. The ASPxPivotGrid was engineered from the ground up to give developers and users the power to create pivot tables and pivot reports that can be integrated into Web applications.

If your users need rows and columns of data that can be filtered, sorted, or grouped by the end user, you can use an ASPxGridView. If your end users need to be able to filter, sort, group, and rearrange the data into hierarchies, interchange rows and columns, and move items between playing the role of a filter item, row item, or column item, you can use an ASPxPivotGrid. In effect, with the ASPxGridView, the developer decides the fundamental arrangement of the data and the user filters that result set; and with the ASPxPivotGrid, the user filters, sorts, and groups data as well as dynamically changes the fundamental arrangement of the result set. The motivation behind the ASPxPivotGrid is to let the user figure out how to mine meaning from that data.

Using Relational Data in an ASPxPivotGrid

The ASPxPivotGrid supports users shaping data to explore the data and understand better what the data mean. For the first sample in this chapter, I returned to the CarsDB.mdb database introduced in Chapter 6, which contains order information. By placing the Customers, Orders, and Cars information in a query and binding that query to an ASPxPivotGrid you can reorganize information to explore order and payment information by model and company. The ASPxPivotGrid can — and does, in the example — show you summary data, support paging and sorting out of the box.

The solution is comprised of a three-table join and an ASPxPivotGrid. The multitable query is bound to an ASPxPivotGrid. The columns in the result set are each associated to the ASPxPivotGrid.Fields collection, and each Fields Area property is set to its purpose. For example, if a field will be used initially as a filter, the Area property is set to `FilterArea`. The available Area values are `RowArea`, `ColumnArea`, `FilterArea`, and `DataArea`.

❑   `RowArea` fields are placed along the vertical axis.

❑   `ColumnArea` values are placed on a horizontal axis.

❑   The intersections of `RowAreas` and `ColumnAreas` represent the `DataArea` for that intersection.

❑   `FilterArea` items are used to manipulate the result set the same basic way that adding a `WHERE` predicate to a query will. An important aspect of how Fields and Areas works is that when you place them at design time, the placement represents an initial organization; the user can grab items from the `FilterArea`, `RowArea`, and `ColumnArea` and move those items to one of the other areas and back.

❑   When fields are moved at runtime, the ASPxPivotGrid is reorganized to reflect the change and the `DataArea` and summary values are updated to contain the new values based on the row and column intersections.

All this happens smoothly with Ajax, letting the user explore the data by moving elements back and forth.

Defining the SQL Query

The data for the sample is from the CarsDB.mdb database. The three tables used are Cars, Customers, and Orders. The Orders table is joined to Customers by `Orders.CustomerID` and `Customers.ID`. The Cars table is joined to the Orders table by `Cars.ID` and `Orders.ProductID`. All the joins are created using an inner join. You can use Visual Studio's Query Designer by right-clicking on the Tables folder in the Server Explorer or by using the query-building capabilities of Microsoft Access. Listing 8-1 contains the query used for the sample.

Listing 8-1: A three-table query containing customer, order, and product (car) information.

```
SELECT Cars.Model, Cars.Price, Orders.PurchaseDate, Orders.PaymentType,
  Orders.PaymentAmount, Orders.Quantity, Customers.Company, Customers.City
FROM (Orders INNER JOIN Customers ON Orders.CustomerID = Customers.ID)
  INNER JOIN Cars ON Orders.ProductID = Cars.ID
```

To kick-start the example, add an `ASPxPivotGrid` from the Data tab of the Toolbox and associate an `AccessDataSource` with the `ASPxPivotGrid` from the Smart tags menu, Choose Data Source item. On the Configure Select Statement step of the Configure Data Source Wizard, choose the Specify a Custom SQL Statement or Stored Procedure option. On the Define Custom Statements or Stored Procedures SELECT statement, enter the query from Listing 8-1. (You can always use the Query Builder button on this step to define the query.) (Refer to Figure 8-1.)

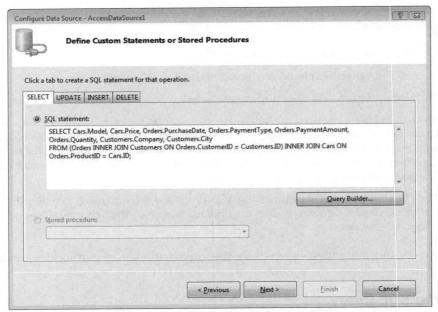

Figure 8-1: Use the query from Listing 8-1 for the SELECT statement of the AccessDataSource.

After the basic configuration of the `AccessDataSource`, the Web page will contain an `ASPxPivotGrid` and `AccessDataSource`. The `ASPxPivotGrid` — as shown in Figure 8-2 — is initially unconfigured and will not reflect any of the data in the result set until you define the Fields properties.

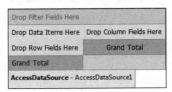

Figure 8-2: The ASPxPivotGrid before you define fields for the control.

Configuring the ASPxPivotGrid Fields

To define the fields to display in the `ASPxPivotGrid`, click the Fields item from the Smart tags menu. Using the Fields Editor Form — see Figure 8-3 — add a field for each of the columns returned from the query in Listing 8-1.

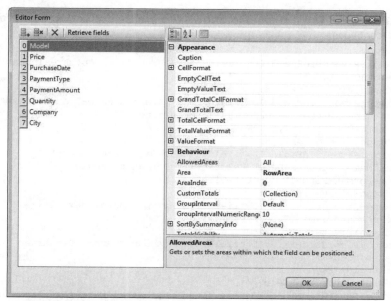

Figure 8-3: The Fields Editor Form assists in defining the Fields for the ASPxPivotGrid.

Listing 8-2: The ASPX for the sample shows the Fields collection used for the sample application.

```
<%@ Page Language="C#" AutoEventWireup="true"  CodeFile="Default.aspx.cs"
Inherits="_Default" %>

<%@ Register assembly="DevExpress.Web.ASPxPivotGrid.v9.1,
Version=9.1.4.0, Culture=neutral, PublicKeyToken=b88d1754d700e49a"
namespace="DevExpress.Web.ASPxPivotGrid" tagprefix="dxwpg" %>

<!DOCTYPE html PUBLIC "-//W3C//DTD XHTML 1.0 Transitional//EN"
"http://www.w3.org/TR/xhtml1/DTD/xhtml1-transitional.dtd">

<html xmlns="http://www.w3.org/1999/xhtml">
<head runat="server">
    <title></title>
</head>
<body>
  <form id="form1" runat="server">
  <div>

    <dxwpg:ASPxPivotGrid ID="ASPxPivotGrid1" runat="server"
    DataSourceID="AccessDataSource1">
    <Fields>
```

Continued

Listing 8-2: The ASPX for the sample shows the Fields collection used for the sample application. *(continued)*

```
            <dxwpg:PivotGridField ID="fieldModel" Area="RowArea" AreaIndex="0"
            FieldName="Model">
            </dxwpg:PivotGridField>
            <dxwpg:PivotGridField ID="fieldPrice" Area="RowArea" AreaIndex="1"
            FieldName="Price" ValueFormat-FormatString="C"
            ValueFormat-FormatType="Numeric">
            </dxwpg:PivotGridField>
            <dxwpg:PivotGridField ID="fieldPurchaseDate" AreaIndex="2"
            FieldName="PurchaseDate" ValueFormat-FormatString="d"
            ValueFormat-FormatType="DateTime">
            </dxwpg:PivotGridField>
            <dxwpg:PivotGridField ID="fieldPaymentType" AreaIndex="1"
            FieldName="PaymentType">
            </dxwpg:PivotGridField>
            <dxwpg:PivotGridField ID="fieldPaymentAmount" Area="DataArea"
               AreaIndex="1"
            FieldName="PaymentAmount">
            </dxwpg:PivotGridField>
            <dxwpg:PivotGridField ID="fieldQuantity" Area="DataArea" AreaIndex="0"
            FieldName="Quantity">
            </dxwpg:PivotGridField>
            <dxwpg:PivotGridField ID="fieldCompany" Area="ColumnArea" AreaIndex="0"
            FieldName="Company">
            </dxwpg:PivotGridField>
            <dxwpg:PivotGridField ID="fieldCity" AreaIndex="0"
            FieldName="City">
            </dxwpg:PivotGridField>
        </Fields>
        <Styles CssFilePath="~/App_Themes/Aqua/{0}/styles.css" CssPostfix="Aqua">
          <MenuStyle GutterWidth="0px" />
        </Styles>
        <OptionsDataField AreaIndex="1" />
        <Images ImageFolder="~/App_Themes/Aqua/{0}/">
          <FieldValueCollapsed Height="15px"
          Url="~/App_Themes/Aqua/PivotGrid/pgCollapsedButton.png" Width="15px" />
          <FieldValueExpanded Height="15px"
          Url="~/App_Themes/Aqua/PivotGrid/pgExpandedButton.png" Width="15px" />
          <HeaderFilter Height="19px"
          Url="~/App_Themes/Aqua/PivotGrid/pgFilterButton.png" Width="19px" />
          <HeaderActiveFilter Height="19px"
          Url="~/App_Themes/Aqua/PivotGrid/pgFilterButtonActive.png" Width="19px" />
          <HeaderSortDown Height="15px"
          Url="~/App_Themes/Aqua/PivotGrid/pgHeaderSortDown.png" Width="11px" />
          <HeaderSortUp Height="15px"
          Url="~/App_Themes/Aqua/PivotGrid/pgHeaderSortUp.png" Width="11px" />
          <FilterWindowSizeGrip Height="12px"
```

```
            Url="~/App_Themes/Aqua/PivotGrid/pgFilterResizer.png" Width="12px" />
          <CustomizationFieldsClose Height="19px"
            Url="~/App_Themes/Aqua/PivotGrid/pcCloseButton.png" Width="19px" />
          <CustomizationFieldsBackground
            Url="~/App_Themes/Aqua/PivotGrid/pcHeaderBack.gif" />
          <SortByColumn Height="14px"
            Url="~/App_Themes/Aqua/PivotGrid/pgSortByColumn.png" Width="15px" />
          </Images>
          <OptionsLoadingPanel Text="">
          </OptionsLoadingPanel>
          <OptionsPager>
            <AllButton>
            <Image Height="19px" Width="27px" />
            </AllButton>
            <FirstPageButton>
            <Image Height="19px" Width="23px" />
            </FirstPageButton>
            <LastPageButton>
            <Image Height="19px" Width="23px" />
            </LastPageButton>
            <NextPageButton>
            <Image Height="19px" Width="19px" />
            </NextPageButton>
            <PrevPageButton>
            <Image Height="19px" Width="19px" />
            </PrevPageButton>
          </OptionsPager>
          </dxwpg:ASPxPivotGrid>
          <asp:AccessDataSource ID="AccessDataSource1" runat="server"
          DataFile="~/App_Data/CarsDB.mdb" SelectCommand="SELECT Cars.Model,
       Cars.Price, Orders.PurchaseDate, Orders.PaymentType, Orders.PaymentAmount,
       Orders.Quantity, Customers.Company, Customers.City
    FROM (Orders INNER JOIN Customers ON Orders.CustomerID = Customers.ID)
     INNER JOIN Cars ON Orders.ProductID = Cars.ID;
    " onselecting="AccessDataSource1_Selecting"></asp:AccessDataSource>

      </div>
      </form>
  </body>
  </html>
```

Using the code in Listing 8-2 as a guide, configure the fields using the Editor Form as described in Table 8-1. For the table elements that are empty, the default settings are used. The AreaIndex property is established based on the order in which an item is assigned to a specific area. (Refer to Figure 8-4 for the design time view of the ASPxPivotGrid based on the field settings in Table 8-1.)

Table 8-1: Add the fields and set the properties for the ASPxPivotGrid according to the contents of the table.

Fieldname	area	value-formatstring	value-formattype
Model	RowArea		
Price	RowArea	C	Numeric
PurchaseDate	FilterArea	D	DateTime
PaymentType	FilterArea		
PaymentAmount	DataArea		
Quantity	DataArea		
Company	ColumnArea		
City	FilterArea		

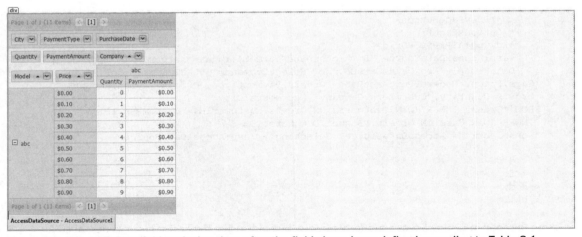

Figure 8-4: The ASPxPivotGrid at design time after the fields have been defined according to Table 8-1.

Given the data source and the ASPxPivotGrid as configured, no code-behind is needed to run the sample. When you run the example, the results should appear to be approximately like the browser client area shown in Figure 8-5. When the sample is running, you can click the City, PaymentType, PurchaseDate, Model, Price, or Company to filter the data shown. You can click any of the fields in the ColumnArea or RowArea to sort based on that field. Finally, you can drag and drop any of the fields from the DataArea (Quantity and Price), FilterArea (City, PaymentType, or PurchaseDate), ColumnArea

(Company), or `RowArea` (Model or Price) (as configured) to reorganize the `ASPxPivotGrid`, and the summary values will be updated.

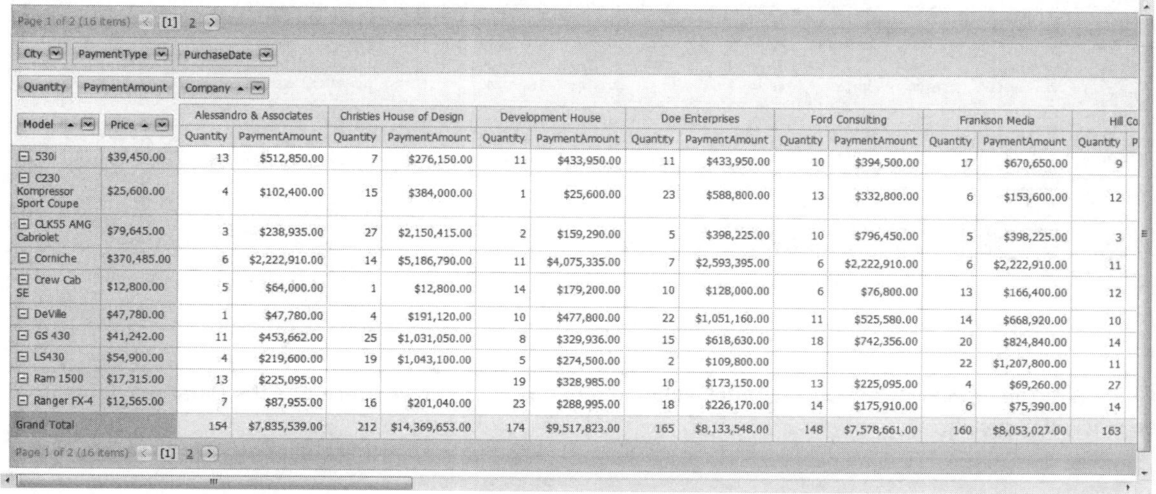

Model	Price	Alessandro & Associates		Christies House of Design		Development House		Doe Enterprises		Ford Consulting		Frankson Media		Hill Co
		Quantity	PaymentAmount	Quantity	PaymentAmount	Quantity	PaymentAmount	Quantity	PaymentAmount	Quantity	PaymentAmount	Quantity	PaymentAmount	Quantity
530i	$39,450.00	13	$512,850.00	7	$276,150.00	11	$433,950.00	11	$433,950.00	10	$394,500.00	17	$670,650.00	9
C230 Kompressor Sport Coupe	$25,600.00	4	$102,400.00	15	$384,000.00	1	$25,600.00	23	$588,800.00	13	$332,800.00	6	$153,600.00	12
CLK55 AMG Cabriolet	$79,645.00	3	$238,935.00	27	$2,150,415.00	2	$159,290.00	5	$398,225.00	10	$796,450.00	5	$398,225.00	3
Corniche	$370,485.00	6	$2,222,910.00	14	$5,186,790.00	11	$4,075,335.00	7	$2,593,395.00	6	$2,222,910.00	6	$2,222,910.00	11
Crew Cab SE	$12,800.00	5	$64,000.00	1	$12,800.00	14	$179,200.00	10	$128,000.00	6	$76,800.00	13	$166,400.00	12
DeVille	$47,780.00	1	$47,780.00	4	$191,120.00	10	$477,800.00	22	$1,051,160.00	11	$525,580.00	14	$668,920.00	10
GS 430	$41,242.00	11	$453,662.00	25	$1,031,050.00	8	$329,936.00	15	$618,630.00	18	$742,356.00	20	$824,840.00	14
LS430	$54,900.00	4	$219,600.00	19	$1,043,100.00	5	$274,500.00	2	$109,800.00			22	$1,207,800.00	11
Ram 1500	$17,315.00	13	$225,095.00			19	$328,985.00	10	$173,150.00	13	$225,095.00	4	$69,260.00	27
Ranger FX-4	$12,565.00	7	$87,955.00	16	$201,040.00	23	$288,995.00	18	$226,170.00	14	$175,910.00	6	$75,390.00	14
Grand Total		154	$7,835,539.00	212	$14,369,653.00	174	$9,517,823.00	165	$8,133,548.00	148	$7,578,661.00	160	$8,053,027.00	163

Figure 8-5: The ASPxPivotGrid with an AccessDataSource containing the query in Listing 8-1 and the Fields settings in Table 8-1.

Using Multiple Data Fields

A cool feature of the `ASPxPivotGrid` is that the values of row and column intersections do not have to be limited to one value. You can add multiple fields to the `DataArea`, as demonstrated in the sample and shown in Figure 8-5. In the sample, each row and column shows the Quantity and PaymentAmount for a given Model and Company. For example, you can see that Newman Systems paid just over a half million dollars for 14 (BMW) 530i automobiles.

The `ASPxPivotGrid` supports an unlimited number of DataArea fields. You can also change where the extra data fields are placed. By default, `DataArea` items are placed side by side under a column. This configuration represents the `OptionsDataField.Area ColumnArea` setting. If you want `DataArea` items side by side under the row area, change the `ASPxPivotGrid`'s `OptionsDataField.Area` setting to `RowArea` (see Figure 8-6). If you want to add more data fields, specify additional columns in the results (or use and existing column) and change the associated field's Area property to `DataArea`.

Page 1 of 4 (32 items) ◁ [1] 2 3 4 ▷

City ▾ | PaymentType ▾ | PurchaseDate ▾

Quantity | PaymentAmount | Company △ ▾

Model △ ▾	Data	Alessandro & Associates	Christies House of Design	Development House	Doe Enterprises	Ford Consulting	Frankson Media	Hill Corporation	Holmes World	James Systems	Jeffers Clinic	Jones & Assoc	Mat...
530i	Quantity	13	7	11	11	10	17	9	10	16	14	8	
	PaymentAmount	$512,850.00	$276,150.00	$433,950.00	$433,950.00	$394,500.00	$670,650.00	$355,050.00	$394,500.00	$631,200.00	$552,300.00	$315,600.00	$19...
C230 Kompressor Sport Coupe	Quantity	4	15	1	23	13	6	12	9	9	9	7	
	PaymentAmount	$102,400.00	$384,000.00	$25,600.00	$588,800.00	$332,800.00	$153,600.00	$307,200.00	$230,400.00	$230,400.00	$230,400.00	$179,200.00	$5E...
CLK55 AMG Cabriolet	Quantity	3	27	2	5	10	5	3	7	13	9	3	
	PaymentAmount	$238,935.00	$2,150,415.00	$159,290.00	$398,225.00	$796,450.00	$398,225.00	$238,935.00	$557,515.00	$1,035,385.00	$716,805.00	$238,935.00	$47...
Corniche	Quantity	6	14	11	7	6	6	11	27	3	11	11	
	PaymentAmount	$2,222,910.00	$5,186,790.00	$4,075,335.00	$2,593,395.00	$2,222,910.00	$2,222,910.00	$4,075,335.00	$10,003,095.00	$1,111,455.00	$4,075,335.00	$4,075,335.00	$1,4...
Crew Cab SE	Quantity	5	1	14	10	6	13	12	10	18	15	16	
	PaymentAmount	$64,000.00	$12,800.00	$179,200.00	$128,000.00	$76,800.00	$166,400.00	$153,600.00	$128,000.00	$230,400.00	$192,000.00	$204,800.00	
Grand Total	Quantity	154	212	174	165	148	160	163	144	160	179	178	
	PaymentAmount	$7,835,539.00	$14,369,653.00	$9,517,823.00	$8,133,548.00	$7,578,661.00	$8,053,027.00	$8,831,991.00	$14,406,099.00	$6,963,765.00	$11,113,011.00	$9,805,240.00	$6,18...

Page 1 of 4 (32 items) ◁ [1] 2 3 4 ▷

Figure 8-6: The ASPxPivotGrid.OptionsDataField.Area property set to RowArea causes the DataArea items to be stacked vertically.

Choosing the Field Summary Type

Each Field object in the ASPxPivotGrid's Fields collection has a SummaryType property, which indicates the kind of aggregation operation that will be performed on all the values for that field. By default, the SummaryType is Sum. Thus, if a field is assigned to the DataArea, its SummaryType operation is performed along both the vertical and horizontal axis. For instance, Quantity is assigned to the DataArea in the sample. This results in the sum of all cars that each customer purchased along the vertical axis. And along the horizontal access the sum of all cars of a given type, spanning all customers, is displayed along the horizontal axis.

Instead of totaling the payment amounts along the vertical and horizontal axis, you could set the SummaryType for PaymentAmount to calculate the average payment per customer along the vertical axis and the average payment amount per automobile for all customers along the horizontal axis. The available choices for SummaryType are Count, Sum, Min, Max, Average, StdDev, StdDevp, Var. Varp, or Custom. If you set the SummaryType to Custom and implement an event handler for the CustomSummary event, you can implement your own aggregation behavior.

Implementing a Custom Summary

In this section, take a moment to think about customers. People who use your product are acting in the capacity of customers. Only a very small percentage of them will be power users — that is, someone that can do substantially more than just use your application. A power user is the kind of person who asks for raw data and access to your database, and who wants to write some kind of custom solution. Again, you're likely to have only a very small number of power users, but they exist.

Consider the CarsDB.mdb database. Suppose that a power user wants to know what the median (or middle of the road payment amount) will be. A power user may be capable of writing a SELECT statement against the raw data like the one in Listing 8-3 and physically examine the data, manually, for the median value.

Listing 8-3: A query that contains the median value in the result set.

```
SELECT Cars.Model, Cars.Price, Orders.PurchaseDate, Orders.PaymentType,
  Orders.PaymentAmount, Orders.Quantity, Customers.Company, Customers.City
FROM ((Orders INNER JOIN
Customers ON Orders.CustomerID = Customers.ID) INNER JOIN
Cars ON Orders.ProductID = Cars.ID)
WHERE (Customers.Company LIKE 'Ales%')
ORDER BY Orders.PaymentAmount
```

The result set returns 55 rows, and the 27 or 28 value is approximately the median payment amount, which happens to be 80,000 in the available sample database. Perhaps a more clever power user can write a slightly more complex Access query and return just the data representing the median value (see Listing 8-4).

Listing 8-4: This query returns just the row containing the single median value.

```
SELECT TOP 1 * FROM
  (SELECT  * FROM
    (SELECT TOP 50 PERCENT Cars.Model, Cars.Price, Orders.PurchaseDate,
    Orders.PaymentType, Orders.PaymentAmount, Orders.Quantity,
    Customers.Company, Customers.City
    FROM ((Orders INNER JOIN
    Customers ON Orders.CustomerID = Customers.ID) INNER JOIN
    Cars ON Orders.ProductID = Cars.ID)
    WHERE (Customers.Company LIKE 'Ales%')
    ORDER BY Orders.PaymentAmount)
  ORDER BY PaymentAmount DESC)
```

The inner SELECT statement returns the TOP 50 PERCENT of records matching the WHERE clause in ascending order. The next outer SELECT statement reverses the order of those results, and the outer SELECT grabs the first record. The result is the median PaymentAmount or 80000 as desired, but there are problems here. The first problem is that it is highly unlikely that you will want to let users query directly against your database. Assuming that you were able to provide access to the data to a power user, such a user could also accidentally or intentionally corrupt the database. An additional problem is that business people will likely want to be able to answer these kinds of questions — such as what is the median value or something similar — but very few of those people will be able to contrive a solution themselves.

The solution really lies in requirements gathering. If, in fact, calculating the median — or anything else — is one of the requirements, providing that aspect of the solution through the application rather than relying on power users and external manipulation of the data is the way to go. This is where a capability of the ASPxPivotGrid, such as calculating custom summary values, comes into play.

The ASPxPivotGrid supports custom summaries, which you can easily add, without the security risks; extra support (because power users ask questions based on solutions they create); and the headache that goes with implicitly expanding requirements. To add a custom summary — in this case, calculating the median PaymentAmount — follow these steps:

1. Change the Caption property of the summary field to cue the user as to what the data mean by changing the PaymentAmount field's caption to "Payment Amount (Median)."

2. Set PaymentAmount's SummaryType to Custom (from the default of Sum).

3. Define the CustomSummary event handler for the ASPxPivotGrid.

4. Add the code to the CustomSummary event that performs the calculation — in this example, finding the median value (see Listing 8-5).

5. Assign the calculated summary value to the event argument property e.CustomValue.

Listing 8-5: This CustomSummary event handler calculates the median PaymentAmount value.

```
protected void ASPxPivotGrid1_CustomSummary(object sender,
  DevExpress.Web.ASPxPivotGrid.PivotGridCustomSummaryEventArgs e)
{
  if (e.FieldName != "PaymentAmount") return;
  // returns records associated with cell being processed
  DevExpress.XtraPivotGrid.PivotDrillDownDataSource source =
    e.CreateDrillDownDataSource();

  // processing summary cells
  var amounts =
    from DevExpress.XtraPivotGrid.PivotDrillDownDataRow row in source
    let val = (decimal)row[e.DataField]
    orderby val
    select val;

  e.CustomValue = amounts.ToArray()[(int)(amounts.Count() / 2)];
}
```

In the sample, a quick check makes sure that the field you are calculating is PaymentAmount. Add if conditions if you have more than one summary to calculate. Next, e.CreateDrillDownDataSource returns a PivotDrillDownDataSource, which contains all the rows used to calculate the value of a given cell. (That is, e.CreateDrillDownDataSource returns an enumerable data source containing all the rows from the database that are used to provide the value for the row and column intersection of a data cell. The LINQ query iterates over the PivotDrillDownDataSource. The range value row in the from clause of the LINQ demonstrates how you can specify the type of the iterator variable, the range variable. The let clause demonstrates how to create a local range value, and this instance it is used to sort the data and create the result data. The value from the LINQ query is an IEnumerable<T>, where, in this case, T is a decimal type. Finally, the result collection amounts are converted to an array, and the middle value is indexed from the array and assigned to e.CustomValue. The results of the caption changes and the summary calculation are reflected in Figure 8-7.

Page 1 of 2 (16 items) [1] 2

City | PaymentType | PurchaseDate

Quantity | Payment Amount (Median) | Company △

Model △	Alessandro & Associates		Christies House of Design		Development House		Doe Enterprises		Ford Consulting		Frankson Media		Hill Corporation	
	Quantity	Payment Amount (Median)	Quantity	Payment Amount (Median)	Quantity	Payment Amount (Median)	Quantity	Payment Amount (Median)	Quantity	Payment Amount (Median)	Quantity	Payment Amount (Median)	Quantity	Payment Amount (Median)
530i	13	$78,900.00	7	$78,900.00	11	$157,800.00	11	$157,800.00	10	$118,350.00	17	$157,800.00	9	$118,35
C230 Kompressor Sport Coupe	4	$102,400.00	15	$76,800.00	1	$25,600.00	23	$76,800.00	13	$76,800.00	6	$128,000.00	12	$76,80
CLK55 AMG Cabriolet	3	$159,290.00	27	$398,225.00	2	$159,290.00	5	$79,645.00	10	$318,580.00	5	$238,935.00	3	$79,64
Corniche	6	$1,111,455.00	14	$740,970.00	11	$1,111,455.00	7	$740,970.00	6	$1,481,940.00	6	$1,481,940.00	11	$1,481,94
Crew Cab SE	5	$12,800.00	1	$12,800.00	14	$64,000.00	10	$51,200.00	6	$51,200.00	13	$51,200.00	12	$51,20
DeVille	1	$47,780.00	4	$143,340.00	10	$95,560.00	22	$143,340.00	11	$191,120.00	14	$143,340.00	10	$95,56
GS 430	11	$164,968.00	25	$123,726.00	8	$123,726.00	15	$164,968.00	18	$164,968.00	20	$164,968.00	14	$206,21
LS430	4	$109,800.00	19	$219,600.00	5	$274,500.00	2	$109,800.00			22	$164,700.00	11	$219,60
Ram 1500	13	$69,260.00			19	$69,260.00	10	$69,260.00	13	$69,260.00	4	$51,945.00	27	$69,26
Ranger FX-4	7	$37,695.00	16	$12,565.00	23	$62,825.00	18	$50,260.00	14	$25,130.00	6	$62,825.00	14	$50,26
Grand Total	154	$80,000.00	212	$128,000.00	174	$86,575.00	165	$82,484.00	148	$86,575.00	160	$109,800.00	163	$79,64

Page 1 of 2 (16 items) [1] 2

Figure 8-7: The ASPxPivotGrid showing the change to the PaymentAmount caption property and the results of the CustomSummary event's median calculation.

Fields are also represented by class variables. For instance, the field PaymentAmount can also be accessed by referring to the variable fieldPaymentAmount or whatever the ID property of the field is. In the code in Listing 8-5, e.DataField is a reference to the field variable fieldPaymentAmount.

Calculating Fields Manually

All the fields demonstrated thus far have been *bound fields*. A bound field (or control) is one whose value is derived or pinned to a data source. For a PivotGridField, this means that the field's FieldName property is assigned to a column in the data source result set and the UnboundType property is set to

`Bound`. If you want to add a manually calculated field, use the Field's Editor Form Add an Item button (see Figure 8-3), set the `UnboundType` to the data type you will be calculating, provide a caption, and implement a handler for the `ASPxPivotGrid.CustomUnboundFieldData` event.

To add a calculated field that applies a discount for cash payments, add an unbound `PivotGridField`, providing the `ID`, `Area`, `Caption`, `UnboundFieldName`, `UnboundType`, `SummaryType`, `TotalCellFormat-FormatString`, and cell formatting for the total cell, total value, and value. The following fragment shows you the unbound field used in the `PivotGridOptionsDataFieldDemo`. Listing 8-6 contains the implementation of the `CustomUnboundFieldData` event handler.

```
<dxwpg:PivotGridField Id="fieldCashDiscount", Area="DataArea" AreaIndex="2"
  Caption="Cash Discount" UnboundFieldName="CashDiscount"
  UnboundType="Decimal" CellFormat-FormatString="n" CellFormat-FormatType="Numeric"
  GrandTotalCellFormat-FormatString="n" GrandTotalCellFormat-FormatType="Numeric"
  SummaryType="Max" TotalCellFormat-FormatString="n"
  TotalCellFormat-FormatType="Numeric" TotalValueFormat-FormatString="n"
  TotalValueFormat-FormatType="Numeric" ValueFormat-FormatString="n"
  ValueFormat-FormatType="Numeric">
</dxwpg:PivotGridField>
```

For the previous code, note the following:

❑   The `ID` property is the variable name in the `Page` class that you can use to refer to the field above directly.

❑   The `Area` property indicates that the cash discount will be placed in the data area.

❑   The `AreaIndex` indicates the position of this field relative to other fields in that grid area.

❑   The `Caption` will be the cell header text.

❑   The `UnboundFieldName` is a string that can be used to test whether the `CustomUnboundFieldData` event was fired for a specific unbound field.

❑   The `UnboundType` indicates the data type of the unbound field.

❑   The hyphenated `FormatString` and `FormatType` properties (for example, `CellFormat-FormatString`) describe how the data for that cell should be formatted.

❑   The format properties used will format the cash discount values as noncurrency decimal values.

❑   The `SummaryType` Max was used because all the discounts are either 0 or 1 percent. Therefore, if any payment is a cash payment, the total discount will be 1 percent. If `SummaryType` were Sum, then for each payment the percentage would go up. For example, two payments would be a discount of 2 percent. Incorrectly using this approach would ultimately result in a discount greater than 100 percent. Here is Listing 8-6.

Listing 8-6: This CustomUnboundFieldData event handler sets the cash discount value of the unbound field if the payment type is cash.

```
protected void ASPxPivotGrid1_CustomUnboundFieldData(object sender,
  DevExpress.Web.ASPxPivotGrid.CustomFieldDataEventArgs e)
{
  if (e.Field.UnboundFieldName == "CashDiscount")
  {
    if (e.GetListSourceColumnValue("PaymentType").ToString() == "Cash")
      e.Value = 0.01M;
    else
      e.Value = 0M;
  }
}
```

In Listing 8-6, the `CustomFieldDataEventArgs.Field.UnboundField` is tested to determine whether the event was called for the `CashDiscount` field. If it was, the `PaymentType` is obtained through the `CustomFieldDataEventArgs.GetListSourceColumnValue`. If the `PaymentType` is `Cash`, the value `0.01M` (where M coerces the value to a decimal type) is assigned to the cell. Because the `SummaryType` Max is used for the `CashDiscount` field, if any payment qualifies for a discount, `0.01` is shown in the discount cell.

> By default, any field can be moved by the user to any area in the ASPxPivotGrid. If you want to limit the areas that a field can be moved to, change the `PivotGridField.AllowAreas` property from `All` and select just the allowable areas. The `AllowedAreas` are any combination of `RowArea`, `ColumnArea`, `DataArea`, and `FilterArea`.

In practice, you probably want to tinker with the approach used here. For example, you can change the discount amount based on the customer, or change the `PaymentAmount` so that only certain customers receive a discount, or the discount varies based on the amount of the payment. Also, instead of showing the Median `PaymentAmount`, you can apply the individual discount directly to the `PaymentAmount` — referred to as rebating by business people — and adjust the displayed `PaymentAmount`. Variations on using custom calculated fields are left as an exercise.

Using the Built-in Summary Variation Feature

The `ASPxPivotGrid` supports trend analysis, too. In *trend analysis*, you can view changes between the data. This used to be supported by the now-obsolete `SummmaryVariation` property, which supported an `Absolute` or `Percent` variation. `SummaryVariation` has been replaced with `SummaryDisplayType`. Property values for `SummaryDisplayType` are `Default`, `AbsoluteVariation`, `PercentVariation`, `PercentOfColumn`, and `PercentOfRow`. By changing the `SummaryDisplayType` property of a field from `Default` to one of the other values, you can let the customer visually compare the corresponding differences between related fields. For example, if the `SummmaryDisplayType` for the median `PaymentAmount` field is set to `PercentVariation`, the `ASPxPivotGrid` will show the percentage differences between median payment amounts (refer to Figure 8-8).

Page 1 of 2 (16 items) ◁ **[1]** 2 ▷

City ▾ | PaymentType ▾ | PurchaseDate ▾

Quantity | Payment Amount (Median) | Cash Discount | Company △ ▾

Model △ ▾	Alessandro & Associates			Christies House of Design			Development House			Doe Enterprises			Ford Consulting		
	Quantity	Payment Amount (Median)	Cash Discount	Quantity	Payment Amount (Median)	Cash Discount	Quantity	Payment Amount (Median)	Cash Discount	Quantity	Payment Amount (Median)	Cash Discount	Quantity	Payment Amount (Median)	Cash Discour
530i	13		0.01	7	0.00 %	0.01	11	100.00 %	0.01	11	0.00 %	0.00	10	-25.00 %	0.0
C230 Kompressor Sport Coupe	4		0.00	15	-25.00 %	0.01	1	-66.67 %	0.00	23	200.00 %	0.01	13	0.00 %	0.0
CLK55 AMG Cabriolet	3		0.01	27	150.00 %	0.01	2	-60.00 %	0.00	5	-50.00 %	0.01	10	300.00 %	0.0
Corniche	6		0.01	14	-33.33 %	0.01	11	50.00 %	0.01	7	-33.33 %	0.01	6	100.00 %	0.0
Crew Cab SE	5		0.01	1	0.00 %	0.00	14	400.00 %	0.01	10	-20.00 %	0.01	6	0.00 %	0.0
DeVille	1		0.01	4	200.00 %	0.01	10	-33.33 %	0.01	22	50.00 %	0.01	11	33.33 %	0.0
GS 430	11		0.01	25	-25.00 %	0.01	8	0.00 %	0.01	15	33.33 %	0.01	18	0.00 %	0.0
LS430	4		0.01	19	100.00 %	0.01	5	25.00 %	0.00	2	-60.00 %	0.00		-100.00 %	0.0
Ram 1500	13		0.01		-100.00 %		19	100.00 %	0.01	10	-25.00 %	0.00	13	33.33 %	0.0
Ranger FX-4	7		0.01	16	-66.67 %	0.01	23	400.00 %	0.01	18	-20.00 %	0.01	14	-50.00 %	0.0
Grand Total	154		0.01	212	60.00 %	0.01	174	-32.36 %	0.01	165	-4.73 %	0.01	148	4.96 %	0.0

Page 1 of 2 (16 items) ◁ **[1]** 2 ▷

Figure 8-8: The ASPxPivotGrid median PaymentAmount with the SummaryDisplayType set to PercentVariation shows the percentage of change between payment amounts.

Because features such as `SummaryDisplayType` are properties, you can easily add elements — such as radio buttons or check boxes — to your solution that permit end users to toggle between different views and states in the ASPxPivotGrid.

Exporting Data to Create Crosstab Reports

The `ASPxPivotGrid` control has an `ASPxPivotGridExporter` control that manages exporting pivot data. The rationale behind some controls having exporters and others not having them revolves around when it makes sense to support multiple export formats. The `ASPxPivotGridExporter` can be associated with any `ASPxPivotGrid` instance and used to send that pivot grid's data to a wide variety of formats, including PDF (Adobe's portable document format), XLS (Microsoft Excel), Text, RTF (Rich Text Format), HTML, and MHT (Microsoft's Mail Extension HTML) format. As with the `ASPxGridViewExporter`, you need to place an `ASPxPivotGridExporter` on the page with an `ASPxPivotGrid`, point the exporter at the grid, and use a stream to send the data to a file.

The example in this section demonstrates how to write the `ASPxPivotGrid`'s data to an Excel-formatted document by calling `ExportToXls`. (To use one of the other formats, call the `ExportToxxx` method correlating to the desired output format; for example, call `ExportToPdf` to send the formatted document to a PDF file.) In the example (see Listing 8-7), the formatted document is sent to the `HttpResponse` stream as an attachment, which results in the end user's being automatically prompted to open or save the document. Here are the steps that add exporting to the PivotGridOptionsDataFieldDemo; these steps are followed by the listing:

1. Add an `ASPxPivotGridExporter` to the page containing the `ASPxPivotGrid`.
2. Set the `ASPxPivotGridExporter's` `ASPxPivotGridID` property to the `ID` of the `ASPxPivotGrid`, `ASPxPivotGrid1` in the sample.
3. Add an `ASPxButton` to the page.
4. For the button's click event, call a function named `Export`.
5. Implement the `Export` behavior, as provided in Listing 8-7. (Refer to Figure 8-9 for an example of the output document.)

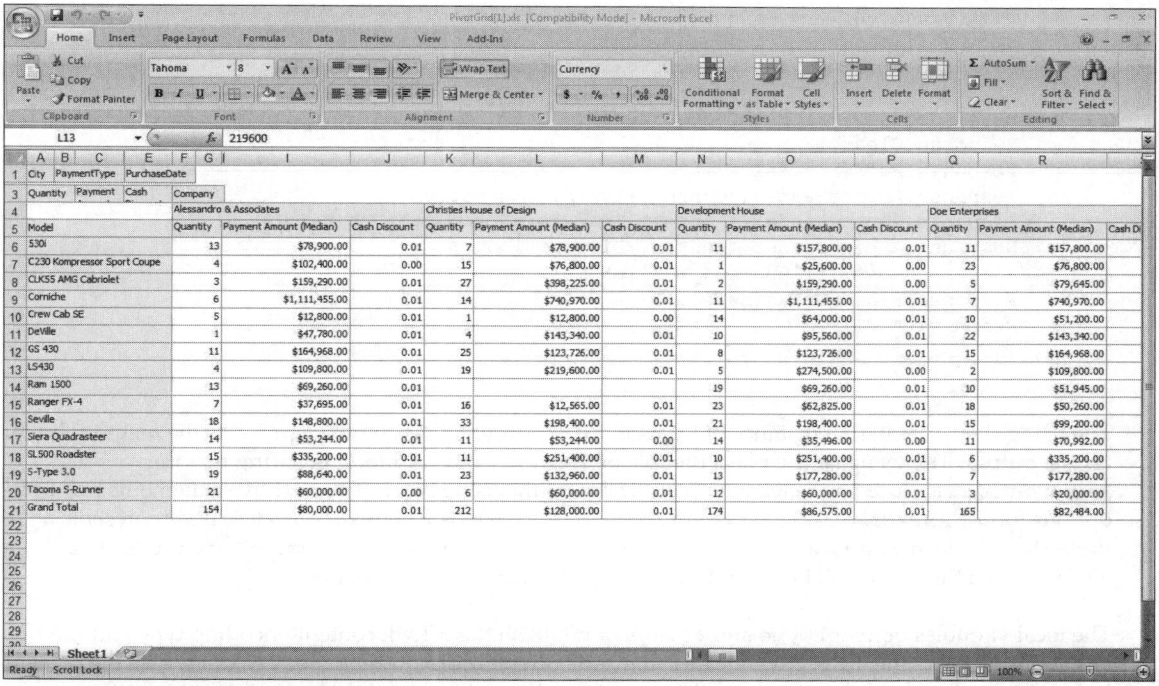

Model	Alessandro & Associates Quantity	Payment Amount (Median)	Cash Discount	Christies House of Design Quantity	Payment Amount (Median)	Cash Discount	Development House Quantity	Payment Amount (Median)	Cash Discount	Doe Enterprises Quantity	Payment Amount (Median)
530i	13	$78,900.00	0.01	7	$78,900.00	0.01	11	$157,800.00	0.01	11	$157,800.00
C230 Kompressor Sport Coupe	4	$102,400.00	0.00	15	$76,800.00	0.01	1	$25,600.00	0.00	23	$76,800.00
CLK55 AMG Cabriolet	3	$159,290.00	0.01	27	$398,225.00	0.01	2	$159,290.00	0.00	5	$79,645.00
Corniche	6	$1,111,455.00	0.01	14	$740,970.00	0.01	11	$1,111,455.00	0.01	7	$740,970.00
Crew Cab SE	5	$12,800.00	0.01	1	$12,800.00	0.00	14	$64,000.00	0.01	10	$51,200.00
DeVille	1	$47,780.00	0.01	4	$143,340.00	0.01	10	$95,560.00	0.01	22	$143,340.00
GS 430	11	$164,968.00	0.01	25	$123,726.00	0.01	8	$123,726.00	0.01	15	$164,968.00
LS430	4	$109,800.00	0.01	19	$219,600.00	0.01	5	$274,500.00	0.00	2	$109,800.00
Ram 1500	13	$69,260.00	0.01				19	$69,260.00	0.01	10	$51,945.00
Ranger FX-4	7	$37,695.00	0.01	16	$12,565.00	0.01	23	$62,825.00	0.01	18	$50,260.00
Seville	18	$148,800.00	0.01	33	$198,400.00	0.01	21	$198,400.00	0.01	15	$99,200.00
Siera Quadrasteer	14	$53,244.00	0.01	11	$53,244.00	0.00	14	$35,496.00	0.00	11	$70,992.00
SL500 Roadster	15	$335,200.00	0.01	11	$251,400.00	0.01	10	$251,400.00	0.01	6	$335,200.00
S-Type 3.0	19	$88,640.00	0.01	23	$132,960.00	0.01	13	$177,280.00	0.01	7	$177,280.00
Tacoma S-Runner	21	$60,000.00	0.00	6	$60,000.00	0.01	12	$60,000.00	0.01	3	$20,000.00
Grand Total	154	$80,000.00	0.01	212	$128,000.00	0.01	174	$86,575.00	0.01	165	$82,484.00

Figure 8-9: The exported Excel pivot grid.

Listing 8-7: The following code exports the ASPxPivotGrid to an Excel format, adding the output document to the HttpResponse as an attachment.

```
private void Export()
{
    using(MemoryStream stream = new MemoryStream())
    {
    ASPxPivotGridExporter1
       .OptionsPrint.PrintHeadersOnEveryPage = true;
    ASPxPivotGridExporter1
       .OptionsPrint.PrintFilterHeaders = DefaultBoolean.True;
    ASPxPivotGridExporter1
       .OptionsPrint.PrintColumnHeaders = DefaultBoolean.True;
    ASPxPivotGridExporter1
       .OptionsPrint.PrintRowHeaders = DefaultBoolean.True;
    ASPxPivotGridExporter1
       .OptionsPrint.PrintDataHeaders = DefaultBoolean.True;

    string contentType = "application/ms-excel";
    string fileName = "PivotGrid.xls";
    ASPxPivotGridExporter1.ExportToXls(stream);

    byte[] buffer = stream.GetBuffer();
    Response.Clear();
    Response.Buffer = false;
    Response.AppendHeader("Content-Type", contentType);
    Response.AppendHeader("Content-Transfer-Encoding", "binary");
    Response.AppendHeader("Content-Disposition",
       "attachment; filename=" + fileName);
    Response.BinaryWrite(buffer);
    Response.End();
    }
}
```

The using clause creates an instance of System.IO.MemoryStream, which represents the memory buffer for the output. The using clause plays the role of the try...finally block, ensuring that the MemoryStream is closed and cleaned up at the end of the using block. The next five statements print options for the ASPxPivotGridExporter. DefaultBoolean is a DevExpress class that represents a three-state Boolean, supporting True, False, or Default. If you set the option to DefaultBoolean .Default, then the value will be taken from the OptionsView property settings.

The local variables contentType and filename establish the HTML content-encoding type and the target output filename, respectively. The call to ASPxPivotGridExporter.ExportToXls writes the content in Excel format to the MemoryStream. The remaining lines of code use the MemoryStream buffer — stream.GetBuffer — to move the buffered data to the HttpResponse stream. (Every age has its own HttpResponse property, Response.) The content type, encoding, and disposition values tell the browser how to handle the additional data. In this example, the HttpResponse will treat the output Excel document as an attachment and prompt the user to open, save, or cancel the attachment. Click Open and the document will be opened with the application type that documents with a specific extension are associated with, in this instance Excel.

The call to `Response.BinaryWrite` writes the data to the `HttpResponseBuffer`, and `Response.End` indicates that the code has finished adding content to the response buffer. As a developer, you can how the application handles output content. You could let the user specify a filename. You could e-mail the content to a logged-in user, or you could save the output to a server location or a database. I leave variations on how the data are saved as an exercise.

Binding to an OLAP Cube

The ASPxPivotGrid is actually promoted at www.devexpress.com as an OLAP Data Mining Control. At the site, choose Products ⇨ ASP.NET Controls ⇨ OLAP Data Mining Control. The motivation for this promotion is that there are compelling reasons for choosing the ASPxPivotGrid over the ASPxGridView. The ASPxPivotGrid is better, for example, for customers who have an OLAP server such as Microsoft Analysis Services or OLAP cube data (exported OLAP data). These types of servers are typically used for data warehousing or data mining. Those of you involved in such work know more about it than I, but basically I define *data warehousing* as managing huge amounts of data in a wide variety of formats and from many sources, and *mining* as figuring out how to derive meaning from that data.

In addition to the ASPxPivotGrid supporting manipulating data and looking at it in user-definable ways, the ASPxPivotGrid supports key performance indicators (referred to as KPI). The ASPxPivotGrid supports associating data items with key performance indicators by configurable graphics. The purpose of the KPI graphics is to permit assigning images to data with the intent of having the images quickly convey meaning to the user, faster than just numbers and dates can.

> *OLPA cube files require an OLE DB provider for Analysis Services which you can download from Microsoft.com. Refer to* www.microsoft.com/downloads/details .aspx?FamilyID=50b97994-8453-4998-8226-fa42ec403d17#ASOLEDB.

Just in case you don't have access to an OLAP server the example in this section uses an exported OLAP cube file based on data converted to a cube from the Northwind sample database. The data file is `Northwind.cub`. The cube file contains Product and Order information by City and Country. You use OLAP data by configuring the ASPxPivotGrid to refer to an OLAP server or cube file through the `OLAPConnectionString` property of the ASPxPivotGrid rather than a data source pointing at a relational database. After you configure the `OLAPConnectionString` using the ASPxPivotGrid, from the developer's and user's point of view, it is the same as using it when configured against a relational database. The following code shows the OLAPConnectionString used for the OlapDemo provided in this book (with Figure 8-10 showing the output from the sample application):

```
protected void Page_Load(object sender, EventArgs e)
{
  string olapConnectionString =
    @"Provider=msolap;Initial Catalog=Northwind;Cube Name=Northwind;" +
    @"Data Source=|DataDirectory|\Northwind.cub";
  ASPxPivotGrid1.OLAPConnectionString = olapConnectionString;
  ASPxPivotGrid1.DataBind();
}
```

City ⌄

| Quantity | Discount | | | | | | | | | | | | | | | | | |

Category Name ▲ ⌄	Products ▲ ⌄	Argentina		Austria		Belgium		Brazil		Canada		Denmark		Finland		France		Qua
		Quantity	Discount	Quantity	Discount	Quantity	Discount	Quantity	Discount	Quantity	Discount	Quantity	Discount	Quantity	Discount	Quantity	Discount	
⊞ Beverages		82	0	982	1.55	272	0.4	968	2.85	303	1	195	0	107	0.25	618	1.9	
⊞ Condiments		45	0	720	1.05	147	0.45	568	1.95	256	0.5	210	0.45	75	0	287	1.25	
⊞ Confections		57	0	575	0.9499999	270	0.45	722	1.8	418	1	185	0.75	89	0.1	566	1.6	
⊞ Dairy Products		54	0	1027	2.1	295	0.25	683	1.75	381	0.95	89	0.2	247	0.6	391	1.05	
⊞ Grains/Cereals		20	0	580	0.5	145	0	315	1.15	207	0.4	15	0.05	110	0.35	312	1.05	
⊞ Meat/Poultry				362	0.9	89	0.2	223	1	141	0.3	146	0.35	93	0.2	243	0.6	
⊞ Produce		33	0	388	0.6	98	0	182	0.85	74	0	100	0.35	73	0.25	259	1.05	
⊞ Seafood		48	0	533	0.95	76	0.4	635	2.15	204	0.65	230	0.95	118	0.25	551	1.65	
Grand Total		339	0	5167	8.6	1392	2.15	4296	13.5	1984	4.800001	1170	3.1	912	2	3227	10.15	

Figure 8-10: The OlapDemo as viewed in the browser's output pane.

If an OLAP cube contains KPI information, the ASPxPivotGrid will automatically display the KPI information and graphic. By default, each field's KPIGraphic is assigned to ServerDefined. You can change the KPIGraphic to one of the available graphics, including Shapes, TrafficLights, RoadSigns, Gauge, Thermometer, or one of the other listed styles. If the cube contains localized versions of KPI graphics, the appropriate graphic is fetched based on the current client culture information. Figure 8-11 provides an illustration from the DevExpress Web site (www.devexpress.com/Products/NET/Controls/ASP/Pivot_Grid/olap.xml) showing how KPI graphics are displayed in an ASPxPivotGrid.

Figure 8-11: A graphic from the DevExpress Web site illustrating how key performance graphics, if available, are displayed in the ASPxPivotGrid.

Creating a Cube File in Excel

Microsoft Office client tools support reading and writing OLAP cube files. You can create a cube file from a spreadsheet by connecting to an external data source from the ribbon for the Data tab (Excel 2007):

1. Click the From Other Sources button on the Data ribbon.

2. On the Import Data step, select PivotTable Report.

3. From the PivotTable Field List, choose the fields to add to the report. When you are finished, the OLAP tools button will be enabled on the Options tab ribbon.

4. Click the OLAP tools button (in Excel) and select Offline OLAP.

5. In the Offline OLAP Settings, click the Create Offline Data File button to create the cube file.

If the OLAP provider does not support offline cube files, the Offline OLAP command will be unavailable. Search Excel help for more on OLAP cube files.

Using an ASPxPivotGrid as a WebChartControl's Data Source

An interesting aspect of the ASPxPivotGrid and the XtraChart Suite is that an ASPxPivotGrid can be used as the data source for a WebChartControl. Set the WebChartControl's DataSourceID to the name of an ASPxPivotGrid and the WebChartControl will derive its content and output from the grid data (see Figure 8-12). Because Chapter 12, "Adding Charts and Graphs to Your Application," provides coverage of the WebChartControl, I don't go into extensive detail on that control here. However, sufficient information to build the sample is provided.

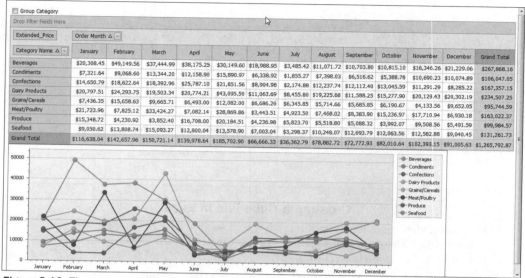

Category Name △	January	February	March	April	May	June	July	August	September	October	November	December	Grand Total
Beverages	$20,308.45	$49,149.56	$37,444.99	$38,175.25	$30,149.60	$18,988.95	$3,485.42	$11,071.72	$10,703.80	$10,815.10	$16,346.26	$21,229.06	$267,868.16
Condiments	$7,321.64	$9,068.60	$13,344.20	$12,158.90	$15,890.97	$6,338.92	$1,855.27	$7,398.03	$6,516.62	$5,388.78	$10,690.23	$10,074.89	$106,047.05
Confections	$14,650.79	$18,622.64	$18,392.96	$25,787.10	$21,851.56	$8,904.98	$2,174.88	$12,237.74	$12,112.40	$13,045.59	$11,291.29	$8,285.22	$167,357.15
Dairy Products	$20,797.51	$24,293.75	$19,503.34	$20,774.21	$43,095.50	$11,063.69	$8,455.80	$19,225.68	$11,588.25	$15,277.90	$20,129.43	$20,302.19	$234,507.25
Grains/Cereals	$7,436.35	$15,658.63	$9,665.71	$6,493.00	$12,082.00	$6,686.26	$6,345.85	$5,714.66	$5,685.85	$6,190.67	$4,133.56	$9,652.05	$95,744.59
Meat/Poultry	$21,723.96	$7,825.12	$33,424.27	$7,082.14	$28,869.86	$3,443.51	$4,923.50	$7,468.02	$8,383.90	$15,236.97	$17,710.94	$6,930.18	$163,022.37
Produce	$15,348.72	$4,230.92	$3,852.40	$16,708.00	$20,184.51	$4,236.98	$5,823.70	$5,518.80	$5,088.32	$3,992.07	$9,508.56	$5,491.59	$99,984.57
Seafood	$9,050.62	$13,808.74	$15,093.27	$12,800.04	$13,578.90	$7,003.04	$3,298.37	$10,248.07	$12,693.79	$12,063.56	$12,582.88	$9,040.45	$131,261.73
Grand Total	$116,638.04	$142,657.96	$150,721.14	$139,978.64	$185,702.90	$66,666.33	$36,362.79	$78,882.72	$72,772.93	$82,010.64	$102,393.15	$91,005.63	$1,265,792.87

Figure 8-12: The output from the sample showing the WebChartControl content based on the ASPxPivotGrid data.

The sample Web application, PivotGridAsXtraChartSource (shown running in Figure 8-12), contains an ASPxPivotGrid, an AccessDataSource, and a WebChartControl. The ASPxPivotGrid is associated with the AccessDataSource, and the WebChartControl's DataSourceID is set to the instance of the ASPxPivotGrid, ASPxPivotGrid1. (Refer to Listing 8-8 for the ASPX for the sample.) The SQL for the ASPxPivotGrid is a SELECT statement against the nwind.mdb (MS-Access instance of the Northwind database) SalesPerson table. Here is the query:

```
SELECT [Extended Price] AS Extended_Price, [CategoryName], [OrderDate]
FROM [SalesPerson]
```

The key here is that the WebChartControl is associated with the ASPXPivotGrid, so changes to the grid at runtime are automatically reflected in the WebChartControl. The code-behind for the sample is provided in Listing 8-9. Here are the steps for reproducing the sample solution:

1. Place an ASPxPivotGrid on a Web page.

2. Use the ASPxPivotGrid's Smart tags menu to configure an AccessDataSource, pointing the AccessDataSource at the nwind.mdb database.

3. In the data source configuration wizard, add the SELECT statement from the preceding SQL code fragment.

4. From the ASPxPivotGrid's Smart tags menu, select Fields.

5. In the Field's Editor Form, click the Retrieve Fields button. (This will retrieve the Extended_Price, CategoryName, and OrderDate fields as defined by the SELECT statement.)

6. Change the OrderDate field's Caption property to Order Month.

7. Set the OrderDate field's GroupInterval property to DateMonth. (This step will cause OrderDate values to be grouped by month rather than show the individual date.)

8. Close the Field's Editor Form by clicking OK.

9. Set the ASPxPivotGrid's OptionsDataSource.ChartDataVertical property to false. (This value is true by default. Setting it to false in this instance moves the CategoryName to the Series and shows Extended_Price values along the vertical axis and months along the horizontal axis of the WebChartControl).

10. Set the ASPxPivotGrid's OptionsDatasource.ShowGrandTotals to false.

11. Add a WebChartControl to the Web page from the DevExpress Data tab of the Toolbox.

12. From the WebChartControl's Smart tags menu, set the data source (Choose Data Source) to the ASPxPivotGrid.

13. Implement the Page_Load event as provided in Listing 8-9.

Listing 8-8: The ASPX for the WebChartControl and the ASPxPivotGrid that is acting as the data source.

```
<%@ Page Language="C#" AutoEventWireup="true"  CodeFile="Default.aspx.cs"
 Inherits="_Default" %>

<%@ Register assembly="DevExpress.XtraCharts.v9.1.Web,
 Version=9.1.4.0, Culture=neutral, PublicKeyToken=b88d1754d700e49a"
 namespace="DevExpress.XtraCharts.Web" tagprefix="dxchartsui" %>
<%@ Register assembly="DevExpress.XtraCharts.v9.1,
 Version=9.1.4.0, Culture=neutral, PublicKeyToken=b88d1754d700e49a"
 namespace="DevExpress.XtraCharts" tagprefix="cc1" %>
<%@ Register assembly="DevExpress.Web.ASPxPivotGrid.v9.1,
 Version=9.1.4.0, Culture=neutral, PublicKeyToken=b88d1754d700e49a"
 namespace="DevExpress.Web.ASPxPivotGrid" tagprefix="dxwpg" %>

<!DOCTYPE html PUBLIC "-//W3C//DTD XHTML 1.0 Transitional//EN"
 "http://www.w3.org/TR/xhtml1/DTD/xhtml1-transitional.dtd">

<html xmlns="http://www.w3.org/1999/xhtml">
<head runat="server">
  <title></title>
</head>
<body>
  <form id="form1" runat="server">
  <div>
    <dxwpg:ASPxPivotGrid ID="ASPxPivotGrid1" runat="server"
    DataSourceID="AccessDataSource1" EnableCallBacks="False"
    onprerender="ASPxPivotGrid1_PreRender">
    <Fields>
      <dxwpg:PivotGridField ID="fieldExtendedPrice" Area="DataArea" AreaIndex="0"
      FieldName="Extended_Price">
      </dxwpg:PivotGridField>
      <dxwpg:PivotGridField ID="fieldCategoryName" Area="RowArea" AreaIndex="0"
      FieldName="CategoryName">
      </dxwpg:PivotGridField>
      <dxwpg:PivotGridField FieldName="OrderDate" ID="PivotGridField1"
```

Continued

Listing 8-8: The ASPX for the WebChartControl and the ASPxPivotGrid that is acting as the data source. *(continued)*

```
            Area="ColumnArea" AreaIndex="0" GroupInterval="DateMonth"
            UnboundFieldName="fieldOrderDate" Caption="Order
            Month"></dxwpg:PivotGridField>
        </Fields>
        <OptionsChartDataSource ChartDataVertical="False" />
        </dxwpg:ASPxPivotGrid>
        <asp:AccessDataSource ID="AccessDataSource1" runat="server"
        DataFile="~/App_Data/nwind.mdb"

        SelectCommand="SELECT [Extended Price] AS Extended_Price,
        [CategoryName], [OrderDate] FROM [SalesPerson]">
        </asp:AccessDataSource>
        <dxchartsui:WebChartControl ID="WebChartControl1" runat="server"
        DataSourceID="ASPxPivotGrid1" Height="300px" Width="1000px">
<SeriesTemplate LabelTypeName="SideBySideBarSeriesLabel"
 PointOptionsTypeName="PointOptions"
 SeriesViewTypeName="SideBySideBarSeriesView">
<View HiddenSerializableString="to be serialized"></View>

<Label HiddenSerializableString="to be serialized"
 LineVisible="True" OverlappingOptionsTypeName="OverlappingOptions">
<FillStyle FillOptionsTypeName="SolidFillOptions">
<Options HiddenSerializableString="to be serialized"></Options>
</FillStyle>
</Label>

<PointOptions HiddenSerializableString="to be serialized"></PointOptions>

<LegendPointOptions HiddenSerializableString=
  "to be serialized"></LegendPointOptions>
</SeriesTemplate>

<FillStyle FillOptionsTypeName="SolidFillOptions">
<Options HiddenSerializableString="to be serialized"></Options>
</FillStyle>
    </dxchartsui:WebChartControl>
  </div>
  </form>
</body>
</html>
```

Listing 8-9: The code-behind for the WebChartControl and ASPxPivotGrid tells the WebChartControl where to get its data from.

```
using System;
using System.Collections.Generic;
using System.Linq;
using System.Web;
using System.Web.UI;
using System.Web.UI.WebControls;
using DevExpress.Web.ASPxPivotGrid;
```

```
using DevExpress.XtraCharts;

public partial class _Default : System.Web.UI.Page
{
  protected void Page_Load(object sender, EventArgs e)
  {

      WebChartControl1.SeriesTemplate.ChangeView(ViewType.Line);
      WebChartControl1.SeriesDataMember = "Series";
      WebChartControl1.SeriesTemplate.ArgumentDataMember = "Arguments";
      WebChartControl1.SeriesTemplate.ValueDataMembers[0] = "Values";
      ASPxPivotGrid1.OptionsChartDataSource.ShowColumnGrandTotals = false;
      ASPxPivotGrid1.OptionsChartDataSource.ShowRowGrandTotals = false;
      WebChartControl1.SeriesTemplate.Label.OverlappingOptions.Mode
        = ResolveOverlappingMode.HideOverlapped;

      WebChartControl1.SeriesTemplate.Label.Visible = false;
  }
}
```

Listing 8-9 tweaks the `WebChartControl` and `ASPxPivotGrid` in the `Page_Load` event and defines the `WebChartControl.SeriesDataMember` and `WebChartControlSeriesTemplate.ValueDataMembers` showing you how easy it is to display `ASPxPivotGrid` data in a `WebChartControl`. (For more information on the `WebChartControl`, refer to Chapter 12, which includes examples demonstrating how to use the Chart Wizard.)

The first statement in `Page_Load` sets the `WebChartControl` view to `ViewTypeLine`. The second statement sets the `SeriesDataMember` to Series, which is used to automatically generate and populate series data. The `WebChartControl.SeriesTemplate.ArgumentMember` is set to Arguments, which specifies the bound data source's field for point values. Set the `ASPxPivotGrid .OptionsChartDataSource.ShowColumnGrandTotals` and `ShowRowGrandTotals` to false. (Grand totals will skew the chart because the totals are substantially larger than other data values.) Finally, the `WebChartControl.SeriesTemplate.ValueDataMembers` collection is set to an array of strings containing the string `Values`. The `ValueDataMembers` collection contains the names of data fields containing data value series points.

The `WebChartControl` is fully configurable. Requirements will determine whether you need to add controls that let the user configure the `WebChartControl` or you simply need to select the data and pick the series arguments that make sense for the business problem you are solving. However, by associating a `WebChartControl` with an `ASPxPivotGrid`, users can interact with the grid and see a visualization of the data in the associated chart. (For an example of an online configurable `WebChartControl` associated with the `ASPxPivotGrid`, check out the ASPxPivotGridDemos project that ships with your copy of ASPxperience.)

Grouping Axis Values

Databases are great at storing detailed information such as transaction dates or individual purchases. For example, in the previous section, the query returned sales for each salesperson. However, a single salesperson makes dozens or more sales in a given day. If a user wanted to get an idea of daily sales to examine trends or compare salesperson results, weekly or monthly sales may be more useful. The

ASPxPivotGrid supports grouping on axis values. Thus, if you have individual sales records by date, for instance, you can group the sales on the date axis and get an overall picture rather than single bits of information.

The ASPxPivotGrid supports grouping on an axis by setting a PivotGridField's GroupInterval property to one of the predetermined group types or by implementing custom grouping. The code in this section extends the PivotGridAsXtraChartSource example, demonstrating automatic and manual grouping.

Grouping Axis Values

The example from the earlier subsection, "Using an ASPxPivotGrid as a WebChartControl's Data Source," contains a query that selects price and order information from the Northwind sample database's SalesPerson table. The OrderDate column from that table has individual dates. Especially for data that may end up in a chart, too many points will do the opposite of conveying meaning. Too many data points will likely result in a grid with too much data and a chart that is hard to decipher.

In the PivotGridAsXtraChartSource sample application, the OrderDate's Caption was changed to Order Month. The GroupInterval property for the OrderDate field was changed to DateMonth. The net effect was that all OrderDate items having the same month and year were aggregated in the same data cell of the ASPxPivotGrid and were represented by the same data point on the WebChartControl. Valid values for the PivotGridField.GroupInterval property includes any of the enum values of the PivotGroupInterval enum type, which includes Alphabetical, Custom, Date, DateDay, DateDayOfWeek, DateDayOfYear, DateMonth, DateQuarter, DateWeekOfMonth, DateWeekOfYear, DateYear, DayAge, Default, Hour, MonthAge, Numeric, WeekAge, and YearAge. For example, if you change the GroupInterval from the default value Default to Alphabetical, the field values are grouped by the starting character of the data values.

Grouping Values Manually

If you want to define custom interval grouping for a field, change that field's GroupInterval to PivotGroupInterval.Custom and implement the ASPxPivotGrid's CustomGroupInterval event handler.

The CustomGroupInterval receives a second argument of PivotCustomGroupIntervalEventArgs. The PivotCustomGroupIntervalEventArgs inherits from EventArgs and introduces additional properties, include Field, GroupValue, and Value.

The revision to Listing 8-8 and Listing 8-9 includes an ASPxCheckBox with AutoPostBack set to true. When the ASPxCheckBox.CheckedChanged event fires, the CheckedChanged event handler changes the fieldCategoryName Caption and GroupInterval. If the ASPxCheckBox is selected, the fieldCatgegoryName GroupInterval is set to PivotGroupInterval.Custom, which in turn causes the CustomGroupInterval event handler to be called and the ASPxPivotGrid and the WebChartControl to be updated. Figure 8-12 already shows the PivotGridAsXtraChartSource sample. Figure 8-13 shows the revised solution running with the CategoryName.PivotGridField. GroupInterval set to Custom and the CustomGroupInterval having consolidated the data further by CategoryName. Listing 8-10 contains the two additional event handlers for the CheckedChanged and CustomGroupInterval events.

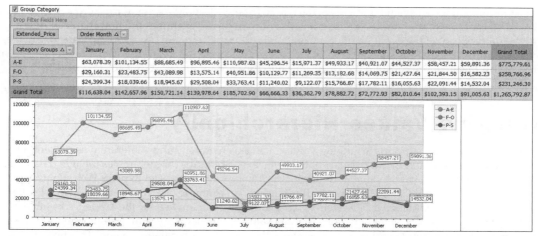

Figure 8-13: The revised sample showing the reduced number of data points as a result of custom grouping on CategoryName.

Listing 8-10: CheckedChanged and CustomGroupInterval toggle custom grouping on the CategoryName PivotGridField.

```
protected void ASPxPivotGrid1_CustomGroupInterval(object sender,
  PivotCustomGroupIntervalEventArgs e)
{
  if(e.Field.FieldName != "CategoryName") return;
    char ch = Convert.ToChar(e.Value.ToString()[0]);
  if(ch < 'F')
    e.GroupValue = "A-E";
  else if ((ch > 'E') && (ch < 'P'))
    e.GroupValue = "F-O";
  else if ((ch > 'O') && (ch < 'T'))
    e.GroupValue = "P-S";
  else
    e.GroupValue = "T-Z";
}
protected void ASPxCheckBox1_CheckedChanged(object sender, EventArgs e)
{
  if (ASPxCheckBox1.Checked)
  {
    fieldCategoryName.GroupInterval =
      DevExpress.XtraPivotGrid.PivotGroupInterval.Custom;
    fieldCategoryName.Caption = "Category Groups";
  }
  else
  {
    fieldCategoryName.GroupInterval =
      DevExpress.XtraPivotGrid.PivotGroupInterval.Default;
    fieldCategoryName.Caption = "Category Name";
  }
}
```

The CheckedChanged event handler sets the GroupInterval and Caption for the CategoryName field based on the state of the checkbox. The CustomGroupInterval examines the first character of the e.Value property of the event handler's PivotCustomGroupIntervalEventArgs. Category names that fall within each of the specified character ranges are slotted into a group for that range. The event handler in this instance consolidates categories into four group ranges: A–E, F–O, P–S, and T–Z.

Arranging Values Hierarchically

The ASPxPivotGrid supports arranging values in an axis hierarchically. A hierarchy is present when more than one PivotGridField is part of the same axis. Scenarios for hierarchies include data that have lookup tables or use a single value in multiple ways. For example, the DevExpress Web site uses a hierarchy that includes Cars, Models, and Trademarks. An example of a Trademark is Mercedes-Benz and a Model is SL500 Roadster. The Models table contains a foreign key for the Trademarks table, which means that Trademarks is a lookup table. In that example, the hierarchy shows all the models for a given trademark. In the example in this section, you use the CarsDB.mdb database again. This time, the OrderDate is used to create a hierarchy.

Creating a Hierarchy

The way to create a hierarchy is to add more than one field bound to the same data value to the ASPxPivotGrid and change the way that data is treated by setting the GroupInterval to different values. For example, a date can be grouped by month, week of the month, and day of the week. The underlying date is the same value, but by varying the GroupInterval, the single date is organized in different ways (see Figure 8-14).

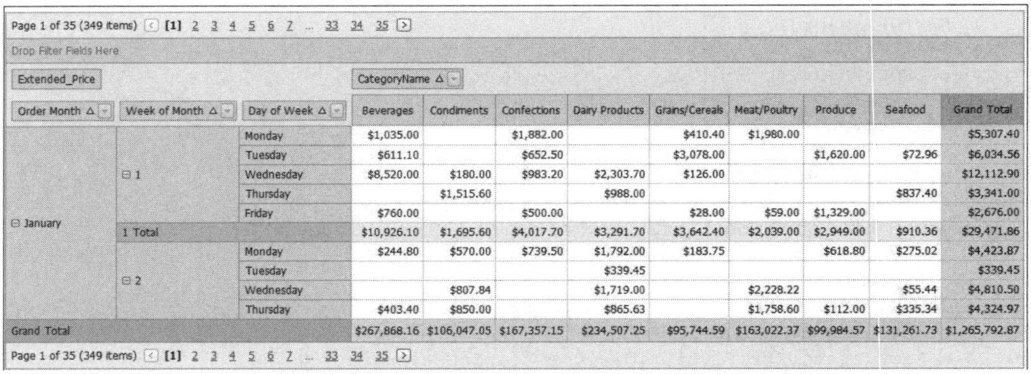

Page 1 of 35 (349 items) [1] 2 3 4 5 6 7 ... 33 34 35											
Drop Filter Fields Here											
Extended_Price				CategoryName △							
Order Month △	Week of Month △	Day of Week △	Beverages	Condiments	Confections	Dairy Products	Grains/Cereals	Meat/Poultry	Produce	Seafood	Grand Total
January	1	Monday	$1,035.00		$1,882.00		$410.40	$1,980.00			$5,307.40
		Tuesday	$611.10		$652.50		$3,078.00		$1,620.00	$72.96	$6,034.56
		Wednesday	$8,520.00	$180.00	$983.20	$2,303.70	$126.00				$12,112.90
		Thursday		$1,515.60		$988.00				$837.40	$3,341.00
		Friday	$760.00		$500.00		$28.00	$59.00	$1,329.00		$2,676.00
	1 Total		$10,926.10	$1,695.60	$4,017.70	$3,291.70	$3,642.40	$2,039.00	$2,949.00	$910.36	$29,471.86
	2	Monday	$244.80	$570.00	$739.50	$1,792.00	$183.75		$618.80	$275.02	$4,423.87
		Tuesday				$339.45					$339.45
		Wednesday		$807.84		$1,719.00		$2,228.22		$55.44	$4,810.50
		Thursday	$403.40	$850.00		$865.63		$1,758.60	$112.00	$335.34	$4,324.97
Grand Total			$267,868.16	$106,047.05	$167,357.15	$234,507.25	$95,744.59	$163,022.37	$99,984.57	$131,261.73	$1,265,792.87

Page 1 of 35 (349 items) [1] 2 3 4 5 6 7 ... 33 34 35

Figure 8-14: A hierarchy created by binding the same column — OrderDate — multiple times and using a unique GroupInterval for each instance.

To recreate the hierarchy shown in Figure 8-14, use the SELECT statement against the SalesPerson table from the MS Access version of the Northwind database:

```
SELECT [OrderDate], [CategoryName], [Extended Price] AS Extended_Price
  FROM [SalesPerson]
```

Based on the query, there are three columns to bind to: OrderDate, CategoryName, and Extended Price. To create a hierarchy, use the Fields Editor Form and follow these steps:

1. In the Fields Editor Form, click Retrieve Fields to retrieve fields for the columns defined by the query.

2. For the OrderDate field, change the Caption to Order Month, set the GroupInterval to DateMonth, and change the Area to RowArea.

3. Change the CategoryName field's Area property to ColumnArea.

4. Change the Extended_Price (the underscore was added automatically) field's Area property to DataArea.

5. Click the Add an Item button to add a new field.

6. Set the Caption of the new field to Week of Month; set the FieldName property to OrderDate; set the GroupInterval to DateWeekOfMonth; and set the Area property to RowArea.

7. Click the Add an Item button again.

8. Set the new field's Caption property to Day of Week; set the FieldName to OrderDate; set the GroupInterval to DateDayOfWeek; and set the Area property to RowArea.

9. Click OK to close the Editor Form.

When you have finished defining the fields, you will have five fields, three of which are based on the OrderDate grouped in three different ways. At this point, you can run the sample. If you drag one of the OrderDate fields — for example, Day of Week — from the RowArea to the ColumnArea, the ASPxPivotGrid will reconfigure its appearance. If you want all the fields based on the OrderDate to move together, you can define a group and add those fields to a group.

Keeping Fields Together

In the example in the preceding section, moving just one of the OrderDate fields from a RowArea to a ColumnArea works fine and the data makes sense. You may elect to treat items in a hierarchy as a single unit. You can do this by defining a group (using the ASPxPivotGrid's Smart tags Groups menu item or the Groups property).

To group the three `OrderDate` fields — representing the month, day of the week, and week of the month — click the ASPxPivotGrid's Smart tags Groups menu item to display the Groups Editor. Using Figures 8-15 and 8-16 as a visual guide, follow the numbered steps to define a group containing all three OrderDate fields:

1. If you haven't already done so, click the ASPxPivotGrid's Groups item from the Smart tags menu to display the Groups Editor form.

2. In that editor, click the Add an Item button (see Figure 8-15).

3. Select the new group and click the Edit button, which opens the Group's Fields Editor.

4. In the Group's Fields Editor, change the Caption to Date Group.

5. From the left list, which contains the ungrouped fields, click each of the Order Month, Week of Month, and Day of Week fields in turn and click the << button to move those fields to the Grouped Fields list (see Figure 8-16).

6. Click OK to close the Group's Fields Editor.

7. Click OK to close the Groups Editor.

Figure 8-15: Use the Groups property to add PivotGridFields to a group, resulting in their staying together as a single unit.

Figure 8-16: The Group's Fields Editor is used to define the PivotGridFields that belong to a group and to be treated as a unit.

When you have finished the preceding numbered steps, the three fields will be treated as a group and will move together at runtime — for instance, when a user drags and drops the group. The visual cue that the fields are part of a group is the thin line connecting each of the fields. The visual line-cue is visible at design time and runtime (see Figure 8-17). Listing 8-11 contains the ASPX for the sample, showing you the field settings that establish the hierarchy.

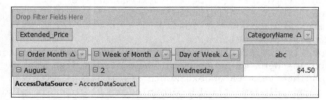

Figure 8-17: When fields are grouped the thin line between the fields — visible at design time and runtime — is the visual cue indicating the membership in a group.

Listing 8-11: Define a hierarchy by binding more than one field to the same FieldName, as demonstrated with OrderDate here.

```
<%@ Page Language="C#" AutoEventWireup="true"  CodeFile="Default.aspx.cs"
 Inherits="_Default" %>

<%@ Register assembly="DevExpress.Web.ASPxPivotGrid.v9.1,↩
 Version=9.1.4.0, Culture=neutral, PublicKeyToken=b88d1754d700e49a"
 namespace="DevExpress.Web.ASPxPivotGrid" tagprefix="dxwpg" %>

<!DOCTYPE html PUBLIC "-//W3C//DTD XHTML 1.0 Transitional//EN"
 "http://www.w3.org/TR/xhtml1/DTD/xhtml1-transitional.dtd">

<html xmlns="http://www.w3.org/1999/xhtml">
<head runat="server">
    <title></title>
</head>
<body>
    <form id="form1" runat="server">
    <div>

      <dxwpg:ASPxPivotGrid ID="ASPxPivotGrid1" runat="server"
        DataSourceID="AccessDataSource1">
        <Fields>
          <dxwpg:PivotGridField ID="fieldOrderDate" Area="RowArea"
            AreaIndex="0"
            Caption="Order Month" FieldName="OrderDate"
            GroupInterval="DateMonth"
            UnboundFieldName="fieldOrderDate" GroupIndex="0"
            InnerGroupIndex="0">
          </dxwpg:PivotGridField>
          <dxwpg:PivotGridField ID="fieldCategoryName"
            Area="ColumnArea" AreaIndex="0"
            FieldName="CategoryName">
          </dxwpg:PivotGridField>
          <dxwpg:PivotGridField ID="fieldExtendedPrice"
            Area="DataArea" AreaIndex="0"
            FieldName="Extended_Price">
          </dxwpg:PivotGridField>
          <dxwpg:PivotGridField ID="field" Area="RowArea" AreaIndex="1"
            Caption="Week of Month" FieldName="OrderDate"
            GroupInterval="DateWeekOfMonth"
            UnboundFieldName="field" GroupIndex="0" InnerGroupIndex="1">
          </dxwpg:PivotGridField>
          <dxwpg:PivotGridField ID="field1" Area="RowArea" AreaIndex="2"
            Caption="Day of Week" FieldName="OrderDate"
            GroupInterval="DateDayOfWeek"
            UnboundFieldName="field1" GroupIndex="0" InnerGroupIndex="2">
          </dxwpg:PivotGridField>
        </Fields>
        <Groups>
          <dxwpg:PivotGridWebGroup Caption="Date Group" />
        </Groups>
      </dxwpg:ASPxPivotGrid>
```

```
<asp:AccessDataSource ID="AccessDataSource1" runat="server"
  DataFile="~/App_Data/nwind.mdb"
  SelectCommand="SELECT [OrderDate], [CategoryName],
  [Extended Price] AS Extended_Price FROM [SalesPerson]">
</asp:AccessDataSource>

  </div>
  </form>
</body>
</html>
```

Calculating Totals

The ASPxPivotGrid is a powerful control for data mining. Thus far, this chapter has covered using relational or OLAP data cubes as data sources for the ASPxPivotGrid. It has discussed groups, hierarchies, keeping fields together, custom summaries, exporting data, and using the ASPxPivotGrid as a data source for a WebChartControl. All these options are available and most require very little coding on your part. Additionally, the ASPxPivotGrid supports custom computations, sorting, a drill-down window, and end-user data filtering. The remaining parts of this chapter briefly demonstrate these features.

Computing Summaries Automatically

The ASPxPivotGrid ships with a summary computation engine. When you see an engine in text think of a class or classes that collaborate to perform some complex behavior to provide some complex behavior. Several examples in this chapter have demonstrated how the automatically enabled aggregation capabilities will update summary values at runtime as users manipulate the orchestration of data displayed in the grid. Examples of the built-in aggregation capabilities of the ASPxPivotGrid include the SummaryType property — set to Sum by default — available for each PivotGridField.

Refer to the section "Choosing the Field Summary Type," earlier in this chapter, for more information. Check out the section "Implementing a Custom Summary" for an example that demonstrates how to define a custom summary based on the median value.

Computing Running Totals

By default, if a data value contains no data, that cell will contain the equivalent of its no-value data. For example, a numeric field will be empty and treated as having a zero value. If you set the RunningTotals to true for a PivotGridField, then along that field's axis, from left to right, the running totals will be fields in the data cells. Examine Figure 8-18, noting that some of the cells are empty. This is the PivotGridHierarchy with no field's RunningTotals set to true. Now, if you change the fieldCategoryName — CategoryName — field's RunningTotals to true (see Figure 8-19), you will see that the default aggregation operation is being performed across categories from left to right.

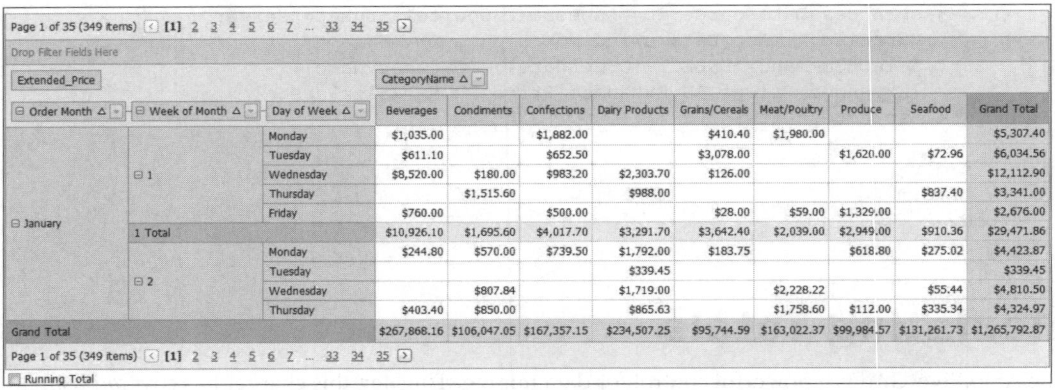

Page 1 of 35 (349 items) [1] 2 3 4 5 6 7 ... 33 34 35

Drop Filter Fields Here

Extended_Price | CategoryName

Order Month	Week of Month	Day of Week	Beverages	Condiments	Confections	Dairy Products	Grains/Cereals	Meat/Poultry	Produce	Seafood	Grand Total
January	1	Monday	$1,035.00		$1,882.00		$410.40	$1,980.00			$5,307.40
		Tuesday	$611.10		$652.50		$3,078.00		$1,620.00	$72.96	$6,034.56
		Wednesday	$8,520.00	$180.00	$983.20	$2,303.70	$126.00				$12,112.90
		Thursday		$1,515.60		$988.00				$837.40	$3,341.00
		Friday	$760.00		$500.00		$28.00	$59.00	$1,329.00		$2,676.00
	1 Total		$10,926.10	$1,695.60	$4,017.70	$3,291.70	$3,642.40	$2,039.00	$2,949.00	$910.36	$29,471.86
	2	Monday	$244.80	$570.00	$739.50	$1,792.00	$183.75		$618.80	$275.02	$4,423.87
		Tuesday				$339.45					$339.45
		Wednesday		$807.84		$1,719.00		$2,228.22		$55.44	$4,810.50
		Thursday	$403.40	$850.00		$865.63		$1,758.60	$112.00	$335.34	$4,324.97
Grand Total			$267,868.16	$106,047.05	$167,357.15	$234,507.25	$95,744.59	$163,022.37	$99,984.57	$131,261.73	$1,265,792.87

Page 1 of 35 (349 items) [1] 2 3 4 5 6 7 ... 33 34 35

Running Total

Figure 8-18: An ASPxPivotGrid with no fields calculating running totals.

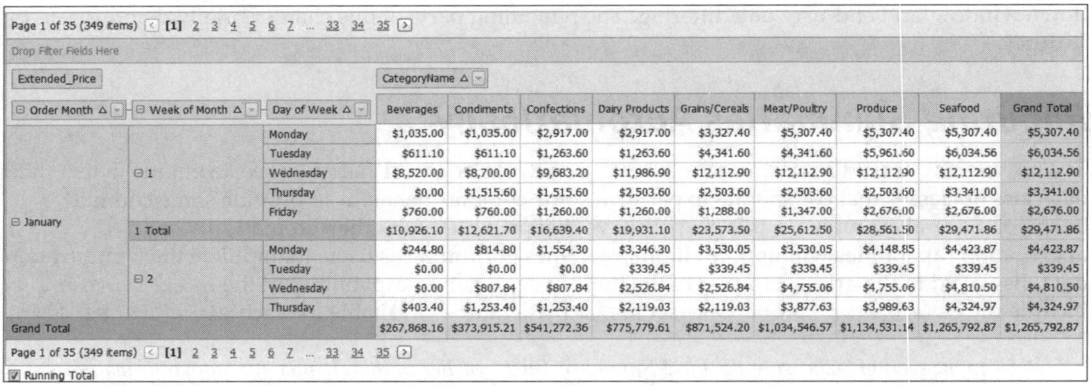

Page 1 of 35 (349 items) [1] 2 3 4 5 6 7 ... 33 34 35

Drop Filter Fields Here

Extended_Price | CategoryName

Order Month	Week of Month	Day of Week	Beverages	Condiments	Confections	Dairy Products	Grains/Cereals	Meat/Poultry	Produce	Seafood	Grand Total
January	1	Monday	$1,035.00	$1,035.00	$2,917.00	$2,917.00	$3,327.40	$5,307.40	$5,307.40	$5,307.40	$5,307.40
		Tuesday	$611.10	$611.10	$1,263.60	$1,263.60	$4,341.60	$4,341.60	$5,961.60	$6,034.56	$6,034.56
		Wednesday	$8,520.00	$8,700.00	$9,683.20	$11,986.90	$12,112.90	$12,112.90	$12,112.90	$12,112.90	$12,112.90
		Thursday	$0.00	$1,515.60	$1,515.60	$2,503.60	$2,503.60	$2,503.60	$2,503.60	$3,341.00	$3,341.00
		Friday	$760.00	$760.00	$1,260.00	$1,260.00	$1,288.00	$1,347.00	$2,676.00	$2,676.00	$2,676.00
	1 Total		$10,926.10	$12,621.70	$16,639.40	$19,931.10	$23,573.50	$25,612.50	$28,561.50	$29,471.86	$29,471.86
	2	Monday	$244.80	$814.80	$1,554.30	$3,346.30	$3,530.05	$3,530.05	$4,148.85	$4,423.87	$4,423.87
		Tuesday	$0.00	$0.00	$0.00	$339.45	$339.45	$339.45	$339.45	$339.45	$339.45
		Wednesday	$0.00	$807.84	$807.84	$2,526.84	$2,526.84	$4,755.06	$4,755.06	$4,810.50	$4,810.50
		Thursday	$403.40	$1,253.40	$1,253.40	$2,119.03	$2,119.03	$3,877.63	$3,989.63	$4,324.97	$4,324.97
Grand Total			$267,868.16	$373,915.21	$541,272.36	$775,779.61	$871,524.20	$1,034,546.57	$1,134,531.14	$1,265,792.87	$1,265,792.87

Page 1 of 35 (349 items) [1] 2 3 4 5 6 7 ... 33 34 35

Running Total

Figure 8-19: With the CategoryName field's RunningTotals set to true, the default aggregation operation (Sum) is being performed from left to right.

Notice that in Figure 8-18, $1,035.00 in beverages was sold in January on the first Monday. Also notice that no condiment sales occurred on the same day. With `RunningTotals` off, the Monday Beverage sales cell contains the value $1,035.00, and the Condiments cell is empty. With `RunningTotals` set to true — see Figure 8-19 — the beverage and condiment sales were accumulated and displayed in the Condiments sales data cell: $1,035.00 + 0 = $1,035.00. The $1,035.00 is added to the $1,882.00 (see Figure 8-18), resulting in the `RunningTotals` of $2,917.00 under confections for the same period.

If you change the SummaryType and RunningTotals, the total value reflects the SummaryType. For example, if fieldCategoryName.RunningTotals is assigned the value true and the fieldExtendedPrice.SummaryType is assigned the value DevExpress.Data.PivotGrid.PivotSummaryType.Count, the totals reflect the number of items.

Using Manually Specified Totals

By default, a Field's SummaryType is Sum. If you want to see more summary information like the Sum, Min, and Max, you can add the field whose totals you want to see more than once in the field's Editor Form. For instance, if you have a query based on SalesPerson that contains Extended Price then you can manually add two additional fields, set the FieldName to Extended Price, and set one field's SummaryType to Min and the other to Max. As a result, the Extended Price data will be summarized in three ways: Sum, Min, and Max. (Other SummaryTypes are available as discussed throughout this chapter.)

> *By default, summary values are displayed along the bottom and right side of the* ASPxPivotGrid. *You can change the summary locations to top and left side by changing the* ASPxPivotGrid.OptionsView.TotalsLocation *from* Far *to* Near.

By default, each PivotGridField's TotalsVisibility property is set to AutomaticTotals. The net effect of AutomaticTotals is that for each axis, the three summary totals are displayed. With an ASPxPivotGrid configured using the following query against the MS Access nwind.mdb database:

```
SELECT [CategoryName], [ProductName], [Extended Price] AS Extended_Price
  FROM [SalesPerson]
```

and the following conditions:

❑   The CategoryName field's Area property is set to RowArea.

❑   The ProductName field's Area property is set to RowArea.

❑   All three Extended Price fields' (Extended Price, Price [Min], and Price [Max] Area properties are set to DataArea.

❑   The ASPxPivotGrid.OptionsDataField.Area is set to RowArea.

The ASPxPivotGrid appears as shown in Figure 8-20. Notice that for each subcategory, represented by ProductName, the three summary values are displayed. However, within a category such as Beverages, there is only one minimum extended price, one maximum extended price, and one sum of extended prices.

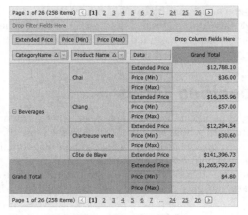

Figure 8-20: With a PivotGridField's TotalsVisibility set to AutomaticTotals (the default), each set of summary values is repeated.

To condense the ASPxPivotGrid's output and display summaries one time by category, change the CategoryName field's TotalsVisibility from AutomaticTotals to CustomTotals and complete the following steps:

1. Assuming that you have five fields in the ASPxPivotGrid — one mapped to CategoryName, one to ProductName, and three to Extended Price with a SummaryType of Sum, Min, and Max, respectively — change the CategoryName field's TotalsVisibility to CustomTotals.

2. Using the Collection Editor Form, modify the CategoryName field's CustomTotals property using Figure 8-21 as a guide, adding a custom total for Sum, Min, and Max.

3. Delete the Extended Price fields with the SummaryType Min and Max, leaving the Extended Price with SummaryType Sum.

4. Close the Collection Editor dialog.

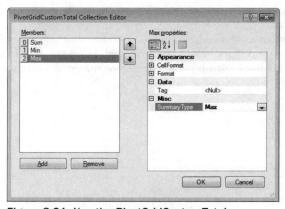

Figure 8-21: Use the PivotGridCustomTotal Collection Editor to define as many custom totals as you want.

If you run the sample after completing the changes in the preceding numbered steps you will see the output similar to Figure 8-22. (Your results will contain more products unless you apply the filter shown at the bottom of Figure 8-22. Refer to the next section for more on end-user filtering.) Notice now that the summary information for each category is displayed just one time at the end of the category. Now, rather than require the user to examine each product and figure out the minimum, maximum, and sum of beverages, just one set of summary values is displayed. For example, if you examine Figure 8-20 and compare the minimum extended price between Chai, Chang, and Chartreuse Verte, you can determine that the minimum beverage price is $30.60. However, in Figure 8-22, only the minimum beverage price is displayed. No code-behind is required for this sample, but the ASPX is provided in Listing 8-12 for reference.

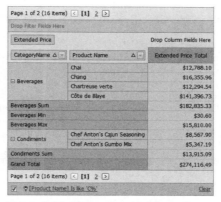

Figure 8-22: The new output based on the CustomTotals reduces unessential clutter, letting the user get answers to questions such as "What is the minimum price for a beverage?" without a lot of manual scanning of data.

Listing 8-12: The ASPX for the PivotGridCustomTotals sample.

```
<%@ Page Language="C#" AutoEventWireup="true"  CodeFile="Default.aspx.cs"
  Inherits="_Default" %>

<%@ Register assembly="DevExpress.Web.ASPxPivotGrid.v9.1,↵
  Version=9.1.4.0, Culture=neutral, PublicKeyToken=b88d1754d700e49a"
  namespace="DevExpress.Web.ASPxPivotGrid" tagprefix="dxwpg" %>

<!DOCTYPE html PUBLIC "-//W3C//DTD XHTML 1.0 Transitional//EN"
  "http://www.w3.org/TR/xhtml1/DTD/xhtml1-transitional.dtd">

<html xmlns="http://www.w3.org/1999/xhtml">
```

Continued

Listing 8-12: The ASPX for the PivotGridCustomTotals sample. *(continued)*

```
<head runat="server">
    <title></title>
</head>
<body>
  <form id="form1" runat="server">
  <div>

    <dxwpg:ASPxPivotGrid ID="ASPxPivotGrid1" runat="server"
    DataSourceID="AccessDataSource1">
    <Fields>
      <dxwpg:PivotGridField ID="fieldCategoryName" Area="RowArea"
      AreaIndex="0"
      FieldName="CategoryName" TotalsVisibility="CustomTotals">
      <CustomTotals>
        <dxwpg:PivotGridCustomTotal />
        <dxwpg:PivotGridCustomTotal SummaryType="Min" />
        <dxwpg:PivotGridCustomTotal SummaryType="Max" />
      </CustomTotals>
      </dxwpg:PivotGridField>
      <dxwpg:PivotGridField ID="fieldExtendedPrice" Area="DataArea"
      AreaIndex="0"
      Caption="Extended Price" FieldName="Extended_Price">
      </dxwpg:PivotGridField>
      <dxwpg:PivotGridField ID="field2" Area="RowArea" AreaIndex="1"
      FieldName="ProductName" Caption="Product Name">
      </dxwpg:PivotGridField>
    </Fields>
    <OptionsDataField Area="RowArea" AreaIndex="2" />
    </dxwpg:ASPxPivotGrid>
    <asp:AccessDataSource ID="AccessDataSource1" runat="server"
    DataFile="~/App_Data/nwind.mdb"
    SelectCommand="SELECT [CategoryName], [ProductName],
    [Extended Price] AS Extended_Price FROM [SalesPerson]">
    </asp:AccessDataSource>

  </div>
  </form>
</body>
</html>
```

End-User Data Filtering

The ASPxPivotGrid supports filtering much as the ASPxGridView does. Integrated into the pivot grid is the ASPxFilterControl. If you click a PivotGridField, a popup menu is displayed. The menu options are Refresh Data, Hide, Show Field List, and Show Prefilter (see Figure 8-23).

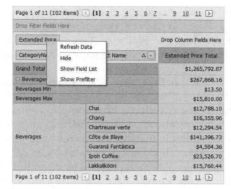

Figure 8-23: Right-click a PivotGridField
at runtime and select Show Prefilter to
visually define a filter for that field.

The PivotGrid Prefilter works just like the `ASPxFilterControl` described in Chapter 1, in the section "Defining Dynamic Predicates with the Filter Bar." To define the filter — [Product Name] is like 'C%' — shown in the Filter Bar at the bottom of the `ASPxPivotGrid` in Figure 8-22, shown previously, right-click one of the `PivotGridFields` at runtime. Select the ProductName field and the `is like` operator; then type **C%** in the data field. (See Figure 8-24, which shows the filter control input that defines the filter.) Return to the aforementioned section in Chapter 1 for a thorough discussion of the filter control.

Figure 8-24: Select the
ProductName field and
the is like operator,
and enter C% to filter
the ASPxPivotGrid on
products beginning with C.

To add the prefilter with code, provide a value for the `ASPxPivotGrid.Prefilter.CriteriaString` or `ASPxPivotGrid.Prefilter.Criteria` properties in code. For example, the following fragment applies a filter identical to the one shown in Figure 8-24 using code instead of the filter control. (You can add the filter using the Properties window or add the code shown to the `Page_Load` event.)

```
ASPxPivotGrid1.Prefilter.CriteriaString = "ProductName like 'C%'";
```

Other kinds of features and filtering are available. For example, you can click the little [-] or [+] buttons to collapse or expand an axis. If you right-click a PivotGridField and click Hide (refer to Figure 8-23), that field will be hidden from the ASPxPivotGrid view. To restore the field, right-click a field, select Show Field List, and drag and drop the field back to the `ASPxPivotGrid`. Finally, the drop-down button will display a filter combo box that has Show All checked by default. If you deselect Show All, you can select individual items to filter on those items. These are mostly automatically available features that you can turn on or off with properties, but you need to know they are present, especially if your Web application commitment to a client has a user training component.

Sorting Data and Displaying Top or Bottom Values

As does the `ASPxGridView`, the `ASPxPivotGrid` has built-in sorting. Click a `PivotGridField` at runtime and the sort order for that field is reversed. Click it a second time and the sort order is restored to the original order. Sorting is an automatic feature managed by the ASPxPivotGrid's `OptionsCustomization.AllowSort` property, which is set to true by default. Change the `OptionsCustomization.AllowSort` to false, and sorting is disabled. The `OptionsCustomization.AllowSortBySummary` feature — also true by default — determines whether a user can sort by summary fields. As shown in Figure 8-25, if you right-click over a summary field, a pop-up menu with summary sorting options is displayed. Click the desired option to sort by that value. When a summary sort is in effect on a field, the opposing triangle icon is displayed next to the field name (see Figure 8-26).

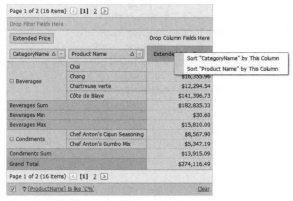

Figure 8-25: If OptionsCustomization.
AllowSortBySummary is true, the user can sort by
summary fields.

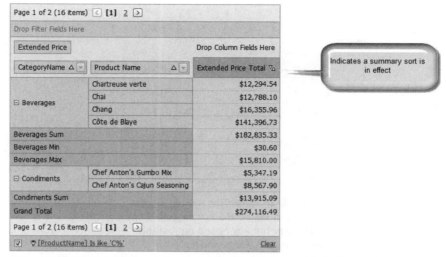

Figure 8-26: The presence of the opposing triangle's graphic indicates that a summary sort is in effect.

Sorting Manually

Sometimes the default sorting behavior may not be the behavior that you desire. For this reason, besides supporting the default sort mode, the ASPxPivotGrid.SortMode property can be set to DisplayText, Key, None, Value, or Custom. The Custom mode lets you write code that ultimately decides how the data elements are ordered.

Suppose you have a data set with key values like A1, A2. . .A10, A11. . .A20, A21, and so on. The default sort would treat these values as strings and order the items A1,A10,A11. . .A2,A20,A21 (see Figure 8-27). This ordering is fine if that is what you want; however, if the numeric aspect of the key value needs to be sorted, you can use a custom sort. To implement a custom sort, set a PivotGridField's SortMode property to PivotSortMode.Custom and implement the ASPxPivotGrid.CustomFieldSort event handler. (The results are shown in Figure 8-28.)

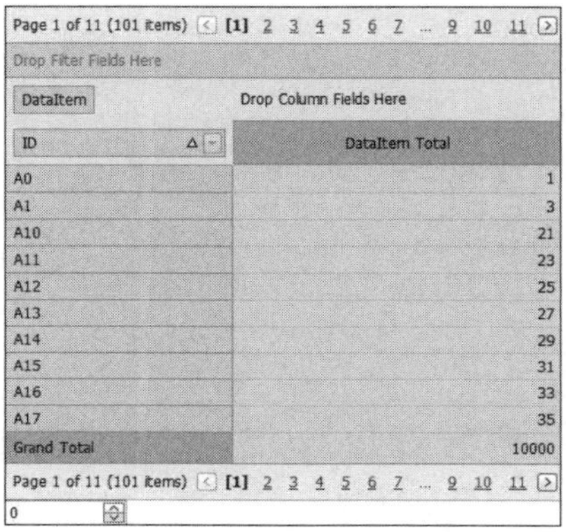

Figure 8-27: Given a set (A1, A2. . .A10, A11) and the default SortMode, here are the results of the sort.

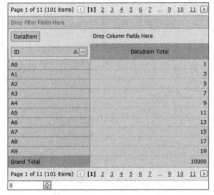

Figure 8-28: Given the same key set as that in Figure 8-27, a custom sort can order the key based on just the numeric part, for instance.

Figure 8-28 shows the revised ordering based on a `SortMode` of `Custom` and a `CustomFieldSort` event handler that strips off alphabetic characters and sorts based on the numeric suffix of the key. Listing 8-13 contains a lot of information. In addition to demonstrating how to implement a `CustomFieldSort`, the listing includes a custom class, programmatic initialization of an `ASPxPivotGrid`, and another example of the `System.Text.RegularExpressions.Regex` class.

Listing 8-13: This code demonstrates a CustomFieldSort based on an alphanumeric key.

```csharp
using System;
using System.Collections.Generic;
using System.Linq;
using System.Web;
using System.Web.UI;
using System.Web.UI.WebControls;
using DevExpress.Web.ASPxPivotGrid;
using DevExpress.XtraPivotGrid;
using System.Text.RegularExpressions;

public partial class _Default : System.Web.UI.Page
{
  private List<Data> list = null;
  protected void Page_Load(object sender, EventArgs e)
  {

    list = new List<Data>();
    for (int i = 0; i < 100; i++)
    {
      list.Add(new Data("A" + i.ToString(), i));
```

```
      list.Add(new Data("A" + i.ToString(), i+1));
  }

  if (!IsPostBack)
  {
    PivotGridFieldBase id = ASPxPivotGrid1.Fields.Add();
    id.Name = "fieldID";
    id.FieldName = "ID";
    id.Area = DevExpress.XtraPivotGrid.PivotArea.RowArea;
    PivotGridFieldBase data = ASPxPivotGrid1.Fields.Add();
    data.Name = "fieldData";
    data.FieldName = "DataItem";
    data.Area = DevExpress.XtraPivotGrid.PivotArea.DataArea;
    id.SortMode = PivotSortMode.Custom;

  }
  ASPxPivotGrid1.CustomFieldSort +=
      new PivotGridCustomFieldSortEventHandler(
        ASPxPivotGrid1_CustomFieldSort);

  ASPxPivotGrid1.DataSource = list;
  ASPxPivotGrid1.DataBind();
}

protected void ASPxSpinEdit1_NumberChanged(object sender, EventArgs e)
{
  ASPxPivotGrid1.Fields["ID"].TopValueCount =
    Convert.ToInt32(ASPxSpinEdit1.Value);
  ASPxPivotGrid1.Fields["ID"].TopValueShowOthers = true;
}

protected void ASPxPivotGrid1_CustomFieldSort(
  object sender,
  DevExpress.Web.ASPxPivotGrid.PivotGridCustomFieldSortEventArgs e)
{
  e.Result = StripAlphaCharacters(e.Value1).CompareTo(
    StripAlphaCharacters(e.Value2));
  e.Handled = true;
}

private int StripAlphaCharacters(object str)
{
  return StripAlphaCharacters(str.ToString());
}

private int StripAlphaCharacters(string str)
{
  return Convert.ToInt32(Regex.Replace(str, "^[A-Z]+", ""));
}

}

public class Data
```

Continued

Listing 8-13: This code demonstrates a CustomFieldSort based on an alphanumeric key. *(continued)*

```
{
  /// <summary>
  /// Initializes a new instance of the Data class.
  /// </summary>
  /// <param name="iD"></param>
  /// <param name="dataItem"></param>
  public Data(string iD, int dataItem)
  {
    this.iD = iD;
    this.dataItem = dataItem;
  }

  private string iD;
  public string ID
  {
    get { return iD; }
    set { iD = value; }
  }

  private int dataItem;
  public int DataItem
  {
    get { return dataItem; }
    set { dataItem = value; }
  }
}
```

The `Data` class exists for demonstration purposes. The `Page_Load` event creates an instance of `List<Data>` to store the sample data. (In practice, you could store such data in `Session`, but doing so isn't relevant to our discussion.) The `for` loop creates instances of the `Data` class and places them in the `List<Data>` object. An unusual alphanumeric key is created for demonstration purposes. (I have seen a lot of projects with alphanumeric keys, especially for legacy databases, but have seldom found a reason to use them for new databases.)

If the page is initializing, two fields are added to the `ASPxPivotGrid` by calling `ASPxPivotGrid1.Fields.Add`. The field `Name`, `FieldName`, and `Area` properties are set for both fields. The `SortMode` property is set to `PivotSortMode.Custom` for the `ID` field. Finally, an event handler is assigned to the `ASPxPivotGrid`'s `CustomFieldSort` event, and the data is bound to the `ASPxPivotGrid`.

The `ASPxPivotGrid1_CustomFieldSort` event handler is called every time a field is shown on the PivotGrid. The `PivotGridCustomFieldSortEventArgs` argument contains several properties and a method. The properties are `Field`, `Handled`, `ListSourceRowIndex1`, `ListSourceRowIndex2`, `Result`, `SortOrder`, `Value1`, and `Value2`. The method is `GetListSourceColumnValue`.

❑   The `Field` property returns the field whose values are being compared.

❑   The `Handled` property is a Boolean. Set it to true to indicate that the event handler completed the comparison; set it to false if you want the default comparison to happen.

❏ `ListSourceRowIndex1` and `ListSourceRowIndex2` return the indexes in the data source of the two items being compared; you can use this information to include other elements of the data source in the comparison.

❏ `Result` is an integer that indicates the comparison result. A `Result` of 0 means that the values are equal; -1 means that value 1 is less than value 2; and a value of 1 means that value 1 is greater than value 2.

❏ `SortOrder` is an instance of `PivotSortOrder` and indicates the current direction of the sort.

❏ `Value1` and `Value2` are object properties and contain the value of the two values being compared.

❏ `GetListSourceColumnValue` accepts an integer representing the index of the item in the data source and a string representing the field name of the desired item from the data source.

`CustomFieldSort` calls the overloaded local method `StripAlphaCharacters` that converts the data to a string and in turn calls the other overloaded `StripAlphaCharacters`. That local method uses a Regular Expression "^[A-Z]+" and the `Regex.Replace` method, which will match any uppercase alphabetic characters, strip them from the input, and convert the remaining value — digits in this instance — to an integer.

Using two overloaded methods `StripAlphaCharacters`, *for example, to perform individual chunks of work — type conversion and data manipulation with a Regular Expression — is a stylistic choice. You could write all the bits of code in the* `CustomFieldSort`, *but I have found time and again that small functions are significantly easier to debug and reuse. Ease of debugging is the greatest motivator for choosing the style of coding demonstrated in Listing 8-13.*

Displaying Top or Bottom Numbers

Users may not be interested in all the available data. In practice, some users will want all the data, some will want a fraction of the top values, and some will want bottom values. I think of top-value, bottom-value, and summary reports (or views of data) as managerial or executive views. A stock trader may want to be aware of bottom performers to help tidy up a portfolio. A manager may want to know who the top sales people are to determine who is eligible for bonuses.

The ASPxPivotGrid supports top and bottom values through the `PivotGridField.TopValueCount` property. If you want:

❏ Top values, sort in ascending order and set the `TopValueCount` for a given field.

❏ Bottom values, sort in descending order and set the `TopValueCount`.

❏ Absolute count, leave the `TopValueType` set to `Absolute`.

❏ The top percentage, change the `TopValueType` to `percent`.

❏ To show the top values and all the other, remaining values as an `Other` line, set `TopValueCount` to the number of items to show and `PivotGridField.TopValueOthers` to true.

The `NumberChanged` event handler in Listing 8-13 demonstrates how you can set the `TopValueCount` (using an `ASPxSpinEdit` control) and `TopValueShowOthers` properties with code. You can also access field properties directly through the instance of a `PivotGridField`, if available. (No such field object exists in the code-behind demo simply because I didn't declare any.)

Using the Drill-Down Window

A neat demo on the DevExpress Web site is the Drill Down demo at `http://demos.devexpress.com/ASPxPivotGridDemos/Features/Drilldown.aspx`. The Drill Down demo illustrates how you can combine DevExpress controls and components to construct useful, advanced solutions while still maintaining a tight leash over the amount of code needed to do so.

The key aspects to the Drill Down demo is a client-side cell click event for the `ASPxPivotGrid` that initiates the JavaScript to display the pop-up window: An `ASPxPivotGrid` with data, and a `CusomCallback` event handler that uses the `ASPxPivotGrid`'s `CreateDrillDownDataSource`. Recall from Listing 8-5 that the `CreateDrillDownDataSource` method returns a data source that represents all the rows from the original data source that are used to compile the data for an axis. Use the drill-down data source to bind to an `ASPxGridView` in the pop-up window and you have a drill-down window. You can look at the code sample that is downloaded with your ASPxperience installation or check out the DevExpress Web site at the aforementioned URL to explore the Drill Down demo. I have included a separate demo here that shows you all the elements of the solution (in case you are reading on a plane or airport without Internet access.) The database used for this final sample for this chapter is the nwind .mdb Access database. Listing 8-14 provides the ASPX for the sample — DrillDownDemo; Listing 8-15 contains the code-behind. (From beginning to end, it took me about 20 minutes to create the demo solution. If you have explored the sample solutions in the preceding chapters up to this point, it shouldn't take you much longer — that's my hope, at least.)

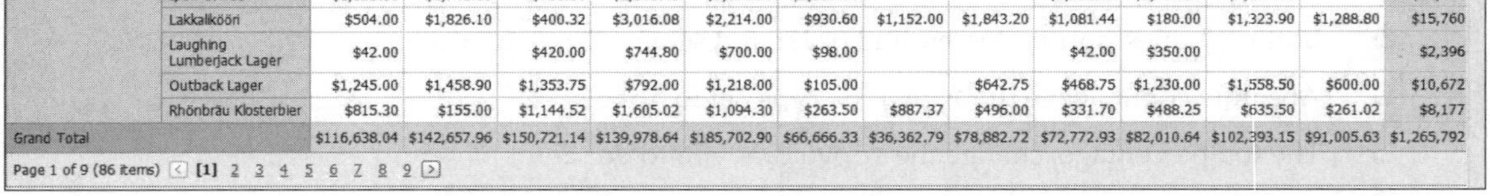

Figure 8-29: The Drill-Down Window shows all of the data for a data cell, including items not displayed in the ASPxPivotGrid.

Listing 8-14: The ASPX for the DrillDownDemo.

```
<%@ Page Language="C#" AutoEventWireup="true"  CodeFile="Default.aspx.cs"
 Inherits="_Default" %>

<%@ Register assembly="DevExpress.Web.ASPxPivotGrid.v9.1,↵
 Version=9.1.4.0, Culture=neutral, PublicKeyToken=b88d1754d700e49a"
 namespace="DevExpress.Web.ASPxPivotGrid" tagprefix="dxwpg" %>
<%@ Register assembly="DevExpress.Web.v9.1, Version=9.1.4.0,↵
 Culture=neutral, PublicKeyToken=b88d1754d700e49a"
 namespace="DevExpress.Web.ASPxPopupControl" tagprefix="dxpc" %>
<%@ Register assembly="DevExpress.Web.ASPxGridView.v9.1,↵
 Version=9.1.4.0, Culture=neutral, PublicKeyToken=b88d1754d700e49a"
 namespace="DevExpress.Web.ASPxGridView" tagprefix="dxwgv" %>
<%@ Register assembly="DevExpress.Web.ASPxEditors.v9.1,↵
 Version=9.1.4.0, Culture=neutral, PublicKeyToken=b88d1754d700e49a"
 namespace="DevExpress.Web.ASPxEditors" tagprefix="dxe" %>

<!DOCTYPE html PUBLIC "-//W3C//DTD XHTML 1.0 Transitional//EN"
 "http://www.w3.org/TR/xhtml1/DTD/xhtml1-transitional.dtd">

<html xmlns="http://www.w3.org/1999/xhtml">
<head runat="server">
  <title></title>
<script type="text/javascript">
  function ShowDrillDown() {
  var mainTable = PivotGrid.GetMainTable();
  DrillDownWindow.ShowAtPos(_aspxGetAbsoluteX(mainTable),
   _aspxGetAbsoluteY(mainTable));
  }
</script>
</head>
<body>
  <form id="form1" runat="server">
  <div>

    <dxwpg:ASPxPivotGrid ID="ASPxPivotGrid1" runat="server"
    ClientInstanceName="PivotGrid" DataSourceID="AccessDataSource1"
    >
    <Fields>
      <dxwpg:PivotGridField ID="fieldOrderID" AreaIndex="0" FieldName="OrderID">
      </dxwpg:PivotGridField>
      <dxwpg:PivotGridField ID="fieldProductName" Area="RowArea" AreaIndex="1"
      FieldName="ProductName">
      </dxwpg:PivotGridField>
      <dxwpg:PivotGridField ID="fieldCategoryName" Area="RowArea" AreaIndex="0"
      FieldName="CategoryName">
      </dxwpg:PivotGridField>
      <dxwpg:PivotGridField ID="fieldOrderDate" Area="ColumnArea" AreaIndex="0"
      FieldName="OrderDate" GroupInterval="DateMonth"
      UnboundFieldName="fieldOrderDate">
      </dxwpg:PivotGridField>
```

Continued

Listing 8-14: The ASPX for the DrillDownDemo. *(continued)*

```
        <dxwpg:PivotGridField ID="fieldExtendedPrice" Area="DataArea" AreaIndex="0"
        FieldName="Extended Price">
        </dxwpg:PivotGridField>
      </Fields>
      <ClientSideEvents CellClick="function(s, e) {
        debugger;
        GridView.PerformCallback('D|' + e.ColumnIndex + '|' + e.RowIndex);
        ShowDrillDown();
      }
}" />
    </dxwpg:ASPxPivotGrid>
    <asp:AccessDataSource ID="AccessDataSource1" runat="server"
    DataFile="~/App_Data/nwind.mdb" SelectCommand="SELECT * FROM [SalesPerson]">
    </asp:AccessDataSource>

  </div>
  <dxpc:ASPxPopupControl ID="ASPxPopupControl1" runat="server"
    HeaderText="Drill Down Window" Height="146px" Width="384px"
    ClientInstanceName="DrillDownWindow">
    <ContentCollection>
<dxpc:PopupControlContentControl runat="server">
  <dxwgv:ASPxGridView ID="ASPxGridView1" runat="server" Width="100%"
  ClientInstanceName="GridView"
OnCustomCallback="ASPxGridView1_CustomCallback">
  </dxwgv:ASPxGridView>
    </dxpc:PopupControlContentControl>
</ContentCollection>
  </dxpc:ASPxPopupControl>
  </form>
</body>
</html>
```

Listing 8-15: The code-behind for the DrillDownDemo contains single event handler, CustomCallback, that binds the data to the pop-up window's ASPxGridView.

```
using System;
using System.Collections.Generic;
using System.Linq;
using System.Web;
using System.Web.UI;
using System.Web.UI.WebControls;

public partial class _Default : System.Web.UI.Page
{
  protected void Page_Load(object sender, EventArgs e)
  {

  }

  protected void ASPxGridView1_CustomCallback(object sender,
    DevExpress.Web.ASPxGridView.ASPxGridViewCustomCallbackEventArgs e)
```

```
    {
        string[] param = e.Parameters.Split('|');
        if (param.Length != 3) return;
        ASPxGridView1.DataSource =
        ASPxPivotGrid1.CreateDrillDownDataSource(
        Int32.Parse(param[1]), Int32.Parse(param[2]));
        ASPxGridView1.DataBind();
        ASPxGridView1.PageIndex = 0;
    }
}
```

The Web GUI is comprised of an ASPxPivotGrid bound to an AcessDataSource. The data source selects all the columns and rows from the nwind.mdb SalesPerson table. Just the CategoryName, ProductName, OrderID, OrderDate, and [Extended Price] are bound to the ASPxPivotGrid. CategoryName and ProductName are placed in the RowArea. OrderDate is placed in the ColumnArea and has a GroupInterval of DateMonth. OrderID is placed in the FilterArea, and Extended Price is located in the DataArea. The ASPxPopupControl is placed on the same Web page and the ASPxPopupControl contains an ASPxGridView.

There are two JavaScript functions in the ASPX: ShowDrillDown and a CellClick function assigned to the ASPxPivotGrid's CellClick client-side event. When the user clicks a data cell, the CellClick function runs on the client. CellClick calls GridView.PerformCallback, passing in the selected Column and RowIndex. PerformCallback is handled by the ASPxGridView's server-side CustomCallback handler (refer to Listing 8-15). The CustomCallback event handler parses the e.Parameters argument, which contains the column and row indexes. These indices are in turn used to obtain the cell's underlying data source rows and bind that data source to the ASPxGridView. The runtime results are reflected in Figure 8-29.

Summary

The ASPxPivotGrid is a powerful control because it lets end users dynamically change what data is displayed and how it is organized. A substantial extra benefit is that the pivot grid can be associated with relational data or OLAP data (using an OLAP server or an offline hypercube file).

As demonstrated in this chapter, you can calculate values automatically or dynamically. Also, you can sort and filter pivot grid data, create drill-down windows, build hierarchies, perform group operations, and even export the pivot grid data into multiple output formats. I hope that by looking at the code listings, you can also tell that a tremendous amount of this functionality is built in, requiring only a modest amount of code labor on your part.

If you have been reading the book from beginning to end, this chapter really demonstrates how you can tie in a variety of skills to this one control and create powerful and compelling ways of letting the user interact with and explore his or her data.

## 9

Using the ASPxHtmlEditor

Sometimes writing yields funny surprises. I was thinking of a demo for this chapter, and a natural choice is an application that supports writing and publishing Web logs. I picked a random name for the demo, blogit, and then thought maybe I should look to see if it had been taken. (Sometimes people get very territorial about names. Yes, blogit was taken.) The funny part is that almost every combination I could imagine was taken — goblog, blogexpress, devblog, superblog, blogx — until I eventually gave up on clever blog names for the sample. The winner is blogsample out of desperation.

The name of the sample application isn't really that important, though. What is important is the powerful editing features of the ASPxHtmlEditor. The ASPxHtmlEditor is a full-featured editor with Design, HTML, and Preview modes. Like the ASPxScheduler, the ASPxHtmlEditor is closer to a subsystem than it is to a control. The ASPxHtmlEditor supports HTML and text input; scripts are disabled by default but supported; performance is enhanced with Ajax; and buttons, toolbars, and context menus make the ASPxHtmlEditor a full-featured editor for all your online editing projects.

Managing ASPxHtmlEditor Features

Like all of the other DevExpress controls the ASPxHtmlEditor can largely be managed by toggling property states. Script support has AllowScripts, IFrame, and Form supports as the AllowIFrames and AllFormElements properties. With a little experimentation with the samples in this chapter or the online demos you can quickly find these features and adjust the ASPxHtmlEditor based on your application's needs.

Enabling or Disabling Scripts

The first thing you will notice when you add an `ASPxHtmlEditor` to a Web page is that the designer inserts a lot of additional content into your project, including a DevExpress folder containing two subfolders and six user controls. Like the `ASPxScheduler`, the `ASPxHtmlEditor` adds these elements because they implement some of the rich features of the control. Refer to Figure 9-1 for an out-of-the-box view of the ASPxHtmlEditor and the Solution Explorer showing the aforementioned user controls.

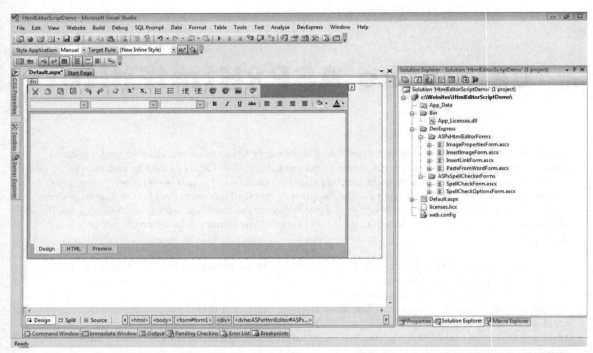

Figure 9-1: The ASPxHtmlEditor at design time, out of the box, is a rich subsystem that supports online editing.

Script injection is a well-known and often exploited security challenge. Permitting users to create HTML online means that all it takes is a single unscrupulous user to write some script that performs a malicious act and all of the positive benefit becomes a big headache. For this reason the `ASPxHtmlEditor` supports scripts, but this support is a turned-off feature — `ASPxHtmlEditor.SettingsHtmlEditing` `.AllowScripts` is set to false. When `AllowScripts` is set to false any script block typed into the editor by the user is stripped out.

If the reason for using the ASPxHtmlEditor is to allow users to create HTML including scripts, you can set AllowScripts to true. When AllowScripts is true, any script blocks typed in by the user will remain in the content.

Allowing IFrames

An iframe is a frame within a Web page that can be used to load other pages. If you set ASPxHtmlEditor.SettingsHmlEditing.AllowIFrames, users can enter <iframe> tags into their online content. Following is an example of an iframe tag. Figure 9-2 shows an instance of the ASPxHtmlEditor focused on the Preview tab with an iframe tag referencing a file named test.html.

```
<iframe src="test.html" scrolling="yes">
</iframe>
```

Figure 9-2: An instance of the ASPxHtmlEditor containing an iframe element focused on the Preview tab.

Occasionally I encounter anecdotal written comments about frames being inherently bad. Something about hacks and injection attacks. The iframe was a poor-cousin replacement for the frame. One drawback to the iframe is that the content in the iframe will not be indexed by search engines. This may or may not be important to you. If you want your page bookmarked by the spiders that index the Internet then use a <div>. If not, try the iframe.

Hack Attacks

If you look in almost any direction it is easy to find an exploit or hack that makes some-one else's life more difficult. For example, in the early 1990s I realized that the command.com — the old MS DOS command line — had a big hole of unused space and that it was easily possible to modify the command.com file. The initial branch statement in command.com could be modified so that some other code could be run — like turning the speaker on or copying the Michelangelo virus to the file system — and branch back to command.com's actual instructions. Using the debug.exe command-line program, some basic instructions, and a little knowledge of MS-DOS BIOS was all it took. (The debug.exe is still installed with Windows Vista.) For me it was more about experimentation than actually wreaking havoc, but the potential for havoc always exists.

Allowing Form Elements

Like script blocks and iframes, form elements are automatically removed from the `ASPxHtmlEditor` unless you change the default `ASPxHtmlEditor.SettingsHtmlEditing.AllowFormElements` from false to true.

Allowing Supported Editor Views

The `ASPxHtmlEditor` has three views enabled by default: Design, HTML, and Preview. You can enable or disable these at design time from the Smart tags menu or the `ASPxHtmlEditor.Settings` property. For example, to disable the HTML tab change the `ASPxHtmlEditor.Settings.AllowHtmlView` to false.

The `ASPxHtmlEditor.Settings` property contains properties for enabling or disabling the editor's context menu, Design view tab, HTML view tab, and Preview tab and for indicating whether or not image URLs from other Web sites can be referenced or are downloaded and cached locally.

Updating Document Elements Automatically

The `ASPxHtmlEditor.SettingsHtmlEditor` has two more properties that you can use to tweak editor content.

❑ The `UpdateDeprecatedElements` property replaces deprecated HTML elements with their valid analogs.

❑ The `UpdateBoldItalic` property causes `<b></b>` (bold) or `<i></i>` (italic) elements to be replaced with the `<strong></strong>` or `<em></em>` elements, respectively.

The underlying reason for having the `<b>` for bold versus `<strong>` also for bold co-existing in the same universe has to do with text-to-speech (or the aural Web). Visually the `<b>` and `<strong>` tags make the text appear to be in a bold font. However, if a Web page's content is converted to speech, there is no aural difference between bold text and normal text, but text marked with the strong tag is also played or read with emphasis.

Defining a Custom ASPxHtmlEditor Toolbar

When you add an ASPxHtmlEditor to a Web page, the standard toolbars are enabled and visible. The standard toolbars contain dozens of options that support all of the favorite features for editing, like redo and undo, superscript and subscript, paste and paste from Word, and insert hyperlink and image. If you open the ASPxHtmlEditor Toolbars Editor — see Figure 9-3 — and click the Create Default Toolbars button, the toolbar items for each of the standard menu items are created and added to the ASPX.

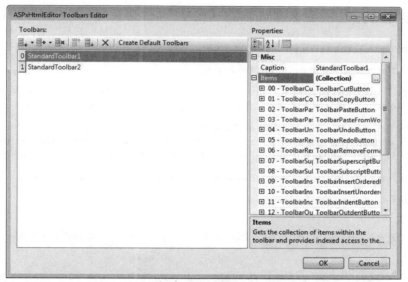

Figure 9-3: The ASPxHtmlEditor Toolbars Editor supports creating and modifying toolbars for the editor.

With the standard toolbars added you can use the ASPxHtmlEditor Toolbars Editor to add and remove items, and modify items, including the Text, Tooltip, and Image. You can set the BeginGroup property of a toolbar item to true, and the group divider is added to indicate a logical grouping.

If you want to create to custom toolbars, use the Add an Item button (on the left end of the toolbar above the left pane) in the ASPxHtmlEditor Toolbars Editor dialog box. The remaining toolbar buttons for the editor (going from left to right above the left pane in Figure 9-3) are Insert an Item, Remove the Item, buttons for moving items up and down, and Remove All Items, as well as the Create Default Toolbars button.

To access the toolbars use the ASPxHtmlEditor.Toolbars property by calling the FindByName method passing in the name of the toolbar (see the following code fragment). FindByName returns an instance of HtmlEditorToolbar, assuming the toolbar exists. HtmlEditorToolbar inherits from ToolbarBase, which supports adding menu items at design time as well as run time.

```
HtmlEditorToolbar toolbar =
        ASPxHtmlEditor1.Toolbars.FindByName("StandardToolbar1");
```

Most scenarios are supported by predefining toolbars and menu items at design time based on the feature set offered to the end user and hiding or revealing the toolbar based on the context. All toolbar buttons are derived from the `HtmlEditorToolbarButtonBase` class. For the extensive list of predefined derived toolbar button types see the table of classes that are derived from `HtmlEditorToolbarButtonBase`. This list includes `CustomToolbarButton`, `DefaultToolbarButton`, and many more, including all of the toolbar buttons shown in Figure 9-1.

To define a custom toolbar, follow these steps:

1. Open the `ASPxHtmlEditor` Toolbars Editor.

2. Click the Add an Item button in the editor.

3. In the Properties window for the new custom toolbar click the button to invoke the Items Editor for the new toolbar. (This step displays the `ASPxHtmlEditor` Items Editor.)

4. In the Items Editor click the Add an Item button to add a `CustomToolbarButton` (see Figure 9-4) or click the drop-down to pick from one of the many predefined buttons (see Figure 9-5). (Use the other toolbar buttons of the Items Editor to construct the layout of your custom menu.)

5. When you are finished defining the toolbar items, click OK to close the Items Editor.

6. Click OK to close the Toolbars Editor.

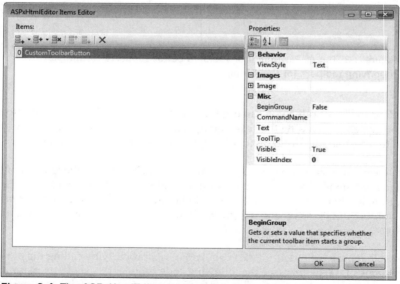

Figure 9-4: The ASPxHtmlEditor Items Editor is used to manage toolbar buttons.

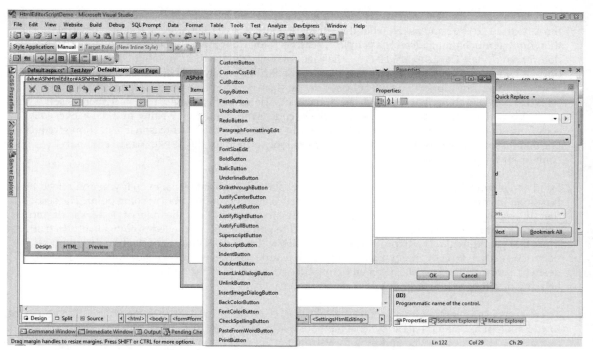

Figure 9-5: The drop-down for the ASPxHtmlEditor Items Editor Add an Item button lists the predefined buttons, which include their associated behaviors.

If you want to execute a command from the client when no toolbar button is present for that command you can invoke `ASPxClientHtmlEditor.ExecuteCommand`. *Pass in the command name, a string containing the parameters for that command, and a Boolean indicating whether or not the command should be placed on the toolbar's undo stack. The list of existing commands is defined as members of* `ASPxClientCommandConsts`.

Toolbar items that have well-defined names like CutButton — see Figure 9-5 — perform the behavior described by the name. You can use the Properties window in the Items Editor to set things like Text, ToolTip, Visibility (the Visible property), the ViewStyle, and Image. The ViewStyle determines if the toolbar button displays text, an image, or both. The `CustomToolbarButton` type also introduces a `CommandName` property. This is a string value. If you define a `CustomToolbarButton` and provide a `CommandName`, you can implement a client-side event for the `CustomCommand`. The `commandName` property of the `e` argument for the `CustomCommand` client-side event can be examined to determine which custom command invoked the behavior.

Adding a Custom Toolbar Item with Code

On real software projects spending several hours trying to figure out something clever can get you into hot water. Doing the same thing on a book project can exacerbate your deadlines, but a book is a much better venue for tinkering with the possible, even if the possible is of questionable, direct use.

I was talking to our developers today and indicated that I wanted a demo for a custom toolbar item for the `ASPxHtmlEditor` and asked what they thought about a Save toolbar item. (I don't think they thought that much of the idea for a couple of reasons aside from the fact that the ASPxHtmlEditor doesn't have one.) The `ASPxHtmlEditor` has a lot of toolbar items that provide rich client functionality, but saving is not one of them. Customers may not be thrilled by saving their data on your server. Second, JavaScript does not support File IO, at least directly. (I suspect some clever tinkerer can figure it out, but IO is just not something that is supported from client-side script.) However, that said, there is something I have learned after two decades — writing clever code is more fun than writing mundane, everyday code, and someone always needs something weird to satisfy an (often) unreasonable customer request. For that reason this section demonstrates a custom toolbar item for the `ASPxHtmlEditor` that saves the contents of the `ASPxHtmlEditor`.

I'd like to mention a couple of points before you get started. The first is that even if you don't need this functionality, my hope is that you may need to create a custom toolbar item at some point. The second is that this example — in the next subsection — demonstrates how to use the older-style Ajax code and how to dynamically inject JavaScript; you may decide you need this knowledge occasionally. In truth I think that generally the DevExpress Ajax capabilities will suffice 99 percent of the time and that the default `ASPxHtmlEditor` menu items provide the features most customers need, but it is those fringe desires that can kill a schedule. (Remembering how to put all of this plumbing together today didn't help my intraday writing schedule, but it was fun.)

To create a custom toolbar item for the `ASPxHtmlEditor`, obtain a reference to the toolbar that you want to add an item to using the `FindByName` method. Instantiate a new instance of the `CustomToolbarButton` type and provide a string for the display text and name. Optionally provide a value for the `ToolTip` property, and set the `ViewStyle` and the `Image.Url` property if you have an image. The snippet from the `Page_Load` sets all of the `Text`, `Name` (through the constructor argument), `ToolTip`, and `CommandName` properties to `Save`. The `ViewStyle` is set to `Image`, and a file named `Save.gif` is associated with the `Image.Url` property of the `CustomToolbarButton`. Finally, the `CustomToolbarButton` is added to the toolbar's `Items` collection.

```
HtmlEditorToolbar toolbar =
  ASPxHtmlEditor1.Toolbars.FindByName("CustomToolbar");
CustomToolbarButton button =
  new CustomToolbarButton("Save", "Save");

button.ToolTip = "Save";
button.CommandName = "Save";
button.ViewStyle = ViewStyle.Image;
button.Image.Url = "~/images/Save.gif";
toolbar.Items.Add(button);
```

Defining CustomCommand Toolbar Behavior and Ajax

Creating instances of classes and setting properties is always the easiest part of code. Defining dynamic behaviors, especially on the client, is more challenging. `HtmlToolbarButton` objects don't have server-side events for commands, so the behaviors have to be initiated on the client at a minimum.

You can invoke a custom client-side behavior in two ways:

❑   Invoke `ASPxClientHtmlEditor.ExecuteCommand` passing a previously undefined command.

❑   Define a `CustomToolbarButton` with a previously undefined `CommandName`.

Both ways require that you provide an implementation for the ASPxHtmlEditor's ClientSideEvents .CustomCommand event handler. Here is the snippet from the aforementioned Page_Load that dynamically assigns a function via the CustomName property to the CustomCommand client-side event:

```
ASPxHtmlEditor1.ClientSideEvents.CustomCommand =
        "function(s, e) { " +
        "if(e.commandName != 'Save') return;" +
        "debugger; " +
        "DoMyCallback(HtmlEditor.GetHtml()); " +
        "}";
```

The preceding code defines a function that will be associated with the CustomCommand event for the ASPxHtmlEditor. The code checks the commandName property to see if it is the Save command. If not, the function returns. If the event was raised by the Save button, the debugger statement gives you a chance to debug the JavaScript, and DoMyCallback sends the HTML content of the editor to a function called DoMyCallback. This is where the older style of Ajax comes into play. Listing 9-1 contains the complete implementation of the Page_Load event and all of the Ajax boilerplate code.

Listing 9-1: Just a few short years ago programmers had to routinely construct Ajax calls using script (this is something that is required much less frequently nowadays).

```
using System;
using System.Collections.Generic;
using System.Linq;
using System.Web;
using System.Web.UI;
using System.Web.UI.WebControls;
using DevExpress.Web.ASPxHtmlEditor;
using System.IO;

public partial class _Default : System.Web.UI.Page,
  ICallbackEventHandler
{
    protected void Page_Load(object sender, EventArgs e)
    {
      //HtmlEditorToolbar toolbar =
      //  ASPxHtmlEditor1.Toolbars.FindByName("StandardToolbar1");

      if(!Request.Browser.SupportsCallback)
        throw new ApplicationException("browser doesn't support callbacks");

      string source = Page.ClientScript.GetCallbackEventReference(
        this, "args", "PlaceHolder", "context", true);

      string script = @"function
        DoMyCallback(args, context){ " +
        source + "; }";

      string placeHolder =
        "function PlaceHolder(result, content) " +
        "{ alert(result);}";

      Page.ClientScript.RegisterClientScriptBlock(this.GetType(),
```

Continued

Listing 9-1: Just a few short years ago programmers had to routinely construct Ajax calls using script (this is something that is required much less frequently nowadays. *(continued)*

```
            "PlaceHolder", placeHolder, true);

        Page.ClientScript.RegisterClientScriptBlock(this.GetType(),
            "DoMyCallback", script, true);

        ASPxHtmlEditor1.ClientSideEvents.CustomCommand =
        "function(s, e) { " +
        "if(e.commandName != 'Save') return;" +
        "debugger; " +
        "DoMyCallback(HtmlEditor.GetHtml()); " +
        "}";

        HtmlEditorToolbar toolbar =
          ASPxHtmlEditor1.Toolbars.FindByName("CustomToolbar");
        CustomToolbarButton button =
          new CustomToolbarButton("Save", "Save");

        button.ToolTip = "Save";
        button.CommandName = "Save";
        button.ViewStyle = ViewStyle.Image;
        button.Image.Url = "~/images/Save.gif";
        toolbar.Items.Add(button);

    }

    #region ICallbackEventHandler Members

    public string GetCallbackResult()
    {
      return "save complete";
    }

    public void RaiseCallbackEvent(string eventArgument)
    {
      string filepath = Server.MapPath("~/output/") + "content.htm";
      StreamWriter stream = File.CreateText(filepath);
      stream.Write(eventArgument);
      stream.Close();
    }
    #endregion
}
```

An *interface* is a contract that indicates that a particular class will implement particular features based on the implicit contract — the *interface definition*. If you want to wire up Ajax code without UpdatePanel or ASPxCallbackPanel controls, you need to implement ICallbackEventHandler. ICallbackEventHandler has two methods: GetCallbackResult and RaiseCallbackEvent. The way Ajax works at a level lower than the ASPxCallbackPanel, for instance, is that an asynchronous callback is initiated by JavaScript on the client. The predetermined RaiseCallbackEvent method is designated as the respondee. RaiseCallbackEvent handles the call and the results are returned by

GetCallbackResult. If you need to update the appearance part of a page, GetCallbackResult needs to contain data or HTML that can be used again on the client to build up part of the page. For example, GetCallbackResult could contain information that is to be placed in predetermined cells of a table or the HTML that is the table itself. In the example in Listing 9-1 RaiseCallbackEvent writes the HTML contents of the ASPxHtmlEditor to a file and GetCallbackResult contains a simple text message indicating that the file was saved. The tricky part is wiring up each of these elements by injecting various bits of script to the client.

The Page_Load event handler demonstrates a way that you can check to see if the current browser supports callbacks. Page.ClientScript.GetCallbackEventReference actually accepts all of the arguments you provide to construct a call to the predefined WebForm_DoCallback method (see the following code snippet). This method is predefined in a script file named something like WebResource .axd. (Files with the .axd extension contain script that is shipped with the .NET Framework.)

```
WebForm_DoCallback('__Page',args,PlaceHolder,context,null,true)
```

The call to GetCallbackEventReference is made using a reference to the calling control, the name of the event arguments, the client callback that handles the return data, the return data parameter, and a Boolean indicating whether or not the callback is asynchronous.

The next string local variable, script, is the wrapper function to inject on the client that will contain the call to WebForm_DoCallback. The local variable placeHolder contains the implementation of the client result handler; in this instance it will just display the return message.

The next statement registers the placeholder script block by calling Page.ClientScript .RegisterClientScriptBlock, and the same method call after that registers the script containing the DoMyCallback method that will be called by the CustomCommand event. The rest of the code was described in the preceding section; it sets up the client-side CustomCommand handler and the CustomToolbarButton.

You have some options here. You could predefine some of the script elements in advance, but this demo shows you how to set up all of the script using injection. You can also use RegisterClientScriptBlock to inject any JavaScript dynamically. RegisterClientScriptBlock is not just for Ajax plumbing. For example, my article "Maintain ASP.NET Tree Position on Postbacks" at www.codeguru.com/csharp/ .net/net_asp/scripting/print.php/c12869 demonstrates how to inject script to scroll to the last position in a Microsoft TreeView. (Of course, using the ASPxTreeList from DevExpress eliminates the need for this technique.)

Applying Custom Styles (CSS)

As a book author one of the things that editors provide are document template files for MS Word. Document template files basically contain many — sometimes a huge number of — styles for every imaginable element of a book. There are styles for bulleted lists, code listings, tips, regular text, chapter and section headers, and much more. Rather than guess about how to format a document element, authors like me look at sample chapters and apply the styles from those provided based on how the sample chapter is formatted. After a while picking the correct style for an element is second nature. Providing styles to choose from for your customers can help them more easily achieve document consistency and apply some nice effects with a lot less effort than if they were left to their own devices.

One of the many cool features of the ASPxHtmlEditor is the ToolbarCustomCssEdit toolbar item. If you add this default item to one of the standard toolbars or a custom toolbar, you can predefine as many styles as you would like to provide for your users. The key is to define one or more custom style sheet (.css) files and add an item to the ToolbarCustomCssEdit toolbar item — a drop down list — for each style a user can choose.

If you need help creating a cascading style sheet choose View CSS Sample from the ASPxHtmlEditor's Smart tags menu and copy the sample style sheet content to a .css file you have added to your project. (Chapter 10 discusses defining and using style sheets in greater detail.) To add custom styles that can be applied to the ASPxHtmlEditor content, follow these steps:

1. Add a style sheet to the Web application from the Website ⇨ Add New Item menu. (For the sample I named the style sheet Sample.css and placed it in a subfolder named CSS.)

2. Add some classes and style information to the Sample.css style sheet. (You can use the sample from the ASPxHtmlEditor's Smart tags menu or copy the style content provided in Listing 9-2.)

3. In Visual Studio's designer, click the ASPxHtmlEditor and open the Properties window.

4. Click the editor button for the ASPxHtmlEditor.CssFiles property to edit the CssFiles collection (see Figure 9-6).

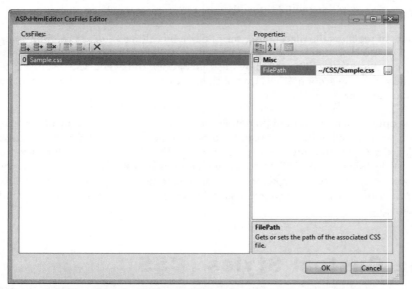

Figure 9-6: The ASPxHtmlEditor CssFiles Editor lets you associate style sheets (.css files) with your application.

5. Under the `CssFiles` list click the Add an Item button.

6. For the CSS file click the editor button for the `FilePath` property and select the `Sample.css` file from the Select URL dialog box (see Figure 9-7).

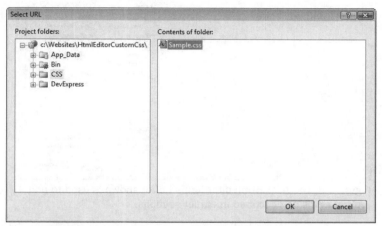

Figure 9-7: The Select URL dialog box lets you associate a style sheet with each style in the CSS Files list.

7. Click OK to close the Select URL dialog box.

8. Click OK to close the `ASPxHtmlEditor` CssFiles Editor dialog box.

9. Again in the Properties window for the `ASPxHtmlEditor` click the editor button for the `ASPxHtmlEditor.Toolbars` property to display the `ASPxHtmlEditor` Toolbars Editor.

10. Under the Toolbars list click Add an Item to add a `CustomToolbar`.

11. For the added `CustomToolbar` click its Items property editor button (a button with an ellipsis, to the right of the Items property).

12. In the ASPxHtmlEditor Items Editor click the Add an Item drop-down and pick the `CustomCssEdit` item (see Figure 9-8).

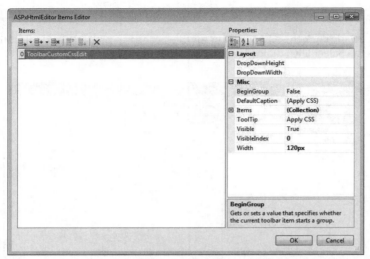

Figure 9-8: The ASPxHtmlEditor Items Editor shown is used to add toolbar items as described in earlier sections.

13. You need only one `ToolbarCustomCssEdit`; click its `Items` property to edit style items (see Figure 9-9).

14. For each item you want to add to the CSS toolbar item click Add an Item and provide the `CssClass` name property and the `Text` property (use Figure 9-9 as a visual guide).

15. Click OK to close the editors when finished.

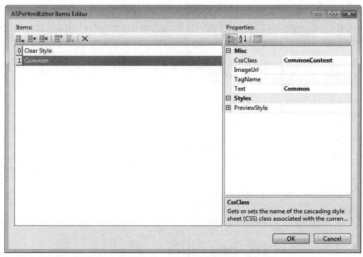

Figure 9-9: The Items Editor for the toolbar items — a ToolbarCustomCssEdit — supports adding the selectable styles.

Listing 9-2: The contents of the Sample.css style sheet used for the sample application in this section.

```css
.CommonTitle {
    color: #3366ff;
    font-family: Tahoma;
    font-size: 20pt;
    font-weight: bold;
    text-align: center;
}
.CommonHeader1 {
    color: #576fa5;
    font-weight: lighter;
    font-size: 170%;
    margin-top: 20px;
    margin-bottom: 10px;
}
.CommonHeader2 {
    color: #576fa5;
    font-weight: lighter;
    font-size: 130%;
    margin-top: 20px;
    margin-bottom: 10px;
}
.CommonContent, div
{
    font-weight: bold;
    color: Red;
}
.CommonFeatures {
    font-weight: 700;
    color: #595d66;
}
.CommonFooter {
    padding-top: 8px;
    color: Black;
    font-size: 12px;
}
.ImageTitle {
    color: #000000;
    line-height: 20px;
}
a.link {
    text-decoration: none;
}
a.link:hover {
    text-decoration: underline;
}
```

The `CssClass` property shown in Figure 9-9 should match the name of a style class in one of the files associated with your application in the `ASPxHtmlEditor`'s `CssFiles` collection. The `Text` property is the name you want to appear in the `ASPxHtmlEditor` styles toolbar item. If you want the styles toolbar item — a drop-down — to reflect the style in the `.css` file associated with the CssClass, use the `PreviewStyle` property in the Items Editor (see Figure 9-9 again).

If you want a style applied whenever a class name is used, create the item for the `ToolbarCustomCssEdit` item as described in the preceding numbered steps. If you define a style for an element like a `<div>` tag, then whenever a user uses that style in the `ASPxHtmlEditor`, the element style will be applied. Listing 9-2 shows a style class called `CommonContent`, which is also defined as the same style for `div` elements.

Given the HTML in the editor shown in the following snippet, the Design tab will appear as shown in Figure 9-10. Notice that when the cursor is on the text that has the `CommonContent` applied, the style toolbar item reflects the applied style. (You can't tell in the black and white pages of the book that the text is red, but the bold font-weight should be evident.) Listing 9-3 contains the ASPX for the sample application for reference, showing you the property settings and attributes configured by Visual Studio's and DevExpress's designers for the `ASPxHtmlEditor`. The standard toolbar items have been elided to shorten the listing.

```
<p class="CommonContent">This text is in a p element with the class="CommonContent"
  Attribute
</p>
<div>This text is inside of a div element.</div>
```

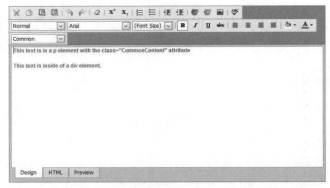

Figure 9-10: The runtime view of the ASPxHtmlEditor with the
HTML shown above in the fragment.

Listing 9-3: The ASPX for the sample applicationDevExpress.

```
<%@ Page Language="C#" AutoEventWireup="true"  CodeFile="Default.aspx.cs"
 Inherits="_Default" %>

<%@ Register assembly="DevExpress.Web.ASPxHtmlEditor.v9.1,↵
 Version=9.1.4.0, Culture=neutral, PublicKeyToken=b88d1754d700e49a"
 namespace="DevExpress.Web.ASPxHtmlEditor" tagprefix="dxhe" %>
<%@ Register assembly="DevExpress.Web.ASPxEditors.v9.1,↵
 Version=9.1.4.0, Culture=neutral, PublicKeyToken=b88d1754d700e49a"
 namespace="DevExpress.Web.ASPxEditors" tagprefix="dxe" %>
<%@ Register assembly="DevExpress.Web.ASPxSpellChecker.v9.1,↵
 Version=9.1.4.0, Culture=neutral, PublicKeyToken=b88d1754d700e49a"
 namespace="DevExpress.Web.ASPxSpellChecker" tagprefix="dxwsc" %>

<!DOCTYPE html PUBLIC "-//W3C//DTD XHTML 1.0 Transitional//EN"
 "http://www.w3.org/TR/xhtml1/DTD/xhtml1-transitional.dtd">

<html xmlns="http://www.w3.org/1999/xhtml">
<head runat="server">
  <title></title>
</head>
<body>
  <form id="form1" runat="server">
  <div>
    <dxhe:ASPxHtmlEditor ID="ASPxHtmlEditor1" runat="server">
    <settingsimageupload>
      <validationsettings allowedcontenttypes=
        "image/jpeg,image/pjpeg,image/gif,image/png,image/x-png">
      </validationsettings>
    </settingsimageupload>
    <Toolbars>
  <!—standard toolbar items removed to shorten the listing -->
      <dxhe:CustomToolbar>
      <Items>
        <dxhe:ToolbarCustomCssEdit Width="120px">
        <Items>
          <dxhe:ToolbarCustomCssListEditItem CssClass=""
          TagName="" Text="Clear Style">
          </dxhe:ToolbarCustomCssListEditItem>
          <dxhe:ToolbarCustomCssListEditItem CssClass="CommonContent" TagName=""
          Text="Common">
          <PreviewStyle ForeColor="Blue">
          </PreviewStyle>
          </dxhe:ToolbarCustomCssListEditItem>
        </Items>
        </dxhe:ToolbarCustomCssEdit>
      </Items>
      </dxhe:CustomToolbar>
    </Toolbars>
    <CssFiles>
```

Continued

Listing 9-3: The ASPX for the sample applicationDevExpress. *(continued)*

```
            <dxhe:HtmlEditorCssFile FilePath="~/CSS/Sample.css" />
          </CssFiles>
          <StylesContextMenu CssFilePath="~/CSS/Sample.css">
          </StylesContextMenu>
          </dxhe:ASPxHtmlEditor>
      </div>
      </form>
  </body>
  </html>
```

All of this online editing power enables your users — with a little imagination for their part — to create compelling documents like the cutout shown from the CustomCss.aspx sample page on the DevExpress Web site at `http://demos.devexpress.com/ASPxHTMLEditorDemos/Features/CustomCSS.aspx` (refer to Figure 9-11).

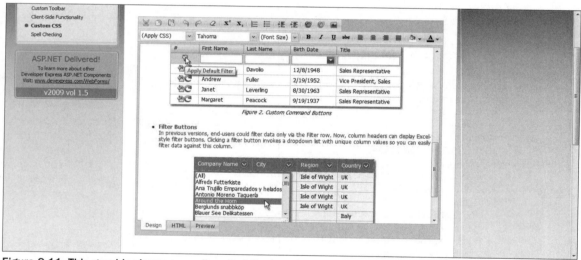

Figure 9-11: This graphic shows a small part of the functional custom CSS sample from the DevExpress Web site with the ASPxHtmlEditor focused on the Design tab.

Enabling Spell Checking

Everyone can be published these days. If you write a blog and people read it, you can become an instant celebrity. Perez Hilton is an example. (The tagline on PerezHilton.com is "Hollywood's Most-Hated Web Site!") I don't read Hilton, but even I have heard of him. So while anyone and everyone can get published and some people achieve some notoriety — waiterrant.net — what is not acceptable is mizpelings [sic: e-intentionally misspelled for fun].

I have a general rule that my personal blogs are okay if there are a few misspelled words and the occasional bad grammar. My blog at DevExpress — `http://community.devexpress.com/blogs/paulk` — has to be written with a little more care. In fact, customers are perfectly willing to write scathing comments if my prose is a little dodgy. With published articles and books obviously even more care is taken to eke out all misspellings and examples of poor grammar. My point is that people are becoming even more increasingly suspicious of misspelled blogs, emails, and sometimes even text messages. (I suspect as soon as spell checking is easier to do on cell phones, text messages that include r u, lmao, rofl, and other shortcut words and acronyms will be frowned upon too.)

With the ASPxSpellChecker and the spell-checking capabilities of the ASPxHtmlEditor you can provide spell checking for your DevExpress-supported Web applications easily. In fact, the first standard toolbar contains ToolbarCheckSpellingButton (a Check Spelling button). Clicking this button before configuring a dictionary displays a message that reminds you that you have to configure spell checking through the `ASPxHtmlEditor.SettingsSpellChecker.Dictionaries` property.

The ASPxSpellChecker (and the spell checking through the ASPxHtmlEditor) supports ISpell and OpenOffice dictionaries. ISpell originated on a PDP-10 — the same computer Bill Gates got his start on in the 1970s — and a lot of Web sites provide dictionaries and tools for creating dictionary files. This site — `www.lasr.cs.ucla.edu/geoff/ispell-dictionaries.html` — at the University of California Los Angeles (UCLA) has a very long list of dictionary files posted for languages from Afrikaans to Wallon. The site includes the dictionary (`.dic`) and affix (`.aff`) files. The dictionary file contains words, and the affix file contains grammatical rules. (You can read more about the open source ISpell project at `http://ficus-www.cs.ucla.edu/geoff/ispell.html`. Similar resources exist for OpenOffice, too.)

To enable spell checking you need a dictionary file, an affix grammar file (`.aff`), and an alphabet file. A dictionary file is generally a variation of correctly spelled words and the grammar rules that are written as a form of regular expressions. Affix means to attach or append. Affix rules are appended to words in the dictionary to provide rules for handling things like punctuation. A dictionary can be created with a text editor, and you can find tools to convert it to a binary form if you wish. The demos that are downloaded when you download ASPxperience contain samples for all of these files, and they are used with the HtmlEditorSpellChecker sample program.

> *The LevensteinDistance is a value used to measure the proximity of words. ISpell supports a LevensteinDistance of 1. This value is used to indicate the maximum number of steps to convert a misspelled word into a suggested word. For background information search on "Levenshtein distance" — note the correct spelling of the last name of Vladimir Levenshtein for which the concept is named.*

To configure spell checking for the ASPxHtmlEditor (or the ASPxSpellChecker) search for the following files: `american.xlg`, `english.aff`, and `EnglishAlphabet.txt` (or supply your versions of these files). These files are generally way too big to list in their entirety here. For example, the `.xlg` text-dictionary file is 83,660 entries. However, abridged versions of samples of these files are provided in listings at the end of this section, so that you have an idea of their contents. When you have the spell-checking files you would like to use, follow these steps to configure spell checking for the ASPxHtmlEditor:

1. Click the ASpxHtmlEditor that you want to configure and open the Properties window.

2. Expand the `SettingsSpellChecker` property.

3. Invoke the Dictionaries Editor Form for the Dictionaries subproperty (see Figure 9-12, which already has a dictionary configured in the graphic).

4. Click the Add an Item drop-down and select the ISpell Dictionary to add an `ASPxSpellCheckerISpellDictionary` to the `Dictionaries` collection.

5. Select the path where you copied the text file for the alphabet. In the example this is Dictionaries/EnglishAlphabet.txt, which contains the alphabetic characters in your language (see Listing 9-4).

Listing 9-4: The contents of EnglishAlphabet.txt.

```
ABCDEFGHIJKLMNOPQRSTUVWXYZ
```

6. Provide a value for caching the dictionary. (In the sample `ispellDic` was used.)

7. Select the Culture value from the drop-down list; this value matches your dictionary's language.

8. Browse for the `.xlg` file to specify the DictionaryPath. (This value can be the `.xlg` or `.dic` files, which contain variations of plain text words and cues for the affix grammar rules file.) (See Listing 9-5.)

Listing 9-5: An extract from the dictionary file american.xlg (the additional characters at the end of some words are affix grammar rules).

```
a
AAA/S
Aachen
Aalborg
Aalesund
aardvark/MS
aardwolf
Aargau
Aarhus
Aaron
Aaronic
AAU
ab
abac
abaca
aback
abacterial
abactinal
```

9. Select the `EncodingName`, which is the human-readable description of the language encoding.

10. Browse the affix grammar file — `Dictionaries/english.aff`. (Refer to Listing 9-6 for an extract from this file.)

11. Click OK to close the Dictionaries Editor Form.

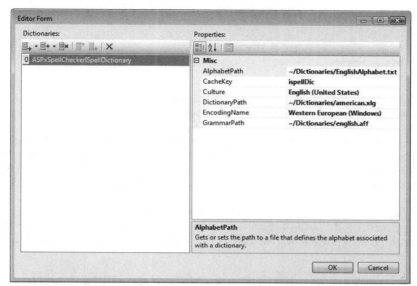

Figure 9-12: Use the Dictionaries Editor Form to configure a dictionary for the ASPxHtmlEditor or ASPxSpellChecker.

Listing 9-6: An extract from the affix grammar file english.aff.

```
nroffchars   ().\\*
texchars     ()\[]{}<\>\\$*.%

# First we declare the character set.  Since it's English, it's easy.
# The only special character is the apostrophe, so that possessives can
# be handled.  We declare it as a boundary character, so that quoting with
# single quotes doesn't confuse things.  The apostrophe is the only
# character that gets such treatment.
#
# We declare the apostrophe first so that "Jon's" collates before "Jonas".
# (This is the way ASCII does it).
#

defstringtype "nroff" "nroff" ".mm" ".ms" ".me" ".man" ".NeXT"

boundarychars '
wordchars [a-z] [A-Z]

altstringtype "tex" "tex" ".tex" ".bib"

# Here's a record of flags used, in case you want to add new ones.
# Right now, we fit within the minimal MASKBITS definition.
#
#           ABCDEFGHIJKLMNOPQRSTUVWXYZ
# Used:     *   *  ****   ** * ***** ***
```

Continued

Listing 9-6: An extract from the affix grammar file english.aff. *(continued)*

```
#              A  D  GHIJ  MN P RSTUV XYZ
# Available:  -- --        --  - -      -
#              BC EF       KL  O Q      W

# Now the prefix table.  There are only three prefixes that are truly
# frequent in English, and none of them seem to need conditional variations.
```

The first time I incorporated spell checking into an application assembling all of these elements seemed a bit challenging. However, as I already noted, the best way to get up and running is to find examples of these files that contain the values you need. DevExpress provides a couple of examples for the sample applications, and you can find more dictionaries at the aforementioned Web site at ucla.edu.

> *To enable the Add a Dictionary button in the Check Spelling dialog box you need to add a Custom Dictionary from the Add an Item drop-down in the Dictionaries editor dialog box. For a demonstration refer to DevExpress TV's online video at* http://tv.devexpress.com/ASPxSpellChecker02. movie.

> *For example, to enable the Add a Dictionary button change the dictionary type in step 4 in the numbered list at the start of this section from an ASPxSpellCheckerISpellDictionary to ASPxSpellCheckerCustomDictionary.*

To use the Check Spelling option, run the sample application containing the ASPxHtmlEditor. Type some text into the editor and click the Check Spelling button (see Figure 9-13). Either you will receive a message indicating that check spelling is complete or the Check Spelling dialog box will provide alternatives for misspelled words (see Figure 9-14). You can configure Spelling Options at design time through the ASPxHtmlEditor.SettingsSpellChecker.SettingsSpelling property or at runtime with code or through the Spelling Options dialog box (see Figure 9-15), which can be initiated from the Check Spelling dialog box's Options button shown in Figure 9-14.

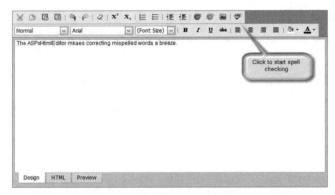

Figure 9-13: The Spell Checking button is an instance of the ToolbarCheckSpellingButton class.

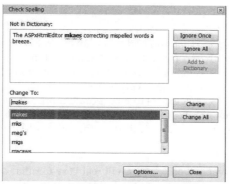

Figure 9-14: Use the Check Spelling dialog box to correct misspelled words, set options, and update the dictionary.

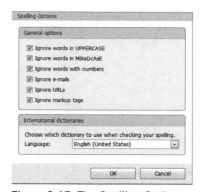

Figure 9-15: The Spelling Options dialog box lets the user configure check spelling options.

To configure elements like the text to display when spell checking is complete or when a word is not found or the caption for the options form or the spell checking dialog box, you can modify the `ASPxHtmlEditor.SettingsText FinishSpellChecking`, `NoSuggestionsText`, `OptionsFormCaption`, or `SpellCheckFormCaption` properties, respectively.

Summary

It didn't seem like all that long ago that you had to use an external editor to format the text, perform spell-checking operations, and then copy and paste that content into a Web application if you wanted to incorporate formatted text into a Web application. With the explosion of social computing applications like Facebook, MySpace, Twitter, and blogs, everyone is interested in putting content on the Web. This naturally encourages and invites developers to incorporate more advanced editing right into the Web application. (Of course, you are not limited to using the ASPxHtmlEditor for social computing applications. I used it more recently on an application that supported spell checking the content of custom medical labels.)

The ASPxHtmlEditor is an advanced editor that will feel very familiar and intuitive to users because it resembles in many ways the most popular editor, MS Word. With the ASPxHtmlEditor you can let your users build content right in your Web application, which includes extensive formatting features, defined styles, and online spell checking (through the embedded ASPxSpellChecker). The ASPxHtmlEditor supports script and iframes through property settings, custom toolbar buttons for programmer-defined tool customizations, and a long list of well-defined editing features, including support for cascading style sheets.

10

Using Themes, CSS, and JavaScript for Customizations and Enhancements

In twenty years of consulting I have worked on projects that had budgets in the tens of thousands of dollars to the tens of millions of dollars at some of the smallest to some of the largest and best known companies in the world. At all but the smallest of these projects — and in my books and articles — I have preached the value of specialization. From Adam Smith's *Wealth of Nations* and my experiences, specialization increases efficiencies substantially. Unfortunately younger industries start with generalists and it takes many business generations to get to the point of specialization. Thus even on the projects with extraordinary budgets there were always plenty of programmers, some DBA types, a manager or two, and occasionally testers. Designated and trained architects were rare, real Web designers were very rare, and CSS and script specialists were nonexistent. Generally, for every job that needed to be done, if it wasn't project management work, then the programmers had to do it, including creating style sheets and writing script.

Not to take anything away from programmers who really know CSS or script, knowing something and specializing in it, or better still, being an expert, are completely different things.

This chapter is provided as a quick reference. This chapter is not a comprehensive missive on CSS and JavaScript because it is possible to fill entire bookshelves on these subjects. Instead this chapter is designed to be used as a reference. In my experience many of you will have to write your own style sheets and script if they are to be present at all. For that reason this chapter includes some things about CSS and JavaScript that I have found useful and that you may find interesting.

Defining and Managing Style Information

The notion of style information refers in large part to setting attributes of HTML and Web server controls to manage how those controls appear, behave, and react. Style information is predominantly a means of applying static — or dynamic — data that determine what an element in a Web page will look like. Common attributes are things like height, width, background color, and borders, and can be as diverse as fonts, position, and layout. Collectively these attributes fall under the heading of style information.

Style information is conveyed or added to your Web applications in four ways. You can manipulate attributes of controls with JavaScript or code-behind at run time to change these attributes. (This is probably the least common way attributes are changed.) You can add inline style information to each control at design time. You can add style information for a single page using the embedded `<style>` tag, or you can link an external style sheet to your Web application and apply style information from a central location. Style information can be defined by element; for example, all of the styles for a `div` or `p` element. Style information can be defined by name and that named block of style information — referred to as a class — can be applied to as many elements as you'd like. Style information can be applied by an ID reference — styles for a control by the control's ID attribute — and you can use "at-rules." At (or @;) rules include items like `@page` and `@import`. The `@page` rule contains style information about the dimensions, orientation, and margins of a page, and `@import` is used to import an external style sheet.

Style information cascades. Cascading rules are rules that determine the precedence in which styles are applied. It is the combination of style information and cascading rules that give style documents their name, cascading style sheets. A cascading style sheet is a text file that contains style information that includes element-based rules, class-based rules, ID-based rules, and at-rule rules. These cascading style sheets can be modified with any text editor and have a .css file extension.

Visual Studio also includes many tools for managing style information. In addition to describing how to define and apply styles, this section demonstrates the integrated Visual Studio tools that support a rich CSS editing experience. These VS tools include the CSS Properties window, the Apply Styles and Manage Styles windows, the Direct Style Application toolbar, the Style Builder dialog box, and the CSS Document Outline window.

Specifying Style Information and Understanding Precedence

This part of the chapter covers two general concepts. Several subsections demonstrate how to set style information for inline styles, page-specific styles, and external cascading style sheets, and there is a brief discussion on style precedence relative to style information in the three aforementioned areas. By the time you have finished reading this section you will have a pretty good understanding of the different levels of style information and the precedence in which the different levels of attribute information is applied.

Creating Inline Styles

If I recall correctly my first company Web site went up in 1995. Our area in Okemos, Michigan had access to high-speed Internet through cable very early, and I was able to host my own Web site and install wireless access throughout the house (using wireless transmitters and receivers the size of paperback books that plugged into the Ethernet cards). That first Web site (which unfortunately can still be viewed on the Wayback Machine) was created using Microsoft FrontPage and HTML. The appearance was managed by writing a lot of HTML and managing the appearance of elements with style information applied to those controls. ASP.NET changed all of that.

ASP.NET introduced Web server controls. Web server controls are HTML engines. A Web server control is a class that wraps the kind of HTML that it emits. For example, if you place a `TextBox` or an `ASPxTextBox` control on a Web page at design time, that Web server control will render an HTML `<input>` element at run time. Every visual Web server control renders its analog HTML control at run time. Web server controls offer many benefits, one of which is that Web server controls can be used and manipulated at design time in a way that was similar to how programmers manipulated WinForms controls; that is, by setting properties and experiencing the results. Web server controls provided a more WYSIWYG experience for developers. The drawback was that while Web server control properties essentially surfaced constituent HTML control attributes — for example, a `Textbox.BackColor` property surfaces the background-color style — and made design-time development easier, adding properties also meant that there were now a couple of ways to accomplish the same objective.

If a `TextBox.BackColor = Red` property is rendered as an `input` element with a `style="background-color:Red;"`, which should a programmer use? The answer isn't straightforward. If you use the Web server properties, your experience will be more Windows-programming like. Unfortunately, if you use Web server control properties, what you are essentially doing is adding inline style elements. The drawback to a simplified design experience is what is euphemistically referred to as *tag soup*. Tag soup is when the elements that make up your presentation layer, or your GUI, all contain their own style information. Every element means every `<div>`, every control, every table, every TextBox, and so on. Adding the style information for each control is labor-intensive, it bloats the size of the page, pages appear more cluttered, and maintaining consistency within and between pages and making changes becomes significantly harder. Here is an example of inline style information for a p element:

```
<p style="font-weight: bold; font-style: italic; color: #FF0000">
```

The preceding p element simply represents a paragraph. A Web application may contain hundreds or thousands of such elements and each has dozens if not hundreds of possible settings. The result is the somewhat derisive tag soup.

The short answer to the question is that although Web server controls were a technological leap forward, managing the appearance of Web controls through properties or inline styles is not the best way to manage the way your Web page or application looks. What I do is use properties or inline style information (for HTML elements) to prototype pages, or the way I want the site to look, and then all of that information is stripped from the inline style attribute and moved to an external cascading style sheet. In this way I get the design time of Web server controls to visualize the appearance of one page and then use a style sheet to skin — make all pages look uniform — the rest of the application, pages, and user controls.

Creating Page-Specific Styles

Inline styles are single item — element, tag, control — specific. If you use the `<style>` block in a page, you are basically defining an embedded style sheet. A `<style>` block applies to the entire page in which it is embedded. The `<style>` block is placed in the `<head>` section — see Listing 10-1 — and can contain all of the style information you would like.

Listing 10-1: An HTML page showing the placement of the <style> block and style for H1 — header level 1 — elements.

```
<!DOCTYPE HTML PUBLIC "-//W3C//DTD HTML 4.0 Transitional//EN">
<html>
  <head>
    <title>HTML 4.0 CSS Element Style Example</title>
      <style type="text/css">
        h1{text-align:center; color:blue;}
      </style>
  </head>
  <body>
    <h1>This text is centered and blue</h1>
  </body>
</html>
```

My first Web site used a combination of inline style elements and definitions defined in a `<style>` block. I don't remember their exact introduction, but style blocks were a measured improvement over inline styles. At least by using a style block you could easily define a single style for an element; for example, an H1 — header level 1 — element would be applied to all elements of that type. You can also define style classes — named styles — and styles for elements by their name or their ID attribute.

Generally, as mentioned before I use the WYSIWYG capabilities afforded by Web server controls and then move the style information to an external cascading style sheet, skipping the page-level style block altogether.

Linking External Cascading Style Sheets

Simple Web sites and prototypes use inline styles quite a bit, but for professional Web sites you will more often than not encounter external cascading style sheets. In fact, external style sheets are so popular that a whole cottage industry aftermarket exists for this approach — referred to as skinning — for commercial portal and application products like DotNetNuke.

> *DotNetNuke is a user- and programmer-configurable base of Web pages and controls that can be downloaded, used, and extended to build your applications, if desired. I generally consider tools like DotNetNuke as a good starting point for portals rather than application developers, but this posture represents a personal bias, not a technical limitation of portal technology.*

To link an external style sheet to a Web page, add a style sheet from the Wesbsite ⇨ Add New Item menu option, choose the Style Sheet template, and drag and drop the style sheet (the .css file) from the Solution Explorer to a Web page. You can also reference the style sheet with a `<link>` tag — see the following code snippet — to the `<head>` section of a page or from Visual Studio's Format ⇨ Attach Style Sheet menu item. (Associating a cascading style sheet with your entire Web application is referred to as *skinning*. You can attach a style sheet to each page or skin the site. Refer to the section "Using Skins and Themes" later in the chapter for more information.) The following fragment represents the `<link>` tag for referencing a single style sheet named styles.css to an individual page:

```
<link rel=stylesheet href="styles.css" type="text/css">
```

Understanding Style Precedence

The cascading part of style information refers to rules that determine the precedence that determine the order in which rules are applied. Inline styles have the highest precedence, followed by rules in an embedded style block, followed by rules in a cascading style sheet. This means that if a style sheet contains the same rule — a value for the same attribute — as a local style, the local style information will be what the user sees. If a local style or embedded style rule exists but is silent, that is, it doesn't contain an attribute value that a style sheet does, on a specific attribute, the local rules are applied and the style sheet rules fill in the blanks.

Assume for example that a style sheet specifies a font for an H1 element and a style attribute contains an inline background color. In this instance the background color indicated in the inline style is applied and the style sheet's font value is applied too. As a general guiding principle I remove all local style information before an application ships and move all style information to the application's style sheet. The result is that all style information can be managed from one location, resulting in a site that has a uniform appearance and all changes are reflected everywhere.

Creating Cascading Style Sheets

A cascading style sheet can contain at-rules, named styles, element styles, ID-based styles, and comments. All of these elements except for comments use the same structure. Each element has a selector, the bracketed block of attributes ({}), and a semicolon-delimited list of attribute names followed by a colon, the attribute's value, and a semicolon following roughly this general structure:

```
selector { property : value ; property2 : value2}
```

The selector is the at-rule name, class-based name, element-based name, or ID-based name with the specific semicolon-delimited name and value pairs within that style's brackets. Here is how an `h1` element might appear in a style sheet with the attribute values for text-align and color indicated:

```
h1 {text-align:center; color:blue;}
```

Where style sheets can involve more advanced rules is by adding comma-delimited selectors that mean the style applies to more than one thing. Let's look at examples of different kinds of style sheet elements, including how to use selectors.

Defining Element-based Styles

An element-based style is a style based on an HTML element such as a `p`, `div`, `table`, `h1`, or `td` element. You can define a style for any or all of these elements using the same `select{property:value;}` structure previously described. The only limitation is that you can only describe supported attribute values. For example, to specify left and right margins for all paragraph tags (`<p>`) you could add a style rule like the following:

```
p { margin-left: 25px; margin-right: 25px }
```

469

This means that every paragraph that uses the style sheet containing the preceding rule will automatically have a 25-pixel left and right margin. If you want to apply this rule to all div and p elements, you can add the div element to the list of selectors, resulting in a style rule that can be written like the following:

```
div, p
{
  margin-left: 25px;
  margin-right: 25px;
}
```

To incorporate a comment that provides clear text describing what the style rule does, use the C-style /* */ commenting style right in the .css file. Here is the preceding style with an associated comment:

```
/* this is a margin rule for div and paragraph elements */
div, p
{
  margin-left: 25px;
  margin-right: 25px;
}
```

Defining Class-based styles

Class-based style rules are constructed just like element-based style rules except that the selector is the name of the rule preceded by a period. For example, to define a style rule that indicates the font-size and color for a class named introduction, add the following rule to your style sheet:

```
.introduction {font-size: small; color: white}
```

To apply this rule in an ASPX page, set the class or CssClass attribute of the element or control to introduction, leaving out the period, as shown here:

```
<asp:TextBox CssClass="introduction" runat="server"
    BackColor="Silver" >This is the text</asp:TextBox>
```

Notice that the preceding snippet references the class name introduction and contains an inline style. Because introduction doesn't specify a background color, the value Silver for BackColor is applied in conjunction with the attributes indicated by the style. Even if the style sheet's introduction class contained a background-color attribute, as long as BackColor is present the inline style will be applied.

```
.introduction
{
  font-size: small;
  color: white;
  /* this is ignored if an inline style for this attribute is present */
  background-color: Black;
}
```

One of the challenges of using style sheets and inline styles together, if you so choose, is to know what properties of a Web server control are mapped to an equivalent in a cascading style sheet.

You can also combine class-based styles with element styles. For example, if the following two styles are present in the same style sheet, all of the styles for the paragraph element (p) are applied to paragraphs that don't have inline style information for the same values.

```
/* this is a margin rule for div and paragraph elements */
div, p
{
  margin-left: 25px;
  margin-right: 25px;
}

.introduction, p
{
  font-size: small;
  color: white;
  /* this is ignored if an inline style for this attribute is present */
  background-color: Black;
}
```

A <p> tag without inline styles in a page that references a cascading style sheet with the preceding style rules will have left and right margins of 25 pixels, use a small font with white text, and have a black background. You can see the results in the center of Figure 10-1.

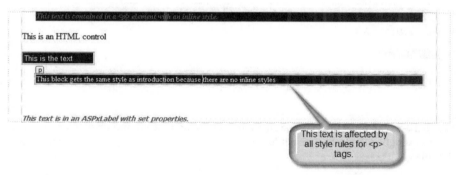

Figure 10-1: The text indicated is inside of the <p>tag so it gets all styles defined by the preceding two blocks of style rules.

Defining ID-based Styles

ID-based styles use the same selector {property:value} syntax as other rules. The difference is that the selector name is preceded with a # character (instead of a period). Use ID-based styles when you want to define styles for a specific item whose ID attribute matches the ID-based style sans the pound character:

```
#footer {background-color: #CCCCCC; margin: 15px}
```

Now everything that has an ID value of `footer` will use the preceding style. Because only one element per page can have the same ID value you use this approach to implement visual consistency for similar types of elements across pages, for example for all footers. And, of course, you can combine styles for names, elements, and IDs by comma-delimiting those selectors.

Defining At-rule Styles

At-rule styles are style sheet elements whose selector begins with an @ followed by the selector name. The at-rule selectors are `@charset`, `@font-face`, `@import`, `@media`, and `@page`. The `@charset` rule defines the character set for an external style sheet. The `@font-face` rule defines the font to embed in the HTML document. The `@import` rule imports an external style sheet. The `@media` rule sets the media types for a style sheet, and the `@page` rule can be used to define the dimensions, orientation, and margins of a page. The basic structure of at-rules is the same as all other rules, which includes the at-rule selector name, the bracket block, and the attributes for that style. The following `@page` rule changes the margins of every page to have a top and bottom margin of 10 pixels and a left and right margin of 0 pixels. Figure 10-2 shows the page box as a dotted line clearly showing the application of the margin rules.

```
@Page
{
   margin: 10px, 10px, 0px, 0px;
}
```

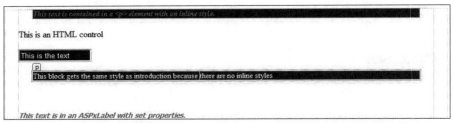

Figure 10-2: The preceding @Page rule adds a top and bottom margin of 10 pixels and a left and right margin of 0 pixels for every page that uses the style sheet containing the rule.

Qualifying Style Rules with Specific Selectors

Element-based, class-based, ID-based, and at-rule selectors are the most common ways to define style rules, but they really just scratch the surface of what you can do with cascading style sheets.

The difference between someone who has to write CSS and a specialist is that a specialist will know about class, element, and ID-based selectors. They will also know how to use equality, existence, hyphen, prefix, substring, suffix, type, universal, whitespace, pseudo-class and pseudo-element selectors as well as combinators. Pseudo-class (like `:hover` and `:link`) and pseudo-element selectors (like `:first-letter` and `:first-line`) are preceded by a semicolon, and combinators (like `Child >`) use special characters like +, >, and ~. Specialists will keep abreast of changes between versions of IE as well as compatibility between browser models, what is CSS compatible, and what is specific to a vendor's browser. A CSS specialist will also know things like how to set browser compatibility modes.

I use common pseudo-class selectors like :active, :hover, :link, and :visited to change the way a link appears, for example after it is has been visited or when the mouse is hovering. The following example illustrates how to apply the pseudo-element selector :hover to an <a> tag to change the mouse pointer (see Figure 10-3):

```
a:hover
{
    cursor:pointer;
}
```

This is an HTML control

This is the text

This block gets the same style as introduction because there are no inline styles

This text is in an ASPxLabel with set properties.
Developer Express Website

Pseudo-element selector :hover used to change the mouse

Figure 10-3: The pseudo-element selector :hover applied to an a element is used (in this example) to change the appearance of the mouse pointer when the user hovers over the hyperlink.

To master CSS experimentation, experience and a good reference book will be immeasurably helpful. To explore CSS in more detail pick up a copy of *Professional CSS: Cascading Style Sheets for Professional Web Design* by Christopher Schmitt, et. al. from Wrox.

Microsoft has always added proprietary features to technologies where it thinks such a decision was useful or helpful to the chagrin or delight of some developers. With IE it has made strides toward greater CSS 2.1 compliance, but some proprietary features for IE8 still remain. A greater exploration of the online and help documentation and CSS as a separate technology will help you discover the similarities and differences between IE development and multi-browser development. For our part DevExpress works hard to make multi-browser support for our controls easier.

If you want to target a specific browser version, you can add meta tags to the <head> section of a Web page similar to the following. The following snippet instructs the page to operate on IE7 emulation mode:

```
<meta http-equiv="X-UA-Compatible" content="IE=EmulateIE7" />
```

Exploring Additional Style Sheet Attributes

Common attributes include things like colors, fonts, positioning, layout, and cursor information. You can provide some additional elements in style sheets that include behaviors, expressions, function calls, filters, accelerators, and zoom information. These can add more depth and richness to your Web applications if you know of their presence and how to use them. I have included a few examples of their richness to give you some ideas. Some, such as the `expression` attribute, have been deprecated in IE8 in favor more CSS-compliant attributes, but they exist for older versions of IE and they will help you learn about some possibilities and perhaps give you some ideas.

This section includes a sample smattering of these attributes, including `expression`, `behavior`, `!important`, `filter`, `accelerator`, and `zoom`. The attributes that are specific to Microsoft Internet Explorer have been renamed in IE8 to include an ms prefix. For example, `zoom` is now `ms-zoom`. For a while both versions will work but only in IE8. As I have been developing software over the years, some applications such as intranet Web applications used internally by a company have stipulated IE support only. Under these circumstances using features available only in Internet Explorer are acceptable. Of course, if you are doing multi-browser development support, using things like `expression` or `filter` to load an ActiveX control will likely be supported with some kind of browser extender or not at all.

The examples in the subsection just scratch the surface of possibilities. For a more comprehensive list of CSS attributes refer to the help subject "CSS Attributes" at the following Visual Studio MSDN help document: `ms-help://MS.VSCC.v90/MS.MSDNQTR.v90.en/css/workshop/author/css/reference/css_ref_attributes_entry.htm`. While you are awaiting Visual Studio 2010 you can explore the CSS section for "What's New in Internet Explorer" at `http://msdn.microsoft.com/en-us/library/cc288472(VS.85).aspx#css`. (Google or Bing will provide you with up-to-date links as Microsoft releases new information.)

Using the Expression Attribute

The `expression` function is one of those items that were supported for older versions of Internet Explorer that let you replace a style value with an expression. For example, rather than express a literal value for the height attribute of a `div` you could supply an expression as demonstrated here:

```
<div style='height: expression(document.body.clientHeight / 2);'>
```

Rather than a specific value like 75% the expression is evaluated to determine the value assigned to the height attribute. Visual Studio does a pretty good job of indicating when deprecated features are no longer supported by listing them as errors and underlining the unsupported feature in the IDE (see Figure 10-4).

```
 5   <!DOCTYPE html PUBLIC "-//W3C//DTD XHTML 1.0 Transitional//EN" "http://www.w3.org/TI
 6
 7   <html xmlns="http://www.w3.org/1999/xhtml">
 8   <head runat="server">
 9       <title></title>
10       <link href="CSS/StyleSheet.css" rel="stylesheet" type="text/css" />
11       |
12   </head>
13   <body>
14       <form id="form1" runat="server" >
15       <div style='height: expression(document.body.clientHeight / 2);'>
16       <p style="font-weight: bold; font-style: italic; color: #FF0000">
17           This text is contained in a &lt;p&gt; element with an inline style.
18       </p>
19       <span>This is an HTML control
20           <br />
21           </span><br />
22
23       <asp:TextBox CssClass="introduction" ID="TextBox1" runat="server"
24       BackColor="silver"
25       >This is the text</asp:TextBox>
26
27           <p>
28           This block gets the same style as introduction because
29           there are no inline styles</p>
30           <br />
31           <br />
32
```

Figure 10-4: If you use an inline style, embedded style, or style sheet feature that is unsupported, Visual Studio indicates that the feature is not supported with a squiggly underline.

Based on several blog comments I have read there are probably just as many developers who want Microsoft to work toward greater compatibility with open standards like CSS as there are those who like having proprietary features. As is true with religion and politics everyone is entitled to their own opinion. It is hard to know for sure whether or not features that start off as proprietary help drive changes in the standard.

Using the Behavior Attribute

The way that open standards like CSS work is that a group of interested parties, including companies such as Microsoft, Sun, HP, and Apple, get together and form a consortium. (Sometimes it seems like the world is comprised of open standards groups against Microsoft, but this isn't really an accurate reflection of reality.) Members of these groups get together — it always seems like these meetings happen in Iceland or Switzerland — and vote on features. In the interim interested parties may incorporate features they'd like to be part of a standard and then hope that the item or feature gets adopted. Microsoft is a big company and clearly has demonstrated strong advocacy for its desire to get items adopted by standards bodies, but it is often one voting member among many and standards decisions are fluid and ongoing.

The behavior attribute is an example of one proposed addition to the CSS standard. The behavior is part of Dynamic HTML (DHTML). The behavior attribute supports indicating the URL of an .htc or .hta file containing script. These files are HTML Component files that support implementing HTML Components script providing dynamic behaviors. For more information refer to the section in this chapter titled "Creating a Behavior Script Component."

As a general rule I don't keep up on a daily, weekly, or even monthly basis with standards bodies, consortiums, and the groups that make open standards decisions for the rest of us. There are too many of them. Instead I look up the Web sites that represent these standards bodies and their decisions when or if I need to know. For example, when I was writing my book *UML DeMystified* from McGraw-Hill/Osborne I spent a lot of time reading the OMG's (Object Management Group) specifications regarding the UML (Unified Modeling Language), but the actual standard was 600 pages. My UML book was about 300 pages. If you want to know about leading-edge open standards, this information is readily available on the Web, but often they are read as thoroughly and as often as the U.S. tax code.

Using the !Important Declaration

The `!important` declaration is added as a suffix to a style rule and increases the weight of a style rule. Normally, for example, an inline style rule attribute overrides an embedded style or style sheet rule for the same attribute, but if you append the `!important` declaration after a rule, that rule can override the same rule further down the cascade chain. For example, if you change the `background-color` rule for the `introduction` class from earlier in the chapter, it will override the inline attribute `BackColor` for any element that refers to the `introduction` class.

```
.introduction, p
{
  font-size: small;
  color: white;
  /* this is ignored if an inline style for this attribute is present */
  background-color: Black!important;
}
```

Given the style sheet `background-color` rule with the `!important` declaration the following TextBox will have a black background even though the `BackColor` attribute is set in the ASPX:

```
<asp:TextBox CssClass="introduction" runat="server"
    BackColor="silver">This is the text</asp:TextBox>
```

The TextBox will have a black background even though the `BackColor` attribute is set to `Silver` because the `!important` declaration overrides the local style. The background color would be overridden even if you used the inline style declaration `style='background-color:Silver'` because setting the `BackColor` property and the inline `background-color` style are effectively the same thing.

If you set redundant style information — for example, the `BackColor` *property and the* `background-color` *style — the property value does not overwrite the style attribute having the same semantic purpose. That is, if* `BackColor='Silver'` *is present and* `style="background-color:Red;"` *is also present, the background color will be* `Red`. *It is this kind of experimentation and tinkering — or reading books that cover such subjects — that is necessary to figure out how rules are applied specifically.*

Defining Filters

The `filter` attribute is now co-named `ms-filter` (in IE8) because it is one of those IE-only features. I like the filter because it can be used to load ActiveX code that can be used to create fun and interesting effects in your Web applications. Granted, style information like the following can only be used if ActiveX is supported by your target browser, but sometimes the target browser may just be browsers that support such features.

```
<img src="Images/microsoft_lego_guys.jpg"
style="filter:progid:DXImageTransform.Microsoft.MotionBlur(strength=50)
 progid:DXImageTransform.Microsoft.BasicImage(mirror=1); height: 473px; width: 553px;"
alt="cone" />
```

The preceding snippet contains an `<img>` tag with an inline style filter attribute. The filter loads two ActiveX controls, MotionBlur and BasicImage, which together based on the arguments passed to the ActiveX controls reverse an image and create a motion effect by blurring the image (see Figure 10-5). The picture is of me, this book's initial cover design, and the Microsoft Visual Studio LEGO guys. The picture is blurry and reversed, which my co-workers will attest is the best possible way — blurry — to view pictures of me. (My dear mother says: *"Honey, God made you useful not pretty; don't complain."*)

Figure 10-5: A picture of me, this book's original cover design, and the Visual Studio LEGO characters with the applied transform that reverses the image and creates a motion effect by blurring the image.

> Attributes like filter are available in style sheets and script. For example, you can refer to a filter with JavaScript by writing object.style.filter where object is the element or control who's filter property you want to get or set in code.

Clearly there is a time and place for such gimmickry. I don't have to tell you that blurry images, graphic effects, scrolling banners, and sounds used extensively exhaust users, but applications sometimes benefit from these kinds of special effects. Many ActiveX programs can be used with the `filter` attribute if you search for them on the Web.

Specifying an Accelerator

The `accelerator` attribute accepts a Boolean true or false. This is the style attribute that supports defining a hotkey (or access key) for controls. For instance, if you happen to be using an `input` HTML element, set the `accelerator` style attribute to true and provide a letter — the key — for the input element's `accesskey` attribute. If you are using a Web server control like the TextBox or preferably the ASPxTextBox, you can achieve the same effect by setting the `AccessKey` property. The following snippet contains a style sheet class named `textbox` followed by an HTML element that defines an access key "C" for the `input` element:

```
.textbox
{
  accelerator:true;
}
```

```
<input class="introduction" accesskey="C" value="Input element"/>
```

Context Counts

Book editors are smart people. Authors like me rely on them to check facts, get alternate technical opinions, help us organize, and ensure that the best book-product possible is produced. Technical people like you and I have to know or learn the highly specialized details that let us solve technical problems. One common thing that happens is an editor will see `AccessKey`, `ACCESSKEY`, and `accesskey` and request that the particular term be made consistent throughout the book. My response is often that it depends on context.

`AccessKey` is correct when referring to the ASPxTextBox property. `ACCESSKEY` is an attribute of the `input` element, so is `accesskey`. Note the difference in case. All of these differences may seem confusing, even to technophiles, but there is an underlying reason. In this instance the case varies because the text is referring to a property — `AccessKey` — and an HTML attribute — `accesskey`. The reason the help documentation may show `ACCESSKEY` and my code fragment shows `accesskey` has to do with the Document Type Definition. ASPX Web pages contain a `!DOCTYPE` element with a reference to the W3 organizations standard. What you don't see in the snippet is the `!DOCTYPE` reference added by default in Visual Studio 2008.

```
<!DOCTYPE html PUBLIC "-//W3C//DTD XHTML 1.0 Transitional//EN"
  "http://www.w3.org/TR/xhtml1/DTD/xhtml1-transitional.dtd">
```

The XHTML 1.0 DTD specification includes, among other things, that tags have an explicit closing tag or are self-closing (`/>`), and that tag and attribute names are lowercase. The DTD document reference will determine the kinds of things that are indicated as errors or warnings in your ASPX code.

I couldn't get a book published without help from the technical people that create the software I am writing about or the editors that help me organize my thoughts. And, it can be challenging for editors and some technical people to understand why simple things like `AccessKey`, `ACCESSKEY`, and `accesskey` appear differently.

Using the Zoom Attribute

Technology features overlap many times. Sometimes software and hardware features overlap. For example, my laser mouse has a button that starts a magnifier. (In a couple more years my aging eyes will appreciate that feature.) The magnifier feature on my mouse works with everything, and this feature overlaps with the `zoom` style attribute. If you provide a value for the `zoom` attribute, you can make a hyperlink or image grow or shrink depending on the value of the `zoom` attribute. The following style sheet snippet shows how to add the `zoom` attribute to the a element style, and the snippet after that shows the same behavior associated with an image's (`img` element's) `onmouseover` event.

```
a:hover
{

cursor:pointer;
zoom: 200%;
}
<img src="Images/microsoft_lego_guys.jpg"
  style="filter:progid:DXImageTransform.Microsoft.MotionBlur(strength=50)
  progid:DXImageTransform.Microsoft.BasicImage(mirror=1); height: 473px; width: 553px;"
  alt="cone" onmouseover="style.zoom='200%'"/>
```

The attribute examples for style sheets can also be accessed through script, as demonstrated in the preceding code snippet. The preceding subsections represent a smattering of the possibilities. The good news is that many books, blogs, articles, and samples have been written on subjects like CSS. Hopefully this section provided some ideas and demonstrated possibilities.

Creating a Behavior Script Component

There is so much technology available that one of the pleasures of writing a book is that I have to think about things that I don't use very often or that I would like to know more about. The process of formulating a book forces me to learn too. I don't have to tell you that authors don't know everything. One such technology that seems to be lurking in the background of my knowledge base is the HTML Component. So I wanted to touch on it here.

An HTML Component is represented by an .htc (HTML Component) file. These files are part of DHTML (Dynamic HTML). As previously mentioned the `behavior` attribute with the URL function can be used to associate an HTML Component file with a style. Using this approach, though I see it employed infrequently on projects, enables you to construct a whole series of behaviors in JavaScript (in the component file) in one location and reference that behavior file. The supported concept here is a separation of concerns. The style sheet contains style information and the script file contains the script that implements the behaviors.

To begin exploring HTML Components follow these steps to associate an ID-based style with an `img` element. The steps, when combined with the style (snippet) and the .htc file in Listing 10-2, will cause the image to zoom in on mouseover and zoom out on mouseout.

1. Use the Visual Studio Website ⇨ Add New Item menu to add a new XML item from the Add New Item dialog box, renaming the .xml file Behaviors.htc and saving the file in a folder called Components.

2. Add the code provided in Listing 10-2.

3. Add the following style snippet to the style sheet document, making sure that the style sheet is referenced by the Web page using a `<link>` tag. The Web page example is provided in Listing 10-3.

```
#ComponentZoom
{
  behavior:url('Components/Behaviors.htc');
}
```

Listing 10-2: An example HTML Component file containing the behaviors — zoom in and zoom out on mouseover and mouseout.

```
<?xml version="1.0" encoding="utf-8" ?>
<component>
<implements type="Behavior">
    <comment>The following implements an HTML component file defining
    a behavior that will set the zoom style attribute
    when the mouse is moved over an element that is associated with
    this behavior.</comment>
    <attach event="onmouseover" handler="do_onmouseover"/>
    <attach event="onmouseout" handler="do_onmouseout"/>
</implements>
<script language="javascript">

function do_onmouseover(){
  //debugger;
  this.style.zoom = "200%";
}

function do_onmouseout() {
  //debugger;
  this.style.zoom = "100%";
}

</script>
</component>
```

The most common two ways that I have seen programmers actually implement behaviors like those shown in Listing 10-2 is a behavior applied in the element's inline style or through JavaScript in the Web page itself. The preceding .htc file essentially attaches the events when the behavior attribute and .htc file are associated with an element, and then the events fire as if you had associated them directly in the ASPX. (You can of course provide an onmouseover and onmouseout event right in the ASPX too.) The difference is that the .htc file can be downloaded and cached on the client, the HTML Component code can be reused, and it offers a convenient way to isolate behaviors from individual aspects of pages.

If, for example, you use a feature like zoom (or any feature) right in the page itself, you get into a pattern of copying and pasting the attributes — in this case onmouseover and onmouseout — and the script that provides those behaviors for every page in which the behavior is supported. Using an HTML Component file supports defining the behavior once and using it many times just by applying the behavior style that loads the component page.

As indicated by the HTML Component file you can also add the debugger statement, which supports debugging the script in the Component file.

By no means is this section more than an introduction to the subject of HTML Component authoring, but it will help you begin your exploration of this subject. Listing 10-3 contains the ASPX with the referenced ID and the `<link>` tag. Imagine how clean the ASPX will look if you move the `filter` attribute out of the ASPX page too. The JavaScript is external in the htc file, the style information is externally contained in the style sheet, and the page becomes less cluttered. The only downside for newer developers is that the page will appear to work as if by magic unless one knows to look in the style sheet and the htc file.

You will see style sheets and htc Component files on projects where the developers are writing and need to reuse common styles, elements, and code repeatedly (for example, in Microsoft's shipped code or DotNetNuke). Also, by reducing tag soup it becomes increasingly easier to skin a Web site with selectable style sheets and behaviors loaded by those style sheets, in effect changing the appearance and behavior of a site by simply picking a new style sheet.

Listing 10-3: The sample Web page that contains an ID-based style associated with an img element.

```
<%@ Page Language="C#" AutoEventWireup="true" CodeFile="Default2.aspx.cs"
 Inherits="Default2" %>

<!DOCTYPE html PUBLIC "-//W3C//DTD XHTML 1.0 Transitional//EN"
 "http://www.w3.org/TR/xhtml1/DTD/xhtml1-transitional.dtd">

<html xmlns="http://www.w3.org/1999/xhtml">
<head runat="server">
    <title></title>
  <link href="CSS/StyleSheet.css" rel="stylesheet" type="text/css" />
</head>
<body>
    <form id="form1" runat="server">
    <div>
    <p>
    <img ID="ComponentZoom" src="Images/microsoft_lego_guys.tif"
    style="filter:progid:DXImageTransform.Microsoft.MotionBlur(strength=50)
 progid:DXImageTransform.Microsoft.BasicImage(mirror=1);
 height: 473px; width: 553px;"

    alt="cone" />
    <!-- inline style for onmouseover
    <img src="Images/microsoft_lego_guys.tif"
    style="filter:progid:DXImageTransform.Microsoft.MotionBlur(strength=50)
 progid:DXImageTransform.Microsoft.BasicImage(mirror=1);
 height: 473px; width: 553px;"
    alt="cone"
    onmouseover="style.zoom='200%'"
    />
    -->
    </p>
    </div>
    </form>
</body>
</html>
```

Managing Style Information with Visual Studio Features

As the notion of skinning Web applications by dynamically changing referenced style sheets becomes more pervasive, developers have expressed more interest in cascading style sheets. To address customers' implicit or expressed interest Microsoft is converging on a greater adherence to open standards like CSS, deprecating IE-only supported features. It's hard to blame Microsoft for driving new features to make its browser a more desirable choice, but the reality is that users do choose other browsers and want to be able to develop in Visual Studio while supporting these other browsers.

To that end IE8 more closely supports CSS 2.1 and has some CSS 3.0 features available. Visual Studio 2008 also has added Manage Styles and Apply Styles windows, the Direct Style Application toolbar, in addition to the CSS Document Outline window that has been in Visual Studio for a couple of generations. The Manage Styles and Apply Styles windows can be accessed in an ASP.NET project from the View menu, and the Direct Application Style toolbar — named Application Style — can be made visible by right-clicking over Visual Studio's toolbar and clicking the Application Style itemit. (Figure 10-6 shows the Manage Styles window on the left and the Application Style toolbar centered.)

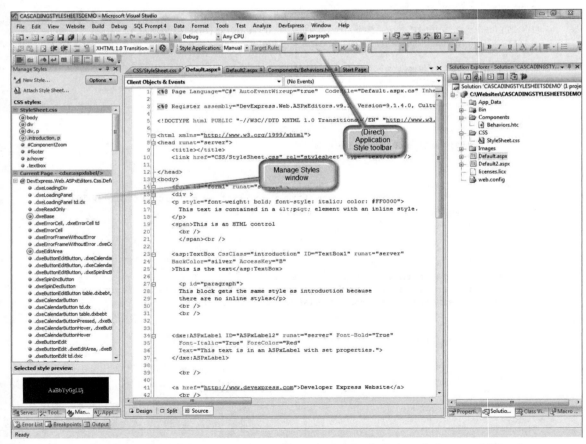

Figure 10-6: Greater CSS support is provided via the Manage and Apply Styles windows and (Direct) Application Style toolbar.

The Apply Styles window lets you apply a single or multiple styles to a page element. The Apply Styles window displays each style based on the style rules and the location of the styles, for example, if it's in the style sheet or the current page. The Manage Styles window displays styles and you re-order styles and move styles between locations such as from a page to a style sheet. For instance, if you use my approach and prototype the appearance of your Web site in a single page, then after you get the page to look the way you want you can drag styles from the list of styles for the page to the style sheet.

Both style windows use icons to indicate how the style is defined. For example, a red dot (see Figure 10-6) indicates an ID-based style. For more information on the style cues see the help topic "How to: Use the Apply Styles and Manage Styles Windows" at ms-help://MS.VSCC.v90/MS.MSDNQTR.v90.en/dv_vwdcon/html/f26c7f35-516a-4369-9ec3-1d6de7220456.htm. In addition to the visual style cues, the Manage Styles window contains a Selected Style Preview window (see Figure 10-6) that lets you preview what the style will look like when rendered on a page.

If you want to modify a style in the style sheet, click that style in the Manage Styles window. This feature is also support by the Manage Styles context menu option Go to Code. If you want to change the style you can go to the style sheet or right-click the style and select Modify Style. Modify Style will display a dialog box with the same name that contains a selector — to pick the style to manage — and supports modifying the style using the dialog box (see Figure 10-7).

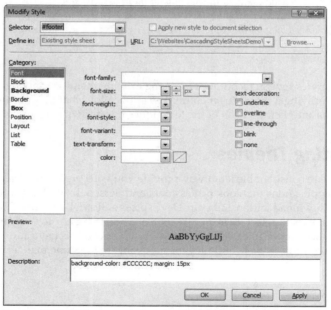

Figure 10-7: Pick the style to modify in the Selector drop-down and visually change the style selected.

With the Manage and Apply Styles windows, the Modify Style and Build Style (which has been around for several VS generations) dialog boxes, the CSS Document Outline, and CSS Properties window and toolbars you now have more features available in Visual Studio for managing styles than ever before.

Using Skins and Themes

All technologies seem to evolve and converge on more organized approaches to accomplishing the same kinds of things. In a rough chronology programmers discovered or invented property settings in HTML, inline and embedded styles and style sheets, followed by skins and themes. I have talked about everything mentioned so far except for skins and themes. Skin files are XML files that contain definitions for individual controls. These definitions look a lot like a control definition in an ASPX Web page, except the settings define attribute values for a given control type and its sub-control types. Skin files can include references to other content files like images. Themes are a collection of folders. Each theme is a folder that contains the skins, style sheets, graphic files, and any other resource that a particular theme is comprised of. In ASP.NET themes are added to a project as a subfolder of the App_Themes folder in your Web site.

> With the release of ASPxperience 9.2 you can omit the App_Themes folder. Instead of deploying all of the individual files that make up DevExpress themes as individual files and folders you can deploy the DevExpress.Web.ASPxThemes.v9.2.dll file usually found in c:\program files\DevExpress 2009.2\ Components\Sources\DevExpress.DLL\. You can also use this DLL in your project at design time. Check out Mehul Harry's blog on the subject at http://community.devexpress.com/blogs/ aspnet/archive/2009/07/22/asp-net-skins-in-dlls-new-devexpress-feature- in-mid-2009-release.aspx.

This section demonstrates several techniques for using existing themes, applying a theme to all of the controls on a page, applying a theme to an entire Web application, changing themes at run time, and defining custom skins and themes. Each of the techniques has its own subsection.

Applying Existing Themes

DevExpress has gone to considerable lengths to provide you with predefined themes that you can pick from to create Web applications that look professional and personalized. These themes are already available when you download and install your DevExpress ASP.NET controls. The easiest way to use these predefined themes is to select them from a control's Smart tags Auto Format menu item and pick the theme you want (see Figure 10-8). (Microsoft's Web server controls have additional themes predefined for those controls as well, and they are accessible in the same manner.)

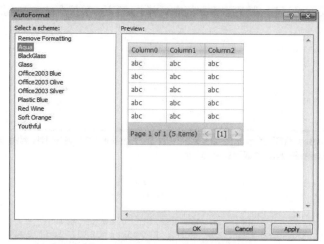

Figure 10-8: Choose one of the predefined themes for a DevExpress control from the AutoFormat dialog box.

When you chose a theme in this manner all the necessary theme folders, skin files, and supporting resources are added to your project's App_Themes folder. The AutoFormat dialog box also causes all of the style information (and style sheets) to be referenced in the Web page as well as required skin content. Listing 10-4 shows an ASPX page containing just an ASPxGridView and then the same page after the Aqua theme has been selected from the AutoFormat dialog box (see Listing 10-5).

Listing 10-4: A Web page containing a single ASPxGridView.

```
<%@ Page Language="C#" AutoEventWireup="true"
CodeFile="Default.aspx.cs" Inherits="_Default" %>

<%@ Register assembly="DevExpress.Web.ASPxGridView.v9.1,
 Version=9.1.4.0, Culture=neutral, PublicKeyToken=b88d1754d700e49a"
 namespace="DevExpress.Web.ASPxGridView" tagprefix="dxwgv" %>
<%@ Register assembly="DevExpress.Web.ASPxEditors.v9.1,
 Version=9.1.4.0, Culture=neutral, PublicKeyToken=b88d1754d700e49a"
 namespace="DevExpress.Web.ASPxEditors" tagprefix="dxe" %>

<!DOCTYPE html PUBLIC "-//W3C//DTD XHTML 1.0 Transitional//EN"
 "http://www.w3.org/TR/xhtml1/DTD/xhtml1-transitional.dtd">

<html xmlns="http://www.w3.org/1999/xhtml">
<head runat="server">
  <title></title>
</head>
<body>
  <form id="form1" runat="server">
  <div>

    <dxwgv:ASPxGridView ID="ASPxGridView1" runat="server">
```

Continued

Listing 10-4: A Web page containing a single ASPxGridView *(continued)*

```
      </dxwgv:ASPxGridView>

    </div>
    </form>
</body>
</html>
```

Listing 10-5: The same ASPX page as shown in Listing 10-4 with the Aqua theme applied from the AutoFormat dialog box.

```
<%@ Page Language="C#" AutoEventWireup="true"
CodeFile="Default.aspx.cs" Inherits="_Default" %>

<%@ Register assembly="DevExpress.Web.ASPxGridView.v9.1,↵
 Version=9.1.4.0, Culture=neutral, PublicKeyToken=b88d1754d700e49a"
 namespace="DevExpress.Web.ASPxGridView" tagprefix="dxwgv" %>
<%@ Register assembly="DevExpress.Web.ASPxEditors.v9.1,↵
 Version=9.1.4.0, Culture=neutral, PublicKeyToken=b88d1754d700e49a"
 namespace="DevExpress.Web.ASPxEditors" tagprefix="dxe" %>

<!DOCTYPE html PUBLIC "-//W3C//DTD XHTML 1.0 Transitional//EN"
 "http://www.w3.org/TR/xhtml1/DTD/xhtml1-transitional.dtd">

<html xmlns="http://www.w3.org/1999/xhtml">
<head runat="server">
  <title></title>
</head>
<body>
  <form id="form1" runat="server">
  <div>

    <dxwgv:ASPxGridView ID="ASPxGridView1" runat="server"
    CssFilePath="~/App_Themes/Aqua/{0}/styles.css" CssPostfix="Aqua">
    <Styles CssFilePath="~/App_Themes/Aqua/{0}/styles.css" CssPostfix="Aqua">
    </Styles>
    <SettingsLoadingPanel Text="" />
    <SettingsPager>
      <AllButton>
      <Image Height="19px" Width="27px" />
      </AllButton>
      <FirstPageButton>
      <Image Height="19px" Width="23px" />
      </FirstPageButton>
      <LastPageButton>
      <Image Height="19px" Width="23px" />
      </LastPageButton>
      <NextPageButton>
      <Image Height="19px" Width="19px" />
      </NextPageButton>
```

```
        <PrevPageButton>
        <Image Height="19px" Width="19px" />
        </PrevPageButton>
    </SettingsPager>
    <Images ImageFolder="~/App_Themes/Aqua/{0}/">
        <CollapsedButton Height="15px"
        Url="~/App_Themes/Aqua/GridView/gvCollapsedButton.png" Width="15px" />
        <ExpandedButton Height="15px"
        Url="~/App_Themes/Aqua/GridView/gvExpandedButton.png" Width="15px" />
        <DetailCollapsedButton Height="15px"
        Url="~/App_Themes/Aqua/GridView/gvDetailCollapsedButton.png" Width="15px" />
        <DetailExpandedButton Height="15px"
        Url="~/App_Themes/Aqua/GridView/gvDetailExpandedButton.png" Width="15px" />
        <HeaderFilter Height="19px"
Url="~/App_Themes/Aqua/GridView/gvHeaderFilter.png"
        Width="19px" />
        <HeaderActiveFilter Height="19px"
        Url="~/App_Themes/Aqua/GridView/gvHeaderFilterActive.png" Width="19px" />
        <HeaderSortDown Height="5px"
        Url="~/App_Themes/Aqua/GridView/gvHeaderSortDown.png" Width="7px" />
        <HeaderSortUp Height="5px"
Url="~/App_Themes/Aqua/GridView/gvHeaderSortUp.png"
        Width="7px" />
        <FilterRowButton Height="13px" Width="13px" />
        <WindowResizer Height="13px"
Url="~/App_Themes/Aqua/GridView/WindowResizer.png"
        Width="13px" />
    </Images>
    <StylesEditors>
        <ProgressBar Height="25px">
        </ProgressBar>
    </StylesEditors>
    <ImagesEditors>
        <CalendarFastNavPrevYear Height="19px"
        Url="~/App_Themes/Aqua/Editors/edtCalendarFNPrevYear.png" Width="19px" />
        <CalendarFastNavNextYear Height="19px"
        Url="~/App_Themes/Aqua/Editors/edtCalendarFNNextYear.png" Width="19px" />
        <DropDownEditDropDown Height="7px"
        Url="~/App_Themes/Aqua/Editors/edtDropDown.png"
        UrlDisabled="~/App_Themes/Aqua/Editors/edtDropDownDisabled.png"
        UrlHottracked="~/App_Themes/Aqua/Editors/edtDropDownHottracked.png"
        Width="9px" />
        <SpinEditIncrement Height="6px"
        Url="~/App_Themes/Aqua/Editors/edtSpinEditIncrementImage.png"
        UrlDisabled="~/App_Themes/Aqua/Editors/edtSpinEditIncrementDisabledImage.png"
        UrlHottracked=
"~/App_Themes/Aqua/Editors/edtSpinEditIncrementHottrackedImage.png"
        UrlPressed=
"~/App_Themes/Aqua/Editors/edtSpinEditIncrementHottrackedImage.png"
        Width="7px" />
        <SpinEditDecrement Height="7px"
        Url="~/App_Themes/Aqua/Editors/edtSpinEditDecrementImage.png"
```

Continued

Listing 10-5: The same ASPX page as shown in Listing 10-4 with the Aqua theme applied from the AutoFormat dialog box. *(continued)*

```
        UrlDisabled="~/App_Themes/Aqua/Editors/edtSpinEditDecrementDisabledImage.png"
        UrlHottracked=
"~/App_Themes/Aqua/Editors/edtSpinEditDecrementHottrackedImage.png"
        UrlPressed=
"~/App_Themes/Aqua/Editors/edtSpinEditDecrementHottrackedImage.png"
        Width="7px" />
        <SpinEditLargeIncrement Height="9px"
        Url="~/App_Themes/Aqua/Editors/edtSpinEditLargeIncImage.png"
        UrlDisabled="~/App_Themes/Aqua/Editors/edtSpinEditLargeIncDisabledImage.png"
        UrlHottracked=
"~/App_Themes/Aqua/Editors/edtSpinEditLargeIncHottrackedImage.png"
        UrlPressed="~/App_Themes/Aqua/Editors/edtSpinEditLargeIncHottrackedImage.png"
        Width="7px" />
        <SpinEditLargeDecrement Height="9px"
        Url="~/App_Themes/Aqua/Editors/edtSpinEditLargeDecImage.png"
        UrlDisabled="~/App_Themes/Aqua/Editors/edtSpinEditLargeDecDisabledImage.png"
        UrlHottracked=
"~/App_Themes/Aqua/Editors/edtSpinEditLargeDecHottrackedImage.png"
        UrlPressed="~/App_Themes/Aqua/Editors/edtSpinEditLargeDecHottrackedImage.png"
        Width="7px" />
      </ImagesEditors>
      </dxwgv:ASPxGridView>

    </div>
    </form>
  </body>
  </html>
```

From the differences between Listings 10-4 and 10-5 you can see that the Visual Studio IDE made a substantial number of changes to the ASPX for you. Style sheet information was added to the grid and individual skin elements were added. For example, the SettingsLoadingPanel skin information includes an empty Text property and skin elements for the SettingsPager, including sizes for the pager buttons.

The skin content added by the AutoFormat designer provides you with some insight on the kinds of elements you will need to add in a hierarchical fashion to define custom skins. (For more on custom skins refer to the section "Defining Custom Skins and Themes" later in this chapter)

To save custom property settings as a new skin, make all of your desired property settings to a control and select Save As AutoFormat from the control's Smart tags menu. All controls of that type can reuse the saved skin. For more on creating and applying a custom theme refer to the section "Defining Custom Skins and Themes" at the end of this section or the DevExpress TV link http://tv .devexpress.com/ASPxperience04.movie, *entitled "Appearance Customization – Creating and Applying a New Theme."*

Applying a Theme to Your Web Application

To easily apply a theme to the whole Web application you will need to make a small modification to the web.config file. Before you do that you need to add an App_Themes folder to your project and add a theme to that folder. You can add the App_Themes folder by selecting the root folder of the Web project and selecting Website ⇨ Add ASP.NET Folder ⇨ Theme or by manually adding a folder named App_Themes (see Figure 10-9). Either way you will need to copy and paste all of the theme folders and subfolders for the theme you want to use to the App_Themes folder. (Hint: Using the Auto Format menu from one control is the easiest way to add App_Themes and the theme files you want to use.)

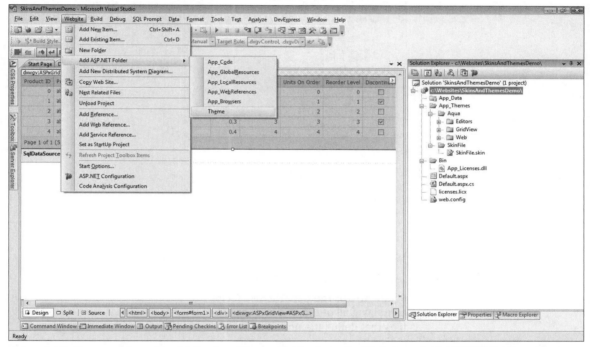

Figure 10-9: You can manually add the App_Themes folder from the Website ⇨ Add ASP.NET Folder ⇨ Theme menu item shown; this menu item is present when the root folder is selected in the Solution Explorer.

The information is a complete set of steps that applies the Aqua theme consistently across a Web application:

1. In the Solution Explorer right-click the root folder and select New Folder from the context menu.

2. Name the folder App_Themes.

3. Navigate to your version of the DevExpress installed files; you should find themes in the default location C:\Program Files\DevExpress 2009.1\Components\Demos\Data\App_Themes.

4. Copy the Aqua folder and paste it into your Web project's App_Themes folder.

5. In the Solution Explorer back in Visual Studio click the refresh button. (The Solution Explorer should contain all of the theme folders and skin files for the Aqua theme.) See Figure 10-10.

6. Modify (or add) a `pages` the tag to the web.config file to include the theme attribute, setting the theme attribute to Aqua. (The `pages` element needs to be in the `<system.web>` section of the web.config file.)

Figure 10-10: The App_Themes folder containing all of the skin and resource files that define the Aqua theme.

Here is snippet showing the complete tag for the `pages` element:

```
<pages theme="Aqua">
```

When you run the Web application you will see that the Aqua theme has been uniformly applied to all of the Web controls for which a skin has been defined. The list of .skin files are present in Figure 10-10. Common resource files for the various skins are contained in the subfolders for the Aqua theme (also visible in Figure 10-10).

Changing a Theme Dynamically

Themes and skins both exist to provide a common way to define how a Web site looks. However, themes do not cascade like style sheets. With style sheets if there is a local style present that is also defined in the style sheet, the local style takes precedence. A theme is designed to make a Web site uniform in appearance. Therefore, if you have a local style and a theme, the theme's settings will be applied. In short, a theme's styles take precedence over the same style applied to a control unless you apply the theme using the styleSheetTheme attribute instead of the theme attribute. If you apply a theme using the styleSheetTheme attribute, local control settings take precedence over theme settings.

Assume, for example, that you have a Web page with a GridView. (The Microsoft GridView is used here because it has fewer properties than the ASPxGridView, making it easier to isolate an attribute for the purposes of contrasting StylesheetTheme and Theme.) Further assume that you used the Smart tags Auto Format menu item to apply the Autumn skin. The grid will have a maroon header and rows that alternate between white and a Stewart's Orange and Cream color. (An excellent carbonated beverage if I say so myself.) All things being equal, the grid will display this color combination at design time and run time. Now, let's assume that you define a .skin file by right-clicking App_Themes and adding a theme subfolder named Custom, and to that folder (from the Theme folder's context menu) you add a skin file. If you defined a skin for the GridView that specified a value for the HeaderStyleBackColor, then how you applied that skin would determine if the GridView displayed the maroon background color or the color in the skin (see Listing 10-6 for the skin file contents). If the skin file's BackColor was red and you applied the Custom theme — which contains the GridView.skin file — using the Theme attribute, the grid would display a header. If you applied the theme using the StylesheetTheme, the grid would display the maroon color defined by the Autumn theme. (Listing 10-6 shows you the contents of the .skin file and the Default2.aspx page from the SkinsAndThemesDemo contains the GridView with the Autumn formatting applied.)

Listing 10-6: A very short .skin file that defines the HeaderStyle's BackColor for a Microsoft GridView Web server control.

```
<%@ Register TagPrefix="asp" Namespace="System.Web.UI.WebControls" %>
<asp:GridView runat="server">
  <HeaderStyle BackColor="Red" />
</asp:GridView>
```

The theme or styleSheetTheme attributes can be applied to a page as attributes of the @Page directive or to the whole Web application using the same attributes of the pages element.

The attributes for the @Page directive are StylesheetTheme and Theme, and for the <pages> tag the attributes are styleSheetTheme and theme. Note the differences in the attribute name's text casing.

The whole purpose of themes is to create a uniform appearance. This means even if you have local settings and forget to remove them the theme's settings will be applied. This also means that if you change a theme at run time, changes will be reflected uniformly. If you want to change the theme of a page dynamically, define a Page_PreInit method and set the Page.Theme property to the name of one of the themes — theme folder — in the App_Themes folder.

```
protected void Page_PreInit(object sender, EventArgs e)
{
  Page.Theme = "Aqua";
}
```

Defining Custom Skins and Themes

Twenty five years ago in February it was my 18th birthday. A recruiter from the army called and asked: "Hey, have you considered the army? Would you like to come down and talk to us about the United States Army?" With five brothers and sisters and seven stepbrothers and sisters — this is a true story, don't laugh — and a stepdad with a fair paying blue collar job there was no extra money for college. My response was, "yeah, sure." Well, when you get down there they say something like, "Do you want to take the test while you are here?" The test is (or was) the ASVAB (Armed Services Vocational Aptitude Battery) test. The ASVAB test is sort of like a "what might you be good at" test. Before I knew it I had taken the test, found myself in a room with other young souls raising my right hand, and voila! I was in the army.

I treated the army like a weird uncle that paid for me to live in Germany and drink beer. The U.S. Army was a good experience. I was a sketchy soldier, but I did my job and got paid a whopping $600 per month to drive a Volkswagen van with Military Police attached to the side with a magnetic sticker, write the occasional traffic ticket, and once even chase a real Russian spy. None of this is the point, but I like the story.

On that ASVAB test I got a score of 123. A 123 is a pretty good score as I was told. You need a 110 to become a general. I certainly wouldn't brag about test scores because I have gotten my share of bad ones, but I was told it was an okay score. I met one guy during my three years in the service that had a higher one. (Young army people talk about ASVAB scores like young college students talk about SAT scores.) This guy was from Alaska and he had scored a 132. His favorite topic of discussion was talking about the specifications of an F16 fighter jet. Now I really like technology, but at parties even I don't talk about code.

In my roundabout way the point of the introduction is that you and I are technophiles. Books like this are read because you and I like to know facts and details, but it is impossible to know facts and details about everything. I spent 30 hours one weekend using Abacus software's CPU simulator to understand how INTEL 80286 processors worked and what the AX, BX, CX, DX, SPP, BP, SI, DI, DS, ES, SS, CS, and IP registers of the microprocessor did and how they were used. Unfortunately, there is more to learn than time permits. The upside is that you get to choose how much you want to know on a subject. Defining skins and themes is one of those subjects you get to decide on. For me organizing the files for a theme, writing a skin file, and designing a theme is not something I have the time to do from scratch. If I want a custom theme I am going to start with an existing theme and tweak it rather than start from scratch, which is the approach described in the remaining subsections. If you want to design a theme from scratch, copying an existing theme and tweaking it is still a good place to start.

Creating a New Skin File

A skin file contains XML-formatted text and can be as simple as the contents of Listing 10-6. By indicating the control, sub-controls, and the properties that are predefined you can define a skin file. Creating skin files from scratch for all of the controls and sub-controls that you are likely to use in an application will be a time-consuming, meticulous endeavor. A good way to create skin files is to start with an existing theme and modify the skin files for that theme. A good way to create skin files from scratch is to visually modify a control, like the ASPxGridView, get it looking the way you want, and then save the format to a skin file. Listing 10-6 provides you with a small stub that shows you how to construct a skin file from scratch. To create a skin file in Visual Studio based on your interactive property settings, follow these steps:

1. Place an ASPxGridView on a Web page.

2. Make some modifications to the grid to change the way it appears. For example, set `Styles.Header.BackColor` to #99CCFF, set `Style.Header.Font.Bold` to true, and set `Styles.AlternatingRow.BackColor` to #CCFFFF (see Figure 10-11). (The colors will appear as gray shading in the book, but that should convey the setting differences.)

3. To create the skin file for the ASPxGridView select Save As AutoFormat from the ASPxGridView's Smart tags menu and save the file wherever you'd like.

4. Open the .skin file in Visual Studio (see Listing 10-7) and delete all of the `<Columns></Columns>` content.

5. Remove the ASPxGridView's `DataSourceID` and `KeyFieldName` properties.

6. Save the skin file. The final results are provided in Listing 10-8.

Product ID	Product Name	Supplier ID	Category ID	Quantity Per Unit	Unit Price	Units In Stock	Units On Order	Reorder Level	Discontinued	Category Name
1	Chai	1	1	10 boxes x 20 bags	18.0000	39	0	10	☐	Beverages
2	Chang	1	1	24 - 12 oz bottles	19.0000	17	40	25	☐	Beverages
3	Aniseed Syrup	1	2	12 - 550 ml bottles	10.0000	13	70	25	☐	Condiments
4	Chef Anton's Cajun Seasoning	2	2	48 - 6 oz jars	22.0000	53	0	0	☐	Condiments
6	Grandma's Boysenberry Spread	3	2	12 - 8 oz jars	25.0000	120	0	25	☐	Condiments
7	Uncle Bob's Organic Dried Pears	3	7	12 - 1 lb pkgs.	30.0000	15	0	10	☐	Produce
8	Northwoods Cranberry Sauce	3	2	12 - 12 oz jars	40.0000	6	0	0	☐	Condiments
10	Ikura	4	8	12 - 200 ml jars	31.0000	31	0	0	☐	Seafood
11	Queso Cabrales	5	4	1 kg pkg.	21.0000	22	30	30	☐	Dairy Products
12	Queso Manchego La Pastora	5	4	10 - 500 g pkgs.	38.0000	86	0	0	☐	Dairy Products

Page 1 of 8 (71 items) [<] **[1]** 2 3 4 5 6 7 8 [>]

Figure 10-11: A bold header font, a header background color, and an alternating row background color make up the basis for the ASPxGridView skin.

For the demonstration I added a SqlDataSource and the Northwind.Products table data. This allowed me to view the grid in the browser to experiment with my grid property settings. However, to create a general skin you won't want specifics like grid columns, so those will have to be removed from the skin file. The original skin file is shown in Listing 10-7. The modified skin file is shown in Listing 10-8.

Listing 10-7: The ASPxGridView.skin file with column data that isn't needed for a general skin because different data sources will have different columns.

```
<%@ Register TagPrefix="asp" Namespace="System.Web.UI.WebControls"
 Assembly="System.Web.Extensions, Version=3.5.0.0,↩
 Culture=neutral, PublicKeyToken=31BF3856AD364E35" %>
<%@ Register TagPrefix="asp" Namespace="System.Web.UI"
 Assembly="System.Web.Extensions, Version=3.5.0.0, ↩
 Culture=neutral, PublicKeyToken=31BF3856AD364E35" %>
<%@ Register TagPrefix="asp" Namespace="System.Web.UI.WebControls.WebParts"
 Assembly="System.Web, Version=2.0.0.0, Culture=neutral,↩
 PublicKeyToken=b03f5f7f11d50a3a" %>
<%@ Register TagPrefix="dxe" Namespace="DevExpress.Web.ASPxEditors"
 Assembly="DevExpress.Web.ASPxEditors.v9.1, Version=9.1.4.0,↩
 Culture=neutral, PublicKeyToken=b88d1754d700e49a" %>
<%@ Register TagPrefix="dxwgv" Namespace="DevExpress.Web.ASPxGridView"
 Assembly="DevExpress.Web.ASPxGridView.v9.1, Version=9.1.4.0,↩
 Culture=neutral, PublicKeyToken=b88d1754d700e49a" %>
<dxwgv:ASPxGridView runat="server" DataSourceID="SqlDataSource1"
 AutoGenerateColumns="False" KeyFieldName="ProductID">
<Styles>
<Header BackColor="#99CCFF" Font-Bold="True"></Header>

<AlternatingRow BackColor="#CCFFFF"></AlternatingRow>
</Styles>
<Columns>
<dxwgv:GridViewDataTextColumn FieldName="ProductID" ReadOnly="True"
 VisibleIndex="0"></dxwgv:GridViewDataTextColumn>
<dxwgv:GridViewDataTextColumn FieldName="ProductName"
 VisibleIndex="1"></dxwgv:GridViewDataTextColumn>
<dxwgv:GridViewDataTextColumn FieldName="SupplierID"
 VisibleIndex="2"></dxwgv:GridViewDataTextColumn>
<dxwgv:GridViewDataTextColumn FieldName="CategoryID"
VisibleIndex="3"></dxwgv:GridViewDataTextColumn>
<dxwgv:GridViewDataTextColumn FieldName="QuantityPerUnit"
 VisibleIndex="4"></dxwgv:GridViewDataTextColumn>
<dxwgv:GridViewDataTextColumn FieldName="UnitPrice"
 VisibleIndex="5"></dxwgv:GridViewDataTextColumn>
<dxwgv:GridViewDataTextColumn FieldName="UnitsInStock"
 VisibleIndex="6"></dxwgv:GridViewDataTextColumn>
<dxwgv:GridViewDataTextColumn FieldName="UnitsOnOrder"
 VisibleIndex="7"></dxwgv:GridViewDataTextColumn>
<dxwgv:GridViewDataTextColumn FieldName="ReorderLevel"
 VisibleIndex="8"></dxwgv:GridViewDataTextColumn>
<dxwgv:GridViewDataCheckColumn FieldName="Discontinued"
 VisibleIndex="9"></dxwgv:GridViewDataCheckColumn>
<dxwgv:GridViewDataTextColumn FieldName="CategoryName"
 VisibleIndex="10"></dxwgv:GridViewDataTextColumn>
</Columns>
</dxwgv:ASPxGridView>
```

Listing 10-8: The modified skin file without the column information.

```
<%@ Register TagPrefix="asp" Namespace="System.Web.UI.WebControls"
 Assembly="System.Web.Extensions, Version=3.5.0.0,
 Culture=neutral, PublicKeyToken=31BF3856AD364E35" %>
<%@ Register TagPrefix="asp" Namespace="System.Web.UI"
 Assembly="System.Web.Extensions, Version=3.5.0.0,
 Culture=neutral, PublicKeyToken=31BF3856AD364E35" %>
<%@ Register TagPrefix="asp" Namespace="System.Web.UI.WebControls.WebParts"
 Assembly="System.Web, Version=2.0.0.0, Culture=neutral,
 PublicKeyToken=b03f5f7f11d50a3a" %>
<%@ Register TagPrefix="dxe" Namespace="DevExpress.Web.ASPxEditors"
 Assembly="DevExpress.Web.ASPxEditors.v9.1, Version=9.1.4.0,
 Culture=neutral, PublicKeyToken=b88d1754d700e49a" %>
<%@ Register TagPrefix="dxwgv" Namespace="DevExpress.Web.ASPxGridView"
 Assembly="DevExpress.Web.ASPxGridView.v9.1, Version=9.1.4.0,
 Culture=neutral, PublicKeyToken=b88d1754d700e49a" %>
<dxwgv:ASPxGridView runat="server"  AutoGenerateColumns="False">
<Styles>
<Header BackColor="#99CCFF" Font-Bold="True"></Header>

<AlternatingRow BackColor="#CCFFFF"></AlternatingRow>
</Styles>
</dxwgv:ASPxGridView>
```

The key to a reusable skin is to remove specific data such as references to data sources, tables, and specific columns. Now that you have a skin file for the grid you can incorporate that skin to build up an entire theme.

To build out an entire theme, repeat the steps in this section for each control you want in your theme. Settings can include graphics for items that have bitmaps and cascading style sheets. If you need some ideas open the files that make up part of an existing theme, like the Aqua theme, and reproduce skin files or even borrow elements from that theme.

Defining a Custom Theme

Application themes are placed in an App_Themes folder in your project. Each theme is an immediate child folder of the App_Themes folder. In each theme folder are the skin files that contain the settings for a control. A skin file can contain multiple skins. A default skin has no SkinID, and subsequent skins can be identified by adding a SkinID attribute. A useful convention is to create a subfolder for each skin and place the additional content — resources, style sheets, and graphics — in those subfolders. (Figure 10-10 shows you a well-organized theme structure.)

To incorporate the skin from the previous section into a custom theme you will need to reproduce the App_Themes structure, add a subfolder for the theme, put the skin file in the theme folder, and reference the theme in the project. The following detailed steps walk you through the process of structuring and using the custom theme, and Listing 10-9 contains the ASPX showing you how to use the theme.

1. In the Solution Explorer right-click the root folder, select Add ASP.NET Folder, and click the Theme item. This adds the App_Themes folder and Theme subfolder.

2. Rename the Theme folder to whatever you want to name the theme, such as MyTheme.

3. Right-click the MyTheme folder and click Open Folder in Windows Explorer.

4. Copy and paste the skin files, .css files, and any resources that you want to make part of your theme. (For this example copy the ASPxGridView.skin created in the prior section, "Creating a New Skin File.")

5. To use the skin return to the project CustomSkinAndTheme and strip out all of the content in the ASPxGridView's `<Styles></Styles>` section including the `<Styles>` tags.

6. Modify the ASPX @`Page` directive referencing your custom theme by setting the Theme attribute to "MyTheme." The finished ASPX content is provided in Listing 10-9 and the results will look just like Figure 10-11.

Listing 10-9: The ASPX shows that no local styles are present in the grid and MyTheme has been applied using the @Page directive.

```
<%@ Page Language="C#" AutoEventWireup="true"  CodeFile="Default.aspx.cs"
Inherits="_Default" Theme="MyTheme"%>
<%@ Register assembly="DevExpress.Web.ASPxGridView.v9.1,↵
Version=9.1.4.0, Culture=neutral, PublicKeyToken=b88d1754d700e49a"
namespace="DevExpress.Web.ASPxGridView" tagprefix="dxwgv" %>
<%@ Register assembly="DevExpress.Web.ASPxEditors.v9.1, Version=9.1.4.0,↵
Culture=neutral, PublicKeyToken=b88d1754d700e49a"
namespace="DevExpress.Web.ASPxEditors" tagprefix="dxe" %>

<!DOCTYPE html PUBLIC "-//W3C//DTD XHTML 1.0 Transitional//EN"
"http://www.w3.org/TR/xhtml1/DTD/xhtml1-transitional.dtd">

<html xmlns="http://www.w3.org/1999/xhtml">
<head runat="server">
  <title></title>
</head>
<body>
  <form id="form1" runat="server">
  <div>

    <dxwgv:ASPxGridView ID="ASPxGridView1" runat="server"
    AutoGenerateColumns="False" DataSourceID="SqlDataSource1"
    KeyFieldName="ProductID">
    <Columns>
      <dxwgv:GridViewDataTextColumn FieldName="ProductID" ReadOnly="True"
      VisibleIndex="0">
      </dxwgv:GridViewDataTextColumn>
      <dxwgv:GridViewDataTextColumn FieldName="ProductName" VisibleIndex="1">
      </dxwgv:GridViewDataTextColumn>
      <dxwgv:GridViewDataTextColumn FieldName="SupplierID" VisibleIndex="2">
      </dxwgv:GridViewDataTextColumn>
      <dxwgv:GridViewDataTextColumn FieldName="CategoryID" VisibleIndex="3">
      </dxwgv:GridViewDataTextColumn>
      <dxwgv:GridViewDataTextColumn FieldName="QuantityPerUnit" VisibleIndex="4">
      </dxwgv:GridViewDataTextColumn>
      <dxwgv:GridViewDataTextColumn FieldName="UnitPrice" VisibleIndex="5">
      </dxwgv:GridViewDataTextColumn>
      <dxwgv:GridViewDataTextColumn FieldName="UnitsInStock" VisibleIndex="6">
```

```
            </dxwgv:GridViewDataTextColumn>
            <dxwgv:GridViewDataTextColumn FieldName="UnitsOnOrder" VisibleIndex="7">
            </dxwgv:GridViewDataTextColumn>
            <dxwgv:GridViewDataTextColumn FieldName="ReorderLevel" VisibleIndex="8">
            </dxwgv:GridViewDataTextColumn>
            <dxwgv:GridViewDataCheckColumn FieldName="Discontinued" VisibleIndex="9">
            </dxwgv:GridViewDataCheckColumn>
            <dxwgv:GridViewDataTextColumn FieldName="CategoryName" VisibleIndex="10">
            </dxwgv:GridViewDataTextColumn>
        </Columns>
        </dxwgv:ASPxGridView>
        <asp:SqlDataSource ID="SqlDataSource1" runat="server"
        ConnectionString="<%$ ConnectionStrings:NorthwindConnectionString %>"
        SelectCommand="SELECT * FROM [Alphabetical list of products]">
        </asp:SqlDataSource>

    </div>
    </form>
</body>
</html>
```

> To create a global theme create your theme folder and add the elements to iisdefaul-troot\aspnet_client I system_web\version\Themes, for example c:\Inetpub \wwwroot. (Notice that the global themes folder is Themes, not App_Themes.)

Making the Most of JavaScript

If you've developed Web applications for any length of time, there would have been a point when you wrote your first bit of JavaScript code (or, as Microsoft would have it, JScript code). You probably wrote just enough to get by and assumed that it was all pretty much Java (that is, C#-like under the hood). Not so. JavaScript is a pretty complete functional language, a not-what-you're-used-to object-oriented language, and altogether fun to write.

When you are using DevExpress's ASP.NET controls, you have some standard opportunities for using JavaScript to interact with the controls on the client side, rather than the server side. Because of this interactivity, it's possible to implement a richer user experience without having to chatter to the server (and thereby introduce delays through latency or just from the speed of the network connection).

Common Client-Side Functionality

In general, the DevExpress ASP.NET controls introduce client-side functionality through a set of four common properties.

❑   **EnableClientSideAPI.** This Boolean property defines whether the control can be manipulated at the client side using JavaScript. In general, this defaults to false and, if set to true, will result in the server sending an extra "API" JavaScript file to the client along with the page. This can result in a slightly larger payload for the page and hence a slightly longer time to render the page in the browser. In general, though, this increased time is not particularly noticeable (and you can

497

use other strategies to reduce the pageload time, such as compression and the like). Some controls, in the later versions of DXperience, assume that this property is, in fact, true, and the property has been marked obsolete.

❑ **ClientVisible.** What it says: is the control visible on the client in the browser or not. The control is hidden through CSS using the `display:none;` attribute. If you enable the API for the control, you will be able to hide or show the control on the client.

❑ **ClientInstanceName.** This is the identifier for the control on the client. What the JavaScript code for initializing the control does is to create a global variable for the object that represents the control when the page is loaded. If you specify a name using ClientInstanceName, that's what will be used; if not, it'll synthesize one using the ID for the control and possibly its parent's name. To be honest, it's probably better to specify your own control names, rather than work out what the synthesized name happens to be. You see more about global variables and name pollution later, but try and make the names you use unique to your application by using some kind of prefix (DevExpress developers use a prefix of "ASPx" in some form for their global objects, for example).

❑ **ClientSideEvents.** These are events that will fire according to what the control is doing or how the user is interacting with the control. Different controls use different events; some have many, some only a couple. In all cases, subscribing to these events will necessitate the use of JavaScript. And, unfortunately, in all cases, the editor to write this JavaScript is very basic, so you should keep your event handlers *short*.

Client-Side Discussion

Let's take an example so we can dissect these properties: the ASPxTimer. This control is not a UI control — it has no visible representation — so it doesn't have a `ClientVisible` property (it would always be false). Also, it is designed to tick on the client side and so it doesn't make sense to have a `EnableClientSideAPI` property because it would always be true.

Drop one on a new form. Set `ClientInstanceName` to something like "timer." Run the application and then view the source for the page in the browser. You should see something like Listing 10-10.

Listing 10-10: A bare ASPxTimer as rendered in a page.

```
<script id="dxss_1664712032" type="text/javascript">
<!--

var dxo = new ASPxClientTimer('ASPxTimer1');
window['timer'] = dxo;
dxo.InlineInitialize();

//-->
</script>
```

The first line of the script creates a new `ASPxClientTimer` called `ASPxTimer1`. `ASPxClientTimer` is a constructor that creates a special JavaScript object to run on the client side that is the equivalent of the server-side `ASPxTimer` control. (If the server-side control is known as ASPxSomething, DevExpress names the client-side version ASPxClientSomething. That's a handy hint for when you're looking for the client-side interface of a control in the help.)

The next line of code sets up a global variable called `timer` to be equal to this object. In JavaScript the `window` variable is the parent of all global variables. If you want to create a global variable called `timer` in JavaScript you can use any one of the following:

```
window['timer'] = somevalue;
window.timer = somevalue;
timer = somevalue;
```

They are all equivalent. The important thing to realize is that, if there already exists a variable of the same name, it will be deleted, thrown away, disposed of. The new variable will overwrite the old. The two variables don't have to be the same type — indeed JavaScript is dynamic and the type of a variable only becomes important at run time. Global variables are dangerous and it's unfortunate that ASP.NET's usage of JavaScript is such that global variables are created ad nauseam.

Finally, the third line of code initializes the object.

Let's now break future code, just by renaming the control. Add a button underneath the timer and change the timer's `ClientInstanceName` to `ASPxClientButton`. If you run this application now, you'll get an error along the lines of "`ASPxClientButton` is not a constructor" (the exact error depends on your IDE/browser combination; this is the error Firebug produces in Firefox, whereas IE8 produces an exception inside the Visual Studio IDE saying "Object doesn't support this action," which is somewhat harder to understand).

What has happened is that the global variable called `ASPxClientButton`, which was a constructor, is now a timer object. You can't use `new` with an object that's not a constructor, and hence the error. So, all in all, beware and heed the recommendation that you use a prefix to name your client instances.

Client-Side Events

Rename your ASPxTimer control to have a client-side name of `timer` and we'll look at the events you can subscribe to on the client side.

The timer control has two possible client-side events you can subscribe to: the `Init` event, which is fired when the control is being created on the client, and the `Tick` event, which is fired when the timer ticks. All events, including these two, have the same signature:

```
function (s, e) {
}
```

and you basically provide the code between the braces. The `s` parameter is the sender object and the `e` parameter the event arguments.

The problem I have is that the editor for adding the code between the braces is basic in the extreme. There is no syntax highlighting, no IntelliSense, no auto-indenting, just a basic text editor. For that reason, I tend to just type in a call to a method of a helper object. This object I will write in a JavaScript file (.js) that I add to the project. Look at an example of that process using the timer control.

First of all, add the `Init` and `Tick` event handlers as shown in Listing 10-11. You'll use a helper object called `timerEngine`.

Listing 10-11: The Init and Tick event handlers.

```
Init="function(s, e) { timerEngine.init(); }"
Tick="function(s, e) { timerEngine.tick(); }"
```

Before you continue with this example, I have to lay some foundations as to what JavaScript is all about.

Quick Language Overview

JavaScript is an interpreted dynamic language. When you declare a variable, you do not declare its type. The JavaScript interpreter will work out the type of a variable at run time, and, if necessary, coerce the variable into the type it expects for a particular statement. This coercion is the source of many bugs.

There is a very small set of types: Boolean (works like you'd expect, can have two values, true and false), number (actually a double type underneath, JavaScript does not have an integer type), string (pretty much like .NET strings), objects, arrays, and functions. The typeof function will return a string representing the type of the variable you pass in. Well, usually. Although arrays have some special semantics, typeof will return object when called on an array.

If you want to declare a variable, use the keyword var. It's not wrong to leave it off though, in which case the variable gets declared on the global object, window, instead. It will be a global variable from that point on.

Classes do not exist in JavaScript. Inheritance is there, but you inherit from other objects. This is known as prototypal inheritance. In other words, given an object, you can create another that looks like it. Inheritance in JavaScript tends to be done by creating some interesting object that has the behavior you want, and then creating clones of it. (Compare this to C#, where you create a class with the interesting behavior, and then use that as a template to create objects.)

Objects are dynamic as well. You can add properties and methods to any object and remove them at will. An object does not have a static definition based upon the class it was created from, because, as you just saw, there are no classes. It's best to think of an object as a hash map between names and values.

Functions are first-class objects in JavaScript. You can assign them to variables, and they can be returned from function calls. JavaScript is a functional language and you can easily do things like currying or producing a closure. In fact, it goes further: the scope of a variable is defined by the function call chain that produced it (this scoping rule is completely different than C#'s). Anonymous functions are very prevalent in JavaScript, especially when creating singleton objects or defining event handlers.

Here's a note on conventions when writing JavaScript: Variable and function names are always in lowercase, or CamelCase with the initial letter as lowercase (timerEngine, init, tick and so on). There are two main exceptions. First, constants are written in all uppercase. The main reason for this is that JavaScript does not have the concept of a constant, and so constants are really variables and can be changed. The uppercasing is a warning to the maintenance programmer that the variable is being used as a constant.

The second exception is constructors where the initial letter is uppercased. The main reason for this is that a constructor is nothing more or less than an ordinary function; it's just that when it is used with the new keyword the function is called with some special semantics (the this variable is the new object and if the function doesn't have a return statement it will return this instead of undefined).

By the way, if you look back at Listing 10.10 where a new timer was being constructed, ASPxClientTimer is not a class, as you'd expect from C#. JavaScript does not have classes like you'd understand from C# or Java. ASPxClientTimer is a function being used as a constructor. It will create and return a new object, and that object will have certain behavior that is inherited from another object, the so-called prototype object.

Creating a Singleton

Back to our example. You want to create a `timerEngine` object and give it some behavior (that is, give it a couple of methods) and some state (an internal field or two, let's say a counter of how many times the timer has ticked). First add a new item to the solution, a JScript file called timerEngine.js. Listing 10-12 then has the initial, draft version of this object's code.

Listing 10-12: An initial stab at writing a timerEngine object.

```
var timerEngine = { };

timerEngine.init = function() {
    this.counter = 0;
};

timerEngine.tick = function() {
    this.counter++;
};
```

The code first creates an empty object called `timerEngine` (this object is global in scope) using the literal syntax and then adds a new property called `init` to it. This is a function, and therefore `init` would be known as a method. This function sets a field of the object called `counter` to zero (`counter` gets created at this point). Then a new property called `tick` is added, also a function, and this function increments the counter.

This code has numerous problems. First of all, it's not encapsulated at all: the object's definition is all over the place. The `counter` property of the object is visible outside the object (there are not private/public keywords in JavaScript). It's ugly in that you have to make reference to the `this` variable in order to reference the object itself: the scope of variables inside the two functions is *not* the object. Scoping rules in JavaScript don't work the same way as in C#.

You could try and encapsulate the object better. Listing 10-13 shows a slightly improved version.

Listing 10-13: An improved timerEngineObject.

```
var timerEngine = {
  counter: 0,

  init: function() {
    this.counter = 0;
  },

  tick: function() {
    this.counter++;
  }
};
```

Here, all you've done is to move the definitions of the methods inside the object declaration (again using the literal syntax), nicely encapsulating it all. The counter variable is still publicly visible. You still have the issue of the `this` variable as well: again the scope of variables inside the methods is not the object itself, despite it looking like it this time around.

How do you change this to have a hidden counter and remove the need for 'this'?

You have to embrace some idiomatic JavaScript. The answer is to write a function to return the object. Executing the function will create not only the object, but also a closure. Local variables referenced by the function will remain in scope, even after the function has completed execution. Listing 10-14 shows this version of the `timerEngine` object.

Listing 10-14: The definitive timerEngine object with a private variable.

```
var timerEngine = function() {
  var counter;

  return {
    getCounter: function() {
      return counter;
    },

    init: function() {
      counter = 0;
    },

    tick: function() {
      counter++;
    }
  };
} ();
```

This looks a bit more complicated, so let's dissect it. First of all, you're declaring a global variable called `timerEngine`. What is `timerEngine`? Reading that first line seems to indicate that it's going to be a function. Not so. If you look at the end brace of the function, you'll see that it is followed by a pair of parentheses: the execution operator. That is, the function is immediately executed. It is never assigned to a variable as a function, it is an anonymous function that's immediately executed, and the return value from that function is assigned to the `timerEngine` variable. This type of code is extremely idiomatic and is something that you'll see over and over again in professional JavaScript. It's usually known as the *module pattern* and was invented by Douglas Crockford of Yahoo!.

So what does this function return when it is executed? It returns an object with three methods: `getCounter` (a getter for the counter field), `init`, and `tick`. The object has no field called `counter`, though; instead the `counter` variable is declared as a local variable of the anonymous function. You might think that this would disappear as soon as the function has completed executing, making the return object flawed, but in reality it's not. Because the returned object methods all reference this variable, the executed function produces a closure and encapsulates the local variable. The variable "lives on" as part of the closure around the object's methods.

Even better, because the variable is local, it is not visible outside the function (or, if you like, the closure). However, due to the scoping rules in JavaScript — which follow the calling function chain — the returned object's methods can see it. That is, because the init function, say, is declared inside the anonymous function, it can see and access all the local variables of that function — and the same goes for the getCounter and tick functions.

This code, in brief, creates an object with hidden state and public methods that control access to that state. The only global variable is the object itself.

Now that you've created the JavaScript file and the code for the timerEngine object, you should add the file to the ASPX file so that the script is actually executed when the page is loaded. To do this easily, the best way is to drag the .js file from the Solution Explorer to the ASPX file's source and drop it inside the body element (I tend to drop it at the end of the body element, just above the closing tag).

Prototypal Inheritance

As mentioned before, JavaScript has no classes. Nevertheless, it has an inheritance mechanism: all objects inherit from another object. This ancestor has as specific name: the prototype object. This lends its name to the kind of inheritance JavaScript supports: prototypal inheritance. In essence, what happens is that you define an object with the kind of behavior you are interested in, and then you create duplicates of that object.

Let's see how it works. Every object in JavaScript is automatically given a property called constructor. This is set by the interpreter to the function (the constructor) that created the object using the new keyword. For objects that are created using the literal syntax with braces, the constructor function is Object. Generally, once you've created an object, you don't particularly care how it was constructed, apart from one thing. Every function has an automatic property called prototype. For an ordinary function, this is an empty object and isn't used, but for a constructor, this property contains the ancestor object from which behavior is inherited.

Listing 10-15 shows a Point constructor, and the code to create such an object. This constructor takes an x and a y value and stores those values as fields of the object being constructed.

Listing 10-15: A simple constructor to create a Point object and one being created.

```
var Point = function(x, y) {
  this.x = x;
  this.y = y;
};
var point = new Point(0, 0);
```

Suppose you wanted now to have a move method on points to effect a mathematical translation operation. Where would you put it? It's inefficient to put it in the constructor as well because every Point object you create would have its own copy of the move method (a function is an object, remember). It would be better instead to place it in the ancestor of all points so that they all can use the same function. And that is the prototype object. For the Point constructor, you haven't set the prototype anywhere and so it has the default value: an empty object. Listing 10-16 shows how to add a move method to the prototype.

Listing 10-16: Adding a move method to the prototype object.

```
var Point = function(x, y) {
  this.x = x;
  this.y = y;
};
Point.prototype.move = function(x, y) {
  this.x += x;
  this.y += y;
};
var point = new Point(0, 0);
point.move(1, 2);
```

So, to recap so far: `Point` is a special function called a constructor. Like all functions, it has a property called prototype. This defines an object from which behavior is inherited. Adding functions to this prototype object means that all objects created from the constructor will share these functions.

Let's finally look at inheritance. Declare a `ColorPoint` constructor. Your intent is that objects created from this constructor will inherit the behavior of `Point` objects — in this case that means you inherit the method called `move`. Listing 10-17 shows this inheritance in action.

Listing 10-17: Inheriting behavior from Point.

```
var ColorPoint = function(x, y, color) {
  this.x = x;
  this.y = y;
  this.color = color;
};
ColorPoint.prototype = new Point(0, 0);

var colorPoint = new ColorPoint(0, 0, "red");
colorPoint.move(1, 2);
```

Notice that you're creating a new `Point` object and assigning it to the `ColorPoint.prototype` property. (In effect, you discard the original to be garbage collected.) When the interpreter reaches the call to the `move` method, it proceeds as follows. First it looks in the `colorPoint` object for a method called `move`. There isn't one. It then finds the prototype object through the constructor function, and looks there. It finds it and executes it on the `colorPoint` object. Note, in particular, that the x and y fields are instance variables created by the `ColorPoint` constructor and so are not shared via the prototype. If the `Point` constructor had created another field called `length`, say, as the vector length from the origin to the point, that field would be shared from the prototype, and would have whatever value it had in from the prototype. The length property would be the same for all `ColorPoint` objects, in other words.

In general, professional JavaScript developers tend not to build deep inheritance structures. Mostly they deal with very shallow inheritance, and objects are very easy to create and modify to suit your needs, without delving into a deep model. Should you want a class-like model, several open source libraries provide such functionality; the most famous is probably Prototype.

JavaScript Debugging

No matter how good we are at writing code or at coding and maintaining tests, at some point we're going to be breaking out the debugger. There's some good and bad news.

First, if your development environment is Visual Studio driving Internet Explorer as the browser and you're debugging at development time, you'll find that this combination is the best. Providing that you've enabled Script Debugging (Other) in the Advanced tab of your Internet Options dialog box, Visual Studio will be the debugger. You will be in a familiar environment where you can browse variables, set breakpoints, and do all those other debugging tasks, even though the target language is JavaScript.

If your JavaScript code is the only code you'll be debugging, you'll be fine. However, if you're using other JavaScript libraries (for example, jQuery, Prototype, and so on), the main issue you'll encounter is that they've been *minified*. This means the code has been compressed such that identifiers are renamed to smaller non-semantic names, whitespace will be removed where possible, and other obfuscation type compression will have been applied. During development, you should locate and use the non-compressed version of the libraries in order to make your debugging session as productive as possible. (This goes the other way, of course: as soon as you've debugged your own JavaScript code, you should minify it using one of the many JavaScript compressors and make sure that you're only serving compressed JavaScript from your production Web server.)

Sometimes a script bug will appear in a production environment. Using a JavaScript debugger, you'll be able to debug the Web page directly in the browser. The best known debugger for JavaScript is part of Firebug, which is an add-in for the Firefox browser. Firebug is an essential tool for the Web developer anyway because you can view and debug your HTML code and styles (or investigate how other sites get their look-and-feel), but its script debugger works extremely well and has the same facilities as Visual Studio. You can set breakpoints and watches, and look at variables and investigate the DOM at a breakpoint.

Internet Explorer 8 also comes with a set of developer tools (press F12 to show the Developer Tools window). Again you can do things like view and debug your HTML and CSS. The script debugger work as you'd expect. Unfortunately, at the time of writing, the capabilities for investigating the real-time DOM are very much less than Firebug's (for example, if you mistakenly create a global object in your code, you'll be able to see that with Firebug, but not with IE8).

Summary

JavaScript, cascading style sheets, and skins and themes are not specific to DevExpress controls. This chapter really constitutes general ASP.NET information; I just hope you will use this information alongside of our controls. Probably the uniformly best way to take advantage of this information is to begin using style sheets and themes and consider using HTML Components for your JavaScript. The net benefit will be that you can reuse a style sheet in its entirety or as a starting point, themes can be reused, and JavaScript files or HTML Components can be reused. Compartmentalizing promotes reuse to a much greater extent than plumbing existing code for embedded elements. Happy programming.

Part III: Ajax, Charting, Reporting, and Cloud Computing

11

Asynchronous Computing for ASP.NET

Asynchronous programming is essentially client-side programming of functionality that doesn't complete immediately (synchronously, in other words) but that is completed some time later. The application is notified, usually through an event, that processing has completed. During the time between firing off the processing request and getting the completed response, the application doesn't block, and the user can continue to interact with it.

This asynchronous behavior is provided with ASP.NET in a couple of ways.

❑   The first is very simple: a timer that ticks at regular intervals, with each tick resulting in an event being triggered. Here there is no processing *per se*, just the requirement that the application be notified of every tick.

❑   The second is more complex and broader in scope: Asynchronous JavaScript and XML (Ajax) and callbacks. The X in Ajax has become less of a requirement these days with simple strings or JSON packets becoming more prevalent.

Ajax is the underlying technology that provides the ability to update part of a Web page from server-provided data without refreshing it all. Using it gives you the opportunity to provide Rich Internet Application (RIA) features in your application.

Ajax has been available officially for ASP.NET since the beginning of 2007, and since that time third-party vendors have been *Ajaxifying* (if there is such a verb) their ASP.NET controls to give them the ability to perform RIA-type services in Web applications. DevExpress is no different in this respect.

The Ajax functionality is provided through the mechanism of *callbacks* rather than the postback we've had since the beginning of ASP.NET. It's best to think of the callback as being a lightweight postback with the differences being that at the client no page refresh occurs and at the server not all the usual postback data may be available. In particular, the usual page cycle, albeit slightly abbreviated, is processed on a callback, just as with a postback.

The support for Ajax in the DevExpress ASP.NET suite is twofold. First of all there are the explicit controls that provide Ajax functionality, ASPxCallBack and ASPxCallbackPanel, and then there is the implicit callback functionality provided with each control.

❏ ASPxCallback is a very simple non-visual control that provides the basic callback functionality. That is, you can set up a callback on the client, send that to the server, and obtain any response sent back from the server. There is a method to determine whether a callback is in progress. On the server side, the callback will trigger an event (and pass to the event handler the callback-specific data from the client).

❏ ASPxCallbackPanel is a visual container control that provides callback functionality to update the controls within the panel.

This chapter is going to take a look at both of the ways that ASP.NET gives you to deal with asynchronous behavior — using a timer and using callbacks. It also shows you how to use the DevExpress controls that deal with displaying multimedia content, an exceptionally easy method of doing asynchronous programming where all the hard asynchronous behavior is hidden.

Controlling Asynchronous Behavior with a Timer

In the DevExpress suite of ASP.NET controls, timing functionality is provided by the ASPxTimer control. This is a simple non-visual control with an uncomplicated API. Nevertheless, you should bear in mind that the API is twofold: client-side and server-side.

In practice, the server-side processing of the timer is rarely used. Two main reasons: First, you get much more control when you process the timer client-side, and second, having the tick occur on the server means that there is a round-trip involved. That's not to say that having the tick event fire on the server is never done: The typical scenario for this is timing out the client after a period of inactivity so that the user gets automatically logged off. The server would then redirect the client to the login page again.

Using the timer on the client exclusively and marrying it up to a callback mechanism to get updated data from the server is the usual development scenario, and you see examples of this approach in this chapter and the next.

For the client-side user of the timer, the essential four properties are Enabled, Interval, ClientInstanceName, and ClientSideEvents. The latter property has two events to write handlers for: Init and Tick. You see their use later on in this chapter.

Controlling Asynchronous Behavior with Callbacks

The ASPxCallback non-visual control is perhaps the simplest encapsulation of callbacks you can use.

The control, like every control that uses Ajax, is split into two parts: client-side and server-side. Client-side, the ASPxCallback control implements several events of which two are paramount: CallbackComplete and CallbackError. The first is triggered when the callback completes (that is, after the client has sent the callback to the server and has received a reply). The second is a catch-all error event and is fired if the callback failed in some way.

Server-side, there's really only one event for which you should implement a handler: Callback. This receives the callback from the control and processes it, returning a result in the EventArgs for the event.

You can use an ASPxCallback control for any functionality for which some kind of quick communication to the server is required without the interruption and refresh of a full postback. You don't even have to use any other DevExpress ASP.NET controls; you can easily use the results from a callback to update individual HTML elements in the current DOM, for example.

Using the ASPxCallback Control

Take a look at a very simple example. You'll write an application that converts a whole number to its Roman numeral equivalent (so 24 would be converted to XXIV, for example). Imagine that this conversion is complex enough that it has to be done server-side (perhaps there's some access required to a database) and conveniently ignore the fact that writing a JavaScript routine to do so is simple enough.

Drop an ASPxTextBox, ASPxLabel, ASPxButton, and an ASPxCallback control onto an ASPxRoundPanel. Set the panel's Header property to "Convert to Roman numerals".

For the textbox, set the EnableClientSideAPI to true, and the ClientInstanceName to "textBox". Set the NullText property to "Enter number" to act as a prompt when the textbox is empty. To make data entry easier (you don't want to go through the pain of manually validating that the input is numeric, and so on), configure the MaskSettings property so that the Mask is "<0..4999>", and the ErrorText is "Invalid whole number". Finally set the MaxLength to 4.

For the label, just set the ClientInstanceName to "label" and EnableClientSideAPI to true.

For the button, it's a little more involved. Set the Text to "Convert". Set the ClientInstanceName to "button" and EnableClientSideAPI to true. The next change is something I missed the first time I wrote this small application: You should set AutoPostBack to false. If you don't, clicking the button will also cause the Web form to be submitted as a postback, causing all kinds of weird effects. The final change is to set up the client-side Click event handler to the code in Listing 11-1. This code will first check that the input in the textbox is valid, and, if so, set the label's text to "Loading..." to indicate that something is happening and then execute the callback control's PerformCallback method, passing the input from the textbox.

Listing 11-1: The client-side Click handler for the button.

```
function(s, e) {
    if (textBox.GetIsValid()) {
        label.SetText("Loading&hellip;");
        callback.PerformCallback(textBox.GetText());
    }
}
```

Finally, you come to the callback control. Set the `ClientInstanceName` to `"callback"`. For the client-side events, set the `CallbackComplete` handler to the code in Listing 11-2, and the `CallbackError` handler to that in Listing 11-3.

Listing 11-2: The client-side CallbackComplete handler for the callback control.

```
function(s, e) {
    label.SetText("Done: " + e.result);
}
```

Listing 11-3: The client-side CallbackError handler for the callback control.

```
function(s, e) {
    label.SetText("Error in conversion callback");
}
```

You must also code the `Callback` event handler for the server-side processing, shown in Listing 11-4. The `EventArgs` for the event has two properties that you should use: `Parameter` is the string sent by the ASPxCallback control, and `Result` is the string you want to send back to the client.

Listing 11-4: The Callback event handler for the ASPxCallback control.

```
protected void ASPxCallback1_Callback(
    object source, DevExpress.Web.ASPxCallback.CallbackEventArgs e) {
  RomanConverter converter = new RomanConverter();
  string result = converter.Convert(int.Parse(e.Parameter));
  if (string.IsNullOrEmpty(result)) {
    e.Result = "Error: number out of range 1 to 4999";
  }
  else {
    e.Result = e.Parameter + " is " + result;
  }
}
```

In this example, you parse the `Parameter` property to an integer and then convert that to a Roman number (Listing 11-5). Finally, you pass back the result of the conversion.

Listing 11-5: One way to convert from an integer value to its Roman representation.

```
class RomanNumberAtom {
  public RomanNumberAtom(int intValue, string romanValue) {
    IntValue = intValue;
    RomanValue = romanValue;
  }
  public int IntValue { get; set; }
  public string RomanValue { get; set; }
}

class RomanConverter {
  private List<RomanNumberAtom> atoms = new List<RomanNumberAtom>();
  public RomanConverter() {
    atoms.Add(new RomanNumberAtom(1000, "M"));
    atoms.Add(new RomanNumberAtom(900, "CM"));
    atoms.Add(new RomanNumberAtom(500, "D"));
    atoms.Add(new RomanNumberAtom(400, "CD"));
    atoms.Add(new RomanNumberAtom(100, "C"));
    atoms.Add(new RomanNumberAtom(90, "XC"));
    atoms.Add(new RomanNumberAtom(50, "L"));
    atoms.Add(new RomanNumberAtom(40, "XL"));
    atoms.Add(new RomanNumberAtom(10, "X"));
    atoms.Add(new RomanNumberAtom(9, "IX"));
    atoms.Add(new RomanNumberAtom(5, "V"));
    atoms.Add(new RomanNumberAtom(4, "IV"));
    atoms.Add(new RomanNumberAtom(1, "I"));
  }
  public string Convert(int value) {
    if (value <= 0) return string.Empty;
    if (value >= 5000) return string.Empty;
    string result = string.Empty;
    for (int i = 0; i < atoms.Count; i++) {
      while (value >= atoms[i].IntValue) {
        result = result + atoms[i].RomanValue;
        value -= atoms[i].IntValue;
      }
    }
    return result;
  }
}
```

Using the listings you can trace the execution of the callback:

1. Clicking the button calls the `Click` event handler; this executes the callback's `PerformCallback` method.

2. This sends the callback request to the server, which is routed to the `Callback` event handler.

3. This converts the number passed to its Roman representation and sets the callback's `Result` argument.

4. This is received by the callback control through the `CallBackComplete` event, which then updates the label to show the result.

Figure 11-1 shows the application in action. The whole process is asynchronous in that the client does not block or wait for the response.

Figure 11-1: The Convert to Roman Numerals application in action.

Using the ASPxCallbackPanel Control

As I intimated at the start, the callback control may be all that you will need, but it does come with some coding required. A better solution in many cases may be the ASPxCallbackPanel control. For this example you are going to use it to create a slideshow-type application.

The slideshow application will have two modes: manual and automatic. In automatic mode, a timer will cause the slideshow of images to advance, picture by picture, once every 5 seconds. In manual mode, the viewer is in charge and uses buttons to show the next (and previous) image, a play button to switch to automatic mode, and a stop button to switch to manual mode. Note that the next/previous buttons will also switch to manual mode.

Regardless of whether the application is in manual or automatic mode, the images are changed using a callback. The server holds all image URLs (presumably in some kind of database), and the client only has the one image to display. In particular, using a callback means that the slideshow will not cause a refresh of the page.

The important thing to grasp about the ASPxCallbackPanel is that it is a non-visual container and every control within that container participates in the callback. Therefore, you want to ensure as much as possible that only controls that need to participate in the callback (because they're going to be updated in some fashion by the callback event handler at the server) are present in the callback panel.

Here are a couple of hints that helped me when I was learning about callbacks and callback panels and was apt to get confused. Just because a control may have explicit client-side behavior (using manually coded JavaScript) doesn't mean that it has to be on a callback panel. Just because a control is calling a method on another control in a callback panel doesn't mean the caller control has to be in that callback panel. The callback panel uses JavaScript under the hood, certainly, but it's only "special" because it does callbacks to the server. That's all.

First, set up the visual aspects of the slideshow application. Drop an ASPxCallbackPanel on the form, then a round panel inside of that, and an ASPxImage inside of that. This means, in effect, that only two controls will be updated by your callbacks: the image and the round panel in which it resides. Everything else you add to your application is not updated by callbacks. Listing 11-6 shows the source for this initial arrangement and the properties you should set.

Listing 11-6: The updatable part of the application as ASPX code.

```
<dxcp:ASPxCallbackPanel ID="callbackPanel" runat="server"
  Width="768px" ClientInstanceName="callbackPanel"
  OnCallback="callbackPanel_Callback" HideContentOnCallback="False"
  ShowLoadingPanel="False">
<PanelCollection>
   <dxp:PanelContent ID="PanelContent1" runat="server">
       <dxrp:ASPxRoundPanel ID="RoundPanel" runat="server"
          Width="768px" HeaderText="Slideshow" ContentHeight="512px">
          <PanelCollection>
            <dxp:PanelContent runat="server">
              <dxe:ASPxImage ID="ImageViewer" runat="server">
              </dxe:ASPxImage>
            </dxp:PanelContent>
          </PanelCollection>
       </dxrp:ASPxRoundPanel>
    </dxp:PanelConten7t>
  </PanelCollection>
</dxcp:ASPxCallbackPanel>
```

In particular, note that I've disabled the HideContentOnCallback and ShowLoadingPanel properties: Doing so reduces the amount of flicker in the application and ensures a smoother user experience.

The next thing to do is to add the four buttons. Drop them all underneath the callback panel (not inside it) and then switch to the Source display to change their properties as shown in Listing 11-7. I've set each button but the last in its own <div> so that I could then float those divs left. This approach ensures that all the buttons are in a horizontal line rather than a column (which is the default layout). I also embedded them all inside another <div> called "buttons" to help in further styling the application, if needed.

Listing 11-7: Adding the buttons to the slideshow application.

```
<div id="buttons">
  <div style="float: left;">
    <dxe:ASPxButton ID="Prev" runat="server"
      Text="Previous" ClientInstanceName="prevButton"
      EnableClientSideAPI="True" AutoPostBack="False">
      <ClientSideEvents
        Click="function(s, e) {slideshowEngine.movePrev();}" />
    </dxe:ASPxButton>
  </div>
  <div style="float: left;">
    <dxe:ASPxButton ID="Play" runat="server"
      Text="Play" ClientInstanceName="playButton"
      EnableClientSideAPI="True" AutoPostBack="False">
      <ClientSideEvents
        Click="function(s, e) {slideshowEngine.play();}" />
    </dxe:ASPxButton>
  </div>
```

Continued

515

Listing 11-7: Adding the buttons to the slideshow application. *(continued)*

```
        <div style="float: left;">
          <dxe:ASPxButton ID="Stop" runat="server"
            Text="Stop" ClientInstanceName="stopButton"
            EnableClientSideAPI="True" AutoPostBack="False">
            <ClientSideEvents
              Click="function(s, e) {slideshowEngine.stop();}" />
          </dxe:ASPxButton>
        </div>
        <dxe:ASPxButton ID="Next" runat="server"
          Text="Next" ClientInstanceName="nextButton"
          EnableClientSideAPI="True" AutoPostBack="False">
          <ClientSideEvents
            Click="function(s, e) {slideshowEngine.buttonMoveNext();}" />
        </dxe:ASPxButton>
      </div>
```

Notice in Listing 11-7 that all the buttons have their client-side API activated and each has a client-side `Click` event handler. Each of the handlers calls a method on some JavaScript object called `slideshowEngine`. You are going to meet `slideshowEngine` in a moment, but right now notice that this is an example of reducing the global identifier pollution that JavaScript is known for. Already in this application you have a whole slew of global names (each control will have a global name, some defined by you, some automatically by the run time), so make sure you add the minimum yourself to avoid name clashes.

Finally, you can add the timer: Drop an ASPxTimer onto the form and set its properties as shown in Listing 11-8. In particular note that the timer is not enabled to begin with, but instead is enabled via its `Init` event handler. This approach enables you to do some extra initialization work in the `slideshowEngine` object.

Listing 11-8: Adding the timer to the slideshow application.

```
<dxt:ASPxTimer ID="ASPxTimer1" runat="server"
  ClientInstanceName="slideshowTimer" Interval="5000"
  Enabled="False">
  <ClientSideEvents
    Tick="function(s, e) {slideshowEngine.tickMoveNext();}"
    Init="function(s, e) {slideshowEngine.play();}"
  />
</dxt:ASPxTimer>
```

The next thing to do is to create the `slideshow.js` file as shown in Listing 11-9. This file contains the code for the `slideshowEngine` object.

Listing 11-9: The definition of the slideshowEngine object.

```
var slideshowEngine = function() {
    var timerOn = false;

    var setTimer = function(enable) {
```

```
            slideshowTimer.SetEnabled(enable);
            timerOn = enable;
        };

        var moveNext = function() {
            if (!callbackPanel.InCallback()) {
                callbackPanel.PerformCallback("next");
            }
        };

        var movePrior = function() {
            setTimer(false);
            if (!callbackPanel.InCallback()) {
                callbackPanel.PerformCallback("prev");
            }
        };

        return {
            tickMoveNext: function() {
                if (timerOn) {
                    moveNext();
                }
            },
            buttonMoveNext: function() {
                setTimer(false);
                moveNext();
            },
            movePrev: function() {
                movePrior();
            },
            play: function() {
                setTimer(true);
            },
            stop: function() {
                setTimer(false);
            }
        };
    } ();
```

The `slideshowEngine` object has been defined as the return value from an anonymous function call (note the calling parentheses on the last line). Doing so enables you to define private members of the object through the closure to help in encapsulation and data hiding.

This style of defining a one-off object with a well-defined public interface and hidden methods doing the work is extremely prevalent in professional JavaScript, so I want to take some time to make sure you understand the code.

Look at the `return` statement first of all. It returns an anonymous object, which is defined by the braces. The object has five methods called `tickMoveNext`, `buttonMoveNext`, `movePrev`, `stop`, and `play`, all methods that you're going to be calling in the event handlers you've already written.

The code *above* the return statement defines a single field (`timerOn`) and three methods (`setTimer`, `moveNext`, and `movePrior`). The important thing to realize is that these members are local variables to the outer, anonymous function. They are visible *only* to other functions defined within that outer function, including the methods of the object returned by the `return` statement. They are not visible outside. They form part of the *closure* of the function call that sets up the `slideshowEngine` object — that is, they live on in the object well after the function has executed. They are, in effect, private members of the returned object. Reading `slideshowEngine.timerOn` or calling `slideshowEngine.moveNext`, for example, results in an error.

So, as an example, looking at the `tickMoveNext` method, you see that it checks the value of the private `timerOn` field, and if true, calls the private `moveNext` method to advance to the next image. This function checks to see if the callback panel (a global object) is already in a callback, and if not, asks it to perform one. The other public methods function in a similar manner by accessing the private members.

Finally, it's time to look at the server-side code. You create a `Callback` event handler for the callback panel, as shown in Listing 11-10.

Listing 11-10: The Callback event handler for the callback panel.

```
private void UpdatePanelContents(int photoId) {
  ImageViewer.ImageUrl = photos[photoId];
  RoundPanel.HeaderText =
    String.Format("Slideshow: {0} of {1} images", photoId + 1, photos.Length);
  Session["photoId"] = photoId;
}
protected void callbackPanel_Callback(
    object sender, CallbackEventArgsBase e) {
  int photoId = (int)Session["photoId"];
  switch (e.Parameter) {
    case "prev":
      if (photoId == 0)
        photoId = photos.Length - 1;
      else
        photoId--;
      break;
    case "next":
      photoId++;
      if (photoId >= photos.Length)
        photoId = 0;
      break;
    default:
      photoId = 0;
      break;
  }
  UpdatePanelContents(photoId);
}
```

You make use of a small `Session` object to hold the current photo number. You read that value and then calculate the next photo number. Finally you call the `UpdatePanelContents` method to update the controls on the callback panel (and the save the current number in the `Session` object again). The round panel's header is changed to show which photo you are looking at in the list of photos, and the image control is updated with the URL.

The photos themselves are added to an images folder on the Web site and the photos array is merely a hard-coded list of those photo URLs. You could easily use something like an XML file (to also include captions for each photo, for example) rather than hard-coding the photo URLs, and doing so would make the whole application more flexible.

Finally, you should make sure that you show the first photo when the application is first run (or is refreshed). Listing 11-11 shows the page load method to do that.

Listing 11-11: Making sure you show a photo when the application is first run.

```
protected void Page_Load(object sender, EventArgs e) {
  if (!IsCallback && !IsPostBack) {
    UpdatePanelContents(0);
  }
}
```

Figure 11-2: The slideshow application in action.

Figure 11-2 shows the application in action.

Displaying Multimedia Content

The DevExpress ASPxperience library of controls also includes a control for displaying multimedia content. Because by the term *multimedia* we generally mean video or audio or both, and because these media types usually involve some kind of asynchronous streaming of data, I want to close off this chapter on asynchronous programming by looking at the functionality provided by the ASPxObjectContainer that enables you to handle just that sort of multimedia content.

The ASPxObjectContainer hosts media objects. In this case, a media object is one of four possible types: a Flash object (that is, an Adobe Flash SWF file, and not some object that happens to be rather ostentatious), an image, a video clip, or an audio clip. As you've just seen in the previous section you have an ASPxImage control at your disposal to cover dealing with images, — but the other objects are the ones that really enable you to provide multimedia capabilities in your Web application.

As an example of how to harness these multimedia capabilities, I want you to take a look at a simple Flash SWF video player to play a video from YouTube.

Creating a YouTube Player

Drop an ASPxObjectContainer onto a new Web form. Switch to Source mode. In a browser, find the video you want to play on YouTube. Select and copy the Embed code from the textbox to the right of the video. Paste it into your source code after the closing HTML tag. This is only temporary — you'll be deleting it in a moment — but it contains some pertinent information you can use.

Go to the Properties page for the object container. Set the ObjectUrl to the value of the src attribute of the embed element of the pasted code. Set the Height and Width properties to the values of the equivalently named attributes of the same pasted embed element. Now delete the pasted code; you no longer need it.

You now need to access the specific properties for the Flash object itself. To do this, set the ObjectProperties property to Flash. As soon as you do, the property becomes an object and you can expand it to show the specific properties that are associated with playing Flash media. Set Loop to false; otherwise, the Flash video will loop once it reaches the final frame. Set Play to false so the video doesn't start playing immediately when the Web page is displayed in the browser.

Listing 11-12 shows the source code for an ASPX page to show a DevExpress video on the Free Silverlight Grid.

Listing 11-12: Basic configuration of an object container to show a Flash video.

```
<dxoc:ASPxObjectContainer ID="ASPxObjectContainer1" runat="server"
  ClientInstanceName="flashVideo"
  Height="344px" Width="425px" ObjectType="Flash"
  ObjectUrl="http://www.youtube.com/v/AuNTLDzH9ds">
  <ObjectProperties Play="False" Loop="False" />
</dxoc:ASPxObjectContainer>
```

At this point you can just run the application; there's no server-side code to write because all the processing is performed by the browser.

Controlling the YouTube Player

The YouTube player comes with a full API (search Google for *YouTube JavaScript Player API*). You can use the API to display the Flash SWF video in a "chromeless" player, that is, one that does not show controls for the user to play the video. In this example you are going to add a couple of buttons to start playing the video and to stop it.

Create a new Web form and drop an ASPxObjectContainer on it. Set the `ObjectUrl` to "`http://www`
`.youtube.com/apiplayer?enablejsapi=1`". Note that you're not specifying the video to play and that you're adding the parameter `"enablejsapi=1"` to enable the control of the player through JavaScript. Set the ID of the control to `"youTubeContainer"`, and set the width and height to 425px and 344px, respectively (the normal size for YouTube videos).

To interact with a chromeless YouTube player, you need to include the SWFObject JavaScript file in your solution. This is open source code that helps with the manipulation of SWF objects client-side, and the chromeless YouTube player needs it to act as the interface between the Flash object and JavaScript.

To find it, go to `http://swfobject.googlecode.com/p/swfobject`. On the right side of the page, you'll see a downloads panel. Download the latest zip file (at the time of writing this is `swfobject_2_`
`2.zip`). This zip file will contain two copies of the JavaScript that instantiates the SWFObject — a minimized one (that is, all spaces removed and identifiers renamed to smaller names) and the full one.

Add the minimized `.js` file to your solution, and then drag that item from the Solution Explorer to your ASPX file to add a script element referencing it. I put it in the head element.

Because you must provide the linkage between the object container and JavaScript, you should initialize it yourself. Add an `Init` client-side event handler to the object container as shown in Listing 11-13. Note it references a function you haven't written yet.

Listing 11-13: The code defining the ASPxObjectContainer instance.

```
<div>
  <dxoc:ASPxObjectContainer ID="youTubeContainer" runat="server"
    Height="344px" Width="425px" ObjectType="Flash"
    ObjectUrl="http://www.youtube.com/apiplayer?enablejsapi=1">
    <ClientSideEvents
      Init="function(s, e) { initObjectContainer(s, e); }" />
  </dxoc:ASPxObjectContainer>
</div>
```

As you did in the slideshow application earlier in the chapter, you add four buttons underneath the object container: Load, Play, Pause, and Stop. With the use of left-floating `div`s, you can arrange them in a row. Listing 11-14 shows the code. Note this time that you're going to be making use of an object called `playerEngine`.

Listing 11-14: The four player control buttons.

```
<div style="float: left;">
  <dxe:ASPxButton ID="LoadButton" runat="server"
    AutoPostBack="False" Text="Load"
    EnableClientSideAPI="True" ClientInstanceName="loadButton">
    <ClientSideEvents
      Click="function(s, e) {
        playerEngine.load(&quot;AuNTLDzH9ds&quot;); }" />
  </dxe:ASPxButton>
</div>
<div style="float: left;">
  <dxe:ASPxButton ID="PlayButton" runat="server"
    AutoPostBack="False" Text="Play"
    EnableClientSideAPI="True" ClientInstanceName="playButton">
    <ClientSideEvents Click="function(s, e) { playerEngine.play(); }" />
  </dxe:ASPxButton>
</div>
<div style="float: left;">
  <dxe:ASPxButton ID="PauseButton" runat="server"
    AutoPostBack="False" Text="Pause"
    EnableClientSideAPI="True" ClientInstanceName="pauseButton">
    <ClientSideEvents Click="function(s, e) { playerEngine.pause(); }" />
  </dxe:ASPxButton>
</div>
<dxe:ASPxButton ID="StopButton" runat="server"
  AutoPostBack="False" Text="Stop"
  EnableClientSideAPI="True" ClientInstanceName="stopButton">
  <ClientSideEvents Click="function(s, e) { playerEngine.stop(); }" />
</dxe:ASPxButton>
```

Finally, add a new JavaScript file to the solution called `playerEngine.js`. Drag that file from the Solution Explorer to the ASPX file to create a script element, this time putting it just above the ending body tag. That's it for the ASPX file.

Now for the fun stuff: the JavaScript code. Open up the new `playerEngine.js` file. The first thing to write is the `initObjectContainer` method, as shown in Listing 11-15. I've chosen to go for the bare minimum here: For instance, if your user doesn't have Flash installed in their browser, they're not going to get prompted to download and install it (for more information on the `embedSWF` method and how to specify the code that prompts the user to install Flash and where to get it, you should peruse the documentation on the Google Code site).

Listing 11-15: Initializing the object container, client-side.

```
var initObjectContainer = function(s, e) {
  var params = { allowScriptAccess: "always" };
  swfobject.embedSWF("http://www.youtube.com/apiplayer?enablejsapi=1",
```

```
    "youTubeContainer", 425, 344, "8.0",
    null, null, params);
};
```

Note that you repeat the URL for the chromeless player, and you define 8.0 as the minimum version of Flash you'll accept (this was the first version that allowed for the interaction of the Flash object and JavaScript, and so it is the earliest version you can accept).

What happens in this code is that the chromeless player gets loaded into the youTubeContainer object, and, once the player is ready to be used, the Flash object calls a function called onYouTubePlayerReady (if one is found) to indicate that videos can be loaded and played. (I have no idea why it was done this way rather than, say, registering an event handler or specifying a callback function in the embedSWF call. Unfortunately, no such luck; you have to write a global function.)

The function is shown in Listing 11-16, and it initializes the playerEngine object.

Listing 11-16: The onYouTubePlayerReady function.

```
var onYouTubePlayerReady = function() {
  playerEngine.init(document.getElementById("youTubeContainer"));
};
```

And now it's time to write the playerEngine object itself. For this kind of singleton, it's best to write it as an anonymous function that is immediately executed and that returns an object with the required methods. Listing 11-17 shows the starting point for the object.

Listing 11-17: The starting point for the playerEngine object.

```
var playerEngine = function() {

  // private code

  return {
    init: function(player) {
      init(player);
    },
    load: function(id) {
      loadVideo(id);
    },
    play: function() {
      playVideo();
    },
    pause: function() {
      pauseVideo();
    },
    stop: function() {
      stopVideo();
    }
  };
} ();
```

All you've done here is to define the public interface of the `playerEngine` object as the `return` object from a still-to-be-filled-in anonymous function. There are five methods to initialize the object, and load, play, pause, and stop a video, and all of them call some inner private functions that have to be written. The `load` method takes an `id` parameter: the id of the video to play (if you look back at the client-side `Click` event handler for the Load button in Listing 11-14, you'll see the `id` hard-coded).

Now it's time for another hack from the YouTube player. The player signals state changes through an event. Instead of providing a reference to a function as with normal JavaScript, you have to specify the *name* of the function as a string. This is passed to the JavaScript `eval` function in order to signal a state change. Because of this situation, the function to be called must be public; in particular, you can't use a private function inside of `playerEngine`. I cheated by adding another public method to the `playerEngine` object called `setState` (see Listing 11-18), but this is obviously breaking the encapsulation of the object. The `setState` method is added just below the `playerEngine` function's `return` statement, above the declaration of the `init` method.

Listing 11-18: The hacky setState method.

```
return {
  setState: function(newState) {
    if (newState !== BUFFERING) {
      state = newState;
    }
  },
  init: function(player) {
  ...as before...
```

Note that you get notified of buffering state changes. For your purposes, knowing about these is not that important, so you ignore them.

Now that you have the state change events taken care of, you can write the private methods of the `playerEngine` object. Listing 11-19 has the details, and this code should be inserted into Listing 11-18 to replace the private code comment. Note that you're enabling/disabling the buttons depending on which state the player is in (so, for example, if there is no video loaded, the only button enabled is the Load button). JavaScript does not have constants, so I've declared the various states as "read-only" variables and uppercased them as a warning for the next developer.

Listing 11-19: The private behavior of the playerEngine object.

```
var
  UNSTARTED = -1,
  ENDED = 0,
  PLAYING = 1,
  PAUSED = 2,
  BUFFERING = 3,
```

```
VIDEOCUED = 5,

state = 99,
youtubePlayer,

init = function(player) {
  youtubePlayer = player;
  youtubePlayer.addEventListener(
    "onStateChange", "playerEngine.setState");
  loadButton.SetEnabled(true);
  playButton.SetEnabled(false);
  pauseButton.SetEnabled(false);
  stopButton.SetEnabled(false);
},

loadVideo = function(id) {
  if (state === UNSTARTED || state === ENDED) {
    youtubePlayer.cueVideoById(id);
    loadButton.SetEnabled(false);
    playButton.SetEnabled(true);
  }
},

playVideo = function() {
  if (state === VIDEOCUED || state === PAUSED) {
    youtubePlayer.playVideo();
    playButton.SetEnabled(false);
    pauseButton.SetEnabled(true);
    stopButton.SetEnabled(true);
  }
},

pauseVideo = function() {
  if (state === PLAYING) {
    youtubePlayer.pauseVideo();
    playButton.SetEnabled(true);
    pauseButton.SetEnabled(false);
    stopButton.SetEnabled(false);
  }
},

stopVideo = function() {
  youtubePlayer.stopVideo();
  playButton.SetEnabled(true);
  pauseButton.SetEnabled(false);
};
```

The application is now ready to be run. The initial display is of a chromeless YouTube player with only the Load button enabled. Clicking this button loads the video, disables the Load button, and enables the Play button. Clicking Play starts the video.

Listing 11-20 shows the completed `playerEngine.js` file, showing the full definition of the playerEngine object as well as the two functions needed by the SWFObject.

Listing 11-20: The full playerEngine code for the chromeless YouTube player application.

```
var playerEngine = function() {

  var
    UNSTARTED = -1,
    ENDED = 0,
    PLAYING = 1,
    PAUSED = 2,
    BUFFERING = 3,
    VIDEOCUED = 5,

    state = 99,
    youtubePlayer,

    init = function(player) {
      youtubePlayer = player;
      youtubePlayer.addEventListener(
        "onStateChange", "playerEngine.setState");
      loadButton.SetEnabled(true);
      playButton.SetEnabled(false);
      pauseButton.SetEnabled(false);
      stopButton.SetEnabled(false);
    },

    loadVideo = function(id) {
      if (state === UNSTARTED || state === ENDED) {
        youtubePlayer.cueVideoById(id);
        loadButton.SetEnabled(false);
        playButton.SetEnabled(true);
      }
    },

    playVideo = function() {
      if (state === VIDEOCUED || state === PAUSED) {
        youtubePlayer.playVideo();
        playButton.SetEnabled(false);
        pauseButton.SetEnabled(true);
        stopButton.SetEnabled(true);
      }
    },

    pauseVideo = function() {
      if (state === PLAYING) {
        youtubePlayer.pauseVideo();
```

```
          playButton.SetEnabled(true);
          pauseButton.SetEnabled(false);
          stopButton.SetEnabled(false);
      }
    },

    stopVideo = function() {
      youtubePlayer.stopVideo();
      playButton.SetEnabled(true);
      pauseButton.SetEnabled(false);
    };


  return {
    setState: function(newState) {
      if (newState !== BUFFERING) {
        state = newState;
      }
    },
    init: function(player) {
      init(player);
    },
    load: function(id) {
      loadVideo(id);
    },
    play: function() {
      playVideo();
    },
    pause: function() {
      pauseVideo();
    },
    stop: function() {
      stopVideo();
    }
  };
} ();

var onYouTubePlayerReady = function() {
  playerEngine.init(document.getElementById("youTubeContainer"));
};


var initObjectContainer = function(s, e) {
  var params = { allowScriptAccess: "always" };
  swfobject.embedSWF("http://www.youtube.com/apiplayer?enablejsapi=1",
                     "youTubeContainer", 425, 344, "8.0",
                     null, null, params);
};
```

Listing 11-21 presents the ASPX file, showing the proper placement of the script elements introducing the two .js files.

Listing 11-21: The ASPX code for the chromeless YouTube player application.

```
<html xmlns="http://www.w3.org/1999/xhtml">
<head runat="server">
  <title></title>

  <script src="swfobject.js" type="text/javascript"></script>

</head>
<body>
  <form id="form1" runat="server">
  <div>
    <dxoc:ASPxObjectContainer ID="youTubeContainer" runat="server"
      Height="344px" Width="425px" ObjectType="Flash"
      ObjectUrl="http://www.youtube.com/apiplayer?enablejsapi=1">
      <ClientSideEvents
        Init="function(s, e) { initObjectContainer(s, e); }" />
    </dxoc:ASPxObjectContainer>
  </div>
  <div style="float: left;">
    <dxe:ASPxButton ID="LoadButton" runat="server"
      AutoPostBack="False" Text="Load"
      EnableClientSideAPI="True" ClientInstanceName="loadButton">
      <ClientSideEvents
        Click="function(s, e) {
          playerEngine.load(&quot;AuNTLDzH9ds&quot;); }" />
    </dxe:ASPxButton>
  </div>
  <div style="float: left;">
    <dxe:ASPxButton ID="PlayButton" runat="server"
      AutoPostBack="False" Text="Play"
      EnableClientSideAPI="True" ClientInstanceName="playButton">
      <ClientSideEvents Click="function(s, e) { playerEngine.play(); }" />
    </dxe:ASPxButton>
  </div>
  <div style="float: left;">
    <dxe:ASPxButton ID="PauseButton" runat="server"
      AutoPostBack="False" Text="Pause"
      EnableClientSideAPI="True" ClientInstanceName="pauseButton">
      <ClientSideEvents Click="function(s, e) { playerEngine.pause(); }" />
    </dxe:ASPxButton>
  </div>
  <dxe:ASPxButton ID="StopButton" runat="server"
    AutoPostBack="False" Text="Stop"
    EnableClientSideAPI="True" ClientInstanceName="stopButton">
    <ClientSideEvents Click="function(s, e) { playerEngine.stop(); }" />
  </dxe:ASPxButton>
  </form>

  <script src="playerEngine.js" type="text/javascript"></script>

</body>
</html>
```

Playing FLV Files

Rather than showing videos from YouTube or similar Web sites, you may decide that you want to show FLV (Flash Video) files that you've created and that are stored on your own Web site. This is slightly more involved in that you have to locate and download an FLV player first. Several are on the market, some commercial and paid for, some open source. The player will itself be an SWF file (Shockwave Flash object). For the purposes of this discussion, I assume that the player is called `player.swf` and that you have a video called `video.flv`, both stored in the Web site's/videos folder. Here's what you do:

1. Start off with a new Web form and drop an ASPxObjectContainer onto it.

2. Set the `ObjectUrl` property to the name of your player, videos/player.swf.

3. Set the `ObjectProperties` to `Flash`, and expand its properties.

4. You need to add some Flash variables. It is the player's documentation that will describe what needs to be added in order to define the file to play. For the freeware JW FLV Player that I used, the `"file"` variable needs to be set to the URL of the FLV file (and relative URLs start from the folder containing the player).

   The Flash variables are entered in the "name=value" format in the `FlashVars` property in the `ObjectProperties` object. For this example, I set the `FlashVars` property to `"file=video.flv"`. If you need to add more Flash variables, they are separated from each other by the `&` character.

5. At this point you can run the application and play the video.

Listing 11.22 shows what the object container looks in the ASPX file.

Listing 11-22: The ASPX code for the object container to show an FLV file.

```
<dxoc:ASPxObjectContainer ID="ASPxObjectContainer1" runat="server"
  ObjectType="Flash" ObjectUrl="videos/player.swf">
  <ObjectProperties FlashVars="file=video.flv" />
</dxoc:ASPxObjectContainer>
```

Summary

This chapter has shown you some of the variety of methods available with DevExpress' controls to provide a rich user experience. We've seen the two main callback controls, ASPxCallback and ASPxCallbackPanel, and why you would use one over the other for given situations.

Along the way we also took a quick look at the timer object ASPxTimer. Although we discussed the timer with respect to fetching images at regular intervals from the server, there are obviously many things that can be done with a timer and JavaScript in the browser without having to communicate with the server.

Finally we looked at a few examples of playing multimedia files in your application, all the way to embedding a chromeless YouTube player.

## 12

Adding Charts and Graphs to Your Applications

Writing business applications will (or maybe that should be *should*), at some point, involve the presentation of data. The data being displayed may be shown in tabular form (such as in the earlier chapters of this book), but oftentimes it's better to show it in some visual illustrative form, following the adage that a picture is worth a thousand words.

One of the simplest ways of showing a picture of your data is to use a graph or chart. Your end users will be able to see at a glance the outliers of your data or any trends that the raw data may be hiding, get an appreciation for the rate of change of the values of the data over time, and perhaps even analyze different views of the data to understand what is important and what is not. These immediate visual insights are more difficult to attain if the data is presented in a list or grid.

DevExpress's charting facilities are provided in the XtraCharts product. Unlike many other products, XtraCharts provides support for both ASP.NET and Windows Forms applications, although this chapter primarily discusses the Web side of the product.

XtraCharts provides the usual gamut of chart types, from the standard two-dimensional ones to the more visually appealing three-dimensional charts. Examples of the types of charts that are available include bar charts, line charts, area views, radar/polar views, pies and doughnuts, and financial type charts.

The Vernacular

Before starting on how to use charts within your application, I should introduce the charting terms I will be using. This will help you both in reading this chapter, but also in searching the documentation provided with the product.

In Figure 12-1 you can see a somewhat stylized representation of a 2-D chart. Nevertheless, it shows the more important attributes and parts of a chart. The graphical representation of the chart is known as the diagram. Also part of the diagram are the axes: There will be at least one x-axis (the horizontal one) and one y-axis (the vertical one). A chart may, however, have secondary axes to provide other variable and data points.

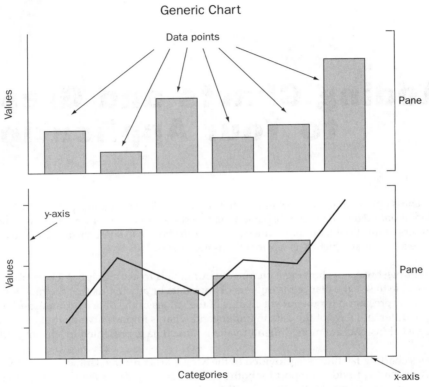

Figure 12-1: An illustration of a generic chart.

An axis will generally have tick marks to show the major/minor values, as well as labels and titles. Some of these have to be explicitly made visible.

The x-axis is sometimes known as the arguments axis, and the y-axis is the values axis. The arguments of the data points that make up the chart are generally separate values or categories (as compared to a scientific graph where their values form a continuous variable).

The diagram may also show more than one pane, that is, a different chart that shares one of the primary axes with the main chart and that is displayed on top or alongside. And along with the diagram you will find a chart title and the legend for each series of data points.

Talking of data points, the data point is the fundamental element of the chart and represents an individual item of data that is plotted. It has two main attributes: the argument (that is, where it appears on the x-axis) and in general, at most one value (the position on the y-axis). (Some data points require more than one value. For example, a data point for a financial stock chart requires four values: the open, close, high, and low prices.)

A set of data points is called a *data series*. The *data series* is plotted in a chart view and it is the view that defines what kind of chart is to be displayed: bar, line, area, pie, and so on. All charts have at least one data series defined for it (otherwise there would be no chart to see). A chart could display several data series if need be, and each series could have a different view. In general, for this situation to work well, all of the data series would have to share the same arguments.

Creating a Chart

From the discussion of the various parts of a chart you just saw, creating a chart seems to involve a lot of configuration. True enough, which is why XtraCharts comes with a setup wizard that helps you create a standard-looking chart very easily.

However, to obtain the maximum flexibility for a chart, you should try to understand the various components and how to set their properties using the property inspector, as well as how to set up the data series for a chart.

As an example, try writing a small application that displays several charts. The chart will be selected by the user from a list and the chart will be displayed in a page control (ASPxPageControl). During the callback you will create the chart from scratch (that is, you won't pre-design it using the designer) and populate the data series for the chart.

One of the reasons for using the page control is that you can configure it in such a way that only the initially displayed page needs to be created. All the other pages — the initially invisible ones — can be created at runtime using a callback, and, once created, they are then available at the client thereafter without another round-trip to the server. So, for "static" pages that only need to be created when the users decide that they want to see them, the page control is ideal.

To create this application, perform the following steps:

1. First create a couple of side-by-side `div`s to hold the content as shown in Listing 12-1. The left-hand `<div>` holds the list box, and the right-hand one holds the page control with the charts.

Listing 12-1: The basic background for the "on-demand" chart application.

```
<div id="list" style="float: left;margin-right:20px;">
  <!-- content -->
</div>
<div id="chart">
  <!-- content -->
</div>
```

2. I decided to use a couple of ASPxRoundPanels to hold the content: they look nice and professional. Drop one on each content div. Give the left one a header of "Chart types", and the right one a header of "Chart display".

3. Drop an ASPxListBox on the left round panel. Set the ID and ClientInstanceName properties to "ChartTypes", and set EnableClientSideAPI to true. Give it three items: "Bar Chart", "Line Chart", and "Pie Chart".

4. Drop an ASPxPageControl in the right round panel. Set the ID and ClientInstanceName properties to "ChartPageControl", and ensure that EnableCallbacks and EnableClientSideAPI are both true. Create three pages in the page control to go along with the three items in the list box. Call them "BarPage", "LinePage", and "PiePage".

5. Now drop a WebChartControl onto each of these three pages. Size them to taste, and name them "BarWebChart", "LineWebChart", and "PieWebChart".

6. Now that you have set up the pages in the page control, turn off the tabs (set the ShowTabs property for the control to false).

Once all the content has been set up, the form should look like Figure 12-2.

Figure 12-2: The layout of the "on-demand" chart application.

You have one final step to make here and that is to write the JavaScript that will cause the page control to issue the callback needed to create the hidden pages.

Click the Smart tag for the list box, select Client-Side Events, and then, in the dialog box that's presented, click ValueChanged. This defines the event handler that will fire when the selected item in the list box is changed. Enter the JavaScript shown in Listing 12-2.

Listing 12-2: The client-side event handler for the list box.

```
function(s, e) {
  var item = s.GetSelectedIndex();
  var tab = ChartPageControl.GetTab(item);
  ChartPageControl.SetActiveTab(tab);
}
```

The s parameter is the sender of the event, and e is the event arguments. So you get the index of the item that the user selected, you use that to get the tab object from the page control (because there's a one-to-one correspondence between the indexes of the items in the list box and the pages in the page control), and then you get the page control to set that tab as the active one. If the page control has already downloaded that page it'll get displayed, otherwise a callback is triggered to the server to get that page. Look at that page load code now with Listing 12-3.

Listing 12-3: Loading the page for the on-demand chart application.

```
protected void Page_Load(object sender, EventArgs e) {
  LoadData();

  if (IsCallback) {
    int item = ChartTypes.SelectedIndex;
    switch (item) {
      case 0:
        CreateBarChart();
        break;
      case 1:
        CreateLineChart();
        break;
      case 2:
        CreatePieChart();
        break;
      default:
        CreateBarChart();
        ChartTypes.SelectedIndex = 0;
        break;
    }
  }
  else {
    CreateBarChart();
    ChartTypes.SelectedIndex = 0;
  }
}
```

First things first: You need to load the data that you'll be using in the charts. After that you test to see if this is a callback. If so, you get the selected index of the item from the list box, and, depending on its value, you create the bar chart, the line chart, or the pie chart. If the index is out of range — not quite sure how, so this is a sanity check — you just create the bar chart and set the selected index to that of the bar chart option.

If it's not a callback at all, so it's either the first time the form is displayed or the user refreshed, you just create the bar chart and make sure the list box has that item selected.

535

For the `LoadData` method, I decided to use some skier visit statistics from the Colorado Ski Country USA Web site. The data shows the number of "skier days" for a set of Colorado ski resorts over several seasons. Because this chapter is more about charting than data access, I hard-coded the data I was going to use.

First I declared a couple of classes to hold the data, as shown in Listing 12-4.

Listing 12-4: The classes needed to hold the ski visitor data.

```
public class SkierDayCount {
  private string season;
  private int count;
  public SkierDayCount(string season, int count) {
    this.count = count;
    this.season = season;
  }
  public SeriesPoint AsSeriesPoint() {
    return new SeriesPoint(season, count);
  }
}

public class ResortData {
  private string name;
  private List<SkierDayCount> skierDayCounts = new List<SkierDayCount>();
  public ResortData(string name) {
    this.name = name;
  }
  public string Name {
    get { return name; }
    set { name = value; }
  }
  public List<SkierDayCount> SkierDayCounts {
    get { return skierDayCounts; }
    set { skierDayCounts = value; }
  }
}
```

Then, as Listing 12-5 shows, all the `LoadData` method has to do is to create a set of resorts and their data.

Listing 12-5: Loading the ski visitor data.

```
List<ResortData> resorts = new List<ResortData>();

private void LoadData() {
  ResortData resort = new ResortData("Copper Mountain");
  resort.SkierDayCounts.Add(
    new SkierDayCount("2004-05", 1046242));
  resort.SkierDayCounts.Add(
    new SkierDayCount("2005-06", 1132021));
  resort.SkierDayCounts.Add(
    new SkierDayCount("2006-07", 1046959));
```

```
      resort.SkierDayCounts.Add(
        new SkierDayCount("2007-08", 934870));
      resorts.Add(resort);

      resort = new ResortData("Breckenridge");
      resort.SkierDayCounts.Add(
        new SkierDayCount("2004-05", 1470961));
      resort.SkierDayCounts.Add(
        new SkierDayCount("2005-06", 1619043));
      resort.SkierDayCounts.Add(
        new SkierDayCount("2006-07", 1650321));
      resort.SkierDayCounts.Add(
        new SkierDayCount("2007-08", 1630106));
      resorts.Add(resort);

      resort = new ResortData("Keystone");
      resort.SkierDayCounts.Add(
        new SkierDayCount("2004-05", 1021069));
      resort.SkierDayCounts.Add(
        new SkierDayCount("2005-06", 1093939));
      resort.SkierDayCounts.Add(
        new SkierDayCount("2006-07", 1170710));
      resort.SkierDayCounts.Add(
        new SkierDayCount("2007-08", 1129608));
      resorts.Add(resort);
    }
```

Once you have the data loaded, you can start writing the code to create the charts. As discussed before, you're going to create the charts on the fly rather than predefine them using the Visual Studio designer. All you've done with the designer is to drop a Web chart control onto the page control, one for each type of chart you're going to create.

The bar chart is first, because it is the default chart for this Web page. Listing 12-6 has the details.

Listing 12-6: Creating the on-demand bar chart.

```
private void CreateBarChart() {
  Series series;

  WebChartControl chart = BarWebChart;

  foreach (ResortData resort in resorts) {
    // create the series for a bar chart
    series = new Series(resort.Name, ViewType.Bar);
    series.Label.Visible = true;

    // Add the data points to the series
    resort.SkierDayCounts.ForEach(
      count => series.Points.Add(count.AsSeriesPoint())
    );

    chart.Series.Add(series);
```

Continued

Listing 12-6: Creating the on-demand bar chart. *(continued)*

```
    }

    // set up the chart axes
    XYDiagram diagram = chart.Diagram as XYDiagram;
    diagram.AxisX.Title.Text = "Season";
    diagram.AxisX.Title.Visible = true;
    diagram.AxisY.Title.Text = "Number of skier days";
    diagram.AxisY.Title.Visible = true;

    // set up the chart title
    chart.Titles.Add(
      new ChartTitle
        { Text = "Colorado Ski Resorts - Skier Days" });
  }
```

The code illustrates the basic concepts of how to configure a chart in code. First of all, you instantiate a `Series` object for each of the data series you want to display, defining its name and its view type.

You can then add the data points for the series (I'm making use of a helper method in the `SkierDayCount` class for this purpose). Finally, you add the series to the chart, for each of the three series you're using.

At the point of adding the first series to the chart control, something important happens internally: The diagram object is created. Prior to this time, the `Diagram` property was null: The chart cannot decide what type of diagram to create (`XYDiagram`, `SimpleDiagram`, `GanttDiagram`, and so on) until the first series has been added. Because you added a series with a bar view, the diagram was created as an `XYDiagram`.

So, once all the series have been added you can manipulate the axes of the chart diagram. Here you're merely setting the title for each axis and making sure that they're visible.

Finally, you add a single title for the chart.

As Listing 12-7 shows, creating the line chart is virtually the same, except that you need to create a line chart instead of the bar chart. This time I also configured the labels to resolve any overlapping text.

Listing 12-7: Configuring the line chart of ski visitors.

```
    private void CreateLineChart() {
      Series series;

      WebChartControl chart = LineWebChart;

      foreach (ResortData resort in resorts) {
        // create the series to show as a bar chart
        series = new Series(resort.Name, ViewType.Line);
        series.Label.Visible = true;
        series.Label.ResolveOverlappingMode =
```

```
        ResolveOverlappingMode.JustifyAllAroundPoint;

      // Add the data points to the series
      resort.SkierDayCounts.ForEach(
        count => series.Points.Add(count.AsSeriesPoint()));

      chart.Series.Add(series);
    }

    // set up the chart axes
    XYDiagram diagram = chart.Diagram as XYDiagram;
    diagram.AxisX.Title.Text = "Season";
    diagram.AxisX.Title.Visible = true;
    diagram.AxisY.Title.Text = "Number of skier days";
    diagram.AxisY.Title.Visible = true;

    // set up the chart title
    chart.Titles.Add(
      new ChartTitle
        { Text = "Colorado Ski Resorts - Skier Days" });
  }
```

Creating the pie chart is similar, but there are some big differences in the way the chart is laid out. For a start, because you can show only one series per pie, you have to have three charts rolled into one diagram. Listing 12-8 shows the code to create these pies.

Listing 12-8: Creating the on-demand pie chart.

```
    public void CreatePieChart() {
      Series series;

      WebChartControl chart = PieWebChart;

      foreach (ResortData resort in resorts) {
        series = new Series(resort.Name, ViewType.Pie);
        series.Label.Visible = true;

        // a series view as a pie chart
        ((PieSeriesView)series.View).Titles.Add(
          new SeriesTitle { Text = resort.Name });

        // Add the data points to the series
        resort.SkierDayCounts.ForEach(
          count => series.Points.Add(count.AsSeriesPoint()));

        ((PieSeriesLabel)series.Label).Position =
          PieSeriesLabelPosition.Inside;
        ((PiePointOptions)series.PointOptions).PointView =
          PointView.Argument;

        chart.Series.Add(series);
```

Continued

Listing 12-8: Creating the on-demand pie chart. *(continued)*

```
    }

    // Set up the pies horizontally, a maximum of 2 in a row
    SimpleDiagram diagram = chart.Diagram as SimpleDiagram;
    diagram.LayoutDirection = LayoutDirection.Horizontal;
    diagram.Dimension = 2;

    // set up the chart title
    chart.Titles.Add(new ChartTitle
      { Text = "Colorado Ski Resorts - Skier Days" });
    chart.Legend.Visible = false;
}
```

The first difference is that you will have a title for each of the pie charts, and so you need to set that up. Also, in order to show the right kind of data for each pie, you set what the labels for each slice of the pie look like (in essence, you use just the argument, which is the data's season) and ensure that the text is drawn inside the slice.

The code that deals with the overall diagram is different too: You have to cast it to a `SimpleDiagram` this time. Using the diagram you can configure the multiple pie charts in a horizontal formation with a maximum of two pies per row.

Now that this code has been written, you can run the application. Notice that the bar chart is initially displayed when the page is first shown, and that the first time you click the Line Chart and Pie Chart items in the list box, there's a slight delay, but that this delay disappears on subsequent clicks because the page control has cached the pages.

Figure 12-3 shows the application in action, displaying the bar chart.

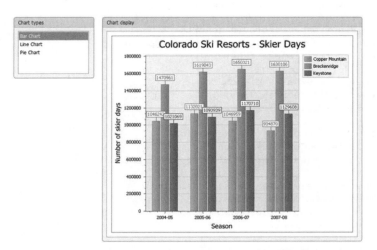

Figure 12-3: The on-demand chart application, showing the bar chart.

Medium Trust

If you experiment with the various options for the charts, you'll notice that although the majority of charts you create will work at the Medium Trust level, some options require more rights. This can be a problem in those Web hosting environments that enforce Medium Trust on the Web sites they host.

The biggest example of this limitation is that all 3-D charts currently require Full Trust in order to create the display. This is because the 3-D charting algorithm used by XtraCharts uses the OpenGL library to render the chart and this is only available in Full Trust environments.

At the time of writing (version v2009.1), a couple of other limitations exist: The algorithm that resolves overlapping labels in data series also uses OpenGL (however, the `HideOverlapped` mode does not and therefore works in Medium Trust, as do the various pie chart label overlapping algorithms); and if you use the HTML text formatting in chart titles and the like, the text is not aligned consistently, again because of the requirement for OpenGL to get it right.

The XtraCharts development team at DevExpress has stated that they are continually working to remove these limitations, and so the exclusion list may already be smaller by the time you read this. Indeed, version v2009.2 has removed the limitations for the resolve overlapping algorithms for the 2-D charts.

Real-time Updates

One of the features not currently provided by XtraCharts is support for real-time updates. Nevertheless, this is relatively easy to implement using callbacks, although the solution does have some downsides.

In the most prevalent case, this type of functionality is required by applications that provide and analyze financial-type data. Basically there is a chart showing the price of a financial instrument (say a bond or a stock) and this chart needs to be updated to follow the changes in price. You have two ways of going about this: using either a push or a pull methodology.

❑   **Push methodology** — The server sends updated data, unbidden, to the client. Presumably the client issues some kind of get operation, and the server satisfies that request only once the data being returned has changed. The problems with this type of solution are many and include having to deal with timeouts (there may be some appreciable time between request and response), and with balancing server loads (we assume that there may be several clients waiting for push data and they will all need servicing at the same time).

❑   **Pull methodology** — This removes several of these issues by placing the burden on the client. In essence, the client application has a timer triggered to fire every second or 5 seconds, say, and every time it fires, the client requests updated data from the server. The issue here is again server load because it's going to get a request from every client at every timer tick to which it has to respond. You'll look to this type of methodology to update your charts in real-time.

First, set up the basic form. Start off by dropping an ASPxRoundPanel on the form as a container for the chart, and then drop a WebChartControl inside it and size it accordingly. You will also need an ASPxTimer control to provide the "tick" for your pull updates, so drop one of those on the form too. Figure 12-4 shows this layout in the running application.

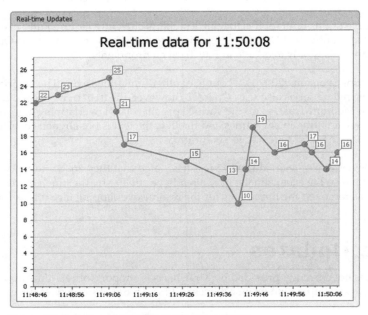

Figure 12-4: A line chart that regularly updates.

Now set some of the properties. For the round panel, just set HeaderText to "Real-time updates". For the WebChartControl, you have a few properties to set: set the ID and ClientInstanceName to "RealTimeChart", EnableClientSideAPI to true, ShowLoadingPanel to false; and then create a CustomCallback event handler (leave it empty for now). For the timer, set the ID and ClientInstanceName to "UpdateTimer", the Interval to 1000 (that is, one second), and set the Tick value for the ClientSideEvents to Listing 12-9.

Listing 12-9: The client-side tick method.

```
function(s, e) {
   RealTimeChart.PerformCallback("");
}
```

At this point the Web form is completely configured, so now it's time to write the code behind the pull-style updating.

What you'll do is mimic a stock ticker. That is, every second, on the callback you'll "get" the latest price of a fictitious stock, add it to the data series, and update the chart. Because the chart would rapidly get unwieldy, you'll limit the number of points on the chart to the last 25.

First, look at the page load method in Listing 12-10. In essence, all it does is call a method to initialize the whole system and especially the configuration of the chart.

Listing 12-10: Configuration for the real-time chart.

```
private string GetTitleText() {
  return String.Format(
    "Real-time data for {0}", DateTime.Now.ToString("h:mm:ss"));
}
private void InitializeSystem() {
  WebChartControl chart = RealTimeChart;

  Series series = new Series("Real-time data", ViewType.Line);
  series.Label.Visible = true;
  series.Label.ResolveOverlappingMode =
    ResolveOverlappingMode.JustifyAroundPoint;
  series.ArgumentScaleType = ScaleType.DateTime;

  series.Points.Add(GetNextPoint(20.0));

  chart.Series.Add(series);
  chart.Titles.Add(new ChartTitle { Text = GetTitleText() });

  XYDiagram diagram = chart.Diagram as XYDiagram;
  AxisX xaxis = diagram.AxisX;


  xaxis.DateTimeMeasureUnit =
    DevExpress.XtraCharts.DateTimeMeasurementUnit.Second;
  xaxis.DateTimeGridAlignment = DateTimeMeasurementUnit.Second;

  xaxis.DateTimeOptions.Format =
    DevExpress.XtraCharts.DateTimeFormat.Custom;
  xaxis.DateTimeOptions.FormatString = "h:mm:ss";
}
```

The page load method merely calls the InitializeSystem method when the page is initially shown (that is, not on a postback or a callback). The InitializeSystem method has all the goodies.

Like before, you set up the series for the chart, add it to the chart, and then you configure the chart itself.

So you create the series for a line chart and ensure that the labels are visible. Because the series is going to be a set of "prices" (y-axis) at given times (x-axis), you need to set the type of the argument axis to date/time.

Rather than pre-populate the chart with a full set of data points, you'll just create the first point based on an initial price of 20 and then you'll let the chart update itself once every second until it's "full."

The final bit of configuration is to set up the x-axis so that it displays data on a timescale of seconds. You'll also set up the formatting of times for the labels on the axis.

The `GetNextPoint` method in Listing 12-11 is where — in theory, at least — you could connect to a Web service or similar to get the next stock price. For this example, though, I've created what might be called an optimistic price generator (the code is written so that, over time, the trend is for the price to rise rather than fall).

Listing 12-11: The method that returns the next price for the stock.

```
public SeriesPoint GetNextPoint(double prevValue) {
  double value;
  Random random = new Random();
  if (random.Next(2) == 0)
    value = prevValue + random.Next(6);
  else
    value = prevValue - random.Next(5);
  return new SeriesPoint(DateTime.Now, value);
}
```

The method calculates a new price based upon a previous one. Half the time, the price will go down and half the time up, but the price rise has the possibility of being slightly more than the price fall. (I would also point out that creating a `Random` object in this manner is not the most efficient use of a random number generator and doing so would normally produce "bad" random number sequences, given that the seed for the new generator is based upon the system time.)

Now you can write the more interesting part of the code: the callback. Listing 12-12 has the details.

Listing 12-12: The callback method that allows the chart to update.

```
protected void RealTimeChart_CustomCallback(
  object sender,
  DevExpress.XtraCharts.Web.CustomCallbackEventArgs e) {

  WebChartControl chart = RealTimeChart;
  SeriesPointCollection points = chart.Series[0].Points;

  SeriesPoint oldValue = points.Last() as SeriesPoint;

  if (points.Count >= 25)
    points.RemoveAt(0);
  points.Add(GetNextPoint(oldValue.Values[0]));

  chart.Titles[0].Text = GetTitleText();
}
```

In reality, this method is extremely simple. You retrieve the chart, and from that, the points collection. If there are already 25 points in the collection, you remove the first one, the oldest. Finally you add the next point, calculated from `GetNextPoint`, and update the chart title to reflect the current time.

Runtime Visual Effects

A popular requirement is the ability to customize charts so that they fit in with a corporate theme. Although the charts in XtraCharts are already pretty customizable (the text for titles and the like, for example, can be rendered with a simple HTML parser, meaning that you can change colors, font sizes, and so on, using simple markup), sometimes you have to roll your sleeves up and write some code.

Let's create a bar chart that displays different colored bars for values that occur in three different bands. So, for example, if the value is in the lowest band the bar is colored red, if the bar is in the middle band the bar is colored orange, and, finally, if the value is in the top band the bar is colored green.

You'll use some more of that skier visit data, but this time you'll look at all the Colorado Front Range ski resorts for a given season. If the number of skier days is below 1 million for the 2007–2008 ski season, you color the bar red; between 1 million and 1.5 million inclusive, orange; and greater than 1.5 million, green.

The key for this type of functionality is to use one of the various `CustomDraw` events. For this particular functionality, you'll go for the `CustomDrawSeriesPoint` event.

Create a new Web application. As you've been doing up to now, drop an ASPxRoundPanel for the container, and set its `HeaderText` property to `"Skier days chart"`. Now drop a WebChartControl in the round panel, set its `ID` to `"BarChart"`, size it appropriately, and then double-click the `CustomDrawSeriesPoint` event to create the stub for the event handler.

Now that you have the design of the application, such as it is, you need to write the code to make it work.

For convenience, create the data class in Listing 12-13 to hold the data for each resort.

Listing 12-13: The class to hold the number of skier days for each resort.

```
public class SkierDayValue {
  private string resort;
  private int count;
  public SkierDayValue(string resort, int count) {
    this.resort = resort;
    this.count = count;
  }
  public SeriesPoint AsSeriesPoint() {
    return new SeriesPoint(resort, count);
  }
}
```

As done previously in this chapter you'll make use of a helper method to convert the data into a `SeriesPoint`.

You now need a method to load the data for the chart. This could be from a database table or XML file, but because this example application is more about chart customization than data access, you'll hard-code the data as shown in Listing 12-14.

Listing 12-14: Loading the data for the multicolored chart.

```
private List<SkierDayValue> skierDays =
  new List<SkierDayValue>();

public void LoadData() {
  skierDays.Add(new SkierDayValue("Beaver Creek", 917863));
  skierDays.Add(new SkierDayValue("Breckenridge", 1630106));
  skierDays.Add(new SkierDayValue("Copper Mountain", 934870));
  skierDays.Add(new SkierDayValue("Keystone", 1129608));
  skierDays.Add(new SkierDayValue("Vail", 1569788));
  skierDays.Add(new SkierDayValue("Winter Park", 1000221));
}
```

Now you can look at the code that creates the chart itself in Listing 12-15.

Listing 12-15: Creating the conditionally colored bar chart.

```
public void CreateChart() {
    WebChartControl chart = BarChart;

    // create the series
    Series series = new Series("Ski Visits", ViewType.Bar);
    series.Label.Visible = true;
    series.ShowInLegend = false;

    // now we can set the position of the label for each bar
    ((SideBySideBarSeriesLabel)series.Label).Position =
      BarSeriesLabelPosition.Center;

    // add the points to the series
    skierDays.ForEach(
      item => series.Points.Add(item.AsSeriesPoint())
    );

    // add the series to the chart (which configures the diagram)
    chart.Series.Add(series);

    // set up the axes
    XYDiagram diagram = chart.Diagram as XYDiagram;
    diagram.AxisX.Title.Text = "Ski resort";
    diagram.AxisX.Title.Visible = true;
    diagram.AxisY.Title.Text = "Number of skier days";
    diagram.AxisY.Title.Visible = true;

    // set up the horizontal constant lines to show the ranges
    diagram.AxisY.ConstantLines.Add(GetLine(1000000, "1.0M"));
    diagram.AxisY.ConstantLines.Add(GetLine(1500000, "1.5M"));

    // set up the chart title
    ChartTitle title = new ChartTitle();
```

```
    title.Text = "Colorado Front Range Ski Resorts";
    chart.Titles.Add(title);

    title = new ChartTitle();
    title.Text = "Skier Days for 2007-08 season";
    Font font = new Font(title.Font.FontFamily, title.Font.Size * 0.90f);
    title.Font = font;
    chart.Titles.Add(title);
}
```

The first thing that happens is that you create the series for the chart to display bars, and ensure that its labels are visible and its legend is not. You cast the series'Label property as a SideBySideSeriesLabel so that you can access its Position property. Set it to Center.

Next, you can quickly add the data points to the series, and the series itself to the chart. This will trigger the chart's Diagram property to be created as an XYDiagram, and you can now access the diagram's properties, such as the axes. Set the axes' titles.

What I'd like to do now is to add a couple of constant lines to the chart to indicate the values at which the bars will change color. For this I make use of the helper method in Listing 12-16 to create a constant line, passing in the axis value to place the line and a title to properly show what the line indicates.

Listing 12-16: Creating a constant line.

```
private static ConstantLine GetLine(int axisValue, string title) {
    ConstantLine line = new ConstantLine();
    line.ShowBehind = true;
    line.AxisValue = axisValue;
    line.ShowInLegend = false;
    line.Color = Color.DarkSeaGreen;
    line.LineStyle.DashStyle = DashStyle.Dot;
    line.Title.Text = title;
    return line;
}
```

Back to the code that creates the chart, you now set the chart's title. This time you will use two titles, as indicated in the code, with the second title in a slightly smaller font size than the first.

Listing 12-17: The page load method for the multicolored chart.

```
protected void Page_Load(object sender, EventArgs e) {
    LoadData();
    CreateChart();
}
```

Add the page load method to call the data load and the chart creation methods (Listing 12-17) and run the code. You'd see the display shown in Figure 12-5.

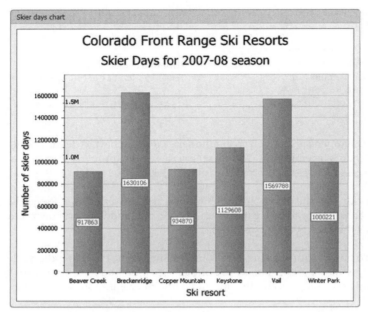

Figure 12-5: The bar chart before any changes have been made to the bars.

The chart looks very good, but is, of course, rather monochromatic. Nevertheless you can see the title fonts work as required, the labels are shown inside the bars, and the constant lines are shown correctly.

Now it's time to fill in the currently empty event handler to custom draw the bars. Listing 12-18 has the details, showing the event handler and a helper method.

Listing 12-18: The custom draw method for coloring the bars conditionally.

```
private static void SetDrawOptions(DrawOptions seriesDrawOptions,
    Color light, Color dark) {
  var drawOptions = (seriesDrawOptions as BarDrawOptions);
  drawOptions.Color = dark;
  drawOptions.FillStyle.FillMode = FillMode.Gradient;
  var options =
    (GradientFillOptionsBase)drawOptions.FillStyle.Options;
  options.Color2 = light;
}
protected void LineChart_CustomDrawSeriesPoint(object sender,
    DevExpress.XtraCharts.CustomDrawSeriesPointEventArgs e) {
```

```
        if (e.SeriesPoint.Values[0] < 1000000) {
          SetDrawOptions(
            e.SeriesDrawOptions, Color.Bisque, Color.Coral);
        }
        else if (e.SeriesPoint.Values[0] > 1500000) {
          SetDrawOptions(
            e.SeriesDrawOptions, Color.Honeydew, Color.YellowGreen);
        }
        else {
          SetDrawOptions(
            e.SeriesDrawOptions, Color.Wheat, Color.Orange);
        }
    }
```

The event handler gets called prior to each series point being plotted on the chart and it's an opportunity to change the parameters for the actual painting. All you're going to do is to change the color of the bar (that is, the series point) according to whether the value being plotted is less than 1 million, greater than 1.5 million, or in between.

You access the e parameter of the event, which contains all the information and structures you need to access and change in order to effect your requirement. The SetDrawOptions method does the actual work: It gets passed the current draw options object, and the two colors — light and dark — for the color gradient.

In SetDrawOptions, you first cast the object to the BarDrawOptions class, so that you can access the required properties. Because you want to draw the bar with a gradient brush, you have to set the FillStyle mode to Gradient, and then cast the fill style options property to GradientFillOptionsBase so that you can provide the second color (the lighter one) for the color gradient.

I will admit that these types of casts can be hard to discover. The best way I found to research this is to use the help documentation. Find the class from which you want to cast and look for the derived classes link at the bottom of the page that shows any descendants. If one of these is relevant to your task — for example, noticing SideBySideBarSeriesLabel when you're researching the type of series.Label, or GradientFillOptionsBase when researching FillStyle.Options — then cast to it, and use IntelliSense to complete your code.

After these changes, the chart now looks like Figure 12-6 when the application is run.

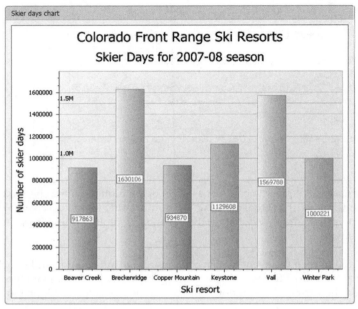

Figure 12-6: Custom painted bars in a chart.

Summary

In this chapter, you've been introduced to some tips and tricks dealing with charting in ASP.NET applications. XtraCharts is broad enough that devoting more pages to this topic would make a book, but using these tips you will be able to create more professional charting for your applications than before.

I would recommend that you experiment with the various charts provided by XtraCharts, and see how to make them more flexible by writing the code to display them rather than relying on the Visual Studio designer.

In particular, you should consider using callback technology (or Ajax, to give it its correct term) to provide responsive Web pages by deferring the creation of charts until the user requests them (or, even more stylishly, by providing self-updating charts).

13

XtraReports For the Web

It was a love of programming reports that started your lifetime devotion to software development, right? Not to worry, I would answer No to that question as well.

This chapter explores the XtraReports suite that allows you to quickly develop high-quality reports in the comfortable and familiar environment of Visual Studio. It looks at how to develop a traditional tabular business report, and then demonstrates the additional features that provide great flexibility in data sources, report organization, presentation, and delivery.

The sample SQL database AdventureWorks available from Microsoft serves as the basis for the sample reports in this chapter, allowing you to follow along with the reports as they are discussed.

XtraReports development is done in Microsoft Visual Studio. The design experience is virtually identical for both Windows Forms and Web projects, differing mainly by the unique requirements of the two environments. Web projects take advantage of the HTML view to review layout and appearance during development.

Creating a Tabular Report

The majority of business reports are fairly standard. One or more tables or views directly serve as the data source to which one or more selection criteria are applied, sometimes provided by the user and other times determined by the report's internal logic.

The detail information is presented in a tabular format, often grouped on a dimension such as Product or Order, preceded by identifying headers and followed by summary totals. Larger reports may begin or end with a separate summary section to provide an overview of the detail. Sound familiar?

This section introduces XtraReports by creating a standard tabular report for a single table to demonstrate a simple scenario.

To get started, create a new ASP.Net Web Application in C# in Visual Studio 2008. Next, select the XtraReport Class template as shown in Figure 13-1.

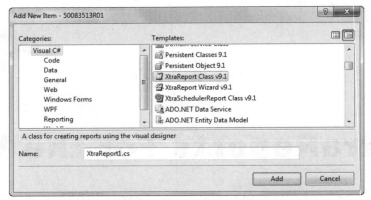

Figure 13-1: Selecting the XtraReport Class template.

Add a data set to the project to serve as the data source. Right-click the DataSet design surface and choose Add TableAdapter. Follow the wizard to connect to the Person.Contact table of the AdventureWorks database, and select the fields FirstName, LastName, EmailAddress, and Phone for the DataSet table.

One of the first things I do after creating a report is to change the report's GridSize *property from the default of 8,8 to a value of 4,4. The finer grid allows more precise control alignment and leads to a more professional appearance. The report's* ReportUnit *property can be set to hundredths of an inch or tenths of a millimeter depending on your preference.*

All XtraReports consist of a series of one or more report bands. By default, the designer appears with only three bands: PageHeader, Detail, and PageFooter. Other bands available are TopMargin, ReportHeader, GroupHeader, GroupFooter, ReportFooter, and BottomMargin. A special band called DetailReport is often used as an alternative to SubReports and is discussed later in this chapter. These bands are accessible in code via the report's XtraReportBase.Bands property.

Report bands serve as containers for the XtraReport controls that collectively constitute the visual elements of the report. The self-explanatory report controls available in the Visual Studio Toolbox when the report designer is selected include XRBarCode, XRChart, XRCheckBox, XRCrossbandBox, XRCrossBandLine, XRLabel, XRLine, XRPageBreak, XRPageInfo, XRPanel, XRPivotGrid, XRRichText, XRShape, XRSubreport, XRTable, and XRZipCode.

For further data representation flexibility, Windows Form controls can be dragged onto the XtraReport design surface, even for Web reports. The ability of XtraReports to accurately render Windows Form controls is dependent on the individual control's architecture. Controls that use the native .NET drawing classes fare better that those that do not. Data can be dynamically represented in the Windows Form control at run time by coding the fill logic in the containing report band's BeforePrint event.

The XtraReport form designer provides three design-time panels to assist with layout and navigation of the report. The Field List panel provides a hierarchical list of the fields that are available via the data source. These fields can be dragged and dropped onto the design surface and will be automatically bound to the data source. The Report Explorer provides a hierarchical view of the report structure. Finally, the Group and Sort panel makes it easy to manage your report's data organization and related report bands.

Access to important report-level tasks, including the ability to choose a data source and maintain report bands, is available from the SmartTag (visually an arrow) in the upper-left corner of the designer as shown in Figure 13-2. The SmartTag is a common access point for functionality throughout the report designer.

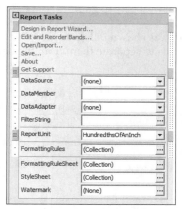

Figure 13-2: The report-level SmartTag.

To identify the report's fields, use the report-level SmartTag to set the DataSource property to the table created in the DataSet earlier in this section. To add fields to the report, drag the XRTable control to the Detail band. Add a fourth column by right-clicking the third column and choosing Insert Column to the Right and resize the columns as desired.

Click the arrow SmartTag on each XRTable cell to use the DataBinding property drop-down to select the corresponding field from the DataSet's Contact table. An alternative to the XRTable is to drag over individual fields from the Field List panel, visible when the report is in design mode.

You can create a report without using any data source. This is useful for quickly creating flyers, wall signs, and so on. Create a new report that has only a Detail band and a single control, the XRRichText control. Format the text as desired. Want multiple copies? Set the `DetailBand.RepeatCountOnEmptyDataSource` *property to the desired number of copies.*

The Preview and HTML View tabs of the report designer do not show an exact representation of your final report but are useful to work out column formatting with live data. For faster previews with large data sets, limit the number of records shown by setting the report's `PreviewRowCount` property to a value that represents a couple pages of data. One special consideration for Web reports is that field overlap is not permitted in HTML. Overlapping two or more fields results in a warning message and a red icon in the top-left corner of the affected fields in the designer.

Page header information should be placed in the PageHeader or TopMargin band. Correspondingly, page footer information should be placed in a PageFooter or BottomMargin band.

A useful technique to create a page header is to use a GroupHeader band to hold an unbound XRTable with the desired column names, or use independent unbound XRLabel fields within the GroupHeader. Set the GroupHeaderBand.RepeatEveryPage *property to true and set the* GroupHeaderBand .GroupUnion *property to the WithFirstDetail value to prevent the header from displaying if there is not sufficient data for the last page. Examples include providing an XRTable heading in the middle of the page for the next table after one just finished, or to serve as a heading for a DetailBand report section.*

To add typical page footer elements as the current date and page counts, use the XtraReports PageInfo control. A "Page x of y" display is created by setting the XRPageInfo control's PageInfo property to NumberOfTotal and setting the Format property to Page {0} of {1}.

The resulting design surface will appear as shown in Figure 13-3. For appearance, I have added a header and footer and a couple XRLine elements to separate them from the detail band.

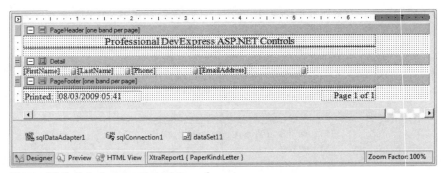

Figure 13-3: Tabular report design surface.

Column summary values are created by dragging the source field into the appropriate report band and setting the Summary properties. Summaries can only be calculated automatically for bound XRLabel controls that are contained in a GroupHeader, GroupFooter, or DetailReport band and is done by setting the XRLabel's Summary.Func property. The scope of the Summary function is set with the Summary .Running property to one of None, Group, Report, and Page, which define the level at which the summary value is reset.

Available Summary.Func options include Avg, Count, DAvg, DCount, DStdDev, DStdDevP, Dsum, DVar, DVarP, Max, Median, Min, Percentage, RecordNumber, RunningSum, StdDev, StdDevP, Sum, Var, and VarP.

If one of the standard Summary.Func options does not suit your needs, you can use the Custom option to define your own summary function for an XRLabel. If you choose Custom, you will need to handle the SummaryReset event to set initial values of your function, handle the SummaryRowChanged event to perform the required calculations every time the current data row is changed, and finally, handle the XRLabel.SummaryGetResult event to return the custom summary value (set e.Result to the custom value and e.Handled = true).

Displaying the Report in an ASP.NET Web Page

XtraReports are displayed using a combination of two XtraReport controls: the ReportToolbar and the ReportViewer control.

To display a report, simply drag over an XtraReports ReportToolbar control and ReportViewer control onto the design surface of a blank ASPX page. To connect the ReportToolbar to the ReportViewer, set the ReportToolbar's `Viewer` property to the ReportViewer control. Next, set the ReportViewer's `Report` property to the XtraReport created in the designer. That is all that is needed to display a basic report in a Web application.

> *Sometimes it is best to set the ReportViewer's `Report` property at run time rather than design time.*
> *If you need to interact with the report via code-behind before it is rendered, be sure to leave the*
> *ReportViewer's `Report` property unset in the designer and also make sure the `Report` and `ReportName`*
> *attributes of the ReportViewer HTML tag are not present in the markup of the viewer page.*

Once rendered, an XtraReport can be exported to a number of formats. Support is automatically provided within the ReportToolBar for export to PDF, HTML, MHT, Text, CSV, XLS, RTF, and image formats.

The report itself is a series of classes compiled into the application's assembly as with any other code. For ASP.NET deployment, a series of assemblies are required on the Web server to support XtraReports functionality (as of version 9.1). See Listing 13-1. A Windows Form application, or one that implements the End-User Designer, would require a different set of assemblies.

Listing 13-1: Required and optional assemblies for an ASP.NET XtraReports deployment.

```
DevExpress.Utils.v9.1.dll
DevExpress.Data.v9.1.dll
DevExpress.XtraPrinting.v9.1.dll
DevExpress.XtraReports.v9.1.dll
DevExpress.Web.v9.1.dll
DevExpress.XtraReports.v9.1.Web.dll
                                            Required:
DevExpress.Web.ASPxEditors.v9.1.dll         if a ReportToolbar control is used
DevExpress.Charts.v9.1.Core.dll             if an XRChart control is used
DevExpress.XtraCharts.v9.1.dll              if an XRChart control is used
DevExpress.XtraPivotGrid.v9.1.Core.dll      if an XRPivotGrid is used
DevExpress.XtraPivotGrid.v9.1.dll           if an XRPivotGrid is used
DevExpress.XtraRichEdit.v9.1.dll            if an XRRichText control is used
```

Using the SQLDataAdapter as a DataSource

An alternative to a DataSet's TableAdapter for querying a database is the SQLDataAdapter component. It has the advantage of allowing default values to be specified for stored procedure parameters or parameterized queries via the `SelectCommand.Parameters.Value` property when used as a report data source. This allows the report designer's Preview and HTML View tabs to continue to display live data for these data sources, based on the default parameter values. Use the Parameters collection of the SQLDataAdapter's SelectCommand property to supply the desired default parameter values.

The SQLDataAdapter is not included in the Visual Studio Toolbox by default. To add it, right-click the Toolbox panel in the Data section and click Choose Items. Navigate to the SQLDataAdapter on the .NET Framework Components tab, found as part of the System.Data assembly. Click OK to add it to the Toolbox. See Figure 13-4.

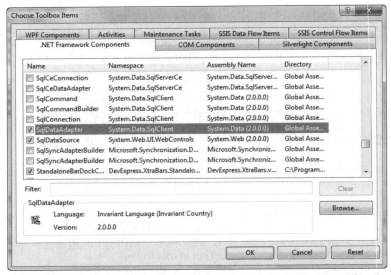

Figure 13-4: Adding the SQLDataAdapter component to the Visual Studio Toolbox.

To use the SQLDataAdapter component, drag and drop it onto the XtraReport design surface. Complete the wizard to set up the desired data environment. Right-click the SQLDataAdapter and choose Generate DataSet and be sure to check the Add This DataSet to the Designer option in the resulting dialog box as shown in the Figure 13-5.

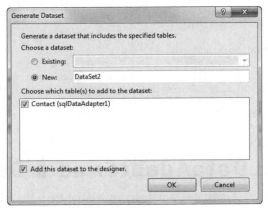

Figure 13-5: Generating the DataSet from SQLDataAdapter.

Fields can be placed onto the XtraReport design surface by dragging them over from the Fields panel.

Using an IBindingList as a DataSource

One of the true tests of a reporting tool is the ease with which it can report custom data sources. If a developer can use custom code to perform complex manipulations as necessary to prepare the data outside of the report, and easily incorporate that data into the report, the reporting tool can be appropriate for virtually any scenario.

XtraReports can bind to any object that supports the IList, ITypedList, or IBindingList interfaces. To demonstrate, Listing 13-2 shows a custom class that implements an IBindingList of InventoryItem objects with a single method GetInventory() to populate the list with sample data.

If you are dynamically setting the report's DataSource property at run time, be sure the Report and ReportName attributes of the ReportViewer HTML tag are not present in the markup of the viewer page. Otherwise the data will be populated when the report is instantiated but before you can set the DataSource to the desired data.

Listing 13-2: The code that returns a custom IBindingList of InventoryItem objects.

```
namespace IBindingListReport
{
    public class DataLayer
    {
        public class InventoryItem
        {
            public int InventoryID { get; set; }
            public string ItemName { get; set; }
            public int Quantity { get; set; }
            public int ReorderQuantity { get; set; }
        }

        public BindingList<InventoryItem> GetInventory ()
        {
            BindingList<InventoryItem> items =
                    new BindingList<InventoryItem>();

            InventoryItem item1 = new InventoryItem();
            item1.InventoryID = 1;
            item1.ItemName = "Inkjet Notecards ";
            item1.Quantity = 15;
            item1.ReorderQuantity = 5;
            items.Add(item1);

            InventoryItem item2 = new InventoryItem();
            item2.InventoryID = 2;
            item2.ItemName = "Composition Notebook ";
            item2.Quantity = 5;
            item2.ReorderQuantity = 8;
            items.Add(item2);

            return items;
        }
    }
}
```

Because the IBindingList is available only at run time, it cannot be used to lay out the report at design time. To compensate for this, you add a DataSet that parallels the structure of the IBindingList, mapping equivalent field names and data types to the project. See Figure 13-6.

Figure 13-6:
DataSet structure
to parallel
IBindingList
structure.

The data fields are now available for use in the report designer once the report's DataSource property is set to DataSet1.xsd.

Because the DataSource will actually be an IBindingList and not a DataSet as indicated at design time, the report's constructor must be modified to directly bind to the DataSource for each of the report field controls. See Listing 13-3.

Listing 13-3: Custom binding to report field elements in the report's constructor.

```
using System;
using System.Drawing;
using System.Collections;
using System.ComponentModel;
using DevExpress.XtraReports.UI;

namespace IBindingListReport
{
    public partial class XtraReport1 : DevExpress.XtraReports.UI.XtraReport
    {
        public XtraReport1()
        {
            InitializeComponent();

            xrlInventoryID.DataBindings.Add(
                    "Text", DataSource, "InventoryID");
            xrlItemName.DataBindings.Add(
                    "Text", DataSource,  "ItemName");
            xrlQuantity.DataBindings.Add(
                    "Text", DataSource,  "Quantity");
            xrlReorderQuantity.DataBindings.Add(
                    "Text", DataSource,  "ReorderQuantity");
        }
    }
}
```

The data is provided to the report at run time via the Page_Load event as shown in Listing 13-4.

Listing 13-4: Providing custom IBindingList data to the report at run time.

```csharp
using System;
using System.ComponentModel;
using System.IO;

namespace IBindingListReport
{
    public partial class _Default : System.Web.UI.Page
    {
        protected void Page_Load(object sender, EventArgs e)
        {
            if (!Page.IsPostBack)
            {
                DataLayer datalayer = new DataLayer();
                BindingList<DataLayer.InventoryItem>
                    items = datalayer.GetInventory();
                XtraReport1 xr = new XtraReport1();
                xr.DataSource = items;
                this.ReportViewer1.Report = xr;
            }
        }
    }
}
```

The resulting report reflects the custom data as shown in Figure 13-7.

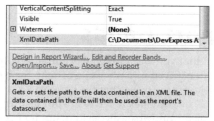

Inventory ID	Name	Quantity	Reorder Quantity
1	Inkjet Notecards	15	5
2	Composition Notebook	5	8
3	Item 0	0	2
4	Item 1	1	3
5	Item 2	2	4

Figure 13-7: Sample report from IBindingList data source.

Using XML as a DataSource

XML is a common format for data exchange. XtraReports directly supports XML as a data source via the report's XMLDataPath property. See Figure 13-8. When supplied with a proper XML data file, the XML elements appear in the Field List panel in the same manner as other data sources.

Figure 13-8: Setting the XmlDataPath property.

XML data can be output directly from SQL Server 2005 or later in a format that is compatible with XtraReports as a data source. See Listing 13-5 for a sample query. Notice that the ELEMENTS XSINIL display keyword breaks each column in the relational table into an individual node and permits representation of NULL values. The ROOT(ContactType) phrase adds a parent element to encapsulate all rows in order to generate a valid XML file as shown in Listing 13-6.

XML as a data source can be useful in scenarios where portability or archive of the data is important. This can be a great way to create a fixed report demo for a client, or save a snapshot report as of a certain date, without maintaining the data in a database. When combined with the End-User Designer discussed later in this chapter, it can be an excellent way to provide moment-in-time ad-hoc reporting to a departmental supervisor or manager.

Listing 13-5: Query to generate XML data from SQL Server for XtraReports.

```
SELECT [ContactTypeID]
     , [Name]
     , [ModifiedDate]
FROM [AdventureWorks].[Person].[ContactType]
FOR XML AUTO, ELEMENTS XSINIL, ROOT('ContactType')
```

Listing 13-6: Resulting XML generated by query in Listing 13-5.

```
<ContactType xmlns:xsi="http://www.w3.org/2001/XMLSchema-instance">
  <AdventureWorks.Person.ContactType>
    <ContactTypeID>1</ContactTypeID>
    <Name>Accounting Manager</Name>
    <ModifiedDate>1998-06-01T00:00:00</ModifiedDate>
  </AdventureWorks.Person.ContactType>
  <AdventureWorks.Person.ContactType>
    <ContactTypeID>2</ContactTypeID>
    <Name>Assistant Sales Agent</Name>
    <ModifiedDate>1998-06-01T00:00:00</ModifiedDate>
  </AdventureWorks.Person.ContactType>
  <AdventureWorks.Person.ContactType>
    <ContactTypeID>3</ContactTypeID>
    <Name>Assistant Sales Representative</Name>
    <ModifiedDate>1998-06-01T00:00:00</ModifiedDate>
  </AdventureWorks.Person.ContactType>
</ContactType>
```

Conditional Report Bands

Suppose you have a report band that you want to display conditionally based on a Boolean value determined by the current data query. You initially write code to the band's BeforePrint event in order to hide the band when the Boolean is true by setting the band's Visible property to false, then set Visible = true when the Boolean evaluates to false. In your testing you see that the band disappears on the first occurrence of the Boolean value true as desired, but it never becomes visible again. Why?

The problem occurs because once the band is no longer visible, the band's `BeforePrint` event never fires again. The preferred approach is simply to cancel the print of the band by setting `PrintEventArgs.Cancel` to true in the band's `BeforePrint` event rather than change the `Visible` property.

Master-Detail Report

A Master-Detail report is a natural way to report tables from a database that have a parent-child relationship such as individual products within a series of product categories. Master-Detail reports can be constructed with the XRSubReport control, but using the DetailBand control as an alternative has several advantages.

To illustrate a Master-Detail report utilizing the DetailBand, create a new Web application project and add a blank XtraReport class. Add a DataSet and then a TableAdapter each for the Product and TransactionHistory tables. Next create a relationship between the Product and TransactionHistory tables of the AdventureWorks database as shown in Figure 13-9.

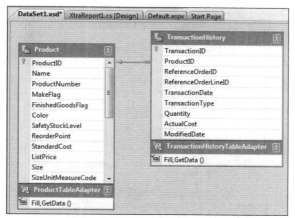

Figure 13-9: Product-TransactionHistory relationship in the DataSet.

Use the report SmartTag to assign the report `DataSource` property to the Product table of DataSet1.xsd. Drag over the fields `ProductID`, `ListPrice`, and `Name`. Right-click the DetailReport band, choose Insert Detail Report, and select the relationship created in the data set as shown in Figure 13-10.

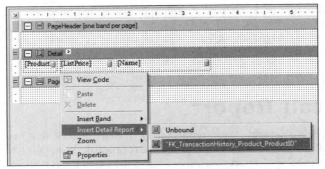

**Figure 13-10: Inserting the DetailBand via the DataSet
relationship.**

To limit the size of the report to a reasonable size, set the XtraReport's `FilterString` property to limit
the report to `ProductID` values of less than 10. See Figure 13-11.

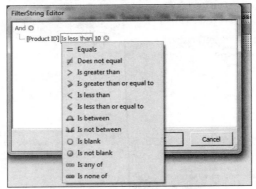

**Figure 13-11: Filtering by ProductID to limit
records returned to the report.**

If the data set is formed correctly, you will see the relationship in the field list of the report as shown in
Figure 13-12. Notice how the DetailReport section is shown in a different color on the screen and has its
own set of report bands. Multiple DetailReport bands can be used with a report to show deep
hierarchical relationships if needed.

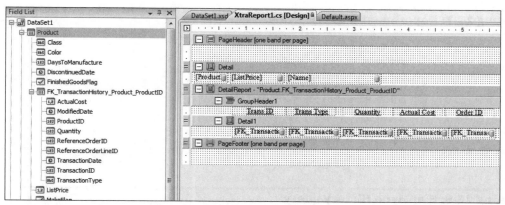

Figure 13-12: Field List panel reflecting the foreign key relationship.

Based on this example, a partial output is shown in Figure 13-13.

		Trans ID	Trans Type	Quantity	Actual Cost	Order ID
		212796	P	3	50.2635	3694
		212963	P	3	50.2635	3773
		213131	P	3	50.2635	3852
		213294	P	3	50.2635	3931
2	0.0000	Bearing Ball				
		Trans ID	Trans Type	Quantity	Actual Cost	Order ID
		104763	P	3	41.9160	425
		106242	P	3	41.9160	504
		107546	P	3	41.9160	587

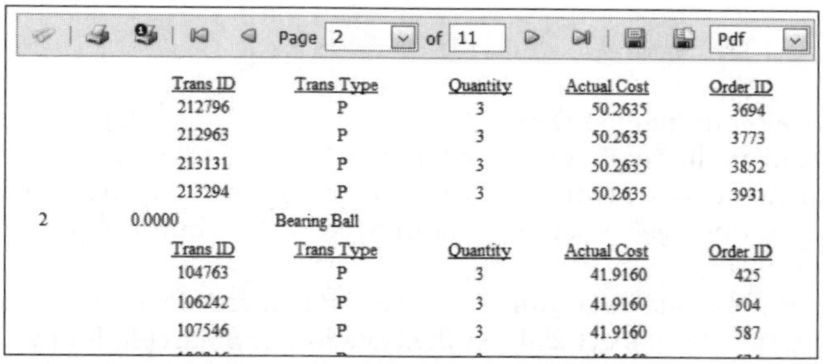

Figure 13-13: Output of Master-Detail report.

Drill-Through Report

A drill-through report provides links that open a separate window with supporting detail for the selected item of the master report.

The AdventureWorks database will be used to create a Departmental report with drill-through to a report of all employees that have historically worked for that department. The EmployeeDepartmentHistory table serves as the base table for both reports. The SQL query for the list of departments is shown in Listing 13-7 and the query for a department's employees, when later filtered by department in the report, is shown in Listing 13-8. Note that each GroupName may contain multiple departments.

Listing 13-7: Departmental query.

```
SELECT
        D.DepartmentID, D.GroupName
FROM
      HumanResources.EmployeeDepartmentHistory EDH
          LEFT JOIN HumanResources.Department D
             on D.DepartmentID = EDH.DepartmentID
GROUP BY
        D.DepartmentID,D.GroupName
ORDER BY
        D.DepartmentID, D.GroupName
```

Listing 13-8: Employee History query.

```
SELECT
      EDH.DepartmentID, E.EmployeeID, C.FirstName, C.LastName, E.HireDate
FROM
      HumanResources.EmployeeDepartmentHistory EDH
          LEFT JOIN HumanResources.Employee E on E.EmployeeID = EDH.EmployeeID
          LEFT JOIN Person.Contact C on C.ContactID = E.ContactID
ORDER BY
      C.LastName, C.FirstName
```

In your project, add an XtraReport named Departments and a second XtraReport named DepartmentEmployees. Add a data set that will contain one TableAdapter for each report. The first TableAdapter "Department" is set to the Departmental query from Listing 13-7 and the second TableAdapter "DepartmentEmployee" is set to the Employee History query shown in Listing 13-8.

Assign each report to the appropriate data source. Set the DataSource SmartTag for the Departments report to the Department table of DataSet1.xsd. Set the DataSource SmartTag for the DepartmentEmployees report to the Employee table of DataSet1.xsd.

On the DepartmentEmployees report, create a calculated field to combine the employee's name into Last,First format. To add a calculated field, right-click the employee table in the Field List and choose Add Calculated Field as shown in Figure 13-14. Set the calculated field's Expression property to [LastName] + ", " + [FirstName] and then drag it over to the report.

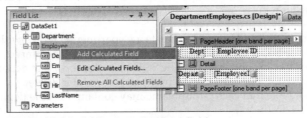

Figure 13-14: Adding a calculated field.

Add two public parameters to the DepartmentEmployees report's Parameters collection, one for the DepartmentID and one for the GroupName. As a convenience to the user, add the parameter fields to the PageHeader band to identify the parameter values used. Set the report's `RequestParameters` property to false to prevent the report from prompting the user for the parameter values.

Limit the display of employees to the `DepartmentID` parameter value by setting the XtraReport's `FilterString` property to `[DepartmentID] = [Parameters.DepartmentID]`.

To have the `DepartmentID` in the Departments report serve as a hyperlink to the DepartmentEmployees report, you must set the `NavigateURL` property for each value of `DepartmentID` in the Departments report as it is being displayed. See Listing 13-9. If you would like the DepartmentEmployees report to open in a new window, set the `txtDeptID`'s Target property to `_blank`.

Listing 13-9: Setting the Department ID's navURL property at report display.

```
private void txtDeptID_BeforePrint(object sender,
System.Drawing.Printing.PrintEventArgs e)
{
    string navURL =  "DepartmentEmployees.aspx?DepartmentID=" +
        GetCurrentColumnValue("DepartmentID") +
        "&GroupName=" + GetCurrentColumnValue("GroupName");

    ((XRLabel)sender).NavigateUrl = navURL;
}
```

To format the `HireDate` field on the DepartmentEmployees report to hide the time value, it is easiest to use the control's `(databindings).Text.FormatString` property to set the format to `{0:MM/dd/yyyy}`.

To illustrate the same operation using the `HireDate`'s `BeforePrint` event, see Listing 13-10. This is a useful technique to perform more advanced custom formatting of any report field.

Listing 13-10: Formatting the HireDate prior to its display on the report.

```
private void txtHireDate_BeforePrint(object sender,
System.Drawing.Printing.PrintEventArgs e)
{
    DateTime hireDate = (DateTime)GetCurrentColumnValue("HireDate");
    ((XRLabel)this.txtHireDate).Text = string.Format("{0:MM/dd/yyyy}",hireDate);
}
```

The resulting report output is shown in Figure 13-15.

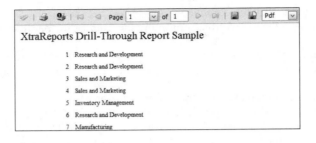

Figure 13-15: Output of Drill-Through report.

Label Report

The XtraReport Wizard template (Add New Items . . .) offers to guide you through the creation of two different types of reports — Standard Report and Label Report. Choosing Label Report displays a screen that allows you to choose from a large number of predefined label formats, organized by manufacturer as shown in Figure 13-16.

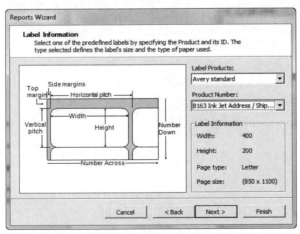

Figure 13-16: Label Wizard Selection panel.

Click Next to get the option to customize the labels as shown in Figure 13-17.

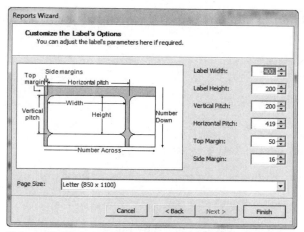

Figure 13-17: Label Wizard Customization panel.

The resulting XtraReport design surface is ready to accept standard report controls to format the label content as desired. The report's SmartTag is set to the desired data source as usual. Each row of the data source will result in another label as defined by the label template.

Mail Merge Report

Mail merge reports are standard reports that use embedded fields in the text of the XRLabel or XRRichText controls. Simply enclose the field name within brackets in the text.

Though you must type the name of the field manually, it is possible to get visual feedback that the field name was typed properly and recognized by the designer. Type the field name in uppercase, lowercase, or any combination that is different from the representation of the field name in the Field List panel. When you exit the field, the field will be updated to match the exact case of the Field List entry if it was recognized.

To have each source row appear on its own page, add a GroupHeader band based on a unique value or combination of values such as the ContactID or FirstName + LastName and set the GroupHeader's PageBreak property to the BeforeBand value. Label reports may be previewed or printed as with any other report type.

Caching the Report

Query performance can quickly become an issue when paging though large report data sets over the Web. You may have noticed in Listing 13-4 that the GetInventory() method is called for each page display. If that is a lengthy data query, the report may slow significantly. Fortunately, the XtraReports ReportViewer control supports the CacheReportDocument and RestoreReportDocumentFromCache events. Listing 13-11 is a revision of Listing 13-4 that supports report caching to Session.

Listing 13-11: Revision to support report caching to a memory stream in Session.

```csharp
using System;
using System.ComponentModel;
using System.IO;

namespace IBindingListReport
{
    public partial class _Default : System.Web.UI.Page
    {
        protected string key = "MyReport1";

        protected void Page_Load(object sender, EventArgs e)
        {
            if (!Page.IsPostBack)
            {
                DataLayer datalayer = new DataLayer();
                BindingList<DataLayer.InventoryItem>
                        items = datalayer.GetInventory();
                XtraReport1 xr = new XtraReport1();
                xr.DataSource = items;
                this.ReportViewer1.Report = xr;
            }
        }

        protected void ReportViewer1_CacheReportDocument(
                object sender, DevExpress.XtraReports.Web.
CacheReportDocumentEventArgs e)
        {
            e.Key = key;
            Session[e.Key] = e.SaveDocumentToMemoryStream();
        }

        protected void ReportViewer1_RestoreReportDocumentFromCache(
            object sender,
            DevExpress.XtraReports.Web.RestoreReportDocumentFromCacheEventArgs e)
        {
            Stream stream = Page.Session[e.Key] as Stream;
            if (stream != null)
                e.RestoreDocumentFromStream(stream);
        }
    }
}
```

Parameterized Stored Procedure Report

Most reports have some ability for the user to select desired criteria such as date range, account number, and so on. The easier option is to use the XtraReports FilterString property to limit the display of records from a SELECT data source with the obvious performance issue of potentially retrieving more data than needed.

The more efficient option is to create a data source with a parameterized query or stored procedure data source and update the data source parameters with the values supplied by the user at run time. This limits the data retrieval to only the needed records, enhancing the report experience for the user.

> *This example does not use the report's Parameters collection; it passes the parameter directly into the report's constructor. To see an example of using the report's Parameters collection, see the "Drill-Through Report" section of this chapter.*

To illustrate, create a report that uses the `upsGetManagerEmployees` stored procedure to list a Manager's employees after prompting the user to select one of several valid Manager ID values.

Create a new Web application and add a blank XtraReport item. Drag a SQLDataAdapter to the report design surface and choose a connection to the AdventureWorks database. Select Existing Stored Procedure as the data source and choose `upsGetManagerEmployees` for the Select command as shown in Figure 13-18.

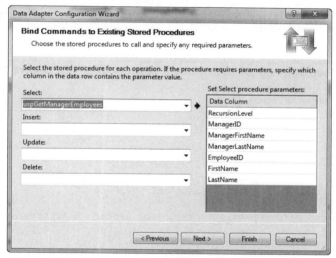

Figure 13-18: Using a stored procedure as the data source.

Right-click the SQLDataAdapter and generate a data set and add it to the designer as shown previously in Figure 13-5. Set the `Value` property to 108 in the `@ManagerID` parameter of the SQLDataAdapter to serve as the default parameter value for the Preview and HTML View tabs. Drag the `ManagerID`, `ManagerFirstName`, and `ManagerLastName` fields into the PageHeader band. Drag the `EmployeeID`, `FirstName`, and `LastName` fields to the Detail band. Format these fields as desired.

On the Default.aspx Web page, create a Panel control that will contain the three `ManagerID` choices of 16, 18, and 21 as radio buttons. Add a button with the text "Manager's Employee Report."

Add a second Panel control that contains the ReportToolbar and ReportViewer controls. Set the `ReportViewer` property of the ReportToolbar control to the ReportViewer control. Be sure to leave the `Report` property of the ReportViewer control blank. Set the `Visible` property to false.

The resulting design screen will appear as in Figure 13-19 as a combined parameter request and report viewer page.

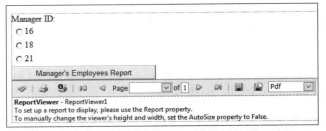

Figure 13-19: Combined parameter request and report viewer Web page.

Next you add the code to the button to determine the selected Manager ID and create the report with that value. To be able to do paging through the report, you need to cache the report as discussed in the "Caching the Report" section of this chapter. The combined code is shown in Listing 13-12.

Listing 13-12: Accepting report parameters and caching the report for proper paging.

```
using System.ComponentModel;
using System.IO;

namespace _50083513R05_Parameter
{
    public partial class _Default : System.Web.UI.Page
    {
        protected string key = "ParameterDrivenReport";

        protected void Button1_Click1(object sender, EventArgs e)
        {
            this.Panel1.Visible = false;
            this.Panel2.Visible = true;
            int ManagerID = 0;
            int.TryParse(RadioButtonList1.SelectedValue, out ManagerID);
            XtraReport1 xr1 = new XtraReport1(ManagerID);
            this.ReportViewer1.Report = xr1;
        }

        protected void ReportViewer1_CacheReportDocument(object sender,
        DevExpress.XtraReports.Web.CacheReportDocumentEventArgs e)
        {
            e.Key = key;
            Session[e.Key] = e.SaveDocumentToMemoryStream();
        }

        protected void ReportViewer1_RestoreReportDocumentFromCache(object
        sender,
        DevExpress.XtraReports.Web.RestoreReportDocumentFromCacheEventArgs e)
```

```
        {
            Stream stream = Page.Session[e.Key] as Stream;
            if (stream != null)
                e.RestoreDocumentFromStream(stream);
        }

    }
}
```

Finally, you need to add the code to the XtraReport's constructor to accept the ManagerID as a constructor parameter and initially fill the DataSet based upon that parameter. See Listing 13-13.

Listing 13-13: Accepting report parameters and caching the report for proper paging.

```
namespace _50083513R05_Parameter
{
    public partial class XtraReport1 : DevExpress.XtraReports.UI.XtraReport
    {
        public XtraReport1(int ManagerID)
        {
            InitializeComponent();

            // Initialize the report data based on the ManagerID parameter
            sqlDataAdapter1.SelectCommand.Parameters["@ManagerID"].Value
                    = ManagerID;
            sqlDataAdapter1.Fill(dataSet11);
        }
    }
}
```

The resulting report for the selected Manager ID of 21 is shown in Figure 13-20.

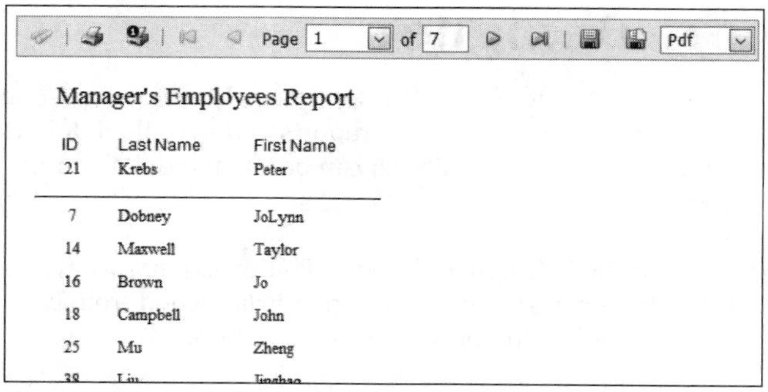

Figure 13-20: Stored-procedure report for user-supplied Manager ID of 21.

Combining Multiple Reports

Executive-level business reports often include an executive summary as the first page, then go into supporting detail as the body of the report, and finally wrap up with a detailed summary report. XtraReports makes it easy to combine multiple reports into a single report. Listing 13-14 combines an introductory report, detail report, and summary report into a single report as presented to the user with continuous page numbering across all three reports.

Listing 13-14: Combining three reports as one report with continuous page numbering.

```
// Create the 1st report and generate its document.
XtraReport1 report1 = new XtraReport1();
report1.CreateDocument();

// Create the 2nd report and generate its document.
XtraReport2 report2 = new XtraReport2();
report2.CreateDocument();

// Create the 3rd report and generate its document.
XtraReport2 report3 = new XtraReport3();
Report3.CreateDocument();

// Add all pages of the 2nd and 3rd reports to the end of the 1st report.
report1.Pages.AddRange(report2.Pages);
report1.Pages.AddRange(report3.Pages);

// Reset all page numbers in the resulting document.
report1.PrintingSystem.ContinuousPageNumbering = true;

// Assign the report to the ReportViewer
this.ReportViewer1.Report = report1;
```

End-User Report Designer

The best report is the one you do not have to write. XtraReports includes the End-User Designer that allows users to customize existing reports or create new reports and save them for later use. Although the End-User Designer is a Windows-only application, it can be used to develop reports for either Windows Forms or ASP.NET.

The End-User Designer provides a report design and customization experience that is very similar to the Visual Studio appearance for the end user. The report designer is launched from code-behind and typically is made available from an application button or menu option.

Database views that combine related tables into logical rows are useful to provide a data source for reporting in the End-User Designer. This simplifies field selection for the end user.

Create a new Windows application and add a single button named button1. Create an XtraReport that has its report DataSource property set to the desired query, stored procedure, or view. In this example, I used the vIndividualDemographics view of the AdventureWorks database. The resulting display is shown in Figure 13-21. Notice the similarity to the Visual Studio designer, which will assist the experienced XtraReports developer in supporting the End-User Designer.

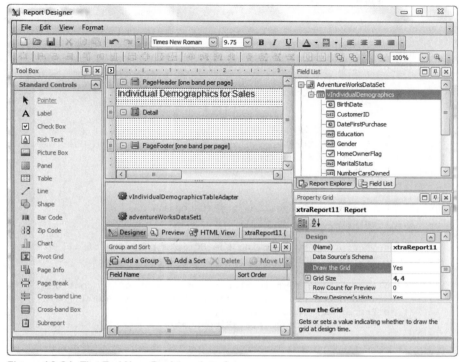

Figure 13-21: The End-User Designer interface.

The code needed to launch the End-User Designer is shown in Listing 13-15.

Listing 13-15: Launching the XtraReport End-User Designer for a report.

```
XtraReport1 xr1 = new XtraReport1();
xr1.ShowDesigner();
```

Scripting in C# or Visual Basic is supported in the End-User Designer. Though most end users may not be comfortable scripting in these languages, it makes it convenient for the developer to easily add custom logic to an End-User report at their request.

Certain features can be restricted in the End-User Designer to protect data integrity or comply with company security policies, for example. Various features can be removed by coding to the static `XtraReport.OnFilterControlProperties` event of the End-User Designer as shown in Listing 13-16.

Listing 13-16: Restricting capabilities within the End-User Designer.

```
using DevExpress.XtraReports.UI;
using DevExpress.XtraReports.UserDesigner;

static void Main()
{
        // Handle the static FilterControlProperties event
        XtraReport.FilterControlProperties +=
        new FilterControlPropertiesEventHandler(OnFilterControlProperties);
        Application.Run(new Form1());
}

private void button1_Click(object sender, System.EventArgs e) {
        // Instantiate the XtraReport1 type and invoke its End-User Designer
        XtraReport1 report = new XtraReport1();
        report.ShowDesigner();
}

static void OnFilterControlProperties(object sender,
FilterControlPropertiesEventArgs e) {

        // Remove scripting by removing the Scripts property of all elements
        e.Properties.Remove("Scripts");

        // Example of hiding certain properties on a specific control
        if (sender is XtraReport1 && e.Control.Name == "xrLabel1") {
                e.Properties.Remove("Name");
                e.Properties.Remove("DataBindings");
        }
}
```

Many organizations may want to hide the data source elements shown in the component tray as shown in Listing 13-17.

Listing 13-17: Hiding Data Source Elements within the End-User Designer.

```
using System;
using System.Windows.Forms;
using DevExpress.XtraReports.UserDesigner;
// ...

private void button1_Click(object sender, EventArgs e) {
        // Create an End-User Designer, hide the component tray
        XRDesignFormEx designForm = new XRDesignFormEx();
        designForm.DesignPanel.ShowComponentTray = false;

        // Open a report and show it in the modified designer
        designForm.OpenReport(new XtraReport1());
        designForm.Show ();
}
```

As you can see, the End-User Designer is a highly customizable tool to empower end users to create or modify their own XtraReports.

Summary

In this chapter you have seen how to use the familiar Visual Studio environment to create reports for deployment on the Web and the rich set of capabilities available for reporting.

We were not able to touch upon many features of XtraReports in this chapter, such as BarCodes, CrossTab reports, custom formatting, and so on. You owe it to yourself to check out all the capabilities of XtraReports.

With only minor differences, the same steps can be used to create and deliver Window Forms reports as well. The ability to learn something once and use it in multiple scenarios is a great boost to productivity and lowers the pain points of reporting.

Understanding How Web Applications Differ from Windows Applications

ASP.NET principles, guidelines, and behaviors are highly important to ASP.NET developers, which includes us at DevExpress. However, this book is primarily about DevExpress's ASP.NET controls and code, and Parts I, II, and III emphasize that fact.

The only reason I've added the general ASP.NET items at all is so that those of you who may not know this material don't have to buy a second book just to get to where you can work with DevExpress's ASP.NET controls, and so that you will understand (if you don't already know) how Ajax works and why incorporating Ajax functionality into DevExpress controls helps us provide a better developer experience and a better end-user experience for your customers.

If you are still reading, you are probably in one of two groups: You have questions about how Web applications differ from Windows applications, or you understand the basic differences between Windows and the Web but are hoping to get some new information. This appendix will address both issues. If you understand Web versus Windows development, just skim the appendix for juicy bits. Or, if you want to master the differences (or are learning about them for the first time), read the whole appendix.

Using ASP.NET Page Lifecycle Events

This section's heading introduces two important concepts: ASP.NET pages have a life cycle, and the life cycle is represented by events. Events for the Web work like events for anything else, but ASP.NET pages have different events than Windows forms do. Also, the life cycle of an ASP.NET page is very different from a lifecycle for a Windows form, and this difference primarily involves the concept of ASP.NET as a disconnected model. Let's start with the idea of disconnectedness.

When you are using a Windows form, objects, behaviors, and the database are all readily accessible because the Windows form is an executing binary, a running application. When you are using an ASP .NET page (or application made of many pages), the opposite is true. When the client sees your Web page (or Web application), the running application is not really your page, it is the consumer's Web browser. In some sense, your page just kind of lies there. Although this isn't strictly true because your page responds to user input via JavaScript, for the most part none of your C# or VB code is even present; your code is back on the server. In short, the client GUI that the customer sees is disconnected from the code you wrote to support it.

When you design a Web page, you put Web server controls on the page (and you can put HTML in the page, too). It is useful to think of Web server controls as little HTML code generators. When one of your pages is requested, the ASP.NET engine emits a server control as HTML, and that HTML is returned to the client. The same thing happens when you use Microsoft's GridView or DevExpress's ASPxGridView — these feature-rich Web server controls render HTML. The code you wrote — generally referred to as *code-behind* — actually runs on your Web server, which, in part, determines elements such as the data that is included in the rendered HTML. The whole lifecycle of each of your pages actually occurs on the Web server from object creation to object destruction before the end-user — some customer peering at your efforts through a browser — ever sees it.

Your job as an ASP.NET programmer is to organize and orchestrate Web server controls to guide the user through some kind of experience. Our job at DevExpress is to produce HTML engines, that is, additional controls that make you more productive and help you achieve a better result.

Mastering Events

Events (also called delegates in .NET) are really just functions that are called. Events generally describe behaviors that can be responded to, such as Click or Load (as in page load). If all you understand about events is that you double-click something, such as a button, after which a Click event handler is generated for you and you fill in some lines of code, then you are missing a big part of the picture. Sure, the IDE will generate some events for you, but you can use events anywhere you want, which is a very powerful concept.

> Event driven programming is a paradigm in which the flow is determined by (user or code) events and responses to those events. You can contrast the event-driven paradigm to another paradigm, batch-driven programming. Batch-driven programming is a series of instructions, and the flow is determined by the programmer who has predetermined the order of execution.

The basic idea of an event is that one party writes some code that says *I will notify your code when something happens* and the other party writes the code that provides the response. Notice that nothing was said about buttons, text boxes, grids, or event controls in general. Events can be and are used everywhere. Because events have evolved, following is a quick history of events.

Basically, computers originally knew about state and behaviors — a lovely duo — but this pair didn't support dynamic behavior, that is, a response to something occurring. Well, everything is ultimately located somewhere in memory in your computer, and that somewhere is generally a location referred to by an address. A function sits somewhere in memory, and so does state information. An event, then, is a placeholder for a future address (or location) of a function to be named, and an event's purpose is to provide a dynamic response to an occurrence. This occurrence is often thought of as an event caused by a user's actions, but no such limitation actually exists. (In fact, it's better if you broaden your view of events in general; you will write better solutions.)

I was first introduced to events as function pointers in 1990 while learning C++. (My guess is that events go back at least as far as Xerox PARC [Palo Alto Research Center] in the 1970s.) A function pointer is literally a pointer typed to the signature of a method as opposed to a pointer to a structure or simple type. The difficulty with this pointer approach is that pointers can be null and only one method could be assigned to the pointer. The Delphi programming language improved on events and reduced the complexity of defining function pointer method signatures. Again, the challenge was how to code more than one respondent (a function) to an event. Anders Hejlsberg is probably the person most responsible for Delphi (and C#) and with C#, events were further refined and dubbed delegates.

.NET introduces the concept of a multicast delegate. A multicast delegate is an event type that internally supports assigning multiple event handlers to a single event. Because events are first-class types in C# (and VB), using them is easier than ever: You declare an event property and assign a method to it. This is exactly the dance that the Visual Studio IDE does. Microsoft programmers define events, and when you click a button, the IDE spits out a method with the right signature and binds the method to the event. When the event occurs, any methods associated with the event are called.

There are thousands of predefined events. Understanding how they work is more important than knowing them all, but let's cover the ones you will routinely encounter, including life-cycle, application-level, and page-level events.

Reviewing the ASP.NET Lifecycle

For the most part, I never spent a lot of time worrying about how ASP.NET and IIS did their respective jobs, and in most cases, you don't have to worry, either. Some changes have occurred for IIS 7, and I cover those here briefly for reference.

For security reasons, the Web server originally code-named Cassini — and now still referred to that way by some — is a local running host for Web applications. Cassini enables developers to work locally on their workstations without installing IIS, thus allaying the concerns of security-conscious wonks. Cassini enables you to create Web sites using the local file system (see Figure A-1).

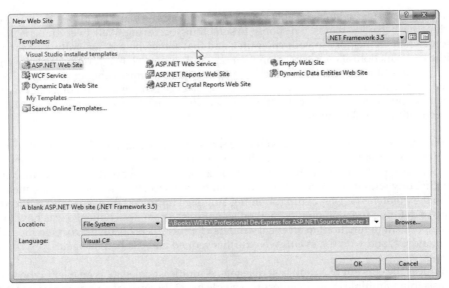

Figure A-1: The Cassini Web host permits creating Web site projects locally without installing IIS.

Visual Studio, in addition to letting you creating Web sites locally, supports using and installing a local copy of IIS, opening a Web site running on a local or remote FTP server, or creating projects on a remote computer running IIS. The Remote Site option requires FrontPage server extensions. Click the Browse button in Figure A-1 to display the Choose Location dialog box shown in Figure A-2.

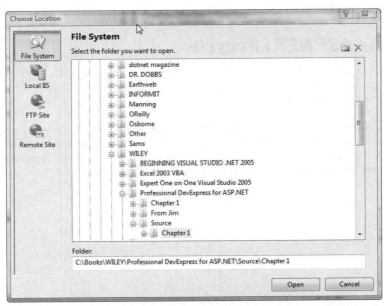

Figure A-2: Create a Web site on the local file system, a local copy of IIS, a local or remote FTP server, or a remote server running IIS with FrontPage Server Extensions.

IIS 6 uses filters for various file types. Some files go to IIS, some go to ASP.NET, and some go to other filters generally based on the file extension. IIS 7 supports classic mode, which behaves like IIS 6 in integrated mode. In IIS 7 in integrated mode, the ASP.NET runtime is integrated with the Web server, providing a unified processing pipeline. In addition to having more events, including `MapRequestHandler`, `LogRequest`, and `PostLogRequest`, IIS 7 in integrated mode raises all `HttpApplication` events; allows support for native and managed code modules to be configured at the Web server, Web site, or Web application level; and lets managed code modules be invoked at any stage. Modules can be registered and enabled or disabled through the application's `web.config` file.

I found upgrading to IIS 7 to be less than intuitive, so I start with the steps for upgrading to IIS 7 and then proceed to an overview of the life-cycle events. If you don't plan on installing IIS, skip the next section.

Upgrading to IIS 7

The instructions in this section apply to Windows Vista and updating from IIS 6 to IIS 7 (or enabling IIS on your Windows Vista workstation). If you are using an older version of IIS or Windows, you may need to perform some additional steps.

Assuming that you have IIS installed locally (on your workstation or laptop) and you'd like to update from IIS 6 to IIS 7, follow these steps:

1. Open the Control Panel by holding the Windows key and pressing R to open the Run dialog box; then, type Control Panel and click OK.

2. If you get lost in the new Control Panel, switch to classic view and double-click Programs and Features. (In the updated Control Panel view, click Programs.)

3. In the Tasks pane on the left, click Turn Windows Features on or off to open the Turn Windows Features on or off dialog box, shown in Figure A-3.

4. Expand the Internet Information Services node.

5. First deselect the highest level (Internet Information Services) node and then re-check it.

6. Click OK.

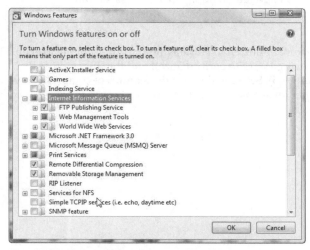

Figure A-3: Use the Turn Windows Features on or off
dialog box to upgrade to IIS 7.

The preceding steps upgrade IIS to IIS 7. Even though these steps seem less than intuitive, you can verify that they worked (the upgrade may take a couple of minutes) by entering **http://localhost** in a browser instance. A successful upgrade will be indicated by the IIS 7 graphic visible in your browser (see Figure A-4).

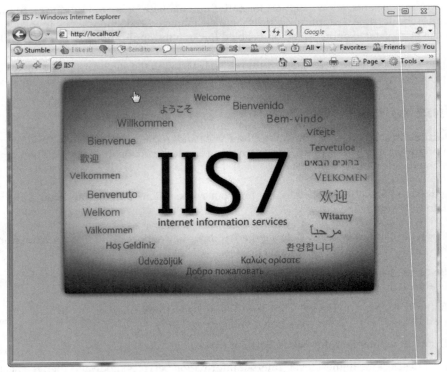

Figure A-4: A successful upgrade to IIS 7 should display the IIS 7 graphic in your browser when you navigate to http://localhost (as shown).

IIS 7 uses the pretty-picture approach to administration. For example, to enable IIS compression (which is a useful tip for improving Web site performance), find the IIS region of IIS Manager and click Compression (see Figure A-5). Select or deselect the features of compression you'd like enabled. You can use a tool such as Fiddler (available at www.fiddlertool.com) to see what compression options do to your served content's size.

Figure A-5: Compression can reduce bandwidth-related charges and improve perceived performance.

When you change an IIS configuration setting for a Web site, be sure to test thoroughly. (Check out *Professional ASP.NET 3.5 in C# and VB* by Bill Evjen, et. al., (Wrox, 2008), for a comprehensive discussion of the benefits and possible pitfalls of IIS compression.)

Reviewing Lifecycle Events

Many of you may still be using IIS 6 in early 2009, but going forward, I hope you are able to update to IIS 7. (Generally, I think, using legacy technology is a decision made by nontechnologists; you and I call these people managers.) All things being equal, I presume that given the chance, many of you would prefer to use newer, if not the newest, technology. This section provides an overview of the IIS 7 life cycle.

The life cycle from a high-level perspective begins when a browser makes a request to the Web server. In IIS 7, the unified pipeline receives the request. An `ApplicationManager` is created; the `ApplicationManager` represents the application domain, providing process isolation. In the application domain, a `HostingEnvironment` class is created. The `HostingEnvironment` class includes such useful information as where the application physically resides. If required, the application is compiled. Compilation includes items in the App_Code folder.

If you are sensitive to possible latency issues caused by first-time request compilation, you can precompile your entire Web site by using the ASP.NET command-line compiler. The following command compiles your Web site into a DLL:

```
aspnet_compiler -v /MowtownJobs -p C:\WebSites\MowtownJobs C:\CompiledWebs
```

The first argument is the virtual path preceded by –v, the second argument is the physical path with the –p switch, and the last argument is the output folder.

Other compiler options and combinations of permissible options are available. You can find these by checking out the ASP.NET Compilation Tool help documentation.

After the application domain and HostingEnvironment class are created, the HttpContext, HttpRequest, and HttpResponse class instances are created. The HttpContext contains objects specific to the current request, including HttpRequest and HttpResponse. The HttpRequest object represents the request including cookie and browser information, and the HttpResponse object represents the server's response. A SubStatusCode is available with IIS 7 in integrated mode, and the Headers and ServerVariables properties of HttpResponse are writeable. SubStatusCode is a programmer-settable value to facilitate request-failure tracing.

The HttpContext supports IsPostNotification and CurrentNotification in IIS 7 integrated mode. IsPostNotification indicates whether all the HttpApplication events have finished processing, and CurrentNotification returns an enumerated value of type RequestNotification that indicates which HttpApplication event is processing.

If a Global.asax file is present, an instance of that class — HttpApplication — is created. (HttpApplication classes might be reused for additional requests.) The HttpApplication performs the numbered tasks that follow. You can check the help documentation if you need to explore these events further, but in general, you will most commonly use the Global.asax application and page events. I cover those in the next two subsections.

The following represents the order of processing steps and events that occur for each page request.

1. The request is validated for malicious markup and script exploits.

2. URL mapping is performed if the UrlMappingsSection of the web.config file contains any URLs.

3. The BeginRequest event is raised.

4. The AuthenticateRequest event is raised.

5. The PostAuthenticateRequest event is raised.

6. The AuthorizeRequest event is raised.

7. The PostAuthorizeRequest event is raised.

8. The ResolveRequestCache event is raised.

9. The `PostResolveCache` event is raised.

10. The `MapRequestEventHandler` event is raised. The handler can be a native-code module, such as `StaticFileModule`, or a managed-code module, such as `PageHandlerFactory`.

11. The `PostMapHandler` event is raised.

12. The `AcquireRequestState` event is raised.

13. The `PostAcquireRequestState` event is raised.

14. The `PreRequestHandlerExecute` event is raised.

15. The `ProcessRequest` method is called (or `IHttpAsyncHandler.BeginProcessRequest`, for asynchronous requests).

16. The `PostRequestHandlerExecute` event is raised.

17. The `ReleaseRequestState` event is raised.

18. The `PostReleaseRequestState` event is raised.

19. Response filtering is performed if the `HttpApplication.Filter` property is defined.

20. The `UpdateRequestCache` event is raised.

21. The `PostUpdateRequestCache` event is raised.

22. The `LogRequest` event is raised.

23. The `PostLogRequest` event is raised.

24. The `EndRequest` event is raised.

25. The `PreSendHeaders` event is raised.

26. The `PreSendRequestContext` event is raised.

To use these events, add a Global Application Class (global.asax) file to your project and define the handler as

```
void Application_eventname(object sender, EventArgs e)
{

}
```

For example, the following method demonstrates how to implicitly add a `BeginRequest` handler to the global.asax file. It is worth noting that the signature of the method must match the event type; in the example, `BeginRequest` is an `EventHandler`, which is the basic event type that accepts an object and `EventArgs` arguments.

```
void Application_BeginRequest(object sender, EventArgs e)
{

}
```

Programming Application-Level Events

Application-level events are defined in the Global.asax (Global Application Class) file. By default, the Global.asax file employs inline code (code residing in the .ASPX file) instead of in the code-behind (source code .cs) file. Inline code means that the source code is contained in the .asax (or.aspx) file inside a <script> block. I generally prefer code-behind files, but there isn't really anything else in .asax files, and inline code supports IntelliSense now. (IntelliSense is the mechanism that displays information about the .NET framework as you code in the IDE.)

When you add a Global.asax file, the inline script will contain event handlers for Application_Start, Application_End, Application_Error, Session_Start, and Session_End, arguably some of the most common events you will want to handle. (As mentioned in the preceding part, you can add more events by prefixing the event name with **Application_**; for instance, typing **Application_BeginRequest** adds a handler for the BeginRequest event.)

Think of the global.asax file as a place to do application-level preparation and housekeeping work. For example, if every user needs a list of slow-to-change data for lookup lists, such as a list of U.S. states, you can cache that information in the global.asax file. If you want to log application level events, the global. asax file is the place to do it. Listing A-1 demonstrates a means of caching information for all users and writing application-level events to the EventLog.

Listing A-1: Caching data for all users at the application level and writing to the EventLog.

```
<%@ Application Language="C#" %>
<%@ Import Namespace="System.Diagnostics" %>

<script runat="server">

    private static readonly string STATE_KEY = "STATES";

    public static System.Collections.Generic.List<State>
      States
    {
      get
      {
        return (System.Collections.Generic.List<State>)
          HttpContext.Current.Cache[STATE_KEY];
      }
    }

    void Application_Start(object sender, EventArgs e)
    {
      //TODO: Comment out when finished testing event log entry
      throw new Exception("Test");
      if(HttpContext.Current.Cache[STATE_KEY] == null)
        HttpContext.Current.Cache[STATE_KEY] = StateHelper.ReadAll();
    }

    void Application_End(object sender, EventArgs e)
```

```
    {
    }

    private static readonly string LOG_SOURCE = "MyApp";
    void Application_Error(object sender, EventArgs e)
    {
      //Note: This approach won't work under Vista.
      //Use an installer instead.
      //if (!EventLog.SourceExists(LOG_SOURCE))
      //   EventLog.CreateEventSource(LOG_SOURCE, "Application");

      EventLog log = new EventLog();
      log.Source = LOG_SOURCE;
      log.Log = "Application";
      log.WriteEntry(Server.GetLastError().Message, EventLogEntryType.Error);
    }

    void Session_Start(object sender, EventArgs e)
    {
        // Code that runs when a new session is started.

    }

    void Session_End(object sender, EventArgs e)
    {
        // Code that runs when a session ends.
        // Note: The Session_End event is raised only
        // when the sessionstate mode
        // is set to InProc in the Web.config file. If session
        // mode is set to StateServer
        // or SQLServer, the event is not raised.

    }

</script>
```

In Listing A-1, two event handlers are implemented: `Application_Start` and `Application_Error`. `Application_Start` adds a collection of State objects — as in City, State, postal code — objects in the `HttpContext`, which makes this information available to all users. For demonstration purposes, the `State` class is a simple entity class and the actual data is hard coded; this approach is beneficial when you have a large amount of data that changes only infrequently or not at all. In this case, the last time the U.S. designated a new state was 1959. `Application_Start` throws an exception to test `Application_Error`. After `Application_Error` is tested, you can comment out the exception.

`Application_Error` writes the error to the Application log using a new source. In the example, the last error is written to the EventLog. The last error can be retrieved by invoking `Server.GetLastError`. You used to be able to use the `SourceExists-CreateEventSource` pairing, but because of security constraints, if you want to use a new source for your application, you need to create an event source. Unfortunately, creating an event source takes a little work. I describe that process in the following subsection.

Writing to the EventLog

Like it or not, the world economy and our lives depend on and are deeply integrated with computers. Regardless of whether it's a CPU fan or a hacker that brings your computer down, the downtime is not only aggravating but also often halts all productive work. Consequently, Microsoft and other security-conscious software vendors keep ratcheting up security, which means you and I have to learn how to do everyday tasks all over again.

If you are using a version of Windows earlier than Vista and a version of .NET earlier than 3.5, you can try to create an EventLog source using code like the following:

```
if (!EventLog.SourceExists(sourcename))
        EventLog.CreateEventSource(sourcename, "Application");
```

The EventLog is a dictionary. Event sources are keys in the dictionary, so when you write **SourceExists** *(sourcename),* the whole registry is checked. The downside is that your Web application won't have permissions to access the Security log, so a security exception may occur, depending on your specific OS and .NET configuration. If that happens, you will need to use an installer and InstallUtil.exe, running with administrative permissions.

Creating an Installer

You use an Installer — a class that inherits from System.Configuration.Install.Installer — for the express purpose of performing custom install actions. To create an EventLog installer, you create a separate class library project, define the class to inherit from Installer, and add the `RunInstaller(true)` attribute to the class. You can create the event source in the public constructor. All these elements are shown in Listing A-2.

Listing A-2: Use an installer to create a custom EventLog source.

```
using System;
using System.Collections.Generic;
using System.Linq;
using System.Text;
using System.Diagnostics;
using System.ComponentModel;
using System.Configuration.Install;

namespace MyEventLogInstaller
{

  [RunInstaller(true)]
  public class MyInstaller : Installer
  {
    private EventLogInstaller installer = null;

    public MyInstaller()
    {
      installer = new EventLogInstaller();
      installer.Source = "MyApp";
      installer.Log = "Application";
      Installers.Add(installer);
```

```
        }

      }
    }
```

In Listing A-2, `MyInstaller` will be invoked by the InstallUitl.exe tool. You will need to add a reference to the System.Configuration.Install.dll. The `EventLogInstaller` class creates the source, indicated in the listing, in the specified log. In the example, the source `MyApp` will be added to the Application log.

Running the Installer

To run the installer, open the Visual Studio 2008 command prompt in Administrative mode. To open the command prompt with administrative privileges, do the following:

1. In Vista, click Start ⇨ All Programs ⇨ Microsoft Visual Studio 2008 ⇨ Visual Studio Tools.

2. Right-click the Visual Studio 2008 command prompt and select Run as Administrator.

3. Change directories to the location of your compiled installer and enter

```
InstallUtil MyEventLogInstaller
```

at the command prompt. You should get some output indicating that the installer succeeded or failed. Take any necessary corrective action as described by the output. Next, test the new event source from your Web application. (You can use the code in Listing A-1 for this purpose.)

Writing to the EventLog from a Web Application

Adding code that writes to the event log is one aspect of what is now commonly referred to as instrumenting your code. *Instrumenting* code means adding extra code that helps you diagnose and observe the overall health of your deployed application.

To test the new event source, run the code from Listing A-1, making sure that the `Application_Error` method is called. If you have already run the code using the Cassini server then you may need to shut down the Cassini server by opening it from the system tray and clicking Stop (refer to Figure A-6).

Figure A-6: Open the Cassini server dialog box from the system tray — found in the lower-right corner of the task bar in Windows — and click Stop to shut down the server.

Viewing the Event Entry in Visual Studio

When you run the code from Listing A-1, an event will be written to the EventLog. You can open the Event Viewer (to do so, press Windows key+R, type **eventvwr**, and click OK) to view your event. Or you can view the written event in Visual Studio from the Server Explorer by following these steps:

1. Open the Server Explorer.

2. Expand the server name.

3. Expand the Event Logs node.

4. Expand the Application node.

5. Find the MyApp source and expand it.

The entries will be listed after the event source (see Figure A-7). You can click any entry and view the contents in the Properties window.

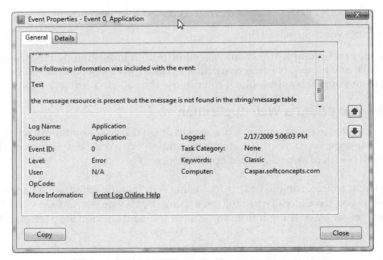

Figure A-7: The event entry shown in the Application log.

Programming Page-Level Events

Every page and user control has page-level events. The most common page-level event, and the one you will probably use for every page, is the Page_Load event. In addition to Page_Load, there are several other page events. They occur each time in a particular order and are usually designed for a general kind of use.

The order of page events is PreInit, InitComplete, PreLoad, Load, LoadComplete, PreRender, Render, and Unload. PreInit is one place to check IsPostBack, although I generally check this Page property in Page_Load. PreInit is also a good place to create or recreate dynamic controls, set the master page dynamically, set the theme dynamically, and read or set profile properties. Init is raised after all the controls have been initialized; this is a good place to read or initialize properties.

InitComplete is a good place for code that requires all Page initialization to be complete. PreLoad is a good place for page or control processing prior to the Load event. Load raises OnLoad for the page and all the page's child controls. LoadComplete is used when all the controls are required to be loaded. PreRender is a good place to use DataBind controls, but I also use these controls in Page_Load quite a bit. The ViewState for all the controls has been written, so changes to controls at this point will effectively be ignored (refer to the next section, "Understanding ViewState," for more information on ViewState.) Render is called. There is no event for Render. Finally, Unload is called for each control and then the Page, the Response, and Request properties are destroyed and final cleanup is performed as the page begins its hop to the requesting client.

Understanding ViewState

When a client computer experiences your application, that computer is not actively connected to your application or server. A request is made, the server satisfies the request, and a page is served to the requestor. If connections were maintained, the bandwidth of the Web would be dramatically limited to the number of concurrent connections your server's hardware could support. When it's disconnected, the server isn't actively keeping track of what is on the client, what's in the controls, or even what the client is doing on his or her end. For instance, when a user puts some data in a TextBox, the server doesn't know about that data until the page is posted back to the server. This means that Web applications need to know what the state of the client (the client view) is between trips to and from the server. ViewState plays the role of storing what's on the page.

ViewState is actually encrypted text stored right in the served page. ViewState is how the server can figure out what the disconnected client did. In a simplistic sense, ViewState can be unencrypted on the server and the state can be compared to the posted page contents, allowing the server to figure out what happened, what the user did. ViewState stores control content and settings and everything on the page participates, whether those controls are Web server controls from Microsoft or controls from DevExpress.

ViewState is actually stored in a hidden <input> field with an encrypted value. You can see ViewState by right-clicking a page and selecting View Source. Here is ViewState for a simple form containing a single TextBox:

```
<input type="hidden" name="__VIEWSTATE" id="__VIEWSTATE"
value="/wEPDwULLTE3NDI1ODEyMjhkZOlex9UvhF08/pa/mN1fNfXfaVdE" />
```

For the most part, you don't care *how* ASP.NET manages ViewState, just that it does. However, if you have a very complex page, ViewState can become very large and impact how long it takes your page to be served to the user. A good strategy for improving performance is to leave ViewState on the server in Session. I cover Session in the next section, and you can learn how to leave ViewState on the server in the follow-up section to that one, "Leaving ViewState on the Server with PageAdapters."

ViewState can be turned on or off at the page level and the control level. For Web server controls, the property you use to turn ViewState on or off is EnableViewState. EnableViewState is True by default. If you don't need ViewState for a particular control or page, you should disable it. The ViewState for a Page is an attribute of the @Page directive, which is a supported directive for Web pages and user controls. To disable `ViewState` for an entire page, modify the `@Page` directive to include the `EnableViewState` attribute, as depicted in the code that follows:

```
<%@ Page Language="C#" AutoEventWireup="true" CodeFile="Default.aspx.cs" Inherits=
"_Default" EnableViewState="false" %>
```

A good strategy for optimizing your Web applications is to defer `ViewState` tweaking until your application is functioning and then make adjustments during optimization by experimenting with `ViewState` at the control, user control, and page levels.

If `ViewState` exceeds the `Page.MaxPageStateFieldLength` value, additional hidden input `ViewState` fields are added automatically as needed. The default value for `Page`
`.MaxPageStateFieldLength` is -1, which means that `ViewState` should not be split.

> `Page.MaxPageStateFieldLength` *does not show up with IntelliSense, but it's there. The fact that it's hidden implies that Microsoft doesn't encourage random fiddling with it. If you use Red-Gate's Reflector and disassemble the* `System.Web.UI.Page.MaxPageStateLength` *property, you will see that it is decorated with the following attributes that conceal it from IntelliSense and Visual Studio, which in turn conceals it from casual users:*
>
> ```
> [DesignerSerializationVisibility(DesignerSerializationVisibility.Hidden),
> EditorBrowsable(EditorBrowsableState.Never), Browsable(false)]
> ```

Why Session Information Is So Important

`ViewState` stores information about the view so that it can be retrieved by the server, but `ViewState` does not store information about noncontrol objects that aren't represented on a Web page or control. Hence, something else is needed to store noncontrol object states. That something is called Session. Every client request is associated by ASP.NET with a `SessionID` (automatically). The `SessionID` is stored in a cookie on the client machine and returned to the server on postbacks to coordinate client requests with a specific client. If cookies are turned off, the `SessionID` is passed as part of the request URL.

> *To experience a cookieless Session, add the* `cookieless="true"` *attribute to the* `<sessionState>` *tag in the* `web.config` `<configuration>` *section, as shown here, followed by the URL containing the* `SessionID`:
>
> ```
> <sessionState cookieless="true"/>
> http://localhost:46691/ViewStateDemo/(S(furoxcvxeuipwiq35fwvbsr3))/default.aspx
> ```

A single user's Session is resolved by the `SessionID` by ASP.NET whether it is stored in a user's cookie or in the URL. Some security-conscious users will have cookies disabled, so it's worth knowing that ASP .NET will still function correctly.

To store or retrieve an object from Session, all you need to do in your code is use a unique string — a key — to access a particular Session variable.

Understanding Session Servers

There are five possible Session state modes, and the one your application is using is expressed in the <sessionState> section of the web.config file. The possible choices are InProc, StateServer, SQLServer, Custom, and Off. The InProc state stores Session state in memory with the Web server. InProc stores references to objects stored in Session, effectively serving as a pointer to your objects. The out-of-process servers are the StateServer and SQL Server. With either of these choices, objects are serialized as XML and stored in the external state server, so serialization is a key element here. StateServer stores Session information in a separate application process called the ASP.NET state server. This approach ensures that state is preserved if the Web application restarts. The InProc Session information dies with the Web application. The SQL Server Session state stores Session information serialized in a SQL Server database.

If you are building a simple Web application, InProc or StateServer are reasonable choices. If you are building a bigger application configured with multiple Web servers, use StateServer and sticky IP — each request goes to the original server — or use SQL Server Session, which permits any server to service the request by restoring Session objects from SQL Server. Custom storage requires that you provide a custom provider, and Off disables Session state.

> **Do not use the InProc Session state server for a multiserver Web farm configuration.**

The first of the following fragments shows you how to configure the StateServer as the Session server, and the next fragment is an example of configuring SQL Server as the state server:

```
<configuration>
  <system.web>
    <sessionState mode="StateServer"
      stateConnectionString="tcpip=SampleStateServer:42424"
      cookieless="false"
      timeout="20"/>
  </system.web>
</configuration>

<configuration>
  <system.web>
    <sessionState mode="SQLServer"
      sqlConnectionString="Integrated Security=SSPI;data source=SampleSqlServer;" />
  </system.web>
</configuration>
```

These fragments were taken from the help files. You can use the StateServer configuration as shown, but the SQL Server version will vary based on your actual SQL Server configuration and installation. (Remember to exclude the <configuration> and <system.web> tags because these are in the web .config file by default.) You do not need to indicate the SQL Server table information for a SQL Server Session. ASP.NET takes care of that for you, but you do need to configure the Session state database (refer to the next subsection).

> For out-of-process state servers, including StateServer and SQL Server, your objects
> must be serializable.

Configuring the SQL Server Session State Database

To use SQL Server Session state, you have to configure a Session state database. By default, this option isn't available on SQL Express, but you can configure SQL Server Session for SQL Server Express with a few extra steps. Because many of you will be configuring Session state management for SQL Server Express, the extra steps are added (but you can skip the SQL script step for non-SQL Server Express additions). Follow these steps to configure SQL Server state management for SQL Server Express:

1. Open Microsoft SQL Server Management Studio (or run the following query statements following step 2 in Visual Studio, using the SQL option).

2. In Microsoft SQL Server Management Studio, click the New Query button, add the following text, and click the Execute button:

```
EXECUTE sp_configure 'show advanced options', 1
RECONFIGURE WITH OVERRIDE
GO

EXECUTE sp_configure 'Agent XPs', 1
RECONFIGURE WITH OVERRIDE
GO

EXECUTE sp_configure 'show advanced options', 0
RECONFIGURE WITH OVERRIDE
GO
```

3. Open the Visual Studio 2008 Command Prompt.

4. At the command prompt, enter the following command:

```
aspnet_regsql.exe -S CASPAR\SQLExpress -E -ssadd -sstype p
```

The preceding steps create a database named ASPState in the SQL Express instance. This database contains two tables named ASPStateTempApplications and ASPStateTempSessions. The first table contains a value indicating the AppId and AppName; the second table holds the serialized Session information. Run the very simple Web application in Listing A-3 to test the Session configuration. The rows from two sample runs are shown in Figure A-8.

> You can run `aspnet_regsql` and walk through the wizard, but doing so creates a database named aspnetdb. Having this database will result in an error when you try to store information in Session because the SQL Server Session server is looking for a database named ASPState. Use the command-line option as described in step 4 previously.

Listing A-3: Contains some simple code that will add a value to the SQL Server Session database.

```
using System;
using System.Collections.Generic;
using System.Linq;
using System.Web;
using System.Web.UI;
using System.Web.UI.WebControls;
using System.Runtime.Serialization;

public partial class _Default : System.Web.UI.Page
{
    protected void Page_Load(object sender, EventArgs e)
    {
      Session["SQL"] = new Dummy(43);
    }
}

[SerializableAttribute]
public class Dummy
{
  public Dummy() { }

  public Dummy(int arg)
  {
    filler = arg;
  }

  private int filler;
  public int Filler
  {
    get { return filler; }
    set { filler = value; }
  }
}
```

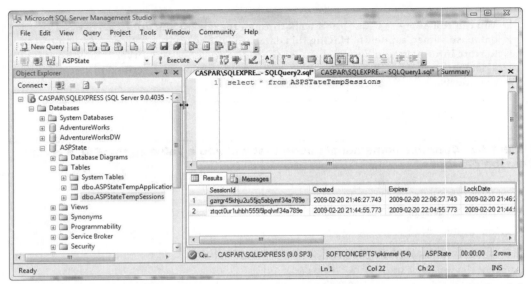

Figure A-8: The Session information (shown in the query result) from running the code in Listing A-3.

The actual web.config settings used for the sample application are shown here:

```
<sessionState mode="SQLServer"
    sqlConnectionString="Integrated Security=True;data source=CASPAR\SQLExpress;"/>
```

The `SerializableAttribute` marks the `Dummy` class as serializable, and the `Page_Load` event puts the information in Session. To read the information from the Session, place the `Session["SQL"]` fragment on the right side of an expression.

> *Attributes are a little funny in their application in .NET in that the Attribute part of all attribute names can be left off. For example, the* `SerializableAttribute` *can be applied as* [Serializable] *or* [SerializableAttribute]. *Both refer to the same class.*

The `Inproc` and `StateServer` Session servers are easier to use and configure, but you need a more robust server such as SQL Server for enterprise or applications of any scale running in a Web farm.

Leaving ViewState on the Server with PageAdapters

`ViewState` keeps track of your application's visual information, and Session keeps track of your custom objects (or any objects that run in the code-behind but aren't represented on the client as rendered controls). If `ViewState` gets to be very large for a particular page, the delivery speed of that page to a client can be affected. To improve the performance of the page, you can store `ViewState` on the server in Session.

Jeff Prosise, an excellent presenter, offers a presentation on tuning ASP.NET. If you get to TechEd or another event, right after you stop by and say hello to me at the DevExpress booth and pick up your free ASP.NET controls, or see Mark Miller's awesome CodeRush presentation, get to Jeff's presentation on ASP.NET. It is one of the best presentations I have seen at any conference.

The code in Listing A-4 uses the `WebClient` class's `DownloadString` method to request current stock quotes from Yahoo! Finance. The URL is `http://download.finance.yahoo.com/d/quotes` `.csv?s={0}&f=nspc s={0}&f=nspc`. The s parameter is the stock symbol. The f parameter indicates the desired fields; the letters `nspc` represent the name, symbol, price, and change fields. (This information is particular to the Yahoo! Finance feature.) The `GetQuote` function sends the symbol to Yahoo!, parses the resultant data, and removes quotation marks.

`InitializeQuotes` uses LINQ to send each string symbol to `GetQuote` and creates an anonymous type from the results specified by the f (fields) parameter. The anonymous type is stored in an enumerable collection. This collection, represented by the variable quotes, is assigned to the `GridView`'s `DataSource`, and `GridView.DataBind` is called. In short, the code in Listing A-4 is a down-and-dirty stock quote page and contains enough information to illustrate using Session to store `ViewState` information. (You will need to add a GridView named GridView1 to the Web page to support the code in Listing A-4.)

Listing A-4: A down-and-dirty stock quote page that uses WebClient and LINQ to query and parse stock quotes from Yahoo! Finance.

```
using System;
using System.Collections.Generic;
using System.Linq;
using System.Web;
using System.Web.UI;
using System.Web.UI.WebControls;
using System.Net;

public partial class _Default : System.Web.UI.Page
{
    protected void Page_Load(object sender, EventArgs e)
    {
      if (!IsPostBack)
      {
        InitializeQuotes();
      }
    }

    private void InitializeQuotes()
    {
      string[] symbols =
        { "GOOG", "MSFT", "DELL", "GM", "F", "C", "PNC" };


      var quotes = from symbol in symbols
                   let values = GetQuote(symbol)
                   select new
```

Continued

Listing A-4: A down-and-dirty stock quote page that uses WebClient and LINQ to query and parse stock quotes from Yahoo! Finance. *(continued)*

```
                            {
                                CompanyName = values[0],
                                Symbol = values[1],
                                Price = Convert.ToDecimal(values[2]),
                                Change = values[3]
                            };

            GridView1.DataSource = quotes;
            GridView1.DataBind();

        }

        private string[] GetQuote(string symbol)
        {
            const string request =
                "http://download.finance.yahoo.com/d/quotes.csv?s={0}&f=nspc";

            WebClient client = new WebClient();
            string result = client.DownloadString(string.Format(request, symbol));
            return result.Replace("\"", "").Split(',');
        }
    }
```

Given the state of the equities markets in 2009, using a stock quote demo is a little awkward, but the quote service from Yahoo! Finance is fun. I am optimistic that markets will correct, stocks will recover, and new opportunities will return eventually.

Run the code in Listing A-4 and select View ➪ Source in Internet Explorer (or the equivalent in your browser). Figure A-9 shows ViewState from Listing A-2 copied into Notepad to give you an idea of how much information this relatively small page returns to the client.

Figure A-9: ViewState from the stock quote sample page.

To store the page state (ViewState) in Session, you need to define a PageAdapter, add a browser file, and add a couple of lines of XML to the .browser file. The .browser file registers the PageAdapter with your application. To implement the PageAdapter add a source code file with a class with about 10 lines of code and about five lines of code in the .browser file. To create a PageAdapter and the necessary .browser file, follow these steps:

1. Add a source code file to your Web application. (Visual Studio places this code in a folder named App_Code.)

2. Modify the source code file to contain the C# from Listing A-5.

3. Add a browser file to the project from the Add New Item dialog box (see Figure A-10). (Visual Studio adds this file in an App_Browsers folder.)

4. Add the XML — the last <browser> tag — shown in Listing A-6.

5. Rerun the sample application from Listing A-4 and view the source; you will see that the input contains substantially less data (see Figure A-11).

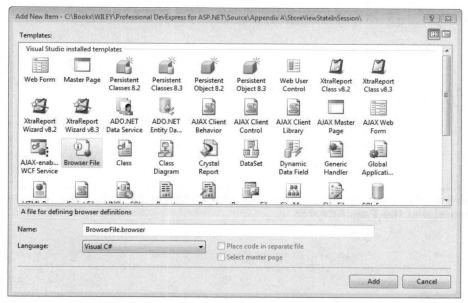

Figure A-10: Add a .browser file from the Add New Item dialog box; the .browser file is used to register the PageAdapter.

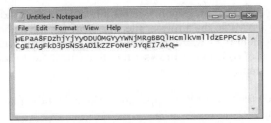

Figure A-11: After the PageAdapter is
incorporated into the application, the ViewState
is substantially smaller than it is without the
PageAdapter.

Listing A-5: This PageAdapter returns SessionPageStatePersister, which is employed by ASP.NET to store ViewState information on the server instead of in the rendered page.

```csharp
using System;
using System.Collections.Generic;
using System.Linq;
using System.Web;
using System.Web.UI;
using System.Web.UI.Adapters;

public class MyPageAdapter : PageAdapter
{
  public override PageStatePersister GetStatePersister()
  {
    return new SessionPageStatePersister(this.Page);
  }
}
```

Listing A-6: This .browser file registers MyPageAdapter by adding the last <browser> tag, describing the PageAdapter.

```xml
<!--
    You can find existing browser definitions at
    <windir>\Microsoft.NET\Framework\<ver>\CONFIG\Browsers
-->
<browsers>
    <browser id="NewBrowser" parentID="Mozilla">
        <identification>
            <userAgent match="Unique User Agent Regular Expression" />
        </identification>

        <capture>
            <userAgent match="NewBrowser (?'version'\d+\.\d+)" />
        </capture>

        <capabilities>
            <capability name="browser" value="My New Browser" />
            <capability name="version" value="${version}" />
```

```
        </capabilities>
    </browser>

    <browser refID="Mozilla">
        <capabilities>
            <capability name="xml" value="true" />
        </capabilities>
    </browser>

    <browser refID="Default">
      <controlAdapters>
        <adapter controlType="System.Web.UI.Page"
             adapterType="MyPageAdapter" />
      </controlAdapters>
    </browser>

</browsers>
```

Because this book is part of Wrox's Professional series, I feel compelled to tell you that individual tuning tips — like using a `PageAdapter` to reduce the amount of `ViewState` sent to the client — are relatively easy to incorporate into your applications (at least sometimes). The best strategy is to defer tuning until after you get the core functionality working. First make your application work and then make it fast. Tuning too early can result in you spinning your wheels but not making significant progress.

Caching Controls, Pages, and Data

Professional guidance varies greatly; very few "experts" agree on a universal set of application development best practices. For example, some will tell you that profiling and tuning should occur early in development because changes cost more later. From my experience, code changes frequently, requirements change frequently, and elements that cause bottlenecks evolve over time. Therefore, I recommend that you get the core functionality working first, let the dust settle on features and requirements, and then profile the application and improve bottlenecks. This section gives you more approaches to improving Web application performance.

Each object, control, user control, and page incurs a creation cost. By reducing the number of times you pay each of these costs, you can improve your application's performance. You will always pay a first-time cost when an object, control, or page is created, but whether (or when) you pay subsequent costs can be controlled by you. Caching permits you to store objects, controls, parts of pages, and whole pages in memory.

> A good rule of thumb is to cache pages and controls that remain relatively unchanged over time and that don't require user input. Blog postings, new sites, static text, and graphic content are all good candidates for caching.

The key to figuring out what to cache is to determine which elements of your pages change frequently and which change infrequently. You can store infrequently changing objects in an instance of the Cache class, and you can cache relatively static user controls and pages using the @OutputCache directive. This section explores page and control caching, adding and removing elements from caching, expressing expiration policies, defining cache dependencies, and caching partial pages.

Using the @OutputCache Directive

Suppose, for argument's sake, that you anticipate adding new clients daily, but your product line changes infrequently and only after long deliberation. Why make your customers wait to query the database and generate a page for data that is relatively static? If you cache the product page after the data is fetched, subsequent users will experience a better response time.

Listing A-1, which appears earlier in this chapter, is a very straightforward page containing an ASPxGridView, and the grid is populated with DevExpress's XpoDataSource and persistent classes. The @OutputCache directive is used to cache the page containing a list of customers. The first request will cache the page, and subsequent requestors will receive the cached page. Listing A-7 contains the Persistent Class Northwind.Products created from the DevExpress Persistent Classes item. (Refer to Chapter 6, "Using the Data that Makes Sense for Your Problem," for detailed information on using persistent classes and XpoDataSources.) Listing A-8 contains the Global.asax file that initializes the Products data, and Listing A-9 contains the .ASPX file showing the @OutputCache directive.

Listing A-7: The Northwind.Products class created with DevExpress's Persistent Classes.

```
using System;
using DevExpress.Xpo;
namespace Northwind {

    public class Products : XPLiteObject {
        int fProductID;
        [Key(true)]
        public int ProductID {
            get { return fProductID; }
            set { SetPropertyValue<int>("ProductID",
                    ref fProductID, value); }
        }
        string fProductName;
        [Size(40)]
        public string ProductName {
            get { return fProductName; }
            set { SetPropertyValue<string>("ProductName",
                    ref fProductName, value); }
        }
        int fSupplierID;
        public int SupplierID {
            get { return fSupplierID; }
            set { SetPropertyValue<int>("SupplierID",
                    ref fSupplierID, value); }
        }
```

```
int fCategoryID;
public int CategoryID {
    get { return fCategoryID; }
    set { SetPropertyValue<int>("CategoryID",
            ref fCategoryID, value); }
}
string fQuantityPerUnit;
[Size(20)]
public string QuantityPerUnit {
    get { return fQuantityPerUnit; }
    set { SetPropertyValue<string>("QuantityPerUnit",
            ref fQuantityPerUnit, value); }
}
decimal fUnitPrice;
public decimal UnitPrice {
    get { return fUnitPrice; }
    set { SetPropertyValue<decimal>("UnitPrice",
            ref fUnitPrice, value); }
}
short fUnitsInStock;
public short UnitsInStock {
    get { return fUnitsInStock; }
    set { SetPropertyValue<short>("UnitsInStock",
            ref fUnitsInStock, value); }
}
short fUnitsOnOrder;
public short UnitsOnOrder {
    get { return fUnitsOnOrder; }
    set { SetPropertyValue<short>("UnitsOnOrder",
            ref fUnitsOnOrder, value); }
}
short fReorderLevel;
public short ReorderLevel {
    get { return fReorderLevel; }
    set { SetPropertyValue<short>("ReorderLevel",
            ref fReorderLevel, value); }
}
bool fDiscontinued;
public bool Discontinued {
    get { return fDiscontinued; }
    set { SetPropertyValue<bool>("Discontinued",
            ref fDiscontinued, value); }
}
public Products(Session session) : base(session) { }
public Products() : base(Session.DefaultSession) { }
public override void AfterConstruction() {
    base.AfterConstruction(); }
    }
}
```

Listing A-8: You use the Globabl.asax file to initialize the data for the Northwind .Products class.

```csharp
<%@ Application Language="C#" %>
<%@ Import Namespace="DevExpress.Xpo" %>
<%@ Import Namespace="DevExpress.Xpo.DB" %>
<%@ Import Namespace="DevExpress.Xpo.Metadata" %>
<%@ Import Namespace="System.Web.SessionState" %>

<script runat="server">

    void Application_Start(object sender, EventArgs e)
    {
      string connectionString =
        MSSqlConnectionProvider.GetConnectionString(
        ".\\SQLExpress", "Northwind");

      XPDictionary dictionary = new ReflectionDictionary();

      IDataStore store = XpoDefault.GetConnectionProvider(
        connectionString,
        AutoCreateOption.SchemaAlreadyExists);

      dictionary.GetDataStoreSchema(typeof(Northwind.Products).Assembly);
      XpoDefault.DataLayer = new ThreadSafeDataLayer(dictionary, store);
      XpoDefault.Session = null;
    }

    void Application_End(object sender, EventArgs e)
    {
        //  Code that runs on application shutdown

    }

    void Application_Error(object sender, EventArgs e)
    {
        // Code that runs when an unhandled error occurs

    }

    void Session_Start(object sender, EventArgs e)
    {
        // Code that runs when a new session is started

    }

    void Session_End(object sender, EventArgs e)
    {
        // Code that runs when a session ends.
        // Note: The Session_End event is raised only when
```

```
        // the sessionstate mode
        // is set to InProc in the Web.config file. If session
        // mode is set to StateServer
        // or SQLServer, the event is not raised.
    }

</script>
```

Listing A-9: The .ASPX code showing the @OutputCache directive.

```
<%@ Page Language="C#" AutoEventWireup="true" CodeFile="Default.aspx.cs"
Inherits="_Default" %>
<%@ Register assembly="DevExpress.Web.ASPxGridView.v8.3, Version=8.3.2.0,
Culture=neutral, PublicKeyToken=b88d1754d700e49a"
namespace="DevExpress.Web.ASPxGridView" tagprefix="dxwgv" %>
<%@ Register assembly="DevExpress.Web.ASPxEditors.v8.3, Version=8.3.2.0,
Culture=neutral, PublicKeyToken=b88d1754d700e49a"
namespace="DevExpress.Web.ASPxEditors" tagprefix="dxe" %>
<%@ Register assembly="DevExpress.Xpo.v8.3, Version=8.3.2.0, Culture=neutral,
PublicKeyToken=b88d1754d700e49a" namespace="DevExpress.Xpo" tagprefix="dxxpo"
%>
<%@ OutputCache Duration="99999" VaryByParam="none" %>

<!DOCTYPE html PUBLIC "-//W3C//DTD XHTML 1.0 Transitional//EN"
"http://www.w3.org/TR/xhtml1/DTD/xhtml1-transitional.dtd">

<html xmlns="http://www.w3.org/1999/xhtml">
<head runat="server">
    <title></title>
</head>
<body>
    <form id="form1" runat="server">
    <div>
      <dxwgv:ASPxGridView ID="ASPxGridView1" runat="server"
        AutoGenerateColumns="False" DataSourceID="XpoDataSource1"
        KeyFieldName="ProductID">
        <Columns>
          <dxwgv:GridViewDataTextColumn FieldName="ProductID" ReadOnly="True"
            VisibleIndex="0">
          </dxwgv:GridViewDataTextColumn>
          <dxwgv:GridViewDataTextColumn FieldName="ProductName" VisibleIndex="1">
          </dxwgv:GridViewDataTextColumn>
          <dxwgv:GridViewDataTextColumn FieldName="SupplierID" VisibleIndex="2">
          </dxwgv:GridViewDataTextColumn>
          <dxwgv:GridViewDataTextColumn FieldName="CategoryID" VisibleIndex="3">
          </dxwgv:GridViewDataTextColumn>
          <dxwgv:GridViewDataTextColumn FieldName="QuantityPerUnit"
VisibleIndex="4">
          </dxwgv:GridViewDataTextColumn>
          <dxwgv:GridViewDataTextColumn FieldName="UnitPrice" VisibleIndex="5">
          </dxwgv:GridViewDataTextColumn>
          <dxwgv:GridViewDataTextColumn FieldName="UnitsInStock" VisibleIndex="6">
          </dxwgv:GridViewDataTextColumn>
```

Continued

605

Listing A-9: The .ASPX code showing the @OutputCache directive. *(continued)*

```
                    <dxwgv:GridViewDataTextColumn FieldName="UnitsOnOrder" VisibleIndex="7">
                    </dxwgv:GridViewDataTextColumn>
                    <dxwgv:GridViewDataTextColumn FieldName="ReorderLevel" VisibleIndex="8">
                    </dxwgv:GridViewDataTextColumn>
                    <dxwgv:GridViewDataCheckColumn FieldName="Discontinued" VisibleIndex="9">
                    </dxwgv:GridViewDataCheckColumn>
                </Columns>
                <SettingsPager PageSize="100" Visible="False">
                </SettingsPager>
            </dxwgv:ASPxGridView>

        </div>
        <dxxpo:XpoDataSource ID="XpoDataSource1" runat="server"
          TypeName="Northwind.Products">
        </dxxpo:XpoDataSource>
        </form>
    </body>
    </html>
```

For detailed steps on using persistent classes and an XpoDataSource, refer to Chapter 6. The following steps summarize how to construct the sample supported by the code in Listings A-7, -8, and -9:

1. Create a Web site.

2. Place an ASPxGridView on the Default.aspx page.

3. From the Add New Item dialog box, add a persistent class to the project and generate a class for the Northwind.Products table using the Persistent Class Wizard.

4. Add an XpoDataSource to the Default.aspx page.

5. Set the ASPxGridView's DataSourceID property to the XpoDataSource component.

6. Finally, disable paging on the grid and set the PageSize to exceed the number of entries.

The code-behind for the .ASPX page is shown in Listing A-9. The date and time value is written to the page. When the output cache is working correctly, the date and time value doesn't change when you refresh the page.

The @OutputCache directive as used in Listing A-9 sets the cache Duration attribute to 99,999 seconds. The Duration attribute describes how long the page is cached. Duration and VaryByParam or VaryByControl are required. VaryByParam contains a comma-delimited list of values that represent URL query parameters. In the example, the value none means that query parameters are ignored.

OutputCache supports Duration, Location, Shared, VaryByControl, VaryByCustom, VaryByHeader, VaryByParam, VaryByContentEncoding, CacheProfile, NoStore, and SqlDependency attributes. Rather than use a random duration for data dependent on the contents of a database, a better choice would be to use a SqlDependency, which will update the cache when the database is changed. (Refer to the subsection "Using Cache Dependencies to Refresh Data," later in this chapter.)

Before you continue to the next section, you should be aware of a few more points about the XPO example in Listings A-7 through A-10. Paging is turned off because when a page is cached, the actual controls don't exist in the code-behind except when the page is actually being rendered. This means that if you try to page — which you do by using Ajax for the ASPxGridView — you will get an error when the Ajax code tries to manipulate the grid. That's also the reason you want to show all the data, which you accomplish by setting the PageSize beyond the size of the data.

Caching Multiple Page Versions

Sometimes you want to cache a page or control that doesn't change very much. You can cache a page or control based on any of the following: a query string, control values posted by the user, HTTP headers, browser versions, or a custom string. The OutputCache's VaryByParam, VaryByControl, VaryByHeader, or VaryByCustom attributes are used for this purpose.

Referring to the example in the previous section, suppose that you want a version of the products page that shows only the products by a supplier. You could add a VaryByParam argument, for example, SupplierID, and use the parameter to return just products for a given supplier. Apply the query string to the ASPxGridView as a filter (see Chapter 1, "Programming with the ASPxGridView," for more information on filters) to modify the result set and cache the supplier-dependant page. You can use the code from Listings A-7 through A-10. Simply modify the OutputCache as shown in the following code snippet and pass the query string on the command line. An example URL showing how to use the query string follows the revised @OutputCache value, and the revised code-behind using the query string is provided in Listing A-10.

```
<%@ OutputCache Duration="1000" VaryByParam="SupplerID;*" %>
```

```
http://localhost:21908/OutputCacheDemo/Default.aspx?SupplierID=6
```

Listing A-10: The new code will use the query string to apply a filter on the grid.

```
using System;
using System.Collections.Generic;
using System.Linq;
using System.Web;
using System.Web.UI;
using System.Web.UI.WebControls;

public partial class _Default : System.Web.UI.Page
{
    private static readonly string SUPPLIER_ID = "SupplierID";

    protected void Page_Load(object sender, EventArgs e)
    {
      Response.Write(DateTime.Now.ToString());
      // Add this code for VaryByParam demo
      if (Request.QueryString[SUPPLIER_ID] != null)
      {
        ASPxGridView1.FilterEnabled = true;
        ASPxGridView1.FilterExpression = "SupplierID='" +
          Request.QueryString[SUPPLIER_ID] + "'";
      }
```

Continued

607

(continued)

```
        else
          ASPxGridView1.FilterEnabled = false;
    }


    protected void Page_Init(object sender, EventArgs e)
    {
      XpoDataSource1.Session = new DevExpress.Xpo.Session();
    }
  }
```

The asterisk in `VaryByParam` will force a re-query if no `SupplierID` is provided or it is removed in subsequent requests.

In Listing A-10, if the `Page_Load` runs — and it will on the first request or when you modify the `SupplierID` query parameter — the ASPxGridView filter is enabled and an expression is applied. This sample will result in having multiple versions of the products page cached, which you can verify by changing `SupplierID`s and examining the timestamp written to the page. Reuse a `SupplierID` and you will see that the timestamp still contains the original timestamp as the original request for that `SupplierID` or until 1,000 seconds pass.

Caching Parts of a Page

A good strategy for making complex pages and reusable elements is to create user controls. User controls can be cached by applying the same rules as Page caching and by placing the `@OutputCache` directive inside the user control's .ASPX. You can define rules for control caching using the same attributes you would use for page caching. `Location`, `CacheProfile`, and `NoStore` are not supported for user controls.

Caching for user controls can be defined declaratively using the `@OutputCache` directive in the .ASPX file or the `PartialCachingAttribute` in the code-behind for the user control. Caching attributes are passed as arguments to the `PartialCachingAttribute` when you apply that attribute to the user control code-behind class.

Caching Application Data

Caching application-level data was introduced in the "Programming Application-Level Events" section, earlier in this chapter. There is more to caching than just inserting and retrieving cached data. Besides adding data to the application cache, you can remove data, create cache dependencies based on SQL Server database tables, define expiration policies, and define events to notify you when an item is removed from the cache.

Each page has a `Cache` property that you can use to access cache data. The remainder of this chapter describes various cache operations and demonstrates how to use them.

Adding Data to and Removing Data from the Application Cache

In Listing A-1, earlier in this chapter, a static property was used to provide access to the cache containing state information. This is a technique I employ sometimes to permit getting at the cached data by a property name from anywhere in my Web applications, but you can also get at the cached data from a page or user control's `Cache` property. All you need to know is the key used to insert the item into the cache.

> Add a wrapper for your cached items. Doing so permits you to refer to cached items by name and localize the typecast in the static property (refer to Listing A-1 for an example).

Because the `Cache` is a dictionary object, cached values are associated with a string dictionary key and stored as objects. The easiest way to insert a value into the cache is to refer to the cache and key pair. Use the same approach to retrieve the value from the cache. Refer to Listing A-1 for an example of adding a value to the cache in this manner.

Caching becomes much more powerful when you combine cache dependencies and expiration policies with caching. The next section briefly covers removing items from the cache. After that, I cover using cache dependencies and expiration polices.

If you want to remove an item from the cache, call the `Cache.Remove` method, passing the key for the item you would like to remove. For example, to remove the states collection from the cache, call

```
Cache.Remove("STATES");
```

Using Cache Dependencies to Refresh Data

Putting data from a database in the cache is a good way to optimize your application relative to expensive database hits, especially for data that may not change frequently. The key is to understand that you really can't guess when the data in the table associated with the cache changes. Fortunately, you do not have to guess. To let SQL Server tell you when it's time to update your table-dependent data, insert the data in the cache with a `SqlDependencyCache` argument.

The `SqlCacheDependency` will clear the cache if the associated table element changes. Your application, checking for a null spot where your data used to be, will know it's time to update the cache. To enable database and table notifications, you will need to call `SqlCacheDependencyAdmin.EnableNotifications` on the database and `SqlCacheDependencyAdmin.EnableNotificationsForTable` on the table (or use the AspNet_regsql.exe command-line utility.) The example in Listing A-11 demonstrates how to create a SQL cache dependency on the `Northwind.Products` table using the `SqlCacheDependencyAdmin` class to enable notifications. The additions to the web.config file are shown in Listing A-12.

Listing A-11: Creating a SQL cache dependency on the Northwind.Products table and enabling cache dependencies with SqlCacheDependencyAdmin.

```csharp
using System;
using System.Collections.Generic;
using System.Linq;
using System.Web;
using System.Web.UI;
using System.Web.UI.WebControls;
using System.Web.Caching;
using System.Configuration;

public partial class _Default : System.Web.UI.Page
{
    private static readonly string PRODUCTS = "Products";
    protected void Page_Load(object sender, EventArgs e)
    {
        if (Cache[PRODUCTS] == null)
        {
            string connectionString = ConfigurationManager.ConnectionStrings[
                "NorthwindConnectionString"].ConnectionString;

            SqlCacheDependencyAdmin.EnableNotifications(connectionString);
            SqlCacheDependencyAdmin.EnableTableForNotifications(connectionString,
                "dbo.Products");

            string selectCommand =
                "SELECT ProductID, ProductName, " +
                "SupplierID, CategoryID, QuantityPerUnit, UnitPrice, " +
                "UnitsInStock, UnitsOnOrder, ReorderLevel, Discontinued " +
                "FROM Products";

            SqlDataSource source =
                new SqlDataSource(connectionString, selectCommand);

            Cache.Insert(PRODUCTS, source,
                new SqlCacheDependency("NorthwindDB", "dbo.Products"));
        }

        ASPxGridView1.AutoGenerateColumns = true;
        SqlDataSource data = ((SqlDataSource)Cache[PRODUCTS]);
        data.FilterExpression = "ProductID > 75";
        ASPxGridView1.DataSource = data;
        ASPxGridView1.DataBind();

    }
}
```

Listing A-12: Add a connectionStrings and caching sections to your web.config file to complete the cache dependency from Listing 11.

```
<connectionStrings>
  <clear/>
    <add name="NorthwindConnectionString" connectionString="Data
Source=WYOMING\SQLEXPRESS;Initial Catalog=Northwind;Integrated
Security=True"/>
</connectionStrings>

<system.web>
  <!-- Add this for caching dependency -->
  <caching>
    <sqlCacheDependency pollTime="1000" enabled="true">
      <databases>
        <add connectionStringName="NorthwindConnectionString" name="NorthwindDB"/>
      </databases>
    </sqlCacheDependency>
  </caching>
...
```

The code in Listing A-11 means that if the cache element associated with key `Products` is null, then initialize a `SqlDataSource` with the Products table data and put the `SqlDataSource` in the cache, using the web.config `connectionString` and `sqlCacheDependency` to establish the change dependency. If the Products table data changes, the cache item will be cleared. Finally, the `SqlDataSource` is retrieved from the cache and used to bind to an `ASPxGridView` with a filter expression.

> Cache dependencies can be created declaratively in user controls and pages using the `@Output` directive.

When you put data in the cache using a `SqlCacheDependency`, use the column names. The asterisk is not permitted. Finally, you need to call `SqlCacheDependencyAdmin.EnableNotifications` and `SqlCacheDependencyAdmin.EnableTableForNotifications` only one time, so you can move this code to `Application_Start` or to an external installer (refer to "Creating an Installer," earlier in this chapter, for an example). You can put anything you want in the cache, so you could easily revise the code to store custom objects instead of a `SqlDataSource`.

Expressing an Expiration Policy

You express an expiration policy by passing an acceptable value to the cache declaratively or in the `Cache.Insert` method. An expiration policy is an expression of time. You can express expiration as a literal `DateTime` and the combination of the cache's `TimeSpan` constant. Expiration policies can be used alone or in conjunction with cache dependencies. The following demonstrates using an absolute expiration of one week and the `NoSlidingExpiration` `TimeSpan` argument:

```
Cache.Insert(PRODUCTS, source,
        new SqlCacheDependency("NorthwindDB", "dbo.Products"),
        DateTime.Now.AddDays(7), Cache.NoSlidingExpiration );
```

When you use a sliding expiration — as shown in the revision from Listing A-11 — you have to use the `Cache.NoSlidingExpiration` property. Sliding expiration means that if the cache is hit, the expiration clock is reset. The preceding example means that this cache item — `Products` — will expire in seven days from the current date and time. (This may be a little long for the average Web application, but Google, Amazon,, and MSN probably run around the clock.)

Receiving Notification of Items Removed from the Cache

If you want to be notified when a cache item has expired and is removed from the cache, pass in an instance of `CacheItemUpdateCallback`. When the item is removed, the callback is invoked, and you can return new cache values in the delegate's out parameters. If you want the item to be removed, return null. The `CacheItemUpdateCallback` will not be called if `Cache.Remove` is called explicitly.

Listing A-13 demonstrates the mechanics of initializing an instance of the `CacheItemUpdateCallback`. The absolute expiration is intentionally set to a short period of time, so you can easily test the callback.

Listing A-13: Using the CacheItemUpdateCallback to re-insert a cache item on expiration.

```csharp
using System;
using System.Collections.Generic;
using System.Linq;
using System.Web;
using System.Web.UI;
using System.Web.UI.WebControls;
using System.Web.Caching;
using System.Diagnostics;

public partial class _Default : System.Web.UI.Page
{
    private static string key;
    private static CacheItemUpdateReason reason;

    private void ItemUpdated(string k,
        CacheItemUpdateReason r, out object o,
        out CacheDependency d, out DateTime dt, out TimeSpan t)
    {
        key = k;
        reason = r;

        o = "New Data";
        d = null;
        dt = DateTime.UtcNow.AddMilliseconds(200);
        t = Cache.NoSlidingExpiration;
    }

    protected void Page_Load(object sender, EventArgs e)
    {
        Response.Write("Key: " + key + "<br />");
        Response.Write("CacheItemUpdateReason: " +
            reason.ToString() + "<br />");
        Cache.Insert("Test", "Test", null,
            DateTime.UtcNow.AddMilliseconds(100),
```

```
        Cache.NoSlidingExpiration,
        new CacheItemUpdateCallback(ItemUpdated));

    System.Threading.Thread.Sleep(200);
    }
}
```

In the example, a simple string value is placed in the cache with a short expiration value — 100 milliseconds. When the cache item expires, `ItemUpdated` is called and new cache values and expirations are returned in the out parameters.

The cache also provides an `Add` method. You can pass in an instance of `CacheItemRemovedCallback` to receive notification when an item is removed. `CacheItemRemovedCallback` does not have out parameters, so your code will just receive information about a removed item.

Summary

The core bit of programming that everyone learns is how to write `for` loops, `if` conditions, and call methods. Professional programming doesn't require that you know everything or even every way to do any one thing. Programming is like practicing any discipline. You expand your repertoire, refine your skills, and add new ones over time.

In this appendix, the application life cycle, events, writing to the event log and creating installers, caching, `ViewState`, Session, and cache dependencies were covered. Possessing these skills will aid you one way or another in writing almost every Web application.

The DevExpress controls will help you create good-looking, cool, powerful applications. Tools such as XPO and persistent classes will help your middleware and make you more productive. Combining DevExpress code with the application management, instrumenting, and tuning capabilities described in this appendix will improve your total application result.

Index

Symbols

A